Rick Steves'

SPAIN
2007

Atlantic Ocean

Ferrol
La Coruña
San Martin
Ribadeo
Canero
La Espina
Gijón
COSTA VERDE
Santander
Santillana del Mar
Altamira Caves

Santiago de Compostela
Lugo
GALICIA
Oviedo
Avilés
ASTURIAS
Cangas
PICOS DE EUROPA
Potes
Comillas
Cillervele

Cabo Fínisterre
Pontevedra
Piedrafita
Fuente Dé
CANTABRIA

RÍAS BAIXAS
Vigo
Redondela
Orense
Ponferrada
León
Aguilar
Burgos

Guillarei
Valença
S. Maria
Becilla
Palencia
Lerma

Viana do Castelo
Braga
Bragança
Benevente
Valladolid
Aranda

DOURO VALLEY
Amarante
Vila Real
Mirandela
Zamora
CASTILE-LEÓN
Medina del Campo

Porto
Pinhão
Vila Nova de Gaia
Mesão Frio
Peso da Régua
Pocinho

Douro
Aveiro
Viseu
Salamanca
Peñaranda
Segovia
La Granja

PORTUGAL
Mondego
Guarda
Ciudad Rodrigo
Valley of the Fallen
Ávila
Barajas

Figueira da Foz
Coimbra
Vilar
Piedranita
El Escorial
Madrid

Conimbriga
Plasencia
Talavera de la Reina
Aranjuez

Batalha
Leiria
Tomar
Castelo Branco
Tajo
Toledo
CASTILE-

Nazaré
Fátima
Valado
Alcobaça
Valencia de Alcántara
Cáceres
Trujillo
La Nava
Almoncid
Consuegra
LA

Óbidos
Entroncamento
Santarém
Portalegre
Zorita
Puerto Lapice
Tomelloso

Cabo da Roca
Sintra
Tejo
Manza-nares
Valde-peñas

Lisbon
Estoril
Cascais
Elvas
Badajoz
Mérida
Don Benito
Ciudad Real
Puertollano

Cromlegue dos Almendres
Setúbal
Cabo Espichel
Escoural
Évora
Anta do Zambujeiro
La Albuera
AVE High-Speed Rail
Linares
Úbeda

Casa Branca
Beja
Llerena
Alcarecejos

Sines
Cercal
ALENTEJO
Galaroza
Medina Azahara
Córdoba
Jaén

Odemira
Funcheira
Italica
Carmona
Écija
ANDALUCÍA

Vila do Bispo
Sagres
ALGARVE
Tunes
Vila Real
Ayamonte
Huelva
Sevilla
Alhambra

Lagos
Loule
Faro
Cacela Velha
Utrera
WHITE HILL TOWNS
Bobadilla
Granada
SIERRA NEVADA

Salema
Albufeira
Tavira
Guadalquivir
Jerez
Arcos
Zahara
Grazalema
Antequera
Málaga
Frigiliana
Nerja
Nerja Caves

Sanlucar
Rota
Cádiz
Benaojan
Ronda
Pileta Caves
Marbella
Torremolinos
Fuengirola
Motril
Salobreña
COSTA DEL SOL

Medina-Sidonia
San Pedro
Costa de la Luz
Vejer
Cabo Trafalgar
Algeciras
La Linea
GIBRALTAR (UK)

Atlantic Ocean
Tarifa
Strait of Gibraltar
CEUTA (Spain)

Tangier
MOROCCO
Tétouan

S P A

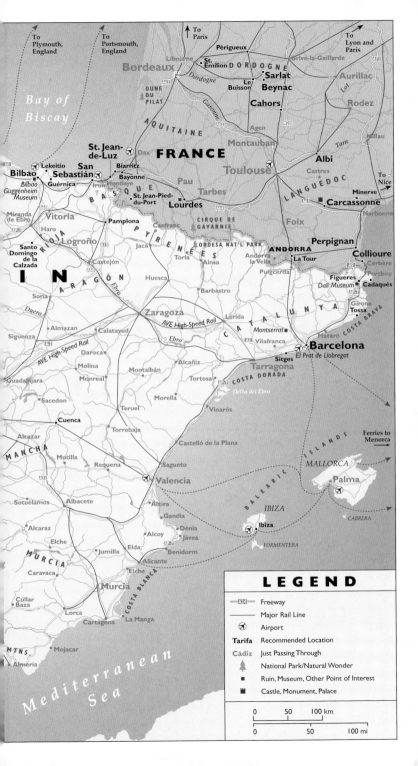

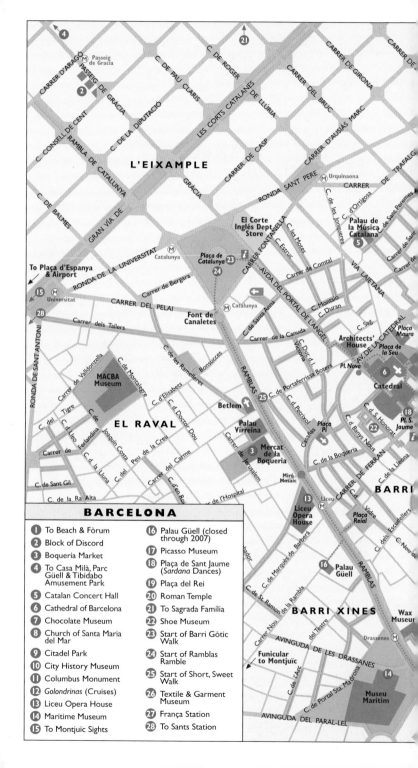

BARCELONA

1. To Beach & Fòrum
2. Block of Discord
3. Boquería Market
4. To Casa Milà, Parc Güell & Tibidabo Amusement Park
5. Catalan Concert Hall
6. Cathedral of Barcelona
7. Chocolate Museum
8. Church of Santa Maria del Mar
9. Citadel Park
10. City History Museum
11. Columbus Monument
12. *Golondrinas* (Cruises)
13. Liceu Opera House
14. Maritime Museum
15. To Montjuïc Sights
16. Palau Güell (closed through 2007)
17. Picasso Museum
18. Plaça de Sant Jaume (*Sardana* Dances)
19. Plaça del Rei
20. Roman Temple
21. To Sagrada Família
22. Shoe Museum
23. Start of Barri Gòtic Walk
24. Start of Ramblas Ramble
25. Start of Short, Sweet Walk
26. Textile & Garment Museum
27. França Station
28. To Sants Station

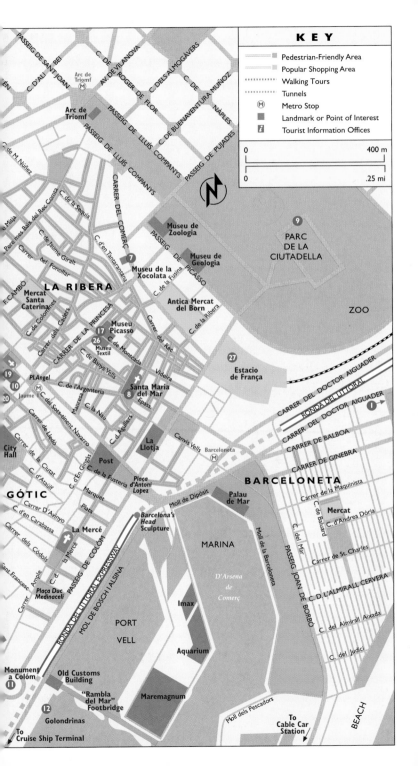

KEY

	Pedestrian-Friendly Area
	Popular Shopping Area
··········	Walking Tours
··········	Tunnels
Ⓜ	Metro Stop
■	Landmark or Point of Interest
i	Tourist Information Offices

0 ———————— 400 m
0 ———————— .25 mi

PASSEIG DE SANT JOAN

C. DE VILANOVA

AV. DE ROGER DE FLOR

C. DELS ALMOGAVERS

C. D'ALI BEI

Arc de Triomf Ⓜ

C. DE

C. DE BUENAVENTURA MUÑOZ

NAPLES

Arc de Triomf

PASSEIG DE LLUÍS COMPANYS

PASSEIG DE PUJADES

C. de M. Núñez

CARRER DEL COMERÇ

PASSEIG DE LLUÍS COMPANYS

⑨

PARC DE LA CIUTADELLA

e Mitja

C. de Jaume Giralt

Pere Ines Baix del Rec Comta

C. del Fonollar

C. de la Sèquia

C. en Tantarantana

PASSEIG DE PICASSO

Museu de Zoologia

Museu de Geologia

⑦ **Museu de la Xocolata**

C. de la Fusina

LA RIBERA

F. CAMBÓ

Mercat Santa Caterina

C. de Colomines

C. dels Cadels

CARRER DE LA PRINCESA

⑰ **Museu Picasso**

㉖ **Museu Textil**

C. de Montcada

C. de Banys Vells

C. de l'Argenteria

Videira

Antica Mercat del Born

CARRER del Rec

C. de la Ribera

Estacio de França ㉗

ZOO

⑲

⑩

⑳

Pl.Angel

Ⓜ Jaume

C. del Sots-tinent Navarro

Manresa

C. la Nau

Santa Maria del Mar ⑧

Epass.

C. d'Aguilers

C. de Lledó

City Hall

C. de la Ciutat

C. d'Arauf

C. d'En Gignas

C. de la Fustería

C. d'Aguilers

La Llotja

Canvis Vells

Barceloneta Ⓜ

CARRER DEL DOCTOR AIGUADER

RONDA DEL LITTORAL

CARRER DEL DOCTOR AIGUADER

CARRER DE BALBOA

CARRER DE GINEBRA

BARCELONETA

ℹ

GÓTIC

Carrer D'Avinyo

C. d'en Carabassa

Carrer dels Codols

Sant Francesc

Carrer Ample

Marquet

Plata

Post

Plaça d'Antoni Lopez

Moll de Dipósit

Palau de Mar

Carrer de la Maquinista

Mercat

C. de Ballard

C. d'Andrea Dória

PASSEIG JOAN DE BORBO

La Mercé

Pza Mercé

Barcelona's Head Sculpture

MARINA

Moll de la Barceloneta

C. del Mar

Carrer de St. Charles

Plaça Duc Medinaceli

PASSEIG DE COLOM

RONDA DEL LITTORAL EXPRESSWAY

MOLL DE BOSCH I ALSINA

D'Arsena de Comerç

C. D. L'ALMIRALL CERVERA

C. del Almirall Aixada

Imax

Monument a Colóm ⑪

Old Customs Building

PORT VELL

Aquarium

C. del Judici

⑫

"Rambla del Mar" Footbridge

Maremagnum

Golondrinas

To Cruise Ship Terminal

Moll dels Pescadors

To Cable Car Station

BEACH

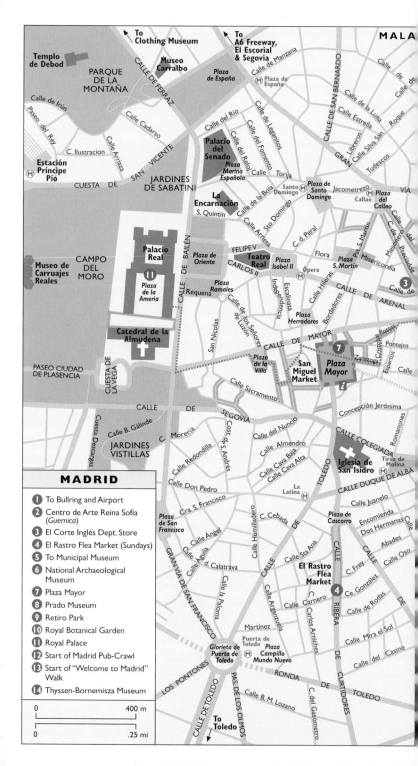

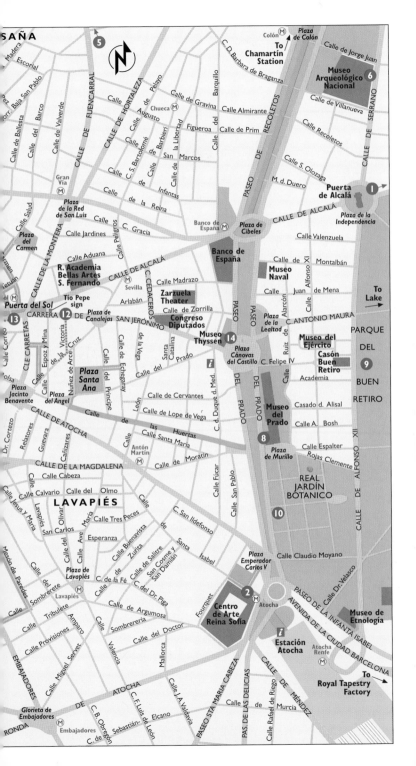

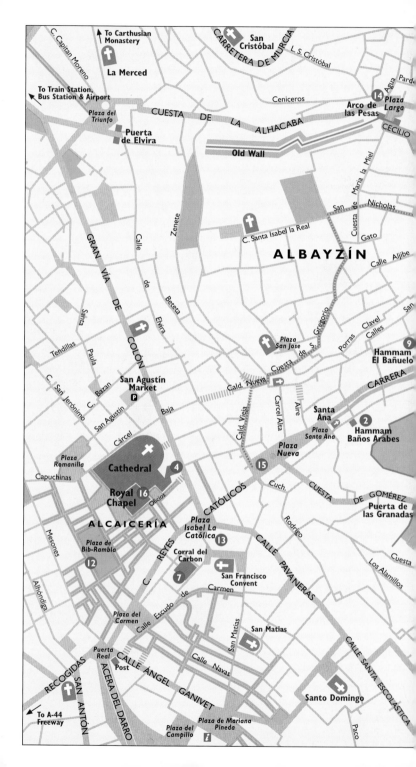

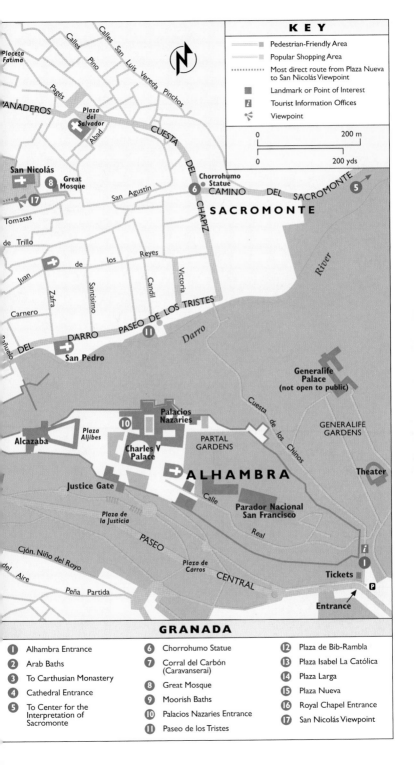

KEY

■ Pedestrian-Friendly Area

■ Popular Shopping Area

⋯⋯⋯ Most direct route from Plaza Nueva to San Nicolás Viewpoint

■ Landmark or Point of Interest

i Tourist Information Offices

✶ Viewpoint

0   200 m

0   200 yds

N

Placeta Fatima

Calles San Luis

Calles Pino

Vereda Pinchos

PANADEROS

Pagés

Plaza del Salvador

Abad

CUESTA

San Nicolás

Great Mosque **8**

San Agustín

DEL

Chorrohumo Statue

6 CAMINO DEL SACROMONTE **5**

CHAPIZ

SACROMONTE

Tomasas

17

de Trillo

de los Reyes

Juan

Zafra

Santísimo

Candil

Victoria

River

Carnero

PASEO DE LOS TRISTES

DARRO

11

Darro

añuelo DEL

San Pedro

Generalife Palace (not open to public)

Cuesta de los Chinos

GENERALIFE GARDENS

Palacios Nazaries

10

Plaza Aljibes

PARTAL GARDENS

Alcazaba

Charles V Palace

ALHAMBRA

Theater

Justice Gate

Calle

Plaza de la Justicia

Parador Nacional San Francisco

Cjón. Niño del Royo

PASEO

Real

i

1

del Aire

Peña Partida

Plaza de Carros

CENTRAL

Tickets

P

Entrance

GRANADA

1 Alhambra Entrance

2 Arab Baths

3 To Carthusian Monastery

4 Cathedral Entrance

5 To Center for the Interpretation of Sacromonte

6 Chorrohumo Statue

7 Corral del Carbón (Caravansarei)

8 Great Mosque

9 Moorish Baths

10 Palacios Nazaries Entrance

11 Paseo de los Tristes

12 Plaza de Bib-Rambla

13 Plaza Isabel La Católica

14 Plaza Larga

15 Plaza Nueva

16 Royal Chapel Entrance

17 San Nicolás Viewpoint

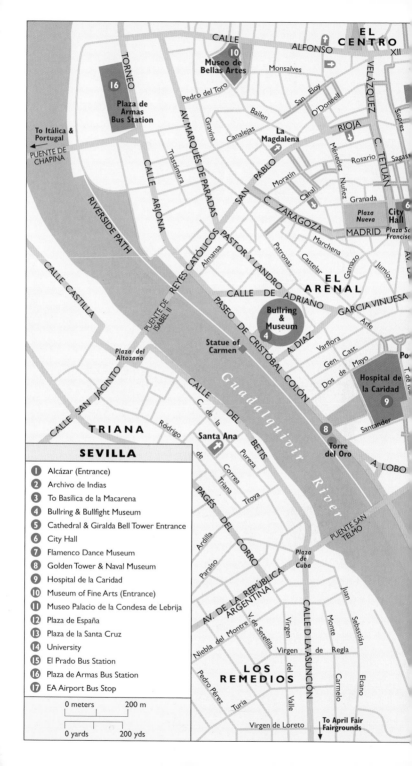

SEVILLA

1. Alcázar (Entrance)
2. Archivo de Indias
3. To Basílica de la Macarena
4. Bullring & Bullfight Museum
5. Cathedral & Giralda Bell Tower Entrance
6. City Hall
7. Flamenco Dance Museum
8. Golden Tower & Naval Museum
9. Hospital de la Caridad
10. Museum of Fine Arts (Entrance)
11. Museo Palacio de la Condesa de Lebrija
12. Plaza de España
13. Plaza de la Santa Cruz
14. University
15. El Prado Bus Station
16. Plaza de Armas Bus Station
17. EA Airport Bus Stop

0 meters   200 m

0 yards   200 yds

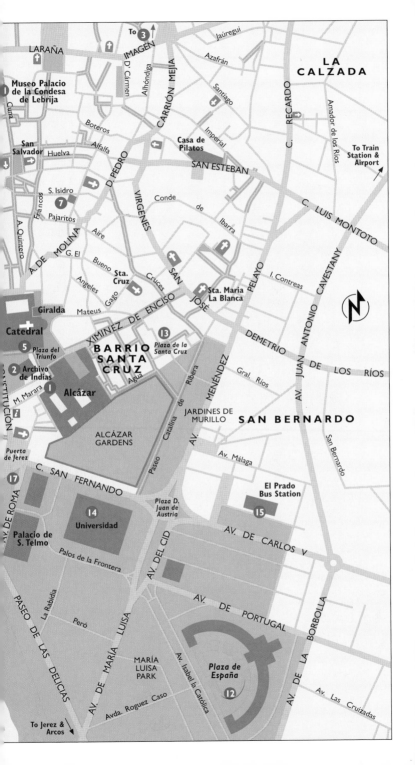

Rick Steves'

SPAIN
2007

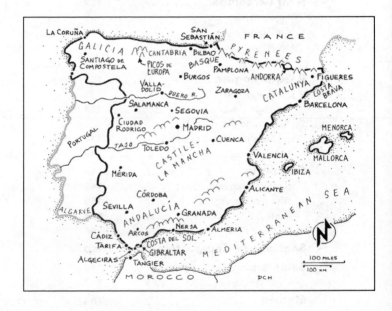

AVALON
TRAVEL

CONTENTS

Top Destinations in Spain

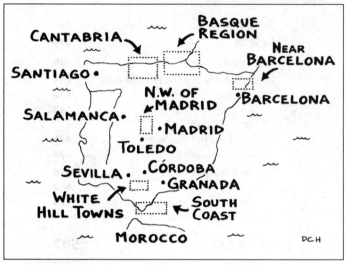

INTRODUCTION

Like a grandpa bouncing a baby on his knee, Spain is a mix of old and new, modern and traditional. Spain can fill your travel days with world-class art, folk life, exotic foods, friendly people, sunshine, and flamenco. And, in spite of its recent economic boom, Spain remains affordable. Tourism is huge here. With 40 million inhabitants, Spain entertains 50 million visitors annually. Spain is very popular—and on your trip, you'll learn why.

This book gives you all the information and opinions necessary to wring the maximum value out of your limited time and money. If you plan a month or less in Spain, this lean and mean little book is all you need.

Experiencing Spain's culture, people, and natural wonders economically and hassle-free has been my goal for three decades of traveling, tour guiding, and writing. With this book, I pass on to you the lessons I've learned, updated for 2007.

Rick Steves' Spain is a tour guide in your pocket, with a balanced, comfortable mix of exciting cities and cozy towns, topped off with an exotic dollop of Morocco. It covers the predictable biggies and stirs in a healthy dose of "Back Door" intimacy. Along with seeing a bullfight, the Prado, and flamenco, you'll greet pilgrims at Santiago de Compostela, visit a bull bar in Madrid, and buy cookies from cloistered nuns in a sun-parched Andalusian town. I've been selective, including only the most exciting sights and experiences. Rather than listing Spain's countless whitewashed Andalusian hill towns, I recommend the top stops: Arcos de la Frontera and Ronda.

The best is, of course, only my opinion. But after spending half my adult life researching Europe, I've developed a sixth sense for what travelers enjoy.

This Information Is Accurate and Up-to-Date

This book is updated every year. Most guidebook publishers can only afford an update once every two or three years (and even then, it's often by e-mail or fax). Since this book is selective, covering only the places that make the best three weeks or so in Spain, it's easy for me to get it updated in person each summer. The telephone numbers and hours of sights listed in this book are accurate as of mid-2006. Even with annual updates, things change. Still, if you're traveling with the current edition of this book, I guarantee you're using the most up-to-date information available in print (for the latest, see www .ricksteves.com/update). Also at our Web site, you'll find a valuable list of reports and experiences—good and bad—from fellow travelers who have used this book (www.ricksteves.com/feedback).

Use this year's edition. People who try to save a few bucks by traveling with an old book learn the seriousness of their mistake... in Spain. Your trip costs about $10 per waking hour. Your time is valuable. This guidebook saves lots of time.

About This Book

This book is organized by destination. Each destination is covered as a mini-vacation on its own, filled with exciting sights and homey, affordable places to stay. In the following chapters, you'll find these sections:

Planning Your Time offers ideas on how to best use your limited time in each destination.

Orientation includes tourist information, city transportation, and easy-to-read maps designed to make the text clear and your arrival smooth.

Sights provides a succinct overview of the most important sights, arranged by neighborhood, with ratings:

▲▲▲—Don't miss;

▲▲—Try hard to see;

▲—Worthwhile if you can make it;

No rating—Worth knowing about.

Sleeping is a guide to my favorite hotels, from budget deals to splurges.

Eating offers good-value restaurants, ranging from inexpensive cafeterias to romantic cafés.

Transportation Connections lays the groundwork for your smooth arrival and departure, explaining connections by bus, train, and plane. It also includes some route tips for drivers, with recommended roadside attractions along the way.

The **appendix** is a traveler's tool kit, with telephone tips, a climate chart, a list of holidays and festivals, and a brief look at Spanish history and culture.

Browse through this book, choose your favorite destinations, and link them up. Then have a great trip! You'll travel like a temporary local, getting the absolute most out of every mile, minute, and euro. As you travel the route I know and love, I'm happy you'll be meeting some of my favorite Spanish people.

PLANNING

Trip Costs

Five components make up your trip cost: airfare, surface transportation, room and board, sightseeing and entertainment, and shopping and miscellany.

Airfare: Don't try to sort through the mess. Find and use a good travel agent. A basic round-trip flight from the US to Barcelona or Madrid should cost $600 to $1,000, depending on where you fly from and when you go. Always consider saving time and money in Europe by flying "open jaw" (into one city and out of another; e.g., into Barcelona and out of Santiago de Compostela, or Lisbon, Portugal).

Surface Transportation: For a three-week whirlwind trip of all my recommended destinations, allow $350 per person for second-class trains and buses ($500 for first-class trains). For a three-week car rental, tolls, gas, and insurance, allow $750 per person (based on two people sharing). It's cheaper to lease (see page 20). A car rental or lease is cheapest when reserved from the US. Train passes are normally sold only outside of Europe. While they are a convenience, you may save money by simply buying tickets as you go (see "Transportation," page 14).

Room and Board: You can thrive in Spain on $90 a day per person for room and board. This allows $10 for lunch, $20 for dinner, and $60 for lodging (based on two people splitting the cost of a $120 double room that includes breakfast). That's doable. If you've got more money, I've listed great ways to spend it. Students and tightwads do it on $30 a day ($15 per hostel bed, $15 for meals and snacks).

Sightseeing and Entertainment: In big cities, figure about $7 per major sight (Barcelona's Picasso Museum, Madrid's Prado), $2 for minor ones (climbing church towers), and about $30 for splurge experiences (flamenco, bullfights). An overall average of $10 a day works for most. Don't skimp here. After all, this category is the driving force behind your trip—you came to sightsee, enjoy, and experience Spain.

Shopping and Miscellany: Figure roughly $1.25 per coffee, beer, ice-cream cone, and postcard. Shopping can vary in cost from nearly nothing to a small fortune. Good budget travelers find that this category has little to do with assembling a trip full of lifelong and wonderful memories.

When to Go

Spring and fall offer the best combination of good weather, light crowds, long days, and plenty of tourist and cultural activities.

July and August are the most crowded and expensive in the coastal areas, and less crowded but uncomfortably hot and dusty in the interior. Air-conditioning is worth the splurge. During these steamy months, lunch breaks can be long, especially in Andalucía.

Off-season, roughly October through April, expect sights to have shorter hours, lunchtime breaks, and fewer activities. Confirm your sightseeing plans locally, especially when traveling off-season.

For weather specifics, see the climate chart in the appendix.

Sightseeing Priorities

Depending on the length of your trip, here are my recommended priorities:

3 days:	Madrid and Toledo
6 days, add:	Sevilla, Granada
10 days, add:	Barcelona, Andalucía (White Hill Towns)
13 days, add:	Costa del Sol, Morocco
15 days, add:	Salamanca, Segovia
17 days, add:	Santiago de Compostela
21 days, add:	Basque Region (San Sebastián and Bilbao), Cantabria (northern Spain)

This includes everything on the map on page 7.

Travel Smart

Your trip to Spain is like a complex play—easier to follow and really appreciate on a second viewing. While no one does the same trip twice to gain that advantage, reading this book in its entirety before your trip accomplishes much the same thing.

Reread this book as you travel, and visit local tourist information offices. Upon arrival in a new town, lay the groundwork for a smooth departure; write down the schedule for the train or bus you'll take when you depart. Buy a phone card and use it for reservations and confirmations. Use taxis in the big cities, bring along a water bottle, and linger in the shade.

Design an itinerary that enables you to visit museums and festivals on the right days. As you read this book, note the days when sights are closed. Saturdays are virtually weekdays with earlier closing hours and no rush hour (though transportation connections can be less frequent than on weekdays). Sundays have the same pros and cons as they do for travelers in the US. Sightseeing attractions are generally open, shops and banks are closed, and public transportation options are fewer. City traffic is light. Rowdy evenings are rare on Sundays.

Plan ahead for banking, laundry, Internet stops, and picnics. To maximize rootedness, minimize one-night stands. Mix intense and relaxed periods. Every trip (and every traveler) needs at least a few slack days. Pace yourself. Assume you will return.

Connect with the culture. Set up your own quest for the best main square, paella, cloister, tapas bar, or whatever. Enjoy the friendliness of the Spanish people. Slow down and ask questions. Most locals are eager to point you in their idea of the right direction. Wear your money belt, pack a pocket-size notebook to organize your thoughts, and practice the virtue of simplicity. Those who expect to travel smart, do.

RESOURCES

Tourist Information Offices

In the US

National tourist offices in the US are a wealth of information. Before your trip, scan their Web sites. If you call, get the free general information packet and request any specific information you want (such as regional and city maps and festival schedules).

Spain Tourist Office: www.okspain.org, www.spain.info, tel. 212/265-8822.

Gibraltar Information Bureau: www.gibraltar.gov.uk, tel. 202/452-1108.

In Spain

Your best first stop in a new city is the Turismo (tourist information office—abbreviated as **TI** in this book). Try to arrive, or at least telephone, before it closes. Get a city map and advice on public transportation (including bus and train schedules), special events, and recommendations for nightlife. Many TIs have information on the entire country or at least the region, so try to pick up maps for towns you'll be visiting later in your trip.

While TIs are eager to book you a room, use their room-finding service only as a last resort (bloated prices, fees, no opinions, and they take a cut from your host). You'll get a far better value by using the listings in this book and booking direct.

Rick Steves' Guidebooks, Public Television Shows, and Radio Shows

With the help of my staff, I produce materials to help you plan your trip and travel smoothly.

Guidebooks: This book is one of a series of 30+ books on European travel that includes country guidebooks, city and regional guidebooks, and my budget-travel skills handbook, *Rick Steves' Europe Through the Back Door.* All are annually updated. My

Whirlwind Three-Week Trip of Spain

Day	Plan	Sleep in
1	Arrive in Barcelona	Barcelona
2	Barcelona	Barcelona
3	AVE train to Madrid	Madrid
4	Madrid	Madrid
5	Day trip to El Escorial/Valley of Fallen	Madrid
6	Toledo	Toledo
7	AVE train to Sevilla	Sevilla
8	Sevilla	Sevilla
9	To Arcos	Arcos
10	To Tarifa	Tarifa
11	Day trip to Morocco	Tarifa
12	To Nerja via Gibraltar	Nerja
13	To Granada	Granada
14	Granada	Granada
15	To Segovia	Segovia
16	To Salamanca via Ávila	Salamanca
17	Salamanca	Salamanca
18	To Santiago	Santiago
19	Santiago	Santiago
20	To Cantabria	Cantabria (Santillana or Comillas)
21	To San Sebastián via Bilbao	San Sebastián
22	San Sebastián	San Sebastián

This itinerary is designed to be done by public transportation, but can be done by car with a few variations. Spain's long distances make the option of flying for at least a portion of the trip worth considering. If you rent a car, it's best for the White Hill Towns (southern Spain), El Escorial/Valley of the Fallen (northwest of Madrid), and Cantabria (northern Spain), where sparse public transportation limits the efficiency of your sightseeing. To mix car and train transportation, consider getting a Spain Rail & Drive pass.

If you're a fan of Salvador Dalí's art, or if you want to make a pilgrimage to the holy site of Montserrat, allot an extra day for Barcelona for day trips. If you want more Moorish sights, stay another day in Sevilla to make a side-trip to Córdoba (45 min on AVE high-speed train). If you're not interested in day-tripping to Tangier, Morocco, you could skip Tarifa and go to Ronda instead.

To allow time to explore Gibraltar, add an extra day between Tarifa (or Ronda) and Nerja.

The above plan assumes you'll fly "open jaw" into Barcelona and out of San Sebastián. If you're returning to Barcelona or Madrid from San Sebastián, it's roughly an eight-hour train ride (night train possible) or a one-hour flight. Or you can cross into France and take the six-hour TGV train to Paris for more adventures!

Two-Week Itineraries: You can end the three-week route (described above) a week early by returning to Madrid from Salamanca and saving northern Spain for another trip.

Here's another alternative, which could include a few car days in southern Spain near the end of your trip: Start in Barcelona (stay two days); train to Madrid (stay five days total, with two days in Madrid and three for side-trips to Toledo, El Escorial, and Segovia or Ávila); train to Granada (two days); bus to Nerja (one day, could rent car here); both Ronda and Arcos for drivers, or just Ronda by train (two days); to Sevilla (drop off car, two days); and then train to Madrid and fly home.

phrase books—for Spanish, Portuguese, French, German, and Italian—are practical and budget-oriented. My other books include *Europe 101* (a crash course on art and history), *European Christmas* (on traditional and modern-day celebrations), and *Postcards from Europe* (a fun memoir of my travels over 25 years). For a complete list of my books, see the inside of the last page of this book.

Public Television and Radio Shows: My television series, *Rick Steves' Europe,* covers European destinations. My weekly public radio show, *Travels with Rick Steves,* features interviews with travel experts from around the world. All the TV scripts and radio shows are at www.ricksteves.com. Listen to the shows at any time—or download them onto your MP3 player to take along on your trip.

Other Guidebooks

Especially if you'll be traveling beyond my recommended destinations, you may want some supplemental information. When you consider the improvements they'll make in your $3,000 vacation, $30 for extra maps and books is money well spent. Especially for several people traveling by car, the extra weight and expense are negligible. One good tip can save the price of an extra guidebook. Note that none of the following guidebooks are updated annually; check the copyright date before you buy.

Lonely Planet's guides to Spain are thorough, well-researched, and packed with good maps and hotel recommendations. The similar *Rough Guide to Spain* is hip and insightful, written by British researchers.

Students and vagabonds like the highly opinionated *Let's Go: Spain & Portugal,* updated by Harvard students. Let's Go is best for backpackers who stay at hostels, use railpasses, and dive into the youth and nightlife scene.

Older travelers enjoy Frommer's Spain guides even though those, like the Fodor's guides, ignore alternatives that enable travelers to save money by dirtying their fingers in the local culture.

The popular, skinny Michelin Green Guides to Spain are excellent, especially if you're driving. They're known for their city and sightseeing maps, dry but concise and helpful information on all major sights, and good cultural and historical background. English editions are sold in Spain. The well-written and thoughtful Cadogan guide to Spain is excellent for "A" students on the road. The encyclopedic Blue Guides to Spain are dry as the plains in Spain, but just right for scholarly types.

The Eyewitness series has about a dozen editions covering Spain, including Barcelona, Madrid, and Sevilla/Andalucía. They're extremely popular for great, easy-to-grasp graphics and photos, 3-D cutaways of buildings, aerial-view maps of historic

Begin Your Trip at www.ricksteves.com

At our travel Web site, you'll find a wealth of free information on European destinations, including fresh monthly news and helpful tips from thousands of fellow travelers.

Our online Travel Store offers travel bags and accessories specially designed by Rick Steves to help you travel smarter and lighter. These include Rick's popular carry-on bags (wheeled and rucksack versions), money belts, totes, toiletries kits, adapters, other accessories, and a wide selection of guidebooks, planning maps, and DVDs.

Choosing the right railpass for your trip—amidst hundreds of options—can drive you nutty. We'll help you choose the best pass for your needs, plus give you a bunch of free extras.

Travel agents will tell you about mainstream tours of Europe, but they won't tell you about Rick Steves' tours. Rick Steves' Europe Through the Back Door travel company offers more than two dozen itineraries and 400+ departures reaching the best destinations in this book...and beyond. You'll enjoy great guides, a fun bunch of travel partners (with small groups of generally around 25), and plenty of room to spread out in a big, comfy bus. You'll find European adventures to fit every vacation length. To get our Tour Catalog and a free Rick Steves Tour Experience DVD (filmed on location during an actual tour), visit www.ricksteves.com.

---

neighborhoods, and cultural background. But the written content in Eyewitness is relatively skimpy, and the books weigh a ton. I simply borrow them for a minute from other travelers at certain sights to make sure I'm aware of that place's highlights. *Time Out* travel guides provide good, detailed coverage of Madrid, Barcelona, and Andalucía, particularly on arts and entertainment.

Recommended Books and Movies

To get the feel of Spain past and present, check out a few of these books or films:

Non-Fiction: *A Traveller's History of Spain* (Juan Lalaguna), *The Basque History of the World* (Mark Kurlansky), *Empire: How Spain Became a World Power* (Henry Kamen), *The Reformation: A History* (Diarmaid MacCulloch), *The New Spaniards* (John Hooper), *Moorish Spain* (Richard Fletcher), *Iberia* (James Michener), *Spain: A History* (Raymond Carr), and *Tapas: The Little Dishes of Spain* (Penelope Casas). Also consider these memoirs: *Spanish Lessons* (Derek Lambert), *Driving Over Lemons: An Optimist in Spain* (Chris Stewart), *On Pilgrimage* (Jennifer Lash),

South from Granada (Gerald Brenan), *The Tomb in Seville* (Norman Lewis), *Homage to Catalonia* (George Orwell), and *Following the Milky Way: A Pilgrimage on the Camino de Santiago* (Elyn Aviva).

Fiction: *The Sun Also Rises, For Whom the Bell Tolls,* and *Death in the Afternoon* (Ernest Hemingway); *Don Quixote* (Miguel de Cervantes); *The Heretic* (Lewis Weinstein); *Stories from Spain* (Genevieve Barlow and William N. Stivers); and *Tales of the Alhambra* (Washington Irving).

Films: *The Mystery of Picasso* (1956), *El Cid* (1961), *Love and Pain and the Whole Damn Thing* (1972), *Carmen* (1983), *Blood Wedding* (1981), *Man of La Mancha* (1972), *Barcelona* (1994), and *Open Your Eyes* (1997). Pedro Almodóvar is probably the most famous Spanish director alive today, with a long list of fine films that includes *All About My Mother, Bad Education,* and *Women on the Verge of a Nervous Breakdown.*

Maps

The black-and-white maps in this book, drawn by Dave Hoerlein, are concise and simple. Dave, who is well-traveled in Spain, has designed the maps to help you locate recommended places and get to the tourist offices, where you can pick up a more in-depth map (usually free) of the city or region. Better maps are sold at newsstands—take a look before you buy to be sure the map has the level of detail you want.

Michelin maps are available—and cheaper than in the US—throughout Spain in bookstores, newsstands, and gas stations. Train travelers can do fine with a simple rail map (such as the one that comes with a train pass) and city maps from the tourist information offices. For drivers, I'd recommend a 1:200,000- or 1:300,000-scale map.

PRACTICALITIES

Red Tape: Currently, Americans need a passport, but no visa or shots, to travel in Spain or Morocco.

Time: In Europe—and throughout this book—you'll be using the 24-hour clock. After 12:00 noon, keep going: 13:00, 14:00, and so on. For anything over 12, subtract 12 and add p.m. (14:00 is 2:00 p.m.).

Spain's time zone is six/nine hours ahead of the East/West coasts of the US. Moroccan time can run up to two hours earlier than Spanish time.

Business Hours: For visitors, Spain is a land of strange and frustrating schedules. Many businesses respect the afternoon siesta. When it's 100 degrees in the shade, you'll understand why.

The biggest museums stay open all day. Smaller ones often close for a siesta. Shops are generally open from 9:00 to 13:00 and from 16:00 to 20:00, longer in touristy places. Small shops are often open on Saturday only in the morning, and are closed all day Sunday.

Discounts: Don't expect youth or senior discounts on sights in Spain. Discounts are generally available only to people who are members of the European Union and "reciprocating countries," meaning countries that offer discounts to European youths and seniors. The US isn't big on giving price breaks to Europeans.

Metric: Get used to metric. A liter is about a quart (four quarts to a gallon). A kilometer is six-tenths of a mile. I figure kilometers to miles by cutting them in half and adding back 10 percent of the original (120 km: 60 + 12 = 72 miles, 300 km: 150 + 30 = 180 miles).

Watt's Up? If you're bringing electrical gear, you'll need a two-prong adapter plug (sold cheap at travel stores) and a converter. Travel appliances often have convenient, built-in converters; look for a voltage switch marked 120V (US) and 240V (Europe).

News: Americans keep in touch in Europe with the *International Herald Tribune* (published almost daily via satellite). Every Tuesday, the European editions of *Time* and *Newsweek* hit the stands with articles of particular interest to travelers in Europe. Sports addicts can get their fix from *USA Today*. Good Web sites include www.europeantimes.com and http://news.bbc .co.uk. Many hotels have CNN or BBC television channels.

Theft Alert: Thieves target tourists throughout Spain, especially in Barcelona, Madrid, Granada, and Sevilla. While hotel rooms are generally safe, thieves break into cars, snatch purses, and pick pockets. Thieves zipping by on motorbikes grab handbags from pedestrians or even from cars in traffic (by reaching through open car windows at stoplights). A fight or commotion is created to enable pickpockets to work unnoticed. Be on guard, use a money belt, and treat any disturbance around you as a smoke screen for theft. Don't believe any "police officers" looking for counterfeit bills. Drivers should read the tips on page 22. When traveling by train, keep your backpack in sight and get a *litera* (berth in an attendant-monitored sleeping car) for safety on overnight trips.

Reservations for Granada's Alhambra: The only sight you might want to reserve tickets for in advance is this remarkable Moorish hilltop stronghold that consists of palaces, gardens, a fortress, and a rich history. You can make reservations for the Alhambra upon arrival in Spain (ideally before you reach Granada), but I mention it here for those who like to nail things down online before they leave home. For more information, see page 334 of the Granada chapter.

MONEY

Banking

Bring plastic (ATM, debit, or credit cards) along with several hundred dollars in hard cash as an emergency backup. Traveler's checks are a waste of time (waiting at banks) and a waste of money (paying to purchase and then cash checks).

To withdraw cash from a bank machine, you'll need a debit card that can withdraw money from your bank account, plus a PIN code (numbers only, no letters on European keypads).

Spain has readily available, easy-to-use, 24-hour ATMs with English instructions. You can travel painlessly throughout Spain with a debit card. Before you go, verify with your bank that your card will work, inquire about fees (can be up to $5 per transaction), and alert them that you'll be making withdrawals in Europe; otherwise, the bank may not approve transactions if it perceives unusual spending patterns. Bring an extra card in case one gets demagnetized or eaten by a temperamental machine.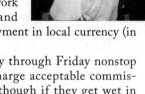

Visa and MasterCard are more commonly accepted than American Express. Just like at home, credit or debit cards work easily at larger hotels, restaurants, and stores, but smaller businesses prefer payment in local currency (in small bills—break large bills at a bank).

Banks are generally open Monday through Friday nonstop from 9:00 to 14:00. Spanish banks charge acceptable commissions for changing traveler's checks (though if they get wet in your money belt, they will be refused). American Express offices

---

Exchange Rate

I list prices in euros throughout the Spain chapters. In the Morocco chapters, I list prices in dirhams (the official currency), although euros and dollars are usually accepted.

1 euro (€) = about $1.20

Like the dollar, the euro is broken down into 100 cents. You'll find coins ranging from 1 cent to 2 euros, and bills from 5 euros to 500 euros. To roughly convert prices in euros to dollars, add 20 percent to Spanish prices: €20 is about $24, €45 is about $55, and so on.

Damage Control for Lost or Stolen Cards

If you lose your credit, debit, or ATM card, you can stop people from using your card by reporting the loss immediately to the respective customer-assistance centers. If you promptly report your card lost or stolen, you typically won't be held responsible for any unauthorized transactions on your account, although many banks charge a liability fee. Call these 24-hour US numbers collect: Visa (tel. 410/581-9994), MasterCard (tel. 636/722-7111), and American Express (tel. 336/393-1111).

At a minimum, have the following information ready: the name of the financial institution that issued you the card, along with the type of card (classic, platinum). Ideally, plan ahead and pack photocopies of your cards—front and back—to expedite their replacement. Providing the following information allows a quicker cancellation of your missing card: full card number, whether you are the primary or secondary cardholder, the cardholder's name exactly as printed on the card, billing address, home phone number, circumstances of the loss or theft, and identification verification (such as your birth date, your mother's maiden name, or your Social Security number—memorize this, don't carry a copy). If you are the secondary cardholder, you'll also need to provide the primary cardholder's identification verification details. You can generally receive a temporary card within two or three business days in Europe.

(found only in big cities) offer mediocre rates but change any type of traveler's check without a commission. Shop around. Sometimes the hole-in-the-wall exchange offices offer better deals than the bank. Better yet, use a cash machine.

You should use a money belt (a pouch with a strap that you buckle around your waist like a belt and wear under your clothes). Thieves target tourists. A money belt provides peace of mind, and allows you to carry lots of cash safely. Change a week's worth of money, stuff it in your money belt, and travel!

VAT Refunds and Customs Regulations

VAT Refunds for Shoppers: Wrapped into the purchase price of your souvenirs is a Value Added Tax (VAT), which is about 14 percent. If you make a purchase of more than €90 in Spain at a store that participates in the VAT refund scheme, you're entitled to get most of that tax back. Personally, I've never felt that VAT refunds are worth the hassle, but if you do, here's the scoop.

If you're lucky, the merchant will subtract the tax when you make your purchase (this is more likely to occur if the store ships the goods to your home). Otherwise, here's what you'll need to do:

• **Get the paperwork:** Have the merchant completely fill out the necessary refund document, called a "cheque." You'll have to present your passport at the store.

• **Get your stamp at the border or airport:** Have your cheque(s) stamped at the border or airport at your last stop in the EU by the customs agent who deals with VAT refunds. It's best to keep your purchases in your carry-on for viewing, but if they're too large or dangerous (such as knives) to carry on, then track down the proper customs agent to inspect them before you check your bag. You're not supposed to use your purchased goods before you leave. If you show up at customs wearing your new flamenco outfit, officials might look the other way—or deny you a refund.

• **Collect your refund:** You'll need to return your stamped documents to the retailer or its representative. Many merchants work with a service, such as Global Refund (www.globalrefund .com) or Premier Tax Free (www.premiertaxfree.com), which have offices at major airports, ports, or border crossings. These services, which extract a 4 percent fee, can refund your money immediately in your currency of choice or credit your card (within two billing cycles). If you have to deal directly with the retailer, mail the store your stamped documents and then wait. It could take months.

Customs Regulations: You can take home $800 in souvenirs per person duty-free. The next $1,000 is taxed at a flat 3 percent. After that, you pay the individual item's duty rate. You can also bring in duty-free a liter of alcohol (slightly more than a standard-size bottle of wine), a carton of cigarettes, and up to 100 cigars. As for food, anything in cans or sealed jars is acceptable. Don't try to bring home meat (even if it's dried and cured), cheeses, and fresh fruits and veggies. To check customs rules and duty rates, visit www.customs.gov.

TRANSPORTATION

By Car or Train?
Cars are best for three or more traveling together (especially families with small kids), those packing heavy, and those scouring the countryside. Trains and buses are best for solo travelers, blitz tourists, and city-to-city travelers.

Overview of Trains and Buses
Public transportation in Spain is getting slick, modern, and efficient. The best option is to mix bus and train travel. Always verify schedules before your departure. Don't leave a station without your next day's schedule options in hand. To ask for a schedule

at an information window, say, *"Horario para* _____ – _____ (fill in names of cities), *por favor."* (The local TI will sometimes have schedules available for you to take or copy.) To study train schedules in advance, visit Germany's excellent all-Europe Web site, http://bahn.hafas.de/bin/query.exe/en, or Spain's site, www.renfe.es. For Comes buses in southern Spain, check www.tgcomes.es.

Trains

While you could save money by purchasing tickets as you go, you may find the convenience of a railpass worth the extra cost, especially if you take some local trains that do not require reservations. You can buy a "flexi" railpass that allows travel for a given number of days over a longer period of time. If your trip also includes neighboring France, consider the France–Spain Pass (see chart on page 16). A Eurail Selectpass lets you travel even farther. Spain also offers a rail-and-drive pass, which gives you the ease of big-city train hops and the flexibility of a car for rural areas such as the Andalusian hill towns. These passes are sold only outside of Europe. For specifics, check the railpass chart on page 16, contact your travel agent, or see my Guide to European Eurail Passes at www.ricksteves.com/rail. Even if you have a railpass, use buses when they're more convenient and direct than the trains. Remember to reserve ahead for the fast AVE trains and overnight journeys. Buy your tickets a day in advance even for short rides; trains sell out.

The long second-class train ride from Madrid to Barcelona costs about $70; from Madrid to either Sevilla or Granada costs about $40–80 each. First class costs 50 percent more—often as much as a domestic flight (for flight fares, check www.iberia.com, www.vueling.com, or www.spainair.com). Using a railpass to cover several long trips can be a good value.

If you're buying point-to-point tickets, note that round-trip tickets are 20 percent cheaper than two one-way tickets. You can get a round-trip discount even if you start with a one-way ticket—as long as you save the ticket and make a return trip. For example, if you buy a one-way ticket from Barcelona to Madrid, visit Madrid, then decide to return to Barcelona, you can bring your one-way Barcelona–Madrid ticket to the train station and get a 40 percent discount on your return trip (this equals a total 20 percent discount for the round trip).

RENFE (the acronym for the Spanish national train system) used to mean "Really Exasperating, and Not For Everyone," but it has moved into the 21st century. To save time, consider buying tickets or reservations at the RENFE offices located in more than 100 city centers. These are more central and multilingual—also

Railpasses

Prices listed are for 2006 and are subject to change. For the latest prices, details, and train schedules (and easy online ordering), see my comprehensive *Guide to Eurail Passes* at www.ricksteves.com/rail.

"Saver" prices are per person for two or more people traveling together. "Youth" means under age 26. The fare for children 4–11 is half the adult individual fare or Saver fare. Kids under age 4 travel free.

SPAIN RAIL & DRIVE PASS

Any 3 rail days and 2 car days in 2 months.

Car Category	1st Class	Extra car day
Economy car	$249	$39
Compact car	262	50
Intermediate car	270	59
Compact automatic	305	95

Prices are per person, two traveling together. Solo travelers pay $50–$75 extra. Third and fourth people sharing car buy only the railpass. Extra rail days (max 2) cost $39 per day.

To order Rail & Drive passes, call your travel agent or Rail Europe at 800-438-7245. *This pass is not sold by Europe Through the Back Door.*

Map key:

Approximate point-to-point one-way second-class rail fares in US dollars. First class costs 50 percent more. Add up fares for your itinerary to see whether a railpass will save you money. Dashed lines are buses.

SPAIN PASS

	1st Class	2nd Class
3 days in 2 months	$234	$182
Extra rail days (max 7)	36	31

SPAIN-PORTUGAL PASS

	Individual 1st Class	Saver 1st Class
3 days in 2 months	$270	$238
Extra rail days (max 6)	37	32

SELECTPASS

This pass covers travel in three adjacent countries. Please visit www.ricksteves.com/rail for four- and five-country options.

	Individual 1st Class	Saver 1st Class	Youth 2nd Class
5 days in 2 months	$383	$325	$249
6 days in 2 months	423	360	275
8 days in 2 months	503	428	325
10 days in 2 months	580	493	375

FRANCE–SPAIN PASS

	Individual 1st Class	Individual 2nd Class	Saver 1st Class	Saver 2nd Class	Youth 2nd Class
4 days in 2 months	$325	$284	$284	$253	$211
Extra rail days (max 6)	36	32	32	28	25

less crowded and confusing—than the train station. Or, for information and reservations, dial RENFE's national number (tel. 902-240-202) from anywhere in Spain.

Spain categorizes trains this way:

The high-speed train called the **AVE** (AH-vay, stands for Alta Velocidad Española) whisks travelers between Madrid and Sevilla in less than three hours. Franco left Spain a train system  that didn't fit Europe's gauge, and AVE trains run on European-gauge tracks. AVE trains can be priced differently according to their time of departure. Peak hours *(punta)* are most expensive, followed by *llano* and *valle* (quietest and cheapest times). AVE is almost entirely covered by the Eurailpass (book ahead, a seat reservation fee from Madrid to Sevilla costs Eurailers about $11 in second class; $29 for first class, includes meal). A new Madrid–Barcelona link is now in operation, and other lines such as Córdoba–Málaga are set to open soon. The AVE line from Toledo to Madrid (only 30 min) effectively makes the old capital of Spain a bedroom community of the new capital.

The **TALGO** is fast, air-conditioned, and expensive, and runs on AVE rails. **Intercity** and **Electro** trains fall just behind TALGO in speed, comfort, and expense. **Rápido, Tranvía, Semidirecto,** and **Expreso** trains are generally slower. **Cercanías** are commuter trains for big-city workers and small-town tourists. **Regional** and **Correo** trains are slow, small-town milk runs. Trains get more expensive as they pick up speed, but all are cheaper per mile than their northern European counterparts. Spain loves to name trains, so you may encounter types of trains not listed here. The names Euromed, Alaris, Altaria, and Arco all indicate faster trains that require reservations.

Salidas means "departures" and *llegadas* is "arrivals." On train schedules, "LMXJVSD" stand for the days of the week in Spanish, starting with Monday. A train that runs "LMXJV-D" doesn't run on Saturdays. *Laborables* can mean Monday through Friday or Monday through Saturday. Most train stations have handy luggage lockers.

Overnight Trains: For long trips, I go overnight on the train or I fly (domestic shuttle flights are generally less than $100). Overnight trains (and buses) are usually less expensive and slower than the daytime rides. Most overnight trains have berths and beds that you can rent (not included in the cost of your train ticket or railpass). A sleeping berth *(litera)* costs about $15. A *coche cama,* or bed in a classy quad compartment, costs about $20; and a bed in a double costs about $25. Night trains are popular, so it's smart to book ahead. Travelers with first-class reservations are entitled to use comfortable "Intercity" lounges in train stations in Spain's major cities.

The term "Hotel Train" *(Trenhotel)* usually means fancy and expensive. The pricey overnight Hotel Train between Madrid and Lisbon is called the "Lusitania" (first class-$120, including a bed in a double compartment; second class-$95 in a quad; pay $30 or more for a sleeper if you have a railpass, additional cost for singles or a shower in your compartment). Unfortunately, no cheaper rail option exists between these two capital cities. You can save money by taking a bus, or save time by taking a plane. Hotel Train prices are at least as high between other major cities, such as Barcelona–Valencia or Barcelona–Madrid.

Overnight Trains to/from Europe: Pricey international Hotel Trains (mentioned above) connect France, Italy, and Switzerland with Spain. All of these spendy overnight trains (known collectively as Elipsos) have names: Francisco de Goya (Madrid–Paris), Joan Miró (Barcelona–Paris), Pau Casals (Barcelona–Zürich), and Salvador Dalí (Barcelona–Milan). Full fares range from $175 in a quad to $440 for a Gran Clase single compartment. Travelers with any railpass that covers at least one country on the route of travel (including Swiss Passes but not Swiss Cards) can use a railpass travel day and pay about half the full fare. For more information on international Hotel Trains, see www.elipsos.com. If you can easily afford to take a Hotel Train, consider flying instead to save time (for flight info, see page 108).

To avoid the expensive luxury of an international Hotel Train, you can take a cheaper train trip that involves a transfer at the Spanish border (at Irún on Madrid–Paris runs, at Cerbère on the eastern side). You'll connect to a normal night train with $20 *literas* (*couchette* berths) on one leg of the trip. This plan is more time-consuming, and may take two days of a flexipass.

Buses

Spain's bus system is confusing. There are a number of different bus companies (though usually clustered within one building), sometimes running buses to the same destinations and using the same transfer points. If you have to transfer, make sure to look for a bus with the same name/logo as the company you bought the ticket from. The larger stations have an information desk with all of the schedules. In smaller stations, check the destinations and schedules posted on each office window. Bus service on holidays, Saturdays, and especially Sundays can be less frequent.

If you arrive in a city by bus and plan to leave by bus, upon your arrival at the bus station check your departure options and buy

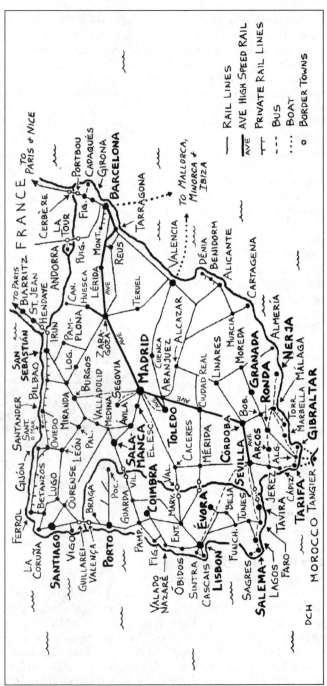

Public Transportation Routes in Iberia

a ticket in advance if necessary (and possible). If you're downtown, need a ticket, and the bus station isn't central, save time by asking at the tourist office about travel agencies that sell bus tickets.

Smoking is no longer allowed on buses, and most people respect this new law. This is the best evidence that Spain isn't stuck in the past—even though people are complaining all way into the future. You can (and most likely will be required to) stow your luggage under the bus. For longer rides, give some thought to which side of the bus will get the most sun, and sit on the opposite side, even if the bus is air-conditioned and has curtains. Your ride will likely come with a soundtrack: taped Spanish pop music, a radio, or sometimes videos. If you prefer silence, bring earplugs.

Drivers and station personnel rarely speak English. Buses generally lack WCs, but they stop every two hours or so for a break (usually 15 min, but can be up to 30). Drivers announce how long the stop will be, but if in doubt, ask the driver, "How many minutes here?" *("¿Cuántos minutos aquí?")* so you know if you have time to get out. Listen for the bus horn as a final call before departure. Bus stations have WCs (rarely with toilet paper) and cafés that offer quick and slightly overpriced food.

Taxis

Most taxis are reliable and cheap. Drivers generally respond kindly to the request, "How much is it to _____, more or less?" *("¿Cuánto cuesta a _____, más o menos?")* Spanish taxis have extra supplements (for luggage, nighttime, Sundays, train-station or airport pickup, and so on). Rounding the fare up to the nearest large coin (maximum of 10 percent) is adequate for a tip. City rides cost $4 to $6. Keep a map in

your hand so the cabbie knows (or thinks) you know where you're going. Big cities have plenty of taxis. In many cases, couples travel by cab for little more than two bus or subway tickets.

Car Rental and Leasing

Car rental is cheapest if arranged in advance from home. Call various companies, look online, or arrange a rental through your hometown travel agent, who can also help you out if anything goes wrong during your trip. The best rates are for renting weekly with unlimited mileage, or leasing (see "Leasing," below). You can pick up and drop off in medium-sized or larger cities. Big companies have offices in more cities and towns. Small rental companies can be cheaper, but aren't as flexible. Almost all rentals are manual by default, so you must specifically request an automatic transmission when renting. You can generally turn in your car at any office on any day (normally with credit for early turn-in or extra charge for extension). Note that rental offices usually close from midday Saturday until Monday.

Some international companies won't rent a car to you unless your driver's license has been valid for at least one year (though most don't seem to check). If your driver's license has been renewed within the last year, play it safe: get an International Driving Permit (see "Driving," below), bring along the old license with your new one, or carry other proof that you've had a license for more than a year.

For peace of mind, consider Collision Damage Waiver insurance (CDW, about $15–25 per day), which limits your financial responsibility in case of an accident. CDW comes with a high deductible (around $1,000–1,500). When you pick up your car, many car-rental companies will try to sell you "super CDW" at an additional cost of $10–20 per day to lower the deductible to zero.

As an alternative, some credit cards offer zero-deductible collision coverage (comparable to CDW) for no charge to their customers. Quiz your credit-card company on the worst-case scenario. You have to choose between the coverage offered by your car-rental company and your credit-card company—this means that if you go with the credit-card coverage, you'll have to decline the CDW offered by the car-rental company. In this situation, some car-rental companies put a hold on your credit card for the amount of the full deductible (which can equal the value of the car). This is bad news if your credit limit is low—particularly if you plan on using that card for other purchases during your trip.

As another alternative, you can buy CDW insurance from Travel Guard ($9/day plus a one-time $3 service fee covers you up to $35,000, $250 deductible, tel. 800-826-4919, www.travelguard.com). It's valid throughout nearly all of Europe, but some car-rental companies refuse to honor it (especially in Italy and the Republic of Ireland). Oddly, residents of Washington State aren't allowed to buy this coverage.

In sum, buying CDW—and the supplemental insurance to buy down the deductible, if you choose—from the car-rental company is the easiest but priciest option. Using the coverage that comes with your credit card is cheaper, but can involve more hassle. If you're taking a short trip, an easy solution is to buy Travel Guard's very affordable CDW. For longer trips, consider leasing.

Leasing: For trips of two and a half weeks or more, leasing (which automatically includes CDW-type insurance with no deductible) is the best way to go. By technically buying and then selling back the car, you save lots of money on tax and insurance.

Leasing provides you with a brand-new car with unlimited mileage and a 24-hour emergency assistance program. You can lease for as little as 17 days to as long as six months. Car leases must be arranged from the US. One of many reliable companies offering affordable lease packages is Europe by Car (US tel. 800-223-1516, www.europebycar.com).

Driving

Driving in Spain is great—sparse traffic and generally good roads. While the International Driving Permit is officially required

(cheap and easy to obtain from the nearest AAA office; bring $10 and two passport-type photos, www.aaa.com), I drive in Spain with only my US driver's license. (The Spanish version of AAA is the Real Automóvil Club.)

Good maps are available and inexpensive throughout Spain. Freeways come with tolls (about $4/hr) but save huge amounts of time. Always pick up a ticket as you enter a toll freeway. On freeways, navigate by direction *(norte, oeste, sur, este)*. Also, since road numbers can be puzzling and inconsistent, navigate by city names. Mileage signs are in kilometers (see page 547 for conversion formula into miles). In smaller towns, following signs to *centro ciudad* will get you to the heart of things.

Drive defensively. If you're involved in an accident, you will be blamed and will be in for a monumental headache. Seat belts are required by law. Expect to be stopped for a routine check by the police (be sure your car-insurance form is up-to-date). Small towns come with speed traps and corruption. Tickets, especially for foreigners, are issued and paid for on the spot. Insist on a receipt, so the money is less likely to end up in the cop's pocket.

Gas and diesel prices are controlled and the same every-

STOP **AND LEARN THESE ROAD SIGNS**

Speed Limit (km/hr)

Yield

No Passing

End of No Passing Zone

One Way

Intersection

Main Road

Freeway

Danger

No Entry

No Entry for Cars

All Vehicles Prohibited

Parking

No Parking

Customs

Peace

Driving in Spain: Distance and Time

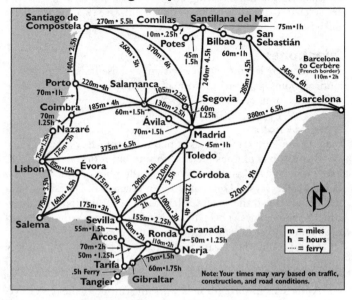

where—about $4.50 a gallon for gas, less for diesel. *Gasolina* is either *normal* or *super;* unleaded *(sin plomo)* is now widely available. Note that diesel is called *diesel* or *gasóleo.*

Choose parking places carefully. Leave valuables in the trunk during the day and leave nothing worth stealing in the car over-night. While you should avoid parking lots with twinkly asphalt, thieves break car windows anywhere, even at stoplights. If your car's a hatchback, take the trunk cover off at night so thieves can look in without breaking in. Try to make your car look locally owned by hiding the "tourist-owned" rental-company decals and putting a local newspaper in your front or back window. Parking attendants all over Spain holler, *"Nada en el coche"* ("Nothing in the car"). And they mean it. Ask your hotelier for advice on parking. In cities you can park safely but expensively in guarded lots.

COMMUNICATING

Language Barrier

Spain presents the English-speaking traveler with the one of the most formidable language barriers in Western Europe. Learn the key phrases. Travel with a phrase book, particularly if you want to interact with local people. You'll find that doors open quicker and with more smiles when you can speak a few words of the language. Use the "Spanish Survival Phrases" in the appendix of this book.

Considering the fun of eating Spanish tapas, the tapas phrase list (see sidebar, page 34) is particularly helpful. Use this and you'll eat much better than the average tourist.

Telephones

Smart travelers learn the phone system and use it daily to book or confirm rooms, get tourist information, confirm tour times, reserve restaurants, or phone home.

Types of Phones

You'll encounter various kinds of phones in your European travels.

Spanish **pay phones** are easy to find but refuse to be rushed. After you *"inserta"* your *"tarjeta"* into the phone, wait until the digital display says *"Marque número"* and then dial. Dial slowly and deliberately. Push the square R button to get a dial tone for a new call. The phone doesn't beep to remind you that you've left the card in, so don't forget to remove it when you're done.

Hotel room phones are fairly cheap for local calls, but pricey for international calls, unless you use an international phone card (see below).

American mobile phones work in Europe if they're GSM-enabled, tri-band (or quad-band), and on a calling plan that includes international calls. (T-Mobile and Cingular have the best deals.) For example, with a T-Mobile phone, you can roam all over Europe using your home number, and pay $1–2 per minute for making or receiving calls. This option is the most convenient—and can be the most expensive.

Some travelers buy a **European mobile phone** in Europe, but if you're on a strict budget, skip mobile phones and use phone cards instead. The cheapest new phones cost around $75, plus $20–50 for the necessary SIM card to make it work (includes some prepaid calling time). A cheapie phone is often "locked" to work afford-ably only in the country where you buy it, but can also roam (for high rates) in other countries. For around $25 more, you can buy an "unlocked" phone that allows you to use different SIM cards in different countries—which saves money if you'll be making lots of calls. If you're interested, stop by any European shop that sells mobile phones; you'll see prominent store-window displays. You aren't required to (and shouldn't) buy a monthly contract—buy prepaid calling time instead. As you use it up, buy additional min-utes at newsstands or mobile-phone shops.

Paying for Calls

You can spend a fortune making phone calls in Spain, or travel smart and call cheap. Here's the skinny on different ways to pay, including the best deals.

Get a **phone card** for your calls. Spanish phone cards come in two types: phone cards that you insert into a pay phone (best for local calls), and international phone cards that come with a code number and can be used from virtually any phone (best for long-distance and international calls). Look for these cards at any post office and most newsstands and tobacco shops, including at train stations and airports. Either type of phone card works only in Spain.

• An **insertable phone card,** called a *tarjeta telefónica,* works in pay phones in public phone booths. These cards are sold at post offices and many newsstand kiosks. To use an insertable card, simply slide it into the slot on the phone, wait for a dial tone and digital readout to show how much value remains on your card, and dial your local, long-distance, or international call. The cost of the call is automatically deducted from your card. These cards are best for making calls within Spain.

• An **international phone card,** called a *tarjeta telefónica con código,* is a better deal for overseas calls. Unlike the official phone cards, an international phone card is *not* inserted into the phone. Instead, you dial the toll-free number listed on the card, reaching an automated operator. When prompted, you dial in a scratch-to-reveal code number, also written on the card. Then dial your number. You can use the cards to make local and domestic long-distance calls as well. Since they're not insertable, you can use them from nearly any phone—including the one in your hotel room (if your phone is set on "pulse," switch it to "tone"). You can buy an international phone card at most kiosks and newsstands, but the best selection is usually at hole-in-the-wall shops catering to immigrants, who are the leading experts on calling home cheaply. These cards, made by numerous (sometimes fly-by-night) companies, offer good rates but don't consistently work well. Try to confirm that the card can be used for calls to America (the sales-clerk may not know), and buy a lower-denomination card in case the card is a dud.

Dialing direct from your hotel room without using an international phone card is usually quite expensive for international calls, but it's convenient. I always ask first how much I'll be charged. Keep in mind that you have to pay for local and occasionally even toll-free calls.

Receiving calls in your hotel room is often the cheapest way to keep in touch with the folks back home—especially if your family has an inexpensive way to call you (either a good deal on their long-distance plan, or a prepaid calling card with good rates to Europe). Give them a list of your hotels' phone numbers before you go. As you travel, send your family an e-mail or make a quick payphone call to set up a time for them to call you, and then wait for the ring.

Metered phones are available in phone offices and sometimes in bigger post offices. You can talk all you want, then pay the bill when you leave—but be sure you know the rates before you have a lengthy conversation.

VoIP (Voice over Internet Protocol), which is pertinent only for those traveling with a laptop computer, allows VoIP users to talk with each other for free via their computers over a fast Internet connection. Look into Skype (www.skype.com) and Google Talk (www.google.com/talk).

US Calling Cards (such as the ones offered by AT&T, MCI, or Sprint) are the worst option. You'll nearly always save a lot of money by paying for your call in any of the other ways described above.

How to Dial

Calling from the US to Spain, or vice versa, is simple—once you break the code. The European calling chart on page 542 will walk you through it. Remember that Spain time is six/nine hours ahead of the East/West coasts of the US.

Dialing Within Spain: Spain has a direct-dial phone system (no area codes). To call anywhere within Spain, just dial the number. For example, one of my recommended Madrid hotels is 915-212-941. To call it from a Madrid train station, just dial 915-212-941. If you call it from Barcelona, it's the same: 915-212-941. All phone numbers in Spain are nine digits.

Dialing International Calls: When calling internationally, dial the international access code (00 if you're calling from Europe, 011 from the US or Canada), the country code of the country you're calling (34 for Spain; see appendix for list of other countries), and the local number. So, to call the Madrid hotel from the US, dial 011 (the US international access code), 34 (Spain's country code), then 915-212-941. To call my office in Edmonds, Washington, from Spain, I dial 00 (Europe's international access code), 1 (the US country code), 425 (Edmonds' area code), and 771-8303.

E-mail and Mail

E-mail: Many travelers set up a free e-mail account with Yahoo, Microsoft (Hotmail), or Google (Gmail). Hotels sometimes have computers in their lobby—usually with slow Internet connections—for guests to use for free or a minimal fee. Cybercafés and hole-in-the-wall Internet-access shops (offering a few computers, no food, and cheap prices) are popular in most cities. E-mail use among Spanish hoteliers is increasing, and most prefer to receive bookings online rather than by fax or phone. I've listed e-mail addresses when available. Some family-run pensions can become overwhelmed by the volume of e-mail they receive, so be patient if you don't get an immediate response.

Wireless access (Wi-Fi) is becoming more common through-out Spain. Telefónica, the Spanish telecom, has begun offering Wi-Fi hotspots at some hotels, restaurants, and cafés (www .telefonicaonline.com/on/es/wifi).

Mail: To arrange for mail delivery, reserve a few hotels along your route in advance and give their addresses to friends. Allow 10 days for a letter to arrive. E-mailing and phoning are so easy that I've dispensed with mail stops altogether.

SLEEPING

Spain offers some of the best accommodation values in Western Europe. Most places are government-regulated, with posted prices. While prices are low, street noise is high (Spaniards are notorious night owls). Always ask to see your room first. Check the price posted on the door, consider potential night-noise problems, ask for another room, or bargain down the price. You can request *con vista* (with a view), or *tranquilo* or *callado* (quiet). In most cases, the view comes with street noise. Most of the year, prices are soft.

In the interest of smart use of your time, I favor hotels (and restaurants) handy to your sightseeing activities. Rather than list hotels scattered throughout a city, I describe my favorite couple of neighborhoods and recommend the best accommodations values in each, from $15 bunks to $330 suites.

All rooms have sinks with hot and cold water. Rooms with private bathrooms are often bigger and renovated, while the cheaper rooms without bathrooms often will be dingier and/or on the top floor. Any room without a bathroom has access to a bath-room on the corridor. You can usually save time by paying your bill the evening before you leave, instead of paying in the busy morn-ing, when the reception desk is crowded with tourists who want to pay up, ask questions, or check in.

Types of Accommodations
Hotels: Don't judge hotels by their bleak and dirty entryways. Landlords, stuck with rent control, often stand firmly in the way of hardworking hoteliers who'd like to brighten up their buildings.

Any regulated place will have a complaint book *(libro de reclama-ciones)*. A request for this book will generally prompt the hotelier to solve your problem to keep you from writing a complaint.

Sleep Code

To help you easily sort through these listings, I've divided the rooms into three categories based on the price for a standard double room with bath:

$$$ **Higher Priced**
$$ **Moderately Priced**
$ **Lower Priced**

To give maximum information in a minimum of space, I use this code to describe accommodations listed in this book. Prices listed are per room, not per person. When there is a range of prices in one category, that means the price will fluctuate with the season; these seasons are posted at the hotel desk. Especially in resort areas, prices go way up in July and August. In Spain, some hotels include the 7 percent I.V.A. tax in the room price; others tack it onto your bill. Hotel breakfasts are rarely included in Spain.

S = Single room (or price for one person in a double).

D = Double or twin. Double beds are usually big enough for nonromantic couples.

T = Triple (often a double bed with a single bed moved in).

Q = Quad (an extra child's bed is usually cheaper).

b = Private bathroom with toilet and shower or tub.

s = Private shower or tub only (the toilet is down the hall).

Unless otherwise noted, you can assume credit cards are accepted and English is spoken. According to this code, a couple staying at a "Db-€90" hotel would pay a total of €90 (about $110) for a double room with a private bathroom. The hotel accepts credit cards or cash in payment, and the staff speaks English.

Hotels are officially prohibited from using central heat before November 1 and after April 1 (unless it's unusually cold); prepare for cool evenings if you travel in spring and fall. Summer can be extremely hot. Consider air-conditioning, fans, and noise (since you'll want your window open), and don't be shy about asking for ice at the fancier hotels. Many rooms come with mini-refrigerators (if it's noisy at night, unplug it). Conveniently, expensive business-class hotels often drop their prices in July and August, just when the air-conditioned comfort they offer is most important.

Most hotel rooms with air-conditioners come with control sticks (like a TV remote, sometimes requires a deposit) that generally have the same symbols and features: fan icon (click to toggle through wind power from light to gale); louver icon (choose steady air flow or waves); snowflake and sunshine icons (heat or cold, depending on season); clock ("O" setting: run x hours before turning off; "I" setting: wait x hours to start); and the temperature control (20° or 21° Celsius is the normal sleeping temperature).

Historic Inns: Spain also has luxurious, government-sponsored, historic inns called *paradores.* These are often renovated castles, palaces, or monasteries, many with great views and stately atmospheres. While full of Old World character, they are usually run in a sterile, bureaucratic way. These are pricey (doubles $100–240), but can be a good deal for younger people (30 and under) and seniors (60 and over), who often get discounted rates; for details, bonus packages, and family deals, see www.parador .es. If you're not eligible for any deals, you'll get a better value by sleeping in what I call (and list in this book as) "poor man's paradors"—elegant, normal places that offer double the warmth and Old World intimacy for half the price.

Rooms in Private Homes: You'll find rooms in private homes, typically in touristy areas where locals decide to open up a spare room and make a little money on the side. These rooms are usually as private as hotel rooms, often with separate entries. Especially in resort towns, the rooms might be in small apartment-type buildings. Ask for a *cama, habitación,* or *casa particular.* They're cheap ($10–25 per bed without breakfast) and usually a good experience.

Hostels and Campgrounds: Spain has plenty of youth hostels and campgrounds, but considering the great bargains on other accommodations, I don't think they're worth the trouble and usually don't cover them in this book. *Hostales* and *pensiones* are easy to find, inexpensive, and, when chosen properly, a fun part of the Spanish cultural experience. If you're on a starvation budget or just prefer camping or hosteling, plenty of information is available in the Let's Go guidebook (see page 8), through the national tourist office, and at local TIs.

Making Reservations

Even though Easter, July, and August are often crowded, you can travel at any time of year without reservations. But given the high stakes and the quality of the gems I've found for this book, I'd reserve ahead, especially for Barcelona.

In peak times or for big cities, you can book long in advance from home. If you prefer more spontaneity, you can grab rooms a few days to a week in advance. If you're traveling without reservations, you'll have greater success of snaring the best rooms if you arrive at your destination early in the day. When you anticipate crowds, call hotels between 9:00 and 10:00 on the day you plan to arrive, when the hotel clerk knows who'll be checking out and just which rooms will be available. Risk-takers on a tight budget can save pocketfuls of euros by traveling with no reservations and taking advantage of the discounted prices hotels offer when it's clear they'll have empty rooms that day. Some of the hotels I recommend offer discounted prices if you have this book; mention it—and claim the discount—when you call to reserve.

I've taken great pains to list telephone numbers with long-distance instructions (see "Telephones," page 24; also see the appendix). Most hotels listed are accustomed to English-only speakers. (If you have difficulty, ask the fluent receptionist at your current hotel to call for you.) A hotel receptionist will usually trust you and hold a room until 16:00 without a deposit, though some will ask for a credit-card number.

If you know where you want to stay each day (and you don't need or want flexibility), reserve your rooms from the US in advance. To book from home, e-mail, phone, or fax your request. Phone and fax costs are reasonable, e-mail is a steal (and preferred by most hotels), and simple English is usually fine. To fax, use the handy form in the appendix (online at www.ricksteves.com /reservation). If you don't get an answer to your faxed request within a week, consider that a "no." (Many little places get many faxes a day after they're full, and they can't afford to respond.)

A two-night stay in August would be "2 nights, 16/8/07 to 18/8/07." (Europeans write the date in this order—day/month/ year—and hotel jargon uses your day of departure.)

If you receive a response from the hotel stating its rates and room availability, it's not a confirmation. You must confirm that you indeed want a room at the given rate. One night's deposit is generally required. A credit-card number will usually be accepted as the deposit (though you may need to send a signed traveler's check or, rarely, a bank draft in the local currency). Be sure to fax your card number (rather than e-mail it) to keep it private, safer, and out of cyberspace. If you use your credit card for the deposit, you can pay with your card or cash when you arrive; if you don't show up, your card will be billed for one night. To make things easier on yourself and the hotel, be sure you really intend to stay at the hotel on the dates you requested. These small, family-run businesses lose money if they turn away customers while holding a room for someone who doesn't show up. Understandably, some hotels bill no-shows for one night. *If you must cancel, give at least two days' notice.* Long distance is cheap and easy from public phone booths. Don't let these people down—I promised you'd call and cancel if for some reason you won't show up.

Reconfirm your reservations a few days in advance for safety, and let them know about what time you'll arrive. Don't needlessly confirm rooms through the tourist office or Web services; they'll take a commission of up to 20 percent. On the small chance that a hotel loses track of your reservation, bring along their faxed confirmation or a printout of their e-mailed confirmation.

EATING

Spaniards eat to live, not vice versa. Their cuisine is hearty and served in big, inexpensive portions. You can eat well in restaurants for €15.

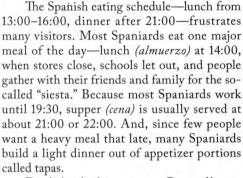

The Spanish eating schedule—lunch from 13:00–16:00, dinner after 21:00—frustrates many visitors. Most Spaniards eat one major meal of the day—lunch *(almuerzo)* at 14:00, when stores close, schools let out, and people gather with their friends and family for the so-called "siesta." Because most Spaniards work until 19:30, supper *(cena)* is usually served at about 21:00 or 22:00. And, since few people want a heavy meal that late, many Spaniards build a light dinner out of appetizer portions called tapas.

Don't buck this system. Generally, no self-respecting *casa de comidas* (house of eating—when you see this label, you can bet it's a good, traditional eatery) serves meals at American hours.

In addition, the Spanish diet—heavy on ham, deep-fried foods (usually fried in olive oil), more ham, weird seafood, and ham again—can be brutal on Americans more accustomed to salads, fruit, and grains.

Survival Tips: To get by in Spain, either adapt yourself to the Spanish schedule and cuisine, or scramble to get edible food in between. Have an early light lunch at a bar. Many Spaniards have a *bocadillo* (sandwich) at about 11:00 to bridge the gap between their coffee-and-roll breakfast and lunch at 14:00 (hence the popularity of fast-food sandwich chains such as Pans & Company). Besides *bocadillos,* bars often have slices of *tortilla* (potato omelet) and fresh-squeezed orange juice.

Then, either have your main meal at a restaurant at 15:00, followed by a light tapas snack for dinner later; or reverse it, having a tapas meal in the afternoon, followed by a late restaurant dinner. Either way, tapas in bars are the key (see page 34).

For just a fresh green salad, most restaurants will offer a simple *ensalada mixta* of iceberg lettuce, tomatoes, tuna and olives. I have even—yes, I confess—patronized fast-food joints such as McDonald's for their simple salads.

Breakfast

Hotel breakfasts are generally about €5 and optional. While they are handy and not expensive, it's easy to start your day with a Spanish flair at the corner bar or at a colorful café near the town market hall. If you like a Danish and coffee in American greasy-spoon joints, you must try the Spanish equivalent: greasy, cigar-shaped fritters called *churros* (or the thicker *porras*) that you dip in warm chocolate pudding.

Here are some key words for breakfast:

café solo	shot of espresso
café con leche	espresso with hot milk
te	tea
zumo de fruta	fruit juice
zumo de naranja (natural)	orange juice (freshly squeezed)
pan	bread
tortilla española	potato omelet (standard dish cooked fresh each morning, served in cheap slices)
sandwich (tostado)	Wonder bread (toasted)
...con jamón/queso/mixto	...with ham/cheese/both
...mixto con huevo	...with ham and cheese topped by an over-easy egg
croissant a la plancha	grilled croissant slathered with butter

Restaurants

In restaurants, don't expect "My name is Carlos and I'll be your waiter tonight" cheery service. Service is often *serio*—it's not friendly or unfriendly...just white-shirt-and-bowtie proficient.

Although not fancy, Spanish cuisine comes with an endless

variety of regional specialties. Two famous Spanish dishes are paella and gazpacho. Paella features saffron-flavored rice as a background for whatever the chef wants to mix in—seafood, sausage, chicken, peppers, and so on. While paella is heavy for your evening meal, jump (like everyone else in the bar) at the opportunity to snare a small plate of paella when it appears hot out of the kitchen in a tapas bar. Avoid the paella shown in pretty pictures on a separate menu—it's from the microwave. Gazpacho, an Andalusian specialty, is a chilled soup of tomatoes, bread chunks,

Tips on Tipping

Tipping in Spain isn't as automatic and generous as it is in the US, but for special service, tips are appreciated, if not expected. As in the US, the proper amount depends on your resources, tipping philosophy, and the circumstance, but some general guidelines apply.

Restaurants: In most restaurants, service is included—your menu typically will indicate this by noting *servicio incluido*. Still, if you like to tip and you're pleased with the service, it's customary to leave up to 5 percent. If service is not included *(servicio no incluido)*, tip up to 10 percent. Leave the tip on the table. It's best to tip in cash even if you pay with your credit card. Otherwise the tip may never reach your server.

Taxis: To tip a cabbie, round up. For a typical ride, round up to the next euro on the fare (to pay a €13 fare, give €14); for a long ride, to the nearest €10 (for a €75 fare, give €80). If the cabbie hauls your bags and zips you to the airport to help you catch your flight, you might want to toss in a little more. But if you feel like you're being driven in circles or otherwise ripped off, skip the tip.

Special Services: Tour guides at public sites sometimes hold out their hands for tips after the tour. If the tour was enjoyable and in English, it's appropriate to give a euro per person. For minivan tours and for private guides, I tip a little more. I don't tip for excursions that simply provide transportation and offer no commentary. Nor do I tip at hotels, but if you do, give the porter a euro for carrying bags, and leave a couple of euros in your room at the end of your stay for the maid if the room was kept clean. In general, if someone in the service industry does a super job for you, a tip of a couple of euros is appropriate...but not required.

When in doubt, ask: If you're not sure whether (or how much) to tip for a service, ask your hotelier or the TI; they'll fill you in on how it's done on their turf.

and spices—refreshing on a hot day and commonly available in the summer. Spanish cooks love garlic and olive oil. The cheapest meal is simply a *bocadillo de jamón* (ham-on-French-bread sandwich), sold virtually anywhere.

For a budget meal in a restaurant, try a *plato combinado* (combination plate), which usually includes portions of one or two main dishes, a vegetable, and bread for a reasonable price; or the *menú del día* (menu of the day, also known as *menú turístico*), a substantial three- to four-course meal that usually comes with a carafe of house wine.

Ordering Tapas

You can often just point to what you want, say *por favor,* and get your food, but these words will help you learn the options and fine-tune your request.

Tapas Terms

pincho	bite-size portion (not always available)
pinchito	tiny *pincho*
tapas	snack-size portions
ración	larger portions—half a meal, occasionally available in a smaller version called a *"1/2 ración" (media ración)*
frito	fried
...a la plancha	grilled
¿Cuánto cuesta una tapa?	How much per tapa?

Sandwich Words

canapé	tiny open-faced sandwich
pulguitas	small closed baguette sandwich
montadito	baguette slice with the tapa "mounted" on top
bocadillos	baguette sandwiches, cheap and basic, a tapa on bread
flautas	sandwich made with flute-thin baguette
pepito	yet one more word for a little sandwich

Typical Tapas

aceitunas	olives
almendras	almonds
atún	tuna
bacalao	cod
banderilla	small skewer of spicy, pickled veggies— eat all at once for the real punch (it's named after the spear matadors use to spike the bull)
bombas	fried meat and potatoes ball
boquerones	fresh anchovies marinated in olive oil, vinegar, and garlic
calamares fritos	fried squid rings
caracoles	snails (May–Sept)
cazón en adobo	salty, marinated dogfish
champiñones	mushrooms
croquetas de...	breaded and fried mashed potatoes, usually with chunks of *jamón* (ham)
empanadillas	pastries stuffed with meat or seafood

ensalada rusa	potato salad with lots of mayo, peas, and carrots
espinacas (con garbanzos)	spinach (with garbanzo beans)
gambas (a la plancha, al ajillo)	shrimp (grilled, with garlic)
gazpacho	cold soup, made with tomato, bread, garlic, and olive oil
guiso	stew
mejillones	mussels
pan	bread
paella	rice dish with saffron, seafood, meat, and/or chicken
patatas bravas	fried chunks of potato with spicy tomato sauce
pescaditos fritos	assortment of fried little fish
picos	little breadsticks
pimiento (relleno)	peppers (stuffed)
pisto	mixed sautéed vegetables
pulpo	octopus
queso	cheese (or a beautiful woman)
queso manchego	sheep-milk cheese
rabas	squid tentacles
rabo de toro	bull-tail stew
revuelto de...	scrambled eggs with...
...setas	...wild mushrooms
tabla serrana	hearty plate of mountain meat and cheese
tortilla española	potato omelet
tortilla de jamón/queso	potato omelet with ham/cheese
variado fritos	typical Andalusian mix of various fried fish

Cured Meats (*Charcutería*)

salchichón	sausage
jamón ibérico	best ham, from acorn-fed baby pigs
jamón serrano	cured ham
chorizo	spicy sausage
lomo	pork tenderloin

Typical Desserts

flan de huevo	crème caramel
arroz con leche	rice pudding
helados (variados)	ice cream (various flavors)
fruta de la estación	fruit in season
queso	cheese

Tapas Bars

You can eat well any time of day in tapas bars. Tapas are small portions, like appetizers, of seafood, salads, meat-filled pastries, deep-fried tasties, and on and on—normally displayed under glass at the bar.

Tapas typically cost about €2, up to €10 for seafood. Most bars push larger portions called *raciones* (dinner-plate-sized) rather than smaller tapas (saucer-sized). Ask for the smaller tapas portions, though many bars simply don't serve anything smaller than a *ración*.

Eating and drinking at a bar is usually cheapest if you eat or drink at the counter *(barra)*. You may pay a little more to eat sitting at a table *(mesa)* and still more for an outdoor table *(terraza)*. Locate the price list (often posted in fine type on a wall somewhere) to know the menu options and price tiers. In the right place, a quiet snack and drink on a terrace on the town square is well worth the extra charge. But the cheapest seats sometimes get the best show. Sit at the bar and study your bartender—he's an artist.

Be assertive or you'll never be served. *Por favor* (please) grabs the guy's attention. Don't worry about paying until you're ready to leave (he's keeping track of your tab). To get the bill ask: *"¿La cuenta?"* (or *la dolorosa*—meaning literally "the sadness"—always draws a confused laugh). Bars come with a formidable language barrier. A small working vocabulary is essential for tapas proficiency (see page 34).

Chasing down a particular bar for tapas nearly defeats the purpose and spirit of tapas—they are impromptu. Just drop in at any lively place. I look for the noisy spots with piles of napkins and food debris on the floor (go local and toss your trash, too), lots of locals, and the TV blaring. Popular television-viewing includes bullfights and soccer games, American sitcoms, and Spanish interpretations of soaps and silly game shows (you'll see Vanna Blanco). While tapas are served all day, the real action begins late—21:00 at the earliest. But for beginners, an earlier start is easier and comes with less commotion.

Get a fun, inexpensive sampler plate. Ask for *una tabla de canapés variados* to get a plate of various little open-face sandwiches. Or ask for a *surtido de* (an assortment of...) *charcutería* (a mixed plate of meat) or *queso* (cheese). *Un surtido de jamón y queso* means a plate of different hams and cheeses. Order bread and two glasses of red wine on the right square—and you've got a romantic (and €8) dinner for two.

Spanish Drinks

Spain is one of the world's leading producers of grapes and that means lots of excellent wine: both red *(tinto)* and white *(blanco)*. Major wine regions include Valdepeñas, Penedès (Cabernet-style wines from near Barcelona), Rioja (spicy, lighter reds from the *tempranillo* grape, from the high plains of northern Spain), and Ribera del Duero (northwest of Madrid). For quality wine, ask for *crianza* (old), *reserva* (older), or *gran reserva* (oldest).

Sherry, a fortified wine from the Jerez region, ranges from dry *(fino)* to sweet *(dulce)*—Spaniards drink the *fino* and export the *dulce*. *Cava* is Spain's answer to champagne. Sangria (red wine mixed with fruit juice) is popular and refreshing.

To get a small draft beer, ask for a *caña* (KAHN-yah). Spain's bars often serve fresh-squeezed orange juice *(zumo de naranja natural)*. For something completely different, try *horchata de chufas*, a sweet, milky beverage made from chufa nuts (a.k.a. earth almonds). If ordering mineral water in a restaurant, request a *botella grande de agua* (big bottle). They push the more profitable small bottles.

Here are some words to help you quench your thirst:

agua con/sin gas	water with/without bubbles
un vasito de agua	glass of tap water
una jarra de agua	pitcher of tap water
refresco	soft drink (common brands are Coca-Cola; Fanta—*limón* or *naranja*; and Schweppes—*limón* or *tónica*)
vino tinto/blanco de la casa	house red/white wine
un tinto	small glass of house red wine
chato	small glass of house wine
tinto de verano	lighter sangria
vermú	vermouth
mucho cuerpo	full-bodied
afrutado	fruity
seco	dry
dulce	sweet
cerveza	beer
caña	small glass of draft beer
doble, tubo	tall glass of beer
¡Salud!	Cheers!

How Was Your Trip?

Were your travels fun, smooth, and meaningful? If you'd like to share your tips, concerns, and discoveries, please fill out the survey at www.ricksteves.com/feedback or e-mail me at rick @ricksteves.com. I personally read and value your feedback. Thanks in advance—it helps a lot.

TRAVELING AS A TEMPORARY LOCAL

We travel all the way to Europe to enjoy differences—to become temporary locals. You'll experience frustrations. Certain truths that we find "God-given" or "self-evident," such as cold beer, ice in drinks, bottomless cups of coffee, hot showers, and bigger being better, are suddenly not so true. One of the benefits of travel is the eye-opening realization that there are logical, civil, and even better alternatives. A willingness to go local ensures that you'll enjoy a full dose of Spanish hospitality.

If there is a negative aspect to the image the Spanish have of Americans, it is that we are big, aggressive, impolite, rich, loud, superficially friendly, and a bit naive. Americans tend to be noisy in public places, such as restaurants and trains. Our raised voices can demolish Spain's reserved and elegant ambience. Talk softly.

While Spaniards look bemusedly at some of our Yankee excesses—and worriedly at others—they nearly always afford us individual travelers all the warmth we deserve.

Judging from all the happy e-mails I receive from travelers who have used this book, it's safe to assume you'll enjoy a great, affordable vacation—with the finesse of an independent, experienced traveler. Thanks, and *buen viaje!*

BACK DOOR TRAVEL PHILOSOPHY
From *Rick Steves' Europe Through the Back Door*

Travel is intensified living—maximum thrills per minute and one of the last great sources of legal adventure. Travel is freedom. It's recess, and we need it.

Experiencing the real Europe requires catching it by surprise, going casual..."Through the Back Door."

Affording travel is a matter of priorities. (Make do with the old car.) You can eat and sleep—simply, safely, and enjoyably—nearly anywhere in Europe for $100 a day plus transportation costs. In many ways, spending more money only builds a thicker wall between you and what you traveled so far to see. Europe is a cultural carnival, and, time after time, you'll find that its best acts are free and the best seats are the cheap ones.

A tight budget forces you to travel close to the ground, meeting and communicating with the people. Never sacrifice sleep, nutrition, safety, or cleanliness in the name of budget. Simply enjoy the local-style alternatives to expensive hotels and restaurants.

Extroverts have more fun. If your trip is low on magic moments, kick yourself and make things happen. If you don't enjoy a place, maybe you don't know enough about it. Seek the truth. Recognize tourist traps. Give a culture the benefit of your open mind. See things as different but not better or worse. Any culture has much to share.

Of course, travel, like the world, is a series of hills and valleys. Be fanatically positive and militantly optimistic. If something's not to your liking, change your liking. Travel is addictive. It can make you a happier American as well as a citizen of the world. Our Earth is home to six and a half billion equally important people. It's humbling to travel and find that people don't envy Americans. Europeans like us, but, with all due respect, they wouldn't trade passports.

Globe-trotting destroys ethnocentricity. It helps you understand and appreciate different cultures. Regrettably, there are forces in our society that want you dumbed down for their convenience. Don't let it happen. Thoughtful travel engages you with the world—more important than ever these days. Travel changes people. It broadens perspectives and teaches new ways to measure quality of life. Rather than fear the diversity on this planet, travelers celebrate it. Many travelers toss aside their hometown blinders. Their prized souvenirs are the strands of different cultures they decide to knit into their own character. The world is a cultural yarn shop. And Back Door travelers are weaving the ultimate tapestry. Join in!

SPAIN

SPAIN

(España)

Spain may seem poor compared to Sweden, but it has a richness—of history, of culture, of people—that has little to do with per capita income. From the stirring *sardana* dance in Barcelona to the sizzling rat-a-tat-tat of flamenco in Sevilla, this country creates its own beat amid the heat. Spaniards are proud and stoic. They can be hard to get to know—but once you've made a connection, you've got a friend for life.

If you fly over Spain, you'll see that parts of the country are parched as red-orange as a desert. But the country thrives, especially in the cool of the evening. Spaniards are notorious night owls. Many clubs and restaurants don't even open until after midnight. The antidote for late nights is a midday nap. Locals—and most businesses—take a siesta (about 13:00–16:00).

Spain is in Europe, but not *of* Europe—it has a unique identity and history, divided from the rest of the Continent by the Pyrenees. For more than 700 years (711–1492), its dominant culture was Muslim, not Christian. And after a brief Golden Age financed by New World gold (1500–1600), Spain retreated into three centuries of isolation (1600–1900). This continued into the 20th century, as the fascist dictator Francisco Franco virtually sealed off the country from the rest of Europe's democracies. But since Franco's death, Spaniards have almost swung to the opposite extreme, becoming extremely open to new trends and technologies. (For more on Spanish history, see the appendix, page 529.)

Spain's relative isolation created a unique country with odd customs—bullfights, flamenco dancing, and a national obsession with ham. It's a land of world-class art (El Greco, Diego Velázquez, Francisco Goya, Salvador Dalí, and Pablo Picasso) and a vibrant contemporary scene in the arts and cinema. The cuisine is hearty and unrefined, ranging from tapas and dry sherry, to paella and sangria, to a full meal of roast suckling pig washed down with spicy Rioja wine.

Spain's topography resembles a giant upside-down bowl, with a coastal lip and a high central plateau. The north is mountainous and rainy; the south is hilly and hot. The large central plain, with

Spain Almanac

Official Name: It's officially the Reino de España (Kingdom of Spain), but locals just call it España.

Population: 40 million. Most speak the official national language of Castilian, but 17 percent speak Catalan, 7 percent Galician, and 2 percent Euskara. The country is 94 percent Roman Catholic.

Latitude and Longitude: 40°N and 4°W (similar latitude to New York City).

Area: 195,000 square miles (15 percent bigger than California). This includes the Canary and Balearic Islands, and small enclaves in Morocco. Spain's long-standing claim to Gibraltar remains a long-standing dispute with Britain.

Geography: The interior of Spain is a high, flat plateau (the Meseta Central), with hot, dry summers and harsh winters. Surrounding the plateau are mountains (including the Pyrenees in the north) and 2,000 miles of coastline.

Agua Agua **Everywhere:** A leader in hydropower and irrigation, Spain, for its size, has more man-made lakes from dams (about 1,400) than any other country. Still, the average Spaniard uses one-third less energy than the average American. Spain's many rivers (1,800) are mostly small, less than 50 miles long. The 600-mile Tajo River (a.k.a. Tagus) runs westward from Toledo through Portugal to the Atlantic. The Guadalquivir irrigates Andalucía and makes Sevilla an ocean-going port city.

Biggest Cities: Madrid (2.8 million; and at more than 2,000 feet in altitude, it's Europe's highest capital), Barcelona (1.5 million),

Madrid in the center, is flat and dry. Along the Mediterranean coast, Spain has an almost Italian feel. Spain has cosmopolitan cities, but at night, when whole families stream out of their apartments to wander the streets, even the biggest city feels like a rural village.

The country hosts several different languages. "Castilian"—what we call "Spanish"—is spoken throughout the country. But in the far north, Euskara (spoken by Basques) is the second language, and Barcelona's natives speak their own Romance language, Catalan. You've heard of Basque nationalists, but every other region of Spain also has its own dialect, customs, and (often half-hearted) separatist movement. Basques, Catalonians, Andalusians, Galicians—even Castilians and Leonese—they're all Spanish second.

The Spanish people have long had a reputation as thrifty, straightforward, and unpretentious. But like much of the world, the allure of consumerism, status symbols, and easy credit is

Valencia (750,000), and Sevilla (700,000). Spaniards are urban dwellers—only one in five lives outside a metropolitan area.

Economy: The Gross Domestic Product is $900 billion (same as the state of New York). The GDP per capita is $23,000 (New York's is $40,000). Major moneymakers include clothes, shoes, olives, wine, oranges, machine parts, ships, and tourism.

Government: Guided symbolically by King Juan Carlos I, Spain is a parliamentary monarchy. José Lopez Rodríguez Zapatero is the left-of-center prime minister. Some of the 600-plus legislators (in two houses) are elected directly, some by regional bodies or political parties. The country is divided into 19 autonomous regions (e.g., Andalucía, Catalunya, Castile-La Mancha, and Madrid).

Flag: Spain's flag has three horizontal bands of red, yellow, and red. To the left of center is the coat of arms—a shield with a crown, framed by the "Pillars of Hercules" that symbolically flank the Straits of Gibraltar.

Soccer: The two perennial powerhouses in "la Liga" (the League) are Real Madrid and FC Barcelona.

The Average José: The average Spaniard is 39 years old, will live to age 79, and resides in a home with one car and one TV. One in four Spaniards uses the Internet, and one in 10 owns a cat. The average Spaniard has one mobile phone, 1.27 kids, and sleeps 40 minutes less every night than the typical European.

changing old ways of life. Once content to own one car and one TV, many Spanish people now save (or borrow) for high-fashion clothes, second cars, and summer chalets. Despite all this, daily lives still focus on friends and family. In fact, the siesta is not so much naptime as it is the opportunity for everyone to shut down their harried public life, and enjoy good food and the comfort of loved ones. Nighttime is for socializing, whether it's cruising the streets or watching the soccer game (Real Madrid or FC Barcelona) on TV in a crowded bar.

While you can see some European countries by just passing through, Spain is a destination. Learn its history and accept it on its own terms. Gain (or just fake) an appreciation for sliced ham, dry sherry, and bull's-tail soup, and the Spanish will love you for it. If you go, go all the way. Immerse yourself in Spain.

BARCELONA

Barcelona is Spain's second city, and the capital of the proud and distinct region of Catalunya. With Franco's fascism now ancient history, Catalan flags wave once again. And the local language and culture are on a roll in Spain's most cosmopolitan and European corner.

Barcelona bubbles with life in its narrow Barri Gòtic alleys, along the grand boulevards, and throughout the chic, grid-planned, new part of town, called Eixample. While Barcelona had an illustrious past as a Roman colony, Visigothic capital, 14th-century maritime power, and—in more modern times—a top Mediterranean trading and manufacturing center, it's most enjoyable to throw out the history books and just drift through the city. If you're in the mood to surrender to a city's charms, let it be in Barcelona.

Planning Your Time

Located in the far northeast corner of Spain, Barcelona makes a good first or last stop for your trip. With the new AVE train, Barcelona is only 4.5 hours away from Madrid.

You could sandwich Barcelona between flights. From the US, it's as easy to fly into Barcelona as it is to land in Madrid, Lisbon, or Paris. Those renting a car can cleverly start here, fly (or train) to Madrid, and see Madrid and Toledo, all before picking up their car—saving on several days' worth of rental fees.

On the shortest visit, Barcelona is worth one night, one day, and an overnight train ride or evening flight out. The Ramblas is two different streets by day and by night. Stroll it from top to bottom in the evening and again the next morning, grabbing breakfast on a stool in a market café. Wander the Barri Gòtic (BAH-ree

Barcelona Overview

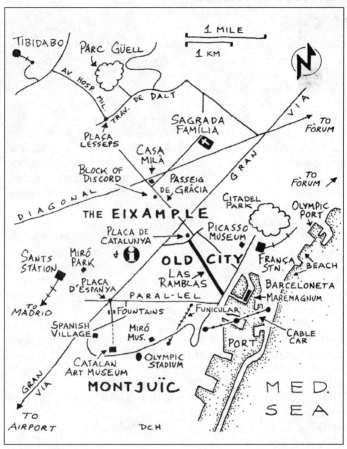

GOH-teek), see the cathedral, and have lunch in the Eixample (eye-SHAM-plah). The top two sights in town, Antoni Gaudí's Sagrada Família church and the Picasso Museum, are usually open until 20:00 during the summer (Picasso closed Mon). The illuminated Magic Fountains on Montjuïc make a good finale for your day (Thu–Sun until 23:00 in summer).

Of course, Barcelona in a day is insane. To better sample the city's ample charm, spread your visit over two or three days.

ORIENTATION

Like Los Angeles, Barcelona is a basically flat city that sprawls out under the sun between the sea and the mountains. It's huge (1.5 million people), but travelers need only focus on four areas: the Old

City, the harbor/Barceloneta, the Eixample, and Montjuïc.

A large square, Plaça de Catalunya, sits at the center of Barcelona, dividing the older and newer parts of town. Sloping downhill from the Plaça de Catalunya is the Old City, with the boulevard named the Ramblas running down to the harbor. Above Plaça de Catalunya is the modern residential area called the Eixample. The Montjuïc hill overlooks the harbor. Outside of the Old City, Barcelona's sights are widely scattered. But with a map and a willingness to figure out the sleek subway system (or a few euros for taxis), all is manageable.

Here are more details per neighborhood:

The **Old City** is where you'll probably spend most of your time. This is the compact soul of Barcelona—your strolling, shopping, and people-watching nucleus. It's a labyrinth of narrow streets that once were confined by the medieval walls. The lively pedestrian drag called the **Ramblas**—one of Europe's great people-watching streets—runs through the heart of the Old City from Plaça de Catalunya down to the harbor. The Old City is divided into thirds by the Ramblas and another major thoroughfare, Via Laietana. To the west of the Ramblas is the **Raval,** enlivened by its university and modern art museum, and infamous in the past for the red lights of its so-called "Chinese Quarter." The Raval is of least interest to tourists. Far better is the **Barri Gòtic** (Gothic Quarter), between the Ramblas and Via Laietana, with the cathedral as its navel. To the east of Via Laietana is the **Ribera** district (a.k.a. "El Born"), centered on the Picasso Museum and the Church of Santa Maria del Mar.

The **harborfront** has been energized since the 1992 Olympics. A pedestrian bridge links the Ramblas with the modern **Maremagnum** shopping/aquarium complex. On the peninsula across the harbor is **Barceloneta,** a traditional fishing neighborhood that's home to some good seafood restaurants and a string of sandy beaches. Beyond Barceloneta, a man-made beach, several miles long, leads east to a new commercial and convention district called the **Fòrum.**

North of the Old City, beyond the bustling hub of Plaça de Catalunya, is the elegant **Eixample** district—its grid plan softened by cut-off corners. Much of Barcelona's Modernista architecture is found here (see sidebar on Modernisme, page 80). To the north is the **Gràcia** district, and beyond that, Antoni Gaudí's **Parc Güell.**

The large hill overlooking the city to the west is **Montjuïc**, home to a variety of attractions including several excellent museums (Catalan Art, Joan Miró) and the Olympic Stadium.

Apart from your geographical orientation, you'll need to orient yourself linguistically to a language distinct from Spanish. While Spanish ("Castilian") is widely spoken, the native tongue in this region is Catalan—as different from Spanish as Italian (see the sidebar on page 52).

Tourist Information

There are several useful **city TIs** in Barcelona: at the **airport** (daily 9:00–21:00, offices in both terminal A and terminal B, tel. 934-784-704); at **Sants Train Station** (Mon–Fri 8:00–20:00, Sat–Sun 8:00–14:00, near track 6); and at **Plaça de Catalunya** (daily 9:00–21:00, on main square near recommended hotels—look for red sign, tel. 932-853-832). Most of these TIs have a room-finding service and sell phone cards and tickets for the Tourist Bus (described in "Getting Around Barcelona," page 51). The TI on Plaça de Catalunya also offers some guided walks (see "Tours," page 54). Throughout the summer, young, red-jacketed tourist-info helpers appear in the most touristy parts of town.

The two **all-Catalunya TIs** work fine for the entire region and even Madrid. You'll find them at **Passeig de Gràcia** (Mon–Sat 10:00–19:00, Sun 10:00–14:00, on Plaça de Joan Carlos I, at the intersection of Diagonal and Passeig de Gràcia, Passeig de Gràcia 107, tel. 932-384-000) and on **Plaça de Sant Jaume** (Mon–Fri 9:00–20:00, Sat 10:00–20:00, Sun 10:00–14:00, in the City Hall/ Ajuntament building).

At any TI, pick up the free, small city map (the large €1.20 map is unnecessary), the brochure on public transport, and the free quarterly *See Barcelona* guide (practical information on museum hours, restaurants, transportation, history, festivals, and so on).

Articket Card: You can get into seven art museums and their temporary exhibits with this ticket, including the recommended Picasso Museum, Casa Milà, Catalan Art Museum, and Fundació Joan Miró (€20, valid for six months, sold at TIs and participating museums, www.articketbcn.org). If you're planning to go to three or more of the museums, this time-saver pays for itself. To skip the line, show your Articket Card to someone at the info desk or to the ticket taker, and they'll help you get your entrance ticket pronto.

Barcelona Card: This card covers public transportation (buses, Metro, Montjuïc funicular, and *golondrina* harbor tour) and includes free admission to minor sights and discounts on major sights (€23/2 days, €28/3 days, €31/4 days, €34/5 days, sold at TIs and El Corte Inglés department store).

Arrival in Barcelona

By Train: Although many international trains use the França Station, all domestic (and some international) trains use Sants  Station. Both França and Sants have baggage lockers and subway stations: França's subway is Barceloneta (2 blocks away), and Sants' is Sants Estació (under the station). Sants Station has a good TI, a world of handy shops and eateries, automated train-ticket vending machines, and a classy, quiet Sala Euromed lounge for travelers with first-class reservations (TV, free drinks, study tables, and coffee bar). Take the Metro or a taxi to your hotel. Most trains traveling to or from France stop at the subway station Passeig de Gràcia, just a short walk from the center (Plaça de Catalunya, TI, hotels); you can get off there.

By Plane: Barcelona's **El Prat de Llobregat Airport,** eight miles southwest of town, has a post office, pharmacy, left-luggage office, plenty of good cafeterias in the gate areas, and ATMs (avoid the gimmicky machines before the baggage carousels; instead, use the bank-affiliated ATMs at the far-left end of the arrivals hall as you face the street).

The airport is connected cheaply and quickly to downtown by **Aerobus** (immediately in front of arrivals lobby, 3/hr until 24:00, 30 min to Plaça de Catalunya, buy €3.75 ticket from driver) or by the RENFE **train** (line 10; at the airport, walk through overpass to train station; 2/hr at about :00 and :30 after the hour, 20 min to Sants Station, 25 min to Passeig de Gràcia, and 30 min to Estació de França, €2.40 or buy a T10 Card at the airport and use it for this trip—see "Getting Around Barcelona," page 51). A **taxi** between the airport and downtown costs about €20. Airport info: tel. 932-983-838.

By Car: Barcelona's parking fees are outrageously expensive (the one behind Boquería market charges €23/day). You won't need a car in Barcelona because the public transportation is so good.

Helpful Hints

Theft Alert: You're more likely to be pickpocketed here—especially on the Ramblas—than about anywhere else in Europe. Most of the crime is nonviolent, but muggings do occur. Be on guard. Leave valuables in your hotel and wear a money belt.

Street scams are easy to avoid if you recognize them. Most common is the too-friendly local who tries to engage you in conversation by asking for the time, talking sports, asking whether you speak English, and so on. If you suspect the person is more interested in your money than your time, ignore him and move on. Beware of thieves posing as lost tourists who ask for your help. A typical street gambling scam is the pea-and-carrot game, a variation on the shell game. The people winning are all ringers, and you can be sure that you'll lose if you play. Also beware of groups of women aggressively selling carnations, people offering to clean off a stain from your shirt, and people picking things up in front of you on escalators. If you stop for any commotion or show on the Ramblas, put your hands in your pockets before someone else does. Assume any scuffle is simply a distraction by a team of thieves.

US Consulate: It's at Passeig Reina Elisenda 23 (for passport services: Mon–Fri 9:00–13:00, closed Sat–Sun, tel. 932-802-227, emergency after-hours tel. 915-872-200).

Emergency Phone Numbers: Police—092, Emergency—061, directory assistance—010.

Pharmacy: A 24-hour pharmacy is near La Boquería market at #98 on the Ramblas.

American Express: The AmEx office is at Las Ramblas 74 (daily 9:00–24:00, banking services only, opposite Liceu Metro station, tel. 900-994-426; for credit-card concerns, call 900-941-413).

Internet Access: EasyInternetcafé—with piles of computers, zippy access (€1.50/hr), drinks, and munchies—has two central locations: One is a half block west of Plaça de Catalunya on Ronda Universitat, and the other is near the seedy bottom of the Ramblas at #31 (both open daily 8:00–24:00).

Getting Around Barcelona

By Public Transit: Barcelona's Metro, among Europe's best, connects just about every place you'll visit. It has five color-coded lines. Rides cost €1.20. Given the excellent Metro service, it's unlikely

you'll take a local bus (also €1.20). The T10 Card for €6.65 gives you 10 tickets (sharable, good for all Metro and local bus lines as well as the separate FGC line and RENFE train lines, including the airport). Full- and multi-day passes are also available (€5/1 day, €9.20/2 days, €13.20/3 days). Pick up the TI's guide to public transport.

    By Tourist Bus: The handy Tourist Bus (Bus Turistic) offers two multi-stop circuits in colorful double-decker buses

"You're not in Spain, You're in Catalunya!"

This is a popular nationalistic refrain you might see on T-shirts or stickers around town. Catalunya is *not* the land of bullfighting and flamenco that many visitors envision when they think of Spain (best to wait until you're in Madrid or Sevilla for those).

The region of Catalunya—with Barcelona as its capital—has its own language, history, and culture, and the people have a proud, independent spirit. Historically, Catalunya has often been at odds with the central Spanish government in Madrid. The Catalan language and culture were discouraged or even outlawed at various times in Spanish history, as Catalunya often chose the wrong side in wars and rebellions against the kings in Madrid. In the Spanish Civil War (1936–1939), Catalunya was one of the last pockets of democratic resistance against the military coup of the fascist dictator Francisco Franco, who punished the region with four decades of repression. During that time, the Catalan flag was banned—but locals vented their national spirit by flying their football team's flag instead.

Three of Barcelona's monuments are reminders of Franco-era suppression: Citadel Park (Parc de la Ciutadella) was originally a much-despised military citadel, constructed in the 18th century to keep locals in line. The Castle of Montjuïc, built for similar reasons, has been the site of numerous political executions, including hundreds during the Franco era. The Sacred Heart Church atop Tibidabo, completed under Franco, was meant to atone for the sins of Barcelonans during the Spanish Civil War—the main sin being opposition to Franco. Although rivalry between Barcelona and Madrid has calmed down in recent times, it rages any time the two cities' football clubs meet.

(red route covers north Barcelona—most Gaudí sights; blue route covers south—Barri Gòtic, Montjuïc) with live multilingual guides (44 stops, 2 hours per route, daily 9:00–22:00 in summer, 9:00–21:00 in winter, buses run every 6–30 min, most frequent in summer). Ask for a brochure (which has a good city map) at the TI or at a pick-up point (buy tickets on bus or at TI). One-day (€18) and two-day (€22) tickets include 10–20 percent discounts on the city's major sights and walking tours, which will likely save you half the cost of the Tourist Bus.

To see real Catalan culture, look for the *sardana* dance (described on page 69) or an exhibition of *castellers*. These teams of human-castle builders come together for festivals throughout the year to build towers of flesh that can reach more than 50 feet high, topped off by the bravest member of the team—a child! The Gràcia festival in August and the Mercè festival in September are good times to catch the *castellers*.

The Catalan language is irrevocably tied to the history and spirit of the people here. Since the end of the Franco era in the mid-1970s, the language has made a huge resurgence. Now most school-age children learn Catalan first and Spanish second. Although Spanish is understood here (and the basic survival words are the same), Barcelona speaks Catalan.

Here are the essential Catalan phrases:

English	Catalan	Pronounced
Hello	*Hola*	OH-lah
Please	*Si us plau*	see oos plow
Thank you	*Gracies*	GRAH-see-es
Goodbye	*Adéu*	ah-DAY-oo
Exit	*Sortida*	sor-TEE-dah
Long live Catalunya!	*¡Visca Catalunya!*	BEE-skah kah-tah-LOON-yah

Most place-names in this chapter are listed in Catalan. Here's a pronunciation guide:

Plaça de Catalunya	PLAS-sah duh cat-ah-LOON-yah
Eixample	eye-SHAM-plah
Passeig de Gràcia	PAH-sage duh grass-EE-ah
Catedral	CAH-tah-dral
Barri Gòtic	BAH-ree GOH-teek
Montjuïc	MOHN-jew-eek

By Taxi: Barcelona is one of Europe's best taxi towns. Taxis are plentiful (there are more than 10,000) and honest (whether they like it or not—the light on top shows which tariff they're charging). They're also reasonable (€1.45 drop charge, €1 per kilometer, these "*Tarif* 2" rates are in effect 6:00–22:00, pay higher "*Tarif* 1" rates off-hours, luggage-€1/piece, other fees posted in window). Save time by hopping a cab (figure €4 from Ramblas to Sants Station).

Barcelona at a Glance

▲▲▲**Ramblas** Barcelona's colorful, gritty pedestrian thorough-fare. **Hours:** Always open.

▲▲▲**Picasso Museum** Extensive collection offering insight into the brilliant Spanish artist's early years. **Hours:** Tue–Sun 10:00–20:00, closed Mon.

▲▲▲**Sagrada Família** Gaudí's remarkable, unfinished cathedral. **Hours:** Daily April–Sept 9:00–20:00, Oct–March 9:00–18:00.

▲▲**Catalan Concert Hall** Best Modernista interior in Barcelona. **Hours:** 50-minute English tours daily every hour 10:00–15:30, plus frequent concerts.

▲▲**Casa Milà** Barcelona's quintessential Modernista building, the famous melting-ice-cream Gaudí creation. **Hours:** Daily 10:00–20:00.

▲▲**Catalan Art Museum** World-class collection of this region's art, including a substantial Romanesque collection. **Hours:** Tue–Sat 10:00–19:00, Sun 10:00–14:30, closed Mon.

▲**Maritime Museum** Housed in an impressive medieval ship-yard, it's a sailor's delight. **Hours:** Daily 10:00–20:00.

▲**Cathedral** Colossal Gothic cathedral ringed by distinctive chapels. **Hours:** Daily 8:00–19:30. It's free except between 13:30–16:45, when you'll pay €4.

TOURS

Walking Tours—The TI at Plaça de Catalunya offers great guided walks through the Barri Gòtic in English only (€9, daily at 10:00, 2 hours, groups limited to 35, departs from the TI, buy your ticket 15 minutes early at the TI desk—not from the guide). A local guide will explain the medieval story of the city as you walk from Plaça de Catalunya through the cathedral neighborhood, finishing at the City Hall on Plaça de Sant Jaume. The TI also offers a 90-minute Picasso walk, taking you through the streets of his youth and early career and finishing in the museum (€11, includes museum admission, Tue–Sun at 10:30, departs from Plaça de Catalunya). There are also gourmet walks (Fri and Sat at 11:00) and Modernisme walks (Fri and Sat at 16:00).

▲***Sardana* Dances** Patriotic dance where proud Catalans join hands in a circle. **Hours:** Every Sun at 12:00, usually also Sat at 18:00.

▲**Church of Santa Maria del Mar** Catalan Gothic church in La Ribera, built by wealthy medieval shippers. **Hours:** Daily 9:00–13:30 & 16:30–20:00.

▲**Block of Discord** Noisy block of competing Modernista facades by Gaudí and his rivals. **Hours:** Always viewable.

▲**Parc Güell** Colorful park at the center of an unfinished Gaudí-designed housing project. **Hours:** Daily 10:00–20:00.

▲**Palau Güell** Exquisitely curvy Gaudí interior. **Hours:** Closed in 2007.

▲**Fundació Joan Miró** World's best collection of works by Catalan Modern artist Joan Miró. **Hours:** May–Sept Tue–Sat 10:00–20:00—but closes at 19:00 Oct–June, Thu until 21:30, Sun 10:00–14:30, closed Mon.

▲**Magic Fountains** Lively fountains near Plaça d'Espanya. **Hours:** Fri–Sat 19:00–21:00, Thu–Sun in summer until 23:00.

▲**Barcelona's Beach** Fun-filled, man-made stretch of sand reaching from the harbor to the Fòrum. **Hours:** Always open.

Local Guides—The Barcelona Guide Bureau is a co-op with about 20 local guides who give personalized four-hour tours starting at €225 (per person price drops as group gets bigger); Joana Wilhelm and Carles Picazo are excellent (Via Laietana 54, tel. 932-682-422 or 933-107-778, www.bgb.es).

SELF-GUIDED WALKS

Most visitors to Barcelona spend much of their time in the twisty, atmospheric Old City. These two walks will give meaning to your wandering. The first begins at Barcelona's main square, and leads you down the city's main drag, and one of Europe's best public spaces: the Ramblas. The second walk starts at the same square, but guides you into the heart of the Barri Gòtic, to the neighborhood around Barcelona's impressive cathedral.

The Ramblas Ramble:
From Plaça de Catalunya down the Ramblas

A ▲▲▲ sight, Barcelona's central square and main boulevard exert a powerful pull. Many visitors spend the majority of their time doing laps on the Ramblas. While the allure of the Ramblas is fading (as tacky tourist shops and fast-food joints replace its former elegance), this is still a fun people zone that offers a good introduction to the city. See it, but be sure to venture further afield. Here's a top-to-bottom orientation walk.

Plaça de Catalunya: This vast central square divides old and new Barcelona. It's also the hub for the Metro, bus, airport shuttle, and both Tourist Bus routes (red northern route leaves from El Corte Inglés—described below, blue southern route from the west side of the square). The grass around its fountain is the best public place in town for serious necking. Overlooking the square, the huge **El Corte Inglés** department store offers everything from bonsai trees to a travel agency, plus one-hour photo developing, haircuts, and cheap souvenirs (Mon–Sat 10:00–22:00, closed Sun, pick up English directory flier, supermarket in basement, ninth-floor terrace cafeteria/restaurant has great city view—take elevator from entrance nearest the TI, tel. 933-063-800).

Four great boulevards radiate from Plaça de Catalunya: the Ramblas, the fashionable Passeig de Gràcia (top shops, noisy with traffic), the cozier, but still fashionable, Rambla de Catalunya (most pedestrian-friendly), and the stubby, shop-filled, and delightful traffic-free Avinguda Portal de l'Angel. Homesick Americans can even find a Hard Rock Cafe. Locals traditionally start or end a downtown rendezvous at the venerable Café Zürich.

• *Cross the street from the café to...*

❶ **The Top of the Ramblas:** Begin your ramble 20 yards down at the ornate fountain (near #129).

More than a Champs-Elysées, this grand boulevard takes you from rich (at the top) to rough (at the port) in a one-mile, 30-minute stroll. You'll raft the river of Barcelonan life past a grand opera house, elegant cafés, retread prostitutes, brazen pickpockets, power-dressing con men, artists, street mimes, an outdoor bird market, great shopping, and people looking to charge more for a shoeshine than what you paid for the shoes.

Grab a bench and watch the scene. Open up your map and read some history into it: You're about to walk right across medieval Barcelona, from Plaça de Catalunya to the harbor. Notice how the higgledy-piggledy street plan of the medieval town was

From Plaça de Catalunya down the Ramblas

contained within the old town walls—now gone, but traced by a series of roads named Ronda (meaning "to go around"). Find the Roman town, occupying about 10 percent of what became the medieval town—with tighter roads yet around the cathedral. The sprawling, modern grid plan beyond the Ronda roads is from the 19th century. Breaks in this urban waffle show where a little town was consumed by the growing city. The popular Passeig de Gràcia was literally the road to Gràcia (once a separate town, now a characteristic Barcelona neighborhood).

Rambla means "stream" in Arabic. The Ramblas used to be a drainage ditch along the medieval wall that once defined what's now called the Barri Gòtic (Gothic Quarter). "Las Ramblas" is plural, a succession of five separately named segments, but address numbers treat it as a single long street.

You're at Rambla Canaletes, named for the fountain. The black-and-gold **Fountain of Canaletes** is the starting point for celebrations and demonstrations. Legend says that a drink from the fountain ensures that you'll return to Barcelona one day. All along the Ramblas, you'll see newspaper stands (open 24 hours, selling phone cards) and ONCE booths (selling lottery tickets that support Spain's organization of the blind, a powerful advocate for the needs of people with disabilities).

Got some change? As you wander downhill, drop coins into the cans of the human statues (the money often kicks them into entertaining gear). Warning: Wherever people stop to gawk, pickpockets are at work.

• *Walk 100 yards downhill to #115 and the...*

❷ **Rambla of the Little Birds:** Traditionally, kids bring their parents here to buy pets, especially on Sundays. Apartment-dwellers find birds, turtles, and fish easier to handle than dogs and cats. If you're walking by at night, you'll hear the sad sounds of little

tweety birds locked up in their collapsed kiosks.

Along the Ramblas, buildings with balconies that have flowers are generally living spaces; balconies with air-conditioners generally indicate offices. The Academy of Science's clock (at #115) marks official Barcelona time—synchronize. The Champion supermarket (at #113) has cheap groceries and a handy deli with cooked food to go.

A recently discovered **Roman necropolis** is in a park across the street from the bird market, 50 yards behind the big, modern Citadines Hotel (go through the passageway at #122). Local apartment-dwellers blew the whistle on contractors, who hoped they could finish their building before anyone noticed the antiquities they had unearthed. Imagine the tomb-lined road leading into the Roman city of Barcino 2,000 years ago.

• *Another 100 yards takes you to Carrer del Carme (at #2), and a...*

❸ **Baroque Church:** The big Betlem church fronting the boulevard is Baroque, unusual in Barcelona. Note the Baroque-style sloping roofline, ball-topped pinnacles, and the scrolls above the entrance. While Barcelona's Gothic age was rich (with buildings to prove it), the Baroque age hardly left a mark. (The city's importance dropped when New World discoveries shifted lucrative trade to ports on the Atlantic.)

The **Bagues** jewelry shop, across Carrer del Carme from the church, is known for its Art Nouveau jewelry (exactingly duplicated from the c. 1898 molds of Masriera displayed in the window; buzz to get inside). At the shop's side entrance, step on the old-fashioned scales (free, in kilos) and head down the narrow lane opposite (behind the church, 30 yards) to a place expert in making you heavier. **Café Granja Viader** (see page 99) has specialized in baked and dairy delights since 1870. (For more sweets, follow "A Short, Sweet Walk"—on page 107—which begins at the intersection in front of the church.)

• *Stroll through the Ramblas of Flowers to the subway stop marked by the red M (near #100), and...*

❹ **La Boquería:** This lively produce market at #91 is an explosion of chicken legs, bags of live snails, stiff fish, delicious oranges, and sleeping dogs (Mon–Sat 8:00–20:00, best mornings after 9:00, closed Sun). Wander through—as local architect Antoni Gaudí used to—and gain inspiration. The Conserves shop sells 25 kinds of olives (straight in, near back on right, 100-gram minimum, €0.20–0.40). Full legs of ham *(jamón serrano)* abound; *Paleta Ibérica de Bellota* are the best, and cost about €120 each (see "Sampling Serrano Ham," page 201). Beware: *Huevos del toro* are bull testicles—surprisingly inexpensive...and oh so good. Drop by a café for an *espresso con leche* or breakfast (*tortilla española*—potato omelet).

For a quick bite, visit the **Pinotxo Bar** (just to the right as you enter the market), where flamboyant Juan and his family are busy feeding shoppers. (Getting Juan to crack a huge smile and a thumbs-up for your camera makes a great shot...and he loves it.) The stools nearby are a great perch for enjoying both your coffee and the people-watching. The market and lanes nearby are busy with great little eateries (see page 103).

The **Museum of Erotica** is your standard European sex museum—neat if you like nudes and a chance to hear phone sex in four languages (€7.50, daily June–Sept 10:00–22:00, shorter hours Oct–May, across from market at #96).

At #100, **Gimeno** sells cigars (appreciate the dying art of cigar boxes). Go ahead, do something forbidden in America but perfectly legal here...buy a Cuban (singles from €1). Tobacco shops sell stamps and phone cards—and plenty of bongs and marijuana gear (the Spanish approach to pot is very casual).

Farther down the Ramblas at #83, the **Art Nouveau Escriba Café** is an ornate world of pastries, little sandwiches, locally popular chocolates, and fine coffee. Opened in 1820 (as shown on the facade), it was remodeled in the Modernista style (daily 8:30–21:00, indoor/outdoor seating, tel. 933-016-027).

Fifty yards farther, find the much-trod-upon anchor mosaic, a reminder of the city's attachment to the sea. Created by noted abstract artist Joan Miró, it marks the midpoint of the Ramblas. (The towering Columbus Monument in the distance—hidden by trees—is at the end of this hike.) From here, walk down to the **Liceu Opera House** (tickets on sale Mon–Fri 14:00–20:30, tel. 902-533-353; 45-minute €6 tour in English daily at 10:00; 20-min €4 version from upper balcony—escorted but not guided, sometimes with no light—daily at 11:30, 12:00, and 13:00; tel. 934-859-914, www.liceubarcelona.com). From the Opera House, cross the Ramblas to Café de l'Opera for a beverage (#74). This bustling café, with Modernista (that is, old-timey) decor and a historic atmosphere, boasts that it's been open since 1929, even during the Spanish Civil War.

• *Continue to #46; turn left down an arcaded lane to a square filled with palm trees...*

❺ **Plaça Reial:** This elegant, Neoclassical square has a colonial (or maybe post-colonial) ambience. It comes complete with old-fashioned taverns, modern bars with patio seating, a Sunday coin and stamp market (10:00–14:00), Gaudí's first public works (the two colorful helmeted lampposts), and characters who don't need the palm trees to be shady. **Herbolari Ferran** is a fine and aromatic shop of herbs, with fun souvenirs such as top-quality saffron, or *safra* (Mon–Sat 9:30–14:00 & 16:30–20:00, closed Sun, downstairs at Plaça Reial 18). The small streets stretching toward the water from the square are intriguing, but less safe.

Back across the Ramblas, **Palau Güell** normally offers an

enjoyable look at a Gaudí interior, but it's closed through 2007 (Carrer Nou de la Rambla 3–5, tel. 933-173-974). This apartment was the first (1886) of Gaudí's innovative buildings, with a parabolic front doorway that signaled his emerging, non-rectangular style. When it reopens, skip the climb to this less-interesting rooftop if you plan to see Casa Milà.

• *Farther downhill, on the right-hand side, is the...*

❻ **Bottom of the Ramblas:** The neighborhood to your right, Barri Xines, is the world's only Chinatown with nothing even remotely Chinese in or near it. Named for the prejudiced notion that Chinese immigrants go hand-in-hand with poverty, prostitution, and drug dealing, the neighborhood's actual inhabitants are poor Spanish, Arab, and Roma (Gypsy) people. At night, the Barri Xines is frequented by prostitutes, many of them transvestites, who cater to sailors wandering up from the port. A nighttime visit gets you a street-corner massage—look out. Better yet—stay out.

The bottom of the Ramblas is marked by the city's giant medieval shipyards (now the impressive Maritime Museum) and the Columbus Monument (both are described under "On the Harborfront, at the Bottom of the Ramblas," page 65). And just beyond the Columbus Monument, **La Rambla del Mar** ("Rambla of the Sea") is a modern extension of the boulevard into the harbor. A popular wooden pedestrian bridge—with waves like the sea—leads to Maremagnum, a soulless Spanish mall with a cinema, huge aquarium, restaurants (including the recommended Tapasbar Maremagnum; see page 104), and piles of people. Late at night, it's a rollicking youth hangout. It's a worthwhile stroll.

The Barri Gòtic:
From Plaça de Catalunya to the Cathedral

Barcelona's Barri Gòtic, or Gothic Quarter, is a bustling world of shops, bars, and nightlife packed between hard-to-be-thrilled-about 14th- and 15th-century buildings. The section near the port is generally dull and seedy. But the area around the cathedral is a tangled-yet-inviting grab-bag of undiscovered courtyards, grand squares, schoolyards, Art Nouveau storefronts, baby flea markets on Thursdays, musty junk shops, classy antique shops (on Carrer de la Palla), street musicians strumming Catalan folk songs, and balconies with domestic jungles behind wrought-iron bars. Go on a cultural scavenger hunt. Write a poem. This self-guided walk gives you a structure, covering the main sights and offering a historical overview before you get lost.

• *Start on Barcelona's bustling main square...*

Plaça de Catalunya: This square is the center of the world for seven million Catalan people. The square (described at the start of my Ramblas self-guided walk, above) is decorated with the likenesses of important Catalans. From this square, walls that contained the city until the 19th century arc around in each direction to the sea. Looking at your map of Barcelona, you'll see a regimented waffle design—except for the higgledy-piggledy old town corralled by these walls.

The city grew with its history. Originally a Roman town, Barcelona was ruled by the Visigoths from the fall of Rome until 714, when the Moors arrived (they were, in turn, sent packing by the French in 801). Finally, in the 10th century, the Count of Barcelona unified the region, and the idea of Catalunya came to be. The area between Plaça de Catalunya and the old Roman walls (circling the smaller ancient town, down by the cathedral) was settled by churches, each a magnet gathering a small community outside the walls (or "extra muro"). Around 1250, when these "extra muro" communities became numerous and strong enough, the king agreed to invest in a larger wall, and Barcelona expanded. This outer wall was torn down in 1859 and replaced by a series of circular boulevards (named Rondas).

• *From Plaça de Catalunya's TI, head downhill, crossing the busy street into a broad pedestrian boulevard called...*

Avinguda Portal de l'Angel: This boulevard is named for the big gate in the medieval wall that once stood here, called the "Gate of the Angel." The gate was crowned by an angel who kept the city safe from plagues and who bid voyagers safe journey as they left the security of the city. Imagine the fascinating scene here at the Gate of the Angel, where Barcelona stopped and the wilds began.

Walking down the Avinguda Portal de l'Angel, you may detour a half block left on **Carrer de Santa Anna,** where a lane on the right leads into a courtyard facing one of those "extra muro" churches, with a fine cloister and simple, typically Romanesque facade.

Continuing down the main boulevard, you reach a fork in the road with a blue-tiled **fountain.** This was once a freestand-ing well—in the 17th century, it was the last watering stop for horses before leaving town. Take the left fork to the cathedral, past the Architects' House with its Picasso-inspired frieze. Enter the square, where you'll stand before two bold towers—the remains of the old Roman wall that protected a smaller Barcino, as the city was called in ancient times. The big stones at the base of the towers are actually Roman. The wall stretches left of the towers, incorporated into the Bishop's Palace (which you'll enter from the other side later).

Barcelona's Old City

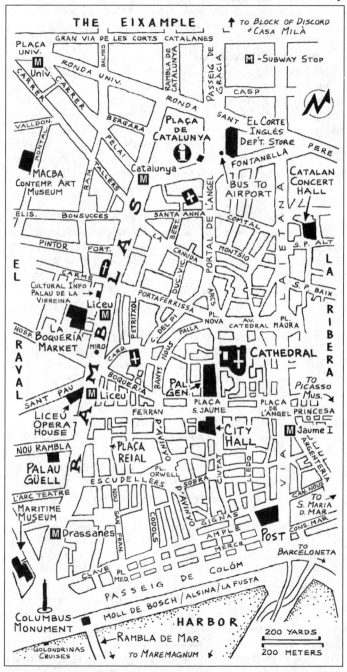

• *The sights from here on are located on the map on page 67. Walk around—past the modern bronze letters* BARCINO *and the mighty facade of the cathedral (which we'll enter momentarily)—and go inside the...*

Bishop's Palace (Palau Episcopal): Visitors are welcome inside this palace, which today functions as the city archives (its front door faces the wall of the church). It's a good example of a Renaissance nobleman's palace. Notice how the century-old palm tree seems to be held captive by urban man. Inside you can see the Roman stones up close. Upstairs affords a good view of the cathedral's exterior—textbook Catalan Gothic (plain and practical, like this merchant community) next to textbook Romanesque (the smaller, more humble church adjacent on the right—which you'll visit entering from the church's cloister later).

• *Now enter the...*

Cathedral of Barcelona (Catedral de Barcelona): This huge house of worship is worth a look. Its vast size, peaceful cloister, and many ornate chapels—each one sponsored by a local guild—are impressive. For a self-guided tour, see "Cathedral of Barcelona" listing on page 66.

• *After visiting the cathedral's cloister, exit and walk to the tiny lane ahead on the right (Carrer de Montjuïc de Bisbe). This leads to the cute...*

Plaça Sant Felip Neri: This square serves as the playground of an elementary school bursting with youthful energy. The Church of Sant Felip Neri, which Gaudí attended, is still pocked with bomb damage from the Civil War. As a stronghold of democratic, anti-Franco forces, Barcelona saw a lot of fighting. The shrapnel that damaged this church was meant for the nearby Catalan government building (Palau de la Generalitat, described below).

Study the medallions on the wall. Guilds powered the local economy, and the carved reliefs here show that this building must have housed the shoemakers. In fact, on this square you'll find a fun little Shoe Museum (see page 69).

• *Circle the block back to the cathedral's cloister and take a right, walking along Carrer del Bisbe to the huge...*

Palau de la Generalitat: For nearly 600 years, this spot has been the home of the Catalan government. Through good times and bad, the Catalan spirit has survived, and this building has housed its capital.

• *Continue along Carrer del Bisbe to...*

Plaça de Sant Jaume (jow-mah): On this stately central square of the Barri Gòtic, once the Roman forum, has been the seat of city government for 2,000 years. Today the two top governmental buildings in Catalunya face each other: the Barcelona City Hall (Ajuntament; free, Sun 10:00–13:30), and the seat of the autonomous government of Catalunya (Palau de la Generalitat, described above). From these balconies, the nation's leaders (and soccer heroes) greet the people on momentous days.

• *Take two quick left turns from the corner of Carrer Bisbe, and climb Carrer del Paridís about 100 yards to the summit of...*

"Mont" Taber: A millstone in the corner marks ancient Barcino's highest elevation, a high spot in the road called Mount Taber. A plaque on the wall says it all: "Mont Taber, 16.9 meters." Step into the courtyard for a peek at a surviving corner of the imposing **Roman temple** (Temple Roma d'August) which once stood here on Mont Taber, keeping a protective watch over Barcino (free, daily 10:00–14:00 & 16:00–20:00).

• *Continue down Carrer del Paridís back to the cathedral, take a right, and go downhill about 100 yards to...*

Plaça del Rei: The Royal Palace sat on this "King's Square" (a block from the cathedral) until Catalunya became part of Spain in the 15th century. Then it was the headquarters of the local Inquisition. In 1493, a triumphant Christopher Columbus, accompanied by six New World natives (whom he called "Indians") and several pure-gold statues, entered the Royal Palace. King Ferdinand and Queen Isabel rose to welcome him home, and honored him with the title "Admiral of the Oceans."

• *Your tour is over. Nearby, just off Plaça del Rei, is another sight—the City History Museum (described on page 69). Or simply wander and enjoy Barcelona at its Gothic best.*

SIGHTS

Barcelona's Old City

I've divided Barcelona's Old City sights into three neighborhoods: near the harbor, at the bottom of the Ramblas; the Cathedral and nearby (Barri Gòtic); and the Picasso Museum and nearby (La Ribera).

On the Harborfront, at the Bottom of the Ramblas

Two great waterfront picnic spots are on the harbor steps or aboard one of the *golondrinas* cruises (described below).

▲**Maritime Museum (Museu Marítim)**—Barcelona's medieval shipyard, the best-preserved in the entire Mediterranean, is an impressive museum covering the salty history of ships and navigation from the 13th to the 20th centuries. Its huge halls evoke the 14th-century days when Catalunya was a naval and shipbuilding power, cranking out 30 huge galleys a winter. As in the US today, military and commercial ventures mixed and mingled as Catalunya built its trading empire. The excellent included audioguide tells the story (€6, €6.70 combo-ticket includes Columbus Monument, daily 10:00–20:00, last entry at 19:00, tel. 933-429-920). Your ticket also gets you into the old-fashioned sailing ship *Santa Eulàlia*, docked in the harbor across the street.

Columbus Monument (Monument a Colóm)— Marking the point where the Ramblas hits the harbor, this 200-foot-tall monument built for an 1888 exposition offers an elevator-assisted view from its top (€2.30, daily June–Sept 9:00–20:30, May and Oct 9:00–20:00, Nov–April 10:00–18:30). It was here in Barcelona that Ferdinand and Isabel welcomed Columbus home after his first trip to America. It's ironic that Barcelona would so honor the man whose discoveries ultimately led to its downfall as a great trading power.

***Golondrinas* Cruises**—At the foot of the Columbus Monument, tourist boats called *golondrinas* offer 30-minute unguided harbor tours (€4, daily 12:00–19:00, tel. 934-423-106, www.lasgolondrinas .com) and longer, 90-minute tours up the coast to the new Fòrum complex and back (€9.70, also unguided, no stops, 6/day, daily 11:30–17:30).

Cathedral of Barcelona

Barcelona's cathedral (Catedral de Barcelona) is worth ▲. Most of the construction on this vast church took place in the 14th century, during the glory days of the Catalan nation. The facade was humble, so in the 19th century, the proud local bourgeoisie redid it in a more ornate neo-Gothic style.

Cost, Hours, Location: Strangely, even though the cathedral is free to enter daily 8:00–13:30 and 17:15–19:30, you have to pay €4 to enter between 13:30–17:15 (cloisters open daily 9:00–13:00 & 17:15–19:00; tel. 933-151-554). The dress code is sometimes strictly enforced; don't wear tank tops, short shorts, or short skirts just in case.

Getting There: The huge, can't-miss-it cathedral is in the center of the Barri Gòtic, on Plaça de la Seu. For an interesting way to reach the cathedral from Plaça de Catalunya, and some commentary on the surrounding neighbor-

Barcelona's Cathedral Neighborhood

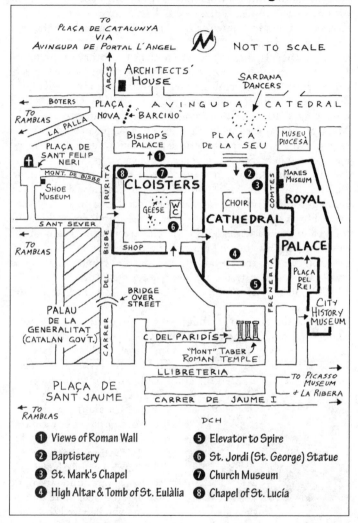

TO
PLAÇA DE CATALUNYA
VIA
AVINGUDA DE PORTAL L'ANGEL

NOT TO SCALE

ARCHITECTS' HOUSE

SARDANA DANCERS

ARCS

BOTERS

PLAÇA A V I N G U D A C A T E D R A L
NOVA BARCINO

TO RAMBLAS

LA PALLA

PLAÇA DE SANT FELIP NERI

BISHOP'S PALACE ❶

PLAÇA DE LA SEU

MUSEU DIOCESÀ

MONT. DE BISBE

SHOE MUSEUM

IRURITA

❽ ❼ CLOISTERS

❷ ❸

MARES MUSEUM

ROYAL

SANT SEVER

GEESE WC

CHOIR CATHEDRAL

COMTES

❻

BISBE

SHOP

❹

PALACE

TO RAMBLAS

DEL

BRIDGE OVER STREET

❺

FRENERIA

PLAÇA DEL REI

PALAU DE LA GENERALITAT (CATALAN GOV'T.)

CARRER

CITY HISTORY MUSEUM

C. DEL PARIDÍS →

"MONT" TABER ROMAN TEMPLE

LLIBRETERIA

TO PICASSO MUSEUM & LA RIBERA

PLAÇA DE SANT JAUME

CARRER DE JAUME I

TO RAMBLAS

DCH

❶ Views of Roman Wall
❷ Baptistery
❸ St. Mark's Chapel
❹ High Altar & Tomb of St. Eulàlia

❺ Elevator to Spire
❻ St. Jordi (St. George) Statue
❼ Church Museum
❽ Chapel of St. Lucía

hood, see my self-guided walk of the Barri Gòtic on page 61.

❍ **Self-Guided Tour:** The cathedral's spacious interior—characteristic of Catalan Gothic buildings—is supported by buttresses. These provide walls for 28 richly ornamented **chapels.** Typical of medieval churches, the cathedral has an "ambulatory" plan—allowing worshippers to amble around to the chapel of their choice. While the main part of the church is fairly plain, the chapels, sponsored by local guilds, show great wealth. Located in the community's most high-profile space, they provided a kind of advertising to illiterate worshippers. Find the logos and symbols of the various trades represented. The Native Americans that Columbus brought to town were supposedly baptized in the first chapel on the left.

The chapels ring a finely carved 15th-century **choir** *(coro)*. For €2, you get a close-up look (with the lights on) of the ornately carved stalls and the emblems representing the various Knights of the Golden Fleece who once sat here. The chairs were folded up, giving VIPs stools to lean on during the standing parts of the Mass. Each was creatively carved and—since you couldn't sit on sacred things—the artists were free to enjoy some secular and naughty fun here. Study the upper tier of carvings.

The **high altar** sits upon the tomb of Barcelona's patron saint, Eulàlia. She was a 13-year-old local girl tortured 13 times by Romans for her faith before finally being crucified on an X-shaped cross. Her X symbol is carved on the pews. Climb down the stairs for a close look at her exquisite marble sarcophagus. Many of the sarcophagi in this church predate the present building.

You can ride the **elevator** to the roof and climb a tight spiral staircase up the spire for a commanding view (€2.20, Mon–Fri 10:30–12:30 & 17:15–18:00, closed Sat–Sun, start from chapel left of high altar).

Enter the **cloister** (through arch, right of high altar). From there, look back at the arch, an impressive mix of Romanesque

and Gothic. A tiny statue of St. George slaying the dragon stands in the garden. Jordi (George) is one of the patron saints of Catalunya, and by far the most popular boy's name here. Cloisters are generally found in monasteries. But this church has one because it needed to accommodate more chapels—to make more money. With so many wealthy merchants in town (who believed that their financial generosity would impress God and win them favor), the church needed more private chapel space. Merchants wanted to be buried close to the altar, and their tombs also spill over into the cloister. On the pavement stones, as in the chapels, notice the symbols of the trades or guilds: scissors, shoes, bakers, and so on.

Long ago the resident **geese**—there are always 13, in memory of Eulàlia—functioned as an alarm system. Any commotion would get them honking, alerting the monk in charge. They honk to this very day.

From the statue of St. Jordi, circle to the right (past a WC

Sardana Dances

The patriotic *sardana* dances are held at the cathedral (every Sun at 12:00, usually also Sat at 18:00). Locals of all ages seem to spontaneously appear. For some, it's a highly symbolic, politically charged action representing Catalan unity—but for most, it's just a fun chance to kick up their heels. Participants gather in circles after putting their things in the center—symbolic of community and sharing (and the ever-present risk of theft). All are welcome, even tourists cursed with two left feet.

Holding hands, dancers raise their arms *Zorba the Greek*–style as they hop and sway gracefully to the band. The band *(cobla)* consists of a long flute, tenor and soprano oboes, strange-looking brass instruments, and a tiny bongo-like drum *(tambori)*. The rest of Spain mocks this lazy circle dance, but considering what it takes for a culture to survive within another culture's country, it is a stirring display of local pride and patriotism.

hidden on the left). The skippable little €1 **museum** (far corner) is one plush room with a dozen old religious paintings. In the corner, built into the cloister, is the dark, barrel-vaulted, Romanesque Chapel of Santa Lucía, a small church that predates the cathedral. People hoping for good eyesight (Santa Lucía's specialty) leave candles outside. Farther along, the Chapel of Santa Rita (her forte: impossible causes) usually has the most candles.

In the Barri Gòtic, near the Cathedral

For an interesting route from Plaça de Catalunya to the Cathedral neighborhood, see my self-guided walk of the Barri Gòtic on page 61. And if you're in town on a weekend, don't miss the *sardana* dances (see sidebar above).

Shoe Museum (Museu del Calçat)—Shoe-lovers enjoy this two-room shoe museum, watched over by a we-try-harder attendant. The huge shoe at the entry is designed to fit the foot of the Columbus Monument at the bottom of the Ramblas (€2.50, Tue–Sun 11:00–14:00, closed Mon, 1 block beyond outside door of cathedral cloister, behind Plaça de G. Bachs on Plaça Sant Felip Neri, tel. 933-014-533).

City History Museum (Museu d'Història de la Ciutat)—For a walk through the history of the city, take an elevator down 65 feet (and 2,000 years) to stroll the streets of Roman Barcelona. You'll see sewers, models of domestic life, and bits of an early Christian church. Then, an exhibit in the 11th-century count's palace shows you Barcelona through the Middle Ages (€4; June–Sept Tue–Sat 10:00–20:00, Sun 10:00–15:00, closed Mon; Oct–May same hours but closed for lunch 14:00–16:00; Plaça del Rei, tel. 933-151-111).

▲▲Catalan Concert Hall (Palau de la Música Catalana)—This concert hall, finished in 1908, features the best Modernista interior in town (by Lluís Domènech i Muntaner). Inviting arches lead you into the 2,000-seat hall. A kaleidoscopic skylight features a choir singing around the sun, while playful carvings and mosaics celebrate music and Catalan culture. Admission is by tour only and starts with a relaxing 20-minute video (€8, 50-min tours in English, daily every hour 10:00–15:30, maybe later, about 6 blocks northeast of cathedral, tel. 932-957-200). To get a spot on an English guided tour, you must reserve in advance: you can drop by earlier in the day or up to a week in advance (ticket office open 9:30–15:30). Ask about concerts (300 per year, inexpensive tickets available, www.palaumusica.org).

Picasso Museum (Museu Picasso)

This is the best collection in the country of the work of Spaniard Pablo Picasso (1881–1973), and—since he spent his formative years (age 14–21) in Barcelona—it's the  best collection of his early works anywhere. The museum is easily worth ▲▲▲. By seeing his youthful, realistic art, you can more fully appreciate the artist's genius and better understand his later, more challenging art. The collection is scattered through several connected Gothic palaces, six blocks from the cathedral in the Ribera district (for more on this area, see "In La Ribera, near the Picasso Museum," below).

Cost, Hours, Location: €6, free on first Sun of month, covered by Articket Card, Tue–Sun 10:00–20:00, closed Mon, Montcada 15, ticket office at #21, Metro: Jaume I, tel. 932-563-000, www.museupicasso.bcn.es. The ground floor has a required bag check, as well as a handy array of other services (bookshop, WC, and cafeteria). This generally crowded museum is quieter at about 14:00 and 18:00.

Hungry? The museum itself has a good café. The café at the Museum of Textiles across the street is good for a light meal in its inviting courtyard. And just down the street is a neighborhood favorite for tapas, El Xampanyet (see page 105).

Background: Picasso's personal secretary amassed a huge collection of his work and bequeathed it to the city. Picasso, happy to have a fine museum showing off his work in the city of his youth, added to the collection throughout his life. (Sadly, since Picasso vowed never to set foot in a fascist, Franco-ruled Spain, and died two years before Franco, the artist never saw the museum.)

● Self-Guided Tour: While the rooms are constantly rearranged, the collection (291 paintings) is always presented chronologically. With the help of thoughtful English descriptions for each stage (and blue-shirted guards who don't let you stray), it's easy to follow the evolution of Picasso's work. The room numbers—though not exact—can help you get oriented in the museum. You'll see his art evolve in these 12 stages:

Rooms 1, 2, 3—Boy Wonder, Age 12–14, 1895–1897: Pablo's earliest art is realistic and serious. A budding genius emerges at age 12 as Pablo moves to Barcelona and gets serious about art. Even this young, his portraits of grizzled peasants show great psychological insight and flawless technique. You'll see portraits of Pablo's first teacher, his father *(Padre del Artista)*. Displays show his art-school work. Every time Pablo starts breaking rules, he's sent back to the standard classic style. The assignment: Sketch nude models to capture human anatomy accurately. Three self-portraits (1896) show the self-awareness of a blossoming intellect. When Pablo was 13, his father quit painting to nurture his young prodigy. Look closely at the portrait of his mother *(Retrato de la Madre del Artista)*. Pablo, then age 15, is working on the fine details and gradients of white in her blouse and the expression in her cameo-like face. Notice the signature. Spaniards keep both parents' surnames, with the father's first, followed by the mother's: Pablo Ruiz Picasso. Pablo was closer to his mom than his dad. Eventually he kept just her name.

Rooms 4, 5, 6—Málaga, Exploration of Nature: During a short trip to Málaga, Picasso dabbles in Impressionism (otherwise unknown in Spain at the time).

Rooms 7, 8—A Sponge, Influenced by Local Painters: As a 15-year-old, Pablo dutifully enters art-school competitions. His first big work—while forced to show a religious subject *(Primera Comunión,* or *First Communion,* Room 7)—is more an excuse to paint his family. Notice his sister Lola's exquisitely painted veil. This painting was heavily influenced by local painters.

In Room 8, *Ciencia y Caridad (Science and Charity),* which won second prize at a fine-arts exhibition, got Picasso the chance to study in Madrid. Now Picasso conveys real feeling. The doctor (Pablo's father) represents science. The nun represents charity and religion. But nothing can help, as the woman is clearly dead (notice her face and lifeless hand). Pablo painted a little perspective trick: Walk back and forth across the room to see the bed stretch and shrink. Four small studies for this painting, hanging in the back of the room, show how this was an exploratory work. The frontier: light.

Picasso travels to Madrid for further study. Finding the stuffy fine-arts school in Madrid stifling, Pablo hangs out in the Prado museum and learns by copying the masters. Notice his nearly perfect copy of Felipe IV by Diego Velázquez.

Rooms 8, 9, 10—Independence, 1899–1900: Having absorbed the wisdom of the ages, in 1898, Pablo visits Horta, a rural Catalan village, and finds his artistic independence. Poor and without a love in his life, he returns to Barcelona. It's 1900, and Art Nouveau is the rage. Upsetting his dad, Pablo quits art school and falls in with the avant-garde crowd. These bohemians congregate daily at Els Quatre Gats ("The Four Cats," slang for "a few crazy people"—see page 101). Further establishing his artistic freedom, he paints portraits—no longer of his family...but of his new friends. Still a teenager, Pablo puts on his first one-man show.

Room 10—Paris, 1900–1901: Nineteen-year-old Picasso arrives in Paris, a city bursting with life, light, and love. Dropping the paternal surname Ruiz, Pablo establishes his commercial brand name: "Picasso." Here, the explorer Picasso goes bohemian and befriends poets, prostitutes, and artists. He paints Impressionist landscapes like Claude Monet, posters like Henri de Toulouse-Lautrec, still lifes like Paul Cézanne, and bright-colored Fauvist works like Henri Matisse. (*La Espera*—with her bold outline and strong gaze—pops out from the Impressionistic background.) It was Cézanne's technique of "building" a figure with "cubes" of paint that inspired Picasso to soon invent Cubism.

Room 11—Blue Period, 1901–1904: The bleak Paris weather, the suicide of his best friend, and his own poverty lead Picasso to his "Blue Period." He cranks out piles of blue art just to stay housed and fed. With blue backgrounds (the coldest color) and depressing subjects, this period was revolutionary in art history. Now the artist is painting not what he sees but what he feels. The touching portrait of a mother and child, *Desamparados* (*Despair*, 1903), captures the period well. Painting misfits and street people, Picasso, like Velázquez and Toulouse-Lautrec, sees "the beauty in ugliness." Back home in Barcelona, Picasso paints his hometown at night from rooftops *(Terrats de Barcelona)*. Still blue, here we see proto-Cubism...five years before the first real Cubist painting.

Room 11—Rose Period, 1904–1907: The woman in pink *(Retrato de la Sra. Canals)*, painted with classic "Spanish melancholy," finally lifts Picasso out of his funk, moving him out of the blue and into a happier "Rose Period" (of which this museum has only the one painting).

Rooms 12, 13, 14—Cubism, 1907–1920: Pablo's invention in Paris of the shocking Cubist style is well-known—at least I hope so, since this museum has no true Cubist paintings. In the age of the camera, the Cubist gives just the basics (a man with a bowl of fruit) and lets you finish it.

Also in Rooms 12, 13, 14—Eclectic, 1920–1950: Picasso is a painter of many styles. We see a little post-Impressionistic Pointillism in a portrait that looks like a classical statue. After a trip to Rome, he paints beefy women, inspired by the three-dimensional sturdiness of ancient statues. To Spaniards, the expressionist horse symbolizes the innocent victim. In bullfights, the horse—clad with blinders and pummeled by the bull—has nothing to do with the fight. To Picasso, the horse symbolized the feminine, and the bull, the masculine. Picasso would mix all these styles and symbols—including this image of the horse—in his masterpiece *Guernica* (in Madrid's Centro de Arte Reina Sofía—see page 238) to show the horror and chaos of modern war. From here, follow the small wall signs directing you to rooms 15–19.

Rooms 15, 16, 17—Picasso and Velázquez, 1957: Notice the print of Velázquez's *Las Meninas* (in Madrid's Prado) that introduces this section. Picasso, who had great respect for Velázquez, painted more than 50 interpretations of this painting that many consider the greatest painting by anyone, ever. These two Spanish geniuses were artistic equals. Picasso seems to enjoy a relationship with Velázquez. Like artistic soulmates, they spar and tease. He dissects Velázquez, and then injects playful uses of light, color, and perspective to horse around with the earlier masterpiece. In the big black-and-white canvas, the king and queen (reflected in the mirror in the back of the room) are hardly seen, while the self-portrait of the painter towers above everyone. The two women of the court on the right look like they're in a tomb—but they're wearing party shoes. In these rooms, see the fun Picasso had playing paddleball with Velázquez's masterpiece—filtering Velázquez's realism through the kaleidoscope of Cubism.

Room 17—Windows, 1957: All his life, Picasso said, "Paintings are like windows open to the world." Here we see the French Riviera—with simple black outlines and Crayola colors, he paints sun-splashed nature and the joys of the beach. He died with brush in hand, still growing. To the end, Picasso continued exploring and loving life through his art. As a child, he was taught to paint as an adult. Now, as an old man (with little kids of his own and an also-childlike artist Marc Chagall for a friend), he paints like a child.

As a wrap-up, notice 41 works in Rooms 18 and 19, representing Picasso's ceramics made during his later years (1947).

In La Ribera, near the Picasso Museum

There's more to the Ribera neighborhood than just the Picasso Museum. While the nearby, waterfront Barceloneta district was for the working-class sailors, La Ribera housed the wealthier shippers and merchants. Its streets are lined with their fine mansions—which, like the much-appreciated Church of Santa Maria del Mar, were built with shipping wealth.

La Ribera (also known as "El Born") is separated from the Barri Gòtic by Via Laietana, a street built through the Old City in the early 1900s to alleviate growing traffic problems. From the Plaça Jaume I (where the nearest Metro stop is), cross this busy street to enter an up-and-coming zone of lively and creative restaurants and nightlife. The Carrer de l'Argenteria (literally, "Goldsmiths Street"—streets in La Ribera are named after the workshops that used to occupy them) runs diagonally from the Plaça Jaume I straight down to the Church of Santa Maria del Mar.

Just beyond the church is a long square, the Passeig del Born (formerly a jousting square, as its shape indicates). This is the neighborhood center and a popular springboard for exploring tapas bars, fun restaurants, and nightspots in the narrow streets all around. Wandering around here at night, you'll find piles of inviting and intriguing little restaurants (I've listed my favorites in "Eating," page 104). Enjoy a glass of wine on the square facing the church, or consider renting a bike here for a pedal down the beach promenade to the Fòrum (described on page 89). From behind the church, the Carrer de Montcada leads two blocks to the Picasso Museum (described above). The street's mansions—built by rich shippers centuries ago—now house galleries, shops, and even museums. In fact, the Picasso Museum itself consists of five such mansions laced together.

▲**Church of Santa Maria del Mar**—This church is the proud centerpiece of La Ribera. "Del Mar" means "of the sea"... and that's where the money came from. The proud shippers built this church in only 55 years, so it has a harmonious style considered pure Catalan Gothic. As you step in, notice the figures of workers carved into the big front doors. During the Spanish Civil War (1936–1939), the Church sided with the conservative forces of Franco against the people. In retaliation, the working class took their anger out on this church, burning all of its wood furnishings and decor (carbon still blackens the ceiling). Today it's stripped down—naked in all its Gothic glory. The tree-like columns inspired Gaudí (their influence on the columns inside his Sagrada Família church is obvious). Sixteenth-century sailors left models of their ships at the foot of the altar for Mary's protection. Even today, there remains a classic old Catalan ship at the feet of Mary (free entry, €3 guidebook explains the church well, buy it by the

Barcelona's La Ribera

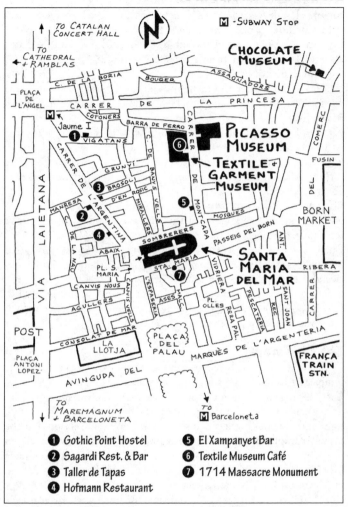

TO CATALAN CONCERT HALL

TO CATHEDRAL + RAMBLAS

M -SUBWAY STOP

CHOCOLATE MUSEUM

C. DE LA BORIA

BOUGER

ASSAONADORS

PLAÇA DE L'ANGEL

CARRER DE LA PRINCESA

CARRER COTONERS

Jaume I

M

❶ VIGATANS

BARRA DE FERRO

PICASSO MUSEUM

❻

TEXTILE + GARMENT MUSEUM

FUSIN

COMERC

GRUNY

CARRER DE L'ARGENTINA

BROSOLI

❸

D'EN ROSIC

MIRALLERS

BAIX'S VELS

❺

MOSQUES

BORN MARKET

MANRESA

❷

DE LA NAU

PASSEIG DEL BORN

DEL

ABAIX.

❹

SOMBRERERS

STA. MARIA

❼

SANTA MARIA DEL MAR

RIBERA

PL. S. MARIA

VIDRIERA

CANVIS NOUS

CANVIS VELLS

L'ESPASERIA

ASES

PESCATERIA

PL. OLLES

REA PAL.

REC

SANT JOAN

CARRER

AGULLERS

MALC.

POST

VIA LAIETANA

CONSOLAT DE MAR

LA LLOTJA

PLAÇA DEL PALAU

MARQUÈS DE L'ARGENTERIA

FRANÇA TRAIN STN.

PLAÇA ANTONI LOPEZ

AVINGUDA DEL

TO MAREMAGNUM + BARCELONETA

TO M Barceloneta

❶ Gothic Point Hostel
❷ Sagardi Rest. & Bar
❸ Taller de Tapas
❹ Hofmann Restaurant

❺ El Xampanyet Bar
❻ Textile Museum Café
❼ 1714 Massacre Monument

main altar, daily 9:00–13:30 & 16:30–20:00).

Exit the church from the side, and you arrive at a square with a modern **monument** to a 300-year-old massacre that's still a part of the Catalan consciousness. On September 11, 1714, the Bourbon king ruling from Madrid massacred Catalan patriots, who were buried in a mass grave on this square. From that day on, the king outlawed Catalan culture and its institutions (no speaking the language, no folk dances, no university, and so on). The eternal flame burns atop this monument, and 9/11 is still a sobering anniversary for the Catalans.

Textile and Garment Museum (Museu Tèxtil i d'Indumentària)—If fabrics from the 12th to the 20th centuries leave you cold, consider a *café con leche* on the museum's beautiful patio (museum entry €3.50, Tue–Sat 10:00–18:00, Sun 10:00–15:00, closed Mon, 30 yards from Picasso Museum at Montcada 12–14, www.museutextil.bcn.es).

It's free to enter the museum's patio—an inviting courtyard with a WC and coffee shop that's outside the museum but within the walls.

On Sunday nights, the museum hosts **jazz concerts** on this patio when the weather permits (21:00–23:00, generally closed in winter). You can stand and listen for free, or sit at the café tables for a pleasant meal (€5–10 salads, couscous, and quiche fare, plus €5 cover charge).

Chocolate Museum (Museu de la Xocolata)—This museum, only a couple of blocks from the Picasso Museum, is a delight for chocolate-lovers. It tells the story of chocolate from Aztecs to Europeans via the port of Barcelona, where it was first unloaded and processed. Even if you're into architecture more than calories, don't miss this opportunity to see the Sagrada Família church finished—and ready to eat (€4, Mon and Wed–Sat 10:00–19:00, Sun 10:00–15:00, closed Tue, Carrer Comerç 36, tel. 932-687-878, www.museuxocolata.com).

The Eixample

Wide sidewalks, hardy shade trees, chic shops, and plenty of Art Nouveau fun make the Eixample a refreshing break from the Old City. Uptown Barcelona is a unique variation on the common grid-plan city. Barcelona snipped off the building corners to create light and spacious eight-sided squares at every intersection. For the best Eixample example, ramble Rambla de Catalunya (unrelated to the more famous Ramblas) and pass through Passeig de Gràcia (described below, Metro for Block of Discord: Passeig de Gràcia, or Metro for Casa Milà: Diagonal).

The 19th century was a boom time for Barcelona. By 1850, the city was busting out of its medieval walls. A new town was planned to follow a grid-like layout. The intersection of three major thoroughfares—Gran Via, Diagonal, and Meridiana—would shift the city's focus uptown.

The Eixample, or "Expansion," was a progressive plan in which everything was made accessible to everyone. Each 20-block-square district would have its own hospital and large park, each 10-block-square area would have its own market and general services, and each five-block-square grid would house its own schools and day-care centers. The hollow space found inside each "block" of apartments would form a neighborhood park.

While much of that vision never quite panned out, the Eixample was an urban success. Rich and artsy big shots bought plots along the grid. The richest landowners built as close to the center as possible. For this reason, the best buildings are near the Passeig de Gràcia. While adhering to the height, width, and depth limitations, they built as they pleased—often in the trendy new Modernista style.

Gaudí's Art and Architecture

Barcelona is an architectural scrapbook of the galloping gables and organic curves of hometown boy Antoni Gaudí (1852–1926). A devoted Catalan and Catholic, he immersed himself in each project, often living on-site. At various times, he called Parc Güell, Casa Milà, and the Sagrada Família home.

▲▲▲**Sagrada Família (Holy Family)**—Gaudí's most famous and persistent work is this unfinished landmark church. He worked on it from 1883 to 1926. Since then, construction has moved forward in fits and starts. (But over 30 years of visits, I've seen considerable progress.) Even today, the half-finished church is not expected to be completed for another 50 years. One reason it's taking so long is that the temple is funded exclusively  by private donations and entry fees. Your admission helps pay for the ongoing construction.

Cost, Hours, Location: €8, €7 with Tourist Bus ticket, €9 combo-ticket includes Gaudí Museum in Parc Güell, daily April–Sept 9:00–20:00, Oct–March 9:00–18:00, Metro: Sagrada Família puts you right on the doorstep, tel. 932-073-031, www .sagradafamilia.org.

Tours: The 50-minute English tours cost €3.50 (6/day April–Oct, Nov–March usually Fri–Mon only). Or rent the good, 70-minute audioguide (also €3.50).

The Construction Project: There's something powerful about an opportunity to feel a community of committed people with a vision working on a church that will not be finished in their lifetime (as was standard in the Gothic age). Local craftsmen often cap off their careers by spending a couple of years on this exciting construction site. The church will trumpet its completion with 18 spires: A dozen "smaller" 330-foot spires (representing the apostles) will stand in groups of four and mark the three entry facades of the building. Four taller towers (dedicated to the four Evangelists) will surround the two tallest, central towers: a 400-foot-tall tower of

Modernista Sights

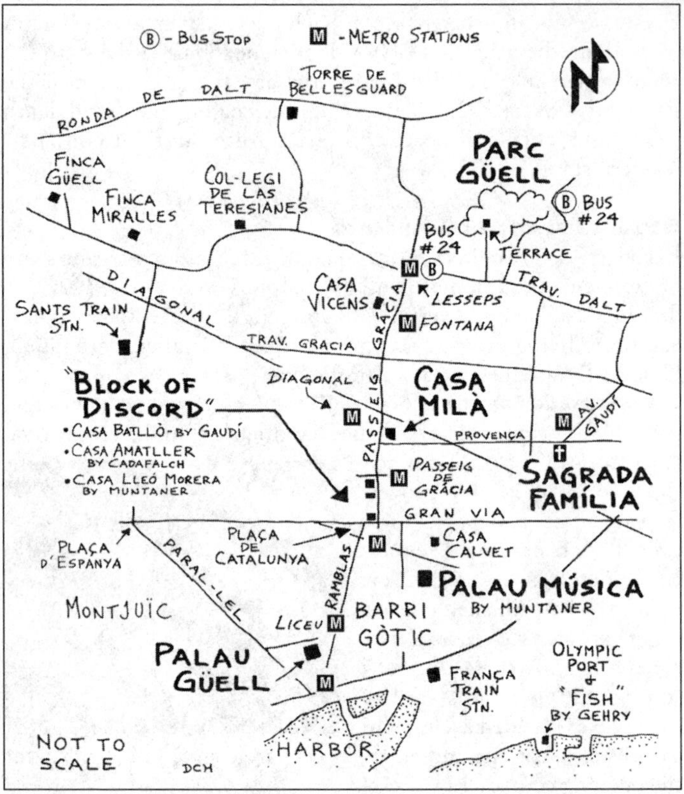

Mary and the grand 550-foot Jesus tower, which will shine like a spiritual lighthouse—visible even from out at sea. A unique exterior ambulatory will circle the building, like a cloister turned inside out. If there's any building on earth I'd like to see, it's the Sagrada Família...finished.

➲ **Self-Guided Tour:** To get the whole story, follow this commentary.

• *Begin facing the western side of the church (where you'll enter).*

Passion Facade: This facade is full of symbolism from the Bible. The story of Christ's Passion unfolds in the shape of a Z, from bottom to top. Find the stylized Alpha and Omega over the door; Jesus—hanging on the cross—with an open book (the word of God) for hair; and the grid of numbers adding up to 33 (Jesus' age at the time of his death). The distinct face of the man below and just left of Christ is a memorial to Gaudí.

When Gaudí died in 1926, only the stubs of four spires stood above the building site. The rest of the church has been inspired

by Gaudí's vision but designed and executed by others. Gaudí knew he wouldn't live to complete the church and recognized that later architects and artists would rely on their own muses for inspiration. This artistic freedom was amplified in 1936, when Civil War shelling burned many of Gaudí's blueprints. Judge for yourself how the recently completed and controversial Passion facade by Josep María Subirachs (b. 1927) fits with Gaudí's original formulation (which you'll see downstairs in the museum).

Now look high above: The colorful ceramic caps of the columns symbolize the mitres (formal hats) of bishops. This is only a side entrance. The nine-story apartment flat to the right will be torn down to accommodate the grand front entry of this church. The three facades—Passion, Nativity, and Glory—will chronicle Christ's life from birth to death to resurrection.

• *Go inside the church, entering the...*

Construction Zone (the Nave): The cranking cranes, rusty forests of rebar, and scaffolding require a powerful faith, but the Sagrada Família offers a fun look at a living, growing, bigger-than-life building. Part of Gaudí's religious vision was a love for nature. He said, "Nothing is invented; it's written in nature." His columns blossom with life, and little windows let light filter in like the canopy of a rain forest, giving both privacy and an intimate connection with God. The U-shaped choir hovers above the nave, tethered halfway up the columns. It's estimated that the proposed central tower (550 feet tall) will require four underground support pylons, each consisting of 8,000 tons of cement. Take the elevator on the Passion side (€2) or the stairs on the Nativity side (free, often miserably congested, most likely closed in hot weather) up to the dizzy lookout that bridges two spires. You'll get a great view of the city and a gargoyle's-eye perspective of the loopy church.

• *Outside, just after exiting the building, you'll encounter the...*

Nativity Facade (east side): This, the only part of the church essentially finished in his lifetime, shows Gaudí's original vision. Mixing Gothic-style symbolism, images from nature, and Modernista asymmetry, it is the best example of Gaudí's unmistakable cake-in-the-rain style. The sculpture shows scenes from the birth and childhood of Jesus, along with angels playing musical instruments. You can love it, hate it, or adopt a love/hate attitude to it, but you can't deny that it is unique.

• *Before leaving, head downstairs (into the church basement, or crypt) to the...*

Modernisme

The Renaixensa (Catalan cultural revival) gave birth to Modernisme (Catalan Art Nouveau) at the end of the 19th century. Barcelona is its capital. Its Eixample neighborhood shimmers with the colorful, leafy, flowing, blooming shapes of Modernisme in doorways, entrances, facades, and ceilings.

Meaning "a taste for what is modern"—things like street-cars, electric lights, and big-wheeled bicycles—this free-flowing organic style lasted from 1888 to 1906. Breaking with tradition, artists experimented with glass, tile, iron, and brick. The structure was fully modern, using rebar and concrete, but the decoration was a clip-art collage of nature images, exotic Moorish or Chinese themes, and fanciful Gothic crosses and knights to celebrate Catalunya's medieval glory days. It's Barcelona's unique contribution to the Europe-wide Art Nouveau movement. Modernisme was a way of life as Barcelona burst into the 20th century.

Antoni Gaudí (1852–1926), Barcelona's most famous Modernista artist, was descended from four generations of metalworkers, a lineage of which he was quite proud. He incorporated ironwork into his architecture and came up with novel approaches to architectural structure and space.

Two more Modernista architects famous for their unique style are Lluís Domènech i Muntaner and Josep Puig i Cadafalch. You'll see their work on the Block of Discord.

Museum: The museum displays physical models used for the church's construction. As you wander, you'll notice that they don't always match the finished product—these are ideas, not blueprints set in stone. Original architectural sketches are in a dimly lit room. Photos show the construction work as it was when Gaudí died in 1926, and how it's progressed over the years. See how the church's design is a fusion of nature, architecture, and religion. The columns seem light, with branches springing forth and capitals that look like palm trees. An exhibition compares nature, waves, shells, mushrooms, and so on to Gaudí's work. Find the hanging model showing how Gaudí used gravity to calculate the perfect parabolas incorporated into the church design (the mirror above this model shows how the right-side-up church is derived from this). You'll also peek into a busy workshop where the slow-and-steady building pace is maintained.

Gaudí lived on the site for more than a decade and is buried in the crypt. A window allows you to look down into the neo-Gothic 19th-century crypt (which is how the church began) to see Gaudí's tomb. There's a move afoot to make Gaudí a saint. Perhaps someday, this tomb will be a place of pilgrimage. Gaudí—a faith-ful Catholic whose medieval-style mysticism belied his Modernista architecture career—was certainly driven to greatness by his pas-sion for God. When undertaking a lengthy project, he said, "My client"—meaning God—"is not in a hurry."

▲▲**Casa Milà (La Pedrera)**—This Gaudí exterior laughs down on the crowds filling Passeig de Gràcia. Casa Milà, also called

La Pedrera (The Quarry), has a much-photographed roller coaster of melting-ice-cream eaves. This is Barcelona's quint-essential Modernista building and Gaudí's last major work (1906–1910) before dedicating his final years to the Sagrada Família.

You can visit three sections of Casa Milà: the apartment, attic, and rooftop. Buy the €8 ticket to see all three (all covered by Articket Card). Two elevators take you up to either the apart-ment or the attic and rooftop. Normally you're directed to the apartment, but if you arrive late in the day, go to the attic/rooftop elevator first, to make sure you have enough time to enjoy Gaudí's works and the views.

The apartment elevator whisks you to the *Life in Barcelona 1905–1929* exhibit (good English descriptions). Then, walk through

the sumptuously furnished Art Nouveau apartment. Upstairs in the attic, wander under parabola-shaped brick arches and enjoy a multimedia exhibit of models, photos, and videos of Gaudí's works. A stairway leads to the fanciful rooftop, where chim-neys play volleyball with the clouds. From here, you can see Gaudí's other principal works: the Sagrada Família to the west, Casa Batlló to the south, and Parc Güell to the north (daily 10:00–20:00, free 60-minute audio-

guide, Passeig de Gràcia 92, Metro: Diagonal, tel. 934-845-530).

At the ground level of Casa Milà, poke into the dream-ily painted original entrance courtyard. The first floor hosts free art exhibits. During the summer, a concert series called "Pedrera by Night" features live music—jazz, flamenco, tango—a glass of champagne, and the chance to see the rooftop illuminated (€10, July–Sept Fri–Sat at 22:00, tel. 934-845-900).

If you're hungry, stop by the recommended La Bodegueta, a

long block away (daily lunch special, see "Eating," below).

▲**Block of Discord**—Four blocks from Casa Milà, you can survey a noisy block of competing late-19th-century facades. Several of Barcelona's top Modernista mansions line Passeig de Gràcia (Metro: Passeig de Gràcia). Because the structures look as though they are trying to outdo each other in creative twists, locals nicknamed the block between Consell de Cent and Arago the "Block of Discord." First (at #43) and most famous is Gaudí's **Casa Batlló,** with skull-like balconies and a tile roof that suggests a cresting dragon's back; Gaudí based the work on the popular St. Jordi (George) legend, in which he slays the dragon (daily 9:00–20:00; €16 includes main floor, roof, and decent audioguide—but entering Casa  Milà is much cheaper and better). By the way, if you're tempted to snap your photos from the middle of the street, be careful—Gaudí died under a streetcar.

Next door, at **Casa Amatller** (#41), check out architect Josep Puig i Cadafalch's creative mix of Moorish- and Gothic-inspired architecture and iron grillwork, which decorates a step-gable like those in the Netherlands.

On the corner (at #35), **Casa Lleó Morera** has a wonderful interior highlighted by the dining room's fabulous stained glass. The architect, Lluís Domènech i Muntaner, also did the Catalan Concert Hall (you'll notice similarities).

The perfume shop halfway down the street has a free and interesting little perfume museum in the back. La Rita restaurant, just around the corner on Carrer Arago, serves a fine three-course lunch for a great price at 13:00 (see "Eating," below).

▲**Parc Güell**—Gaudí fans enjoy the artist's magic in this colorful park. Gaudí intended this 30-acre garden to be a 60-residence housing project—a kind of gated community. As a high-income housing development, it flopped. But as a park, it's a delight, offering another peek into the eccentric genius of Gaudí. Notice the mosaic medallions that say "park" in English, reminding folks that this is modeled on an English garden.

Cost, Hours, Location: Free, daily 10:00–20:00, tel. 932-130-488. The red Tourist Bus or bus #24 from Plaça de Catalunya leaves you a few blocks away, or a €6 taxi drops you right at the gate.

If you're taking the Metro (which is likely if you're coming from Sagrada Família), get off at the Lesseps stop; to avoid the 20-minute tiring, uphill walk to the park, don't follow the *Parc*

Güell 1300 metros sign; instead, exit left out of the Metro station, cross the streets Princep d'Astúries and Gran de Grácia, and catch bus #24 (on Gran de Grácia), which takes you to the park's side entrance in five to 10 minutes.

◐ Self-Guided Tour: As you wander the park, imagine living here a century ago—if this gated community succeeded and was filled with Barcelona's wealthy. Stepping past fancy gate houses (which now hold a good bookshop), you walk by Gaudí's wrought-iron gas lamps (1900–1914)— his dad was a blacksmith, and he always enjoyed this medium.

Climb the grand stairway past the ceramic dragon fountain. At the top, drop by the "Hall of 100 Columns," housing a produce market for the neighborhood's 60 mansions. The fun columns—each different, made from concrete and rebar, topped with colorful ceramic, and studded with broken bottles and bric-a-brac—add to the market's vitality.

After shopping, continue up. Look left, down the playful "pathway of columns" that support a long arcade. Gaudí drew his inspiration from nature, and this arcade is like a surfer's perfect tube. From here, continue up to the terrace. Sit on a colorful bench—designed to fit your body ergonomically—and enjoy one of Barcelona's best views. Look for the Sagrada Família church in the distance. Gaudí was an engineer as well. He designed a water-catchment system by which rain hitting this plaza would flow into and through the columns from the market below and power the park's fountains.

When considering the failure of Parc Güell as a community development, also consider that it was an idea a hundred years ahead of its time. Back then, high-society ladies didn't want to live so far from the cultural action. Today, the surrounding neighborhoods are some of the wealthiest in town, and a gated community here would be a big hit.

The skippable **Center for Interpretation of Parc Güell** (Centre d'Interpretació), at the park's main entrance, shows Gaudí's building methods plus maps, photos, and models of the park (€2, daily 11:00–15:00, tel. 933-190-222).

The small **Gaudí Museum** in the middle of the park is more worthwhile than the Center. While sparse, it comes with some interesting Gaudí furniture and a chance to wander through a model home used to sell the others. Gaudí lived here for 20 years, until his father died. His humble artifacts are mostly gone (€4, €9 combo-ticket includes Sagrada Família, daily April–Sept 10:00–20:00, Oct–March 10:00–18:00).

▲**Palau Güell**—This building, closed through 2007, will offer a good chance to see a Gaudí interior when it reopens. Curvy.

Montjuïc

Montjuïc ("Mount of the Jews"), overlooking Barcelona's hazy port, has always been a show-off. Ages ago it had an impressive fortress. In 1929, it hosted an international fair, from which most of today's sights originated. And in 1992, the Summer Olympics directed the world's attention to this pincushion of attractions once again.

Getting to Montjuïc: You have several options. The simplest is to take a **taxi** directly to your destination (about €7).

Here are more ways to reach Montjuïc, all of which drop you off at the base of a funicular below the Castle of Montjuïc: the **blue Tourist Bus** route (see "Getting Around Barcelona," page 51); by **public bus** (take #50 from the corner of Gran Via and Passeig de Gràcia, or #55 from Plaça de Catalunya, next to Caja de Madrid building); or by **Metro** (to the Paral-lel stop, exit direction Non de la Rambla for the funicular).

By bus or Metro, you'll arrive at the base of **funicular**—take it up to Montjuïc (covered by a Metro ticket, every 10 min, 9:00–22:00, the number of minutes until next departure posted at start of entry tunnel). From the top of the funicular, it's a two-minute walk to the Joan Miró museum and a 10-minute stroll to the Catalan Art Museum.

The **bus** marked *Parc Montjuïc* also loops around the sights, starting at Plaça d'Espanya, and going to the Catalan Art Museum, the Joan Miró museum, the funicular, and the Castle of Montjuïc.

From the port, the most scenic way to Montjuïc is via the **cable car**, called the 1929 Transbordador Aereo (closed until May 2007 or possibly later, rates and schedules to be determined on opening, tel. 934-430-859).

I've listed the two museums in a logical sightseeing order—from higher up (Fundació Joan Miró, reach by funicular) to lower down (Catalan Art Museum)—but note that if you want to visit only the Catalan Art Museum, you can skip the funicular and instead take the Metro to Plaça d'Espanya and ride the escalators up to the museum.

▲**Fundació Joan Miró**—Showcasing the talents of yet another Catalan artist, this museum has the best collection of Joan Miró

Montjuïc

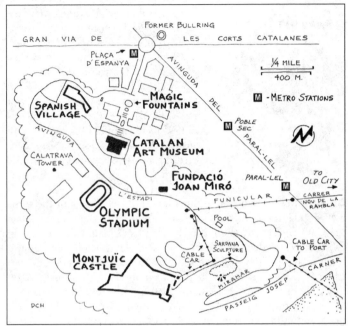

art anywhere. You'll also see works by other Modern artists (such as *Mercury Fountain* by the American sculptor Alexander Calder). If you don't like abstract art, you'll leave here scratching your head, but those who love this place are not faking it...they understand the genius of Miró and the fun of abstract art.

As you wander, consider this: Miró believed that everything in the cosmos is linked—colors, sky, stars, love, time, music,

dogs, men, women, dirt, and the void. He mixed childlike symbols of these things creatively, as a poet uses words. It's as liberating for the visual artist to be abstract as it is for the poet: Both can use metaphors rather than being confined to concrete explanations. Miró would listen to music

and paint. It's interactive, free interpretation. He said, "For me, simplicity is freedom."

Here are some tips to help you enjoy and appreciate Miró's art: 1) meditate on it; 2) read the title (for example, *The Smile of a Tear*); 3) meditate on it again. Repeat the process until you have an

COPA DEL MUNDO DE FUTBOL ESPAÑA 82

epiphany. There's no correct answer—it's pure poetry. Devotees of Miró say they fly with him and don't even need drugs. You're definitely much less likely to need drugs if you take advantage of the wonderful audioguide, included with admission (€7.50, covered by Articket Card, May–Sept Tue–Sat 10:00–20:00—but closes at 19:00 Oct–June, Thu until 21:30, Sun 10:00–14:30, closed Mon, 200 yards from top of funicular, Parc de Montjuïc, tel. 934-439-470, www.bcn.fjmiro.es).

Olympic Stadium (Estadi Olímpic)—For two weeks in the summer of 1992, the world turned its attention to this stadium (between the Catalan Art Museum and the Fundació Joan Miró at Passeig Olímpic 17). Redesigned from an earlier 1929 version, the stadium was updated, expanded, and officially named for Catalan patriot Lluís Companys i Jover. The XXV Olympiad kicked off here on July 25, when an archer dramatically lit the Olympic torch—which still stands high at the end of the stadium overlooking the city skyline—with a flaming arrow. Over the next two weeks, Barcelona played host to the thrill of victory (mostly at the hands of Magic Johnson, Michael Jordan, Larry Bird, and the rest of the US basketball "Dream Team") and the agony of defeat (i.e., the nightmares of the Dream Team's opponents). Hovering over the stadium is the memorable, futuristic Calatrava Communications Tower, used to transmit Olympic highlights and lowlights around the world. Aside from the memories of the medals, today's Olympic Stadium offers little to see today...except when it's hosting a match for Barcelona's soccer team, RCD Espanyol, or a game of the NFL Europe's Barcelona Dragons.

▲▲Catalan Art Museum (Museu Nacional d'Art de Catalunya)—The big vision for this wonderful museum is to showcase Catalan art from the 10th century through about 1930. Often called "the Prado of Romanesque art" (and "MNAC" for short), its highlight is Europe's best collection of Romanesque frescos (€8.50, includes audioguide, covered by Articket Card, free first Sun of month, open Tue–Sat 10:00–19:00, Sun 10:00–14:30, closed Mon; in massive National Palace building above Magic Fountains, near Plaça d'Espanya—take escalators up; tel. 936-220-376, www.mnac.es).

As you enter, pick up a map (helpful for such a big and confusing building). The left wing is Romanesque, and the right wing is Gothic, exquisite Renaissance, and Baroque. Upstairs is more

Baroque, plus modern art, photography, and more.

The MNAC's rare, world-class collection of **Romanesque** art came mostly from remote Catalan village churches in the Pyrenees (saved from unscrupulous art dealers—including many Americans). The Romanesque wing features frescoes, painted wooden altar fronts, and ornate statuary. This classic Romanesque art—with flat 2-D scenes, each saint holding his symbol, and Jesus (easy to identify by the cross in his halo)—is impressively displayed on replicas of the original church ceilings.

In the **Gothic** wing, fresco murals give way to vivid 14th-century wood-panel paintings of Bible stories. A roomful of paintings by the Catalan master Jaume Huguet (1412–1492) deserves a look, particularly his altarpiece of Barcelona's patron saint, George.

For a break, glide under the huge dome (which once housed an ice-skating rink) over to the air-conditioned cafeteria. This was the prime ceremony room and dance hall for the 1929 International Exposition. Then, from the big ballroom, ride the glass elevator upstairs, where the **Modern** section takes you on a delightful walk from the late 1800s to about 1930—kind of a Catalan Musée d'Orsay, showing off the best of local art during this exciting period. You start with Modernisme (furniture complements the empty spaces you likely saw in Gaudí's buildings), then Impressionists, *fin de siècle* fun, and Art Deco. It's refreshing to be introduced to Catalan artists.

Upstairs you'll also find photography (with a bit on how photo-journalism came of age covering the Spanish Civil War), seductive sofas, and the chic Oleum restaurant, with vast city views.

▲**Magic Fountains (Font Màgica)**—Music, colored lights, and huge amounts of water make an artistic and coordinated splash on summer nights at Plaça d'Espanya (20-min shows start on the half-hour Fri–Sat 19:00–21:00, Thu–Sun in summer until 23:00; from the Espanya Metro station, walk toward the towering National Palace).

Spanish Village (Poble Espanyol)—This tacky five-acre model village uses fake traditional architecture from all over Spain as a shell to contain gift shops. Craftspeople do their clichéd thing only in the morning (not worth your time or €7.50, www.poble -espanyol.com). After hours, it's a popular local nightspot.

Castle of Montjuïc—The castle offers great city views from its fortress (€1, April–June daily 10:00–14:00, July–Sept daily 10:00–20:00, Oct–March Sat–Sun only 10:00–14:00) and a military museum (€2.50, Tue–Sun 10:00–20:00, closed Mon). The seemingly endless museum houses a dull collection of guns, swords, and toy soldiers. An interesting section on the Spanish-American War of 1898 covers Spain's valiant fight against American aggression (from its perspective). Unfortunately, there are no English descriptions. Those interested in Jewish history will find a fascinating collection of ninth-century Jewish tombstones.

The castle itself has a fascist past rife with repression. It was built in the 18th century by the central Spanish government to keep an eye on Barcelona and stifle citizen revolt. When Franco was in power, the castle was the site of hundreds of political executions.

Near the Waterfront, East of the Old City and Harbor

Citadel Park (Parc de la Ciutadella)—Barcelona's biggest, greenest park, originally the site of a much-hated military citadel, was transformed in 1888 for a World's Fair (Universal Exhibition). The stately Triumphal Arch at the top of the park, celebrating the removal of the much hated citadel, was built as the main entrance. Inside, you'll find wide pathways, plenty of trees and grass, the zoo, and the geology and zoology museums. Barcelona, one of Europe's most densely populated cities, suffers from a lack of real green space. This park is a haven, and especially enjoyable on weekends when it teems with happy families. Enjoy the ornamental fountain that the young Antoni Gaudí helped design, and consider a jaunt in a rowboat on the lake in the center of the park (€1.20 per person for 30 min). Check out the tropical Umbracle greenhouse and the Hivernacle winter garden, which has a pleasant café-bar (daily 8:00–20:00, Metro: Arc de Triomf, east of França Train Station).

▲Barcelona's Beach, from Barceloneta to the Fòrum—Barcelona has created a summer tourist beach trade by building

a huge stretch of beaches east from the town center. Before the 1992 Olympics, the zone was an industrial wasteland nicknamed the "Catalan Manchester." Not anymore. The industrial zone was demolished and dumped into the sea, while sand was dredged out of the sea bed to make the pristine beaches locals enjoy today. The scene is great for sunbathing and for an evening paseo before dinner.

Bike the Beach: For a break from the city, rent a bike (in La Ribera or Citadel Park, listed above, bike rentals described below) and take the following little ride: Explore Barcelona's "Central Park"—Citadel Park—filled with families enjoying a day out (described above). Then roll through Barceloneta (an artificial peninsula, once the home of working-class sailors and shippers). From the Barceloneta beach, head west to the Olympic Village, where the former apartments for 13,000 visiting athletes now house permanent residents. The village's symbol, Frank Gehry's striking "fish," shines brightly in the sun. A bustling night scene keeps this stretch of harborfront busy until the wee hours. From here you'll come to a series of man-made, crescent-shaped beaches, each with trendy bars and cafés. If you're careless (down by Platja de la Mar Bella), you might find yourself pedaling through a nudist beach (locals say that when you see the Pakistanis lined up gawking, you're very close). In the distance, you see the huge solar panel marking the site of the Fòrum shopping and convention center (described below).

There are plenty of **bike rental** places around Citadel Park and La Ribera's Church of Santa Maria del Mar. **Un Cotxe Menys** ("One Car Less"), near the Church of Santa Maria del Mar, is handy, giving out proposed biking routes and leading tours (€11/4 hrs, Mon–Sat 10:00–19:00, Sun 10:00–14:00, leave €150 or photo ID for deposit, Espaseria 3, tel. 932-682-105, www.bicicletabarcelona.com). **Classic Rent A Bike** is three blocks downhill from Plaça de Catalunya (€11/4 hrs, €16/24 hrs, daily 9:30–14:00 & 15:30–20:00, Carrer Tallers 45, tel. 933-171-970). To rent a bike on the Barceloneta beach, consider **Biciclot** (€5/hr, €13/3 hrs, €18/24 hrs; Mon–Thu 10:00–20:00, Fri–Sun 10:00–14:00; in winter Sat–Sun 10:00–15:00 only; on the sand 300 yards from Olympic Village towers at Passeig Maritime 33, tel. 932-219-778). Note that while biking is great in the park and along the beach, it's terrible in the city center, where pedestrians and cars rule.

The Fòrum—The original vision for the enlargement of Barcelona from 1860 had the boulevard called Diagonal continuing right to the sea. They finally realized this goal nearly a century and a half later, with the opening of the Fòrum. Go here for a taste of today's Barcelona: nothing Gothic, nothing quaint, just big and modern—a mall and a convention center. In 2004, Barcelona hosted the first "Forum of the Cultures," an attempt to create a world's fair that recognized not states, but peoples. Roma (Gypsies), Basques, Māoris, Native Americans, and Catalans all assembled here in a global celebration of cultural diversity, multiculturalism, peace, and sustainability.

The Fòrum also tries to be an inspiration for environmental engineering. Waste is burned to create heat. The giant solar panel creates perfectly clean and sustainable energy. The festival was a moderate success and will be a once-every-four-years bash for this planet's "nations without states." Local government officials hoped the event—like other "expos"—would goose development...and it did. Barcelona now has a new modern part of town.

You can get out to the Fòrum by bike, bus, or taxi via the long and impressive new beach. Or the Metro zips you there in just a few minutes from the center (yellow line, Fòrum station). Once there, browse around the modern shopping zone.

Away from the Center

Tibidabo—Tibidabo comes from the Latin for "to thee I shall give," the words the devil used when he was tempting Christ. It's still an enticing offer: At the top of Barcelona's highest peak, you're offered the city's oldest fun-fair (€22, erratic hours, tel. 932-117-942, www.tibidabo.es), the neo-Gothic Sacred Heart Church, and—if the weather and air quality are good—an almost limitless view of the city and the Mediterranean.

Getting there is part of the fun: Start by taking the FGC line—similar to, but separate from, the Metro (also covered by the T10 Card, see "Getting Around Barcelona," page 51)—from the Plaça de Catalunya station (under Café Zürich) to the Tibidabo stop. The red Tourist Bus stops here, too. Then take Barcelona's only remaining tram—the Tramvía Blau—from Plaça John F. Kennedy to Plaça Dr. Andreu (€3.50 round-trip, 2–4/hr). From there, take the funicular to the top (€3, tel. 906-427-017).

NIGHTLIFE

Refer to the *See Barcelona* guide (free from TI) and ask about the latest at a TI. Major sights open until 20:00 include the Picasso Museum (closed Mon), Gaudí's Sagrada Família (open daily, until 18:00 Nov–March), Casa Milà (daily), and Parc Güell (daily). On Thursday, Montjuïc's Joan Miró museum stays open until 21:30 (otherwise open May–Sept Tue–Sat until 20:00).

Many lesser sights also stay open until 20:00, such as La Boquería market (Mon–Sat), the Maritime Museum (daily), Columbus Monument (daily May–Oct), City History Museum (Tue–Sat), Church of Santa Maria del Mar (daily), Casa Batlló (daily), Gaudí Museum (daily April–Sept), the Castle of Montjuïc (daily July–Sept), and Citadel Park (daily). The Magic Fountains on Plaça d'Espanya make a splash on weekend evenings (Fri–Sat, plus Thu in summer). The Tourist Bus (Bus Turístic) runs until 22:00 every day in summer.

For music, consider a performance at Casa Milà ("Pedrera by Night" summer concert series, see page 81), the Liceu Opera House (page 60), or the Catalan Concert Hall (page 70). There are many nightspots around Plaça Reial (such as the popular Jamboree).

Palau de la Virreina, an arts-and-culture TI, offers information on Barcelona cultural events—music, opera, and theater (Mon–Sat 10:00–20:00, Sun 10:00–15:00, Ramblas 99, see map on page 57).

SLEEPING

Book ahead. Barcelona is Spain's most expensive city. Still, it has reasonable rooms. Cheap places are more crowded in summer; fancier business-class hotels fill up in winter and offer discounts on weekends and in summer. When considering relative hotel values, you can often get modern comfort for about the same price (€100) as you'll pay for ramshackle charm (and only a few minutes' walk from the Old City action). The TI at Plaça de Catalunya has a room-finding service, though it's cheaper to go direct.

Business-Class Comfort near Plaça de Catalunya

These hotels have sliding glass doors leading to plush reception areas, air-conditioning, and perfectly sterile modern bedrooms. Most are on big streets within two blocks of Barcelona's exuberant central square. As business-class hotels, they have hard-to-pin-down prices that fluctuate wildly. I've listed the average rate you'll pay. But in summer and on weekends, it seems the supply often far exceeds the demand, and many of these places lower prices to around €100—always ask for a deal.

$$$ **Hotel Catalonia Albinoni,** the best located of all, elegantly fills a renovated old palace with wide halls, hardwood floors, and 74 rooms. It overlooks a thriving pedestrian boulevard. Front rooms have views; balcony rooms on the back are quiet and come with sun terraces (Db-€170, extra bed-€35, family rooms, great

---

Sleep Code

(€1 = about $1.20, country code: 34)
S = Single, **D** = Double/Twin, **T** = Triple, **Q** = Quad, **b** = bathroom,
s = shower only. Unless otherwise noted, credit cards are accepted, English is spoken, and prices listed do not include the 7 percent tax or breakfast (ranging from simple €3 spreads to €18 buffets).

To help you easily sort through these listings, I've divided the rooms into three categories, based on the price for a standard double room with bath (during high season):

$$$ **Higher Priced**—Most rooms €150 or more.
$$ **Moderately Priced**—Most rooms between €100–150.
$ **Lower Priced**—Most rooms €100 or less.

While many of my recommendations are on pedestrian streets, night noise can be a problem (especially in cheap places, which have single-pane windows). For a quiet night, ask for "*tranquilo*" rather than "*con vista.*"

buffet breakfast free when you book direct and show this book in 2007, air-con, elevator, a block down from Plaça de Catalunya at Avinguda Portal de l'Angel 17, tel. 933-184-141, fax 933-012-631, www.hoteles-catalonia.com, albinoni.reservas@hoteles-catalonia.es).

$$$ Hotel Duques de Bergara boasts four stars. It has splashy public spaces, slick marble and hardwood floors, 150 comfortable rooms, and a garden courtyard with a pool a world away from the big-city noise (Sb-€155, Db-€192, Tb-€227, air-con, elevator, a half block off Plaça de Catalunya at Carrer de Bergara 11, tel. 933-015-151, fax 933-173-442, www.hoteles-catalonia.es, duques@hoteles-catalonia.es).

$$$ Nouvel Hotel, in an elegant, Victorian-style building on a handy pedestrian street, is less business-oriented and offers more character than the others listed here. It boasts royal lounges and 78 comfy rooms (Sb-€97, Db-€160, includes breakfast, manager Roberto promises 10 percent discount on these prices when booking direct with this book in 2007, air-con, Carrer de Santa Ana 18, tel. 933-018-274, fax 933-018-370, www.hotelnouvel.com, info@hotelnouvel.com).

$$ Hotel Occidental Reding, on a quiet street a five-minute walk west of the Ramblas and Plaça de Catalunya action, is a slick place renting 44 rooms at a very good price (Db-€120, extra bed-€59, air-con, elevator, near Metro: Universitat, Gravina 5–7, tel. 934-121-097, fax 932-683-482, www.occidental-hoteles.com, reding@occidental-hoteles.com).

$$ Hotel Duc de la Victoria, with 156 rooms, is professional yet friendly, buried in the Barri Gòtic just three blocks off the Ramblas (Db-€100–150 depending on occupancy, superior rooms—bigger and on a corner with windows on 2 sides—are worth €15 extra, air-con, elevator, Duc de la Victoria 15, tel. 932-703-410, fax 934-127-747, www.nh-hotels.com, nhducdelavictoria@nh-hotels.com).

$$ Hotel Lleó is well-run, with 90 big, bright, and comfortable rooms and a great lounge (Db-€120 but flexes way up with demand, summer Db special-€100, extra bed-about €25, air-con, elevator, Wi-Fi and Internet in lounge, 2 blocks west of Plaça de Catalunya at Carrer de Pelai 22, tel. 933-181-312, fax 934-122-657, www.hotel-lleo.com, reservas@hotel-lleo.es).

$$ Hotel Atlantis is solid, with 50 rooms and great prices for the location (Sb-€90, Db-€107, Tb-€125, breakfast-€8, air-con, elevator, Wi-Fi and Internet in lobby, Carrer de Pelai 20, tel. 933-189-012, fax 934-120-914, www.hotelatlantis-bcn.com, info@hotelatlantis.com).

Hotels with "Personality"
on or near the Ramblas

The first three hotels—Hotel Continental Barcelona, Hotel Toledano, and Hostal Residencia Capitol—overlook the Ramblas and are in the same building at the top of the Ramblas, very near Plaça de Catalunya. They offer classic, tiny-view balcony opportunities if you don't mind the noise.

My last three listings—España, Peninsular, and Opera—are a few blocks away, on a seedy but safe street about halfway down the Ramblas. These places are generally family-run, with ad-lib furnishings, more character, and much lower prices. Only the Jardí offers a quaint square buried in the Barri Gòtic ambience—and you'll pay for it.

$ Hotel Continental Barcelona has an inviting lounge with a great Ramblas-view balcony. Its comfortable rooms come with double-thick mattresses, wildly clashing carpets and wallpaper, and perhaps one too many clever ideas (they're laden with microwaves, fridges, and strange Tupperware drawers). Choose between your own little Ramblas-view balcony or a quieter back room (S-€75, Db-€85, twin Db-€95, Db with balcony-€105, extra bed-€20, includes tax, air-con, elevator, Internet in lobby, Ramblas 138, tel. 933-012-570, fax 933-027-360, www.hotelcontinental .com, barcelona@hotelcontinental.com). José's free breakfast and all-day snack-and-drink bar makes this a better deal than the price suggests.

$ Hotel Toledano, overlooking the Ramblas, is stark and basic, popular with backpackers and dust-bunnies. Small, folksy, but with unpredictable plumbing, it's warmly run by Albert Sanz, his father Juan, Dani, and trusty Daniel on the night shift (Sb-€39, Db-€64, Tb-€81, Qb-€90; front rooms have petite Ramblas-view balconies, back rooms have no noise—request your choice when you call; some rooms have air-con, free Internet in lobby, Rambla de Canaletas 138, tel. 933-010-872, fax 934-123-142, www.hoteltoledano .com, reservas@hoteltoledano.com). The Sanz family also runs **Hostal Residencia Capitol** one floor above—quiet, plain, no air-conditioning, cheaper, and also appropriate for backpackers (S-€28, D-€41, Ds-€47, Q-€61, 5-bed room-€69).

$ Hostería Grau is homey, family-run, and almost alpine. Its 25 clean and woody rooms are a few blocks off the Ramblas in the colorful university district (S-€33, D-€57, Db-€80, 2-bedroom family suites-€120, fans, air-con planned for summer 2007, Internet in lobby, 200 yards up Carrer dels Tallers from the Ramblas at Ramelleres 27, tel. 933-018-135, fax 933-176-825, www .hostalgrau.com, reservas@hostalgrau.com, Monica). The first two floors have ceilings a claustrophobic seven feet high, then things get tall again.

Hotels near the Ramblas

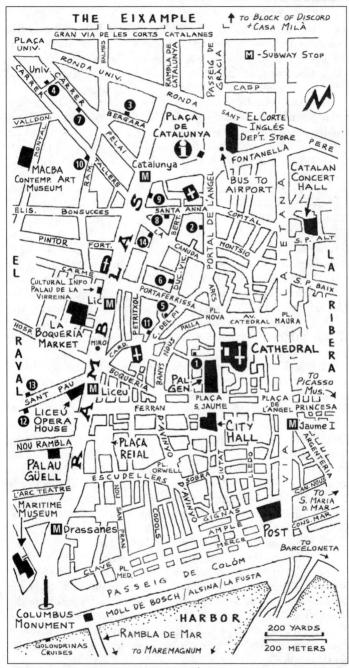

Hotel Key

❶ Hotel Neri	❾ Hotel Continental Barcelona, Hotel Toledano & Hostal Residencia Capitol
❷ Hotel Catalonia Albinoni	
❸ Hotel Duques de Bergara	❿ Hostería Grau
❹ Hotel Occidental Reding	⓫ Hotel Jardí
❺ Hostal Malda	⓬ Hotel España
❻ Hotel Duc de la Victoria	⓭ Hotel Peninsular & Hostal Opera
❼ Hotels Lleó & Atlantis	
❽ Nouvel Hotel	⓮ Hostal Campi

$ Hotel Jardí offers 40 clean, remodeled rooms on a breezy square in the Barri Gòtic. Many of the tight, plain, comfy rooms come with petite balconies (€15 extra) and enjoy an almost Parisian ambience. It's a good deal only if you value the cute square location. Book well in advance, as this family-run place has an avid following (Sb-€70, small interior Db-€80, Db-€86, Db with square-view terrace-€96, extra bed-€12, breakfast-€6, air-con, elevator, halfway between Ramblas and cathedral at Plaça Sant Josep Oriol 1, tel. 933-015-900, fax 933-425-733, www.hoteljardi-barcelona.com, reservations@hoteljardi-barcelona.com).

$ Hotel España is in a big, creaky, circa-1900 building with 84 rooms and lavish public spaces still sweet with Art Nouveau decor by locally popular Modernista architect Domènech i Muntaner. While it's 50 yards off the Ramblas on a borderline-seedy street, it feels safe (Sb-€55–65, Db-€90–105, Tb-€105–135, includes tax and breakfast, air-con, elevator, near Metro: Liceu at Carrer Sant Pau 9, tel. 933-181-758, fax 933-171-134, www.hotelespanya.com, hotelespanya@hotelespanya.com).

$ Hotel Peninsular, farther down the same creepy-at-night street, is a unique and thoughtfully run value in the old center. A former convent, the 80 still-basic and thinly furnished rooms—once nuns' cells—gather prayerfully around a bright, peaceful courtyard (Sb-€54, Db-€75, Tb-€90, prices include tax and breakfast and are the same year-round, air-con, elevator, Carrer Sant Pau 34, tel. 933-023-138, fax 934-123-699, www.hpeninsular.com, reservas@hpeninsular.com, Alex and Augustin).

$ Hostal Opera, with 70 stark rooms 20 yards off the Ramblas, is clean, simple, and modern (Sb-€43, Db-€63, no breakfast, air-con only in summer, elevator, Internet in lobby, Carrer Sant Pau 20, tel. 933-188-201, www.hostalopera.com, info@hostalopera.com). The street can feel seedy at night, but it's safe, and the hotel is very secure.

Chic and Posh, Deep in the Barri Gòtic

$$$ Hotel Neri is sophisticated, with 22 rooms spliced into the ancient stones of the Barri Gòtic overlooking an overlooked square a block from the cathedral. Opened in 2003, it has big plasma-screen TVs, pricey modern art on the bedroom walls, and dressed-up people in its gourmet restaurant (Db-€250, suites-€360, breakfast-€22, air-con, elevator, rooftop tanning deck, St. Sever 5, tel. 933-040-655, fax 933-040-337, www.hotelneri.com, info @hotelneri.com).

Humble, Cheaper Places Buried in the Old City

$ Hostal Campi is big, quiet, and ramshackle. This easygoing, old-school spot rents 24 rooms a few doors off the top of the Ramblas. The streets can be noisy, so request a quiet room in the back (D-€48, Db-€56, T-€65, Tb-€76, no breakfast but you're welcome to picnic in their fine salon, Canuda 4, tel. & fax 933-013-545, hcampi@terra.es, friendly Sonia, Margarita, and Nando).

$ Hostal Malda rents the best cheap beds I found in the old center. With 25 rooms above a small shopping mall near the cathedral, it's a time-warp—quiet and actually charming. Good-natured Aurora speaks no English and takes no reservations...good luck (S-€15, D-€30, T-€45, 100 yards up Carrer del Pi from delightful Plaça Sant Josep Oriol, Carrer del Pi 5, tel. 933-173-002).

$ Gothic Point Hostel is youthful, fun, and super-efficient, with 150 beds in the trendy Ribera district a block from the Picasso Museum. Rooms are coed, with eight to 12 beds. Each bunk bed has a little curtained area for privacy with a locker (€20 per bed, sheets-€2, includes breakfast, free Internet in lobby, open 24 hours but quiet after 23:00, roof terrace, Carrer Vigatans 5, tel. 932-687-808, www.gothicpoint.com). **Sea Point Hostel** is their sister hostel, on the beach nearby (Plaça del Mar 4, tel. 932-247-075, www .seapointhostel.com).

In the Eixample

For an uptown, boulevard-like neighborhood, sleep in the Eixample, a 10-minute walk from the Ramblas action.

$$ Hotel Granvía, filling a palatial 1870s mansion, offers Botticelli and chandeliers in the public rooms; a sprawling, peaceful sun garden; and 54 spacious, comfy, quiet, air-conditioned rooms. Its salon is plush and royal, making the hotel an excellent value for romantics (Sb-€75, Db-€120, or €110 July–Aug, Tb-€145, Juan promises these rates with this book in 2007 if you reserve directly by phone or e-mail—not Web site—and mention Rick Steves' name, breakfast-€10, air-con, elevator, Internet in lobby, Gran Via de les Corts Catalanes 642, tel. 933-181-900, fax 933-189-997, www.nnhotels.es, hgranvia@nnhotels.es, Juan Gomez).

Hotels in Barcelona's Eixample

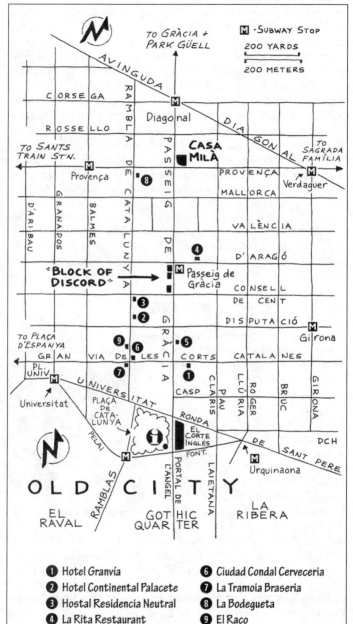

1. Hotel Granvía
2. Hotel Continental Palacete
3. Hostal Residencia Neutral
4. La Rita Restaurant
5. "QU QU" Quasi Queviures
6. Ciudad Condal Cerveceria
7. La Tramoia Braseria
8. La Bodegueta
9. El Raco

$$ Hotel Continental Palacete, with 19 rooms, fills a 100-year-old chandeliered mansion. With flowery wallpaper and cheap but fancy furniture under ornately gilded stucco, it's gaudy in the city of Gaudí. But it's friendly, clean, quiet, and well-located. Guests have unlimited access to the extravagant, "cruise-inspired" fruit, veggie, and drink buffet—worth factoring into your comparison-shopping (Sb-€95, Db-€135, Tb-€180, €20 more for bigger and brighter view rooms, 5 percent discount with this book in 2007, includes breakfast, air-con, 2 blocks north of Plaça de Catalunya at corner of Carrer Diputació, Rambla de Catalunya 30, tel. 934-457-657, fax 934-450-050, www.hotelcontinental.com, palacete@hotelcontinental.com).

$ Hostal Residencia Neutral, with a classic Eixample address and 28 very basic rooms, is a family-run time-warp and a fine value (tiny Ss-€30, Ds-€48, Db-€55, extra bed-€15, €6 breakfast in pleasant breakfast room, request a back room to avoid street noise, thin walls, fans, elevator, elegantly located 2 blocks north of Gran Via at Rambla de Catalunya 42, tel. 934-876-390, fax 934-876-848, hostalneutral@arrakis.es, owner Ramón, Fernando works the night shift).

EATING

Barcelona, the capital of Catalan cuisine—featuring seafood—offers a tremendous variety of colorful eateries. Because of their common struggles, Catalans seem to have an affinity for Basque culture—so you'll find a lot of Basque tapas places here, too. Most of my listings are lively spots with a busy tapas scene at the bar, along with restaurant tables for *raciones*. A regional specialty is *pa amb tomaquet* (pah ahm too-MAH-kaht), bread topped with a mix of crushed tomato and olive oil.

I've listed mostly practical, characteristic, colorful, and affordable restaurants. The city is thriving with trendy and chic new eateries, and foodies will do well to get local advice or explore the Ribera area for a fine dinner. Many restaurants close in August (or July), when the owners take a vacation.

Eating Simply yet Memorably near the Ramblas

Taverna Basca Irati serves 40 kinds of hot and cold Basque *pintxos* for €1.60 each. These are open-faced sandwiches—like sushi on bread. Muscle in through the hungry local crowd. Get an empty plate from the waiter, and then help yourself. Every few minutes, a waiter prances proudly by with a platter of new, still-warm munchies. Grab one as they pass by...it's addictive. You pay on the honor system: you're charged by the number of toothpicks left on your plate when you're done. Wash it down with a €2 glass of Rioja (full-bodied red wine), €2.40 Txakolí (sprightly Basque white wine), or €1.60 *sidra* (apple wine) poured from on high to add oxygen and bring out the flavor (daily 11:00–24:00, a block off the Ramblas, behind arcade at Carrer Cardenal Casanyes 15, Metro: Liceu, tel. 933-023-084).

Restaurant Elisabets is a happy little neighborhood eatery packed with antique radios and popular with locals for its "home-cooked," three-course €8 lunch special. Stop by for lunch, survey what those around you are enjoying, and order what looks best (Mon–Sat 13:00–16:00, closed Sun, 2 blocks west of Ramblas on far corner of Plaça Bonsucces at Carrer Elisabets 2, tel. 933-175-826, run by Pilar).

Café Granja Viader is a quaint time-capsule place, family-run since 1870. They boast to be the first dairy business to bottle and distribute milk in Spain. This feminine place—specializing in baked and dairy delights, toasted sandwiches, and light meals—is ideal for a traditional breakfast (note the "Esmorzars" specials posted). Try a glass of *orxata* (or *horchata*—*chufa* nut milk, summer only), *llet mallorquina* (Majorca-style milk with cinnamon, lemon, and sugar), *crema catalana* (crème brûlée, their specialty), or *suis* ("Switzerland"—hot chocolate with a snowcap of whipped cream). It's a block off the Ramblas behind El Carme church (and an easy stop along my Ramblas walk, page 56; Sun–Mon 17:00–20:45, Tue–Sat 9:00–13:45 & 17:00–20:45, Xucla 4, tel. 933-183-486).

La Poma is popular with tired tourists for its good pizza, pasta, and salads in a bright, modern setting at the top of the Ramblas. Enjoy the comfortable views of all the Ramblas action, from street level or upstairs (daily 9:00–24:00, Ramblas 117, tel. 933-019-400).

Veggie Options: See "Vegetarian Eateries near Plaça de Catalunya and the Ramblas," below.

Picnics: Shoestring tourists buy groceries at **El Corte Inglés** (Mon–Sat 10:00–22:00, closed Sun, supermarket in basement, Plaça de Catalunya) and **Champion Supermarket** (Mon–Sat 10:00–22:00, closed Sun, Ramblas 113).

Dining (Real Restaurants) in the Barri Gòtic

Popular Chain Restaurants: Barcelona is enjoying a chain of five bright, modern restaurants (all with different names). These are a hit for their modern, artfully presented Spanish and Mediterranean cuisine, crisp ambience, and unbeatable prices. Because of their three-course €8 lunches and €15–20 dinners (both with wine), all

Barcelona's Barri Gòtic Restaurants

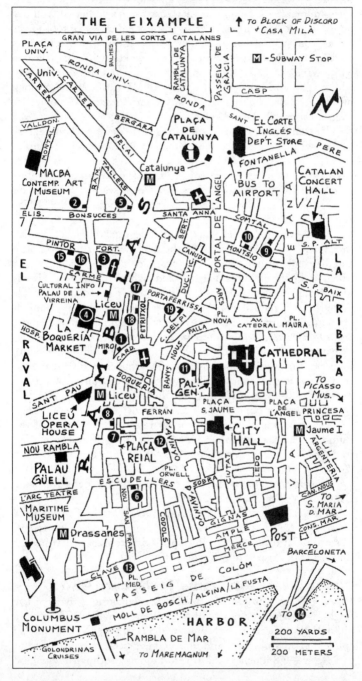

Restaurant Key

❶ Taverna Basca Irati & Juicy Jones	❿ Els Quatre Gats
❷ Restaurant Elisabets	⓫ El Pintor Restaurante
❸ Café Granja Viader	⓬ Agut d'Avignon Restaurante
❹ La Boquería Market Eateries	⓭ Carrer Mercè Tapas Bars
❺ La Poma & Champion Supermarket	⓮ To Tapasbar Maremagnum
❻ La Fonda	⓯ Biocenter Veggie Rest.
❼ Les Quinze Nits	⓰ Fresc Co Veggie Cafeteria
❽ La Crema Canela	⓱ Casa Colomina Sweet Shop
❾ La Dolça Herminia	⓲ La Pallaresa Granja-Xocolateria
	⓳ Fargas Chocolate Shop

are crowded with locals and in-the-know tourists. My favorite of the bunch is **La Crema Canela,** which feels cozier than the others and is the only one that takes reservations (daily 13:30–15:45 & 20:00–23:30, Passatge de Madoz 6, 30 yards north of Plaça Reial, tel. 933-182-744). The rest don't take reservations and are notorious for long lines at the door—arrive 30 minutes before opening, or be prepared to wait. The first two (along with La Crema Canela) are within a block of the Plaça Reial; the third is near the Catalan Concert Hall: **La Fonda** (daily 13:00–15:30 & 20:30–23:30, Carrer dels Escudellers 10, tel. 933-017-515); **Les Quinze Nits** (daily 13:00–15:45 & 20:30–23:30, on Plaça Reial at #6—you'll see the line, tel. 933-173-075); and **La Dolça Herminia** (2 blocks toward Ramblas from Catalan Concert Hall at Carrer de les Magdalenes 27, tel. 933-170-676). The fifth restaurant in the chain, **La Rita,** is described under "In the Eixample," below.

Els Quatre Gats, Picasso's hangout (and where he first showed off his paintings), retains its bohemian feel and serves quality, good-value meals in spite of its tourist crowds. Before Els Quatre Gats was founded in 1897, the idea of a café for artists was mocked as a place where only *quatre gats*—"four cats," meaning "crazies"—would go. Today diners enjoy a vaguely Parisian ambience with a rollicking crowd (of mostly tourists) surrounded by mementos from the Art Nouveau era (€10 three-course lunch, €10 salads, €15 plates, daily 8:30–24:00, live piano from 21:00, Carrer de Montsió 3, tel. 933-024-140).

El Pintor Restaurante serves one of the best €30 dinners in town. Dining here, you'll enjoy Catalan cuisine under medieval arches and rough brick, with candles and friendly service (daily 13:30–16:30 & 20:00–24:00, reserve ahead for evening, from Plaça de Sant Jaume walk north on Carrer Sant Honorat to #7, tel. 933-014-065).

Agut d'Avignon Restaurante has a country elegance and serves traditional Catalan and North Spanish cuisine to a dressy local clientele that knows good food (€11.50 fixed-price lunch offered Mon–Fri, €10–20 plates, daily 13:00–15:30 & 21:00–23:30, reservations smart, a block from Plaça de Sant Jaume in a dead-end alley off Carrer d'Avinyó 8 at Calle de la Trinidad 3, tel. 933-026-034).

Tapas on Carrer Mercè in the Barri Gòtic

Barcelona boasts great *tascas*—colorful local tapas bars. Get small plates (for maximum sampling) by asking for "tapas," not the bigger "raciones." Glasses of *vino tinto* go for about €0.50. While trendy uptown restaurants are safer, better-lit, and come with English menus and less grease, these places will stain your journal. The neighborhood's dark, the regulars are rough-edged, and you'll get a glimpse of a crusty Barcelona from before the affluence hit.

From the bottom of the Ramblas (near the Columbus Monument), hike east along Carrer Clave. Then follow the small street that runs along the right side of the church (Carrer Mercè), stopping at the *tascas* that look fun. For a montage of edible memories, wander Carrer Mercè west to east and consider these spots, stopping wherever looks most inviting:

La Pulpería serves up fried fish, octopus, and *patatas bravas*, all with Galician Ribeiro wine. Tapas at the tables in back cost €1 extra. A few steps down the street, at **Casa del Molinero,** you can sauté your chorizo *al diablo* ("devil sausage"). It's great with *pa amb tomaquet* (tomato bread). Across the street, **La Plata** keeps things wonderfully simple, serving extremely cheap plates of sardines (€1.25), little salads (€1.10), and small glasses of keg wine (€0.50). **Tasca el Corral** serves mountain favorites from northern Spain, such as *queso de cabrales* (very moldy cheese) and chorizo (spicy sausage) with *sidra* (apple wine sold by the €4 bottle). **Sidrería Tasca La Socarrena** (at #21) is the only place that serves hard cider by the glass. At the end of Carrer Mercè, **Cerveceria Vendimia** serves up tasty clams and mussels (hearty *raciones* for €3 a plate—they don't do smaller portions, so order sparingly). Their *pulpo* (octopus) is more expensive and is the house specialty. Carrer Ample and Carrer Gignas, the streets parallel to Carrer Mercè inland, have more refined bar-hopping possibilities.

In and near La Bouqería Market

Try eating at La Boquería market at least once (#91 on the Ramblas). Like all farmers' markets in Europe, this place is ringed

by colorful, good-value eateries. Lots of stalls sell fun take-away food—especially fruit salads and fresh-squeezed fruit juices. There are several good bars around the market busy with shoppers munching at the counter (breakfast, tapas all day, coffee). The market, and most of the eateries listed here (unless noted), are open Monday through Saturday from 8:00 until 20:00 and closed on Sunday.

Pinotxo Bar is just to the right as you enter the market. It's a great spot for coffee, breakfast (spinach tortillas, or whatever's cooking with toast), or tapas. Fun-loving Juan and his family are La Boquería fixtures. Grab a stool across the way to sip your drink with people-watching views.

Kiosko Universal Bar is popular for its great prices on wonderful fish dishes (€10 fixed-price meals with different fresh-fish options, better before 12:30 but always packed, tel. 933-178-286). As you enter the market from the Ramblas, it's all the way to the left on the first alley. If you see people waiting, ask who's last in line *("¿El último?")*.

Restaurant la Gardunya, at the back of the market, offers tasty meat and seafood meals made with fresh ingredients bought directly from the market (€12.50 fixed-price lunch includes wine and bread, €15.50 dinner specials don't include wine, Mon–Sat 13:00–16:00 & 20:00–24:00, closed Sun, mod seating indoors or outside watching the market action, Carrer Jerusalem 18, tel. 933-024-323).

Casa Guinart is an "I love food and wine" kind of place serving fine light meals and great wine by the glass since 1899. The menu lists *flautas* (flute-sized sandwiches) and *xapatas* (bigger sandwiches). Check for the day's posting of wines. Some of the tables come with fine Ramblas views (Mon–Sat 9:00–21:00, closed Sun, on uphill corner of the market facing the Ramblas at Ramblas 95, tel. 933-178-887).

Bar Terrace Restaurant Ra is a lively terrace immediately behind the market with outdoor tables offering a view of the parking lot and happy eaters. At lunch they serve one great salad/pasta/wine meal for €11. If you feel like eating a big salad under an umbrella...this is it (daily 10:00–12:30 & 13:30–16:00 & 21:00–24:00, fancier menu at night, tel. 615-959-872).

Out at Sea—Maremagnum

Tapasbar Maremagnum is a big, rollicking, sports-bar kind of tapas restaurant, great for large groups. It's a fun way to end your Ramblas walk, featuring breezy harbor views and good local food with an emphasis on the sea (daily 11:00–24:00, a 10-minute stroll past the Columbus Monument straight out the dock on Moll d'Espanya, tel. 932-258-180).

In the Ribera District, near the Picasso Museum

La Ribera, the hottest neighborhood in town, sparkles with eclectic and trendy as well as subdued and classy little restaurants hidden in the small lanes surrounding the Church of Santa Maria del Mar. While I've listed a few well-established tapas bars that are great for light meals, to really dine, simply wander around for 15 minutes and pick the place that tickles your gastronomic fancy. I think anyone saying they know what's best in this area is kidding themselves—it's changing too fast and the choices are too personal. One thing's for sure: There are a lot of talented and hardworking restaurateurs with plenty to offer. Consider starting your evening off with a glass of fine wine at one of the *enotecas* on the square facing the Church of Santa Maria del Mar. Sit back and admire the pure Catalan Gothic architecture. My first three listings are all on the main drag, Carrer de l'Argenteria.

Sagardi offers a wonderful array of Basque goodies—tempting *pinchos* and *montaditos* at €1.30 each—along its huge bar. Ask for a plate and graze. You can sit on the square with your plunder for a few cents extra. Wash it down with Txakolí, a Basque white wine poured from the spout of a huge wooden barrel into a glass as you watch. Sagardi's back restaurant features excellent grilled meats and is a worthwhile splurge (bar open daily 12:00–24:00, restaurant open daily 12:00–16:00 & 19:30–24:00, Carrer de l'Argenteria 62–4, tel. 933-199-993).

Taller de Tapas ("Tapas Workshop") is an upscale, trendier tapas bar and restaurant that dishes up more sophisticated morsels and light meals in a medieval-stone yet mod setting or on the square. This is favored by local office workers who aren't into the Old World Gothic stuff (little sandwiches until 12:30, then tapas, Mon–Sat 8:30–24:00, Sun 12:00–24:00, Carrer de l'Argenteria 51, tel. 932-688-559).

Hofmann is a renowned cooking school with an excellent if pricey restaurant. The four-course, €32 lunches are made up of just what the students are working on that day—so there's no choice. Dinners can easily cost twice as much. Save room (and euros) for the incredible desserts. Reservations are recommended, because locals love this place (Mon–Fri 13:30–15:15 & 21:00–23:15, closed Sat–Sun and Aug, Carrer de l'Argenteria 74–78, tel. 933-195-889, www.hofmann-bcn.com). When your meal's done, ask for a tour of the impressive kitchen.

El Xampanyet, a characteristic and often congested family-run bar with a fun-loving staff, specializes in tapas and anchovies. A *sortido* (assorted plate) of *carne* (meat) or *pescado* (fish) costs about €6 with *pa amb tomaquet* (bread topped with tomato). While it's filled with tourists during the sightseeing day, it's a local favorite after dark (Tue–Sat 12:00–16:00 & 19:00–23:30, Sun 12:00–16:00, closed Mon, a half block beyond the Picasso Museum at Montcada 22, tel. 933-197-003). Don't be put off by the seafood from a tin... Catalans like it this way.

Vegetarian Eateries near Plaça de Catalunya and the Ramblas

Biocenter, a Catalan soup-and-salad restaurant popular with local vegetarians, takes its cooking very seriously and feels a bit more like a real restaurant than most (€8 lunches, Mon–Sat 13:00–17:00, Thu–Sat also 20:00–23:00, closed Sun, 2 blocks off the Ramblas at Pintor Fortuny 25, Metro: Catalunya, tel. 933-014-583).

Fresc Co, bright and cheery, offers a healthy buffet in a sleek and efficient cafeteria. For one cheap price (€8 until 18:00, then €10), you get a drink (one alcoholic or unlimited soft drinks) and all the salad (some with chicken or turkey), pasta, soup, pizza, and dessert you want. The hearty buffet is more appetizing than most. Choose between two locations (both open daily 12:30–24:00, tel. 933-016-837): west of Plaça de Catalunya at Ronda Universitat 29, or a block off the Ramblas (near La Boquería market) at Carme 16.

Juicy Jones is a tutti-frutti vegan/vegetarian eatery with garish colors, a hip veggie menu (served downstairs), and a stunning array of fresh-squeezed juices served at the bar (lunch and dinner fixed price meal-€8, daily 13:00–24:00, Carrer Cardenal Casanyes 7). Pop in for a quick €3 "juice of the day."

In the Eixample

The people-packed boulevards of the Eixample (Passeig de Gràcia and Rambla de Catalunya) are lined with appetizing eateries fea-

turing breezy outdoor seating. Many trendy and touristic tapas bars offer a cheery welcome and slam out the appetizers. The first listing is a normal restaurant. The next three are upscale tapas bars, most with plenty of seating and a restaurant feel.

La Rita is a fresh and dressy little restaurant serving Catalan cuisine near the Block of Discord. Their lunches—three courses with wine for €8 (served Mon–Fri from 13:00)—and dinners (€15, à la carte, daily from 20:30) are a great value (a block from Metro: Passeig de Gràcia, near corner of Carrer de Pau Claris and Carrer Arago at Arago 279, tel. 934-872-376). Like its four sister restaurants—described under "Dining (Real Restaurants) in the Barri Gòtic," above—it takes no reservations and its prices attract long lines, so arrive just before the doors open...or wait.

"QU QU" Quasi Queviures serves upscale tapas, sandwiches, or the whole nine yards—classic food served fast from a fun menu with modern decor and a high-energy sports-bar ambience. Walk through their enticing kitchen to get to the tables in back (daily 7:00–24:00, between Gran Via and Via Diputació at Passeig de Gràcia 24, tel. 933-174-512).

Ciudad Condal Cerveceria brags it serves the best *montaditos* (sandwiches) and beers in Barcelona. It's an Eixample favorite, with an elegant bar and tables plus good seating out on the Rambla de Catalunya for all that people-watching action. While it has no restaurant-type menu, the list of tapas and *montaditos* is easy, fun, and comes with a great variety (including daily specials). This place is a cut above your normal tapas bar, but with reasonable prices (daily until 24:00, facing the intersection of Gran Via and Rambla de Catalunya at Rambla de Catalunya 18, tel. 933-181-997).

La Tramoia is a *braseria* (lots of grilled specialties) with piles of cheap *montaditos* and tapas at the downstairs bar. The brasserie-style restaurant upstairs bustles with happy local eaters enjoying great food and Gran Via views (€8–12 plates, open daily, also facing the intersection of Gran Via and Rambla de Catalunya at Rambla de Catalunya 15, tel. 934-123-634).

La Bodegueta is an unbelievably atmospheric below-street-level bodega serving hearty wines, homemade vermouth, *anchoas* (anchovies), tapas, and *flautas*—sandwiches made with flute-thin baguettes. Its daily €8.50 lunch special of three courses with wine is served 13:00–16:00 (Mon–Sat 8:00–24:00, Sun 19:00–24:00, at intersection with Provenza, Rambla de Catalunya 100, Metro: Diagonal, tel. 932-154-894). A long block from Gaudí's Casa Milà, this makes a fine sightseeing break.

El Raco is a local favorite for pasta, pizza, crêpes, and salads (about €6 each) in a modern, air-conditioned, lively setting (daily 13:00–24:00, Rambla de Catalunya 25, tel. 933-175-688).

Sandwich Shops

Bright, clean, and inexpensive sandwich shops are proudly holding the cultural line against the fast-food invasion hamburger-izing the rest of Europe. You'll find great sandwiches at **Pans & Company** and **Bocatta,** two chains with outlets all over town.

Catalan sandwiches are made to order with crunchy French bread. Rather than butter, locals prefer *pa amb tomaquet* (tomato bread). Study the instructive multilingual menu fliers to understand your options.

A Short, Sweet Walk

Let me propose this three-stop dessert. You'll try a refreshing glass of *orxata*, munch some *churros con chocolate*, and visit a fine *xocolateria*, all within a three-minute walk of each other in the Barri Gòtic just off the Ramblas. Start at the corner of Carrer Portaferrissa midway down the Ramblas. For the best atmosphere, begin your walk at about 18:00.

Orxata **at Casa Colomina:** Walk down Carrer Portaferrissa to #8. Casa Colomina, founded in 1908, sells ice cream and the refreshing *orxata* (or *horchata*—a drink made from the *chufa* nut). Order a glass (€1.15) and ask to see and eat a *chufa* nut (a.k.a. earth almond or tiger nut). In winter, they sell homemade *turrón*—a variation of nougat made with almond, honey, and sugar, brought to Spain by the Moors 1,200 years ago. They sell it in big €6 slabs, but if you ask nicely, they might give you a sample *(muestra)* of *blando, duro,* and *yema*—soft, hard, and yolk (Mon–Sat 10:00–20:30, Sun 12:30–20:30, tel. 933-122-511).

Churros con Chocolate **at La Pallaresa Granja-Xocolateria:** Continue down Carrer Portaferrissa, taking a right at Carrer Petrixol to this fun-loving *xocolateria*. Older, elegant ladies gather here for the Spanish equivalent of tea time—dipping their greasy *churros* into pudding-thick cups of hot chocolate (€4 for 5 *churros con chocolate*, daily 9:00–13:00 & 16:00–21:00, Carrer Petritxol 11, tel. 933-022-036).

Homemade Chocolate at Fargas: For your last stop, head for the ornate Fargas chocolate shop (Mon–Sat 9:30–13:30 & 16:00–20:00, closed Sun, continue down Carrer Petritxol to the square, hook left and up Carrer del Pi; it's on the corner of Portaferrissa and Carrer del Pi, tel. 933-020-342). Since the 19th century, gentlemen with walking canes have dropped by here for their chocolate fix. Founded in 1827, this is one of the oldest and most traditional chocolate places in Barcelona. Ask to see the old chocolate mill *("¿Puedo ver el molino?")*. They sell even tiny quantities (one little morsel) by the weight—don't be shy. A delicious chunk of the house specialty costs €0.40 (tray by the mill).

TRANSPORTATION CONNECTIONS

From Barcelona by Train to: Madrid (6/day, 4.5–6.5 hrs, about €60, plus 2 night trains, 9 hrs, about €35–45 plus berth cost; new high-speed AVE reduces time but increases cost, reservation required), **Paris** (1/day, 12 hrs, about €130, night train, reservation mandatory), **Sevilla** (3/day, 8.5–11 hrs, about €50), **Granada** (2/day, 12 hrs, about €50), **Málaga** (2/day, 14 hrs, about €55), **Lisbon** (no direct trains, head to Madrid and then catch night train to Lisbon, 17 hrs, about €130), **Nice** (1/day, 12 hrs, about €65, change in Cerbère, or about €95 for change in Montpellier), **Avignon** (5/day, 6–9 hrs, about €40, or about €65 for change in Montpellier). Train info: tel. 902-240-202, www.renfe.es.

By Bus to: Madrid (18/day, 8 hrs, half the price of a train ticket, departs from station Barcelona Nord at Metro: Marina, tel. 902-260-606). Sarfa buses serve all the coastal resorts (tel. 902-302-025).

By Plane: Check the reasonable flights from Barcelona to Sevilla or Madrid. Vueling is Iberia's most popular discount airline (e.g., Barcelona–Madrid flights as low as €30 if booked in advance, tel. 902-333-933, www.vueling.com). Iberia (tel. 902-400-500, www.iberia.com) and Air Europa (tel. 902-401-501 or 932-983-907, www.aireuropa.com) offer €80 flights to Madrid. Also, for flights to other parts of Europe, consider British Airways (tel. 902-111-333, www.britishairways.com) and easyJet (tel. 902-299-992, www.easyjet.com). Airport info: tel. 932-983-838. For details on getting between downtown Barcelona and the airport, see "Arrival in Barcelona—By Plane," page 50.

NEAR BARCELONA

Figueres, Cadaqués, Sitges, and Montserrat

Four fine sights are day-trip temptations from Barcelona. Fans of Surrealism can combine a fantasy in Dalí-land with a classy but sleepy port-town getaway by spending a day or two in Cadaqués (pictured above), with a stop at the Dalí Theater-Museum in Figueres (an hour from Cadaqués and two hours from Barcelona). For the consummate day at the beach, head 45 minutes south to the charming and free-spirited resort town, Sitges. And pilgrims with hiking boots head an hour into the mountains for the most sacred spot in Catalunya: Montserrat.

Figueres

The town of Figueres (feeg-YEHR-ehs)—conveniently connected by train to Barcelona—is of sightseeing interest only for its Salvador Dalí Theater-Museum. In fact, the entire town seems Dalí-dominated.

Getting to Figueres: Figueres is an easy day trip from Barcelona, or a handy stopover en route to France (trains between Barcelona and France stop in Figueres; lockers at station). Trains to Figueres from Barcelona depart from Sants Station or from the RENFE station at Metro: Passeig de Gràcia (hourly, 2 hours, €15 round-trip). For bus connections to Cadaqués, see page 114.

Arrival in Figueres: From the train station, simply follow *Museu Dalí* signs (and the crowds) for the five-minute walk to the museum.

SIGHTS

Dalí Theater-Museum (Teatre-Museu Dalí)

Easily worth ▲▲▲, this is *the* essential Dalí sight—and, if you like Dalí, one of Europe's most enjoyable museums, period. Inaugurated in 1974, the museum is a work of art in itself. Ever the entertainer and promoter, Dalí personally conceptualized, designed, decorated, and painted it to showcase his life's work. The museum is also a kind of mausoleum to Dalí's creative spirit.

Dalí had his first public art showing at age 14 here in this building, a former theater, and he was baptized in the church just across the street. The place was sentimental to him. After the theater was destroyed in the Spanish Civil War, Dalí struck a deal with the mayor: Dalí would rebuild the theater as a museum to his works, Figueres would be put on the sightseeing map...and the money's been flowing in ever since.

Even from the outside—painted pink, studded with golden loaves of bread, and topped with monumental eggs and a geodesic dome—the building exudes Dalí's outrageous public persona.

Cost, Hours, Information: €10, July–Sept daily 9:00–19:45 & maybe 22:00–24:00; Oct–June Tue–Sun 10:30–17:45, closed Mon; last entry 30 min before closing; tel. 972-677-500, www.salvador-dali.org. The free bag check has your bag waiting for you at the exit.

Coin-Op Tip: Much of Dalí's art is movable and coin-operated—bring a few €0.20 coins.

Visiting the Museum: The museum has two parts—the theater/mausoleum and the "Dalí's Jewels" exhibit in an adjacent building. There's no logical order for a visit (that would be un-Surrealistic). And, naturally, there's no audioguide. Dalí said there are two kinds of visitors: those who don't need a description, and those who aren't worth a description.

➋ Self-Guided Tour: At the risk of offending Dalí, I've written this loose commentary to attach some meaning to your visit.

Stepping into the **theater** (with its audience of statues), face the stage—and Dalí's unmarked crypt. You know how you can never get a cab when it's raining? Pop a coin into Dalí's personal 1941 Cadillac, and it rains inside the car. Look above, atop the tire tower: That's the boat enjoyed by Dalí and his soulmate, Gala—his emotional life-preserver, who kept him from going overboard. When she died...so did he (for his last seven years). Below the boat

Near Barcelona

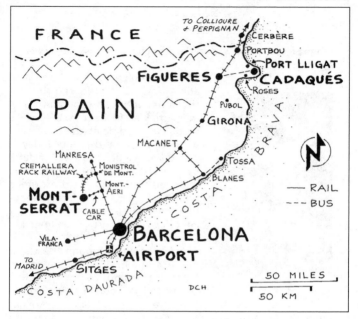

drip blue tears made of condoms.

Up on the **stage,** squint at the big digital Abraham Lincoln, and president #16 comes into focus. Approach the painting to find that Abe's facial cheeks are Gala's butt cheeks. Under the painting, a door leads to the **Treasures Room,** with the greatest collection of actual Dalí original oil paintings in the museum. (Much of what hangs on the walls is just prints.) You'll see Cubist visions of Cadaqués and dreamy portraits of Gala. Crutches—a recurring Dalí theme—represent Gala, who kept him supported whenever a meltdown threatened.

The famous **Homage to Mae West room** is a tribute to the sultry seductress. Dalí loved her attitude. Saying things like, "Why marry and make one man unhappy, when you can stay single and make so many so happy?" Mae West was to conventional morality what Dalí was to conventional art. Climb to the vantage point where the sofa lips, fireplace nostrils, painting eyes, and drapery hair come together to make the face of Mae West.

Dalí's art can be playful, but also disturbing. He was passionate about the dark side of things, but, with Gala for balance, he managed never to go off the deep end. Unlike Pablo Casals (the Catalan cellist) and Pablo Picasso (another local artist), Dalí didn't go into exile under Franco's dictatorship. Pragmatically, he accepted both Franco and the Church, and was supported by the

Salvador Dalí
(1904–1989)

When Salvador Dalí was asked, "Are you on drugs?" he replied, "I am the drug... take me."

Labeled by various critics as sick, greedy, paranoid, arrogant, and a clown, Dalí produced some of the most thought-provoking and trailblazing art of the 20th century. His erotic, violent, disjointed imagery continues to disturb and intrigue today.

Born in Figueres to a well-off family, Dalí showed talent early. He was expelled from Madrid's prestigious art school—twice—but formed long-time friendships with the playwright Federico García Lorca and filmmaker Luis Buñuel.

After a breakthrough art exhibit in Barcelona in 1925, Dalí moved to Paris. He hobnobbed with fellow Spaniards Picasso and Miró, and with a group of artists exploring Sigmund Freud's theory that we all have a hidden part of our mind, the unconscious "id," that surfaces when we dream. Dalí became the best-known spokesman for this group of Surrealists, channeling his id to create photorealistic dream images (melting watches, burning giraffes) set in bizarre dreamscapes.

His life changed forever in 1929, when he met an older, Russian, married woman named Gala who would become his wife, muse, model, manager, and emotional compass. Dalí's

dictator. Apart from the occasional *sardana* dance (see page 69), you won't find a hint of politics in Dalí's art.

Wander around. You can spend hours here, wondering, is it real or not real? Am I crazy, or is it you? Beethoven is painted with squid ink applied by a shoe on a stormy night. Jesus is made with candle smoke and an eraser. It's fun to see the Dalí-ization of art classics. Dalí, like so many modern artists, was inspired by the masters—especially Velázquez.

The former theater's **smoking lounge** is a highlight, with portraits of Gala and Dalí (with a big eye, big ear, and a dark side) bookending a Roman candle of creativity. The fascinating ceiling painting shows the feet of Gala and Dalí as they zoom into heaven. Dalí's drawers are wide open and empty, indicating he gave everything to his art.

popularity spread to the US, where he (and Gala) weathered the WWII years.

In his prime, Dalí's work became less Surrealist and more classical, influenced by past masters of painted realism (Velázquez, Raphael, Ingres) and by his own study of history, science, and religion. He produced large-scale paintings of historical events (e.g., Columbus discovering America, the Last Supper) that were collages of realistic scenes floating in a surrealistic landscape, peppered with thought-provoking symbols.

Dalí—an extremely capable technician—mastered many media, including film. *An Andalusian Dog* (1929, with Buñuel) was a cutting-edge montage of disturbing, eyeball-slicing images. For Alfred Hitchcock, he designed the big-eye backdrop for the dream sequence of *Spellbound* (1945). He made jewels for the rich and clothes for Coco Chanel, wrote a novel and an autobiography, and pioneered what would come to be called "installations." He also helped develop "performance art" by showing up at an opening in a diver's suit or by playing the role he projected to the media—as a super-confident, waxed-mustached artistic genius.

In later years, Dalí's over-the-top public image contrasted with his ever-growing illness, depression, and isolation. He endured the scandal of a dealer overseeing "limited editions" of his work. When Gala died in 1982, Dalí retreated to his hometown, living his last days in the Torre Galatea of the Theater-Museum complex, where he died of heart failure.

Dalí's legacy as an artist includes his self-marketing persona, his exceptional ability to draw, his provocative pairing of symbols, and his sheer creative drive.

Leaving the theater, keep your ticket and pop into the adjacent **"Dalí's Jewels"** exhibit. It shows sketches and paintings of jewelry Dalí designed, and the actual pieces jewelers made from those surreal visions: a mouth full of pearly whites, golden finger corset, fountain of diamonds, and the breathing heart. Explore the ambiguous perception worked into the big painting entitled *Apotheosis of the Dollar.*

Cadaqués

Since the late 1800s, Cadaqués (kah-dah-KEHS) has served as a haven for intellectuals and artists alike. The fishing village's craggy coastline, sun-drenched colors, and laid-back lifestyle inspired Fauvists such as Henri Matisse and Surrealists such as René

Magritte, Marcel Duchamp, and Federico García Lorca. Even Picasso, drawn to this enchanting coastal haunt, painted some of his Cubist works here.

Salvador Dalí, raised in nearby Figueres, brought international fame to this sleepy Catalan port in the 1920s. As a kid, Dalí spent summers here in the family cabin, where he was inspired by the rocky landscape that would later be the backdrop for many Surrealist canvases. In 1929, he met his future wife Gala in Cadaqués. Together, they converted a fisherman's home in nearby Port Lligat into their semi-permanent residence, dividing their time between New York, Paris, and Cadaqués. And it was here that Dalí did his best work.

In spite of its fame, Cadaqués is mellow and feels off the beaten path. If you want a peaceful beach-town escape near Barcelona,  this is a good place. From the moment you descend into the town, taking in whitewashed buildings and deep blue waters, you'll be struck by the port's tranquility and beauty. Join the locals playing chess or cards at the cavernous Casino Coffee House (harborfront, with games and Internet access). Have a glass of *vino tinto* or *cremat* (a traditional rum-and-coffee drink served flambé-style) at one of the seaside cafés. Savor the lapping waves, brilliant sun, and gentle breeze. And, for sightseeing, the reason to come to Cadaqués is the Dalí House, a 20-minute walk from the town center at Port Lligat.

Tourist Information: The TI is at Carrer Cotxe 2 (Mon–Sat 9:00–14:00 & 16:00–21:00, Sun 10:30–13:00, less off-season, tel. 972-258-315).

Getting to Cadaqués

Reaching Cadaqués is very tough without a car. There are no trains and only a few buses a day.

By Car: It's a twisty 45-minute drive from Figueres. In Cadaqués, drivers should park in the big lot just above the city—don't try to park near the harborfront. To reach the Dalí House, follow signs near Cadaqués to Port Lligat (easy parking).

By Bus: Cadaqués is connected by Sarfa buses to **Figueres** (3/day, 60 min, €4) and to **Barcelona** (2/day, 2.5 hours, €18, a few more in July–Aug). Bus info: Barcelona tel. 902-302-025, Cadaqués tel. 972-258-713, Figueres tel. 972-674-298, www.sarfa.com.

SIGHTS

In Port Lligat, near Cadaqués

▲▲▲**Salvador Dalí House (Casa Museu Salvador Dalí)**—Once Dalí's home, this house gives fans a chance to explore his laby-

rinthine compound. This is the best artist's house I've toured in Europe. It shows how a home can really reflect the creative spirit of an artistic genius and his muse. The ambience both inside and out is perfect for a Surrealist hanging out with his creative playmate. The bay is ringed by sleepy islands. Fishing boats are jumbled on the beach. After the fisher-men painted their boats, Dalí asked them to clean their brushes on his door—creating an abstract work of art he adored (which you'll see as you line up to get your ticket).

The interior is left almost precisely as it was in 1982, when Gala died and Dalí moved out. See Dalí's studio (the clever easel cranks up and down to allow the artist to paint while seated, as he did eight hours a day); the bohemian-yet-divine living room (complete with a mirror to reflect the sunrise onto their bed each morning); the phallic-shaped swimming pool, which was the scene of orgiastic parties; and the painter's study (with his favorite moustaches all lined up). Like Dalí's art, his home is offbeat, pro-vocative, and fun.

Cost and Hours: €8; mid-June–mid-Sept daily 10:30–21:00; mid-March–mid-June and mid-Sept–early Jan Tue–Sun 10:30–18:00, closed Mon; closed early Jan–mid-March.

Touring the House: Reservations are mandatory—call ahead to book a time (tel. 972-251-015). Only 8–10 people are allowed in (no large groups) every 10 minutes. You must arrive 30 minutes early to pick up your ticket or they'll sell it—no exceptions. Once inside, there are four sections, each with a guard who gives you a brief explanation in English, and then turns you loose for a few minutes. The entire visit takes 40 minutes.

Getting There: The house is a 20-minute walk over the hill from Cadaqués to Port Lligat.

SLEEPING

$$ Hotel Llane Petit, with 37 spacious rooms (half with view balconies), is a small, resort-like hotel with its own little beach, a 10-minute walk south of the town center (Db–€65–122, air-con, elevator, Dr. Bartomeus 37, tel. 972-251-020, fax 972-258-778,

---

Sleep Code

(€1 = about $1.20, country code: 34)
S = Single, **D** = Double/Twin, **T** = Triple, **Q** = Quad, **b** = bathroom,
s = shower only. Unless otherwise noted, credit cards are accepted and English is spoken.
   To help you easily sort through these listings, I've divided the rooms into two categories, based on the price for a standard double room with bath (during high season):

   $$ Higher Priced—Most rooms €75 or more.
   $ Lower Priced—Most rooms less than €75.

---

www.llanepetit.com, info@llanepetit.com).

$ Hotel Nou Estrelles is a big, concrete exercise in efficient, economic comfort facing the bus stop, a few blocks in from the waterfront. With 15 rooms, it's family-run and a great value (Sb-€30–40, Db-€50, €75 July–Aug, Tb-€60–85, air-con, elevator, Carrer Sant Vicens, tel. 972-259-100, nouestrelles@yahoo.es, Emma).

$ Hostal Marina is cheap, with a great location a block from the harborfront main square (D-€35–50, Db-€45–60 depending on season, Riera 3, tel. & fax 972-258-199).

EATING

For a fine dinner, try **Casa Anita,** down a narrow street from Hotel La Residencia. Sitting with others around a big table, you'll enjoy house specialties such as *calamares a la plancha* (grilled squid) and homemade *helado* (ice cream). Muscatel from a glass *porrón* finishes off the tasty meal (Calle Miquel Roses 16, tel. 972-258-471, Juan and family).

Sitges

Sitges (SEE-juhz) is one of Catalunya's most popular resort towns. It's long been famous for its free spirit and is a world-renowned vacation destination among the gay community. Despite its jet-set status, the old town has managed to retain its charm. Nine beaches extend about a mile southward from town. Stroll

down the seaside promenade, which stretches from the town to the end of the beaches. About halfway, the crowds thin out, and the beaches become more intimate and cove-like. Along the way, restaurants and *chiringuitos* (beachfront bars) serve tapas, paella, and drinks. Take time to explore the old town's streets and shops. On the waterfront, you'll see the 17th-century Sant Bartomeu i Santa Tecla Church. It's a quick hike up for a view of town, sea, and beaches.

Getting to Sitges: Southbound trains depart Barcelona from Sants Station (2/hr, 35–40 min, €4.20 round-trip; easy connections from RENFE station at Plaça de Catalunya to Sants Station).

Montserrat

Montserrat—the "serrated mountain"—rockets dramatically up from the valley floor northwest of Barcelona. With its unique rock

formations, a dramatic mountaintop monastery (also called Montserrat), and spiritual connection with the Catalan people and their struggles, it's a popular day trip. This has been Catalunya's most important pilgrimage site for a thousand years. Hymns explain how the mountain was carved by little angels with golden saws. Geologists blame nature at work.

A hundred million years ago, there was no mountain. A river flowed here, laying down silt that hardened into sedimentary layers of hard rock. Ten million years ago, the continents shifted, and the land around the rock massif sank, exposing this series of peaks that reach upwards to 4,000 feet. Over time, erosion pocked the face with caves and cut vertical grooves near the top, creating the famous serrated look.

The monastery is nestled in the jagged peaks at 2,400 feet, but it seems higher because of the way the rocky massif rises out of nowhere. The air is certainly fresher than in Barcelona. In a day, you can view the mountain from its base, ride a funicular up to the monastery, tour the basilica and museum, touch a Black Virgin's orb, hike down to a sacred cave, and listen to Gregorian chants by the world's oldest boys' choir.

Montserrat's monastery is Benedictine, and its 30 monks carry on its spiritual tradition. Since 1025, the slogan *"ora et labora"* ("prayer and work") pretty much sums up life for a monk here.

The Benedictines welcome visitors—both pilgrims and tourists—and offer this travel tip: Please remember that the most important part of your Montserrat visit is not enjoying the architecture, but rather discovering the religious, cultural, historical, social, and environmental values that together symbolically express the life of the Catalan people.

Getting to Montserrat

By Car
Once drivers get out of Barcelona, it's a short 30-minute drive to the base of the mountain, then a 10-minute series of switchbacks to the actual site (where you can find parking for €4 per day). It may be easier to park your car down below and ride the cable car up (see below).

By Train
Trains leave hourly for Montserrat from Barcelona's Plaça d'Espanya, and take you to the base of the mountain. From there, you can take a cable car (the most fun way), or a rack railway up the mountain. For most travelers, it's simplest to buy a package ticket.

Package Tickets: You can buy one of two special **package tickets** in Barcelona from the train company. The €18.40 **Trans Montserrat** combo-ticket includes your Metro ride in Barcelona to the train station, the train trip, the ride on the cable car or Cremallera rack railway, unlimited trips on the two funiculars up on Montserrat, and entrance to the audiovisual presentation. The €31 **Tot Montserrat** ticket includes all of this, plus the museum and a self-serve lunch. If you plan to do it all, you'll save at least €5 with either ticket. Buy your tickets in Barcelona at any of these three places: at the TI kiosk on Plaça d'Espanya; at the uncrowded FGC La Molina office next to Plaça de Catalunya (Tue–Sat 11:00–14:00 & 16:30–20:30, Mon 16:30–20:30, closed Sun, see map on page 100 for location, Pelai 17–39 Triangle, tel. 933-664-553, helpful Rosa); or at the TI kiosk at Plaça de Catalunya (though it sells only the Trans Montserrat ticket).

On Your Own: If you don't plan on taking either funicular at Montserrat, simply buy a train ticket to Montserrat (€12.90 round-trip, includes the cable car *or* rack railway, cash only, Eurailpass not valid, tel. 932-051-515, www.fgc.es). The train—which takes you as far as the base of the mountain—has two potential stops to choose from: either the **Montserrat-Aeri** stop, where you'll catch the cable car up (see "Cable Car to/from the Monastery," below) or the **Monistrol de Montserrat** stop, which is for the rack railway (see "Cremallera Rack Railway to/from the Monastery," below). When you buy your ticket, you must specify which combination you would like: TransMontserrat-Aeri-cable car or TransMontserrat-Cremallera-rack railway.

Departing Barcelona: Whether you have a package ticket or

The History of Montserrat

The first hermit monks built huts at Montserrat around A.D. 900. By 1025, a monastery was founded. The Montserrat Escolania, or Choir School, soon followed, and is considered to be the oldest music school in Europe (they still perform—see "Choir Concert" on page 123).

Legend has it that in medieval times, some shepherd children saw lights and heard songs coming from the mountain. They traced it to a cave (now called the Sacred Cave, or Santa Cova), where they found the Black Virgin statue (La Moreneta), making the monastery a pilgrim magnet.

In 1811, Napoleon's invading French troops destroyed Montserrat's buildings, though the Black Virgin survived, hidden away by monks. Then, in the 1830s, the Spanish royalty— tired of dealing with the pesky religious orders—dissolved the monasteries and convents.

But in the 1850s, the monks returned as part of Catalunya's (and Europe's) renewed Romantic appreciation for all things medieval and nationalistic. (Montserrat's revival coincided with other traditions born out of rejuvenated Catalan pride: the much-loved Football Club Barcelona, Barcelona's Palace of Catalan Music, and even the birth of local champagne, *cava*.) Montserrat's basilica and monastery were reconstructed and became, once more, the strongly beating spiritual and cultural heart of the Catalan people.

Then came Franco, who wanted a monolithic Spain. To him, Montserrat represented Catalan rebelliousness. During Franco's rule, the *sardana* dance was still illegally performed here (but with a different name), and literature was published in the outlawed Catalan language. In 1970, 300 intellectuals demonstrating for more respect for human rights in Spain were locked up in the monastery for several days by Franco's police.

But now Franco is history. The 1990s brought another phase of rebuilding (after a forest fire and rain damage), and the Montserrat community is thriving once again, unafraid to display its pride for the Catalan people, culture, and faith.

a train ticket, you'll leave Barcelona from the same place and on the same train. In Barcelona, take the Metro to Plaça d'Espanya. Follow signs showing a picture of a train to the FGC (Ferrocarrils de la Generalitat de Catalunya) underground station, then look for train line R5 (direction: Manresa, departures at :36 past each hour, 45 min).

Cable Car to/from the Monastery: At the Montserrat-Aeri stop, the cable car awaits (4/hr, 9:24–13:45 & 14:20–18:45—note the lunch break). On the way back down, departures from the monastery at :25 past the hour make the Barcelona-bound trains leaving at :39 past the hour. The last efficient departure is at 18:25. Although there's a later cable-car departure from the monastery, at 18:45 (17:45 off-season), it entails almost an hour-long wait for the next train.

Cremallera Rack Railway (Mountain Train) to/from the Monastery: Get off the train at the Monistrol de Montserrat stop (one stop after Montserrat-Aeri) and catch the Cremallera rack railway (€4 one-way, €6.30 round trip, included with your train or package ticket, hourly 9:38–18:38, until 20:38 in summer, www.cremalladrademontserrat.com). On the way back, departures from the monastery at :06 past the hour will get you to the Barcelona-bound train (which departs at :33 past each hour).

ORIENTATION

When you arrive at the base of the mountain, look up the rock face to find the cable-car line, the tiny monastery near the top, and the tiny building midway up, marking the Sacred Cave.

However you make your way up to the Montserrat monastery, it's easy to get oriented. Everything is within a few minutes' walk of your entry point. The parking lot, cable-car station, rack railway terminal, and Sant Joan funicular whisking hikers to the ridge top all meet at a long square below the basilica (where you'll also find the TI—see below). There's a humble farmers' market here each morning selling traditional produce. Arrive early or late, as tour groups mob the place midday.

Tourist Information

The square below the basilica houses a helpful TI (daily 9:00–19:40, tel. 938-777-701, www.abadiamontserrat.net). A good audioguide, available only at the TI, describes the general site, basilica, and museum (€5, includes book). If you're a hiker, request the *Six Itineraries from the Monastery* brochure. Trails offer spectacular views (on clear days) to the Mediterranean and even (on clearer days) to the Pyrenees.

The audiovisual center (next to TI) offers some cultural and historical perspective. The lame interactive exhibition—nowhere near as exciting as the mountains and basilica outside—includes computer touch-screens and a short video, covers the mountain's history and gives a glimpse into the daily lives of the monastery's resident monks (€2, daily 9:00–20:00).

SELF-GUIDED SPIN-TOUR

From the monastery's main square, Plaça de Santa Maria, face the main facade and take this spin tour, moving from right to left: Like a good pilgrim, face Mary, the centerpiece of the facade. Below her to the left is St. Benedict, the sixth-century monk who established the rules that came to govern Montserrat's monastery. St. George, the symbol of Catalunya, is on the right (amid victims of Spain's Civil War).

Five arches line the base of the church. The one on the far right leads pilgrims to the high point of any visit, the Black Virgin (a.k.a. La Moreneta, described below). The center arch leads into the basilica, and the arch second from left directs you to a small votive chapel filled with articles representing prayer requests or thanks.

Left of the basilica, the delicate arches mark the old monks' cloister. Below that are four trees the monks plant, hoping to harvest only their symbolism (palm = martyrdom, cypress = eternal life, olive = peace, and laurel = victory). Next to the trees is a public library and peaceful reading room. The big archway is the private entrance to the monastery. Then comes the modern hotel and, below that, the modern, white museum. Other buildings provide cells for pilgrims. The Sant Joan funicular lifts hikers up to the trailhead (you can see the tiny building at the top). From there, you can take a number of fine hikes (described below). Another funicular station descends to the Holy Cave (see below). And, finally, five arches separate statues of founders of the great religious orders. Step over to the arches for a commanding view (on a clear day) of the Llobregat River, meandering all the way to the Mediterranean.

SIGHTS AND ACTIVITIES

Basilica—While there's been a church here since the 11th century, the present church was built in the 1850s, and the facade only dates from 1968. The decor is neo-Romanesque, so popular with the Romantic artists of the late 19th century. The basilica itself is ringed with interesting chapels, but the focus is on the Black Virgin sitting high above the main altar.

Montserrat's top attraction is **La Moreneta,** the small wood statue of the Black Virgin, discovered in the Sacred Cave in the 12th century. Legend says she was carved by St. Luke (the Gospel writer and supposed artist), brought to Spain by St. Peter, hidden away in the cave during the Moorish invasions, and miraculously discovered by shepherd children. (Carbon dating says she's 800 years old.) While George is the patron saint of Catalunya,

La Moreneta is its patroness, having been crowned as such by the pope in 1881. "Moreneta" is usually translated as "black" in English, but the Spanish name actually means "tanned." The statue was originally lighter, but darkened over the centuries from candle smoke, humidity, and its original varnish darkening with age. Pilgrims shuffle down a long and ornate passage leading alongside the church for their few moments alone with the virgin (free, daily 8:00–10:30 & 12:00–18:30 & 19:30–20:15).

Join the line of pilgrims. While Mary's behind a protective glass case, the royal orb she cradles in her hands is exposed. Pilgrims touch Mary's orb with one hand and hold their other hand up to show that they accept Jesus. Newlyweds in particular seek Mary's blessing.

Immediately after La Moreneta, turn right into the delightful neo-Romanesque prayer chapel, where worshippers sit behind the Virgin and continue to pray. Don't miss the sumptuous ceiling painted in the Modernista style in 1898 by Joan Llimona: Jesus and Mary are high in heaven. The trail connecting Catalunya with heaven seems to lead through these serrated mountains. The figures depicted lower are people symbolizing Catalan history and culture.

You'll leave walking along the Ave Maria Path, which thoughtfully integrates nature and the basilica. Thousands of colorful votive candles are all busy helping the devout with their prayer needs. Before reaching the square, pop into the little room with the many votive offerings where people leave personal belongings (wedding dresses, baby's baptism outfits, wax body parts in need of healing, and so on) as part of a prayer request or as a thanks for divine intercession.

Museum of Montserrat—The bright, shiny, and cool collection of paintings and artifacts was mostly donated by devout Catalan Catholics. While it's nothing really earth-shaking, you'll enjoy an air-conditioned wander past lots of antiquities and fine Modernista paintings, plus works by El Greco, Caravaggio, Monet, Picasso, and Dalí (€6.30, daily 10:00–19:00).

Sant Joan Funicular—This funicular climbs 820 feet above the monastery (€4 one-way, €6.30 round-trip). At the top of the funicular, you are at the starting point of a 20-minute walk that takes you to the Sant Joan Chapel. The trailhead by the funicular is also where numerous hikes described in the TI's *Six Itineraries from the Monastery* brochure begin. For a quick and easy chance to get out into nature, simply ride up and follow the most popular hike, a 45-minute downhill loop through mountain scenery back down to the monastery. For this route, go left from the funicular station; the trail—marked *Monestir Montserrat*—will first go up to a rocky point before heading downhill.

Sacred Cave (Santa Cova)—The Moreneta was originally discovered in the Sacred Cave (or Sacred Grotto), a 40-minute hike down from the monastery. The path (c. 1900) was designed by devoted and patriotic Modernista architects, including Gaudí and Josep Puig i Cadafalch. It's lined with Modernista statues depicting scenes from the life of Christ. While the original Black Virgin statue is now in the basilica, a replica sits in the cave. A three-minute funicular ride cuts 20 minutes off the hike (€1.70 one-way, €2.60 round-trip, daily April–Oct 10:30–17:15, Nov–March 11:30–16:15).

If you're here on a late afternoon, check the funicular schedule before you head into the Sacred Cave to make sure you don't miss the final ride down. Missing the last ride could mean you'd catch a train back to Barcelona later than you had planned.

Choir Concert—Montserrat's Escolania, or Choir School, has been training voices for centuries. Fifty young boys, who live and study in the monastery itself, make up the choir, which performs daily except Saturday (Mon–Fri at 13:00, Sun at 12:00 and 18:45, choir on vacation in July). The boys sing for only 10 minutes, the basilica is jam-packed, and you'll likely actually see almost nothing. Also note that if you attend the evening performance, you'll miss the last funicular down the mountain.

SLEEPING

An overnight here gets you monastic peace and a total break from the modern crowds. There are ample rustic cells for pilgrim visitors, but tourists might prefer this place:

$$ Hotel Abat Cisneros, a three-star hotel with all the comforts, is low-key and appropriate for a sanctuary (Sb-€30–50, Db-€53–89, depending on season, includes breakfast, half- and full-board available, tel. 938-777-701, fax 938-777-724, www.abadiamontserrat.net, reserves@larsa-montserrat.com).

BASQUE REGION

(Euskadi/País Vasco/Le Pays Basque)

Straddling Spain and France on the Atlantic Coast is a land that's both famous for its sunny beaches and scintillating modern architecture, and infamous for its feisty, independent natives. This is Basque country, or in Spanish, *País Vasco*. The Basque region stretches 100 miles from Bilbao north to Bayonne, France. And in some ways, the *País Vasco* has more in common with the neighboring *Pays Basque* in France than it does with Spain. The Spanish and French Basque regions share a Union Jack–style flag (green, red, and white), cuisine, and common language (Euskara), spoken by about a half million Spaniards and French.

Insulated from mainstream Europe for centuries, the plucky Basques have just wanted to be left alone for more than 7,000 years. For 40 years, Generalissimo Franco did his best to tame the separatist-minded Basques. The bombed city of Guernica (Gernika), halfway between San Sebastián and Bilbao, survives as a tragic example of his efforts to suppress Basque independence.

Today the Basque terrorist organization, ETA (which stands for the Euskara phrase *Euskadi Ta Askatasuna*, or "Basque Country and Freedom"), is supported by a tiny minority of the population. Although the group periodically has been in the news for attacks on the Spanish government (and is blamed for 800 deaths since 1968), members have focused their anger on political targets and have been largely unnoticed by tourists. Hoping to promote a democratic process in the Basque region, the ETA imposed a "permanent ceasefire" in March of 2006.

Even though the region was technically bilingual (Euskara and Spanish), Franco so effectively blunted Basque expression that the language was primarily Spanish by default. But after several

Basque Region

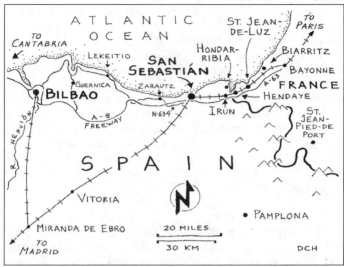

Franco-free decades, there's a renewed awareness of the importance of the Basque language (which is absolutely unrelated to any other). Look for it on street signs, menus, and signs in shops.

Similarly, today's Basque lands are undergoing a 21st-century renaissance, as the dazzling new architecture of the Guggenheim Bilbao modern-art museum (pictured on previous page) and the glittering resort of San Sebastián are drawing enthusiastic crowds. For small-town fun, drop by the fishing village of Lekeitio (near Bilbao) and little Hondarribia near the border, providing a good last (or first) stop in Spain.

San Sebastián

Shimmering above the breathtaking bay of La Concha, elegant and prosperous San Sebastián ("Donostia" in Euskara) has a favored location with golden beaches, capped by twin peaks at either end,

and a cute little island in the center. A delightful beachfront promenade runs the length of the bay, with an intriguing Old Town at one end and a smart shopping district in the center. It has 180,000 residents and almost that many tourists in high season (July–Sept). With a romantic setting, a soaring statue of Christ gazing over the city, and a late-night lively Old Town, San Sebastián has a Rio de Janeiro aura. While there's no compelling museum to visit, the scenic city provides a pleasant introduction to Spain's Basque country.

In 1845, Queen Isabel II's doctor recommended she treat her skin problems by bathing here in the sea. Her visit mobilized Spain's aristocracy, and soon the city was on the map as a seaside resort. By the turn of the 20th century, Donostia was the toast of the belle époque, and a leading resort for Europe's beautiful people. Before World War I, Queen María Cristina summered here and held court in her Miramar Palace overlooking the crescent beach. Hotels, casinos, and theaters flourished. Even Franco enjoyed 35 summers in a place he was sure to call San Sebastián, not Donostia.

Planning Your Time

San Sebastián is worth a day. Stroll the two-mile-long promenade and scout the place you'll grab to work on a tan. The promenade leads to a funicular that lifts you to the Monte Igueldo viewpoint (described below). After exploring the Old Town and port, walk up to the hill of Monte Urgull. A big part of any visit to San Sebastián is enjoying tapas in the Old Town bars.

ORIENTATION

The San Sebastián we're interested in surrounds Concha Bay (Bahía de la Concha), and can be divided into three areas: Playa de la Concha (best beaches), the shopping district (called Centro Romántico), and the skinny streets of the grid-planned Old Town (called Parte Vieja, to the north of the shopping district). The Centro Romántico, just east of Playa de la Concha, has beautiful turn-of-the-20th-century architecture, but no real sights.

It's all bookended by mini-mountains: Monte Urgull to the north and east, Monte Igueldo to the south and west. The river (Río Urumea) divides central San Sebastián from the district called Gros (which has a lively night scene and surfing beach).

Tourist Information

San Sebastián's TI, a block from the river on the boulevard that separates the Centro Romántico from the Old Town, has information on city and regional sights, as well as bus and train schedules.

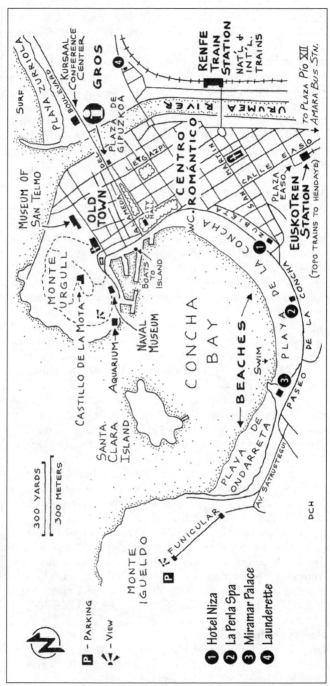

San Sebastián

300 YARDS
300 METERS

P – PARKING
🔱 – VIEW

1 Hotel Niza
2 La Perla Spa
3 Miramar Palace
4 Launderette

Pick up the excellent town booklet, which has English descriptions of the three walking tours—the Old Quarter/Monte Urgull walk is best (July–Sept Mon–Sat 9:00–20:00, Sun 10:00–14:00 & 15:30–19:00; Oct–June Mon–Sat 9:00–13:30 & 15:30–19:00, Sun 10:00–14:00; just off Zurriola bridge at Calle Reina Regente 3, tel. 943-481-166, www.sansebastianturismo.com). Skip the **San Sebastián Card** unless you plan to use the bus a lot (€10 for 3 days of free bus transport plus minor sightseeing discounts). Ask about occasional English **walking tours** (€10, usually June–mid-Sept Tue–Sat at 11:00, depart from town hall), and consider renting an **audioguide** (€10, 2 hours).

Arrival in San Sebastián

By Train: If you're coming on a regional Topo train from Hendaye ("Hendaia" in Euskara) on the French border, get off at the EuskoTren station (end of the line, called Amara). Nearby Continental Auto provides luggage storage (€2/day, Mon–Sat 7:00–13:00 & 15:00–20:30, Sun 7:00–12:00 & 15:00–20:30, tel. 943-469-074). It's a level 15-minute walk to the center; exit the station and walk across the long plaza, then walk eight blocks down Calle Easo to the beach. The Old Town will be ahead on your right, with Playa de la Concha to your left. To speed things up, catch bus #26 or #28 along Calle Easo and take it to the Boulevard stop, near the TI at the bottom of the Old Town.

If you're arriving by train from elsewhere in Spain (or from France with a transfer in Irún), you'll get off at the main RENFE station (luggage lockers available, daily 7:00–22:00). It's just across the bridge (Puente María Cristina) from the Centro Romántico shopping district. To reach the beach, cross the bridge, take your first right along the river, then first left on Calle San Martín, then right on Calle Easo.

By Bus: If you're arriving by bus from Hondarribia, hop off at pretty Plaza de Gipuzkoa (first stop after crossing the river, in shopping area, near TI). To reach the TI, walk down Legazpi, cross Alameda del Boulevard, and turn right.

By Car: Take the Amara freeway exit, follow *Centro Ciudad* signs into the city center, and park in a pay lot (many are well-signed). If you're picking up or returning a rental car, "The Big Autorental"—which includes Hertz (Zubieta 5, tel. 943-461-084) and Avis (Triunfo 2, tel. 943-461-527)—is near Hotel Niza, and Europcar is at the RENFE train station (tel. 943-322-304).

Helpful Hints

Useful Telephone Numbers: For the police, dial 943-538-920. For flight information, call San Sebastián's airport (in Hondarribia, 12 miles away) at tel. 943-668-500.

Internet Access: There are many places in the Old Town; the handiest is **Donosti-NET** (daily 9:00–23:00, Calle Narrika 3 Bajo, tel. 943-429-497). They also sell cheap phone cards for calling home, offer expensive luggage storage, and can arrange car rentals with Avis or National.

Bookstore: Bilintx, near several recommended restaurants in the Old Town, has a wide selection, including some guidebooks in English (daily, closed 14:00–16:00, Calle Fermín Calbetón 21, tel. 943-420-080).

Laundry: Wash & Dry is in the Gros neighborhood, across the river behind the train station (self-service daily 8:00–20:00, drop-off service Mon–Fri 9:30–13:00 & 16:00–20:00, Iparragirre 6, tel. 943-293-150). There's also a **self-service launderette** in the Old Town (Mon–Fri 9:30–13:00 & 16:00–19:30, Sat 10:00–14:00, closed Sun, near Plaza de la Constitución at Calle de Inigo 14).

Bike and Scooter Rental: Try **Bicicletas Alai,** behind the Amara bus station (Avenida de Madrid 24, tel. 943-470-001), or **Bici Rent Donosti** (Avenida de Zurriola 22, 3 blocks across the river from the TI, tel. 943-290-854).

Local Guide: The **Just Follow Me** company offers guide services and excursions in the Basque region by foot, bike, or minivan (tel. 685-757-601, www.justfollowme.com).

Getting Around San Sebastián

By Bus: At Alameda del Boulevard, along the bottom edge of the Old Town, you'll find a line of public buses ready to take you anywhere in town; give any driver your destination, and he'll tell you the number of the bus to catch (€1, pay driver).

Some handy bus routes: #26 and #28 connect the bus and EuskoTren stations to the TI (get off at the Boulevard stop); #16 begins at the Boulevard/TI stop, goes along Playa de la Concha and through residential areas, and eventually arrives at the base of the Monte Igueldo funicular. The TI has an excellent bus-route map, if you want to see exactly where you're going (www.ctss.es).

By Taxi: Taxis start at €3, then charge €0.50 per kilometer. You'll do better calling one or finding a taxi stand (such as along Alameda del Boulevard, described above) rather than trying to hail one (tel. 943-464-646 or 943-404-040).

By Tour: Two tours are available, but they're not necessary in this walkable city: The **"txu-txu"** tourist train (€4.40, daily July–Aug 11:00–19:00, Sept–June 11:00–13:00 & 16:00–19:00, 40-min round-trip, tel. 943-422-973) and the **Donosti** hop-on, hop-off bus tour (€10, 60 min, ticket good for 24 hours, leaves from theater across from TI, tel. 696-429-847). Both do similar routes with minimal commentary along the Playa de La Concha, toward

Monte Igueldo, and back through Centro Romántico—but only the bus tour goes up Monte Igueldo and also crosses the river into the Gros neighborhood (neither tour goes into the Old Town).

SIGHTS AND ACTIVITIES

The Beach

▲▲**La Concha Beach and Promenade**—The shell-shaped Playa de La Concha, the pride of San Sebastián, has one of Europe's

loveliest stretches of sand. Lined with a two-mile-long promenade, it allows even backpackers to feel aristocratic. While pretty empty off-season, in summer, sunbathers pack its shores. But year-round, it's surprisingly devoid of eateries and money-grubbing businesses. There are free showers, and *cabinas* provide lockers, showers, and shade for a fee. The Miramar palace and park, which divides the crescent in the middle, was where Queen María Cristina held court when she summered here. Her royal changing rooms are used today as inviting cafés, restaurants, and a fancy spa (La Perla, described below). For a century, the lovingly painted wrought-iron balustrade that stretches the length of the promenade has been a symbol of the city; it shows up on everything from jewelry to headboards.

La Perla Spa—The spa attracts a less royal crowd today and appeals mostly to visitors interested in sampling "the curative properties of the sea." You can enjoy its Talaso Fitness Circuit, featuring a hydrotherapy pool, relaxation pool, panoramic Jacuzzi, cold-water pools, seawater steam sauna, dry sauna, and a relaxation area. For those seriously into spas, they offer additional services, from Dead Sea mud wraps to massages to day-long "personalized programs" (€19 for 105-min fitness circuit, €24 for 3-hour circuit, daily 8:00–22:00, caps and towels rented/sold, bring or buy a swimsuit, on the beach at the center of the crescent, Paseo de La Concha, tel. 943-458-856, www.la-perla.net).

Old Town (Parte Vieja)

Huddled in the shadow of its once-protective Monte Urgull, the Old Town (worth ▲▲) is where San Sebastián was born about 1,000 years ago. The grid plan of streets hides heavy Baroque and Gothic churches, surprise plazas, and fun little shops, including venerable pastry stores, rugged produce markets, Basque-independence souvenir shops, and seafood-to-go delis. "THC shops" offer the latest from the decriminalized marijuana scene in Spain—adults are allowed to grow two plants. Be sure to wander out to the port to see the fishing industry in action. The Old Town's main square, Plaza de la Constitución (where bullfights used to be held—notice the seat numbering on the balconies) features inviting café tables spilling from all corners. The highlight of the Old Town is its incredibly lively tapas bars—though here, these snacks are called *pintxos* (PEEN-chohs; see "Eating," page 135).

Museum of San Telmo—This humble museum displays exhibits and paintings in rooms arranged around the peaceful cloister of a former Dominican monastery. There are a few exhibits on Basque folk life, and a small collection of 19th- and 20th-century paintings by Basque artists that offer an interesting peek into the spirit, faces, and natural beauty of this fiercely independent region (free, other featured artists include El Greco and Rubens, minimal English information, Tue–Sat 10:30–13:30 & 16:00–19:30, Sun 10:30–14:00, closed Mon, Plaza Zuloaga 1, tel. 943-481-580).

The Port

At the west end of the Old Town, protected by Monte Urgull, is the port. To reach the first three sights, take the passage through

the wall at the appropriately named Calle Puerto, and jog right along the level, portside Paseo del Muelle. You'll pass fishing boats unloading the catch of the day (while hungry locals look on), salty sailors' pubs, and fisherfolk mending nets. The trails to Monte Urgull are just above this scene, near Santa María Church (or climb up the stairs next to the aquarium).

Cruise—Small boats cruise from the Old Town's port to the island in the bay (Isla Santa Clara), where you can hike the trails and have lunch at the lone café (€3.10 round-trip; July–Sept 10:00–20:30, departures every 30 min; June 10:00–20:00, departures hourly; boats don't run Oct–May).

▲**Aquarium**—San Sebastián's impressive aquarium exhibits include a history of the sea, fascinating models showing various drift-netting techniques, a petting tank filled with nervous fish, a huge whale skeleton, and a 45-foot-long tunnel that allows you to look up at floppy rays and menacing sharks (€10, €6 for kids under 13; April–June daily 10:00–20:00; July–Aug daily 10:00–21:00; Sept–March Mon–Fri 10:00–19:00, Sat–Sun 10:00–20:00; ongoing renovations may close some exhibits, Paseo del Muelle 34, tel. 943-440-099, www.aquariumss.com).

Naval Museum (Museo Naval)—Located at the port, this museum's two floors of exhibits describe the seafaring city's history, revealing the intimate link between the Basque culture and the sea (€1.20, borrow the English translation booklet, Tue–Sat 10:00–13:30 & 16:00–19:30, Sun 11:00–14:00, closed Mon, just before aquarium at Paseo del Muelle 24, tel. 943-430-051).

▲**Monte Urgull**—The once-mighty castle (Castillo de la Mota) atop the hill deterred most attackers, allowing the city to prosper in the Middle Ages. The museum located within the castle features San Sebastián history and is mildly interesting. The best views from the hill are not from the statue of Christ, but from the ramparts on the left side (as you face the hill), just above the port's aquarium. Café El Polvorín, nestled in the park, is a friendly place with salads, sandwiches, and good sangria. The path is technically open only from sunrise to sunset (generally daily May–Sept 8:00–21:00, Oct–April 8:00–19:00). Why are some of the directional signs defaced? Because you're in the land of Euskadi, not Spain—and to remind you, some proud Basque has spray-painted over the Spanish.

More Sights

Monte Igueldo—For commanding city views (if you ignore the tacky amusements on top), ride the funicular up Monte Igueldo, a mirror image of Monte Urgull. The views over San Sebastián, along the coast, and into the distant green mountains are sensational day or night. The entrance to the funicular is on the road behind the tennis club on the far western end of Playa de Ondarreta, which extends from Playa de la Concha to the west (funicular-€2; July–mid-Sept daily 10:00–22:00; April–June and mid-Sept–Oct daily 11:00–20:00; Nov–March Mon–Fri 11:00–18:00, Sat–Sun 11:00–20:00, closed Wed). If you drive to the top, you'll pay €1.50 to enter. The #16 bus takes you here from the Old Town in about 10 minutes, stopping at the funicular station.

SLEEPING

$$$ Hotel Niza, set on the western edge of Playa de la Concha, is understandably often booked well in advance. Half of its 40 rooms (some with balconies) overlook the bay. From its chandeliered and plush lounge, a classic elevator takes you to its comfortable, pastel rooms with wedding-cake molding (Db-€108–128, view rooms cost the same—requests with reservation considered...but no promises, extra bed-€20, only streetside rooms have air-con, great buffet breakfast-€9.30, Internet access, free Wi-Fi, parking-€13/day—must reserve in advance, Zubieta 56, tel. 943-426-663, fax 943-441-251, www.hotelniza.com, niza@hotelniza.com).

Sleep Code

(€1 = about $1.20, country code: 34)
S = Single, **D** = Double/Twin, **T** = Triple, **Q** = Quad, **b** = bathroom,
s = shower only. You can assume these places accept credit
cards and speak English unless otherwise noted. Breakfast is
generally not included (unless noted), but you have plenty of
churrerías and cafeterias to choose from in the Old Town.

To help you sort easily through these listings, I've divided
the rooms into three categories based on the price for a standard double room with bath in peak season:

$$$ **Higher Priced**—Most rooms €90 or more.
 $$ **Moderately Priced**—Most rooms between €60–90.
  $ **Lower Priced**—Most rooms €60 or less.

The breakfast room has a sea view and doubles as a bar with light
snacks throughout the day (Bar Biarritz, daily 7:00–24:00, food
service ends at 22:30). The cheap and cheery restaurant downstairs,
called La Pasta Gansa, serves good pizzas and salads (Wed–Mon
13:30–15:30 & 20:30–24:00, closed Tue).

$$$ Hotel Parma is a business-class place with 27 fine
rooms and family-run attention to detail and service. It stands on
the edge of the Old Town, away from the bar-scene noise, and
overlooks the river and a surfing beach (Sb-€56–75, windowless
interior Db-€82–113, view Db-€100–125, air-con, modern lounge,
Paseo de Salamanca 10, tel. 943-428-893, fax 943-424-082, www
.hotelparma.com, hotelparma@hotelparma.com; Iñaki, Arantxa,
Quique, and Ibon).

$$ Pensión Gran Bahía offers 10 good rooms, all with air-
conditioning. You'll enjoy the rich, dark-wood floors polished to a
slippery shine. Teresa—with no English, quite a personality, and
lots of rules—is very proud of her fine *pensión* (June–Sept: Db-
€85, Tb-€118; Oct–May: Sb-€39, Db-€49, Tb-€73; prices soft
off-season, 7 percent tax not included, tries to be non-smoking,
Embeltrán 16, tel. 943-420-216, fax 943-428-276, www.paisvasco
.com/granbahia, reservas@pensiongranbahia.com).

$$ Pensión Edorta elegantly mixes wood, brick, and color into
12 modern, stylish rooms (S-€30–50, D-€40–60, Sb/Db-€60–80,
extra bed-€20–25, elevator, Calle Puerto 15, tel. 943-423-773, fax
943-433-570, www.pensionedorta.com, info@pensionedorta.com).

$$ Pensión Anne is a tiny, well-run place on a relatively quiet
lane in the Old Town, with six rooms sharing two bathrooms. Its sim-
ple rooms are bright and clean but have no sinks (S-€38–46, D-€49,
Db-€64, Esterlines 15, tel. 943-421-438, www.pensionanne.com,

San Sebastián's Old Town

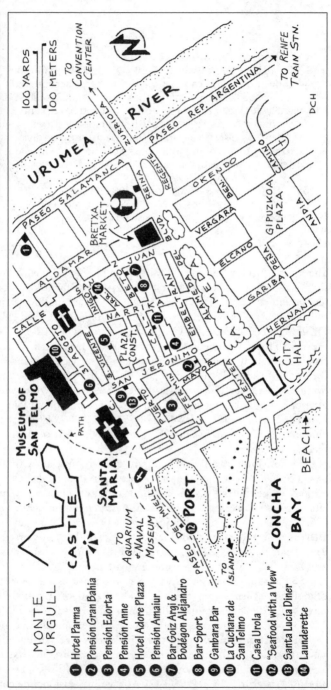

100 YARDS
100 METERS

TO CONVENTION CENTER

URUMEA RIVER

PASEO SALAMANCA

PASEO REP. ARGENTINA

TO RENFE TRAIN STN.

BRETXA MARKET

MONTE URGULL

CASTLE

MUSEUM OF SAN TELMO

SANTA MARIA

TO AQUARIUM + NAVAL MUSEUM

PORT

PASEO DEL MUELLE

TO ISLAND

CONCHA BAY

BEACH

CITY HALL

DCH

1 Hotel Parma
2 Pensión Gran Bahia
3 Pensión Edorta
4 Pensión Anne
5 Hotel Adore Plaza
6 Pensión Amaiur
7 Bar Goiz Argi & Bodegón Alejandro
8 Bar Sport
9 Ganbara Bar
10 La Cuchara de San Telmo
11 Casa Urola
12 "Seafood with a View"
13 Santa Lucía Diner
14 Launderette

pensionanne@yahoo.es, Anne).

$ Pensión Amaiur Ostatua is a popular hangout with the *Let's Go* backpacker crowd, but don't let that scare you. It's a flowery and inviting place buried deep in the Old Town, with great-value rooms. Kind Virginia gives the place a homey warmth, and the colorful pension is absolutely spotless. Her 13 rooms share seven bathrooms (S-€24–37, D with balcony-€38–55, quiet interior D-€33–47, T-€51–75, Q-€63–90, family room, kitchen facilities, Internet access, next to Santa María Church at Calle 31 de Agosto 44, tel. 943-429-654, www.pensionamaiur.com, reservas @pensionamaiur.com).

$ Adore Plaza, run by young and energetic Santi, offers frumpy but good-value rooms overlooking the Old Town's centerpiece, Plaza de la Constitución. Seven rooms—including four with balconies and views of the plaza—share four bathrooms (D-€50–60, one Db-€75, beds in 4-bed room with lockers-€20–25 per person, Plaza de la Constitución 6, tel. & fax 943-422-270, mobile 610-521-092, www.adoreplaza.com, adoreplaza@yahoo.es).

EATING

On menus, you'll see *bacalao* (salted cod), best when cooked *à la bizkaina* (with tomatoes, onions, and roasted peppers); *merluza* (hake, a light whitefish prepared in a variety of ways); and *chipirones en su tinta* (squid served in their own black ink). Carnivores will find plenty of lamb (try *chuletas,* massive lamb chops). Local brews include *sidra* (hard apple cider), *txakolí* (cha-koh-LEE, a local, light, sparkling white wine—often theatrically poured from high above the glass for aeration), and *izarra* (herbal-flavored brandy). Spanish wine is generally served by the glass; red *crianza* spends one year in oak kegs and is *con cuerpo* (full-bodied). If you ask for *una copa de tinto*, they'll likely give you the local wine, bottled without a label. Surprisingly, *rosados* (rosés) have become very popular lately, as Spanish wineries have increased their production.

Bar-Hopping

Txiquiteo (chih-kee-TAY-oh) is the word for hopping from bar to bar, enjoying characteristically small sandwiches and tiny snacks (*pintxos,* PEEN-chohs) and glasses of wine. Local competition drives small bars to lay out the most appealing array of *pintxos,* and the selection is amazing. Later in the evening, the best spreads get picked over (20:30 is prime time). As the night progresses, bars get more crowded and bartenders bounce around. If you can't get the bartender's attention to serve you a particular *pintxo,* don't be shy—just grab it and a napkin, and munch away. If it comes with a toothpick, don't throw it on the ground (it's how they keep track of how many tasty tapas you've had).

Do the *Txiquiteo* Tango: San Sebastián's Old Town provides the ideal backdrop for tapas-hopping; just wander the streets and straddle up to the bar in the liveliest spot. Calle Fermín Calbetón has about the best concentration of bars (don't miss Bar Goiz Argi, described below); the streets San Jerónimo and 31 de Agosto are also good.

Bar Goiz Argi serves its tiny dishes with pride and attitude. Advertising *pintxos calientes,* they cook each treat for you, allowing you a montage of petite gourmet snacks; try their *tartaleta de txan-gurro* (spider-crab spread on bread). Wash it all down with a glass of whichever wine you like—open bottles are clearly priced and displayed on the shelf. You stand at the bar since there are no chairs (closed Mon–Tue, Calle Fermín Calbetón 4, tel. 943-425-204).

Next, make your way down to the nearby **Bar Sport** for more action. They may offer to *calentar* (heat up) some of your selections, such as the toothpick-towering *jamón* and mushroom *pintxo.* They have a few tables, but don't expect service. Order at the bar and take it to your table...if you're lucky enough to get one (closed Mon, Calle Fermín Calbetón 10, tel. 943-426-888).

For top-end tapas, seek out these two bars—each packed with locals rather than tourists: **Ganbara Bar** serves the typical little sandwich *pintxos,* but also heaps piles of peppers and mushrooms—whatever's in season—on its bar, and sautées tasty *raciones* for a steep price (see the dry-erase board, closed Mon, San Jerónimo 21, tel. 943-422-575). **La Cuchara de San Telmo**—with cooks taught by a big-name Basque chef—is a cramped place that devotes as much space to its thriving kitchen as its bar. It has nothing pre-cooked and set on the bar—you order your mini-gourmet plates with a spirit of adventure from the constantly changing blackboard (€3 *pintxos,* closed Mon, tucked away on a lonely alley behind Museo San Telmo at 31 de Agosto 28, tel. 943-420-840).

Restaurants, Picnics, and *Churros*

Bodégon Alejandro is a good spot for modern Basque cuisine in a dark and traditional setting (three-course fixed-price meal-€30, from 13:00 and 21:00, closed Mon, no dinner Sun and Tue, in the thick of the Old Town on Calle Fermín Calbetón 4, tel. 943-427-158). **Casa Urola,** a block away, is *the* place in the Old Town for a good, traditional, sit-down Basque meal (more expensive, reservations smart from 13:00 and 20:00, Calle Fermín Calbetón 20, tel. 943-423-424).

For **seafood** with a view, check out the half-dozen hardworking, local-feeling restaurants that line the harbor on the way to the aquarium.

For **picnics,** drop by one of the countless tiny grocery stores or the Bretxa public market at Plaza Sarriegi (down the modern escalator) near the TI. Then head for the beach or up Monte Urgull.

Santa Lucía, a '50s-style Basque diner, is ideal for a cheap Old Town breakfast or *churros* break (*churros* are like deep-fried, sweet French fries that can be dipped in pudding-like hot chocolate). Photos of 20 different breakfasts decorate the walls, and plates of fresh *churros* with sugar keep patrons happy (daily 8:00–22:00, Calle Puerto 6, tel. 943-425-019). Grease is liberally applied to the grill...from a squeeze bottle. To counteract this place's heart-attack potential, get a glass of O.J., fresh-squeezed by the clever machine.

TRANSPORTATION CONNECTIONS

From San Sebastián by Train: Remember that San Sebastián has two train stations: RENFE and EuskoTren (described in "Arrival in San Sebastián," page 128). The station you use depends on your destination. The RENFE station handles long-distance destinations within Spain, including **Barcelona** (1/day, 8.5 hrs; 1/night except Sat, 10 hrs), **Madrid** (3/day, 6–8.5 hrs, or 10.5-hr night train), and **Santiago de Compostela** (4/day, 11–14 hrs, night train available). If you're going into France, it's best to take the regional Topo train (which leaves from the EuskoTren station) over the French border into **Hendaye** (2/hr, 30 min, departs EuskoTren station at :15 and :45 after the hour 7:15–21:45). From Hendaye, connect to France's SNCF network, including **Paris** (from Hendaye: 4/day, 5.5 hrs, or 8.5–hr night train). Also leaving from San Sebastián's EuskoTren station are regional trains to other destinations in Spain's Basque region, including **Bilbao** (hourly, 2.75 hrs—but the bus is much better, described below; EuskoTren info: tel. 902-543-210, www.euskotren.es). Note that all trains to Barcelona, Madrid, and Paris require reservations.

By Bus: There is no real bus station in San Sebastián—it's more a congregation of bus parking spots, called Amara, on Plaza Pío XII (on the river, three blocks below EuskoTren station). Buy your tickets in advance at any of the bus companies with offices facing the river. Pesa, which serves St. Jean-de-Luz, is located on the opposite side, along Avenida de Sancho el Sabio (www.pesa.net). From San Sebastián, buses go to **Bilbao** (2/hr, hourly on weekends, 6:30–22:00, 1.25 hrs, get €9 ticket from office, departs from Amara, bus tel. 902-101-210; once in Bilbao, buses leave you at Termibús stop about a 30-minute walk away from the Guggenheim Museum) and **St. Jean-de-Luz,** France (2/day direct, at 9:00 and 14:30, 45 min, €4 one-way, €7.45 round-trip, runs only 1/week off-season, departs from Amara, tel. 902-101-210).

Hondarribia

For a taste of small-town *País Vasco*, dip into this enchanting, seldom-visited town. Much smaller and easier to manage than San Sebastián, and also closer to France (across the Bay of Txingudi from Hendaye), Hondarribia allows travelers a stress-free opportunity to enjoy Basque culture. While it's easy to think of this as a border town (between France and Spain), culturally it's in the middle of Basque country.

The town comes in two parts: the lower port town and the historic, balcony-lined streets of the hilly and walled upper town. The **TI** is located between the two parts, two blocks up from the port on Jabier Ugarte 6 (Mon–Fri 9:00–13:30 & 16:00–18:30, Sat 10:00–14:00, closed Sun, tel. 943-645-458). You can follow their self-guided tour of the old town (English brochure available) or just lose yourself within the walls. Explore the plazas of the upper city.

Today, Charles V's odd, squat castle is a parador inn (Db-€195, Plaza de Armas 14, tel. 943-645-500, fax 943-642-153, hondarribia@parador.es). Tourists are allowed to have sangria in the *muy* cool bar, though the terraces are for guests only. In the modern lower town, straight shopping streets serve a local clientele and a pleasant walkway takes strollers along the beach.

TRANSPORTATION CONNECTIONS

From Hondarribia by Bus to: San Sebastián (3/hr, 45 min to go 12 miles), **Hendaye** on the French border (2/hr, 20 min, June–Sept only). A bus stop in Hondarribia is across from the post office, one block below the TI.

By Boat to: Hendaye (4/hr, 15 min, runs about 11:00–19:00 or until dark).

Bilbao and the Guggenheim Museum

In recent years, the cultural and economic capital of the *País Vasco*, Bilbao (pop. 500,000), has seen a transformation like no other Spanish city. Entire sectors of the industrial city's long-depressed port have been cleared away to allow construction of a new opera house, convention center, and the stunning Guggenheim Museum. Still, the city will always be a Marseille-like port; for most, it's worth a visit only for its incredible modern-art museum.

ORIENTATION

Tourist Information

Bilbao's handiest TI is across from the Guggenheim (July–Aug Mon–Sat 10:00–19:00, Sun 10:00–15:00; Sept–June Tue–Sat 11:00–18:00, Sun 11:00–14:00, closed Mon; Avenida Abandoibarra 2, central TI tel. 944-795-760, www.bilbao.net). If you're interested in anything besides the Guggenheim, pick up a map, the bimonthly *Bilbao Guide* newsletter, and the museum brochure (describing museums dedicated to everything from Basques and bullfighting to Holy Week processionals).

Arrival in Bilbao

Thanks to a perfectly planned tram system (EuskoTran), getting to the museum is a snap. From any point of entry, simply buy a

€1 single-ride ticket at a user-friendly green machine, hop on a tram, and head for the Guggenheim stop (only one line so you can't get lost, trams come every 10–15 min, www.euskotran.es). When you buy your ticket, validate it at the machine (follow the red arrow), since you can't do it once on board. An all-day pass costs €3.

The Metro system, designed by prominent architect Lord Norman Foster, is a work of art...but not practical for most visitors.

If you get lost, ask: *"¿Dónde está el museo Guggenheim?"* (DOHN-day ay-STAH el moo-SAY-oh "Guggenheim").

By Train: Bilbao's **RENFE station** (trains from most parts of Spain) is on the river in central Bilbao. Ask for a city map at the train information office. To reach the tram to the Guggenheim, use the exit marked *Hurtado de Amézaga,* and go right to find the BBK bank. Go inside, find the *Automatikoa* door on the right, and buy your ticket at the green machine marked *Abando.* Leave the bank, continuing right around the corner, and take a tram marked *San Mamés/Basurtu* (headed in the direction you just came from).

Trains coming from San Sebastián arrive at the riverside **Atxuri station,** southeast of the museum. Buy and validate your ticket, hop on a tram, and follow the river to the Guggenheim stop.

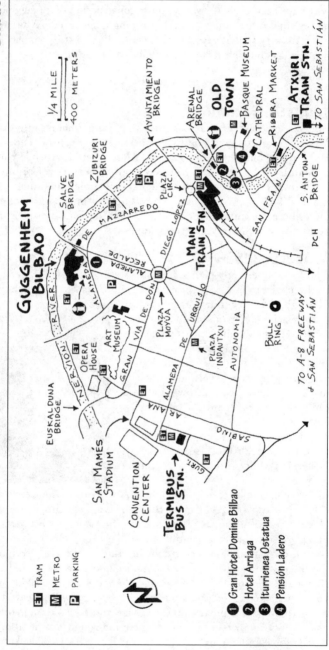

Bilbao

GUGGENHEIM BILBAO

¼ MILE
400 METERS

TRAM
METRO
PARKING

1 Gran Hotel Domine Bilbao
2 Hotel Arriaga
3 Iturrienea Ostatua
4 Pensión Ladero

By Bus: Buses stop at the **Termibus station** on the western edge of downtown, about a mile southwest of the museum. Take the tram (direction: Atxuri) to Guggenheim.

By Car: Parking at the museum itself is a hassle; the closest option is the garage two blocks in front (Calle Iparraguirre 18). But to avoid stressful city traffic and frustrating one-ways, the best plan is this: Use the expressway exit marked *Centro*, following signs to Guggenheim. You'll pass the long train station on your right; continue straight through the traffic circle, veer left at the river, and park at the big garage (called Pío Baroja). Walk 10 minutes to the museum, or hop on the tram (direction: San Mamés/Basurtu).

SIGHTS

Guggenheim Bilbao

While the collection of art in this ▲▲▲ museum is no better than that in Europe's other great modern-art museums, the building itself—designed by Frank Gehry and opened in 1997—is the reason why so many travelers happily splice Bilbao into their itineraries.

Gehry's triumph offers a fascinating look at 21st-century architecture. Using cutting-edge technologies, unusual materials, and daring forms, he created a piece of sculpture that smoothly integrates with its environment and serves as the perfect stage for some of today's best art.

This limestone and titanium-tile-clad building looks like a huge, silvery fish, and connects the city with its river. Gehry meshed many visions. To him, the building's multiple forms jostle like a loose crate of bottles. They also evoke sails heading out to sea. Gehry keeps returning to his fish motif, reminding visitors that, as a boy, he was inspired by carp...even taking them into the bathtub with him. The building's skin—shiny, metallic, fish-like scales—is made of thin titanium, carefully created to give just the desired color and reflective quality.

A great way to really enjoy the exterior is to take a circular stroll up and down each side of the river along the handsome promenade and over the two modern pedestrian bridges.

Guarding the **main entrance** is artist Jeff Koons' 42-foot-tall West Highland Terrier. Its 60,000 plants and flowers, chosen to blossom in concert, grow through steel mesh. A joyful structure, it brings viewers back to their childhood...perhaps evoking humankind's relationship to God...or maybe it's just another notorious Koons hoax. One thing is clear: It answers to "Puppy."

Inside, just beyond the turnstile, you come upon the **atrium.** This is clearly the heart of the building, pumping visitors from various rooms on three levels out and back, always returning to this central area before moving on to the next. Only the floor is straight. The architect invites you to caress the sensual curves of the walls. Notice the sheets of glass that make up the elevator shaft: They overlap like scales on a fish. The various glass and limestone panels are each unique, designed and shaped by a computer—as will likely be standard in constructing the great buildings of the future.

From the atrium, step out onto the riverside **terrace.** The shallow pool lets the river lick at the foundations of the building. Notice the museum's commitment to public spaces: On the right, a grand and public staircase leads under a big green bridge to a tower designed to wrap the bridge into the museum's grand scheme.

As you enter, pick up the English brochure explaining the architecture and the monthly bulletin detailing the art currently on display. Because this museum is part of the Guggenheim "family" of museums, the collection perpetually rotates among the sister Guggenheim galleries in New York, Venice, and Berlin. The best approach to your visit is simply to immerse yourself in a modern-art happening, rather than to count on seeing a particular piece or a specific artist's works. Gehry designed the vast **ground floor** mainly to show off the often-huge modern-art installations. Computer-controlled lighting adjusts for different exhibits. Surfaces are clean and bare, so you can focus on the art.

The museum offers excellent audioguides (sometimes included with admission, sometimes a few euros extra), which give descriptions of current exhibits and fascinating information about the building's architecture. For guided tours in English, call 944-359-080 for the schedule (entry price varies depending on exhibit, generally €10–13; July–Aug daily 10:00–20:00; Sept–June Tue–Sun 10:00–20:00, closed Mon; café, no photos, tram stop: Guggenheim, Metro stop: Moyua, Avenida Abandoibarra 2, tel. 944-359-080, www.guggenheim-bilbao.es).

SLEEPING

(€1 = about $1.20, country code: 34)
Bilbao merits an overnight stay. Even those who are only interested in the Guggenheim find that there's much more to this historic yet quickly changing city. Here are a few options. The first one is across from the Guggenheim, the others are in the Old Town (Casco Viejo), which offers a bustling, pedestrians-only Old World

ambience and lots of dining options. To reach this district, turn right out of the RENFE train station and follow the tram tracks across the river. The 7 percent tax is not included in the prices listed below.

$$$ Gran Hotel Domine Bilbao is *the* place for wealthy modern-art fans looking for a handy splurge. It's right across the street from the Guggenheim, with decor clearly inspired by Gehry's masterpiece. Its 135 plush rooms are all postmodern class (standard Db-€145–230, super-swanky "executive" Db-€160–260, but prices very soft; ask about promotional rates, especially on weekends, when you'll pay closer to €155/€170; elevator, Alameda Mazarredo 61, tel. 944-253-300, fax 944-253-301, www.granhoteldominebilbao .com, reception@granhoteldominebilbao.com).

$$ Hotel Arriaga offers 21 old-fashioned but well-maintained rooms (Sb-€48, Db-€60–64, extra bed-€11, some rooms overlook a busy street—request a quiet back room, Calle Ribera 3, tel. 944-790-001, fax 944-790-516). As you cross the bridge from the station, it's just behind the big theater of the same name.

$$ Iturrienea Ostatua, on a quiet pedestrian street in the Old Town, has 21 rooms packed with brick, stone, and antiques (Sb-€50, Db-€60–66, Tb-€80, prices include taxes, breakfast-€4, Santa María Kalea 14, tel. 944-161-500, fax 944-158-929). From the station, cross the bridge and go past the big theater. Where the river bends, turn left, up quaint Santa María Kalea.

$ Pensión Ladero is a fine budget option in the Old Town. They don't accept reservations, but you can call when you arrive to check availability (S-€32, D-€34, T-€40–45, Q-€45–50, up 4 flights of stairs; 7 rooms share 1 bathroom up a very tight spiral staircase, but 14 rooms use the other 3 bathrooms on the main floor; cash only, Lotería 1, tel. 944-150-932). You'll find the *pensión* just before the big church at the center of the Old Town. This is a better value than the more prominent Pensión Roquefer across the street.

TRANSPORTATION CONNECTIONS

From Bilbao by Bus to: San Sebastián (2/hr, 6:00–22:30, 70 min, departs Bilbao's Termibus station, arrives in San Sebastián at Plaza Pío XII), **Santander** (hourly, 90 min, transfer there to bus to **Santillana del Mar** or **Comillas**—see Cantabria chapter).

Lekeitio

A small fishing port with an idyllic harbor and a fine beach, Lekeitio is an hour by bus from Bilbao and an easy stop for drivers. It's protected from the Bay of Biscay by a sand spit that leads to the lush and rugged little San Nicolás Island. Hake boats fly their Basque flags and proud Basque locals black out the Spanish translations on street signs.

Lekeitio is a teeming resort during July and August (when its population of 7,000 triples as big-city Basque folks move in to their vacation condos), and it's a sleepy backwater the rest of the year. It's isolated from the modern rat race by its location down a long, windy little road.

While sights are humble here, the 15th-century St. Mary's Parish Church is a good example of Basque Gothic with an impressive altarpiece. The town's back lanes are reminiscent of old days when fishing was the only industry. Fisherwomen sell their husbands' catches each morning from about 10:30 at the tiny Plaza Arranegi market (a block off the harbor). The golden crescent beach is as inviting as the sandbar, which—at low tide—challenges you to join the seagulls out on San Nicolás Island.

The **TI** faces the fish market next to the harbor (mid-June–mid-Sept daily 10:00–14:00 & 16:00–20:00; off-season Tue–Sat 10:30–13:30 & 16:00–19:00, Sun 10:00–14:00, closed Mon; tel. 946-844-017). While buses connect Lekeitio with Bilbao hourly (and San Sebastián 4/day), this stop is most logical for those with a car.

The TI recommends Lekeitio as a base for car explorations of the area (coastal and medieval hill villages). The nearby town of **Guernica** (Gernika in Euskara, nine miles toward Bilbao) is near and dear to Basques and pacifists alike for good reason. This is the site of the Gernikako Arbola (oak tree of Gernika), which marked the ancient assembly point where the Lords of Bizkaia (Basque leaders) met through the ages to assert their people's freedom. Long the symbolic heart of Basque separatism, this was a natural target for Franco in the Spanish Civil War. His buddy Hitler agreed to use Guernica as a kind of target practice in 1937. This historic "first air raid"—a prelude to the horrific aerial bombings of World War II—was made famous by Picasso's epic work, *Guernica* (now in Madrid).

Sleeping: **$$ Emperatriz Zita Hotel** is the obvious best bet for your beach-town break. It's named for Empress Zita (who lived here in exile after her Hapsburg family lost World War I and was booted from Vienna). While Zita's mansion burned down, this 1930s rebuild still has a belle époque aristocratic charm, solid classy furniture in 42 spacious rooms, real hardwood floors, and an elegant spa in the basement. Located on the beach a few steps from the harbor, with handy parking and a view restaurant, it's a fine value (Sb-€42–51, Db-€56–69, Db suite-€86–99, views—ask for *vistas del mar*—are worth the extra euros, high prices are for July–Aug, extra bed-€19, breakfast-€7, elevator, Santa Elena Etorbidea, tel. 946-842-655, fax 946-243-500, www.aisiahoteles.com, ezita @aisiahoteles.com). Room prices include a thermal seawater pool and Jacuzzi; the full-service spa is available at reasonable prices.

Eating: Although it's sleepy in the off-season, the harbor promenade is made-to-order in summer for a slow meal or a tapas crawl. For fancy seafood, the local favorite is Restaurante Zapirain (€20 plates, Igualdegi 3, tel. 946-840-255). *Txangurro* (baked, stuffed crabs) is a specialty worth asking for.

CANTABRIA

If you're connecting the Basque Country and Galicia (Santiago de Compostela), you'll go through the provinces of Cantabria and Asturias. Both are interesting, but Cantabria (kahn-TAH-bree-ah) has a few villages and sights that are especially worth a visit. The quaint town of **Santillana del Mar** makes a fine home base for visiting the prehistoric **Altamira Caves** replica. **Comillas** is a pleasant beach town.

The dramatic peaks of the **Picos de Europa** and their rolling foothills define this region, giving it a more rugged feel than the "Northern Riviera" ambience of the Basque region. A drive through the Cantabrian countryside is rewarded with glimpses of endless charming stone homes. Though it's largely undiscovered by Americans, Cantabria is heavily touristed by Europeans in July and August, when it can get very crowded.

Planning Your Time

Cantabria doesn't rank high on the list of sightseeing priorities in Spain. Don't go out of your way to get here. However, if you're passing through on the way between the Basque region and Santiago de Compostela, there are some charming diversions along the way. A night or two in this region breaks up the long drive from Bilbao to Santiago (figure over six hours straight through).

Assuming you're coming from San Sebastián, this is a good plan:

Day 1: Leave San Sebastián early for the Guggenheim in Bilbao (trip takes about an hour by expressway, longer along the coast). After seeing the museum, continue on to explore (and sleep in) Santillana del Mar or Comillas.

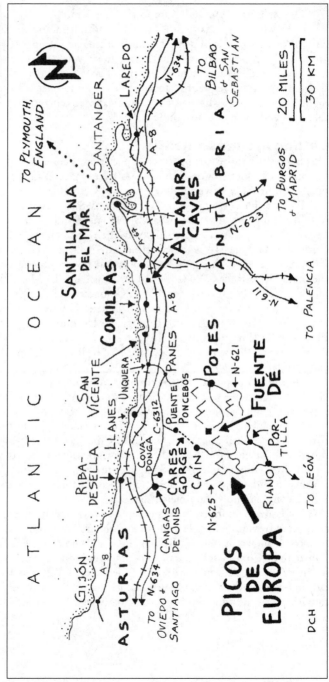

Day 2: Troglodytes will want to visit the Altamira Caves replica right when it opens (9:30). Hikers and high-mountain fans will make a beeline for Fuente Dé in the Picos de Europa. If you get an early start on either of these attractions, you can still make it to Santiago de Compostela by the end of a very long day (figure six hours from this region to Santiago). It's saner to sleep a second night in this area, in which case it's conceivably possible to do both the caves and the mountains on Day 2.

Getting Around Cantabria

This region is best by car; public transportation is complicated, so the payoffs are not so great. Unless you have a special interest in prehistoric art, non-drivers will want to skip Cantabria.

By Car: Drivers enjoy Cantabria. The A-8 expressway runs roughly along the coast from San Sebastián to Gijón, where it becomes an express two-lane highway the rest of the way to A Coruña in Galicia. To reach Santillana del Mar and Comillas, follow signs to A-67 (a jog off the expressway towards Santander), then take the exit for CA-131 (signed for Santillana del Mar). This highway takes you through Santillana, Comillas, and San Vicente de la Barquera. After San Vicente, in Unquera, CA-131 intersects with N-621, which leads south through La Hermida Gorge into the Picos de Europa (follow signs for Potes). If you want to go directly to the Picos, there's an exit for N-621 directly off the A-8 expressway.

By Bus: Without a car, you'll rely on the bus from the port city of Santander—Cantabria's capital and transportation hub. Buses run from Santander to Santillana del Mar, Comillas, and San Vicente de la Barquera (5–7/day each way, about 35 min from Santander to Santillana, then 15 min to Comillas, then 15 more min to San Vicente, tel. 942-720-822, www.santandereabus.com).

A different bus goes from Santander to Potes in the Picos de Europa (2–3/day, 2.25 hours, tel. 942-880-611). There's also a bus from León, but only in summer (1/day, 3 hours).

By Train: Santander, the region's public transportation hub, is connected by train with **Madrid** (4/day, 6 hours, overnight option 9 hours, Chamartín station), **Bilbao** (3/day, 2.75 hours on FEVE), **Santiago de Compostela** (3/day, 13 hours, overnight option, transfer in Palencia). A scenic train line called the FEVE runs from Bilbao to Santander and to Ovideo, but it's not particularly helpful for visiting the destinations in this chapter (www.feve.es).

Santillana del Mar

Every guidebook imparts the same two tidbits about Santillana del Mar: One is that it's known as the "town of three lies," as it's neither holy *(santi)*, nor flat *(llana)*, nor on the ocean *(del Mar)*. The other is that the existentialist philosopher Jean-Paul Sartre once called it the "prettiest village in Spain."

The town is worth the fuss. Santillana is a proud little stone village, with charming time-warp qualities that have (barely) survived the stampede of multinational tour groups here to visit the nearby Altamira Caves. Despite it all, the town is what Spaniards would call *preciosa*.

Santillana is three cobbled streets and a collection of squares, climbing up over mild hills from where the village meets the main road. While Santillana has several sights that cater to the tourist throngs (including a much-promoted zoo), the only sight that makes a visit worthwhile—aside from the town itself—are the cave paintings of Altamira in the nearby countryside (see "Altamira Caves," below).

Tourist Information: The modern TI is right at the entrance to the town (daily July–mid-Sept 9:00–21:00, off-season 9:30–13:30 & 16:00–19:00, Jesús Otero 20, tel. 942-818-251). Only residents (and guests of hotels that offer parking) are allowed to drive in the center—leave your car in the big lot by the TI (pay in-season, free off-season).

SLEEPING

Santillana makes a good home base for visiting the region and the caves. My listings are right in town; you'll find the first three places on Santillana's main square, Plaza Ramón Pelayo. The fourth is farther up, just around the corner (to the right) from the big Collegiate Church.

$$$ Paradores: Two swanky, arrogant *paradores* hold court on the main square—**Parador de Santillana** (Sb-€107–116, Db-€134–144, breakfast-€12, Plaza Ramón Pelayo 11, tel. 942-818-000, fax 942-818-391, santillana@parador.es) and **Parador de Santillana Gil Blas** (Sb-€120–128, Db-€150–160, breakfast-€13, same address, tel. 942-028-028, fax 942-818-391, santillanagb@parador.es).

Sleep Code

(€1 = about $1.20, country code: 34)
S = Single, **D** = Double/Twin, **T** = Triple, **Q** = Quad, **b** = bathroom, **s** = shower only. Unless otherwise noted, English is spoken and credit cards are accepted. Prices include tax and vary with season (highest July–Aug and Holy Week). I've listed shoulder- and peak-season rates.

To help you sort easily through these listings, I've divided the rooms into three categories based on the price for a standard double room with bath:

$$$ **Higher Priced**—Most rooms €90 or more.
$$ **Moderately Priced**—Most rooms between €60–90.
$ **Lower Priced**—Most rooms €60 or less.

$$ Hotel Altamira offers 32 well-priced rooms in an atmospheric 16th-century palace on the main square (Sb-€47–58, standard Db-€66–97, big Db with sitting room a great value at €71–109, extra bed-€17–25, breakfast-€8, Calle Cantón 1, tel. 942-818-025, fax 942-840-136, www.hotelaltamira.com, info@hotelaltamira.com).

$ Hospedaje Octavio is a fine budget option with 11 comfortable, wood-beamed rooms (Db-€30–36, €3 less without bathroom, Plaza Las Arenas 4, tel. & fax 942-818-199, Octavio and Milagros don't speak English but their sons do).

Altamira Caves

Not far from Santillana del Mar is a replica of a cave containing some of the best examples of prehistoric art anywhere. In 1879, the daughter of a local archaeologist discovered several 14,000-year-old paintings in a limestone cave. By the 1960s and 1970s, it became a tremendously popular tourist destination. All of the visitors got to be too much for the delicate paintings, and the cave was closed in 1979. But now a replica cave and museum have opened near the original site, allowing visitors to once again experience these pieces of prehistoric artwork, in something approximating their original setting.

Cost, Hours, Location: €2.40, June–Sept Tue–Sat 9:30–19:30, Sun 9:30–15:00, closed Mon; Oct–May Tue–Sat 9:30–17:00, Sun 9:30–15:00, closed Mon; last tour leaves 30 min before closing (tel. 942-818-815, http://museodealtamira.mcu.es). The caves are on a ridge in the countryside a little over a mile southwest of

Santillana del Mar. There's no public transportation to the site. To get from Santillana del Mar to the caves, it's either a 30-minute walk or a taxi ride (mobile 608-483-441). Bolder travelers hitch a ride with a friendly tour bus.

Visiting the Caves: While you can't actually visit the original caves, prehistoric-art fans will still find Altamira worth the trip. Your visit has two parts: First, there's a fine museum with good English descriptions, featuring models and reproductions of the cave dwellers who made these drawings (and their clothes, tools, and remains). Videos and illuminated pictures help bring these people to life. The second part is a 30-minute guided tour of the highly detailed replica cave.

While it's theoretically possible to take an English tour, English speakers get little respect here. Assume you'll tour with a Spanish-speaking guide (and follow along with the self-guided tour below, which is better than the measly posted English info). English tours are scheduled twice a day in summer (June–Sept generally around 11:00 and 16:25, confirm time in advance by calling 942-818-102). From October through May, English tours are unlikely.

Note that if all you're really interested in is the art itself, other replicas are on display in the National Archaeological Museum in Madrid (just the paintings, not the cave experience); see page 240. Remember—what you'll see at Altamira are replicas, too.

Reservations: Only 240 people are allowed to enter the replica caves each hour (20 people/tour, tours leave every 5 min—or when enough people gather, never more than a 30-min wait). This means that in the busy summer season, spaces fill up fast. In July and August, they recommend getting to the museum when it opens (9:30) to claim your tour appointment.

Better yet, make an advance reservation (no extra charge) through the bank Santander Centro Hispano—drop by a branch, or even easier, call them (tel. 942-818-102, wait through recording and ask for English speaker). You can also make a reservation (for Tue–Sat) on the museum Web site using a credit card; look for the link to the bank. Request a specific date and time (one-hour window) for your tour. In summer, ask to join the scheduled English tour when you reserve (but no guarantees). At the caves, pass any wait time by exploring the museum.

SELF-GUIDED TOUR

You'll begin the tour by watching a four-minute film about the various inhabitants of the cave, the discovery of the paintings in 1879, and the era of over-visitation. Then the guide leads you into the first part of the cave, where (unless you manage to join an English tour) you're on your own for information. The English descriptions that the guide eagerly points out are marginally helpful. Even better, here's what your guide is talking about:

1. In the Cave

Remember that this isn't the actual cave. It's a painstaking replica (called *Neocueva*, or "Neo-cave"), achieved with special computers, so that the cave art can still be enjoyed without endangering the actual paintings. The Neo-cave also simulates the original cave's temperature, sounds, and humidity.

About 14,000 years ago, hunters, gatherers, and fishermen lived in these caves. They huddled around a fire, protected from the elements. They liked the location because of its proximity to the ocean and a river.

2. Excavation Site

This area displays tools used by modern scientists to dig up relics from various periods. We're talking about the Upper Paleolithic era—the time of Cro-Magnon cave people, with big hands and high foreheads. The Upper Paleolithic is divided into three periods, and this cave was inhabited, on two separate occasions, during two of those periods: the Solutrean (about 18,500 years ago) and the Magdalenian (14,000 years ago). You'll see that there are three layers to the excavation: On the bottom are artifacts from Solutrean cavemen (hunting tools and chips of flint); above that is mostly clay, with the remains of a cave bear you'll see in a few minutes; and the top layer holds hearths and tools from the Magdalenian period.

As you continue on to the next stop, you'll pass the bones of a cave bear that once lived in Altamira. Nearby, look for his paw prints.

3. Artists' Workshop

See the tools used by the prehistoric artists, as well as a video showing how the paintings were created. The most dramatic paintings—all the red buffaloes—were made with reddish ochre dissolved in water, outlined in black charcoal. Marrow-burning stone lamps provided light. Many of the images were engraved into the surface of the cave (using flint) before being painted. The reproductions in this Neo-cave were done using the same techniques.

4. Art!

Finally we reach the paintings themselves. While most tourists gasp, some hum the *Flintstones* theme.

This part of the cave has various names, including the "Great

Hall," the "Polychrome Room," or even "the Sistine Chapel of Prehistoric Art." The ledge with the lights shows the floor level of the original cave. This didn't give the cavemen much room to paint, making their creations even more remarkable. Among the fauna in this room are 16 bison, a couple of running boars, some horses, and a giant deer—plus a few handprints and several mysterious symbols.

Unfortunately, the posted English information ends here. These are some of the things to look for (as your guide is pointing them out to the ooh-ing and ahh-ing Spaniards in your group):

Bumps and Cracks: Notice that the artists incorporated the ceiling's many topographical features into their creations (see the bison with the large, swollen back, or the one with the big head).

Overlap: Some paintings actually overlap onto each other. These were painted during two different eras. (The most impressive batch—including all those bison—is thought to be by the same artist.)

Detail: While a few paintings are incomplete, others are finished. Check out the bison with the highly detailed hooves and beard.

The "Old Horse": The horse with its back against the wall is probably among the oldest in the cave.

The "Great Deer": The biggest painting of all (over seven feet across) is the deer with the little black bison under his chin. Notice it's not quite in proportion; due to the tight quarters, the artist couldn't take a step back to survey his work.

Symbols: The strange hieroglyphic-like symbols scattered around the cave, called tectiforms, are difficult to interpret. Scientists have found very similar symbols in caves that were far apart, and wondered if they were some sort of primitive written language (for example, an outline of a horse with a particular symbol might be how to set traps for hunting).

Behavior: The artists captured not only the form, but also the behavior of the animals they depicted. Notice the lowing bison; the curled-up bison; the bison turning its head; and the running boars (with the extra legs).

What's amazing about these paintings is to think they were made by Cro-Magnon cave people. And yet, the artists had an amazing grasp on delicate composition, depicting these animals with such true-to-life simplicity. Some of them are mere outlines, a couple of curvy lines—masterful abstraction that could make Picasso jealous.

So why did they make these paintings? Nobody knows for sure. General agreement is that it's not simply for decoration, and that it must have served some religious or shamanistic purpose.

5. Final Cave

The most impressive paintings were discovered in a single room (whose replica you just visited). However, beyond that room, the cave extended another several hundred feet, though that area was not reproduced. As you leave this replica cave, you'll see a few more replicas—mostly carvings—that came from other parts of the original cave. Most of them are those mysterious symbols, but at the very end you'll also see three masks carved into the rock.

And with that, your cave visit is over. Yabba dabba doo!

Comillas

Just 15 minutes beyond Santillana del Mar, perched on a hill overlooking the Atlantic, you'll find quirky Comillas. Comillas presides over a sandy beach, but feels more like a hill town, with twisty lanes clambering up away from the sea. Comillas is not as undeniably charming as Santillana—it would do well to go traffic-free, as its neighbor has. But it makes for a fine home base if you prefer beach access and a more lived-in feel to touristy quaintness.

Most notably, Comillas also enjoys a surprising abundance of striking Modernista architecture. Three buildings line up along a ridge at the west end of town (just beyond the town center and parking lot, over the big park). Antoni Gaudí, Barcelona's favorite son, designed a villa here called El Capricho—now a restaurant (see below). Next door is the pointy spire of a 17th-century church, and at the end of the row is the Palace of Sobrellano, by Gaudí's mentor Joan Martorell, which hints at early Barcelona-style Modernisme. Peering back at these buildings from a parallel ridge is the huge Pontifical University building, decorated by yet another early-20th-century Catalan architect, Lluís Domènech i Muntaner. These Modernista masterpieces are compliments of Don Antonio López y López, who left Spain to find fortune in America. He returned to Barcelona (where he acquired a taste for Gaudí and company) and eventually became the Marquis of Comillas.

While the beachside road below is lined with tacky tourist hotels, the town center, up on the hill, is much more pleasant—with an odd jumble of squares surrounding the big Parochial Church.

Tourist Information: The westernmost square, Plaza Joaquín de Piélagos, is where you'll find the TI (July–Aug daily 9:00–21:00;

Sept–June Mon–Sat 10:30–13:30 & 16:30–19:30, Sun 10:30–13:30; Calle Aldea 6, tel. 942-720-768).

SLEEPING

($1 = about €1.20, country code: 34)
Both of these listings are in the town center, south of the big Parochial Church, near the long, skinny, restaurant-lined Plaza de Primo de Rivera (also known as "El Corro"). The first hotel is the big red building a block off the south end of the square; the other is a few blocks above the square, on the uphill street with the blue-trimmed railing.

$$$ Hotel Marina de Campíos offers 20 modern, colorful rooms, each one named for a different opera (standard Sb-€64–102, "junior" Db-€86–120, "senior" Db-€128–150, breakfast-€7, elevator, Calle General Piélagos 14, tel. 942-722-754, fax 942-722-749, www.marinadecampios.com, reservas@marinadecampios.com).

$ Pasaje San Jorge, with 11 basic but comfortable rooms in a hundred-year-old house, hovers just over the town center (Db-€45–54, includes breakfast, Calle Carlos Díaz de la Campa 16, tel. & fax 942-720-915, www.pasajesanjorge.com, pasajesanjorge @pasajesanjorge.com).

EATING

El Capricho is a surprising piece of Antoni Gaudí architecture hiding on a ridge above Comillas' center. The sunflower-dappled exterior alludes to Gaudí's plan for the building: His "sunflower design" attempted to maximize exposure to sunshine by arranging rooms so that they would get sun during the part of the day that they were most used. Today, the building is an exclusive-feeling restaurant serving traditional Spanish cuisine. Look around the back for the sculpture of the architect admiring his work. Don't even try to get inside if you're not eating here. Reservations are smart, especially in season (€15–20 entrees, €25 fixed-price meal, Mon–Sat 13:00–15:30 & 21:00–23:00, Sun 13:00–15:30 only, tel. 942-720-365). There are two roads to this hard-to-find restaurant; both are at the west end of town, and both are sometimes closed—ask locally for directions.

Near Comillas: San Vicente de la Barquera

As you continue west from Comillas, the road becomes bumpy and follows the coast, soon crossing a wide bay over a long, dramatic bridge to San Vicente de la Barquera. This salty seaside resort overlooks a boat-filled harbor, with glimpses of the dramatic Picos de Europa in the distance.

Picos de Europa

The Picos de Europa—one of Spain's most popular national parks—are a relatively small stretch of cut-glass mountain peaks (the steepest in Spain, some taller than 8,500 feet) just 15 miles inland from the ocean. These dramatic mountains are home to goats, brown bears, eagles, vultures, wallcreepers (rare birds), and happy hikers. Outdoorsy types could spend days exploring this dramatic patch of Spain, which is packed with visitors in the summer. For our purposes, we'll focus on the two most important excursions: taking the Fuente Dé funicular up to a mountaintop, and hiking the yawning chasm of the Cares Gorge.

ORIENTATION

The Picos de Europa are a patch of mountains covering an area of about 25 miles by 25 miles. They're located where three of Spain's regions converge: Cantabria, Asturias, and León. (Frustratingly, each region's tourist office pretends that the parts of the park in the other regions don't exist—so it's very hard to get information, say, about Asturias' Cares Gorge in Potes, Cantabria.) In addition to three regions, the park comprises three different limestone massifs, or large masses of rock, separated by rivers.

As you venture into the Picos de Europa, pick up a good map; the green 1:80,000-scale map that you'll see is handy,

featuring roads, trails, and topographical features. Serious hikers will want a guidebook (I like the Sunflower guide, published by a British company—www.sunflowerbooks.co.uk). These resources, along with a wide variety of other maps and books, are available locally.

I'll focus on the Cantabrian part of the Picos, which contains the region's most accessible and enjoyable bits: the scenic drive through La Hermida

Gorge; the charming mountain town of Potes; and the sky-high views from the top of the Fuente Dé cable car. This part of the Picos is doable as a long day trip from Santillana del Mar or Comillas (but is easier if you stay in Potes). The next best activity (in León and Asturias, not Cantabria) is the Cares Gorge hike—deeper in the park and requiring another full day.

Getting Around the Picos de Europa

The Picos de Europa are best with a car. If you don't have wheels, skip it, because bus connections are sparse, time-consuming, and frustrating (see "Getting Around Cantabria," page 148).

The A-8 expressway squeezes between the Picos and the north coast of Spain; roads branch into and around the Picos, but beware: Many of them traverse high-mountain passes—often on bad roads—and can take longer to drive through than you expect. *Puerto* means "pass" (slow going) and *desfiladero* means "gorge" (quicker but often still twisty).

Assuming you're most interested in Potes and Fuente Dé, you'll focus on the east part of the park, approaching from the A-8 expressway (or from Santillana del Mar and Comillas). You'll go through Unquera and catch the N-621 into the park (follow signs for Potes). Wind your way through La Hermida Gorge (Desfiladero de la Hermida) en route to Potes.

The Cares Gorge can be approached from either the south (the village of Caín, deep in the mountains beyond Potes) or the north (Puente Poncebos, with easier access).

If you're really serious about tackling the region, and want to do both Fuente Dé and the Cares Gorge, the most sensible plan is this: On Day 1, drive from Comillas/Santillana del Mar to Potes and do the Fuente Dé cable car and hike (sleep in Potes); on Day 2, day-trip to the Cares Gorge hike via Caín (sleep in Potes); and on Day 3, move on to your next destination.

SIGHTS

I've arranged these sights as you'll come to them if you approach from the northeast (that is, from the expressway, Santillana del Mar, or Comillas).

Potes—This quaint mountain village, at the intersection of four valleys, is the hub of Cantabria's Picos de Europa tourist facilities. It's got an impressive old convent and a picturesque stone bridge spanning the Río Deva. It's a good place to buy maps and books. Check in at the **TI** with any travel questions (July–Sept daily 10:00–14:00 & 16:00–20:00; less off-season—often closed Sun–Mon afternoons and all day Tue; Independencia 12, tel. 942-730-787).

Sleeping in Potes: **$ Casa Cayo** has 17 cozy rooms and a fine restaurant that overlooks the river (Sb-€30, Db-€50, Tb-€65, breakfast not included, closed Christmas–Feb, Calle Cántabra 6, tel. 942-730-150, fax 942-730-119, www.casacayo.com, informacion @casacayo.com).

▲▲**Fuente Dé Cable Car (Teleférico Fuente Dé)**—Perhaps the single most thrilling activity in Picos de Europa is to take the cable car at Fuente Dé. The longest, single-span cable car in Europe zips you up 2,600 feet in just four ear-popping minutes. Once at the top (altitude 6,000 feet), you're rewarded with a breathtaking panorama of the Picos de Europa. The huge, pointy, Matterhorn-like peak on your right is Peña Remoña (7,350 feet). The cable-car  station on top has WCs, a cafeteria (commanding views, miserable food), and a gift shop (limited hiking guides—equip yourself before you ascend).

Once you're up there, those with enough time and strong knees should consider hiking back down. From the cable-car station at the top, follow the yellow-and-white signs to Espinama, always bearing to the right. You'll hike gradually uphill (gain about 300 feet), then down (3,500 feet) the back side of the mountain, with totally different views than the cable-car ride up: green, rolling hills instead of sharp, white peaks. Once in Espinama, you'll continue down along the main road back to the parking lot at the base of the cable car (signs to Fuente Dé). Figure about four hours total (nine miles) from the top back to the bottom. Note that the trails are covered by snow into April, and sometimes even May; ask at the ranger station near Potes about conditions before you hike (see "Information," below).

Cost, Hours, Location: €12.50 round-trip, €7 one-way (if you're hiking down), every 30 minutes (or with demand), daily in summer 9:00–20:00, in winter 10:00–18:00, closed Jan. When it's busy, there are constant departures. Note that this is a very popular destination in summer, and you may have to wait in long lines both to ascend and to descend (up to 2.5 hours in early Aug, 1 hour in late July; quieter in June, early July, and Sept—if you're concerned, call ahead to find out how long the wait is before you make the 14-mile drive from Potes). The road dead-ends at Fuente Dé, so you'll have to backtrack to return to Potes. If you're relying on public transportation, you can take the bus from Potes to Fuente Dé (2/day)—but it runs only in summer.

Information: Cable car tel. 942-736-610. The Picos de Europa National Park runs a helpful information kiosk in the parking lot during peak season (July–Aug), with handouts and advice on hikes (including the one described above). Even better, stop at the bigger National Park office on the way to Fuente Dé from Potes; about a mile after you leave Potes, look on the right for the green *Picos de Europa* signs (daily in summer 9:00–14:00 & 17:00–18:30, in winter 9:00–14:00 & 16:00–18:30, tel. 942-730-555).

▲**Cares Gorge (Garganta del Cares)**—This impressive gorge hike—surrounded on both sides by sheer cliff walls, with a long-distance drop running parallel to (and sometimes under) the trail—is ideal for hardy hikers. The trail was built in the 1940s to maintain the hydroelectric canal that runs through the mountains, but today it has become an extremely popular summer-hiking destination. The trail follows the Río Cares seven miles between the towns of Caín (in the south) and Camarmeña (near Puente Poncebos, in the north). Along the way, you'll cross harrowing bridges and take trails burrowed into the rock face. Because it's deeper in the mountains and requires a good six hours (13 miles round-trip, with some ups and downs), it's best left to those who are really up for a hike and not simply passing through the Picos. Visitors who just want a glimpse will hike only partway in before heading back.

Getting There: To reach Caín from Potes, you'll drive on rough, twisty roads (N-621) over the stunning Puerto de San Gloria pass (5,250 feet, watched over by a sweet bronze deer), into a green, moss-covered gorge. Just past the village of Portilla de la Reina, turn right (following signs for Santa Marina de Valdeón) to reach Caín. Note that this is a very long day trip from Potes, and almost brutal if home-basing in Comillas or Santillana del Mar.

The approach to the gorge from the north (Puente Poncebos) is easier, but won't take you near Potes and Fuente Dé. You can reach Puente Poncebos via the AS-114 to Las Arenas, then follow the Cares River on the AS-264 to Puente Poncebos.

SANTIAGO DE COMPOSTELA

The best destination in the northwestern province of Galicia, Santiago de Compostela might well be the most magical city in Spain. This place has long had a powerful and mysterious draw on travelers—as more than a thousand years' worth of pilgrims have trod the desolate trail across the north of Spain to just peer up at the facade of its glorious cathedral.

But there's more to this city than pilgrims and the remains of St. James. Contrary to what you've heard, the rain in Spain does *not* fall mainly on the plain—it falls in Galicia. This "Atlantic Northwest" of Spain is like the Pacific Northwest of the United States: hilly, lush terrain that enjoys far more precipitation than the interior, plus dramatic coastal scenery, delicious seafood, fine local wines, and an easygoing ambience. The Spanish interior might be arid, but the northwest requires rain gear. Even the tourists here have a grungy vibe: Packs of happy hippie pilgrims seek to find themselves while hiking the ancient Camino de Santiago from France. Santiago has a generally festive atmosphere, as travelers from every corner of the globe celebrate the end of a long journey.

There's something vaguely Irish about Galicia—and it's not just the mossy stonework and green, rolling hills. The region actually shares a strain of Celtic heritage with their cousins across the Cantabrian Sea. People here are friendly, and if you listen hard enough, you might just hear the sound of bagpipes.

Planning Your Time

Santiago's biggest downside is its location: a very long car, train, or bus trip from any other notable stop in Spain. But if you decide to visit, you—like a millennium's worth of pilgrims before you—will

Galego

Like Catalunya and the Basque Country, Galicia has its own distinctive language. Galego (called *gallego* in Spanish, and sometimes called "Galician" in English) is a mix between Spanish and Portuguese. Historically, Galego was closer to Portuguese. But Queen Isabel imported Spanish to the region in the 15th century, and ever since, the language has gradually come to sound more and more like Spanish. In an attempt at national unity, Franco banned Galego in the mid-20th century (along with Catalan and the Basque language, Euskara). During these trying times, Galicians spoke Spanish in public—and Galego at home. Since the end of the Franco era, Galego is a proud part of this region's cultural heritage. Street signs and sight names are posted in Galego, and I've followed suit in this chapter.

If you don't speak Spanish, you'll hardly notice a difference. Most apparent is the change in articles: *el* and *la* become *o* and *a*—so the big Galician city La Coruña is known as A Coruña around here. You'll also see a lot more *x*'s, which are pronounced "sh" (such as "Xacobeo," shah-koh-BAY-oh, the local word for St. James' pilgrimage route). The Spanish greeting *buenos días* becomes *bos días* in Galego. The familiar *plaza* becomes *praza*. And if you want to impress a local, say *graciñas* (grah-THEEN-yahs)—a super-polite thank you.

find it's worth the trek. You can get a good feel for Santiago in a day, but a second day relaxing on the squares makes the long trip here more worthwhile.

The city has one real sight: the cathedral, with its museum and the surrounding squares. The rest of your visit is for munching seafood, pilgrim-watching, and killing time in small museums. The highlight of a visit just may be hanging out on the cathedral square at about 10:00 to welcome pilgrims completing their long journey.

ORIENTATION

Santiago is built on hilly terrain, with lots of ups and downs. The tourist's Santiago is small: You can walk across the historic center, or Zona Monumental, in about 15 minutes. There you'll find the city's centerpiece—the awe-inspiring cathedral—as well as several other churches, a maze of pretty squares, a smattering of small museums, a bustling restaurant scene, and all of my recommended hotels.

The historic center is circled by a busy street that marks the former location of the town wall (easy to see on a map). Outside of that is the commercial city center, which is a modern, urban district called Céntrico. A 10-minute walk through Céntrico takes you to the train station.

Tourist Information

There are two different tourist information facilities within a few steps of each other in the center of town (near the cathedral, on Rúa do Vilar). Both are worth a visit.

For information specific to Santiago, stop by the **city TI** (daily June–Sept 9:00–21:00, Oct–May 9:00–14:00 & 16:00–19:00, Rúa do Vilar 63, tel. 981-555-129, www.santiagoturismo.com). The TI also runs walking tours and rents MP3 player audioguides (see "Tours," page 165).

Santiago's several exhibition halls host temporary exhibits. Ask the TI what's going on when you're in town, and grab a free monthly copy of *Culturall* and the free annual *AgendaCultural07* publication.

The **Pilgrim's Information Center,** also called the Office for Pilgrims (Oficina do Peregrino), has tons of tips and maps for those planning to do the Camino de Santiago by foot, bike, or horse (Mon–Fri 10:00–20:00, closed Sat–Sun, Rúa do Vilar 30–32—marked *Xacobeo,* tel. 902-332-010, www.xacobeo.es).

Arrival in Santiago de Compostela

By Train: Santiago's train station is on the southern edge of the modern Céntrico district. You'll find ATMs, a cafeteria, a helpful train information office, and luggage storage (€3/small locker, €4.50/large locker). Computer screens show upcoming departures. To reach the center of town, leave the station and walk up the grand granite staircase, jog right, cross the busy Avenida de Lugo, and walk uphill for 10 minutes on the Rúa do Hórreo to Praza de Galicia. A taxi to your hotel will cost about €5.

By Bus: The bus station is about a 15-minute walk northeast of the cathedral. Hop on local bus #5 (€0.85) and take it to the Praza de Galicia, a few steps from the historical center.

Helpful Hints

Closed Days: Many museums are closed on Mondays. The colorful produce market is closed on Sunday, slow on Monday, and busy on Thursday and Saturday mornings.

Church Hours: Most churches in Santiago are open 9:00–21:00

The Symbols of Santiago

This city and the pilgrim route leading to it are rife with symbolism. Here are a few of the key items you'll see adorning Santiago's facades and souvenir-shop windows.

- **The Scallop Shell (*Vieira*):** Since scallops are so abundant on the Galician coast, their shells are associated with Santiago throughout Europe. While medieval pilgrims only carried shells with them on the return home—to prove they'd been here, and to scoop water from wells— today's pilgrims also carry them on the way *to* Santiago. The yellow sideways shell that looks like a starburst is used to mark the route for bikers.

- **The Gourd:** Gourds were used by pilgrims to drink water and wine.

- **The Tomb and Star:** St. James' tomb (usually depicted as a simple coffin or box), and the stars that led to its discovery, appear throughout the city, either together or separately.

- **The Yellow Arrow:** These arrows direct pilgrims (on foot) at every intersection from here to France.

- **The Red Cross:** This long, skinny cross with curly ends represents the Knights of Santiago, once affiliated with the Knights of Malta—Holy Land Crusaders who guarded pilgrims along the Camino de Santiago.

- **Shield with Five Stars:** This symbolizes Alonso de Fonseca, a wealthy 15th-century nobleman who founded Santiago's university (and many buildings that still bear his seal).

- **"Nunca Máis":** Galego for "never again," this message of protest captures the anger of local residents towards the tragic oil tanker accident in November of 2002 that spilled black crude all along the Galician coast—their main source of both tourist and fishing income. Locals blame governmental bungling for the accident, and have put strong pressure on Spain to improve safety measures to ensure it will never happen again. These words usually appear on a black field with a light-blue diagonal sash—a somber, oil-stained variation on the Galician flag, which is normally white and blue.

without a siesta. There are special Masses for pilgrims daily at noon in the cathedral. The big Masses on Sunday are at 10:00 and noon.

Holy Year: On years that the Feast of St. James (July 25) falls on a Sunday, it's a special Compostela Holy Year (Ano Xacobeo in Galego)—with 25 percent more pilgrims than usual coming to Santiago, and more special services in the cathedral. But cooleth thy jets: The next one isn't until 2010.

Music, Festivals, and Celebrations: You'll likely hear **bagpipes** *(gaitas)* being played in the streets of Santiago. Nobody knows for certain how this unlikely instrument caught on in Galicia, but the tradition has supposedly been passed down since the Celts lived here. Some singers use bagpipes, too, including Milladoiro (a group popular with Galicians in their 40s and 50s) and Carlos Nuñez (trendy with younger people today). Caped university students, called *tunas*, can be seen singing traditional songs around town every night during the summer (Thu–Sat in the winter).

July is the big party time in Santiago. During that time, the city hosts a world music festival and impromptu concerts all over town, and the royal family attends Mass in Santiago. The second-most important musical event in town—several days of free concerts—occurs around **Ascension** (May 17 in 2007).

Galician Folk-Music Concerts: While the summertime is lively with folk-music concerts (ask for details at the TI), the rest of the year is not. One good bet is to drop by a practice session of the troupe called Cantigas e Agarimos (meets Wed and Fri at 21:30 for an hour, maybe at Rúa da Algalia de Arriba 11 or possibly playing at a nearby location—check their schedule at www.cantigaseagarimos.com). Since 1921, this group has shared the traditional Galician culture with visitors in performances throughout the year. Tall Oscar Cobos is a group leader who lived in New York City for five years. Now he's clearly found his niche as a dancer and dance teacher here in what he calls "the kingdom of far, far away."

Internet Access: You'll see signs around the historic center. The handiest and best-equipped is **Cyber Nova 50** (Mon–Sat 9:00–24:00, Sun from 10:00; copying, faxing, phones, and other computer services; Rúa Nova 50, tel. 981-575-188). Nearby is **Mundonet** (daily 9:00–24:00, further up and a few steps off Rúa Nova at Rúa de Xelmírez 19). There are literally dozens of cafés all over town (look for window signs) that offer free Wi-Fi access with a purchase.

Laundry: You'll find a self-service *lavandería* a 20-minute walk from the historic center (Mon–Fri 10:00–14:00 & 17:00–22:00, Sat 10:00–14:00, closed Sun, €4/load, €6.50 for full service, tel. 981-942-110). To get there, go down Rúa do Franco until you reach the big Alameda park, walk along Avenida de Xoán Carlos I with park on your right, continue on the avenue as it becomes Avenida de Rosalía de Castro, to #116 on the right.

Shopping: Jet, the black gemstone (called *azabache* in Spanish) similar to onyx, is believed to keep away evil spirits—and to bring in tourist euros. Along with jet, the silver trade has long been important in Santiago...and continues to be a popular item for tourists. Although the Galicians are a superstitious people and have beliefs about good and bad witches, the made-in-Taiwan witches you see in souvenir shops around the city are a recent innovation.

Best Views: There are beautiful views back towards the cathedral from the Alameda park. From the cathedral, follow Rúa do Franco away from the cathedral to the end. Swing right into the park and continue up Paseo de Santa Susana to the viewpoint *(mirador)* along Paseo da Ferradura. There is another excellent view from the very top of the park (clearly marked on TI maps).

TOURS

A free English-language **walking tour** covers the cathedral and the surrounding plazas (daily June–Sept at 16:00, meet at Praza do Obradoiro, ask for more info at the city TI, listed above). Or you can rent an **MP3 player audioguide** at the city TI, and follow the suggested three-hour route (€12/24-hour rental). Either tour is better than taking the silly **tourist train** (€3.40, 30 min, meet at College of Medicine on Rúa San Francisco).

In this compact city, it's easy to visit the cathedral on your own with the information in this book. If you have the extra cash, you could hire a **local guide** (for 3.5 hours: €70 Mon–Fri, €80 Sat–Sun). Patricia Furelos is good (mobile 630-781-795, pfben @latinmail.com), or contact the Association of Professional Guides of Galicia (tel. 981-589-890, fax 981-553-329, guiasgalicia@ctv.es).

SIGHTS

The Cathedral

Santiago's cathedral isn't the biggest in Spain, nor is it the most impressive. Yet it's certainly the most mystical, exerting a spiritual magnetism that attracts people from all walks of life and from all

corners of the globe. A visit here is worth ▲▲.

Exploring one of the most important churches in Christendom, you'll do some time travel, putting yourselves in the well-worn shoes of the millions of pilgrims who have trekked many miles to this powerful place.

• *Begin facing the cathedral's main facade, in the big square called...*

Praza do Obradoiro

Find the pavement stone with the scallop shell right in the middle of this square. For more than a thousand years, this spot has been where millions of tired pilgrims have taken a deep breath and thought to themselves: "I made it!" To maximize your chance of seeing pilgrims, be here at about 10:00—the last stop on the Camino is two miles away, and pilgrims try to get to the cathedral in time for the 12:00 Mass. (If they've taken the French route, they've entered through the Porta do Camiño; other routes enter the old town through different points.) It's great fun to chat with pilgrims who've just completed their journey. They seem to be very centered and content with the experience, and tuned in to the important things in life...like taking time to talk with others. You'll likely see pilgrims arrive separately who met previously along the way, and then leave together, having reunited at the grand finale.

Before heading into the cathedral, take a spin around the square (start facing the cathedral).

To your left is the **Hospital of the Catholic Kings** (Hostal dos Reis Católicos). Isabel and Ferdinand came to Santiago in 1501

to give thanks for successfully forcing the Moors out of Granada. When they arrived, they found many sick pilgrims at the square. (Numerous pilgrims came to Santiago to ask for help in overcoming an illness, and the long walk here often only made their condition worse.) Isabel and Ferdinand decided to build this hospital to give pilgrims a place to recover on arrival (you'll see their coats-of-arms flanking the intricately carved entryway). It was free, and remained open until 1952 (many locals were actually born here)—when it was converted into a fancy parador and restaurant (see "Sleeping" and "Eating" sections). The modern white windows with the old granite facade might seem jarring—but this contrast is very common in Galicia, maximizing the brightness provided by any sun breaks in this notoriously rainy region.

Another 90 degrees to the left is the Neoclassical **City Hall** (Concello). Notice the equestrian statue up top. That's St. James, riding in from heaven to help the Spaniards defeat the Moors. All over town, Santiago's namesake and symbol—a Christian evangelist on a horse, killing Muslims with his sword—is out doing his

Santiago de Compostela

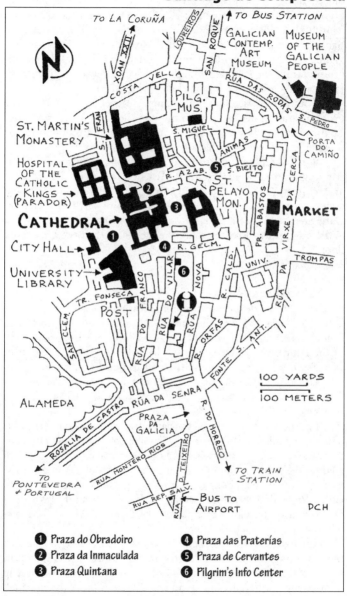

TO LA CORUÑA

↑ TO BUS STATION

LOUREIROS

SAN ROQUE

GALICIAN CONTEMP. ART MUSEUM

MUSEUM OF THE GALICIAN PEOPLE

XOAN XXIII

COSTA VELLA

RUA DAS RODAS

S. PEDRO

PILG. MUS.

S. MIGUEL

PORTA DO CAMIÑO

ST. MARTIN'S MONASTERY

S. FRAN.

ANIMAS

DA CERCA

HOSPITAL OF THE CATHOLIC KINGS (PARADOR) →

R. AZAB.

⑤ S. BIEITO

ST. PELAYO MON.

PR. ABASTOS

MARKET

CATHEDRAL →

②

③

①

④ R. GELM.

VIRXE

CITY HALL →

R. CALD.

UNIV.

TROMPAS

UNIVERSITY LIBRARY →

⑥

RUA NOVA

RUA DA

TR. FONSECA

RUA DO FRANCO

RUA DO VILAR

POST

SAN CLEM.

R. ORFAS

FONTE S. ANT.

ALAMEDA

RÚA DA SENRA

R. DO HORREO

ROSALIA DE CASTRO

PRAZA DA GALICIA

TO TRAIN STATION

RUA MONTERO RIOS

P. TEIXEIRO

TO PONTEVEDRA + PORTUGAL

RUA REP. SALV.

BUS TO AIRPORT

DCH

① Praza do Obradoiro
② Praza da Inmaculada
③ Praza Quintana
④ Praza das Praterías
⑤ Praza de Cervantes
⑥ Pilgrim's Info Center

bloody thing. See any police on the square? Security here has been on high alert since September 11, 2001—and even more so since March 11, 2004, when Madrid's commuter trains were bombed. Santiago's cathedral, as the third most important Christian pilgrimage site in the world (after Jerusalem and Rome), is a high-profile target for Islamic fundamentalists. It doesn't help that St. James seems to take such joy in butchering Muslims.

Completing the square (90 more degrees to the left) is the original **University** building, now just the library. Santiago has Spain's third-oldest university, with more than 30,000 students (medicine and law are especially popular).

You'll likely see Spanish school groups on the square, field-tripping from all over the country. Teachers love to use this spot for an architecture lesson, since it features four different architectural styles (starting with the cathedral and spinning left): 18th-century Baroque; 16th-century Plateresque; 18th-century Neoclassical; and 15th-century Romanesque (the facade around the University door).

• *Now take a look at the...*

Cathedral Facade

Twelve hundred years ago, a monk followed a field of stars (probably the Milky Way) to the little Galician village of San Fiz de Solovio, and discovered what appeared to be the long-lost tomb of St. James. On July 25, 813, the local bishop declared that St. James' relics had been found. They set to building a church here, and named the place Santiago (St. James) de Compostela (*campo de estrellas*, or "field of stars," for the celestial bodies that guided the monk).

For the last 12 centuries, the cathedral you see today has gradually been added on to the original simple chapel. By the 11th century, the church was overwhelmed by the crowds. Construction of a larger cathedral began in 1075, and the work took 150 years. (The granite workers who built it set up shop on this very square—still called Praza do Obradoiro, literally, "Workers' Square.") Much of the design is attributed to a palace artist named Maestro Mateo, whom you'll meet a little later.

The exterior of the cathedral you see today is *not* the one that medieval pilgrims saw (though the interior is much the same). In the mid-18th century, Santiago's bishop—all fired up from a trip to Baroque-slathered Rome, and wanting to protect the original, now-deteriorating facade—decided to spruce up the building with a new Baroque facade. He also replaced the simple stonework in the interior with gaudy gold.

Scrutinize the facade. Atop the middle steeple is St. James. Beneath him is his tomb, marked by a star—one of the many symbols you'll see all over the place (see "The Symbols of Santiago" on page 163). On either side of the tomb are Theodorus and Athanasius, James' disciples who brought his body back to Santiago. On the side pillars are, to the left, James' father Zebedee, and to the right, his mother Salomé.

What a beautiful facade! Don't you wish you had a miniature replica to carry around with you? Actually, you probably do. Check your pocket for a copper-colored euro coin worth €0.01, €0.02, or €0.05. There it is! Of all the churches in Spain, they chose this one as their representative in Euroland. It's even more important when you consider the significance of the images depicted on Spain's other euro coinage: a portrait of the author of *Don Quixote*, Miguel de Cervantes, Spain's greatest contributor to world literature, and the current king, Juan Carlos I. Sevilla and Toledo may have bigger cathedrals, but Santiago has the symbolism to propel its church into this powerful triumvirate.

The cathedral also houses a museum with three parts; as you face this facade, the door to the main museum is to the right, the entry to the crypt is dead ahead (under the staircase), and the door on the left leads to the Gelmírez Palace (and the cathedral rooftop, both part of the Cathedral Museum, described later in this chapter).

• *But that's for later. Head up the stairs to the cathedral and go inside. As you enter, you're face-to-face with the...*

Portico of Glory

Take a step back in time (remember, this used to be the main facade of the cathedral—sculpted in about 1180 by Maestro Mateo). You're a medieval pilgrim, and you've just walked 500 miles from the Frankish lands to reach this cathedral. You're here to request the help of St. James in recovering from an illness or to give thanks for a success. Maybe you've come to honor the wish of a dying relative or to be forgiven for your sins. Whatever the reason, you came here on foot.

You can't read, but you can tell from the carved images that this magnificent door represents the Final Judgment. There's Jesus, front and center, surrounded by Matthew, Mark, Luke, and John. Beside them are angels carrying tools for the Crucifixion—the cross, the crown of thorns, the spear, and a jug of vinegar. Arching above them are 24 musicians playing celestial music—each one with a different medieval instrument. Under Jesus sits St. James, and below him, a column with the genealogy of Jesus (with Mary near the top, and above her, the Holy Trinity: Father, Son, and a dove representing the Holy Spirit).

At the bases of the columns are monsters—being crushed by the glory of God. Atop the columns to the left are prophets

El Camino de Santiago (The Way of St. James)

In 951, Godescalco, the Bishop of Le Puy in France, walked to Santiago de Compostela to pay homage to the relics of St. James. More than a thousand years later, people are still following in his footsteps.

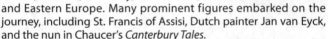

The Camino de Santiago began informally. But in the 12th century, Pope Callistus II decreed that any person who walked to Santiago in a Holy Year, confessed their sins, and took communion here would be forgiven. This opportunity for a cheap indulgence made the Camino de Santiago one of the most important pilgrimages in the world.

In the Middle Ages, pilgrims came to Santiago from all over Europe—mostly from France, but also from Portugal, Italy, Britain, Holland, Germany, Scandinavia, and Eastern Europe. Many prominent figures embarked on the journey, including St. Francis of Assisi, Dutch painter Jan van Eyck, and the nun in Chaucer's *Canterbury Tales*.

By 1130, the trek was so popular that it prompted a French monk named Aimery Picaud to write a chronicle of his journey, including tips on where to eat, where to stay, the best way to get from place to place, and how to pack light. This *Codex Calixtinus* was the world's first guidebook—the great-great-granddaddy of the one you're holding right now.

As Europe emerged from the Middle Ages, and the Black Death swept across the continent, the Camino de Santiago was virtually forgotten. As recently as the 1980s, only a few hardy souls still followed the route.

But following the success of the 1992 Expo in Sevilla, the Spanish government decided to pour funds into reviving the tradition for the Holy Year in 1993. They made Santiago a high-profile destination, and shelled out big pesetas for concerts by stars like the Rolling Stones, Bruce Springsteen, and Julio Iglesias (whose father was born in Galicia).

The plan worked, and now—aided by European Union funding—the route has enjoyed a huge renaissance of interest, with 100,000 pilgrims each year trekking to Santiago. Even Shirley

MacLaine has made the journey (her book *The Camino: A Journey of the Spirit* is popular among pilgrims). Cyclists and horse riders are now joining hikers on the journey, and these days it's "in" to follow the seashells to Santiago.

While there are many routes for approaching Santiago—including one from Portugal—the most popular has always been the French Road. This 500-mile-long route begins in the rugged Pyrenees, in the town of St. Jean-Pied-de-Port. After crossing the mountains to Pamplona, the route wanders through the rough, arid plains of northern Spain—to Burgos, then León. The path crosses into Galicia in the stony mountain village of O Cebreiro, where the terrain changes, becoming lush and green. This last leg of the journey is the most popular. Pilgrims pass simple farms, Romanesque churches, apple orchards, flocks of sheep, eucalyptus forests...and plenty of other pilgrims.

The procedure for walking the Camino has remained the same throughout history. The gear includes a cloak; a pointy, floppy hat; a walking stick; and a gourd (for drinking from wells). The route of the Camino is marked with yellow arrows (for hikers) or seashells (for cyclists) at every intersection.

Doing the entire French Road of the Camino takes about three weeks (averaging 12–15 miles per day). The walk itself is a type of hut-hopping—at regular intervals along the route, you'll encounter humble little hostels called *albergues,* where pilgrims can get a bunk for the night (free, €2–3 donation requested outside of Galicia, hostels subsidized by the government). Pilgrims carry a sort of a passport, which they get stamped at various *albergues* along the way, to prove that they walked the whole Camino. Those who complete the walk get a special certificate (called a *compostela*) when they reach the cathedral.

Imagine the jubilation pilgrims have felt through the ages when—four miles out of town—the spire of the cathedral comes into view.

of the Old Testament, and to the right, the apostles of the New Testament—all barefoot in the presence of God. The gang's all here. The guy with the biggest smile is Daniel.

Take an earthly diversion from your religious journey for a minute: Locals say Daniel is grinning because he's looking at the carved statue of a beautiful, voluptuous woman immediately across from him. The story continues that the priest thought she was

too buxom, and instructed the sculptor to make her less shapely. He did, but the people didn't like being denied a simple pleasure. To get even, ever since, Santiago has made its popular cheese, called *tetilla*, in the shape of what they liked on the statue (you can buy the cheese at the market, listed on page 179).

Return to the spiritual plane. As a pilgrim, you would walk to the column in the middle of the entryway. Squint down the nave to the end, and you'll see the stone statue of St. James that

marks his tomb. Trembling with excitement at the culmination of your long journey, you'd place your hand into the well-worn finger holes on the column and bow your head, giving thanks to St. James for safe passage. (You may see other pilgrims doing the same even today, but—regrettably—this post may be covered by protective glass.) Go around to the other side of the post and, at knee level, see Maestro Mateo, who carved this fine facade. What a smart guy! Kneel and tap your head against his three times—to help improve your intelligence.

• *Now wander down the...*

Nave

Look up, noticing the barrel vault and the heavy, dark Romanesque design of the church. Up near the top, notice the gallery. This is where sweaty, smelly pilgrims sleep (and their animals, too). Man, it stinks in here.

• *Continue up the nave until you reach the high altar, where you'll see a thick rope hanging from a pulley system high in the dome, which is sometimes attached to the...*

Botafumeiro

This huge, silver incense burner (120 pounds and about the size of a small child) is suspended from the ceiling during special Masses (occurring about 25 times a year; ask at the TI if one is scheduled during your visit) or when a pilgrim pays to see it (250 medieval shekels...or about 250 21st-century euros). Supposedly the custom of swinging this giant incense dispenser began in order to counteract the stench of the pilgrims. And to enhance the good mood of the congregation—already giddy for having completed the Camino de Santiago—priests were once said to add a pinch of cannabis to the mixture. After communion, eight men (called *tiraboleiros*) pull on the rope, and this huge contraption swings in a wide arc up and down the transept, spewing sweet-smelling smoke. A replica is on display in the cathedral library (see "Cathedral Museum," below).

• *Stand in the center of the nave, in front of the...*

Altar

You'll have to cheat with time travel for this section, since the original medieval choir and altar were replaced with this gilded

Baroque piece in the 18th century (fragments of the original stone choir can be seen in the Cathedral Museum). Look all the way back, at the big gold altar, to see all three representations of St. James in one place (see "The Three Santiagos" on page 177): up top, on a white horse, is James the *Matamoros*— Moor Slayer; below that (just under the canopy) is pilgrim James; and below that is the original stone Apostle James by Maestro Mateo—still point-ing down to his tomb after all these centuries.

The dome over the altar was added in the 16th century to bring some light into this dark Romanesque church.

On the columns up and down the nave and transept, notice the symbols carved into the granite. These are the markings of the masons who made the columns—to keep track of how many they'd be paid for.

• *Now head back to the Middle Ages. The finale of your long pilgrimage is just ahead. Go down the ambulatory on the left side of the altar— passing where the* botafumeiro *rope is moored to the pillar—and walk down the little stairway (see the green light, on your right) to the level of*

St. James

Santiago is Spanish for "St. James." James and his brother John, sons of Zebedee and Salomé, were well-off fishermen on the Sea of Galilee. One fateful day, a charismatic visionary came and said to them, "Come with me, and I will make you fishers of men." They threw down their nets and became apostles.

Along with Peter, James and John were supposedly Jesus' favorites—he called them the "sons of thunder." Some historians even think Jesus and James might have been related. (This close relationship makes James an even more appealing object of worship.)

After Jesus' death, the apostles spread out and brought his message to other lands. St. James spent a decade as a missionary in Spain, then part of the Roman Empire. The legend goes that as soon as he returned home to the Holy Land in A.D. 44, James was beheaded by Herod Agrippa. Before his body and head could be thrown to the lions—as was the custom in those days—they were rescued by two of his disciples, Theodorus and Athanasius.

These two brought his body back to Spain in a small boat and entombed it in the hills of Galicia—hiding it carefully so it would not be found by the Roman authorities. There it lay hidden for almost eight centuries. In 813, a monk—supposedly directed by the stars—discovered the tomb, and the local bishop proudly exclaimed that St. James was in Galicia. Santiago de Compostela was born.

But is this the *real* story? Historians figure the "discovery" of the remains of St. James in Spain provided a necessary way to rally Europe against the Moors, who had invaded Spain and were threatening to continue into Europe. With St. James—the Moor slayer—in Iberia, all of Europe could rise up to push the Muslims back into Africa...which, after a centuries-long "Reconquista," they finally did in 1492.

Sure, the whole thing's likely a propaganda hoax to get a local populace to support a war. But yesterday's and today's pilgrims may not care whether the body of St. James actually lies in this church. The pilgrimage to Santiago is a spiritual quest powered through the ages by faith.

the earlier, 10th-century church and the...

Tomb of St. James

There he is, in the little silver chest, marked by a star—Santiago de Compostela. You kneel in front of the tomb and make your request or say your thanks. Then you continue through the little passage and trudge up the stairs. Turn left and wander around the ambulatory, noticing the various chapels (built by noblemen who wanted to be buried close to St. James).

• *At the very back of the church (behind the altar) is the...*

Holy Door

This special door is open only during Holy Years. The door, sculpted in 2004 by a local artist, shows six scenes from the life of St. James: the conversion moment when Jesus invited those Galilean fishermen to become "fishers of men"; Jesus with the 12 apostles (James is identified by his scallop shell); James doing his "fishing" in Spain; his return to Jerusalem in A.D. 44 to be beheaded; the ship taking his body back to Spain; and the discovery of James' body by the local bishop in 813. At the bottom, the little snail is the symbol of the pilgrim...slow and steady, with everything on its back.

There's one more pilgrim ritual to complete. Find the little door near where you came out from the tomb (perhaps with a line of pilgrims—10 yards away, occasionally closed). Climb the stairs under the huge babies, find Maestro Mateo's stone statue of St. James—gilded and caked with precious gems—and embrace him from behind.

• *This is your finale. Congratulations, pilgrim! You have completed the Camino de Santiago. Now go in peace.*

Cathedral Museum

The museum, worth ▲, has three parts: The Museum-Cloister (enter through door on the right, as you face main facade); the crypt (under the main staircase in front); and the Gelmírez Palace, where the archbishop traditionally resides (door on the left, as you face main facade). All three parts are covered by the same €5 ticket and have the same hours (daily June–Sept 10:00–14:00 & 16:00–20:00, Oct–May 10:00–13:30 & 16:00–18:30, tel. 981-560-527). Some parts of the museum may be closed during services.

The **Museum-Cloister** (Museo da Catedral) is the most interesting part. On the main floor, you'll find the remaining pieces of Maestro Mateo's original stone choir (stone seats for priests; these seats filled the center of the nave in the 12th century), pieced together as part of a new replica. A miniature model of the choir is in the next room. You'll also see fragments of Roman settlements, dating from before the tomb of St. James was discovered here.

On the first floor up, find a statue of a pregnant Mary. While this theme is unusual in most of Europe, it's common in

Galicia. The coin collection shows off examples of money that pilgrims brought with them from all over Europe (see the displayed map). The dirham coin in the center case is dated 387. Muhammad became a prophet in 612; therefore, this is from the year 997 on the Christian calendar.

On the second floor up, you'll come to the cloister. The tombs lining the cloister floor hold the remains of priests from the cathedral. In the courtyard, you'll see a fountain (which once stood in front of the cathedral and was used by pilgrims to cleanse themselves) and the original church bells (replaced with new models in 1989). As you walk left around the cloister, the first door leads to the Royal Chapel, with a beautiful-smelling cedar altar that houses dozens and dozens of relics. The centerpiece (eye level) holds the remains (likely the skull) of St. James the Lesser (the *other* Apostle James). Look up to find St. James riding heroically out of the woodwork to rally all Europe to reconquer the Iberian Peninsula. This altarpiece was re-carved after a fire around 1900.

Cross the hall to the treasury, which has fine vestments. The fancy solid-gold monstrance is used for carrying the communion host around the cathedral on Corpus Christi (the wafer sits in the little round window in the middle).

The library (near where you first entered the cloister) is where they store old books, a funky rack for reading those huge tomes ("turn pages" by spinning the rack), and the *botafumeiro* (gigantic incense burner). The next room shows how tapestries could warm a stone palace.

Up one more floor (passing a stairwell shrine to St. Salomé—St. James' mother), you'll find more tapestries—including some from cartoons by Rubens and Goya (last room). Look for the painted wood altar depicting the tale of St. James—including his beheading, and his body being brought back to Galicia. From here, if the doors are open, enjoy views from a fine balcony overlooking Praza do Obradoiro.

Leaving the museum, the next two doors take you to the crypt and palace—neither very interesting (but included in your admission). Since the church was built on a too-small hill, the **crypt** was constructed to support the part of the nave that hung over. While the crypt, under a Maestro Mateo-decorated Romanesque vault, is as about as dead as its residents, it does display interesting models of the medieval instruments featured in the heavenly angels' combo in the Portico of Glory.

The **Gelmírez Palace** (Pazo de Xelmírez) requires lots of walking through the stark and stony rooms of a now-empty medieval home. From the Gelmirez Palace, you can buy tickets to tour the **rooftop,** though the experience offers little more than a fine view and a chance to burn your clothes at the cross—a once-

The Three Santiagos

You'll see three different depictions of St. James in the cathedral and throughout the city:

1. Apostle James: James dressed in typical apostle robes, often indiscernible from the other apostles (sometimes with a pilgrim's stick or shell).

2. Pilgrim James: James wearing some or all of the traditional garb of the Camino de Santiago pilgrim: a brown cloak, floppy hat, walking stick, shell, gourd, and sandals. Among pilgrims, he's the one carrying a book.

3. Crusader James: Centuries after his death, the Spaniards called on St. James for aid in various battles against the Moors. According to legend, St. James appeared from the heavens on a white horse and massacred Muslim foes. Locals don't particularly care for this depiction—especially these days, when the rising tide of Islamic fundamentalists could justifiably find it provocative.

common practice for pilgrims (€10, escorted in Spanish, departing hourly 10:00–14:00 & 16:00–20:00).

Cathedral Squares

There is a square on every side of the cathedral, and each one is lined with interesting sights and other tidbits. You've already visited Praza do Obradoiro, in the front. Here are the other three, working clockwise (to reach the first one, go up the passage—which street musicians appreciate for its acoustics—to the left as you're facing the main cathedral facade).

Praza da Inmaculada—This was the way that most medieval pilgrims using the French Road actually approached the cathedral. Across the square is **St. Martin's Monastery** (Mosteiro de San Martiño Pinario), one of two monasteries that sprang up around the church to care for pilgrims. Today, it houses a museum of ecclesiastical artifacts and special exhibits. To the left of the monastery's main door is a fun multimedia exhibit called "Galicia Dixital" (see page 180).

Walk to the corner of the square with the arcade, and go to the post with the sign for Rúa Acibechería (next to the garbage can, under the streetlight). If you look to the roof of the cathedral, between the big dome and the tall tower, you can make out a small green cross. This is where the clothes of medieval pilgrims were ritually burned when they finally arrived at Santiago. This ritual was created for hygienic reasons in an age of frightful diseases... and filthy pilgrims.

• *Continue along the arcade and around the corner, and you'll enter...*

Praza Quintana—The door of the cathedral facing this square is the Holy Door, which is only opened during Holy Years (next in

2010). There's St. James, flanked by the disciples who brought his body back to Galicia. Below them are the 12 apostles and 12 prophets. Tip: Old Testament prophets hold scrolls. New Testament apostles hold books.

Across the square from the cathedral, you'll see the huge **St. Pelayo Monastery** (Mosteiro San Paio). The windows of its cells (now used by Benedictine sisters) face the church. The church at the north end of this monastery is worth a peek. It has a frilly Baroque altar and a statue with a typical Galician theme: a pregnant Mary (to the left as you face main altar). Just off this sanctuary is the entrance to the monastery's **Sacred Art Museum** (Museo de Arte Sacra), with a small but interesting collection and an opportunity to chat with a happy nun (€1.50, Mon–Fri 10:30–13:30 & 16:00–19:00, Sat 11:00–14:00 & 16:00–19:00, closed Sun, some posted English-language information, pick up translations of labels as you enter).

• *Continue around to the...*

Praza das Praterías—This "Silversmiths' Square" is where Santiago's silver workers used to have their shops (and some still do). Overlooking the square is a tall tower that was once a fortress for keeping locals—who were fed up with high taxes—at bay, and for fending off invading enemies over the years, including Normans, Moors, English pirates, and Napoleon's army. An 18th-century bishop added the Baroque top and the bells. At the very top of the tower is a powerful light, most noticeable at night, that serves as a beacon to pilgrims.

The cathedral door facing this square actually combines elements of two different stone doors that were damaged over the centuries. That's why it's a hodgepodge of religious figures and motifs.

Take a look at the **fountain**. Notice the woman sitting on St. James' tomb, holding aloft a star—a typical city symbol. Under her are animals that seem to be half-horse, half-fish. This is the way that Portuguese pilgrims approached Santiago—some by land, others by sea. The mansion behind with the impressive Galician Baroque facade is very skinny—built to give the square an architectural harmony. Its centerpiece even copies the fountain's star.

Cross the street beyond the fountain (Rúa do Vilar) and on the left, you'll see the **Pilgrim's Information Office** (listed in "Tourist Information" at the beginning of this chapter). But first, at the gift shop next door, look for the *compostela*—the certificate issued by the office to those who can prove they finished the entire Camino—with the pilgrim's name in Latin, the date, and the priest's signature. In the shop's window is a life-size replica of the *botafumeiro*, the giant incense burner. Wander into the office. Upstairs is a notice board reminiscent of pre-e-mail days—a reminder of the friendships forged on the long trail to Santiago. Also while you're upstairs, you're likely to see happy pilgrims receiving their diplomas.

Other Sights
▲▲**Market (Praza de Abastos)**—This wonderful market, housed in Old World stone buildings, offers a fine opportunity to do some serious people-watching (Mon–Sat 9:00–14:00, closed Sun). Monday's the least interesting day, since the fishermen don't go out on Sunday. It's definitely busiest and best on Thursday and Saturday (go early).

The market was built in the 1920s (to consolidate Santiago's many small markets) in a style perfectly compatible with the medieval wonder that surrounds it. Today it offers an opportunity to get up close and personal with some still-twitching seafood. Keep an eye out for the specialties you'll want to try later—octopus, shrimp, crabs, lobsters, and expensive-as-gold *percebes* (barnacles; see seafood sidebar on page 186). You'll also see the local spicy sausage.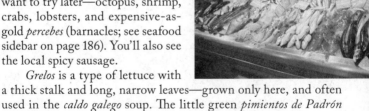

Grelos is a type of lettuce with a thick stalk and long, narrow leaves—grown only here, and often used in the *caldo galego* soup. The little green *pimientos de Padrón* (in season June–Oct) look like jalapeños, but lack the kick...sometimes.

In the cheese cases, you'll see what look like huge yellow Hershey's Kisses (or, to some, breasts). For the story on how they got this shape, see "Portico of Glory," page 169. Among typical Galician cheeses are *tetilla* (white, creamy) and *San Simón* (yellow, smoked). If you linger long enough, they'll offer you a taste.

▲Museum of Pilgrimages (Museo das Peregrinacións)—This fine museum examines various aspects of the pilgrimage phenomenon. You'll see a map of pilgrimage sites around the world, and then learn more about the pilgrimage that brings people to Santiago. There are models of earlier versions of the cathedral, explanations of the differing depictions of St. James throughout history (apostle, pilgrim, and Crusader), and coverage of the various routes to Santiago and stories of some prominent pilgrims. This well-presented place lends historical context to all of those backpackers you see in the streets. While exhibits are not described in English, the loaner translation you'll pick up as you enter and the sheets available throughout the museum are well worth reading (€2.40, free most of the year during special exhibitions, also free Sat afternoon and Sun morning, Tue–Fri 10:00–20:00, Sat 10:30–13:30 & 17:00–20:00, Sun 10:30–13:30, closed Mon, Rúa de San Miguel 4, tel. 981-581-558, www.mdperegrinacions.com).

Galicia Dixital—Housed in the Monastery of St. Martin, this futuristic, kid-friendly exhibit uses various kinds of technology to explore Galicia and Santiago in virtual reality. You'll visit several exhibits, accompanied by a Spanish guide (English groups unlikely, but call ahead to see if an English-speaking group is coming that you can join). First you'll take a 3-D, surround-sound tour of the squares around the cathedral (including a surprise thunderstorm). Then you go on *A Vertixe*—which means "the vertigo," as you'll soon learn. A motion-simulator 3-D "rollercoaster" ride zips you around the top of the cathedral, then underground (keep hands inside your chair, which jerks around wildly). You can don a *casco virtual* ("virtual helmet") and wander through the cathedral. Other 3-D movies include a submarine trip though Galicia's waterways for a look at sea life, as well as an animated tour of the cathedral with a strange little pilgrim creature. While enjoyable, you can't shake the feeling that you could step outside and see most of this stuff in person. Still, it's an enjoyable enough way to get out of the sun for an hour. It ain't Disney World, but it's not bad (free, daily 10:30–14:00 & 16:00–20:30; must go on 1-hour guided visits, which leave regularly—may have to wait a few minutes for more people to show up; last visits begin at 13:00 and 19:30, tel. 981-554-048).

Museum of the Galician People (Museo do Pobo Galego)—If you're intrigued by this very traditional part of Spain, this museum will give you more insight into rural Galician life. As you tour this collection, remember that if you side-trip a few miles into the countryside, you'll find traditional lifestyles thriving even today. Beautifully displayed around an 18th-century cloister, the museum springs from a unique triple staircase, which provided privacy to various hierarchies of the monks who lived here, depending on

which stairway you climbed. The collection shows off boat-building and fishing techniques, farming implements and simple horse-drawn carts, tools of trade and handicrafts (including carpentry, pottery, looms, and baskets), traditional costumes, and a collection of musical instruments that stars the bagpipes *(gaitas)*. If the farm tools seem old-fashioned, there's a reason: Old inheritance laws mean that plots are increasingly smaller, so modern farming machinery is impractical—keeping traditional equipment alive. There's virtually no English, except for a helpful €1.50 guidebook (free entry, Tue–Sat 10:00–14:00 & 16:00–20:00, Sun 11:00–14:00, closed Mon, at northeast edge of historical center in monastery of San Domingos de Bonaval, just beyond Porta do Camiño, tel. 981-583-620, www.museodopobo.es). Behind the museum is a plush and peaceful park—once crowded with tombstones.

Next door, in the striking modern building, is the **Galician Contemporary Art Museum** (Centro Galego de Arte Contemporánea), with continually rotating exhibits—mostly by local artists (free, Tue–Sun 11:00–20:00, closed Mon, tel. 981-546-619, www.cgac.org).

SLEEPING

Thanks to all those pilgrims, Santiago has a glut of cheap, excellent accommodation. Since the Camino was resurrected in 1993, new hotels are popping up all the time—many of them subsidized by the EU. There aren't many affordable big hotels in town for tour groups, so they tend to stay along the Rías Baixas (fjord-like estuaries) about an hour to the south, where beds are cheap. That means many of Santiago's visitors are day-trippers, arriving at about 10:30 and leaving in the afternoon. After dark, it's just you, the locals, the pilgrims, and St. James.

$$$ Hotel Virxe da Cerca is a wonderful splurge just on the edge of the historical center, across the street from the market. Its standard rooms are in a modern building, but some of its "superior" and all of its "special" historic rooms—with classy old stone and hardwoods—are in a restored 18th-century monastery. All 43 rooms surround a lush garden oasis (standard Sb-€75, superior Sb-€85, bigger "special" Sb-€95, standard Db-€85, superior Db-€95, bigger "special" Db-€105, extra bed-€20, breakfast buffet-€8, beautiful glassed-in breakfast room overlooks garden, elevator, Internet in lobby, Rúa Virxe da Cerca 27, tel. 902-405-858, fax 981-586-925,

---

Sleep Code

(€1 = about $1.20, country code: 34)
S = Single, **D** = Double/Twin, **T** = Triple, **Q** = Quad, **b** = bathroom,
s = shower only. You can assume credit cards are accepted and English is spoken unless otherwise noted.

To help you easily sort through these listings, I've divided the rooms into three categories, based on the price for a standard double room with bath:

$$$ **Higher Priced**—Most rooms €80 or more.
 $$ **Moderately Priced**—Most room between €45–80.
  $ **Lower Priced**—Most rooms €45 or less.

High season is roughly Easter through September; most places charge more during this time. When I list a range of prices, it represents low season to high season. Any single prices listed are an average (mid-season). The hostales speak enough English to make a reservation by phone (though sometimes not much more). IVA tax (7 percent) is not included in these rates, and there is no breakfast, unless I've noted otherwise.

---

www.pousadasdecompostela.com, info@pousadasdecompostela.com).

$$$ Altaïr Hotel is owned by the Liñares family (see Costa Vella listing below), but caters to a different clientele. Located in a renovated three-story residence, its mod design can best be described as "rustic minimalist." Exposed stone walls and open beams mix with sleek design to provide a unique yet surprisingly affordable experience in Santiago (Sb-€60, Db-€100, suite-€120, extra bed-€20, breakfast-€6, Rúa dos Loureiros 12, tel. & fax 981-554-712, www.altairhotel.net, info@altairhotel.net).

$$$ Hostal dos Reis Católicos brags that it's the oldest hotel in the world. Founded by the Catholic Kings at the beginning of the 16th century to care for pilgrims arriving from the Camino, it was converted into an upscale parador 50 years ago. This grand building surrounds a series of four courtyards packed with Santiago history (but not tourists—only guests are allowed to wander). It has the best address in Santiago...and prices to match (standard Db-€200, many fancier options, includes breakfast, Praza do Obradoiro 1, tel. 981-582-200, fax 981-563-094, santiago@parador.es). This place still remembers its roots, offering a free breakfast to pilgrims who've hiked the Camino (the first 10 to arrive each day).

$$ Hotel Residencia Costa Vella is my favorite spot in Santiago (book as far in advance as possible), with 14 comfortable

Santiago Hotels and Restaurants

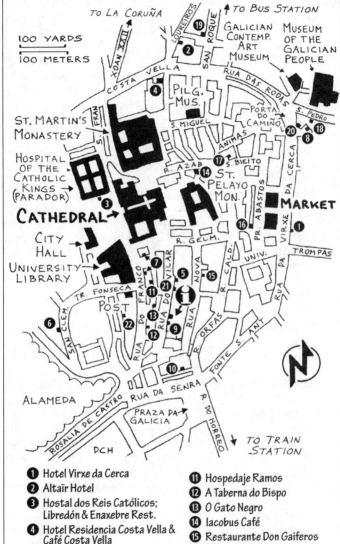

1. Hotel Virxe da Cerca
2. Altaïr Hotel
3. Hostal dos Reis Católicos; Libredón & Enaxebre Rest.
4. Hotel Residencia Costa Vella & Café Costa Vella
5. Hotel Arias Nunes
6. Hotel San Clemente
7. Hostal Residencia Libredon Barbantes (2 Buildings)
8. Hostal Residencia Gaidas
9. Hostal Suso
10. Hostal Residencia Mapoula
11. Hospedaje Ramos
12. A Taberna do Bispo
13. O Gato Negro
14. Iacobus Café
15. Restaurante Don Gaiferos
16. Bar Rest. La Churrasquita
17. Restaurante Casa Manolo
18. O Dezaseis Restaurant
19. La Bodeguilla de San Roque
20. Ambitus Veter Bar
21. Café Casino
22. Café Terra Nova

rooms combining classic charm and modern comforts. The glassed-in breakfast room and lounge terrace overlook a peaceful garden, with lovely views of a nearby church and monastery and into the countryside beyond. They deserve a feature in *Better Stones and Tiles* magazine (Sb-€42–48, standard Db-€59–66, Db with balcony-€75–80, breakfast-€5, Rúa da Porta da Pena 17, tel. 981-569-530, fax 981-569-531, www.costavella.com, hotelcostavella @costavella.com, friendly José).

$$ Hotel Airas Nunes and **Hotel San Clemente** are both affiliated with Hotel Virxe da Cerca, above. They're equally good, stress-free, safe, and professional-feeling. Both have 10 rooms in restored old buildings with classy touches, and both can be reserved through the same office (www.pousadasdecompostela .com). Hotel Airas Nunes is on a peaceful, centrally located street a few blocks in front of the cathedral (Sb-€65, Db-€75, extra bed-€20, breakfast-€6, Rúa do Vilar 17, reception tel. 981-554-706); Hotel San Clemente—about €5 less—is just outside the historical center (Sb-€60, Db-€70, extra bed-€20, breakfast-€5, Rúa San Clemente 28, reception tel. 981-569-260).

$$ Hostal Residencia Libredon Barbantes consists of two *hostales* that face each other across a square, a block from the cathedral. They share a reception desk and both have clean, modern, Scandinavian-design rooms that are an excellent value for the near-perfect location. Barbantes' 17 rooms (Sb-€38–43, Db with 1 big bed-€43–54, twin Db-€54–65, Rúa do Franco 3) and Libredon's 19 rooms (Ss-€27–30, Sb-€38–43, Db with 1 big bed-€43–54, Db-€54–65, Praza do Fonseca 5) are about equal in comfort (reception for both at Libredon, generally open 9:00–21:00, closed Sun afternoon, tel. 981-576-520, www.libredonbarbantes.com).

$ Hostal Residencia Gaidas, tucked away just beyond the market, faces a tidy little square as if it owns it. The Gaidas family runs a small café/bar and rents eight rooms upstairs. The rooms are charming, in spite of the slanted floors and linoleum "hardwood" (Sb-€25–28, Db-€42–44, Tb-€56–59, elevator, next to Porta do Camiño at Praza do Matadoiro 2, tel. 981-587-071, delightful Lola).

$ Hostal Suso, run by the friendly Quintela family, offers 10 ridiculously cheap, new-feeling rooms around an airy atrium over a cheery—if smoky—little bar in the heart of Santiago (Sb-€18–20, Db-€34–39, Rúa do Vilar 65, tel. 981-586-611).

$ Hostal Residencia Mapoula offers 11 clean, bright rooms on a little lane on the edge of the historical center (Sb-€25–30, Db-€30–39, Tb-€40–48, elevator plus a few stairs, laundry service available, Entremurallas 10, tel. 981-580-124, fax 981-584-089, www.mapoula.com, mapoula@mapoula.com, Manuel). Of all of my accommodations listings, this one is closest to the train station.

$ Hospedaje Ramos is a good bet for a rock-bottom budget, renting 10 big, plain, clean rooms with lots of stairs right in the center of town (Sb-€20, Db-€33, prices include tax, Rúa da Raíña 18, tel. 981-581-859).

EATING

Santiago offers a wide range of excellent seafood (see sidebar). It's frustrating to try to eat before the locals do. If you find a restaurant serving before 14:00 or 21:00, you'll be all alone with a few sorry-looking tourists. Early-bird eaters should know that ordering a drink at any bar will generally get you a free tapa—Santiago is one of the few places in Spain that still honors this tradition.

Seafood and More in the Old Center

The easiest area to get your Santiago seafood fix is on two streets just south of the cathedral: **Rúa do Franco** and **Rúa do Vilar.** These lanes are lined with literally dozens of touristy seafood eateries. Even the places that seem "local" probably aren't—the Spanish-speaking clientele are mostly tourists from other parts of the country. Go for a stroll, examine the window display cases, and pop into the restaurant that looks best. You've got a wide range of options: atmospheric mid-range spots; high-end, white-table-cloth splurges; and grumpy, simple, stripped-down joints actually frequented by locals. Generally, these places feel interchangeable—follow your nose.

A Taberna do Bispo is a lively Barcelona-style tavern serving *montaditos* (little €1 baguette slices with various toppings) at the bar, *raciones* at the tables, and good wine by the glass (Tue–Sun 13:00–2:00 in the morning, closed Mon, Rúa do Franco 37, tel. 981-586-045). You might pick up a sandwich to go here before exploring the other Rúa do Franco options.

O Gato Negro is a smoky, no-frills tapas bar stuck in the past and filled with loyal locals (daily 11:00–15:00 & 19:00–23:00, near Rúa do Franco at Rúa da Raíña).

Hostal dos Reis Católicos, the fancy old hospital sharing the square with the cathedral, has two fine restaurants (both down-stairs). The main restaurant, **Libredón,** fills a former stable under a dramatic stone vault, offering international dishes—often with live piano—for €12–30 (plus a variety of interesting €30 fixed-price meals). It's as atmospheric as it gets, with stiff tuxedoed service, white tablecloths, and not a hint of fun (daily 13:30–16:00 & 20:30–23:00, reservations smart, Praza do Obradoiro 1, tel. 981-582-200). A few steps away, **Enaxebre** offers a livelier, easygoing-tavern vibe, good traditional Galician food, and lower prices (€5–12 dishes, daily 13:00–16:00 & 20:00–23:30, tel. 981-050-527).

Galician Cuisine

Strolling through the streets of Santiago is like visiting a well-stocked aquarium: Windows proudly display every form of edible sea life, including giant toothy fish, scallops and clams of every shape and size, monstrous shrimp, and—most importantly—octopus. The fertile fjords of the Galician coast are just 20 miles away, and the region's many fishing villages keep the capital city swimming in seafood. As the seafood is so fresh, the focus here is on purity rather than sauces. The seafood is served simple—generally just steamed or grilled, and seasoned only with a little olive oil, onions, and peppers.

Tasting octopus *(pulpo)* is obligatory in Galicia; it's most often prepared *a la gallega* (also  called *pulpo a feira*): After the octopus is boiled in a copper pot, its tentacles are snipped into bite-size pieces with scissors. It's topped with olive oil, garlic, salt, and paprika, and served on a round wooden plate. Eat it with toothpicks, never a fork.

If you're more adventurous, splurge for *percebes*. These barnacles are a delicacy; since they grow only on rocks that see a lot of dangerous waves, it takes a team of two fishermen to collect them—one with a rope tied to his waist, the other spotting him from above. The danger factor raises the price. You'll pay about €10 per 100 grams, but two beers and a small 100-grams plate to split are a wonderful snack. The price includes instructions on how to eat them (twist, rip, and bite). I ask for toasted bread on the side.

Not a fan of seafood? You can slurp the *caldo galego* soup, a traditional broth that originally came from the leftover stock used to prepare an elaborate Sunday feast (cabbage, potatoes, and so on—not too exciting, but providing comfort on a rainy day). Also look for *pimientos de Padrón*—miniature green peppers sautéed in olive oil with a heavy dose of salt.

For a quick meal on the go, grab a traditional meat pie, or *empanada,* which comes *de carne* (with beef), *de bonito* or *de atún* (tuna), *de bacalao* (cod)—and these days, even *de pulpo* (octopus).

And for dessert: Locals enjoy cheese with honey at the end of a meal. In the tourist zones, bakeries push samples of *tarta de Santiago,* the local almond cake. Historically, the cake was (and still is) cooked by sisters in Santiago's convents. If you're sampling each place, don't fake like it's your first...they know the trick.

Iacobus began by offering a variety of foreign coffees—and, according to the owner, the best *churros* in Santiago—back in 1995. Success led them to open a few other locales, including one in the old center that has a good choice of wine and above-average food (especially for such a touristy area). End your meal with a cool, crisp *chupito de licor de hierbas*—a locally-produced, Mountain Dew–colored herb liqueur (€12 main dishes, daily 13:00–16:00 & 20:00–23:00, Azabachería 5, tel. 981-582-804).

Restaurante Don Gaiferos is a classy, highly regarded splurge under a mighty stone vault (€15–20 main dishes, Tue–Sat 13:15–15:45 & 20:15–23:15, Sun–Mon 13:15–15:45 only, Rúa Nova 23, tel. 981-583-894).

Bar Restaurante La Churrasquita is a colorful place facing the little church just behind the market. At the bar, the local gang watches TV and tosses things on the floor. At the little restaurant in the back, women meet after doing their market chores (€5–10 meals, open all day, full meals served 13:00–16:00 & 21:00–23:00, Plazuela de San Felix 6, tel. 981-582-657).

Restaurante Casa Manolo is where students on a tight budget go for a classy meal out. This smart little eatery combines sleek contemporary design, good Galician and Spanish food, and excellent prices. The service is rushed, but the value is unbeatable (€7 fixed-price meal gives you two very generous courses, plus water, bread, and dessert; Mon–Sat 13:00–16:00 & 20:30–23:30, Sun 13:00–16:00, at the bottom of Praza de Cervantes, tel. 981-582-950).

Just outside the Historical Center, near the Museum of the Galician People

O Dezaseis (literally, "The Sixteen") is every local's favorite: a friendly, laid-back cellar with stone walls, heavy beams, and interesting art, strewn with old farm implements (€4–9 *raciones*, €10–12 meat and fish dishes, Mon–Sat 14:00–16:00 & 20:30–24:00, closed Sun, Rúa de San Pedro 16, tel. 981-564-880).

La Bodeguilla de San Roque offers enormous portions of local specialties in a relaxed, neighborhood atmosphere. If the upstairs restaurant is full, have a drink at the bar to pass the time. The wine list occupies most of the menu, so order a bottle of crisp *albariño* wine to accompany your *pulpo a feira* (€9 *raciones* fill two people, Rúa da San Roque 13, Mon–Sat 14:00–16:00 & 20:00–23:30, closed Sun, tel. 981-564-379).

Ambitus Veter Bar is a street-side, smoky place lively with locals, greasy tapas, and cheap meals (Rúa Aller Ulloa 3).

Cafés

Café Costa Vella, actually the breakfast room and garden of a highly recommended hotel (see "Sleeping," page 182), welcomes non-guests for coffee and a relaxing break in a poetic, time-warp garden with leafy views (daily 8:00–23:00, Rúa da Porta da Pena 17, tel. 981-569-530).

Café Casino, a former private club, is a tired taste of turn-of-the-20th-century elegance with occasional live piano music. Local tour guides recommend this smoky café to their timid British groups, who wouldn't touch an octopus with a 10-foot pole (€4 salads, €6 pizzas, daily 9:00–23:00, Rúa do Vilar 35).

Café Terra Nova really is the "new land" for four men from Houston. These *quatro hombres de Téxas* (Matt, Troy, Scott, and Brian) relocated here with their families to run a fine and friendly café three minutes from the cathedral. This can be a welcoming place to hang out with expat Americans to learn more about Santiago (daily 9:00–24:00, Wi-Fi access, just across from the police station at Rodrigo de Padrón 2, tel. 981-573-490).

TRANSPORTATION CONNECTIONS

From Santiago de Compostela by Train to: Madrid (3/day, 8.5–13 hrs, overnight train departs at 22:30, arrives in Madrid Atocha at 8:30), **Salamanca** (2/day, take Madrid-bound train, transfer in Medina del Campo, 9 hrs), **León** (1/day, 6 hrs), **Bilbao** (2/day, 11–13 hrs), **San Sebastián** (4/day, 11–14 hrs), **Santander** (3/day, 13 hrs, overnight option, transfer in Palencia), **Porto, Portugal** (2/day, 5 hrs, with transfers). Train info: tel. 902-240-202.

By Bus to: Madrid (6/day, 7–9 hrs, includes night bus 21:30–6:30, arrives at the southern Méndez Álvaro station), **Salamanca** (1/day, 6.5 hrs), **León** (1/day, 6.5 hrs), **Bilbao** (3/day, 2 continue to **San Sebastián**, includes 1 night bus, 11 hrs), **Porto,** Portugal (3–4/week, 4 hrs). Bus info: tel. 981-542-416. All Spain destinations are served by the Alsa bus company (tel. 902-422-242, www.alsa.es).

SALAMANCA

This sunny sandstone city boasts Spain's grandest plaza, its oldest university, and a fascinating history, all swaddled in a strolling, college-town ambience. Salamanca—a youthful and untouristy Toledo—is a series of monuments and clusters of cloisters. The many students help keep prices down. Take a paseo with the local crowd down Rúa Mayor and through Plaza Mayor. The young people congregate until late in the night, chanting and cheering, talking and singing. When I asked a local woman why young men all alone on the Plaza Mayor suddenly break into song, she said, "Doesn't it happen where you live?"

Planning Your Time

Salamanca, with its art, university, and atmospheric Plaza Mayor,

is worth a day and a night, but it is stuck out in the boonies. It's feasible as a side-trip—though not a day trip—from Madrid (it's 2.5 hours one-way from Madrid by car, bus, or train). If you're bound for Santiago de Compostela or Portugal, Salamanca is a natural stop.

ORIENTATION

Tourist Information

The main TI is on **Plaza Mayor** (Mon–Fri 9:00–14:00 & 16:30–20:00, Sat 10:00–20:00, closes Mon–Sat at 18:30 in winter, Sun

10:00–14:00, Plaza Mayor 19, tel. 923-218-342). Pick up the free map, city brochure, and current list of museum hours. Another TI at **Casa de Las Conchas** on Rúa Mayor serves the region and province, as well as the city (June–Sept Sun–Thu 9:00–20:00, Fri–Sat 9:00–21:00; Oct–May daily 9:00–14:00 & 17:00–20:00, tel. 923-268-571). Summertime-only TIs spring up at the train and bus stations. There's little in the way of organized tourism for the English-speaking visitor.

Arrival in Salamanca

From either Salamanca's train or bus station to Plaza Mayor, it's a 25-minute walk, an easy bus ride (€0.75, pay driver), or a €5 trip by taxi. Day-trippers can store bags in either station's lockers (*consignas*, bus station-€2, at bay level facing main building on your left; train station: small locker-€3, large locker-€4.50).

By Train: To walk to the center, exit left and walk down to the ring road, cross it at Plaza de España, then angle slightly left up Calle Azafranal. Or you can take bus #1 from the train station, which lets you off at Plaza del Mercado (the market), next to Plaza Mayor.

By Bus: To walk to the center, exit right and walk down Avenida Filiberto Villalobos; take a left on the ring road and the first right on Ramón y Cajal, head through Plaza de las Augustinas, and continue on Calle Prior to reach Plaza Mayor. Or take bus #4 (exit station right, catch bus on same side of the street as the station) to the city center; the closest stop is on Gran Vía, about two blocks east of Plaza Mayor (ask the driver or a fellow passenger, "*¿Para Plaza Mayor?*").

By Car: Drivers will find a handy underground parking lot at Plaza Santa Eulalia (€1/hr, €9.80/day, open 24/7). Two other convenient lots are Parking Plaza Campillo (€8.20/day) and Lemans (€12/day).

Helpful Hints

Book Ahead in Fall: A religious festival in fall (Sept 1–Oct 12) can fill up hotels and increase room prices.

Internet Access: Cyberplace Internet is at Plaza Mayor 10 (Mon–Fri 11:00–24:00, Sat–Sun 11:00–23:00, first floor, tel. 923-264-281). **Over The Game,** with 40 computers and a starry galaxy theme, is at Varillas 24 (daily 11:00–24:00, tel. 923-216-991). Perhaps your most efficient Internet access is at the laundry (see below).

Laundry: It's a five-minute walk from Plaza Mayor to the self-serve laundry (€6.50 for wash and dry, Mon–Fri 9:30–14:00 & 16:00–20:00, Sat 10:00–14:00, closed Sun and Aug 15–30, Pasaje Azafranal 18, located in passageway a half-block north

Salamanca Area

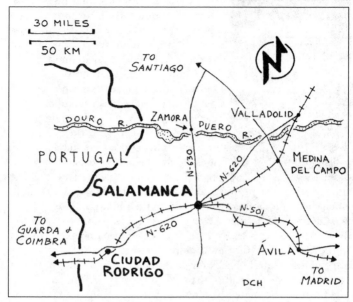

of Plaza Santa Eulalia). Cleverly, it has five online computers (€2/hr, helpful Juan Carlos).

Travel Agency: Viajes Salamanca, which books flights, trains, and some buses, including buses to Coimbra, Portugal, is on Plaza Mayor at #11 (tel. 923-211-414).

Local Guide: Ines Criado Velasco, a good English-speaking guide, is happy to tailor a town walk to your interests (€75/2 hrs—a special rate for readers of this book in 2007, €90/3–5 hrs, €150/day, for groups of 1–30, tel. 923-207-414, mobile 609-557-528, inescriado@yahoo.es).

SIGHTS

▲▲**Plaza Mayor**—Built from 1729 to 1755, this ultimate Spanish plaza is a fine place to nurse a cup of coffee (try the venerable Art Nouveau–style Café Novelty) and watch the world go by.

The town hall, with the clock, grandly overlooks the square. The Arco del Toro (built into the eastern wall) leads to the covered market. While most European squares honor a king or saint, this golden-toned square—ringed by famous Castilians—is for all the people. The square niches above the colonnade surrounding the square depict writers (Miguel de Cervantes), and heroes and conquistadors (Christopher Columbus and Hernán Cortés), as well as numerous kings and dictators (Franco).

Plaza Mayor has long been Salamanca's community living room. The most important place in town, it seems to be continually hosting some kind of party. Imagine the excitement of the days (until 1893), when bullfights were held in the square. Now old-timers gather here each day, remembering an earlier time when the girls would promenade clockwise around the colonnade while the boys cruised counterclockwise, looking for the perfect *queso* (cheese), as they'd call a cute dish. Perhaps the best time of all for people-watching is Sunday after Mass (13:00–15:00) when the grandmothers gather here in their Sunday best.

▲▲**Cathedrals, Old and New**—These cool-on-a-hot-day cathedrals share buttresses, and are both richly ornamented. You get to the old through the new. Before entering the new church, check out its ornate front door (west portal on Rúa Mayor). The **facade** is decorated Plateresque, with masonry so intricate it looks like silverwork. It's Spain's version of Flamboyant Gothic. At the side door (around the corner to the left as you face the main entrance), look for the astronaut added by a capricious restorer in 1993. This caused an outrage in town, but now locals shrug their shoulders and say, "He's the person closest to God." I'll give you a chance to find him on your own. Otherwise, look at the end of this listing for help.

The **"new" cathedral** was built from 1513 to 1733, and is a spacious, towering mix of Gothic, Renaissance, and Baroque. Fancy stone trim is everywhere, and the dome decoration is particularly wonderful. Occasionally the music is live, not recorded. The *coro*, or choir, blocks up half of the church (normal for Spanish Gothic), but its wood carving is sumptuous; look up to see the recently restored, elaborate organ (free, daily April–Sept 9:00–20:00, Oct–March 9:00–13:00 & 16:00–18:00).

The entrance to the **old cathedral** (12th-century Romanesque) is near the rear of the new one (€3.50, free English leaflet, daily April–Sept 10:00–19:30, Oct–March 10:00–12:30 & 16:00–17:30; during Mass the old cathedral is free, but the cloister isn't). Sit in a front pew to study the altarpiece's 53 scenes from the lives of Mary and Jesus (by the Italian Florentino, 1445) surrounding a precious

Salamanca

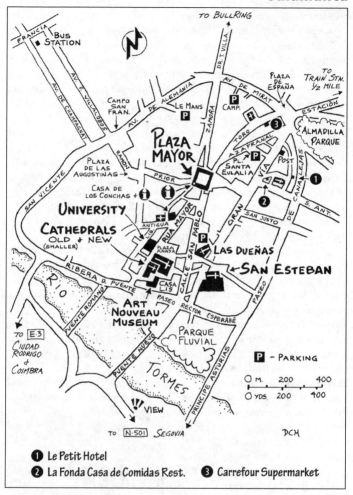

❶ Le Petit Hotel
❷ La Fonda Casa de Comidas Rest.
❸ Carrefour Supermarket

12th-century statue of the Virgin of the Valley. High above, notice the dramatic Last Judgment fresco of Jesus sending condemned souls into the literal jaws of hell.

Head into the **cloister** (off the right transept) and explore the chapels, notable for their unusual tombs, ornate altarpieces, and ceilings with leering faces. In the Capilla de Santa Barbara (second on the left as you enter), you can sit like students did for their tests. During these final exams, a stern circle of professors formed around the student at the tomb of the Salamanca bishop, who founded the University of Salamanca around 1230. (The university originated with a group of teacher/priests who met in this room.)

As you continue through the cloister, you'll see the chapter-house *(salas capitulares)*, contained in three rooms on your left, with a gallery of 15th-century Castilian paintings. Next is the Capilla de Santa Catalina, with two rows of spooky saint statues and two original gargoyles from the cathedral, in the form of a seahorse and a frog. The Capilla de Anaya, farthest from the cloister entrance, has a gorgeously carved 16th-century alabaster tomb (with the dog and lion at its foot making peace—or negotiating who gets to eat the worried-looking rabbit) and a wooden, 16th-century Mudejar organ. (Mudejar is the Romanesque-Islamic style Moorish design made in Spain after the Christian conquest.)

For a fantastic view of the upper floors and terraces of both cathedrals and a look at the inside passages, visit the **tower** (marked *Jerónimos*). It was sealed after Lisbon's 1755 earthquake to create structural support, and reopened in 2003. Exit the cathedral to the left to find a separate entrance around the corner (€2.50, daily 10:00–19:15).

Finally, go find that astronaut: He's just a little guy, about the size of a Ken-does-Mars doll, entwined in the stone trim to the left of the door, roughly 10 feet up. If you like that, check out the dragon (an arm's length below). Historians debate whether he's eating an ice cream cone or singing karaoke.

Tourist Tram—The small tram you might see waiting at the cathedral does 20-minute loops throughout the town with a Spanish narration (€3, daily 10:00–14:00 & 16:00–20:00, departs every 20 min from cathedral, mobile 649-625-703).

▲▲**University**—The University of Salamanca, the oldest in Spain (est. 1230), was one of Europe's leading centers of learning for 400 years. Columbus came here for travel tips. Today, while no longer so prestigious, it's laden with history and popular with Americans, who enjoy its excellent summer program. The old lecture halls around the cloister, where many of Spain's Golden

Age heroes studied, are open to the public (€4, free Mon mornings, Mon–Fri 9:30–13:30 & 16:00–19:30, Sat until 19:00, Sun 10:00–13:30, last entry 30 min before closing, enter from Calle Libreros, tel. 923-294-400, ext. 1150).

The ornately decorated grand **entrance** of the university is a great example of Spain's Plateresque style. The people studying the facade aren't art fans. They're trying to find a tiny frog on a skull that students looked to for good luck.

But forget the frog. Follow the facade's symbolic meaning. It was made in three sections by Charles V. The bottom celebrates the Catholic monarchs. Ferdinand and Isabel saw that the university had no buildings befitting its prestige, and granted the money for this building. The Greek script says something like "From the monarchs, this university. From the university, this tribute as a thanks."

The immodest middle section celebrates the grandson of Ferdinand and Isabel, Charles V. He appears with his queen, the Hapsburg double-headed eagle, and the complex coat of arms of the mighty Hapsburg empire. Since this is a Renaissance structure, it features Greek and Roman figures in the shells. And, as a statement of educational independence from medieval Church control, the top shows the pope flanked by Hercules and Venus.

After paying admission, you get a free English-language leaflet full of details; to follow it, go left (clockwise around the courtyard) upon entering.

In the **Hall of Fray Luís de León,** the narrow wooden beam tables and benches—whittled down by centuries of studious doodling—are originals. Professors spoke from the Church-threatening *cátedra,* or pulpit. It was here that free-thinking brother Luís de León returned, after the Inquisition jailed and tortured him for five years for challenging the Church's control of the word of God by translating part of the Bible into Castilian. He started his first post-imprisonment lecture with, "As we were saying..." Such courageous men of truth believed the forces of the Inquisition were not even worth acknowledging.

The altarpiece in the chapel on the opposite side of the courtyard depicts professors swearing to Mary's virginity. (How did they know?) Climb upstairs for a peek into the oldest library in Spain. Outside the library, look into the courtyard at the American sequoia, brought here 150 years ago and standing all alone. Notice also the big nests in the bell tower. Storks stop here from February through August on their annual journey from northern Europe to Morocco. There are hundreds of such stork nests in Salamanca.

As you leave the university, you'll see the statue of Fray Luís de León. Behind him, to your left, is the entrance to a peaceful courtyard. Within the courtyard is the Museum of the University, notable for Gallego's fanciful 15th-century *Sky of Salamanca* (free, Sun–Mon 10:00–14:00, Tue–Sat 10:00–14:00 & 16:00–20:00, no photos allowed).

Can't forget about the frog? It's on the right pillar of the facade, nearly halfway up, on the leftmost of three skulls.

▲**Art Nouveau Museum (Museo Art Nouveau y Art Deco)**— Located in the Casa Lis, this museum—with its beautifully displayed collection of stained glass, vases, furniture, jewelry, cancan statuettes, and toy dolls—is a refreshing change of pace. Nowhere else in Spain will you enjoy an Art Nouveau collection in a building from the same era. Find the stunning sculptures of Josephine Baker and Carmen Miranda, along with lots of pieces by René Lalique. The museum is a donation of a private collection. The English brochure contains a translation of the Spanish text posted in each room of the collection (€3, Tue–Fri 11:00–14:00 & 17:00–20:00, Sat–Sun 11:00–20:00, closed Mon, strictly no photos—required camera check at ticket counter, between the new/old cathedrals and the river at Calle Gibraltar 14, tel. 923-121-425, www.museocasalis.org).

Church of San Esteban—Dedicated to St. Stephen (Esteban) the martyr, this complex contains a recently restored cloister, tombs, museum, sacristy, and church. Tour it in this order: fancy facade outside, altarpiece in main nave, upstairs to sit in the choir, and finally a browse through the museum.

Before you enter, notice the Plateresque facade and its bas-relief of the stoning of St. Stephen. The crucifixion above is by Benvenuto Cellini. Once inside, follow the free English pamphlet. The nave is overwhelmed by a 100-foot, 4,000-piece wood altarpiece by José Benito Churriguera (1665–1725) that replaced the original Gothic one in 1693. You'll see St. Dominic on the left, St. Francis on the right, and a grand monstrance holding the Communion wafers in the middle, all below a painting of St. Stephen being stoned. This is a textbook example of the intricately detailed churrigueresque style that influenced many South American mission buildings. Quietly ponder the dusty, gold-plated cottage cheese, as tourists shake their heads and say "too much" in their mother tongue.

Upstairs, step into the balcony choir loft for a fine overview of the nave. The staircase itself is architecturally unique, built without any interior support; the staircase is still standing, but you'll notice when you walk, you definitely lean inward. The big spinnable book holder in the middle of the room held big music books—large enough for all to chant from in an age when there weren't enough books for everyone.

The museum next door has temperature-controlled glass cases that preserve illustrated 16th-century Bibles and choir books. Notice also how the curved ivory Filipino saints all look like they're carved out of an elephant's tusk. And don't miss the fascinating "chocolate box reliquaries" on the wall from 1580. Survey whose bones are collected between all the inlaid ivory and precious woods (€2, daily 10:00–14:00 & 16:00–20:00, closes at 18:00 in winter, tel. 923-215-000).

Convento de las Dueñas—Located next door to the Church of San Esteban, the much simpler *convento* is a joy. It consists of a double-decker cloister with a small museum of religious art. Check out the stone meanies exuberantly decorating the capitals on the cloister's upper deck (€1.50, daily 10:30–12:45 & 16:30–18:45, closes 17:30 in winter, no English info). The nuns sell sweets daily except Sunday (€3/small box of specialty *amarillos*—almond, egg white, and sugar; €1/small bag of cookies, no assortments possible even though their display box raises hopes).

Roman Bridge—Historians enjoy the low-slung Roman Bridge (Puente Romano), much of it original, spanning the Río Tormes. The *ibérico* (ancient pre-Roman) faceless bull blindly guards the entrance to the bridge; you'll find this symbol of Salamanca on every city coat-of-arms in town. Nearby, at Parque Fluvial, you can rent rowboats (June–Sept only).

▲Tuna Music—Traditionally, Salamanca's poorer students earned money to fund their education by singing in the streets. This 15th- to 18th-century tradition sur- vives today, as musical groups of students (representing the various faculties)—dressed in the traditional black capes and leggings—play mando- lins, guitars, and sing. They serenade the public in the bars on and around the Plaza Mayor. The name *tuna*, which has nothing to do with fish, refers to a vagabond student lifestyle, and later was applied to the music these students sing. They're out only on summer weeknights (sing- ing for tips from 22:00 until after midnight), because they make more serious money performing for weddings on weekends.

SLEEPING

Salamanca, a student town, has plenty of good eating and sleep- ing values. All but one of my listings (Le Petit Hotel) are on or within a three-minute walk of the Plaza Mayor. Directions are given from the Plaza Mayor, assuming you are facing the building with the clock (e.g., 3 o'clock is 90 degrees to your right as you face the clock).

$$$ Petit Palace Las Torres, on Plaza Mayor, is a remodeled place with 53 modern, spacious rooms and all the amenities. Its rooms with Plaza Mayor views cost the same as viewless rooms (Sb-€55–100, Db-€70–140, Tb-€100–170, low-range prices for weekdays, 30 percent more Sept 1–Oct 12 during religious festival, breakfast-€8, air-con, elevator, parking-€10/day at nearby Lemans lot, hotel entry just off square at Calle Concejo 4 or from the square at Plaza Mayor 26, exit the plaza at 11 o'clock, tel. 923-212-100, fax 923-212-101, www.hthotels.com, tor@hthotels.com).

$$$ Hotel Don Juan, a block off Plaza Mayor, has 16 classy,

Sleep Code

(€1 = about $1.20, country code: 34)
S = Single, **D** = Double/Twin, **T** = Triple, **Q** = Quad, **b** = bathroom,
s = shower only. Unless otherwise noted, credit cards are accepted, English is spoken, and the IVA tax (7 percent) and breakfast are not included.

To help you easily sort through these listings, I've divided the rooms into three categories, based on the price for a standard double room with bath during high season:

$$$ **Higher Priced**—Most rooms €70 or more.
$$ **Moderately Priced**—Most rooms between €40–70.
$ **Lower Priced**—Most rooms €40 or less.

comfy rooms and an attached restaurant (Sb-€53, Db-€72, Tb-€97, 20 percent cheaper in Nov–Feb, air-con, elevator, valet parking in their own private lot-€10/day—give them 10 min to bring your car, exit Plaza Mayor at about 5 o'clock and turn right to Quintana 6, tel. 923-261-473, fax 923-262-475, www.hoteldonjuan-salamanca .com, info@hoteldonjuan-salamanca.com, David or Livia).

$$$ Hotel Salamanca Plaza del Mercado, across the street from the covered market, is a business-class hotel that rents 38 shiny, modern rooms (Sb-€50, Db-€90, Tb/Qb-€100–125, air-con, elevator, parking-€9/day, Plaza del Mercado 16, about 4 o'clock from Plaza Mayor, tel. 923-272-250, fax 923-270-932, www .salamancaplaza.com, reservas@salamancaplaza.com).

$$ Hostal Plaza Mayor, with 19 finely decorated but small rooms, has a good location a block southwest of Plaza Mayor (Sb-€36, Db-€60, Tb-€90, air-con, most rooms served by elevator, exit Plaza Mayor at 7 o'clock, Plaza del Corrillo 20, attached restaurant, tel. 923-262-020, fax 923-217-548, hostalplazamayor @hotmail.com).

$$ Le Petit Hotel, while away from the characteristic core, faces a peaceful park and a church, two blocks east of Gran Vía. It rents 23 spotless and homey yet modern rooms. The rooms with views of the church are brightest; ask for a *vista de iglesia* (Sb-€36, Db-€49, Tb-€59, Qb-€69, breakfast-€3.50, cash only, air-con, elevator, no one at desk at night, Ronda Sancti Spiritus 39, about 6 blocks east of Plaza Mayor; exit Plaza Mayor at 3 o'clock and continue east, turn left on Gran Vía, right on Sancti Spiritus at Banco Simeon, and left after the church; tel. 923-600-773, no fax, www .lepetithotel.net, reserve by simply calling and leaving your name and time of arrival no more than 15 days in advance, Hortensia doesn't speak English).

Central Salamanca

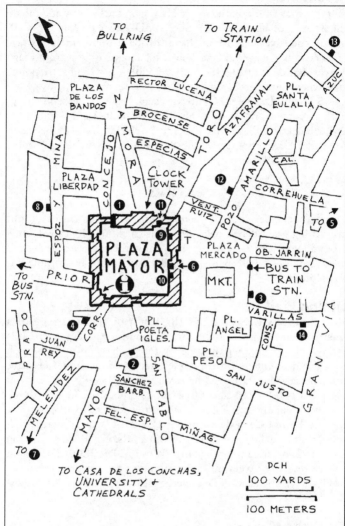

1. Petit Palace Las Torres
2. Hotel Don Juan
3. Hotel Salamanca Plaza del Mercado
4. Hostal Plaza Mayor
5. To Le Petit Hotel &
   Rest. La Fonda Casa de Comidas
6. Hostal Los Angeles & Internet Café
7. To Hostal Las Vegas Centro
8. Restaurante Chez Victor
9. Café Real
10. Cervantes Bar Restaurant
11. Café Novelty
12. Restaurante Isidro &
    Restaurante Comercio
13. Launderette & Internet Access
14. Internet Café

$ Hostal Los Angeles rents 15 simple but cared-for rooms, four of which overlook the square. Stand on the balcony and inhale the essence of Spain (S-€14, Sb-€20, D-€26, Db-€50, Tb-€60, more expensive view rooms have full bathrooms, includes tax, breakfast on plaza-€4, Plaza Mayor 10, about 3 o'clock from Plaza Mayor, tel. & fax 923-218-166, Orlando). View rooms are popular—when you reserve, request *"Con vista, por favor."*

$ Hostal Las Vegas Centro is clean, bright, quiet, and cheap, with 17 cozy rooms (S-€18, Sb-€20, Db-€30–36, Tb-€50, Qb-€65, 2 blocks off Plaza Mayor, about 7 o'clock, toward cathedral at Meléndez 13, first floor, tel. & fax 923-218-749, www.lasvegascentro.com, lasvegas@ono.com).

EATING

Local specialties include *serrano* ham, which is in just about everything (see sidebar, page 201), roast suckling pig (called *tostón* around here), and *sopa de ajo*, the local garlic soup. *Patatas meneadas* (potatoes with Spanish paprika and bacon) is a simple but tasty local tapa.

Dining Well

Restaurante Chez Victor is the result of the marriage of a Castilian chef (Victor) and a French food-lover (Margarite). This family-run place, elegantly decorated with a feminine French touch and bouquets on the tables, serves modern and creative Franco/Castilian fare—perhaps your best €35–40 meal in town (Tue–Sat 14:00–15:30 & 21:00–23:30, Sun 14:00–15:30, closed Sun eve and Mon, air-con, Espoz y Mina 26, tel. 923-213-123).

La Fonda Casa de Comidas is a dark, woody place with solid, traditional cuisine that caters to locals. You'll happily spend about €22 for three courses (daily 13:30–16:30 & 21:00–23:30, a bit smoky, reserve on weekends, 15 yards down the arcade from corner of Gran Vía and Cuesta de Sancti Spiritus at La Reja 2, tel. 923-215-712).

On Plaza Mayor

Here you can enjoy a meal sitting on the finest square in Spain, and savor some of Europe's best people-watching. The bars, with little tables spilling onto the square, serve *raciones* and €2 glasses of wine. A *ración de la casa* (house specialty of hams, sausages, and cheese), a *ración* of *patatas bravas* (chunks of potatoes with tomato sauce), and two glasses of wine makes a nice dinner for two for about €25—one of the best eating values in all of Europe. For dessert, stroll with an ice cream cone from Café Novelty.

Café Real serves bar snacks in a tapas style (open daily).

Sampling Serrano Ham

Jamón serrano is cured in the *sierras* (mountains) of Spain. While there are many variations of this cured ham from dif-  ferent regions of Spain, Spanish people have a special appreciation for *jamón ibérico*, made with the back legs of black pigs fed mainly on acorns. Originating in Spain, these black pigs are fatter and happier (slaughtered much later than regular pigs). Spaniards treasure memories of grandpa thinly carving a *jamón*, supported in a *jamonero* (ham holder) during Christmas just as we savor the turkey-carving at Thanksgiving. To sample this delicacy without the high price tag you'll find in bars and restaurants, go to the local market, ask for 100 grams (*cien gramos de jamón ibérico extra;* about €70/kilo) and enjoy it as a picnic with red wine and bread.

Cervantes Bar is more of a restaurant, with a wide selection of meals, €7 salads, and sandwiches. They also have an indoors section, overlooking Plaza Mayor from one floor up; it's a popular student hangout (tapas daily 10:00–21:00, meals from 12:30, tel. 923-217-213).

Café Novelty is Plaza Mayor's Art Nouveau cafe. It dates from 1905—and has some customers who look like they've been there since it opened. It's filled with character and literary memories. The metal sculpture depicts a famous local writer, Torrente Ballester (daily 8:00–24:00). Their ice cream sweetens a stroll around the plaza.

Eating Simply, But Well

There are plenty of good, inexpensive restaurants between Plaza Mayor and Gran Vía, and as you leave the Plaza Mayor toward Rúa Mayor. The tapas places along and around Rúa Mayor are abundant and often overrun with students.

Restaurante Isidro is a thriving local favorite—a straight-forward, hard-working eatery run by Alberto—offering a good assortment of fish and specialty meat dishes (€9 fixed-price meal, also à la carte €15–20 dinners, Mon–Sat 13:00–16:00 & 20:00–24:00, Sun 13:00–16:00, big portions, good roasts, seating available in its *comedor,* quick and friendly service, Pozo Amarillo 19, about a block north of covered market near Plaza Mayor, tel. 923-262-848).

Restaurante Comercio, next door, has tasty food and is warmly decorated with old photos of the square. Their specialities include *sopa del obispo* (hearty soup) and oxtail stew. The €9 fixed-price meal also works for dinner, or consider their €15–20 à la carte meals (daily 12:30–16:00 & 19:30–24:00, Pozo Amarillo 23, tel. 923-260-280).

The **Pans & Company** sandwich chain is always fast and affordable, with a branch on Calle Prior across from Burger King and another on Rúa Mayor (daily 10:00–24:00).

Picnics: The covered *mercado* (market) on Plaza Mercado has fresh fruits and veggies (Mon–Sat 8:00–14:30, closed Sun, on east side of Plaza Mayor). A small El Arbol grocery, three blocks east of Plaza Mayor, has just the basics (Mon–Sat 9:30–21:00, closed Sun). For variety, the big Carrefour Express Supermercado is your best bet, but it's a six-block walk north of Plaza Mayor on Toro (Mon–Sat 9:00–21:30, closed Sun, across from Plaza San Juan de Sahagún and its church).

If you always wanted seconds at Communion, buy a bag of giant Communion wafers, a local specialty called *obleas.*

TRANSPORTATION CONNECTIONS

From Salamanca by Train to: Madrid (6/day, 2.5 hrs, Chamartín station), **Ávila** (6/day, 1 hr), **Barcelona** (2/day, 8:00 and 20:25 departure, 10 hrs), **Santiago** (2/day, 9 hrs, transfer in Medina del Campo), **Lisbon,** Portugal (1/day, 5 hrs, departs Salamanca station at about 4:50 in the morning, no kidding; you can catch a taxi to the train station at any hour from Plaza Mercado—a few steps east of Plaza Mayor—and from Plaza Poeta Iglesias, which is across from the Gran Hotel, immediately south of Plaza Mayor, taxi ride costs €4 during day, €5 at night; for **Coimbra,** see below). Train info: tel. 902-240-202.

By Bus to: Madrid (€15, hourly express, 2.5 hrs, arrives at Madrid's Conde de Casal station, Auto-Res buses, www.auto-res .com), **Segovia** (2/day, 3 hrs; consider a brief visit to Ávila en route, Auto-Res or La Sepulvedana buses), **Ávila** (4/day, 1.5 hrs Auto-Res buses), **Ciudad Rodrigo** (nearly hourly, 1 hr, El Pilar buses), **Santiago** (1/day, 6.5 hrs), **Barcelona** (2/day, 11 hrs, Alsa buses), **Coimbra,** Portugal (1/day, departs at 12:00, 5.25 hrs, same bus continues to **Lisbon** in 9 hrs, Alsa buses, tel. 902-422-242, www .alsa.es). Bus info: tel. 923-236-717.

Ciudad Rodrigo

Ciudad Rodrigo is worth a visit only if you're driving from Salamanca to Coimbra, Portugal (although buses connect Salamanca and Ciudad Rodrigo with surprising efficiency in about an hour).

This rough-and-tumble old town of 16,000 people caps a hill overlooking the Río Agueda. Spend an hour wandering among the Renaissance mansions that line its streets and exploring its cathedral and Plaza Mayor. Have lunch or a snack at **El Sanatorio** (Plaza Mayor 14). The tapas are cheap, the crowd is local, and the walls are a Ciudad Rodrigo scrapbook, including some bullfighting that makes the Three Stooges look demure.

Ciudad Rodrigo's cathedral—pockmarked with scars from Napoleonic cannon balls—has some entertaining carvings in the choir and some pretty racy work in its cloisters. Who says, "When you've seen one Gothic church, you've seen 'em all"?

The **TI** is two blocks from Ciudad Rodrigo's Plaza Mayor, just inside the old wall near the cathedral (Mon–Fri 9:00–14:00 & 17:00–19:00, Sat–Sun 10:00–12:00 & 17:00–20:00, Plaza Ameyuelas 5, tel. 923-460-561). They can recommend a good hotel, such as **Hotel Conde Rodrigo** (34 rooms, Sb-€70, Db-€75, Tb-€93, air-con, elevator, Plaza San Salvador 9, tel. 923-461-404, www.conderodrigo.com, info@conderodrigo.com).

MADRID

Today's Madrid is upbeat and vibrant, still enjoying a post-Franco renaissance. You'll feel it. Even the living-statue street performers have a twinkle in their eyes.

Madrid is the hub of Spain. This modern capital—Europe's highest, at more than 2,000 feet—has a population of 2.8 million. Like its people, the city is relatively young. In 1561, King Philip II decided to move the capital of his empire from Toledo to Madrid. One hundred years ago, Madrid had only 400,000 people—so the majority of today's Madrid is modern sprawl surrounding an intact, easy-to-navigate historic core.

The city's ambitious plans include the creation of a pedestrian street crossing the city from the Prado to the Royal Palace (the section from the Prado to Plaza Ángel has been completed) and a new macro-train station near Puerta del Sol (which will keep that subway station under construction until 2008). By installing posts to keep cars off sidewalks, making the streets safer after dark, and restoring old buildings, Madrid is working hard to make the city more livable...and fun to visit. In an effort to win the 2012 Olympics, Madrid began some massive city improvement building projects. Even though they lost out, the construction—which many locals believe is profitable for corrupt city officials who are getting kickbacks—continues as if they won.

Tourists are the real winners. Dive headlong into the grandeur and intimate charm of Madrid. The lavish Royal Palace, with its gilded rooms and frescoed ceilings, rivals Versailles. The Prado has Europe's top collection of paintings. The city's huge Retiro Park invites you for a shady siesta and a hopscotch through a mosaic of lovers, families, skateboarders, pets walking their masters, and expert bench-sitters. Save time for Madrid's elegant shops and people-friendly pedestrian zones. On Sundays, cheer for the bull at a bullfight or bargain like mad at a mega-size flea market. Lively Madrid has enough street-singing, bar-hopping, and people-watching vitality to give any visitor a boost of youth.

Planning Your Time

Divide your time between Madrid's top three attractions: the Royal Palace (worth a half day), the Prado museum (also worth a half day), and its bar-hopping contemporary scene. On a Sunday (Easter–Oct), consider allotting extra time for the flea market and/or a bullfight.

Madrid is worth two days on even the fastest trip. I'd spend them this way:

Day 1: Take a brisk, 20-minute good-morning-Madrid walk from Puerta del Sol to the Prado (from Puerta del Sol, walk three blocks south to Plaza del Ángel, then take the pedestrian walkway to the Prado along Huertas street). Spend the rest of the morning at the Prado, then take an afternoon siesta in Retiro Park, or tackle modern art at the Centro de Arte Reina Sofía (Picasso's *Guernica*) and/or the Thyssen-Bornemisza Museum. Have dinner at 20:00, with tapas around Plaza Santa Ana.

Day 2: Follow my "Welcome to Madrid" self-guided walk (see page 215), tour the Royal Palace, and have lunch near Plaza Mayor. Your afternoon is free for other sights, shopping, or a side-trip to El Escorial (open until 19:00 April–Sept, until 18:00 Oct–March—see next chapter). Be out at the magic hour—before sunset—when beautifully lit people fill Madrid.

Note that many top sights are closed on Monday, including the Prado, Thyssen-Bornemisza Museum, and El Escorial; sights remaining open on Monday include the Royal Palace (open daily) and Centro de Arte Reina Sofía (closed Tue). For good day-trip possibilities from Madrid, see the next two chapters (Northwest of Madrid and Toledo).

ORIENTATION

Puerta del Sol marks the center of Madrid. No major sight is more than a 20-minute walk or a €4 taxi ride from this central square. The Royal Palace (to the west) and the Prado Museum and Retiro Park (to the east) frame Madrid's historic center. This zone can be covered on foot. Southwest of Puerta del Sol is a 17th-century district with the slow-down-and-smell-the-cobbles Plaza Mayor and memories of pre-industrial Spain. North of Puerta del Sol runs Calle de Gran Vía, and between the two are lively pedestrian shopping streets. Gran Vía, bubbling with expensive shops and

Madrid

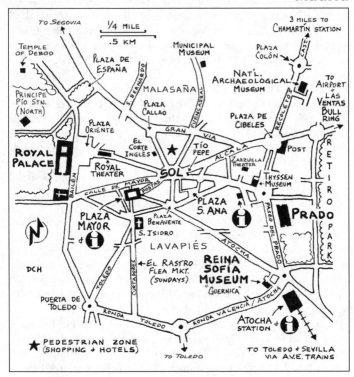

cinemas, leads to the modern Plaza de España. Between Puerta del Sol and the Atocha Train Station stretches the colorful, up-and-coming multiethnic Lavapiés district (see the "The Lavapiés District Tapas Crawl," page 263).

Tourist Information

Madrid has five TIs: on **Plaza Mayor** (daily 9:00–20:30, air-con, four Internet terminals, tel. 915-881-636); near the **Prado Museum** (Mon–Sat 9:00–20:00, Sun 9:00–14:00, Duque de Medinaceli 2, behind Palace Hotel, tel. 914-294-951); at **Chamartín Train Station** (Mon–Sat 8:00–20:00, Sun 8:00–15:00, tel. 913-159-976); at the **Atocha Train Station** (daily 9:00–21:00); and at the **airport** (daily 8:00–20:00, at Terminal 1 in arrival hall and Terminal 2 in baggage area before you go through customs, tel. 913-058-656). During the summer, small temporary stands pop up at touristed places such as Puerta del Sol and Plaza de España.

The general tourist information number is 915-881-636 (or pricier toll call: tel. 902-100-007; www.munimadrid.es).

At any TI, pick up a map and confirm your sightseeing plans.

The TI's free *Public Transport* map is very well-designed for travelers' needs, and has the most detailed map of the center. Get this and use it. TIs have the latest on bullfights and zarzuela (light Spanish opera). Only the most hyperactive travelers could save money buying the **Madrid Card,** which covers 40 museums and the Madrid Vision bus tour mentioned in "Tours," below (€38/24 hrs, €48/48 hrs, €58/72 hrs).

For entertainment listings, the TI's printed material is not very good. Pick up the Spanish-language weekly entertainment guide *Guía del Ocio* (€1, sold at newsstands). It lists daily live music ("Conciertos"), museums ("Museos"—with the latest times and special exhibits), restaurants (an exhaustive listing), kids' activities ("Los Ninos"), TV schedules, and movies ("*V.O.*" means original version, "*V.O. en ingles sub*" means a movie is played in English with Spanish subtitles rather than dubbed).

If you're heading to **other destinations in Spain,** ask any Madrid TI for free maps and brochures (ideally in English). Since many small-town TIs keep erratic hours and run out of these pamphlets, get what you can in Madrid. You can get schedules for buses and some trains, and thus avoid unnecessary trips to the various stations. The TI's free and amazingly informative *Mapa de Comunicaciones España* is a road map of Spain that lists all the tourist offices and highway SOS numbers. (If they're out, ask for the route map sponsored by the Paradores hotel chain, the camping map, or the golf map.)

For tips on sightseeing, hotels, and more, visit www.madridman.com, run with passion by American Scott Martin.

Arrival in Madrid

By Train: Madrid's two train stations, Chamartín and Atocha, are both on subway lines with easy access to downtown Madrid. Each station has all the services. Chamartín handles most international trains. Atocha generally covers southern Spain, including the AVE trains to Sevilla and Toledo. Both stations offer long-distance trains *(largo recorrido)* as well as smaller, local trains (*regionales* and *cercanías*) to nearby destinations. To travel between Chamartín and Atocha, skip the subway (which involves a transfer); the *cercanías* trains are faster (6/hr, 12 min, €1.20, free with railpass or any train ticket to Madrid—show it at ticket window in the middle of the turnstiles, departs from Atocha's track 2 and generally Chamartín's track 2 or 3—but check the *Salidas Inmediatas* board to be sure).

Chamartín Station: The **TI** is opposite track 19. The impressively large Centro de Viajes/Travel Center customer-service office is in the middle of the building. You can relax in the Sala VIP Club if you have a first-class railpass and first-class seat or sleeper reservations (near track 12, next to Centro de Viajes). The station's

Metro stop is Chamartín. (If you arrive by Metro at Chamartín, signs to *Información* lead to the lobby. Signs to *Vías* send you directly to the platforms.)

Atocha Station: The station is split into two halves: an AVE side (mostly long-distance trains) and a *cercanías* side (mostly local trains, nearest the Metro). These two parts are connected by a corridor of shops. Each side of the station has separate schedules and customer-service offices. The **TI,** which is in the AVE side, offers tourist info, but no train info (daily 9:00–21:00). There are three ticket offices at Atocha: The *cercanías* side has a small office for local trains and a big one for major trains (such as AVE). The AVE side has a pleasant, airy *Taquillas* office which also sells tickets for AVE and other long-distance trains. If the line at one office is long, check the other offices.

Atocha's **AVE side,** which is in the towering old-station building, is remarkable for the lush, tropical garden filling its grand hall. It has the slick AVE trains, other fast trains (Grandes Líneas), a pharmacy (daily 8:00–22:00), a cafeteria, and the wicker-elegant Samarkanda restaurant (Mon–Fri 13:00–20:00, Sat–Sun 11:00–20:00). In the departure lounge on the upper floor, TV monitors announce track numbers. For information, try the *Información* counter (daily 6:30–22:30), next to Centro Servicios AVE (which handles only AVE changes and problems). The *Atención al Cliente* office deals with problems on Grandes Líneas (daily 6:30–23:30). Also on the AVE side is the Club AVE, a lounge reserved solely for AVE business-class travelers and for first-class ticket-holders or Eurailers with a first-class reservation (upstairs, past the security check on right; free drinks, newspapers, showers, and info service).

On the *cercanías* **side** of Atocha Station, you'll find the local *cercanías* trains, *regionales* trains, some eastbound faster trains, and the Metro stop named "Atocha RENFE." (Note that the stop named simply "Atocha" is a different Metro stop in Madrid—not at the train station.) The *Atención al Cliente* office in the *cercanías* section has information only on trains to destinations near Madrid.

The terrorist bombing of March 11, 2004, took place in Atocha. Security is understandably tight here. There's a small memorial at the entry level (near where you exit the Metro, above the ticket sales booths) with computer terminals allowing visitors to leave a handprint and message and watch a memorial video (www.mascercanos.com).

Buying Tickets: Since station ticket offices can get really crowded, it's often quicker to buy your ticket at an English-speaking travel agency, such as the El Corte Inglés Travel Agency at Atocha (Mon–Fri 7:00–22:00, Sat–Sun only for urgent arrangements, on ground floor of AVE side at the far end) or at the El

Greater Madrid

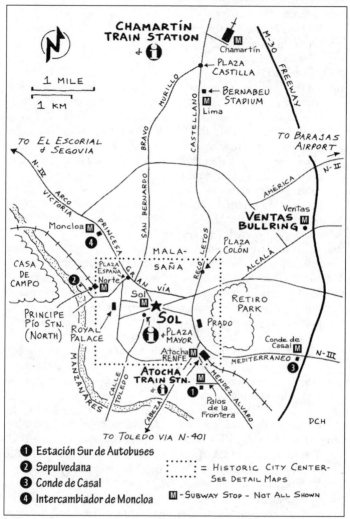

1 Estación Sur de Autobuses
2 Sepulvedana
3 Conde de Casal
4 Intercambiador de Moncloa

⋯⋯⋮ = HISTORIC CITY CENTER-
          SEE DETAIL MAPS

Ⓜ = SUBWAY STOP - NOT ALL SHOWN

Corte Inglés department store at Puerta del Sol (see "Helpful Hints," below). AVE passengers can avoid the trip to the station by reserving ahead by phone: Call 902-240-202 three days in advance, make a reservation, and pick up your ticket just before departure.

By Bus: Madrid's three key bus stations, all connected by the Metro are: Sepulvedana (for buses to Segovia; Metro: Príncipe Pío, garage next to Florida Norte Hotel); Estación Sur Autobuses (for Toledo, Ávila, and Granada; on top of Metro: Méndez Álvaro, tel. 902-222-282); and Estación Intercambiador (for El Escorial; in

Metro: Moncloa). For details, see "Transportation Connections" near the end of this chapter.

By Plane: For information on Madrid's Barajas Airport, see the end of this chapter.

Helpful Hints

Theft Alert: Be wary of pickpockets, anywhere, anytime. Areas of particular risk are Puerta del Sol (the central square), El Rastro (the flea market), Gran Vía (the paseo zone: Plaza del Callao to Plaza de España), the Ópera Metro station (or anywhere on the Metro), the airport, and any crowded streets. Assume a fight or any commotion is a scam to distract people about to become victims of a pickpocket. Wear your money belt. The small streets north of Gran Vía are particularly dangerous, even before nightfall. Muggings occur, but are rare. Victims of theft can call 902-102-112 for help (English spoken, once you get connected to a person).

Prostitution: Diverse by European standards, Madrid is spilling over with immigrants from South America, North Africa, and Eastern Europe. Many young women come here, fall on hard times, and end up on the streets. While it's illegal to make money from someone else selling sex (i.e., pimping), prostitutes get away with selling it directly on the street (€27, FYI). Calle de la Montera (leading from Puerta del Sol to Plaza Red de San Luís) is lined with what looks like a bunch of high-school girls skipping out of school for a cigarette break. Again, don't stray north of Gran Vía—while the streets may look inviting...it's a meat-eating flower.

Embassies: The US Embassy is at Serrano 75 (tel. 915-872-200); the Canadian Embassy is at Nuñez de Balboa 35 (tel. 914-233-250).

One-Stop Shopping: The dominant local department store is **El Corte Inglés,** which takes up several huge buildings in the commercial pedestrian zone just off Puerta del Sol (Mon–Sat 10:00–22:00, closed Sun, navigate with the help of the info desk near the door of the main building—the tallest building with the biggest sign). They give out fine, free Madrid maps. In the main building, you'll find two handy travel agencies (see listing below), a post office, and a supermarket with a fancy "Club del Gourmet" section in the basement. Across the street is its Librería branch—a huge bookstore and six floors of music and home electronics, with a box office for tickets to whatever's on in town. Locals figure you'll find anything you need at El Corte Inglés.

Internet Access: There are plenty of centrally located places to check your e-mail. Consider **NavegaWeb** (daily 9:00–24:00, Gran Vía 30) and the noisy, coin-operated **Zahara** (Mon–Fri

9:00–24:00, Sat–Sun 9:00–24:00, corner of Gran Vía and Mesoneros). Near Plaza Santa Ana (and great if you're waiting for the tapas crawl action to heat up), **Cyber Total** has plenty of fast terminals (€2/hr), disk-burning services, and helpful staff (daily 10:00–22:00, Calle Espoz y Mina 17, tel. 915-322-622). If you'd like to simultaneously wash clothes and surf, see "Laundry," below.

Bookstores: For books in English, try **NFAC Callao** (Calle Preciados 8, tel. 915-956-100), **Casa del Libro** (English on ground floor in back, Gran Vía 29, tel. 915-212-219), and **El Corte Inglés** (guidebooks and some fiction, in its Librería branch kitty-corner from main store, fronting Puerta del Sol—see listing above).

Laundry: Onda Blu will wash, dry, and fold your laundry for €5, including soap (Mon–Fri 9:30–22:00, Sat–Sun 10:30–19:00, self-service available, change machine, four Internet terminals, León 3, east of Plaza Santa Ana, tel. 913-695-071, Ana).

Travel Agencies: The grand department store, El Corte Inglés, has two travel agencies (air and rail tickets, but not reservations for railpass-holders, €2 fee, on first and seventh floors, Mon–Sat 10:00–22:00, closed Sun, just off Puerta del Sol, tel. 915-213-858).

Getting Around Madrid

If you want to use Madrid's excellent public transit, my two best tips are: Pick up and study the fine *Public Transit* map/flier (available at TIs), and take full advantage of the cheap 10-ride Metrobus ticket deal (see below).

By Metro: The city's broad streets can be hot and exhausting. A subway trip of even a stop or two saves time and energy. Madrid's Metro is simple, speedy, and cheap (€1.50/ride, runs 6:00–1:30 in the morning, www.metromadrid.es or www.ctm-madrid.es). The 10-ride Metrobus ticket can be shared by several travelers and works on both the Metro and buses (€6.15, sold at kiosks, tobacco shops, and in Metro). Insert your ticket in the turnstile (it usually shows how many rides remain on it), then retrieve it as you pass through. Stations offer free maps *(Madrid by Underground)*. Navigate by subway stops (shown on city maps). To transfer, follow signs to the next subway line (numbered and color-coded). The names of the end stops are used to indicate directions. Green *Salida* signs point to the exit. Using neighborhood maps and street signs to exit smartly can save lots of walking. And watch out for thieves.

By Bus: City buses, while not as easy as the Metro, can be useful (€1 tickets sold on bus, or €6.15 for a 10-ride Metrobus ticket—see above; bus maps at TI or info booth on Puerta del Sol, buses run 6:00–24:00).

Madrid at a Glance

▲▲▲Prado Museum One of the world's great museums, loaded with masterpieces by Diego Velázquez, Francisco de Goya, El Greco, and Hieronymus Bosch. **Hours:** Tue–Sun 9:00–20:00, closed Mon.

▲▲Bullfight Spain's controversial pastime. **Hours:** Sundays and holidays March–mid-Oct, plus daily May–early June.

▲▲Royal Palace Spain's sumptuous, lavishly furnished national palace. **Hours:** April–Sept Mon–Sat 9:00–19:00, Sun 9:00–16:00; Oct–March Mon–Sat 9:30–18:00, Sun 9:00–15:00.

▲▲Puerta del Sol Madrid's lively central square. **Hours:** Always bustling.

▲▲Thyssen-Bornemisza Museum A great complement to the Prado, with lesser-known yet still impressive works and an especially good Impressionist collection. **Hours:** Tue–Sun 10:00–19:00, closed Mon.

▲▲Centro de Arte Reina Sofía Modern-art museum featuring Picasso's epic masterpiece *Guernica*. **Hours:** Mon and Wed–Sat 10:00–21:00, Sun 10:00–14:30, closed Tue.

▲▲Zarzuela Madrid's delightful light opera. **Hours:** Evenings.

▲Plaza Mayor Historic cobbled square. **Hours:** Always open.

▲Retiro Park Festive green escape from the city, with rental rowboats and great people-watching. **Hours:** Always open.

By Taxi: Madrid's 15,000 taxis are reasonably priced and easy to hail. Threesomes travel as cheaply by taxi as by Metro. After the €1.75 drop charge, the per-kilometer rate depends on the time: *Tarifa 1* (€0.75/kilometer) should be charged Mon–Sat 6:00–22:00; *Tarifa 2* (€0.90/kilometer) is valid after 22:00 and on Sundays. If your cabbie uses anything rather than *Tarifa 1* on weekdays (shown as an isolated "1" on the meter), you're being cheated. Rates can be higher if you go outside of Madrid. Other legitimate charges include the €4.50 supplement for the airport, the €2.40 supplement for train or bus stations, and €13.50 per hour for waiting. A ride from the Royal Palace to the Prado costs about €4.

▲**National Archaeological Museum** Traces the history of Iberia through artifacts, plus a replica of the Altamira Caves. **Hours:** Tue–Sat 9:30–20:30, Sun 9:30–15:00, closed Mon.

▲**El Rastro** Europe's biggest flea market. **Hours:** Sundays 9:00–15:00, best before 11:00.

▲**Clothing Museum** A clothes look at the 18th–21st centuries. **Hours:** Tue–Sat 9:30–19:00, Sun 10:00–15:00, closed Mon.

▲**Chapel of San Antonio de la Florida** Church with Goya's tomb, plus frescoes by the artist. **Hours:** Tue–Fri 10:00–14:00 & 16:00–20:00, Sat–Sun 10:00–14:00, closed Mon.

Royal Botanical Garden A relaxing museum of plants, with specimens from around the world. **Hours:** Daily 10:00–21:00, until 18:00 in winter.

Naval Museum Seafaring history of a country famous for its Armada. **Hours:** Tue–Sun 10:00–14:00, closed Mon.

Municipal Museum Experience Madrid's history via paintings, models, and a movie. **Hours:** Tue–Fri 9:30–20:00, Sat–Sun 10:00–14:00, closed Mon.

Royal Tapestry Factory See traditional tapestries being made. **Hours:** Mon–Fri 10:00–14:00, closed Sat–Sun and Aug.

Cable Car Dangle over Madrid's city park. **Hours:** April–Aug daily from noon, Sept–March Sat–Sun only.

TOURS

Madrid Vision Hop-On, Hop-Off Bus Tours—Madrid Vision offers three different hop-on, hop-off circuits of the city: historic, modern, and monuments. Buy a ticket from the driver (€14.50/1 day, €19/2 days) and you can hop from sight to sight and route to route as you like, listening to a recorded English commentary along the way. Each route has about 15 stops and takes about 90 minutes, with buses departing every 10 or 20 minutes. The three routes intersect at the south side of Puerta del Sol and in front of Starbucks across from the Prado (daily 10:00–21:00, longer in summer, shorter in winter, tel. 917-791-888).

Walking Tours—British expatriate Stephen Drake-Jones gives entertaining, informative walks of historic old Madrid almost nightly. A historian with a passion for the memory of the Duke of Wellington (the man who stopped Napoleon), Stephen is the founder and chairman of the Wellington Society. For €30, you become a member of the society for one year and get a free two-hour tour that includes stops at two bars for local drinks and tapas (morning and evening departures). Chairman Stephen takes you back in time to sort out Madrid's Hapsburg and Bourbon history. Eccentric Stephen likes his wine—if that's a problem, skip the tour. Tours start at the statue of García Lorca at the lower end of Plaza Santa Ana (maximum 10 people, call 609-143-203 to confirm tour and reserve a spot, chairman@wellsoc.org). Members of the Wellington Society can also take advantage of Stephen's helpline (if you're in a Spanish jam, call him to translate and intervene) and assistance by e-mail (for questions on Spain, your itinerary, and so on). Stephen also does specialized walks, private tours, play-by-play bullfight visits, and day trips to great spots in the countryside for small groups (about €275 per couple, €350 per small group, see www.wellsoc.org for details).

LeTango Tourist Services—Carlos Galvin, a Spaniard who speaks flawless English (and has led tours for my groups since 1998) and his American wife, Jennifer, offer private tours in Madrid and other parts of Spain. Carlos mixes a market walk in the historic center with a culinary-and-tapas crawl to get close to the Madrileños, their culture, and their food. His walk gives a fine 2.5-hour orientation and introduction to the fascinating and tasty culture of Madrid (€75 per person including tapas and drinks, minimum 2 people, alcohol-free version, family-friendly). Carlos also offers an array of comprehensive travel services that include organizing itineraries and booking hotels, bullfights, admissions, and tours anywhere in Spain (tel. 915-223-928, mobile 661-752-458, www.letango.com, info@letango.com).

Private Guides—Inés Muniz Martin is a good local guide (€130 for up to 3.5 hours, or €165 on weekends and holidays, tel. 912-366-471, www.immguidedtours.com, info@immguidedtours.com). Hernan Amaya Satt directs a group of guides who take individuals on Madrid walks (€140/5 hrs for up to 8 people, mobile 680-450-231, www.madridmuseumtours.com, info@easygoing.org).

Big-Bus City Sightseeing Tours—Julia Travel offers standard guided bus tours departing from Gran Vía 68 (near Plaza de España, no reservations required—just show up 15 min before departure, tel. 915-599-605, www.juliatravel.com). Their city tours include a three-hour Madrid tour with a live guide in two or three languages (€17, one shopping stop, no museum visits, daily at 9:15 and 15:00) and "Madrid by Night" (€12.50, 2-hour floodlit overview, Mon–Sat at 20:30, none Sun).

Julia Travel also runs multiple day-trip tours to destinations near Madrid. The Valley of the Fallen and El Escorial tour is particularly efficient, given the lousy bus connections for this route (€43, 4.5 hours, makes the day trip easy—blitzing both sights with a commentary en route and no time-stealing shopping stops, Tue–Sun at 9:00 and most days at 15:00, none Mon). Three trips include Toledo: one of the city itself (€55, full day, daily departure at 9:15, return by 17:30), one of Madrid and Toledo together (€45, half-day in Toledo plus panoramic 3-hour Madrid tour, daily at 9:00), and a marathon tour of El Escorial, Valley of the Fallen, and Toledo (€87, full day, Tue–Sun at 9:00, none Mon). Note that the rushed Toledo tours skip the town's one must-see sight, the cathedral... but not the long shopping stops, because the shops give kickbacks to the guides. And even though the buses are air-conditioned, the all-day Toledo trip is just too hot to enjoy in summer (June–Sept).

SELF-GUIDED WALK

Welcome to Madrid:
From the Puerta del Sol to the Royal Palace

Connect the sights with the following commentary. Allow an hour for this half-mile walk. Begin at Madrid's central square, Puerta del Sol (Metro: Sol).

Puerta del Sol: Named for a long-gone medieval gate with the sun carved onto it, bustling Puerta del Sol is worth ▲▲. It's a hub for the Metro, buses, political demonstrations, and pickpockets.

• *Stand by the statue of King Charles III and survey the square.*

Because of his enlightened urban policies, Charles III (who ruled until 1788) is affectionately called "the best mayor of Madrid." He decorated the city squares with fine fountains, got those meddlesome Jesuits out of city government, established the public school system, made the Retiro a public park rather than a royal retreat, and generally cleaned up Madrid.

Look behind the king. The statue of the bear pawing the berry bush and the *madroño* trees in the big planter boxes are symbols of the city. Bears used to live in the royal hunting grounds outside Madrid. And the *madroño* trees produce a berry that makes the traditional *madroño* liqueur.

The king faces a red-and-white building with a bell tower.

From Puerta del Sol to the Royal Palace

1. Puerta del Sol
2. Governor's Office
3. Salon La Mallorquina Pastry Shop
4. Calle de Postas
5. Plaza Mayor
6. Torre del Oro Bar Andalú
7. Mesones (Cave Bars)
8. Mercado de San Miguel
9. Convent Pastries
10. Former City Hall
11. Real Estate Office
12. Royal Palace

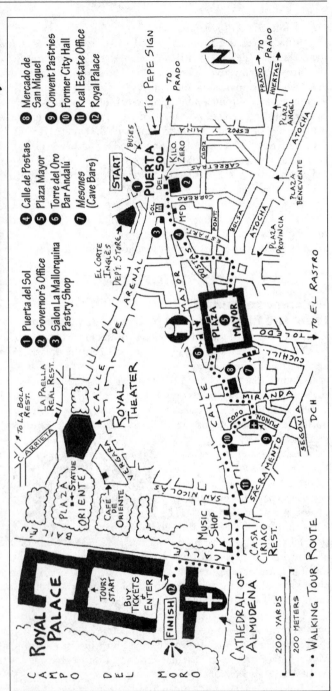

This was Madrid's first post office, established by Charles III in the 1760s. Today, it's the governor's office, though it's notorious for having been Francisco Franco's police headquarters. An amazing number of those detained and interrogated by the Franco police "tried to escape" by jumping out the windows to their deaths. Notice the hats of the civil guardsmen at the entry. It's said the reason the hats have square backs so the men can lean against the wall while enjoying a cigarette.

Appreciate the harmonious architecture of the buildings that circle the square. Crowds fill the square on New Year's Eve as the rest of Madrid watches the action on TV. As Spain's "Big Ben" atop the governor's office chimes 12 times, Madrileños eat one grape for each ring to bring good luck through the coming year.

• *Cross the square, walking to the governor's office.*

Look at the curb directly in front of the entrance to the governor's office. The scuffed-up marker is "kilometer zero," the very center of Spain. Near the entrance are two plaques expressing thanks from the regional government to its citizens for assisting in times of dire need. To the left of the entrance, a plaque on the wall honors those who helped during the terrorist bombing of March 11, 2004. A similar plaque on the right marks the spot where the war against Napoleon started in 1808.

Napoleon wanted his brother to be king of Spain. Trying to finagle this, he brought nearly the entire Spanish royal family to France for negotiations. An anxious crowd gathered outside this building awaiting word of the fate of their royals. This was just after the French Revolution, and there was a general nervousness between France and Spain. When the people of Madrid heard that Napoleon had appointed his own brother as the new king of Spain, they gathered angrily in the streets. The French guard simply massacred the mob. Painter Francisco de Goya, who worked just up the street, observed the event and captured the tragedy in his paintings *Second of May, 1808* and *Third of May, 1808,* now in the Prado (for more on Goya, see page 235).

Walking from Puerta del Sol to Plaza Mayor: On the corner of Calle Mayor and Puerta del Sol (downhill end of Puerta del Sol, across from McDonald's) is the busy confitería Salon La Mallorquina (daily 9:00–21:15). Go inside for a tempting peek at racks with goodies hot out of the oven. The shop is famous for its sweet, cream-filled Napolitana pastry (€1). Or sample the Madrid specialty, *rosquillas* (*tontas* means "silly"—plain, and *listas* means

"all dressed up"—with icing, €0.50 each).

From inside the shop, look back toward the entrance and notice the tile above the door with the 18th-century view of Puerta del Sol. Compare this with today's view out the door. This was before the square was widened, when a church stood where the *Tío Pepe* sign stands today. The French used this church to detain local patriots awaiting execution. (The venerable *Tío Pepe* sign, advertising a famous sherry for more than 100 years, was Madrid's first billboard.)

• *Cross busy Calle Mayor, round McDonald's, and veer up the pedestrian alley called Calle de Postas.*

The street sign shows the post coach heading for that famous first post office. Medieval street signs included pictures so the illiterate could "read" them. Fifty yards up the street, at Calle San Cristóbal, is Pans & Company, a popular sandwich chain. While Spaniards consider American fast food unhealthy—both culturally and physically—the local fast-food chains seem to be more politically and nutritionally correct.

• *From here, hike up Calle San Cristóbal.*

Within two blocks, you'll pass the local feminist bookshop (Librería Mujeres) and reach a small square. At the square, notice the big, brick 17th-century Ministry of Foreign Affairs building (with the pointed spire)—originally a jail for rich prisoners who could afford the cushy cells.

• *Turn right, and walk down Calle de Zaragoza under the arcade into the…*

Plaza Mayor: This square, rated ▲, was built in 1619. It's a vast, cobbled, traffic-free chunk of 17th-century Spain. Each side of the square is uniform, as if a grand palace were turned inside out. The statue is of Philip III, who ordered the square's construction. Upon this stage, much Spanish history has been played out: bullfights, fires, royal pageantry, and events of the gruesome Inquisition. Reliefs  serving as seatbacks under the lampposts tell the story. During the Inquisition, many were tried here—suspected heretics, Protestants, Jews, and Muslims whose "conversion" to Christianity was dubious. The guilty were paraded around the square before their execution, wearing billboards listing their many sins (bleachers were built for bigger audiences, while the wealthy rented balconies). Some were slowly strangled as they held a crucifix, hearing the reassuring words of a priest as this life was squeezed out of them. Others were burned.

The square is painted a democratic shade of burgundy—the result of a citywide vote. Since Franco's death in 1975, there's been a passion for voting here. Three different colors were painted as samples on the walls of this square, and the city voted for its favorite.

A stamp-and-coin market bustles here on Sundays from 10:00

to 14:00; on any day, it's a colorful and affordable place to enjoy a cup of coffee. Throughout Spain, lesser *plazas mayores* provide peaceful pools in the river of Spanish life. The TI (daily 9:00–20:30, wonderfully air-conditioned with free Internet access) is under the building on the north side of the square, the Casa de la Panadería, decorated with painted figures (it once housed the Bakers' Guild).

• For some interesting, if gruesome, bullfighting lore, drop by the...

Torre del Oro Bar Andalú: This bar is a good spot for a drink to finish off your Plaza Mayor visit (northwest corner of square, to the left of the Bakers' Guild). The bar has *Andalú* (Andalusian) ambience and an entertaining staff. Warning: They push expensive tapas on tourists. But buying a beer is safe and painless—just order a *caña* (small beer, shouldn't cost more than €2.30). The price list posted outside the door makes your costs perfectly clear. Consider taking a break at one of their sidewalk tables (or at any café/bar terrace facing Madrid's finest square). The scene is well worth the extra euro you'll pay for the drink.

The interior of the Torre del Oro bar is a temple to bullfighting, festooned with gory decor. Notice the breathtaking action captured in the many photographs. Look under the stuffed head of Barbero the bull. At eye level, you'll see a *puntilla,* the knife used to put a bull out of his misery at the arena. This was the knife used to kill Barbero. The plaque explains: weight, birthdate, owner, date of death, which matador killed him, and the location. Just to the left of Barbero, there's a photo of Franco with a very famous bullfighter. This is Manuel Benítez Pérez—better known as El Cordobés, the Elvis of bullfighters and a working-class hero. At the top of the stairs to the WC, find the photo of El Cordobés and Robert Kennedy—looking like brothers. At the end of the bar in a glass case is the "suit of lights" the great El Cordobés wore in his ill-fated 1967 fight. With Franco in attendance, El Cordobés went on and on, long after he could have ended the fight, until finally the bull gored him. El Cordobés survived; the bull didn't. Find another photo of Franco with El Cordobés at the far end, to the left of Segador the bull. Under the bull is a photo of El Cordobés' illegitimate son kissing a bull. Disowned by El Cordobés senior,

Heart of Madrid

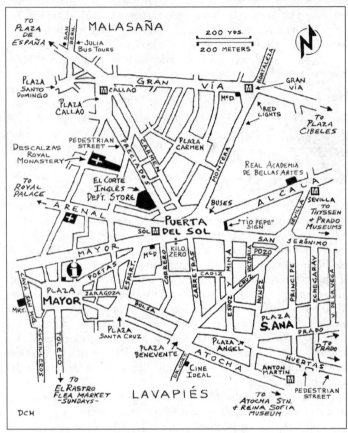

yet still using his dad's famous name after a court battle, the new El Cordobés is one of this generation's top fighters.

Strolling from Plaza Mayor to the Royal Palace: Leave Plaza Mayor on Calle Ciudad Rodrigo (to your right as you exit the bull bar). You'll pass a series of fine turn-of-the-20th-century storefronts and sandwich joints, such as Casa Rúa, famous for their cheap *bocadillos de calamares*—fried squid-rings on a roll.

From the archway, you'll see the covered Mercado de San Miguel (green iron posts, on left). Before you enter the market, look left down the street called Cava de San Miguel. If you like sangria and singing, come back at about 22:00 and visit one of the *mesones* that line the street. These cave-like bars stretch way back and get packed with locals out on cheap dates who—emboldened by sangria, the setting, and Spain—might suddenly just start singing. It's a lowbrow, electric-keyboard, karaoke-type ambience, best on Friday and Saturday nights.

Wander through the produce market and consider buying some fruit (Mon–Fri 9:00–14:30 & 17:15–20:15, Sat 9:00–14:30, closed Sun).

• *Leave the market on the opposite (downhill) side and follow the pedestrian lane left. At the first corner, turn right and cross the small plaza to the modern brick convent.*

The door on the right says *venta de dulces* (sweets for sale). To buy goodies from the cloistered nuns, buzz the *monjas* button, then wait patiently for the sister to respond over the intercom. Say *"dulces"* (DOOL-thays), and she'll let you in (Mon–Sat 9:30–13:00 & 16:00–18:30, closed Sun). When the lock buzzes, push open the door and follow the sign to *torno,* the lazy Susan that lets the sisters sell their baked goods without being seen (smallest quantity: half, or *medio,* kilo—around €6). Of the many choices (all good), *galletas* (orange shortbread cookies) are the least expensive.

• *Follow Calle del Codo (where those in need of bits of armor shopped—see the street sign) uphill around the convent to Plaza de la Villa, the square where City Hall is located until 2007 (when it moves to Plaza de Cibeles).*

The statue in the garden is of Don Bazán—mastermind of the Christian victory over the Turkish Ottomans at the naval battle of Lepanto in 1571. This pivotal battle, fought off the coast of Greece, ended the Turkish threat to Christian Europe. This square was the heart of medieval Madrid, though little remains of the 14th-century town.

From here, busy Calle Mayor leads downhill for a couple more blocks to the Royal Palace. Halfway down (on the left), at #75, a real-estate office *(inmobiliaria)* advertises apartments for rent (*piso* is a large apartment or condo, priced by the month—in the hundreds or low thousands of euros) and condos for sale (with six-digit prices). To roughly convert square meters to square feet, multiply by 10. Notice how for large items, locals still think in terms of *pesetas* ("pts").

A few steps further down, on a tiny square opposite the recommended Casa Ciriaco restaurant (at #84—see page 256), a statue memorializes the 1906 anarchist bombing that killed 23 people as the royal couple paraded by on their wedding day. While the crowd was throwing flowers, an anarchist (what terrorists used to be called) threw a bouquet lashed to a bomb from a balcony of #84 (the building was a hotel at the time). Gory photos of the event hang inside the restaurant (to the right of the entrance).

• *Continue down Calle Mayor. Within a couple of blocks, you'll come to a busy street, Calle de Bailen.*

The Garrido-Bailen music store is *the* place to stock up on castanets, unusual flutes, and Galician bagpipes. Across the busy street is Madrid's Cathedral of Almudena, built between 1883 and 1993. Its exterior is a contemporary mix, and its interior is neo-Gothic, with a refreshingly modern and colorful ceiling, glittering 5,000-pipe organ, and the 12th-century coffin (empty, painted leather on wood, in a chapel behind the altar) of Madrid's patron saint, Isidro. Isidro, a humble peasant, loved the handicapped and performed miracles. Forty years after he died, this coffin was opened and his body was found miraculously preserved, which convinced the pope to canonize him as the patron saint of Madrid and of farmers, with May 15 as his feast day.

Next to the cathedral is the **Royal Palace.** Visit the palace now, using my self-guided tour (see below).

• *When you're finished, you may want to...*

Return to Puerta del Sol: With your back to the palace, face the equestrian statue of Philip IV and (beyond the statue) the Neoclassical **Royal Theater** (Teatro Real, rebuilt in 1997). On your left, the **Madrid Tower** skyscraper marks the Plaza de España. Walk behind the Royal Theater (on the right, passing Café de Oriente—a favorite with theatergoers) to another square, where you'll find the Ópera Metro stop and Calle de Arenal, which leads back to Puerta del Sol.

SIGHTS

Royal Palace (Palacio Real)

Europe's third-greatest palace (after Versailles and Vienna's Schönbrunn), with arguably the most sumptuous original interior, is packed with tourists and royal antiques. It's worth ▲▲.

After a fortress burned down on this site in the 18th century, King Philip V commissioned this huge palace as a replacement. Though he ruled Spain for 40 years, Philip V was very French. (The grandson of Louis XIV, he was born in Versailles, and preferred speaking French.) He ordered this palace to be built as his own Versailles (although his wife's Italian origin had a tremendous impact in the style). It's big—more than 2,000 rooms, with tons of luxurious tapestries, a king's ransom of chandeliers, priceless porcelain, and bronze decor covered in gold leaf. While these days the royal family lives in a mansion a few miles away, this place still functions as a royal palace, and is used for formal state receptions, royal weddings, and tourists' daydreams.

The lions you'll see throughout were symbols of power. The Bourbon kings considered previous royalty not up to European par, and this palace—along with their establishment of a Spanish porcelain works and tapestry works—was their effort to raise the bar.

Cost, Hours, Location: €8 without a tour, €9 with a 60-minute tour; April–Sept Mon–Sat 9:00–19:00, Sun 9:00–16:00; Oct–March Mon–Sat 9:30–18:00, Sun 9:00–15:00; last tickets sold one hour before closing. The palace can close without warning if needed for a royal function; you can call a day ahead to check: tel. 914-548-800. The palace is most crowded on Wednesdays, when it's free for locals. Arrive early to minimize lines. To get to the palace, take bus #3 from Puerta del Sol, or if arriving by Metro, get off the Ópera stop. At the palace, there's a WC just past the ticket booth (men will enjoy the beer-stein urinals—all the rage in Madrid).

Touring the Palace: A simple one-floor, 24-room, one-way circuit is open to the public. You can wander on your own or join an English-language tour (check time of next tour and decide as you buy your ticket; the English-language tours depart about every 20 min, not worth a long wait). The tour guides, like the museum guidebook, show a passion for meaningless data. The €2.30 audioguides are much more interesting, and complement what I describe below (but they'd never mention beer-stein urinals). If you enjoy sightseeing cheek-to-check, crank up the volume and share the audioguide with your companion. The armory (€3.40, described below) and the pharmacy (included in your ticket) are in the courtyard.

◑ Self-Guided Tour: If you tour the palace on your own, here are a few details beyond what you'll find on the little English descriptions posted in each room:

1. The Palace Lobby: In the old days, horse-drawn carriages would drop you off here. Today, a sign divides the visitors waiting for a tour and those going in alone. The modern black bust in the corner is of the current, very popular constitutional monarch—King Juan Carlos I.

2. The Grand Stairs: Fancy carpets are rolled down (notice the little metal bar-holding hooks) for formal occasions. At the top of the first landing, the blue-and-red coat of arms represents Juan Carlos. While Franco chose him to be his successor, J. C. knew Spain was ripe for democracy. Rather than become "Juan the Brief" (as some were nicknaming him), he turned real power over to the parliament. You'll see his (figure) head on the back of the Spanish €1 and €2 coins. At the top of the stairs (before entering first room, right of door) is a white marble bust of J. C.'s great-great-g-g-g-great-grandfather Philip V, who began the Bourbon dynasty in Spain in 1700.

3. Guard Room: The palace guards used to hang out in this relatively simple room. Notice the fine clocks in this room. Charles IV, a great collector, amassed more than 700. The 150 displayed in this palace are all in working order. Look up, and see the first ceiling fresco in a series by the great Venetian painter Giambattista (or G. B.) Tiepolo (also see "Throne Room," below).

4. Hall of Columns: Originally a ballroom and dining room, today this room is used for formal ceremonies. (For example, this is where Spain formally joined the European Union in 1985—see plaque on far wall.) The tapestries (like most you'll see in the palace) are 17th-century Belgian, from designs by Raphael.

5. Throne Room: Red velvet walls, lions, and frescoes of Spanish scenes symbolize the monarchy in this Rococo riot. The chandeliers are the best in the house. While the room is decorated in the 18th-century style, the throne dates only from 1977. This is where the king's guests salute the king prior to dinner. He receives them relatively informally...standing at floor level, rather than seated up on the throne.

The ceiling fresco (1764) is the last great work by Italian master G. B. Tiepolo, who died in Madrid in 1770. This painting celebrates the days of the vast Spanish empire—upon which the sun also never set. Find the Native American (hint: follow the rainbow to the macho, red-caped conquistador).

The next several rooms were the living quarters of King Charles III (ruled 1759–1788).

6. Antechamber: The four paintings are of King Charles IV (looking a bit like a dim-witted George Washington) and his wife, María Luisa (who wore the pants in the palace)—all originals by Francisco de Goya. To meet the demand for his work, he made copies of these (which you'll see in the Prado). The clock—showing Cronus, god of time, in porcelain, bronze, and mahogany—sits on a music box. The gilded decor you see throughout the palace is bronze with gold leaf. Velázquez's famous painting *Las Meninas* (which you'll marvel at in the Prado) originally hung here.

7. Gasparini Room: This was meant to be Charles III's bedroom, but was unfinished when he died. Instead, with its painted stucco ceiling and inlaid Spanish marble floor (restored in 1992), it was the royal dressing room. It's a triumph of the Rococo style, with exotic motifs that were in vogue during that period. Note the fine stucco ceiling and the micro-mosaic table—a typical royal or aristocratic souvenir from any visit to Rome in the mid-1800s. The Asian influence was also trendy at the time. For a divine monarch, dressing was a public affair. The court bigwigs would assemble here as the king, standing on a platform—notice the height of the mirrors—would pull on his leotards and toy with his wig.

In the next room, the silk wallpaper is new; notice the *J.C.S.* initials of King Juan Carlos and Queen Sofía.

• *Pass through the silk room to reach...*

8. Charles III Bedroom: This room is dedicated to Charles III, known as one of the enlightened monarchs, who died here in his bed in 1788. His grandson, Ferdinand II, commissioned the optimistic fresco on the ceiling, showing how the glories of his grandfather's virtuous life earned him a hero's welcome in heaven. Decorated in 19th-century Neoclassical style, the chandelier is in the shape of the fleur-de-lis (symbol of the Bourbon family). The thick walls separating each room hide service corridors for servants, who scurried about generally unseen.

9. Porcelain Room: The 300 separate plates that line this room were disassembled for safety during the Spanish Civil War. (Find the little screws in the greenery that hide the seams.)

The Neoclassical Yellow Room was a study for Charles III. Notice the fine chandelier, with properly cut crystal that shows all the colors of the rainbow.

10. Gala Dining Room: Up to 12 times a year, the king entertains as many as 150 guests at this bowling-lane-size table, which can be extended to the length of the room. Find the two royal chairs. (Hint: With the modesty necessary for 21st-century monarchs, they are only a tad higher than the rest.) The parquet floor was the preferred dancing surface when balls were held in this fabulous room, decorated with vases from China and a fresco depicting the arrival of Christopher Columbus in Barcelona. Imagine the lighting when the 15 chandeliers (and their 900 bulbs) are fired up. The table in the next room would be lined with an exorbitantly caloric dessert buffet.

11. Cinema Room (Sala de Monedas y Medallas): In the early 20th century, the royal family enjoyed "Sunday afternoons at the movies" here. Today, this room stores glass cases filled with coins and medals.

12. Silver Room: This collection of silver tableware dates from the 19th century. The older royal silver was melted down by Napoleon's brother to help fund wars of the Napoleonic age. If you look carefully, you can see quirky royal necessities, including a baby's silver rattle.

13. Stradivarius Room: The queen likes classical music. When you perform for her, do it with these precious 350-year-old violins. About 300 Antonius Stradivarius–made instruments survive. This is the only matching quartet: two violins, a viola, and a cello. The next room was the children's room—with kid-size musical instruments.

14. China Rooms: Several collections of china from different kings (some actually from China, others from royal workshops in Europe such as Sèvres and Meissen) are displayed in this room. This room illustrates how any self-respecting royal family in Europe would have had its own porcelain works.

• *Exit to the hallway. Between statues of the giants of Spanish royal history (Isabel and Ferdinand), you'll enter the...*

15. Royal Chapel: The Royal Chapel is used for private concerts and funerals. The royal coffin sits here before making the sad trip to El Escorial to join the rest of Spain's past royalty (see next chapter).

16. Queen's Boudoir: This room was for the ladies, unlike the next...

17. Billiards and Smoking Rooms: The billiards room and the smoking room were for men only. The porcelain and silk of the smoking room imitates a Chinese opium den, which, in its day, was furnished only with pillows.

18. Charles IV Bedroom: Small for a king's room, the Neoclassical, Wedgwood-like decoration stands out.

19. Fine Woods Room: Fine 18th- and 19th-century French inlaid-wood pieces decorate this room.

You'll exit down the same grand stairway you climbed 24 rooms ago. To exit, cross the big courtyard, go to the gift shop where you entered, and follow *salida* signs.

Facing the courtyard is the **armory** (€3.40), which displays the armor and swords of El Cid (Christian warrior who fought the Moors), Ferdinand (husband of Isabel), Charles V (ruler of Spain at its peak of power), and Philip II (Charles' son, who watched Spain start its long slide downward). At the exit is an air-conditioned cafeteria and a bookstore, which has a good variety of books on Spanish history.

As you leave the palace, walk around the corner to the left, along the palace exterior, to the grand yet people-friendly Plaza de Oriente. Throughout Europe, energetic governments are turning formerly car-congested wastelands into public spaces like this. Madrid's last mayor was nicknamed "The Mole" for all the digging he did. Where's all the traffic? Under your feet.

Madrid's Museum Neighborhood

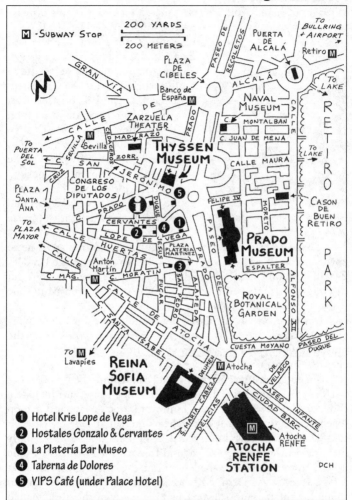

Ⓜ -Subway Stop

200 YARDS
200 METERS

① Hotel Kris Lope de Vega
② Hostales Gonzalo & Cervantes
③ La Platería Bar Museo
④ Taberna de Dolores
⑤ VIPS Café (under Palace Hotel)

Madrid's Museum Neighborhood

Three great museums, all within a 10-minute walk of each other, cluster in east Madrid: El Prado (Europe's top collection of paintings), the Thyssen-Bornemisza Museum (a baron's collection of European art, from the old masters to the moderns), and the Centro de Arte Reina Sofía (modern art, including Picasso's famous *Guernica*). Note that the Prado and Reina Sofía are free on Sunday (and anytime for those under 18); the Prado and Thyssen-Bornemisza are closed Monday; and the Reina Sofía is closed Tuesday.

Prado Museum

With more than 3,000 canvases, including entire rooms of masterpieces by superstar painters, the Prado (PRAH-doh) is overwhelming. But if you use the free English floor plan (pick up as you enter) and follow the self-guided tour (see below), you'll be impressed. Rated ▲▲▲, the Prado is *the* place to enjoy the great Spanish painter, Francisco de Goya, and it's also the home of Diego Velázquez's *Las Meninas*, considered by many to be the world's finest painting, period. In addition to Spanish works, you'll find paintings by Italian and Flemish masters, including Hieronymus Bosch's delightful *Garden of Delights* altarpiece.

Cost and Hours: €6, free all day Sun, and free anytime to anyone under 18 and non-Americans over 65 (because the US does not offer Spanish seniors any discounts, Yankee seniors don't get discounts here). Open Tue–Sun 9:00–20:00, closed Mon, last entry 30 min before closing.

Location: It's at the Paseo del Prado. The Banco de España and Atocha Metro stops are each a five-minute walk from the museum. Cabs picking you up at the Prado are likely to overcharge—insist on the meter.

Special Exhibits and the Prado Expansion: The Prado prides itself on its grand special exhibits. In 2007, these will include a show on the Venetian master Tintoretto (until May) and one on Joachim Patinir (Flemish landscape painter and friend of Albrecht Dürer, June–Sept). While special exhibit admission is generally included in the museum price (and free on Sun, when the Prado is free), you must endure the longer lines by entering from the top floor of the Goya (north) entrance. Special exhibits cause curators to jumble the museum's layout, making many of the directions to my self-guided tour (below) inaccurate. The expansion project in the works now will give special exhibits their own wing, finally bringing stability to the museum's permanent collection. In the meantime, pick up a detailed map when you enter the museum, consider renting the audioguide recommended below, and enlist the help of a guard if you're unable to find a particular work of art.

Crowd-Beating Tips: The self-guided tour described below starts at the Goya (north) entrance, though the Murillo (south) entrance—at the end closest to the Atocha Train Station—often has shorter lines. If lines are long, enter at the south end and go straight through the building to start the tour at the north end.

Prado Museum Overview

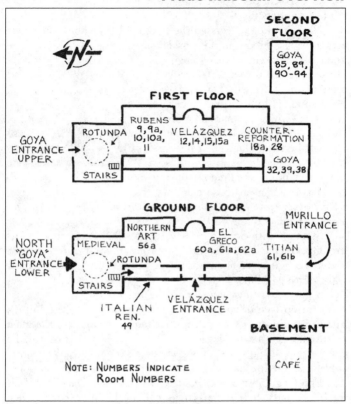

SECOND FLOOR

GOYA
85, 89,
90-94

FIRST FLOOR

ROTUNDA
GOYA ENTRANCE UPPER
STAIRS
RUBENS 9, 9a, 10, 10a, 11
VELÁZQUEZ 12, 14, 15, 15a
COUNTER-REFORMATION 18a, 28
GOYA 32, 39, 38

GROUND FLOOR

MURILLO ENTRANCE
NORTHERN ART 56a
MEDIEVAL
ROTUNDA
NORTH "GOYA" ENTRANCE LOWER
STAIRS
EL GRECO 60a, 61a, 62a
TITIAN 61, 61b
ITALIAN REN. 49
VELÁZQUEZ ENTRANCE

BASEMENT

CAFÉ

NOTE: NUMBERS INDICATE ROOM NUMBERS

Note that special exhibits (see above) can make it tricky for you to choose where you enter the museum. Lunchtime (14:00–16:00) is less crowded.

Tours: Take a tour, rent the €3 audioguide, buy a guidebook, or use my self-guided commentary (below). Given the ever-changing locations of paintings (making my self-guided tour tough to follow), the audioguide (with 120 paintings described) is a good investment, allowing you to wander. When you see a painting of interest, simply punch in the number and enjoy the description. You can drop the audioguide off at all three exits. And, if you're on a tight budget, remember that two can crank up the volume, listen cheek-to-cheek, and share one machine.

Services and Information: Your bags will be scanned (just like at the airport) before you leave them at the free and mandatory baggage check (no water bottles allowed inside). Photos are allowed, but no flash and no tripods. There's a cafeteria in the basement (at Murillo end). Tel. 913-302-800, http://museoprado.mcu.es.

Self-Guided Tour: Thanks to Gene Openshaw for writing the following tour.

New World gold funded the Prado (PRAH-doh), the great-est painting museum in the world. You'll see world-class Italian Renaissance art (especially Titian), Northern art (Bosch, Rubens, Dürer), and Spanish art (El Greco, Velázquez, and Goya). This huge museum is not laid out chronologically, so this tour will not be chronological. Instead, we'll hit the highlights with a mini-

mum of walking. The Prado frequently moves its collection around. If you can't find a particular painting, ask.

• *Start at the Goya (north) entrance, on the ground floor. Just past the entrance rotunda is Room 50.*

Start off with Spain's medieval roots. This art features noth-ing but saints and Bible scenes—appropriate for a country whose extreme religious devotion was forged in seven centuries of bloody war against Muslims.

• *Continue into the long main gallery, Room 49.*

Italian Renaissance: During its Golden Age (the 1500s), Spain was Europe's richest country, but Italy was still the most cultured. Spain's kings loved how Renaissance artists captured a three-dimensional world on a two-dimensional canvas, bringing Bible scenes to life and celebrating real people and their emotions.

Fra Angelico's *The Annunciation (La Anunciacion)* is half medieval piety, half Renaissance realism. In the crude Garden

of Eden scene (on the left) a scrawny, sinful First Couple hovers unrealistically above the foliage, awaiting eviction. The angel's Annunciation to Mary (right side) is more Renaissance, both with its upbeat message (that Jesus will be born to redeem sinners like Adam and Eve) and in the budding photorealism, set beneath 3-D arches. (Still, aren't the receding bars of the porch's ceiling a bit off? Painting three dimensions wasn't that easy.)

In the *Death of the Virgin (El Transito de la Virgen)*, Mantegna masters Renaissance 3-D. The apostles mourn in a crowded room, while the floor tiles recede into the distance, creating the sub-conscious effect of carrying Mary's soul out the window into the serene distance.

Raphael's *Christ Falls on the Way to Calvary (Caida en el Camino del Calvario)* is a study in contrasts. Below the crossbar, Christ and the women swirl in agonized passion. Above, bored soldiers mill about on the bleak hill where Jesus will die.

• *To find works by Titian, continue on into the next long gallery (Room 75). Midway down, turn left into Room 61b.*

Titian (c. 1490–1576): Naked people abound as Titian captures the lusty spirit of his hometown of Venice. *Danae*, from Greek

mythology, opens her legs to receive Zeus, the lecherous king of the gods, who descends as a shower of gold. Danae is helpless with rapture, while her servant tries to catch the holy spurt with a towel.

In *Venus with the Organ Player (Venus Recreándose en la Música)*, a musician turns around to leer at a naked woman while keeping both hands at work on his organ.

• *Continue into the adjoining Room 61.*

Titian also painted portraits of Spain's two Golden Age kings—both staunch Catholics—who amassed this racy collection. *Charles V on Horseback (El Emperador Carlos V en la Batalla de Muhlberg)* rears on his horse, raises his lance, and rides out to crush an army of Lutherans. Charles, having inherited many kingdoms and baronies through his family connections, was the world's most powerful man in the 1500s. His son, *Philip II (Felipe II)*—looking pale, suspicious, and lonely—was scholarly and complex. He built the austere, monastic Escorial Palace, but also indulged himself with Titian's bevy of Renaissance Playmates.

• *El Greco's works are nearby in Rooms 60a, 61a, and 62a.*

El Greco (1541–1614): El Greco was born in Greece (his name is Spanish for "the Greek"), trained in Venice, then settled in Toledo—60 miles from Madrid. His paintings are like Byzantine icons drenched in Venetian color and fused in the fires of Spanish mysticism. (For more on El Greco, see page 312 and visit Toledo.)

In *Christ Carrying the Cross (Cristo Abrazado a la Cruz)*, Jesus accepts his fate, trudging toward death with blood running down his neck. He hugs the cross and directs his gaze along the crossbar. His upturned eyes (sparkling with a streak of white paint) lock onto his next stop—heaven.

The Adoration of the Shepherds (La Adoracion de los Pastores), originally painted for El Greco's own burial chapel in Toledo, has El Greco's typical two-tiered composition—heaven above, earth below. The long, skinny shepherds are stretched unnaturally in between, flickering like flames toward heaven.

The Nobleman with His Hand on His Chest (El Caballero de la Mano al Pecho) is an elegant and somewhat arrogant man whose hand has the middle fingers touching—El Greco's trademark way of expressing elegance (or was it the 16th-century symbol for "Live long and prosper"?). The signature is on the right in faint Greek letters—"Doménikos Theotokópoulos," El Greco's real name.

• *To find Bosch and other Northern art: Return to the main gallery (Room 75), backtrack to Italian Renaissance art (Room 49), turn right into Room 56b, then continue straight into Room 56a.*

Northern Art: Hieronymous Bosch (c. 1450–1516), in his cryptic triptych *The Garden of Delights*, relates the message that the pleasures of life are fleeting, so we'd better avoid them or we'll wind up in hell. The large altarpiece has so many interesting small figures that it helps to "frame off" small sections to catch the details. Here's the big picture: In the central panel, men on horseback ride round and round, searching for but never reaching the elusive Fountain of Youth. Others frolic in earth's "Garden," oblivious to where they came from (Paradise, left panel) and where they may end up (Hell,

right panel). On the left, innocent Adam and Eve get married, with God himself performing the ceremony. The right panel is Hell, a burning wasteland where genetic-mutant demons torture sinners. Everyone gets their just desserts, like the glutton who is eaten and re-eaten eternally. In the center, hell is literally frozen over. A creature with a broken eggshell body, tree-trunk legs, and a witch's cap stares out—it's the face of Bosch himself.

Pieter Brueghel (BROY-gull) the Elder chronicled the 16th century's violent Catholic-Protestant wars in *The Triumph of Death (El Triunfo de la Muerte)*. The painting is one big, chaotic battle, featuring skeletons attacking helpless mortals. Breughel's message is simple and morbid—no one can escape death.

• *Find Dürer's work nearby.*

Albrecht Dürer's *Self-Portrait (Autorretrato)* is possibly the first true self-portrait. The artist, age 26, is dolled up in a fancy Italian hat and permed hair. He'd recently returned from Italy, and

wanted to impress his fellow Germans with his sophistication. But Dürer wasn't simply vain. He'd grown accustomed, as an artist in Renaissance Italy, to being treated like a prince. Note Dürer's signature, the pyramid-shaped "A.D." (D inside the A) on the windowsill.

Dürer's *Adam and Eve* (two separate panels) are the first full-size nudes in Northern European art. Like Greek statues, they pose in their separate niches, with three-dimensional, anatomically correct bodies. This was a bold humanist proclamation that the body is good, man is good, and the things of the world are good.

• *From here, we head upstairs to the first floor: Return to the north entrance and go up the stairs. Enter the long gallery (Room 25) and turn left into Room 9b and the adjoining Room 9.*

Peter Paul Rubens of Flanders painted Baroque-style art meant to play on the emotions, titillate the senses, and carry you away. *Diana and Her Nymphs Discovered by a Satyr (Diana y sus Ninfas Sorprendidas por Sátiros)* ripples from left-to-right with a wave of figures, as the nymphs flee from the half-human sex predators. But Diana, queen of the hunt, turns to bravely face the satyrs with her spear. All of Rubens' trademarks are here—sex, violence, action, emotion, bright colors, fleshy bodies—with the wind-machine set on 10.

Rubens' *The Three Graces (Las Tres Gracias)* celebrate cellulite. Their ample, glowing bodies intertwine as they exchange meaningful glances. The Grace at left is Rubens' young second wife, who shows up fairly regularly in his paintings.

• *Velázquez is midway down the long*

gallery in the large lozenge-shaped Room 12 and adjoining rooms.

Velázquez (1599–1660): Diego Velázquez (vel-LAHSS-kes) was the photojournalist of court painters, capturing the Spanish king and his court with a blend of formal portrait and candid snapshot.

His *Las Meninas (Maids of Honor)* is a behind-the-scenes look at his own job. One hot summer day in 1656, Velázquez (at

left, with paintbrush and Dalí moustache) stands at his easel and stares out at the people he's painting—the king and queen. They would have been standing about where we are, and we see only their reflection in the mirror at the back of the room. Their daughter (blonde hair, in center) watches her parents being painted, joined by her servants *(meninas)*, dwarfs, and the family dog. Also, at that very moment, a man happens to pass by the doorway at back and pauses to look in.

This frozen moment is lit by the window on the right, splitting the room into bright and shaded planes that recede into the distance. The main characters look right at us, making us part of the scene, seemingly able to walk around, behind, and among the characters. This is art come to life.

Velázquez's *The Drinkers (Los Borrachos)* is a cell-phone snapshot in a blue-collar bar, with a couple of peasants mugging for a photo-op with a Greek god—Bacchus, the god of wine.

• *Find more Velázquez in Rooms 14, 15, and 15a.*

Velázquez's boss, King Philip IV, had an affair, got caught, and repented by commissioning the *Crucifixion (Cristo crucificado)*. Christ hangs his head, humbly accepting his punishment, while Philip is left to stare at the slowly dripping blood, contemplating how long Christ had to suffer to atone for Philip's sins.

Prince Balthazar Carlos on Horseback (El Príncipe Baltasar Carlos, a Caballo) is exactly the kind of portrait Velázquez was called on to produce. The prince prances like a Roman emperor—only this "emperor" is just a cute little five-year-old acting oh so serious. Get up close and notice that his remarkably detailed costume is nothing but a few messy splotches of pink and gold paint—the proto-Impressionism Velázquez helped pioneer.

The Surrender of Breda (La Rendicion de Breda) is a piece of artistic journalism, chronicling Spain's victory over the Dutch. The defeated Dutchman starts to kneel, but the Spaniard stops him—no need to rub salt in the wounds. Twenty-five lances silhouetted against the sky reinforce the optimistic calm-after-the-battle mood.

• *Continue into Room 18a.*

Spanish Counter-Reformation Art: In the 1600s, when Europe was torn between Protestant and Catholic ideologies, devoted Spanish artists used images to bolster the Catholic faithful and explain abstract church doctrines. So Francisco Zurbarán's *St. Peter Crucified Appearing to Peter Nolasco (Aparición de San Pedro a San Pedro Nolasco)* renders the mystical vision absolutely literally. Bam, there's the Apostle Peter on an upside-down cross right in front of us. Nolasco looks as shocked as we'd be.

• *Find Murillo back out in the long main gallery, Room 28.*

Bartolomeo Murillo's *Immaculate Conception (La Inmaculada "de el Escorial")* puts a human face on the abstract Catholic doctrine that Mary was conceived and born free of original sin. Floating in a cloud of Ivory-Soap purity, this "immaculate" virgin radiates youth and wholesome goodness. (You'll find more of their work in Sevilla's Museo de Bellas Artes, page 396.)

• *Exit the far end of the gallery into the round Room 32.*

Francisco de Goya (1746–1828): Follow this complex man through the stages of his life—from dutiful court painter, to political rebel and scandal-maker, to the disillusioned genius of his Dark Paintings.

The Family of Charles IV (La Familia de Carlos IV) is all decked

out in their Sunday best for this group portrait. Goya himself stands to the far left, painting the court (a tribute to Velázquez in *Las Meninas*)...and revealing the shallow people beneath the royal trappings. King Charles, with his ridiculous hairpiece and goofy smile, was a vacuous, henpecked husband. His domineering queen upstages him, arrogantly stretching her swan-like neck. The other adults, with their bland faces, are bug-eyed with stupidity.

• *Find the staircase near Room 39 and head up to the second floor.*

Rooms 90–94 display canvases that were Goya's designs to make tapestries for nobles' palaces. The scenes make it clear that, while revolution was brewing in America and France, Spain's lords and ladies played—picnicking, dancing, flying kites, playing

paddleball, playing Blind Man's Bluff, or just relaxing in the sun—the well-known *The Parasol (El Quitasol)* is in Room 85.

• *Still on the second floor, find Room 89.*

Rumors flew that Goya was fooling around with the vivacious Duchess of Alba, and he may have painted her in a scandalous pose in the two similar paintings, the *Nude Maja (La Maja Desnuda)* and *Clothed Maja (La Maja Vestida)*. A *maja* was the name for a trendy, working-class girl. Whether she's a duch-

ess or *maja*, Goya had painted a naked lady, incurring the wrath of the Inquisition. The *Nude* stretches in a Titianesque pose to display her charms, the pale body highlighted by cool green sheets. The two paintings may have been displayed in a double frame, with the *Clothed Maja* sliding over the front to hide the Nude from Inquisitive minds.

• *Head back downstairs to the first floor, Room 39.*

Goya became a political liberal, a champion of democracy. He was crushed when France's hero of the Revolution, Napoleon, morphed into a tyrant and invaded Spain. On the *Second of May, 1808*, Madrid's citizens were protesting the occupation in Puerta del Sol, when the French sent in their dreaded Egyptian mercenaries. They plow through the dense tangle of Madrileños, who have

nowhere to run. The next day, the *Third of May, 1808*, the French rounded up ringleaders and executed them. The colorless firing squad—a faceless machine of death—mows them down, and they fall in bloody, tangled heaps. Goya throws a harsh, prison-yard floodlight on the main victim, who spreads his arms Christ-like to ask, "Why?"

In his seventies, Goya—disillusioned, widowed, exiled, and going deaf—retreated to a villa and smeared the walls with his "Dark Paintings"...dark in color and in mood. The style is considered Romantic—emphasizing emotion over beauty—but it foreshadows 20th-century Surrealism with its bizarre imagery and Expressionism, with the thick brushstrokes and cynical outlook.

• *To find the Dark Paintings, silently flagellate yourself, then go to Room 38.*

Dark forces convened continually in Goya's dining room, where *The Witches' Sabbath (El Aquelarre)* hung. The crones swirl in a frenzy around a dark, Satanic goat in monk's clothing who presides over the obscene rituals. The main witch exudes wild-eyed adoration and lust, while a noble lady (right of center) folds her hands primly in her lap ("I thought this was a Tupperware party!").

In the *Battle to the Death (Duelo a Garrotazos)*, two giants stand face to face, buried up to their knees, and flail at each other with clubs. It's a standoff between superpowers in the never-ending cycle of war.

In *Saturn Devouring One of His Sons (Saturno)*, we see Saturn—fearful that his sons would overthrow him as king of the Roman gods—eating one of them. Saturn, also known as Cronus (Time) may symbolize how time devours us all.

• *Hungry? Relax after your Prado tour in the cafeteria, two floors beneath you in the basement.*

Thyssen-Bornemisza Museum

Locals call this stunning museum simply the Thyssen (TEE-sun). Rated ▲▲, it displays the impressive collection that Baron Thyssen (a wealthy German married to a former Miss Spain) sold to Spain for $350 million. It's basically minor works by major artists and major works by minor artists (major works by major artists are in the Prado). But art-lovers appreciate how the good baron's art complements the Prado's collection by filling in where the Prado is weak (such as Impressionism).

Each floor is divided into two separate areas: the permanent collection (numbered rooms) and additions from the Baroness since the 1980s (lettered rooms). The museum recently opened a new wing (creating an L-shaped museum) to house even more of the Baroness' collection, including works by Impressionists (Monet's *Charing Cross Bridge*), Post-Impressionists, and Picasso. After purchasing your high-tech barcode ticket, continue down the wide main hall past larger-than-life paintings of King Juan Carlos and Queen Sofía, alongside the Baron (who died in 2002) and his art-collecting Baroness, Carmen. Pick up two museum maps (one for numbered rooms, another for lettered rooms) at the info desk. Ascend to the top floor and work your way down, taking a delightful walk through art history. Visit the rooms on each floor in numerical and alphabetical order, from Primitive Italian (Room 1) to Surrealism and Pop Art (Room 48). Afterwards, if you're heading to Centro de Arte Reina Sofía and you're tired, hail a cab at the gate to zip straight there.

Cost and Hours: €6 (€9 if there's a special exhibition); children under 12 free, Tue–Sun 10:00–19:00, closed Mon, last entry 30 min before closing.

Location: The museum is kitty-corner from the Prado at Paseo del Prado 8 in Palacio de Villahermosa (Metro: Banco de España).

Services and Information: Free baggage check, €4 audioguide, café, shop, no photos, tel. 914-203-944, www.museothyssen.org.

Centro de Arte Reina Sofía

This former public hospital (Madrid's first) shows off an exceptional collection of modern art, rated ▲▲. The permanent collection of modern art is on the second and fourth floors; the rotating exhibits are on the first and third floors. Ride the fancy glass elevator to the second floor and follow the room numbers for art chronologically displayed from 1900 to 1940. The fourth floor continues the collection, from 1940 to 1980.

The museum is most famous for Pablo Picasso's *Guernica* (second floor, Room 6), an epic painting showing the horror of modern war (see sidebar on page 240). Notice the two rooms of studies Picasso did for *Guernica*, filled with iron-nail tears and screaming mouths. *Guernica* was displayed at the Guggenheim in New York City until Franco's death, and now it reigns as Spain's national piece of art. After pondering the destruction of war, visit the room furthest back from the painting (confusingly, also numbered 6) to see photos of Picasso creating this masterpiece.

The museum also houses an easy-to-enjoy collection by other modern artists, including more of Picasso and a mind-bending room of works by Salvador Dalí (Room 10). Room 12 is a treat for movie buffs: Two films by Surrealist director Luis Buñuel (who had help from friends Dalí and the poet Federico García Lorca) play continuously. Enjoy a break in the shady courtyard before leaving.

Cost and Hours: €6, free Sat afternoon after 14:30 and all day Sun, always free to those under 18 and over 65. Even if admission is free when you visit, grab a ticket anyway—guards at the elevator check for them. The museum is open Mon and Wed–Sat 10:00–21:00, Sun 10:00–14:30, closed Tue.

Location: It's across from the Atocha Train Station at Santa

Isabel 52; look for the exterior glass elevators (Metro: Atocha).

Services and Information: Good brochure, no tours in English, hardworking audioguide-€4, no photos, free baggage check. The *librería* on the first floor has a larger selection of Picasso and Surrealist reproductions than the main gift shop at the entrance. Tel. 914-675-062, www.museoreinasofia.es.

Near the Prado
▲Retiro Park (Parque del Buen Retiro)—Once the private domain of royalty, this majestic park has been a favorite of Madrid's commoners since Charles III decided to share it with his subjects in the late 18th century. Siesta in this 300-acre, green-and-breezy escape from the city. At midday on Saturday and Sunday, the area around the lake becomes a street carnival, with jugglers, puppeteers, and lots of local color. These peaceful gardens offer great picnicking and people-watching. From the Retiro Metro stop, walk to the big lake (El Estanque), where you can cheaply rent a rowboat. Past the lake, a grand boulevard of statues leads to the Prado.

Royal Botanical Garden (Real Jardín Botánico)—After your Prado visit, you can take a lush and fragrant break in this sculpted park. Wander among trees from around the world. The flier in English explains that this is actually more than a park—it's a museum of plants (€2, daily 10:00–21:00, until 18:00 in winter, entry opposite Prado's Murillo/south entry, Plaza de Murillo 2).

Naval Museum (Museo Naval)—This museum tells the story of Spain's navy, from the Armada to today, in a plush and fascinating-to-boat-lovers exhibit (free, no English anywhere, Tue–Sun 10:00–14:00, closed Mon, a block north of the Prado across boulevard from Thyssen-Bornemisza Museum, Paseo del Prado 5, tel. 915-239-884, www.museonavalmadrid.com). Because this is a military facility, you'll need to show identification (your passport) to get in.

Elsewhere in Madrid
Descalzas Royal Monastery (Monasterio de las Descalzas Reales)—Madrid's most visit-worthy monastery was founded in the 16th century by Philip II's sister, Joan of Hapsburg (also known as Joanna and Juana). She's buried here. The monastery's chapels are decorated with fine art, Rubens-designed tapestries, and the heirlooms of the wealthy women who joined the order (the nuns were required to give a dowry). Because this is still a working Franciscan monastery, tourists can visit only when the nuns vacate the cloister (€8, Tue–Thu 10:30–12:45 & 16:00–17:45, Sat 10:30–12:45, closed Sun–Mon & Fri, Plaza de las Descalzas Reales 3, near the Ópera Metro stop and just a short walk from Puerta del Sol, Metro: Ópera, tel. 914-548-700).

Guernica

Perhaps the single most impressive piece of art in Spain is Pablo Picasso's *Guernica*. The monumental canvas—one of Europe's must-see sights—is not only a piece of art but a piece of history, capturing the horror of modern war in a modern style.

Pablo Picasso (1881–1973), a Spaniard, was in Paris in 1937, preparing an exhibition of paintings for its world's fair. Meanwhile, a bloody Civil War was being fought in his own country. The legally elected democratic government was being challenged by traditionalist right-wing forces under Francisco Franco. Franco would eventually win and rule the country with an iron fist for three decades.

On April 27, 1937, Guernica—a proud Basque village in northern Spain—was the target of the world's first saturation-bombing raid. Franco gave permission to his Fascist ally, Hitler, to use the town as a guinea pig to try out Germany's new air force. The raid leveled the town, causing destruction that was unheard of at the time (though by 1944 it would be commonplace).

News of the bombing reached Picasso in Paris. He scrapped earlier plans and immediately set to work sketching scenes of the destruction as he imagined it. In a matter of weeks, he put these bomb-shattered shards together into a large mural (286 square feet). For the first time, the world could see the destructive force of the rising fascist movement—a prelude to WWII.

The bombs are falling, shattering the quiet village. A woman looks up at the sky (far right), horses scream (center), and a man falls from the horse and dies, while a wounded woman drags

▲**National Archaeological Museum (Museo Arqueológico Nacional)**—This fine museum gives you a chronological walk on one convenient floor through the story of Iberia. With a rich collection of artifacts (but a maddening refusal to describe anything in English), it shows off the wonders of each age: Celtic pre-Roman, Roman, a fine and rare Visigothic section, Moorish, Romanesque, and beyond (€3, free Sat afternoon and Sun; open Tue–Sat 9:30–20:30, Sun 9:30–15:00, closed Mon; Calle Serrano herself through the streets. She tries to escape, but her leg is too thick, dragging her down, like trying to run from something in a nightmare. On the left, a bull—a symbol of Spain—ponders it all, watching over a mother and her dead baby...a modern *pietà*. A woman in the center sticks her head out to see what's going on. The whole scene is lit from above by the stark light of a bare bulb. Picasso's painting threw a light on the brutality of Hitler and Franco, and suddenly the whole world was watching.

Picasso's abstract, Cubist style reinforces the message. It's as if he'd picked up the shattered shards and pasted them onto a canvas. The black and white tones are as gritty as the black-and-white newspaper photos that reported the bombing. The drab colors create a depressing, almost nauseating mood.

Picasso chose images with universal symbolism, making the work a commentary on all wars. Picasso himself said that the central horse, with the spear in its back, symbolizes humanity succumbing to brute force. The fallen rider's arm is severed and his sword is broken, more symbols of defeat. Near the bull, the dove of peace can do nothing but cry.

The bombing of Guernica—like the entire Spanish Civil War (1936–1939)—was an exercise in brutality. As one side captured a town, it might systematically round up every man, old and young—including priests—line them up, and shoot them in revenge for atrocities by the other side.

Thousands of people attended the Paris art fair, and *Guernica* caused an immediate sensation. They could see the horror of modern war technology, the vain struggle of the Spanish Republicans, and the cold indifference of the Fascist war machine. After the Paris exhibition, *Guernica* was exiled to America until Franco's death. Picasso also vowed to never return to Spain while Franco ruled. (Franco outlived him.)

With each passing year, the canvas seemed more and more prophetic—honoring not just the thousand that died in Guernica, but also the 600,000 victims of Spain's bitter Civil War, and the 80 million worldwide that perished in World War II. Picasso put a human face on what we now call "collateral damage."

13, Metro: Serrano or Colón, tel. 915-777-912). Outside, underground in the museum's garden, is an underwhelming replica of northern Spain's Altamira Caves (big on bison), giving you a faded peek at the skill of the cave artists who created the originals 14,000 years ago. For more on the Altamira Caves, see page 150 in the Cantabria chapter.

Municipal Museum (Museo Municipal)—Follow the history of Madrid in old paintings and models (but no English). As you enter, notice Pedro de Ribera's fine Baroque door featuring St. James the Moor Slayer. The 10-minute video (continually playing, no words) gives a relaxing and vivid visual trip through the city's story (free, Tue–Fri 9:30–20:00, Sat–Sun 10:00–14:00, closed Mon, Calle Fuencarral 78, Metro: Tribunal or Bilbao, tel. 915-888-672).

▲**Clothing Museum (Museo del Traje)**—This new museum shows the history of clothing from the 18th century until today. In a cool and air-conditioned chronological sweep, the museum's one floor of exhibits includes regional ethnic costumes, a look at how bullfighting and the French influenced styles, accessories through the ages, and Spanish flappers. The only downside of this marvelous modern museum is that it's a long way from anything else of interest (€3, Tue–Sat 9:30–19:00, Sun 10:00–15:00, closed Mon, Avenida Juan Herrera 2; Metro: Moncloa and a longish walk, bus #46, or taxi; tel. 915-497-150).

▲**Chapel of San Antonio de la Florida**—In this simple little Neoclassical chapel from the 1790s, Francisco de Goya's tomb stares up at a splendid cupola filled with his own proto-Impressionist frescoes. He frescoed this using the same unique technique that he used for his "dark paintings." Use the mirrors to enjoy the drama and energy he infused into this marvelously restored masterpiece (free, Tue–Fri 10:00–14:00 & 16:00–20:00, Sat–Sun 10:00–14:00, closed Mon, Glorieta de San Antonio de la Florida, tel. 915-420-722). This chapel is a five-minute walk down Paseo de San Antonio de la Florida from Metro Príncipe Pío and the Sepulvedana bus station (which serves Segovia). If you're day-tripping to Segovia from Madrid, it's easy to stop by before or after your trip.

Royal Tapestry Factory (Real Fábrica de Tapices)—Have a look at traditional tapestry-making (€3, Mon–Fri 10:00–14:00, closed Sat–Sun and Aug, some English tours, Calle Fuenterrabia 2, Metro: Menendez Pelayo, take Gutenberg exit, tel. 914-340-550). You can actually order a tailor-made tapestry (starting at $10,000).

Temple de Debod—In 1968, Egypt gave Spain its own ancient temple. It was a gift of the Egyptian government, which was grateful for Franco's help in rescuing monuments that had been threatened by the rising Nile waters above the Aswan Dam. Consequently, Madrid is the only place I can think of in Europe where you can actually wander through an intact original Egyptian temple—complete with fine carved reliefs from 200 B.C. (free; April–Sept Tue–Fri 10:00–14:00 & 18:00–20:00, Sat–Sun 10:00–14:00, closed Mon; Oct–March Tue–Fri 9:45–13:45 & 16:15–18:15, Sat–Sun 10:00–14:00, closed Mon). Set in a romantic park that locals love for its great city views (especially at sunset), the temple—as well as its art—is well-described. Popular as the view may be, the uninspiring "grand Madrid view" only causes me to wonder why anyone would build a city here.

Cable Car (Teleférico)—For city views, ride this cable car from downtown over Madrid's sprawling city park to Casa de Campo (€3.25 one-way, €4.65 round-trip, April-Aug daily from noon, Sept–March Sat-Sun only, departs from Paseo del Pintor Rosales, a short walk from Metro: Plaza de España, tel. 915-417-450, www.teleferico.com). Do an immediate round-trip to skip Casa de Campo's strange mix of rental rowboats, prostitutes, addicts, a zoo, and an amusement park. The family-friendly bits of the park are far from the cable-car terminus.

EXPERIENCES

▲▲**Bullfight**—Madrid's Plaza de Toros hosts Spain's top bull-fights on Sundays and holidays from March through mid-October, and nearly every day during the San Isidro festival (May through early June—often sold out long in advance). Fights start between 17:00 and 21:00 (early in spring and fall, late in summer). The bullring is at the Ventas Metro stop (a direct 10-min Metro ride to the end of the  line from Puerta del Sol, tel. 913-562-200, www.las-ventas.com). For info on the "art" of bullfighting, see page 219.

Bullfight tickets range from €3.50 to €100. There are no bad seats at the Plaza de Toros; paying more gets you in the shade and/or closer to the gore. (The action often intentionally occurs in the shade to reward the expensive-ticket holders.) To be close to the bullring, choose areas 8, 9, or 10; for shade: 1, 2, 9, or 10; for shade/sun: 3 or 8; for the sun and cheapest seats: 4, 5, 6, or 7. Note these key words: *corrida*—a real fight with professionals; *novillada*—rookie matadors and younger bulls. Getting tickets through your hotel or a booking office is convenient, but they add 20 percent or more and don't sell the cheap seats. There are two booking offices; call both before you buy: at Plaza del Carmen 1 (daily 9:30–13:00 & 16:30–19:00, tel. 915-312-732, run by English-speaking José, who also sells soccer tickets) and at Calle Victoria 3 (daily 10:00–14:00 & 17:00–19:00, tel. 915-211-213). To save money (20 percent), you can stand in the ticket line at the bullring. Except for important bullfights—or during the San Isidro festival—there are generally plenty of seats available. About a thousand tickets are held back to be sold in the five days leading up to a fight, including the day of the fight. Scalpers hang out before the popular fights at the Calle Victoria booking office. Beware: Those buying scalped tickets are breaking the law, and can lose the ticket with no recourse.

For a dose of the experience, you can buy a cheap ticket and just stay to see a couple of bullfights. Each fight takes about 20 minutes, and the event consists of six bulls over two hours.

Madrid's **Bullfighting Museum** (Museo Taurino) is not as good as Sevilla's or Ronda's (free, Tue–Fri and Sun 9:30–14:30, closed Sat and Mon and early on fight days, at the back of bullring, tel. 917-251-857).

Football—Madrid, like most of Europe, is enthusiastic about soccer (which they call football). The Real Madrid team plays to a spirited local crowd Saturdays and Sundays from September through May (tickets from €30—sold at bullfight box offices listed above, stadium at Metro: Bernabeu).

SHOPPING

Shoppers focus on the colorful pedestrian area between Gran Vía and Puerta del Sol. The giant Spanish department store El Corte Inglés, a block off Puerta del Sol, is a handy place to pick up just about anything you need (Mon–Sat 10:00–22:00, closed Sun, see page 210).

El Rastro: Europe's biggest flea market is a sight in itself, worth ▲. It's a field day for shop-pers, people-watchers, and thieves (Sundays only, 9:00–15:00, best before 11:00). Thousands of stalls titillate more than a million brows-ers with mostly new junk. Locals lament the tattiness of El Rastro lately—you'll find cheap under-wear and bootleg CDs, but no real treasures. Start at the Plaza Mayor, with its stamp- and coin-collectors market (see below), and head south or take the Metro to Tirso de Molina. Walk downhill, finishing at Metro stop Puerta de Toledo. El Rastro offers a fascinating chance to see gangs of young thieves overwhelming and ripping off naive tourists with no police any-where in sight. Seriously: Don't even bring a wallet. The pickpocket action is brutal, and tourists are targeted.

While the flea market can be a downer, Europe's biggest stamp and coin market, thriving simultaneously on Plaza Mayor, is a genteel delight. Watch the old-timers paging lovingly through each other's albums, looking for win-win trades.

Classical Guitars: Guitar-lovers know that the world's finest classical guitars are made in Spain. Several of the top workshops are within an easy walk of Puerta del Sol, and offer inviting little showrooms with a peek at their craft and an opportunity to strum the final product. Consider the workshops of José Romero (Calle de Espoz y Mina 30, tel. 915-214-218) and Paul Martinez (Calle de la Paz 8, tel. 915-314-229). Union Musical is a popular guitar shop off Puerta del Sol (Carrera de San Jerónimo 28, tel 914-293-877). If you're shopping, be prepared to spend €1,000.

NIGHTLIFE

Disco dancers may have to wait until after midnight for the most popular clubs to even open, much less start hopping. Spain has a reputation for partying very late, not ending until offices open in the morning. If you're people-watching early in the morning, it's actually hard to know who is finishing their day and who's just starting it. Even if you're not a party animal after midnight, make a point to be out with the happy masses, luxuriating in the cool evening air between 22:00 and midnight. The scene is absolutely unforgettable.

▲▲▲**Paseo**—Just walking the streets of Madrid seems to be the way the Madrileños spend their evenings. Even past midnight on a hot summer night, whole families with little kids are strolling, enjoying tiny beers and tapas in a series of bars, licking ice cream, and greeting their neighbors. A good area to wander is along Gran Vía (from about Metro: Callao to Plaza de España). Or start at Puerta del Sol, and explore in the direction of Plaza Santa Ana. See "The Madrid Pub-Crawl Dinner (for Beginners)" on page 259.

▲▲**Zarzuela**—For a delightful look at Spanish light opera that even English-speakers can enjoy, try zarzuela. Guitar-strumming Napoleons in red capes; buxom women with masks, fans, and castanets; Spanish-speaking pharaohs; melodramatic spotlights; and aficionados clapping and singing along from the cheap seats, where the acoustics are best—this is zarzuela...the people's opera. Originating in Madrid, zarzuela is known for its satiric humor and surprisingly good music. You can buy tickets at Theater Zarzuela, which alternates between zarzuela, ballet, and opera throughout the year (€10–30, box office open 12:00–18:00 for advance tickets or until showtime for that day, Jovellanos 4, near the Prado, Metro: Banco de España, tel. 915-245-400, http://teatrodelazarzuela.mcu.es). Madrid puts on live zarzuela events in the Royal Palace gardens summer evenings (ask the TI for details). The TI's monthly guide has a special zarzuela listing.

▲**Flamenco**—While Sevilla is the capital of flamenco, Madrid has two easy and affordable options.

Taberna Casa Patas attracts big-name flamenco artists. You'll quickly understand why this intimate (30-table) and smoky venue is named "House of Feet." Since this is for locals as well as tour groups, the flamenco is contemporary and may be jazzier than your notion—it depends on who's performing (€26 for Mon–Thu at 22:30, €31 for Fri–Sat at 21:00 and 24:00, closed Sun, 75–90 min, price includes cover and first drink, reservations smart, no flash cameras, Cañizares 10, tel. 913-690-496, www.casapatas.com). Its restaurant is a logical spot for dinner before the show (€30 dinners, Mon–Sat from 20:00). Or, since it's three blocks south of the recommended Plaza Santa Ana tapas bars, this could be your post-tapas-crawl entertainment.

Las Carboneras, more downscale, is an easygoing, folksy little place a few steps from Plaza Mayor with a nightly hour-long flamenco show (€29 includes an entry and a drink, €52 gets you a table up front with dinner and unlimited cheap drinks if you reserve ahead, the manager Enrique promises a €5 per person discount if you book direct and show this book in 2007, Mon–Thu at 22:30 and often at 21:00, Fri–Sat at 21:00 and 23:00, closed Sun, earlier shows possible if a group books, reservations recommended, Plaza del Conde de Miranda 1, tel. 915-428-677).

Regardless of what your hotel receptionist may want to sell you, other flamenco places—such as Arco de Cuchilleros (Calle de los Cuchilleros 7), Café de Chinitas (Calle Torija 7, just off Plaza Mayor), Corral de la Morería (Calle de Morería 17) and Torres Bermejas (off Gran Vía)—are filled with tourists and pushy waiters.

Mesones—Just west of Plaza Mayor, the lane called Cava de San Miguel is lined with *mesones:* long, skinny, cave-like bars famous for drinking and singing late into the night. If you were to toss lowbrow locals, Spanish karaoke, electric keyboards, crass tourists, cheap sangria, and greasy calamari into a late-night blender and turn it on, this is what you'd get. It's generally lively only on Friday and Saturday, but you're welcome to pop in to several bars (such as Guitarra, Tortilla, or Boquerón) and see what you can find.

Late-Night Bars—If you're just picking up speed at midnight, and looking for a place filled with old tiles and a Gen-X crowd, power into **Bar Viva Madrid** (daily 13:00–3:00 in the morning, downhill from Plaza Santa Ana on Calle Manuel Fernández y González, tel. 914-293-640). The same street has other late-night bars filled with music. Or hike on over to **Chocolatería San Ginés** (described below) for a dessert of *churros con chocolate*.

Movies—During Franco's days, movies were always dubbed into Spanish. Movies in Spain remain about the most often dubbed in Europe. To see a movie with its original soundtrack, look for *V.O.* (meaning "original version"). **Cine Ideal,** with nine screens, is a good place for the latest films in V.O. (€7, 5-min walk south of Puerta del Sol at Calle del Dr. Cortezo 6, tel. 913-692-518 for info). For extensive listings, see the *Guía del Ocio* entertainment guide (€1 at newsstands) or a local newspaper.

SLEEPING

Madrid has plenty of centrally located budget hotels and *pensiones*. You'll have no trouble finding a sleepable double for €35, a good double for €70, and a modern, air-conditioned double with all the comforts for €100. Prices are the same throughout the year, and it's almost always easy to find a place. Anticipate full hotels only during May (the San Isidro festival, celebrating Madrid's patron saint with bullfights and zarzuelas—especially around his feast day on May 15) and the last week in September (conventions). In July and August, prices can be softer—ask about promotional deals. All of the accommodations I've listed are within a few minutes' walk of Puerta del Sol.

With all of Madrid's street noise, I'd request the highest floor possible. Also, twin-bedded rooms are generally a bit larger than double-bedded rooms for the same price. Madrid hoteliers rarely offer a cash discount. During slow times, drop-ins can often score a room in business-class hotels for just a few euros more than the budget hotels (which don't have prices that fluctuate as wildly with demand).

Fancier Places in the Pedestrian Zone Between Puerta del Sol and Gran Vía

Reliable and away from the seediness, these hotels are good values for those wanting to spend a little more. Their formal prices may be inflated, but some offer weekend and summer discounts when

---

Sleep Code

(€1 = about $1.20, country code: 34)
S = Single, **D** = Double/Twin, **T** = Triple, **Q** = Quad, **b** = bathroom, **s** = shower only. Unless otherwise noted, credit cards are accepted, English is spoken, and breakfast is *not* included. In Madrid, the 7 percent IVA tax is sometimes included in the price.

To help you easily sort through these listings, I've divided the rooms into three categories, based on the price for a standard double room with bath during high season:

$$$ **Higher Priced**—Most rooms €100 or more.
$$ **Moderately Priced**—Most rooms between €70–100.
$ **Lower Priced**—Most rooms €70 or less.

Madrid's Center—Hotels and Restaurants

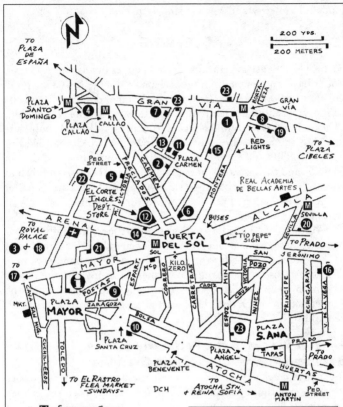

M -SUBWAY STOP

For eateries near Plaza Mayor and Plaza Santa Ana, please see those maps.

1 Hostal Res. Louis XV & Hostal Metropol

2 Hotel Liabeny

3 To Hotel Opera

4 Hotel Preciados

5 Hotel Carlos V

6 Hotel Europa & Cafeteria

7 Hotel Regente

8 Hostal Aliste & Pension Marina Santa

9 Petit Palace Posada del Peine

10 Hotel Plaza Mayor

11 Hostales at Calle de la Salud 13

12 El Corte Inglés Cafeteria

13 Restaurante Puerto Rico

14 Casa Labra Taberna Restaurante

15 Artemisia II Veggie Rest.

16 Artemisia I Veggie Rest.

17 To Casa Ciriaco & La Paella Real Rest.

18 To La Bola Taberna

19 La Gloria de Montera Rest. & Fresc Co Buffet

20 La Finca de Susana

21 Chocolatería San Ginés

22 Chocolatería Valor

23 Internet Cafés (3)

it's slow. Drivers will pay about €24 a day in garages. Use Metro: Sol for all but Hotel Opera (Metro: Ópera). For locations, see the map on page 248.

$$$ Hotel Regente is big and traditional, with 154 tastefully decorated and comfortable air-conditioned rooms, generous public spaces, a great location, and a good value (Sb-€63, Db-€105, Tb-€128, 20 percent cheaper Fri–Sun, tax not included, breakfast-€8, midway between Puerta del Sol and Plaza del Callao at Mesonero Romanos 9, tel. 915-212-941, fax 915-323-014, www.hotelregente .com, info@hotelregente.com).

$$$ Hotel Liabeny rents 220 plush, spacious, business-class rooms offering all the comforts (Sb-€100, Db-€130, Tb-€155, 10 percent cheaper mid-July–Aug and Fri–Sat, tax not included, breakfast-€13, air-con, sauna, gym, off Plaza del Carmen at Salud 3, tel. 915-319-000, fax 915-327-421, www.liabeny.es, reservas @hotelliabeny.es).

$$$ Hotel Preciados, a four-star business hotel, has 73 fine, sleek, and modern rooms, as well as a breakfast room and elegant lounges. It's well-located and reasonably priced for the luxury it provides (Db-€130, prices are often soft, checking Web specials or dropping in will likely snag a room for around €100, just off Plaza de Santo Domingo at Calle Preciados 37, tel. 914-544-400, fax 914-544-401, www.preciadoshotel.com, preciadoshotel @preciadoshotel.com).

$$$ Hotel Opera, a serious and modern hotel with 79 classy rooms, is located just off Plaza Isabel II, a four-block walk from Puerta del Sol toward the Royal Palace (Sb-€100, Db-€134, Db with big view terrace-€147, Tb-€175, tax not included, buffet breakfast-€10, air-con, elevator, free Internet in lobby, ask for a higher floor—there are eight—to avoid street noise, Cuesta de Santo Domingo 2, Metro: Ópera, tel. 915-412-800, fax 915-416-923, www .hotelopera.com, reservas@hotelopera.com). Hotel Opera's cafeteria is understandably popular. Also consider their "singing dinners"—great operetta music with a delightful dinner—offered nightly at 22:00 (average price-€60, reservations wise, call 915-426-382).

$$ Hotel Carlos V, a Best Western with 67 classy, high-ceiling rooms and an elegant breakfast and lounge, is a fair value. Its central location off Preciados pedestrian street makes it convenient—but ask for an inside room to avoid street noise (Sb-€80–90, standard Db-€90, larger "superior" view Db–€112, Tb-€130, air-con, elevator, Maestro Victoria 5, tel. 915-314-100, fax 915-313-761, www.hotelcarlosv.com, recepcion@hotelcarlosv.com).

$$ Hotel Europa, with sleek marble, red carpet runners along the halls, happy Muzak charm, and an attentive staff, is a tremendous value. It rents 103 squeaky-clean rooms, many with balconies overlooking the pedestrian zone or an inner courtyard (Sb-€64, Db-€80–100, Tb-€113, Qb-€129, Quint/b-€144, tax and breakfast not included, air-con, elevator, easy phone reservations with credit card, Calle del Carmen 4, tel. 915-212-900, fax 915-214-696, www.hoteleuropa.net, info@hoteleuropa.net, run by Antonio and Fernando Garaban and their helpful and jovial staff, Javi and Jim). The convenient Europa cafeteria/restaurant next door is a lively and convivial scene—fun for breakfast, and a fine value any time of day.

$$ **Petit Palace Posada del Peine** feels like part of a big modern chain (which it is), but fills its well-located old building with fresh, efficient character. Behind the ornate and sparkling Old World facade is a comfortable and modern business-class hotel with 69 rooms just a block from Plaza Mayor (Db-€85–130 depending on demand, tax not included, air-con, Calle Postas 17, tel. 915-238-151, fax 915-232-993, www.hthoteles.com, pos @hthoteles.com).

$$ **Hotel Plaza Mayor,** with 34 solidly outfitted rooms, is tastefully decorated and beautifully situated a block off Plaza Mayor (Sb-€60, Db-€80, bigger Db corner room-€90, Tb-€110, buffet breakfast-€8, 5 percent discount if you reserve directly by e-mail or fax and mention this book, air-con, elevator, Wi-Fi, Calle Atocha 2, tel. 913-600-606, fax 913-600-610, www.h-plazamayor .com, info@h-plazamayor.com).

Cheaper Bets near Puerta del Sol and Gran Vía

These accommodations are also in or near the handy pedestrian zone between Puerta del Sol and Gran Vía. The first two (Acapulco and Triana) are by far the best (and priciest). The Isabel, Arcos, Aliste, and Marina Santa are your best cheap-bed options (with youth-hostel prices, yet hotel privacy).

At Calle de la Salud 13

These are all in the same building at Calle de la Salud 13, overlooking Plaza del Carmen—a little square with a sleepy, almost Parisian ambience.

$ **Hostal Acapulco** rents 16 bright rooms with air-conditioning and all the big hotel gear. The neighborhood is quiet enough that it's smart to request a room with a balcony (Sb-€45, Db-€55, Tb-€73, elevator, free Internet access in lobby, fourth floor, tel. 915-311-945, fax 915-322-329, www.hostalacapulco.com, hostal _acapulco@yahoo.es, Ana and Marco).

$ **Hostal Triana,** also a fine deal, is bigger—with 40 rooms— and offers a little less charm for a little less money (Sb-€37, Db-€50, Tb-€65, includes taxes, rooms facing the square have air-con and cost €3 extra, other rooms have fans, elevator, free Wi-Fi, first floor, tel. 915-326-812, fax 915-229-729, www.hostaltriana.com, triana@hostaltriana.com, Victor González).

Old-Fashioned, Granny-Run Places: These two tiny, five-room *pensiones*—both run by non-English-speaking little old ladies—reek of the 1950s (their business cards have the new phone codes penned in, and there's no hint of e-mail or even fax). You can reserve by phone only a day in advance, and you must pay in cash. They're clean, quiet, reasonably friendly, and air-conditioned. Both are located on the third floor, which is served by an elevator, and you step right out onto a great square. If you're looking for cheap beds in a great locale, assuming you can communicate enough to reserve a room, these places are unbeatable: **$ Hostal Isabel** (Sb-€35, Db-€43, Tb-€45, tel. 915-217-326, Beatrice) and **$ Pension Arcos,** which has a tiny roof terrace, a nice little lounge, and has been in the Hernández family since 1936 (Db-€36, tel. 915-324-994, Anuncia and Sabino).

More Cheap Sleeps

At Caballero de Gracia 6: These two *hostales* (which share the same building near Gran Vía Metro) are quiet, plain, and dreary, yet safe, on a quiet street a block past the unthreatening prostitutes of Calle de la Montera: **$ Hostal Aliste** (11 rooms on third floor, Sb-€30, D-€30–33, Db-€40–43, extra bed-€10, air-con €5 extra, elevator, tel. 915-215-979, h.aliste@teleline.es, Manuela's son Edward speaks English) and the humble **$ Pension Marina Santa** (nine rooms on second floor, D-€30, Db-€40, elevator, tel. 915-327-074, Lydia).

$ Hostal Residencia Louis XV is a big, plain, well-run, and clean place offering a good value. It's on a quiet eighth floor (there's an elevator). You'll find it where prostitute-lined Calle de la Montera hits noisy Gran Vía. It can be smoky, so if that's an issue, request a non-smoking room. They also run the 36-room Hostal Jerez—similar in every way except the name—located on the floor below (Sb-€42, Db-€55, Tb-€70, includes tax, air-con, elevator, Calle Montera 47, seventh floor, tel. 915-221-350, fax 915-221-021, www.hrluisxv.net, reservas@hrluisxv.net).

$ Hostal Metropol is a big, colorful, and very youthful youth hostel with 130 beds beautifully located at the noisy corner of Calle de la Montera and Gran Vía a few minutes' walk from Puerta del Sol (bed-€18, 3–5 beds per room, includes sheets and breakfast, free Internet access, Calle de la Montera 47, first floor, tel. 915-212-935, fax 915-212-934, www.metropolhostel.com, info@metropolhostel .com).

Near the Prado

To locate the following three places, please see "Madrid's Museum Neighborhood" map on page 227.

$$$ Hotel Kris Lope de Vega is your best business-class hotel value near the Prado. A four-star place that opened in 2000, it's a "cultural-themed" hotel inspired by the 17th-century writer Lope de Vega. With 60 rooms, it feels cozy and friendly for a formal business-class hotel (Sb-€108, Db-€140, Tb-€182, one child sleeps free, prices about 20 percent lower Fri–Sun and during most of the summer, air-con, elevator, Internet access in lobby, parking-€18/day, Calle Lope de Vega 49, tel. 913-600-011, fax 914-292-391, www.krishoteles.com, krislopedevega@krishoteles.com).

At Cervantes 34: Two fine budget *hostales* are at Cervantes 34 (Metro: Anton Martín—but not handy to Metro). Both are homey, with inviting lounge areas; neither serve breakfast. **$ Hostal Gonzalo**—with 15 spotless, comfortable rooms, well-run by friendly and helpful Javier—is deservedly in all the guidebooks. Reserve in advance (Sb-€45, Db-€52, Tb-€63, elevator, third floor, tel. 914-292-714, fax 914-202-007, www.hostalgonzalo.com, hostal@hostalgonzalo.com). Downstairs, the nearly as polished **$ Hostal Cervantes,** also with 15 fine rooms, is likewise good (Sb-€45, Db-€55, Tb-€70, includes tax, cheaper when slow and for longer stays, Wi-Fi and Internet access, second floor, tel. 914-298-365, fax 914-292-745, www.hostal-cervantes.com, correo@hostal-cervantes.com, Fabio and Christian).

EATING

In Spain, only Barcelona rivals Madrid for tastebud thrills. You have three dining choices: an atmospheric sit-down meal in a well-chosen restaurant; an unmemorable, basic sit-down meal; or a stand-up meal of tapas in a bar or four. Many restaurants are closed in August (especially through the last half). Madrid has famously good tap water, and waiters willingly serve it free—just ask for *agua del grifo.*

Eating Cheaply North of Puerta del Sol

See the map on page 248 for locations.

Restaurante Puerto Rico fills a long, congested hall by serving good meals for great prices to smart locals (€8.50 three-course fixed-price meal, Mon–Sat 13:00–16:30 & 20:30–24:00, closed Sun, Chinchilla 2, between Puerta del Sol and Gran Vía, tel. 915-219-834).

Hotel Europa Cafetería is a fun, high-energy scene with a mile-long bar, traditionally clad waiters, great people-watching, local cuisine, and a fine €10 fixed-price lunch (daily 7:30–24:00, next to Hotel Europa—listed on page 249, 50 yards off Puerta del Sol at Calle del Carmen 4, tel. 915-212-900). The menu lists three price levels: bar, table, or outside, on the terrace. While you pay a premium for the outdoor seating, it's a big hit with people-watchers.

El Corte Inglés' seventh-floor cafeteria is fresh, modern, and understated. While not particularly cheap, it's popular with locals (Mon–Sat 10:00–22:00, closed Sun, non-smoking section, just off Puerta del Sol at intersection of Preciados and Tetuán, see "One-Stop Shopping," page 210).

Casa Labra Taberna Restaurante is famous as the birthplace of the Spanish Socialist Party in 1879...and as a spot for great cod. Packed with Madrileños, it's a wonderful scene with three distinct sections: the stand-up bar (cheapest, with two lines: one for munchies, the other for drinks), a peaceful little sit-down area in back (a little more expensive but still cheap; good €6 salads), and a fancy restaurant (€20 lunches). Their tasty little €1 *Tajada de Bacalao* (cod) dishes put it on the map. The waiters are fun to joke around with (Mon–Sat 11:00–15:30 & 18:00–23:00, closed Sun, a block off Puerta del Sol at Calle Tetuán 12, tel. 915-310-081).

La Gloria de Montera Restaurante, a mod Spanish bistro with white tablecloths and a minimalist-library ambience, serves good food to locals (€7 fish and meat plates, daily 13:15–16:00 & 20:30–23:45, no reservations—arrive early or put your name on the list, a block from Gran Vía and Metro: Red de San Luis at Caballero de Gracia 10, tel. 915-234-407). Their sister restaurant, **La Finca de Susana,** is also extremely popular for the same reasons (daily 13:00–15:45 & 20:30–23:45, go early—line starts forming at about 20:00, just east of Puerta del Sol at Calle Arlabán 4, tel. 913-693-557).

Fresc Co is the place for a cheap, modern, fast, and buffet-style meal. It's a chain with a winning plan: a long, appealing salad and buffet bar with one cheap price for all-you-can-eat, including dessert and a drink (€8 lunch, €10 dinner, daily 12:30–24:00, air-con, Caballero de Gracià 8, tel. 915-216-052).

Vegetarian: **Artemisia II** is a hit with vegetarians who like good, healthy food in a smoke-free room without the typical hippie-ambience that comes with most veggie places (great €10.50 three-course fixed-price lunch Mon–Fri only, open daily 13:30–16:00 & 21:00–24:00, 2 blocks north of Puerta del Sol at Tres Cruces 4, a few steps off Plaza del Carmen, tel. 915-218-721). **Artemisia I,** II's older sister, is located two blocks east of Plaza Santa Ana at Ventura de la Vega 4, off San Jerónimo (same hours, tel. 914-295-092).

On or near Plaza Mayor

Madrileños enjoy Plaza Mayor (without its high costs) by grabbing a bite to go from a nearby bar and just planting themselves somewhere on the square to eat (squid sandwiches are popular—described below). But for many tourists, dinner at a sidewalk café

Eating near Plaza Mayor

1. Sobrino del Botín
2. Mercado de San Miguel
3. Torre del Oro Bar Andalú
4. Casa Rúa
5. Posada de la Villa
6. Giangrossi Helado Artesanal Ice Cream
7. Julian de Tolosa
8. Taberna Los Lucio
9. Casa Lucio
10. Taberna Tempranillo
11. El Madroño
12. Taberna Los Austrias
13. Taberna de los 100 Vinos
14. Las Carboneras (Flamenco)
15. Mesones (Cave Bars)

right on the Plaza Mayor is worth paying a premium for (consider Cervecería Pulpito, southwest corner of the square at #10).

Squid Sandwich: Plaza Mayor is famous for its *bocadillos de calamares.* For a tasty €2 squid-ring sandwich, line up at **Casa Rúa** at Plaza Mayor's northwest corner, a few steps up Calle Ciudad Rodrigo (daily 9:00–23:00). Hanging up behind the bar is a photo-advertisement of Plaza Mayor from the 1950s, when the square contained a park.

Bullfighting Bar: The **Torre del Oro Bar Andalú** on Plaza Mayor has walls lined with grisly bullfight photos (read the gory description on page 219). While this place is good for drinks, you pay a premium for the tapas and food...the cost of munching amidst all that bullephenalia while enjoying their excellent Plaza Major outdoor seating (daily 8:00–15:00 & 18:00–24:00).

Hemingway Haunt: **Sobrino del Botín** is a hit with many Americans because "Hemingway ate here" (daily 13:00–16:00 & 20:00–24:00, Cuchilleros 17, a block downhill from Plaza Mayor, tel. 913-664-217). It's touristy, pricey (€30 average meals), and the last place Papa would go now...but still, people love it, and the food is excellent (roast suckling pig is the specialty). If phoning to make a reservation, choose between the downstairs (for dark, medieval-cellar ambience) or upstairs (for a still-traditional, but airier and lighter elegance). While this restaurant boasts that it's the oldest in the world (dating from 1725), a nearby restaurant teases, "Hemingway never ate here."

On Calle Cava Baja, South of Plaza Mayor

Few tourists frequent this traditional neighborhood—Barrio de los Austrias, named for the Hapsburgs. It's three minutes south of Plaza Mayor, or a 10-minute walk from Puerta del Sol. Lined with a diverse array of restaurants and tapas bars, the street called Cava Baja is clogged with Madrileños out in search of a special meal. I've listed a few standards, but there are always excellent new eateries opening up. For a good, authentic Madrid dinner experience, take time to survey the many options along this street—between the first and last listings described below—and choose your favorite. A key wine-drinking phrase: *mucho cuerpo* (full-bodied).

Posada de la Villa serves Castilian cuisine in a 17th-century posada. This sprawling, multi-floor restaurant has dressy tables under open beams, which give it a rustic elegance. Peek into the big oven to see the baby pigs about to make some diner happy (roast suckling pig and lamb are the house specialties; €30 meals, Mon–Sat 13:00–16:00 & 20:00–24:00, closed Sun and Aug, Calle Cava Baja 9, tel. 913-661-860). If you're not going to Toledo or Sevilla, this is the place to try roast suckling pig or lamb.

Julian de Tolosa is classy, pricey, elegantly simple, and popular with natives who know good food. They offer a small, quality menu of Navarra's regional cuisine, from T-bone steak *(chuletón)* to red *tolosa* beans in a spacious, dressy, and sane setting (€40 meals, Mon–Sat 13:30–16:00 & 21:00–24:00, Sun 13:30–16:00, Calle Cava Baja 18, tel. 913-658-210).

Taberna Los Lucio is a jam-packed bar serving good tapas, salads, *huevos estrellados* (scrambled eggs with fried potatoes), and wine (Wed–Mon 13:00–16:00 & 20:30–24:00, closed Tue, Calle Cava Baja 30, tel. 913-662-984). Their basement is much less atmospheric.

Casa Lucio is a favorite splurge among power-dressing Madrileños. While the king and queen of Spain eat in this elegant place, it's accessible to commoners. This could be the best place in town for a special night out and a full-blown meal (€40 for dinner, daily 13:00–16:00 & 21:00–24:00, Calle Cava Baja 35; unless you're the king or queen, reserve several days in advance—and don't even bother on weekends; tel. 913-653-252).

Taberna Tempranillo, ideal for hungry wine-lovers, offers tapas and 250 kinds of wine. Wines available by the glass are listed on the board. With a phrasebook in hand or a spirit of adventure, use their fascinating menu to assemble your dream meal. It's packed and full of commotion—the crowds can be overwhelming. Arrive by 20:00 or plan to wait (daily 13:00–15:30 & 20:00–24:00, closed Aug, Cava Baja 38, tel. 913-641-532).

Ice Cream Finale: **Giangrossi Helado Artesanal** is a popular chain considered to serve some of Madrid's best ice cream. This Giangrossi—which has a plush white leather lounge and lots of great flavors—is a fun way to finish your dining experience in this area. It's just 50 yards from the La Latina Metro stop (Cava Baja 40, tel. 902-444-130).

Near the Royal Palace

Casa Ciriaco is popular with Madrileños who appreciate good traditional cooking (€30 meals, Thu–Tue 13:30–16:00 & 20:30–24:00, closed Wed and Aug, air-con, halfway between Puerta del Sol and the Royal Palace at Calle Mayor 84, tel. 915-480-620). It was from this building in 1906 that an anarchist bombed the royal couple on their wedding day (for details, see page 221; for location, see map on page 216). A photo of the carnage is inside the front door.

La Bola Taberna, touristy but friendly and tastefully elegant, specializes in *cocido Madrileño*—Madrid stew. The €18 stew consists of various meats, carrots, and garbanzo beans in earthen jugs. It's big enough to split—which they'll let you do, as long as the second person orders something small, like a salad. The stew is served as two courses: First you enjoy the broth as a soup, then you dig into the meat and veggies (Mon–Fri lunch seatings 13:30–15:30, evenings 20:30–23:00, closed Sat–Sun, cash only, midway between the Royal Palace and Gran Vía at Calle Bola 5, tel. 915-476-930).

La Paella Real Restaurante ("Royal Paella Restaurant") is considered a top spot for "a proper paella." While you'll see this saffron-rice specialty from Valencia served all over town, paella requires a special oven and big pan in order to cook it correctly. For your paella experience, enjoy this venerable and dressy spot (€14 per person for hearty portions—minimum of two, Tue–Sun 13:00–16:00 & 19:30–22:30, closed Mon, allow a good 30 min for your meal to arrive, between Puerta del Sol and the palace at Plaza  de la Ópera, Arrieta 2, see map on page 216 for location, tel. 915-420-942).

Near the Prado

Each of the three big art museums has a decent cafeteria. Or choose from these restaurants, all within a block of the Prado. To locate the following three places, please see "Madrid's Museum Neighborhood" map on page 227.

La Platería Bar Museo is a hardworking little café/wine bar with a good menu for tapas, light meals, and hearty salads (listed as *raciones* and *1/2 raciones* on the chalkboard). Its tables spill onto the leafy little Plaza de Platerías de Martínez (daily 8:00–24:00, air-con, directly across busy boulevard Paseo del Prado from Atocha end of Prado, tel. 914-291-722).

Taberna de Dolores, a winning formula since 1908, is a commotion of locals enjoying €2.50 *canapés* (open-face sandwiches), tasty *raciones* of seafood, and *cañas* (small beers) at the bar or at a few tables in the back (daily 11:00–24:00, Plaza de Jesús 4, tel. 914-292-243).

VIPS is a bright, popular chain restaurant, handy for a cheap and filling salad. Engulfed in a big bookstore, this is a high-energy, no-charm eatery (daily 9:00–24:00 in the morning, across the boulevard from northern end of Prado, under Palace Hotel). In 2001, Spain's first Starbucks opened next door.

> ## Breakfast in Madrid
>
> As most hotels don't include breakfast (and many don't even serve it), you may be out on the streets first thing looking for a place. Non-touristy places only offer a hot drink and a pastry, with perhaps a potato omelet and sandwiches (toasted cheese, ham, or both). Touristy places will have a *desayuno* menu with various ham and eggs deals. Try *churros* once (see below). Starbucks, a temptation to many for its familiarity, is always nearby. Get advice from your hotel staff for their favorite breakfast place.

Fast Food and Picnics

Fast Food: For an easy, light, cheap meal, try **Rodilla**—a popular sandwich and salad chain with a shop on the northeast corner of Puerta del Sol at #13 (Mon–Fri 9:30–23:00, Sat 10:00–23:00, Sun 11:00–23:00). **Pans & Company,** with shops throughout Madrid and Spain, offers healthy, tasty sandwiches and pre-packaged salads (daily 9:00–24:00, locations at Puerta del Sol, on Plaza Callao, at Gran Vía 30, and many more).

Picnics: The department store **El Corte Inglés** has well-stocked meat and cheese counters downstairs (Mon–Sat 10:00–22:00, closed Sun, see "One-Stop Shopping" on page 244). Downtown Madrid's neighborhood market, **Mercado de San Miguel,** is a perfect place to assemble a cheap picnic. How about breakfast surrounded by early-morning shoppers in the market's café? (Mon–Fri 9:00–14:30 & 17:15–20:15, Sat 9:00–14:30, closed Sun; to reach the market from Plaza Mayor, face the colorfully painted building and exit from the upper left-hand corner.)

Churros con Chocolate

Those not watching their cholesterol will want to try the deep-fried doughy treats called *churros* (or the thicker *porras*), best enjoyed by dipping them in pudding-like hot chocolate. While many *chocolaterías* offer the dunkable fritters, *churros* are most delicious when consumed fresh out of the greasy cauldron.

Chocolaterías Valor is a modern chain that does *churros* with pride and gusto. A few minutes' walk from nearly all my hotel recommendations, it's a fine place for breakfast (€3.50 *churros con chocolate*, Mon–Fri 8:00–24:00, Sat–Sun 9:00–24:00, a half-block below Plaza Callao and Gran Vía at Postigo de San Martín 7, tel. 915-229-288). With a Web address like www.amigosdelchocolate.com, you know where their heart is.

Chocolatería San Ginés is a classy institution, much loved by Madrileños for its *churros con chocolate* (€3). Dunk your *churros* into the chocolate pudding, as locals have done here for more than 100 years. While quiet before midnight, it's packed with the disco crowd in the wee hours; the popular dance club Joy Eslava is next door (Mon–Tue 18:00–7:00 in the morning, Wed–Sun 9:30–7:00 in the morning; from Puerta del Sol, take Calle de Arenal 2 blocks west, turn left on book-lined Pasadizo de San Ginés, and you'll see the café—it's at #5; tel. 913-656-546).

Tapas

Tapa-Hopping on Calle del Nuncio (near Calle Cava Baja)

El Madroño ("The Berry Tree," a symbol of Madrid) is a fun tapas bar that preserves a bit of old Madrid. A tile copy of Velázquez's famous *Drinkers* grins from its facade. Inside, look above the stairs for photos of 1902 Madrid. Study the coats of arms of Madrid through the centuries as you try a *vermut* on tap and a €2 sandwich. Or ask to try the *licor de madroño;* a small glass *(chupito)* costs €1.20 (€8.20 fixed-price lunch, quieter tables in the back, Tue–Sun 9:00–17:00 & 20:00–24:00, closed Mon, Plaza Puerta Cerrada 7, tel. 913-645-629). While indoor seating is bright and colorful, the sidewalk tables come with great people-watching.

Taberna Los Austrias, two blocks away, serves tapas, salads, and light meals on wood-barrel tables (daily 12:00–16:00 & 20:00–24:00, more formal seating in back, Calle Nuncio 17).

Taberna de los 100 Vinos, the "Tavern of 100 Wines," is extremely hip and popular. This classy wine bar serves top-end tapas and fine wine by the glass—see the chalkboard. Eat creative, non-traditional delicious €3.75 *pinchos* standing up, or sit down for excellent €15 *raciones*. For those in search of some fine local wine, this is the place (Tue–Sat 13:00–16:00 & 20:00–24:00, closed Sun–Mon, Calle Nuncio 17).

The Madrid Pub-Crawl Dinner (for Beginners)

For maximum fun, people, and atmosphere, go mobile for dinner: Do the "tapas tango," a local tradition of going from one bar to the next, munching, drinking, and socializing. Tapas are the toothpick

appetizers, salads, and deep-fried foods served in most bars. Madrid is Spain's tapas capital—tapas just don't get any better. Grab a toothpick and stab something strange—but establish the prices first, especially if you're on a tight budget or at a possible tourist trap. Some items are very pricey, and most bars push larger *raciones,* rather than

Plaza Santa Ana Pub Crawl

1. La Taurina Cervecería Bar
2. Museo del Jamón Bar & Lhardy Pastelería
3. La Casa del Abuelo Bar
4. Oreja de Oro Bar
5. Casa Toni Bar
6. Cervecería de Santa Ana & La Moderna Bars
7. Bar Viva Madrid
8. Artemisia I Veggie Restaurant
9. Taberna Casa Patas Flamenco
10. Vinoteca Barbechera
11. Gonzalez Wine & Cheese Shop
12. Launderette
13. Internet Café

smaller tapas. The real action begins late (around 20:00). But for beginners, an earlier start, with less commotion, can be easier. In good old-fashioned bars, a drink comes with a free tapa. The litter on the floor is normal; that's where people traditionally toss their trash and shells. Don't worry about paying until you're ready to go. Then ask for *la cuenta* (the bill).

If done properly, a pub crawl can be a highlight of your trip. Before embarking upon this culinary adventure, study and use the tapas tips on page 34. Your ability to speak a little Spanish will get you a much better (and less expensive) experience.

Prowl the area between Puerta del Sol and Plaza Santa Ana. There's no ideal route, but the little streets (in this book's map) between Puerta del Sol, San Jerónimo, and Plaza Santa Ana hold tasty surprises. Nearby, the street Jesús de Medinaceli is also lined with popular tapas bars. Below is a six-stop tapa crawl. These places are good, but don't be afraid to make some discoveries of your own. The more adventurous should read this crawl for ideas, and skip directly to the advanced zone (Lavapiés), described below.

• *From Puerta del Sol, walk east a block down Carrera de San Jerónimo to the corner of Calle Victoria. Across from the Museo del Jamón (Museum of Ham), you'll find...*

1. La Taurina Cervecería: This is a bullfighters' Planet Hollywood (daily 8:00–24:00, air-con). Wander among trophies and historic photographs. Each stuffed bull's head is named, along with his farm, awards, and who killed him. Among the many gory photos, study the first post: It's Che Guevara, Orson Welles, and Salvador Dalí, all enjoying a good fight. Around the corner, the Babe Ruth of bullfighters, El Cordobés, lies wounded in bed. The photo above and below shows him in action. I enjoyed the art. Then, inspired, I went for the *rabo de toro* (bull-tail stew, €12.50)— and regretted it. A good, basic dish here is *chorizos a la sidra* (spicy sausage in cider, €7) with a beer. If a fight's on, it'll be packed with aficionados gathered around the TV.

• *Across the street, just left of the Museo del Jamón, is the...*

2. Lhardy Pastelería: Offering a taste of Old World charm in this district of rowdy pubs, this place has been a fixture since 1839 for Madrileños wanting to duck in for a cup of soup or a light snack with a fortified wine. Step right in, and pretend you're an aristocrat back between the wars. Serve yourself. You'll pay as you leave (on the honor system). Help yourself to the silver water dispenser (free), a line of elegant bottles (each a different Iberian fortified wine: sherry, port, and so on, €1.80 per glass), a revolving case of meaty little pastries (€0.80 each), and a fancy soup dispenser (chicken broth consommé-€1.80, or €2.30 with a splash of sherry... local style—bottles in the corner, help yourself; daily 9:30–15:00 & 17:00–21:30, Carrera de San Jerónimo 8).

• *Now duck into the...*

3. Museo del Jamón (Museum of Ham): This frenetic, cheap, stand-up bar (with famously rude service) is an assembly line of fast and simple *bocadillos* and *raciones*. It's tastefully decorated—unless you're a pig (or a vegetarian). Take advantage of the easy photo-illustrated menus that show various dishes and their prices. The best ham is the pricey *jamón ibérico*—from pigs who led stress-free lives in acorn-strewn valleys. Just point and eat, but be specific: A plate of low-end *jamón blanco* portion costs only €2, while *jamón ibérico* costs €12. For a small sandwich, ask for a *chiquito* (€0.70, or

€3.10 for *ibérico*). If on a budget, don't let them sell you the *ibérico* (daily 9:00–24:00, sit-down restaurant upstairs, air-con).

• *Next, forage halfway up Calle Victoria to the tiny...*

4. La Casa del Abuelo: This is where seafood-lovers savor sizzling plates of tasty little *gambas* (shrimp) and *langostinos* (prawns). Try *gambas a la plancha* (grilled shrimp, €6.50) or *gambas al ajillo* (ahh-HHEEE-yoh, shrimp version of escargot, cooked in oil and garlic and ideal for bread dipping, €7) and a €1.80 glass of sweet red house wine (daily 11:30–15:30 & 18:30–23:30, Calle Victoria 12).

• *Across the street is...*

5. Oreja de Oro: The "Golden Ear" is named for what it sells—sautéed pigs' ears (*oreja*, €3). While oinker ears are a Madrid specialty, this place is Galician (see "Galician Cuisine," page 186), so people also come here for *pulpo* (octopus, €12), *pimientos de Padrón* (sautéed miniature green peppers—my favorite plate of the entire crawl, €3.50), and the distinctive *ribeiro* (ree-BAY-roh) wine, served Galician-style, in characteristic little ceramic bowls (to disguise its lack of clarity). Jaime is a frantic one-man show who somehow gets everything just right. Have fun here.

• *For a finale, continue uphill and around the corner to...*

6. Casa Toni: This is the spot for refreshing bowls of gazpacho—the cold tomato-and-garlic soup (€1.80, available all year but only popular when temperatures soar). Their specialties are *berenjena* (deep-fried slices of eggplant, €4) and *champiñones* (sautéed mushrooms, €4.50; open daily 11:30–16:00 & 18:00–23:30, closed July, Calle Cruz 14).

More Options: If you're hungry for more, and want a trendy, up-to-date, pricier tapas scene, head for Plaza Santa Ana, with lively bars spilling out onto the square. Survey the entire scene. Consider **Cervecería de Santa Ana** (tasty tapas with two zones: rowdy, circa-1900 beer-hall and classier sit-down) and **La Moderna** (wine, good tapas, pâté, and cheese plates—all with quality ingredients). **Naturbier** is a local microbrewery. **Vinoteca Barbechera,** at the downhill end of the square, has an inviting menu of tapas and fine wines by the glass (indoor and outdoor seating).

Gonzalez, a venerable gourmet cheese and wine shop with a circa 1930s interior, offers a genteel opportunity to enjoy a plate of first-class cheese or meat and a fine glass of wine with friendly service and a fun setting. Their assortment of five Spanish cheeses—more than enough for two—is a cheese lover's treat (Tue–Sat 9:00–24:00, closed Sun–Mon, three blocks past Plaza Santa Ana at Calle Leon 12, tel. 914-295-618).

The Lavapiés District Tapas Crawl (for the Adventurous)

A neighborhood called Lavapiés is emerging as a colorful magnet for people-watching. This is where the multiethnic tapestry of Madrid society enjoys pithy, cheap, seedy-yet-fun-loving life on the streets. Neighborhoods like this typically experience an evolution: initially they're so cheap that only the immigrants, downtrodden, counter-culture types live there. The diversity and color they bring attracts those with more money. Businesses erupt to cater to those bohemian/trendy tastes. Rents go up. Those who gave the area the colorful liveliness in the first place can no longer afford to live there. They move out and here comes Starbucks. For now, Lavapiés is edgy yet comfortable enough for most.

This district has almost no tourists. Old ladies with their tired bodies and busy fans hang out on their tiny balconies as they have for 40 years watching the scene. Shady types lurk on side streets (don't venture off the main drag, don't show your wallet or money, and don't linger on Plaza Lavapiés).

For food, you'll find all the various kinds of tapas bars described earlier in "The Madrid Pub-Crawl Dinner (for Beginners)," plus great Indian and Moroccan eateries. I've listed a couple of places that appealed to me...but explore your options. I'd recommend taking the entire walk once, then backtracking and eating at the place or places that appeal to you.

From the Anton Martin Metro stop (or Plaza Santa Ana), walk down Calle Ave Maria (on its way to becoming Calle Ave Allah) to Plaza Lavapiés (where old ladies hang out with the swarthy drunks and a mosaic of cultures treat this square as a communal living room; Metro station here), and then up Calle de Lavapiés to the newly remodeled square, Plaza Tirso de Molina (Metro stop). This square was once plagued by druggies. Now with flower kiosks and a playground, it's homey and inviting. This is a fine example of the vision for Madrid's public spaces.

On Calle Ave Maria: **Bar Melos** is a thriving dive jammed with a hungry and nubile local crowd. It's famous for its giant patty melts called *Zapatillas de Lacon y Queso* (because they're the size and shape of a *zapatilla* or slipper, €7 feeds at least two, Ave Maria 44, smoky tables in back). **Nuevo Café Barbieri,** one of a dying breed of smoky mirrored cafés with a circa-1940 ambience, offers classical music in the afternoon and jazz in the evening. Coffee sippers enjoy a menu of loaner books (Ave Maria 45).

On Calle de Lavapiés: At Calle de Lavapiés 44, consider a fun cluster of three places: **Indian Restaurant Shapla** (good €8 fixed-price meal), **Tetería Lakutubia** (atmospheric tea house), and **Montes Wine Bar** (countless wines open and served by the glass, good tapas, crawl under the bar to get to the WC).

TRANSPORTATION CONNECTIONS

By Train

Remember that Madrid has two main train stations: Chamartín and Atocha. At the Atocha Station, AVE and other long-distance trains depart from a different area than local *cercanías* trains (see "Arrival in Madrid," page 207).

AVE Trains: Spain's AVE (AH-vay) bullet train opens up some good itinerary options. Currently the AVE is handiest for visiting **Sevilla** (and, on the way, **Córdoba**). The basic Madrid–Sevilla second-class AVE fare is €47 to €71, depending upon departure time (the almost-as-fast TALGO is €12 less; first-class AVE costs €101 and comes with a meal). Consider this exciting day trip to Sevilla from Madrid: 7:00-depart Madrid, 8:45–12:40-in Córdoba, 13:30–21:00-in Sevilla, 23:30-back in Madrid. AVE also runs most of the route between Madrid and **Barcelona;** as tracks are completed, minutes are shaved off that journey (and euros are added to the price). You can now zip to Toledo in 30 minutes by AVE (€8). For the latest, pick up the AVE brochure at the station, or check out www.renfe.es/ave. Prices vary with times and class, and Eurailpass-holders get a big discount (e.g., Madrid to Sevilla is only €9 second-class, only at RENFE ticket windows). Reserve each AVE segment ahead (tel. 902-240-202 for Atocha AVE info).

From Madrid by Train to: Toledo (nearly hourly, 30-min AVE from Atocha), **El Escorial** (hourly, but bus is better—see below), **Segovia** (9/day, 2 hrs, both Chamartín and Atocha stations), **Ávila** (hourly, 1.5–2 hrs, from Chamartín and Atocha), **Salamanca** (6/day, 2.5 hrs, from Chamartín), **Santiago** (3/day, 8.5–13 hrs, includes night train, from Atocha), **Barcelona** (6/day, 4.5–6.5 hrs, mostly from Atocha, plus 2 night trains, 9 hrs; new high-speed AVE connection reduces time but increases cost), **Granada** (2/day, 6 hrs), **Sevilla** (hourly, 2.5 hrs by AVE; 2 slower TALGO trains/day, 3.5 hrs; both from Atocha), **Córdoba** (18 AVE trains/day, 2 hrs, from Atocha, 12 TALGO trains/day, 2 hrs), **Málaga** (7/day, 4 hrs, from Atocha), **Lisbon** (1/day departing at 22:45, 10 hrs, pricey overnight Hotel Train from Chamartín), **Paris** (1/day, 13.5 hrs, 1 direct overnight—a €130 Hotel Train, €119 in winter, from Chamartín). General train info: tel. 902-240-202.

By Bus

Madrid has four major bus stations, all connected by Metro.

Estación Sur de Autobuses (South Bus Station): From here, you can catch buses to **Toledo** (€4 one-way, 2/hr, 1–1.25 hrs, Continental Auto bus company at office #45, tel. 915-272-961), **Ávila** (8/day, 4 on weekends, 1.5 hrs, €11 round-trip), **Santiago**

(6/day, 7–9 hrs, includes 24:00–8:30 night bus), and **Granada** (13/day, 5.25 hrs, €15 one-way, Continental Auto, tel. 915-272-961). The station sets squarely on top of Metro: Méndez Álvaro (has TI, tel. 914-684-200, www.estaciondeautobuses.com).

Sepulvedana Station: This station serves **Segovia** (€6 one-way, €10 round-trip, 2/hr departing on half hour, 75 min, first departure at 6:30, last return at 21:30). From Metro: Príncipe Pío, follow signs to *autobus estacion* at Paseo de la Florida 11. It's a block away next to Florida Norte Hotel (tel. 915-598-955, www.lasepulvedana .es). The Príncipe Pío station is the old North Train Station, which has now morphed into a trendy mall. Buy a ticket from the window. Reservations are rarely necessary.

Conde de Casal Station: Buses depart here for **Salamanca** (hourly express, 2.5 hrs, €15). The station is at Calle Fernández Shaw 1 (Metro: Conde de Casal), and the buses are run by Auto-Res (tel. 902-020-052, www.auto-res.net).

Intercambiador de Moncloa Station: This station, in Metro: Moncloa, serves **El Escorial** (see below).

To El Escorial (by Bus, Train, and Car)

El Escorial is a popular day trip from Madrid (see next chapter). **Buses** leave from the Intercambiador de Moncloa Station in the basement of Madrid's Moncloa Metro stop and drop you in the El Escorial center (€3 one-way, buy ticket from driver, 4/hr, 45 min, in Madrid take bus #664 or slower #661 from Intercambiador's platform 3, Herranz Bus, tel. 918-969-028). One bus each day (except for Mon, when sights are closed) is designed to let travelers do the Valley of the Fallen as a side-trip from El Escorial (€3.20 round-trip). This tourist bus leaves El Escorial at 15:20 (15-min trip) and leaves the Valley of the Fallen at 17:30. **Trains** run hourly to El Escorial, but let you off a 20-minute walk (or a shuttle-bus ride, 2/hr) from the monastery and city center. By **car**, it's easy to visit El Escorial and the Valley of the Fallen on the way to Segovia (but note that sights are closed Mon).

Route Tips for Drivers

Avoid driving in Madrid. Rent your car when you depart. To leave Madrid from Gran Vía, simply follow signs for A6 (direction Villalba or Coruña) for Segovia, El Escorial, or the Valley of the Fallen (see next chapter for details). It's cheapest to make car-rental arrangements before you leave home. In Madrid, consider **Europcar** (central reservations tel. 902-105-030, San Leonardo 8 office tel. 915-418-892, Chamartín Station tel. 913-231-721, airport tel. 913-937-235), **Hertz** (central reservations tel. 902-402-405, Gran Vía 88 tel. 915-425-805, Chamartín Station tel. 917-330-400, airport tel. 913-937-228), **Avis** (Gran Vía 60 tel. 915-472-048, airport tel. 913-937-223), and **Alamo** (central reservations tel. 902-100-515). Ask about free delivery to your hotel. At the airport, most rental cars are returned at Terminal 1.

Madrid's Barajas Airport

Ten miles east of downtown, Madrid's modern airport has four terminals (1, 2, and 3 are connected by long indoor walkways, an 8-minute walk apart; 4 is a bus ride away). The Metro is in Terminal 2. To get to the new Terminal 4, take the 10-minute shuttle-bus trip (see below) from the other terminals and bus and subway stops. T-4 also has a satellite, T-45.

Get the right terminal: International flights use T-1 or T-4. T-1 is served by British Midland, Continental, Delta, easyJet, KLM, Lufthansa, SAS, US Airways, and others. T-4 has American, British Air, Iberia, Virgin Express, Vueling, and more.

At Terminal 1, you'll find a helpful English-speaking **TI** (marked *Oficina de Información Turística*, Mon–Sat 8:00–20:00, Sun 9:00–14:00, tel. 913-058-656); **ATMs**; a **flight info office** (marked simply *Information* in airport lobby, open 24 hours daily, tel. 902-353-570); a **post-office** window; a **pharmacy**; lots of **phones** (buy a phone card from the nearby machine); a few scattered **Internet** terminals (small fee); **eateries**; a **RENFE office** (where you can get train info and buy long-distance train tickets, daily 8:00–21:00, tel. 902-240-202); and on-the-spot **car-rental agencies** (see above). The new, super-modern Terminal 4 offers essentially the same services (www.aena.es).

A **green shuttle bus** connects terminals 1, 2, and 3 with Terminal 4 (free, leaves from departure level, 6/hr, 10 min). A new Metro station is in the works to T-4 (may be completed in 2007).

Iberia, Spanair, and Air Europa are Spain's airlines, connecting a reasonable number of cities in Spain, as well as international destinations (ask for best rates at travel agencies). Vueling is the most popular discount airline in Iberia (e.g., Madrid–Barcelona flight as cheap as €30 if booked in advance, tel. 902-333-933, www.vueling.com).

Getting Between the Airport and Downtown

By Public Bus: The new bus line #200 shuttles travelers between airport terminals 1, 2, and 3 (departing from arrival level every 10 minutes, runs 6:00–24:00) and the Metro stop Avenida de América (northeast of historical center) in about 20 minutes. From the Metro stop, you can connect to your hotel by taking the Metro or hopping a taxi. Bus #204 serves Terminal 4 the same way. The trip costs only €1 (buy ticket from driver; or get a shareable 10-ride Metrobus ticket for €6.15 at a tobacco shop—for more info, see "Getting Around Madrid," page 211).

By Minibus Shuttle: The AeroCity shuttle bus provides door-to-door transport in a seven-seat minibus with up to three hotel stops en route. The €19 fee covers up to three people per trip, and is a good value for two or three people with luggage that they don't want to haul on public transportation. Extra passengers pay more (runs 24 hours, price includes 1 piece of luggage and 1 carry-on per person, payment in cash, tel. 917-477-570, www.aerocity.com). They also offer a €36 private shuttle service for up to three people (your hotel can book it for you).

By Metro: The subway costs the same as the public bus, but involves two transfers (€1; or use a ticket from the 10-ride, €6.15 Metrobus ticket). The airport's futuristic Aeropuerto Metro stop (notice the cash machines, subway info booth, and huge lighted map of Madrid) is in Terminal 2. Access the Metro at the check-in level; to reach the Metro from Terminal 1's arrivals level, stand with your back to the baggage claim, then go to your far right, up the stairs, and follow red-and-blue Metro diamond signs to the station (8-min walk). To get to Puerta del Sol, take line #8 for 12 minutes to Nuevos Ministerios, then continue on line #10 to Tribunal, then line #1 to Puerta del Sol (30 min more total); or exit at Nuevos Ministerios and take a €5 taxi or bus #150 straight to Puerta del Sol.

By Taxi: For a taxi between the airport and downtown, allow €25 during the day *(Tarifa 1)* or €35 at night and on Sundays *(Tarifa 2)*. Insist on the meter. The €4.50 airport supplement is legal. Plan on getting stalled in traffic. For more on taxis—and corrupt cabbies—see "Getting Around Madrid," page 211.

NORTHWEST OF MADRID

Before slipping out of Madrid, consider several fine side-trips northwest of Spain's capital city, all conveniently reached by car, bus, or train.

Spain's lavish, brutal, and complicated history is revealed throughout Old Castile. This region, where the Spanish language originated, is named for its many castles—battle scars from the long-fought Reconquista.

An hour from Madrid, tour the imposing and fascinating palace at **El Escorial,** headquarters of the Spanish Inquisition. Nearby at the awe-inspiring **Valley of the Fallen,** pay tribute to the countless victims of Spain's bloody civil war.

Segovia, with its remarkable Roman aqueduct (pictured above) and romantic castle, is another worthwhile side-trip. At **Ávila,** you can walk the perfectly preserved medieval walls.

Planning Your Time

See El Escorial and the Valley of the Fallen together in less than a day (but not on Mon, when sights are closed). By car, do them en route to Segovia; by bus, make it a day trip from Madrid.

Segovia is worth a half day of sightseeing and is a joy at night. Ávila, while it has its charm, merits only a quick stop (if you're driving and in the area, 1.5 hrs from Madrid) to marvel at its medieval walls and, perhaps, check out St. Teresa's finger.

In total, these sights are worth two days if you're in Spain for less than a month. If you're in Spain for just a week, I'd still squeeze in a quick side-trip from Madrid to El Escorial and the Valley of the Fallen.

Northwest of Madrid

El Escorial

The Monasterio de San Lorenzo de El Escorial is a symbol of power rather than elegance. This 16th-century palace, 30 miles northwest of Madrid, gives us a better feel for the Counter-Reformation and the Inquisition than any other building. Built at a time when Catholic Spain felt threatened by Protestant "heretics," its construction dominated the Spanish economy for a generation

(1563–1584). Because of this bully in the national budget, Spain has almost nothing else to show from this most powerful period of her history.

The giant, gloomy building made of gray-black stone looks more like a prison than a palace. About 650 feet long and 500 feet wide, it has 2,600 windows, 1,200 doors, more than 100 miles of passages, and 1,600 overwhelmed tourists.

Four hundred years ago, the enigmatic, introverted, and extremely Catholic King Philip II (1527–1598) ruled his bulky empire and directed the Inquisition from here. To Philip, the building embodied the wonders of Catholic learning, spirituality, and arts. To 16th-century followers of Martin Luther, it epitomized the evil of closed-minded Catholicism. To architects, the building—built on the cusp between styles—exudes both Counter-Reformation grandeur and understated Renaissance simplicity. Today, it's a time capsule of Spain's "Golden Age," packed with history, art, and Inquisition ghosts. (And at an elevation of nearly 3,500 feet, it can be friggin' cold.)

The building was conceived by Philip II to serve several purposes: as a grand mausoleum for Spain's royal family, starting with his father, Charles V (known as Carlos I in Spain); as a monastery to pray (a lot) for the royal souls; as a small palace to use as a Camp David of sorts for Spain's royalty; and as a school to embrace humanism in a way that promoted the Catholic faith.

The Monasterio looks confusing at first, but you simply follow the *visita* arrows and signs in one continuous walk-through. This is the general order you'll follow (though some rooms may be closed for renovation):

The **Chamber of the Honor Guards** is hung with 16th-century tapestries including fascinating copies of Hieronymus Bosch's most famous and preachy paintings (which Philip II fancied). Don't miss El Greco's towering painting of the *Martyrdom of St. Maurice*. This was the artist's first commission after arriving in Spain from Venice. It was too subtle and complex for the king, so El Greco moved on to Toledo to find work.

Pass through the security scanner, then continue downstairs past the *consigna* bag check (Sala 1) to the fascinating **Museum of Architecture** (Museo de Arquitectura). It has long parallel corridors of fine models of the palace and some of the actual machinery and tools used to construct it. Huge stone-pinching winches, fat ropes, and rusty mortar spades help convey the immensity of this 21-year project involving 1,500 workers. At the big model, notice the complex is shaped like a grill, and recall how San Lorenzo—St. Lawrence, a Christian Spaniard martyred by pagan Romans (A.D. 258)—was burned to death on a grill. Throughout the palace, you'll see this symbol associated with the saint. The grill's "handle" was the palace, or residence of the royal family. The monastery and school gathered around the huge basilica.

Backtrack to the security scanner, then continue past the WCs in the patio to the **Hall of Battles** (Sala de Batallas). Its paintings celebrate Spain's great military victories—including the

El Escorial—Ground Floor

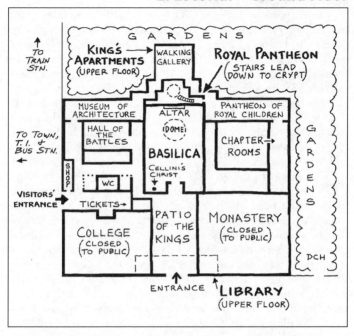

Battle of San Quentin over France (1557) on St. Lawrence's feast day that inspired the construction of El Escorial. The sprawling series, painted in 1590, helped teach the new king all the elements of warfare. Stroll the length for a primer on army skills.

From here, a corridor lined with various family trees (some scrawny, others lush and fecund) leads into the royal living quarters (the building's grill handle). Immediately inside the first door, find the small portrait of Philip II flanked by two large portraits of his daughters. The palace was like Philip: austere. Notice the simple floors, plain white walls, and bare-bones chandelier. This was the bedroom of one of his daughters. Notice the sheet warmer beside her bed—often necessary during the winter. Bend down to see the view from her bed...of the high altar in the basilica next door. The entire complex of palace and monastery buildings was built around that altar.

In the next room, notice the reclinable sedan chair that Philip II, thick with gout, was carried in (for 7 days) on his last trip from Madrid to El Escorial. He wanted to be here when he died.

The **Audience Chamber** is now a portrait gallery filled with Hapsburg royals painted by popular local artists. The portraits of unattractive people that line the walls provide an instructive peek at the consequences of inbreeding among royals—a common problem throughout Europe in those days.

The Spanish emperor Charles V (1500–1558) is over the fireplace mantel. Charles, Philip II's dad, was the most powerful man in Europe, having inherited not just the Spanish crown, but also Germany, Austria, the Low Countries (Belgium and the Netherlands), and much of Italy. When he announced his abdication in 1555, his son Philip II inherited much of this territory... plus the responsibility of managing it. Philip's draining wars with France, Portugal, Holland, and England—including the disastrous defeat of Spain's navy, the Spanish Armada, by England's Queen Elizabeth I (1588)—knocked Spain from its peak of power and began centuries of decline.

The guy with the good-looking legs next to Charles was his illegitimate son, Don Juan de Austria—famous for his handsome looks, thanks to a little fresh blood. Many other portraits show the unhappy effects of mixing blue blood with more of the same blue blood. When one king married his niece, the result was Charles II (1665–1700, opposite Charles V). His severe underbite (an inbred royal family trait) was the least of his problems. An epileptic before that disease was understood, poor "Charles the Mad" would be the last of the Spanish Hapsburgs. He died without an heir in 1700, ushering in the continent-wide War of the Spanish Succession and the dismantling of Spain's empire.

In the **Walking Gallery,** the royals got their exercise privately, with no risk of darkening their high-class skins with a tan. Study the 16th-century maps that line the walls. The slate strip on the floor is a sundial from 1755. It lined up with a (now plugged) hole in the wall so that at noon a tiny beam hit the middle of the three lines. Palace clocks were set by this. Where the ray crossed the strip indicated the date and sign of the zodiac.

As you enter the King's Antechamber, look back to study the fine inlaid-wood door (a gift from the German emperor that celebrates the exciting humanism of the age).

Philip II's bedroom is austere, like his daughter's. Look at the king's humble bed...barely queen-size. He too could view Mass at the basilica's high altar without leaving his bed. The red box next to his pillow holds the royal bedpan. But don't laugh—the king's looking down from the wall behind you. At age 71, Philip II, the gout-ridden king of a dying empire, died in this bed (1598).

From here, his body was taken to the **Royal Pantheon** (Panteón Real), the gilded resting place of 26 kings and queens... four centuries' worth of Spanish monarchy. All the kings are included—but only those queens who became mothers of kings.

There is a post-mortem filing system at work in the Pantheon. From the entrance, kings are on the left, queens on the right. (The only exception is Isabel II, since she was a ruling queen and her husband was a consort.) The first and greatest, Charles V and his Queen Isabel, flank the altar on the top shelf. Her son, Philip II, rests below Charles and opposite (only) one of Philip's four wives, and so on. There is a waiting process, too. Before a royal corpse can rest in this room, it needs to decompose for several decades. The three empty niches are already booked. The bones of the current king Juan Carlos' grandmother, Victoria Eugenia (who died in 1964), are ready to be moved in, but the staff can't explain why they haven't been transferred yet. Juan Carlos' father, Don Juan (who died in 1993), is also on the waiting list...controversially. Technically, he was never crowned king of Spain—Franco took control of Spain before Don Juan could ascend to the throne, and he was passed over for the job when Franco reinstituted the monarchy. Juan Carlos' mother is the most recent guest in the rotting room. So where does that leave Juan Carlos and Sofía? This hotel is *todo completo.*

The next rooms are filled with the tombs of lesser royals: Each bears that person's name (in Latin), relationship to the king, and slogan or epitaph. They lead to the wedding-cake **Pantheon of Royal Children** (Panteón de los Infantes) that holds the remains of various royal children who died before the age of seven (and their first Communion).

Head past the mini-gift shop and continue upstairs to the **Chapter Rooms** (Salas Capitulares). These rooms, where the monks met to do church business, are lined with big-name paintings: José Ribera, El Greco, Titian, and Velázquez. (More great paintings are in the monastery's Museum of Painting.) Continue to the final room to see some atypical Bosch paintings and the intricate, portable altar of Charles V. The **cloister** glows with bright, newly restored paintings by Pellegrino Tibaldi. Off the cloister is the **Old Church** (Iglesia Vieja),  which they used from 1571 to 1586, while finishing the basilica. During that time, the bodies of several kings, including Charles V, were interred here. Among the many paintings you'll see, look for the powerful *Martyrdom of Saint Laurence* by Tiziano (Titian) above the main altar.

Follow the signs to the **basilica.** In the center of the altar wall, find the flame-engulfed grill that features San Lorenzo (the same St. Lawrence from the painting) meeting his famous death—and taking "turn the other cheek" to new extremes. Lorenzo was so cool, he reportedly told his Roman executioners: "You can turn me over now—I'm done on this side." With your back to the altar, go to the right corner for the artistic highlight of the basilica: Benvenuto Cellini's marble sculpture *The Crucifixion.* Jesus' features are supposedly modeled after the Shroud of Turin. Cellini carved this from Carrara marble for his own tomb in 1562 (according to the letters under Christ's feet).

Last comes the immense **library** *(biblioteca)*—where it's clear that education was a priority for the Spanish royalty. Savor this room. The ceiling (by Tibaldi, depicting various disciplines labeled in Latin, the lingua franca of the multinational Hapsburg empire) is a burst of color. At the far end of the room, the elaborate model of the solar system looks like a giant gyroscope, revolving unmistakably around the

Earth, with a misshapen, under-explored North America. As you leave, look back above the wooden door. The plaque warns *"Excomunión..."*—you'll be excommunicated if you take a book without checking it out properly. Who needs late fees when you hold the keys to Hell?

Cost and Hours: Admission to the palace is €8 for the works *(completa),* or €7 for a *principal* ticket, which skips the Chapter Rooms and Royal Pantheon (April–Sept Tue–Sun 10:00–19:00, closed Mon, Oct–March closes at 18:00, last entry 60 min before closing, tel. 918-905-904). It's worth the extra euro to see it all. But be warned that if you arrive less than 90 minutes before closing, you can get only the cheaper ticket. There's also a €10 combo-ticket that includes Valley of the Fallen (buy ticket before 15:00 April–Sept or 14:00 Oct–March), but this makes sense only for drivers, since people taking the bus to the Valley of the Fallen have the site admission included in the cost of transportation.

Guidebook and Tours: You'll find scanty captions in English within the palace. For more information, get the *Guide: Monastery of San Lorenzo El Real de El Escorial,* which follows the general route you'll take (€7.50, available at any of several shops in the palace). While you can pay €9 for admission with a guided **tour** (ask at ticket office for next English tour), I'd rent the €2.30 **audioguide** instead (for €3, you also get a voucher for the audioguide at Valley of the Fallen).

Eating: To shop for a picnic, stop by the Mercado Público on Calle del Rey 9, a four-minute walk from the palace (Mon–Fri 9:00–14:00 & 17:00–20:00, Sat 10:00–14:00, closed Thu and Sat afternoons and Sun). There are restaurants with *menú del día* options on the nearby squares, but if you want a change from

El Escorial Town

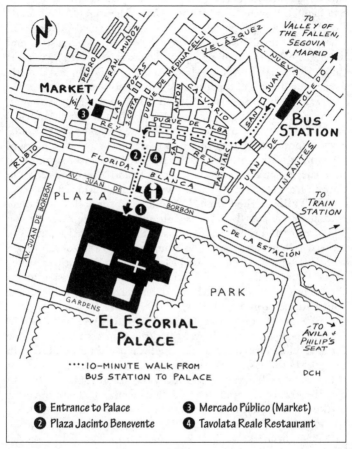

····10-MINUTE WALK FROM
BUS STATION TO PALACE

DCH

❶ Entrance to Palace   ❸ Mercado Público (Market)

❷ Plaza Jacinto Benevente   ❹ Tavolata Reale Restaurant

Spanish fare, get pizza at Tavolata Reale (Tue–Sun 11:00–16:00 &
20:00–24:00, closed Mon, inside a mini-shopping gallery off Plaza
Jacinto Benevente, tel. 918-904-591).

TRANSPORTATION CONNECTIONS

Coming from Madrid: Buses leave from Madrid's Moncloa
Metro stop and drop you in the town center of San Lorenzo de
El Escorial, a 10-minute walk from the Monasterio (4/hr, 45 min,
hourly on weekends, none Sun 15:00–17:30, in Madrid take faster
bus #664 or #661).

Once in El Escorial, it's a pleasant 10-minute stroll from the
station through the town of San Lorenzo de El Escorial. Exit the
bus station from the back ramp that leads over the parked buses,

turn left, and follow the newly cobbled pedestrian lane, Calle San Juan. This street veers to the right and becomes Calle Juan de Leyra. In a few short blocks, it dead-ends at Duque de Medinaceli, where you'll turn left and see the palace. Stairs lead past several decent eateries, through a delightful park, past the **TI** (Mon–Fri 10:00–18:00, Sat–Sun 10:00–19:00, tel. 918-905-313), and directly to the tourist entry of the immense palace/monastery.

Taking the **train** from Madrid is less convenient. Although trains (*Cercanías* line C-8a) leave twice hourly from Madrid's Atocha and Chamartín stations, you'll have to choose your secondary transportation into town. From the train station, it's a pleasant 20-minute walk (through Casita del Príncipe park, straight up from the station), a €4 taxi ride, or a €1 shuttle-bus ride (2/hr) to the San Lorenzo de El Escorial town center and Monasterio.

To Valley of the Fallen: Without a car, the easiest way there is to negotiate a deal with a taxi (to take you there, wait for you 30–60 min, and then bring you back to El Escorial, about €30). Otherwise one bus a day (#660) connects the Valley of the Fallen with El Escorial (15 min, leaves El Escorial at 15:15, leaves Valley of the Fallen at 17:30, €7.80 round-trip includes admission to the site, no bus on Mon when El Escorial monastery and Valley of the Fallen are closed).

By Car: It's quite simple. Taxi to your car-rental office in Madrid (or ask if they'll deliver the car to your hotel). Pick up the car by 8:30 and ask directions to highway A6. From Gran Vía in central Madrid it's easy: Follow signs to A6 (direction *Villalba* or *A Coruña*). The freeway leads directly out of town. Stay on the A6 past the first El Escorial exit. At kilometer 37, you'll see the cross marking the Valley of the Fallen ahead on the left. Exit 47 takes you to both the Valley of the Fallen (after a half mile, a granite gate on right marks *Valle de los Caídos* turn-off) and El Escorial (follow signs to San Lorenzo del Escorial).

The nearby **Silla de Felipe** (Philip's Seat) is a rocky viewpoint where the king would come to admire his palace as it was being built. From El Escorial, follow directions to Ávila, then M505 to Valdemorillo; look for a sign on your right after about a mile.

When you leave El Escorial for Madrid, Toledo, or Segovia, follow signs to *A6 Guadarrama*. After about six miles, you pass the Valley of the Fallen and hit the freeway.

Valley of the Fallen

Six miles from El Escorial, high in the Guadarrama Mountains, is the Valley of the Fallen (Valle de los Caídos). A 500-foot-tall granite cross marks this immense and powerful underground monument to the victims of Spain's 20th-century nightmare—its civil war (1936–1939).

Approaching by car or bus, you enter the sprawling park through a granite gate (€5, or €7.80 to include round-trip bus from El Escorial; €10 for combo-ticket with El Escorial—makes sense only for drivers, since Valley of the Fallen admission is included with bus ticket; April–Sept Tue–Sun 10:00–19:00, closed Mon, last entry 60 min before closing, basilica closes 30 min before

site closes, Oct–March closes at 18:00, tel. 918-905-611). The best views of the cross are from the bridge (but note that it's illegal to stop anywhere along this road). To the right, tiny chapels along the ridge mark the Stations of the Cross, where pilgrims stop on their hike to this memorial.

In 1940, prison workers dug 220,000 tons of granite out of the hill beneath the cross to form an underground basilica, then used the stones to erect the cross (built like a chimney, from the inside). Since it's built directly over the dome of the subterranean basilica, a seismologist keeps a careful eye on things.

The stairs that lead to the imposing monument are grouped in sets of tens, meant to symbolize the Ten Commandments (including "Thou shalt not kill"—hmm). The emotional *pietà* draped over the basilica's entrance is huge—you could sit in the palm of Christ's hand. The statue was sculpted by Juan de Ávalos, the same artist who created the dramatic figures of the four Evangelists at the base of the cross. It must have had a powerful impact on mothers who came here to remember their fallen sons.

A solemn silence and a stony chill fill the basilica. At 300 yards long, the basilica was built to be longer than St. Peter's...but

the Vatican had the final say when it blessed only 262 of those yards. Many Spaniards pass under the huge, foreboding angels of fascism to visit the grave of General Franco—an unusual place of pilgrimage, to say the least.

After walking through the two long vestibules, stop at the iron gates of the actual basilica. The line of torch-like lamps adds to the shrine ambience. Franco's prisoners, the enemies of the right, dug this memorial out of solid rock from 1940 to 1959. (While it looks like there's bare rock still showing on the ceiling, it's just a clever design.) The sides of the

The Spanish Civil War
(1936–1939)

Thirty-three months of warfare killed 200,000 Spaniards. Unlike America's Civil War, which split America roughly north and south, Spain's war was between classes and ideologies, dividing every city and village, and many families. It was especially cruel, with atrocities and reprisals on both sides.

The war began as a military coup to overthrow the democratically elected Republic, a government too liberal and disorganized for the army and conservative powers. The rebel forces, called the Nationalists *(Nacionalistas)*, consisted of the army, monarchy, Catholic church, big business, and rural estates, with aid from Germany, Italy, and Portugal. Trying to preserve the liberal government were the Republicans *(Republicanos)*, also called Loyalists: the government, urban areas, secularists, small business, and labor unions, with aid from the United States (minimal help), and the "International Brigades" of communists, socialists, and labor organizers.

In the summer of 1936, the army rebelled and took control of their own garrisons, rejecting the Republic and pledging allegiance to General Francisco Franco (1892–1975). These Nationalists launched a three-year military offensive to take Spain region by region, town by town. The government ("Republicans") cobbled together an army of volunteers, local militias, and international fighters. The war pitted conservative Catholic priests against socialist factory workers, rich businessmen against radical students, sunburned farmers loyal to the old king against upwardly mobile small businessmen. People suffered. You'll notice that nearly any Spaniard in his or her 70s is very short—a product of growing up during these hungry and very difficult Civil War years.

Spain's Civil War attracted international attention. Adolf Hitler of Germany and Benito Mussolini of Italy sent troops and supplies to their fellow fascist, Franco. It was Hitler's Luftwaffe that helped Franco bomb the town of Guernica (April 1937), an event captured on canvas by the artist Picasso (see page 240). On the Republican side, hundreds of Americans (including Ernest Hemingway) steamed over to Spain to fight for democracy as part of the "Abraham Lincoln Brigade."

By 1939, only Barcelona and Madrid held out. But they were no match for Franco's army. On April 1, 1939, the war ended, beginning 37 years of iron-fisted rule by Franco.

monument are lined with copies of 16th-century Brussels tapestries of the Apocalypse, and side chapels contain alabaster copies of Spain's most famous statues of the Virgin Mary.

Interred behind the high altar and side chapels (marked "RIP, 1936–1939, died for God and country") are the remains of the approximately 50,000 people, both *Republicanos* and Franco's *Nacionalistas*, who lost their lives in the war. Regrettably, the urns are not visible, so it is Franco who takes center stage. His grave, strewn with flowers, lies behind the high altar. In front of the altar is the grave of José Antonio Primo de Rivera (1903–1936), the founder of Spanish fascism, who was killed by Republicans during the Civil War. Between these fascists' graves, the statue of a crucified Christ is lashed to a timber Franco himself is said to have felled. The seeping stones seem to weep for the victims.

As you leave, stare into the eyes of those angels with swords and two right wings and think about all the "heroes" who keep dying "for God and country," at the request of the latter. A Mass closes off the entire front of the basilica (altar and tombs) to the public daily from 11:00 to 12:05. The resident boys' choir (the "White Voices"—Spain's answer to the Vienna Boys' Choir) generally sings during the Mass (you can sit through the service, but not sightsee during this time). The €2 audioguide is heavy on the theological message of the statues and tapestries and ignores Franco.

The expansive view from the monument's terrace includes the peaceful, forested valley and sometimes snow-streaked mountains. For an even better view, consider taking a **funicular** trip—with a short commentary in English—to the base of the cross (€1.50 one-way, €2.50 round-trip, pay fare at machine, April–Sept Tue–Sun 11:00–18:30, closed Mon, 3/hr; Oct–March Tue–Sun 11:00–16:30, closed Mon, 2/hr, has restaurant and public WC). You can hike back down in 25 minutes. If you have a car, you can drive up past the monastery and hike from the start of the trail marked *Sendero a la Cruz.*

Near the parking lot and bus stop at Valley of the Fallen is a small snack bar and picnic tables. Basic overnight lodging is available at the **monastery** behind the cross (100 rooms, Sb-€42, Db-€44, includes meals, tax, and a pass to enter and leave the park after hours, tel. 918-905-494, fax 918-961-542, no English spoken). A meditative night here is good mostly for monks.

For information on how to reach the Valley of the Fallen from El Escorial by bus, see "Transportation Connections" in El Escorial, above.

Segovia

Fifty miles from Madrid, this town of 55,000 boasts a thrilling Roman aqueduct, a grand cathedral, and an historic castle. Since the city is more than 3,000 feet above sea level and just northwest of a mountain range that leaves it exposed to northern breezes, people from Madrid come here for a break from the summer heat.

Day-Tripping from Madrid: Considering the easy bus connections, Segovia makes a fine day trip from Madrid. The disadvantages are that you spend the coolest hours of the day (early and late) on the bus; you miss the charming evening scene in Segovia; and you'll pay more for your hotel in Madrid than in Segovia. Still, Segovia offers a rewarding and convenient break from the big-city intensity of Madrid.

ORIENTATION

Segovia is a medieval "ship" ready for your inspection. Start at the stern—the aqueduct—and stroll up Calle de Cervantes and Calle Juan Bravo to the prickly Gothic masts of the cathedral. Explore the tangle of narrow streets around the playful Plaza Mayor and then descend to the Alcázar at the bow.

Tourist Information

Segovia has two TIs: The one on Plaza Mayor covers both Segovia and the surrounding region (at #10, daily 9:00–20:00, tel. 921-460-334). The other TI, at Plaza del Azoguejo at the base of the aqueduct, specializes in Segovia and has lots of friendly staff, WCs, and a gift shop (daily 10:00–20:00, see wooden model of Segovia, tel. 921-466-720, www.aytosegovia.com).

Arrival in Segovia

If you arrive by bus, it's a 10-minute walk to the town center (exit left out of the bus station, continue straight across the street, and Avenida Fernández Ladreda leads to the aqueduct). Day-trippers can store luggage at the train station, but not at the bus station. To reach the center from the train station, walk 35 minutes; catch bus #6 or 8; or take a taxi. If arriving by car, see "Transportation Connections," page 290.

Helpful Hints

Shopping: If you buy handicrafts such as tablecloths from street vendors, make sure the item you're buying is the one you actually get; some unscrupulous vendors substitute inferior goods at the last minute.

Local Guide: Elvira Valderrama Rascon, a hardworking young woman, is a good English-speaking guide (€95/half-day tour, ask for Rick Steves discount, mobile 636-227-949, elvisvalrras @yahoo.com).

SELF-GUIDED WALK

Welcome to Historic Segovia

This 15-minute walk is all downhill from the city's main square along the pedestrian-only street to the Roman aqueduct. It's most enjoyable just before dinner, when it's cool and filled with strolling locals.

Start on Segovia's inviting **Plaza Mayor**—once the scene of executions, religious theater, and bullfights with spectators jamming the balconies. In the 19th century, the bullfights were stopped. When locals complained, they were given a more gentle form of entertainment—bands in the music kiosk. Today the very best entertainment is simply enjoying a light meal, snack, or drink in your choice of the many restaurants and cafés lining the square. The Renaissance church opposite the City Hall and behind the TI was built to replace the church where Isabel was proclaimed Queen of Castile in 1474. The symbol of Segovia is the aqueduct—find it in the seals on the Theater Juan Bravo and atop the City Hall. Head down Calle de Isabel la Católica (downhill, to right of Hotel Infanta Isabel) and tempt yourself with the pastries in the window display of the corner bakery.

After 100 yards, at the first intersection, you'll see the Corpus Christi Convent on the right. For €1.50, you can pop in to see the Franciscan church (with lots of art featuring St. Francis), which was once a synagogue, which was once a mosque. (While sweet and peaceful, the church is skippable.)

After another 100 yards, you come to the complicated Plaza de San Martín, a commotion of history surrounding a striking statue of Juan Bravo. When Charles V, a Hapsburg who didn't even speak Spanish, took power, he imposed his rule over Castile. This threatened the local nobles, who—inspired and led by Juan

Segovia

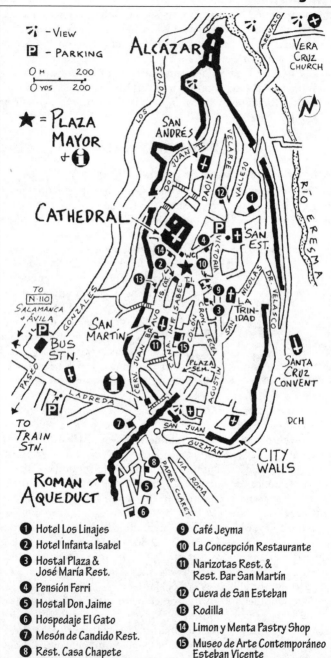

- **1** Hotel Los Linajes
- **2** Hotel Infanta Isabel
- **3** Hostal Plaza & José María Rest.
- **4** Pensión Ferri
- **5** Hostal Don Jaime
- **6** Hospedaje El Gato
- **7** Mesón de Candido Rest.
- **8** Rest. Casa Chapete
- **9** Café Jeyma
- **10** La Concepción Restaurante
- **11** Narizotas Rest. & Rest. Bar San Martín
- **12** Cueva de San Esteban
- **13** Rodilla
- **14** Limon y Menta Pastry Shop
- **15** Museo de Arte Contemporáneo Esteban Vicente

Bravo—revolted in 1521. While Juan Bravo lost the battle—and his head—he's still a symbol of Castilian pride. This statue was erected in 1921 on the 400th anniversary of his death.

On the same square, the 12th-century Church of St. Martín is Segovian Romanesque in style (a mix of Christian Romanesque and Moorish styles). The 14th-century Tower of Lozoya, behind the statue, is one of many fortified towers that marked the homes of feuding local noble families. Clashing loyalties led to mini civil wars. In the 15th century, as Ferdinand and Isabel centralized authority in Spain, nobles were required to lop their towers. You'll see the once-tall, now-stubby towers of 15th-century noble mansions all over Segovia.

In front of the Juan Bravo statue (downhill end of square) stands the bold and bulky House of Siglo XV. Its fortified *Isabelino* style was typical of 15th-century Segovian houses. Later, in a more peaceful age, the boldness of these houses was softened with the decorative stucco work—Arabic-style floral and geometrical patterns—that you see today (for example, in the big house across the street). At Plaza del Platero Oquendo, 50 yards farther downhill on the right, you'll see a similar once-fortified, now-softened house with a cropped tower.

At the next corner, find the "house of a thousand beaks" with another truncated tower. This building, maintaining its original Moorish design, has a wall just past the door, which blocks your view from the street. This wall, the architectural equivalent of a veil, hid this home's fine courtyard—Moors didn't flaunt their wealth. Step inside; there may be art students at work and perhaps an exhibit on display.

From here, stroll 100 yards, and you'll see the Roman aqueduct, which marks the end of this walk.

SIGHTS

▲**Roman Aqueduct**—Segovia was a Roman military base and needed water. So Emperor Trajan's engineers built a nine-mile aqueduct to channel water from the Río Frío to the city, culminating at the Roman castle (which is the Alcázar today). The famous and exposed section of the 2,000-year-old *acueducto romano* is 2,500 feet long and 100 feet high, has 118  arches, was made from 20,000 granite blocks without any mortar, and can still carry a stream of water. It actually functioned until the late 19th century. On Plaza del Azogüejo, a grand stairway leads from the base of the aqueduct to the top—offering close-up looks at the imposing work.

▲ **Cathedral**—Segovia's cathedral, built in Renaissance times (1525–1768, the third on this site), was Spain's last major Gothic

building. Embellished to the hilt with pinnacles and flying buttresses, the exterior is a great example of the final, overripe stage of Gothic, called Flamboyant. Yet the Renaissance is arriving—as evidenced by the fact that the cathedral is crowned by a dome, not a spire.

The dark, spacious, and elegantly simple interior provides a delightful contrast to the frilly exterior. The **choir** features finely carved wooden stalls from the previous church (1400s). The *catedra* (bishop's chair) is in the center rear of the choir. The many side chapels are mostly 16th century, and come with big locking gates—a reminder that they were the private sacred domain of the rich families and guilds who "owned" them. They could enjoy private Masses here with their names actually spoken in the blessings, and a fine burial spot close to the altar. Find the **Capilla La Concepción** (a chapel in the rear that looks like a mini art gallery). Its many 17th-century paintings hang behind a mahogany wood gate imported from colonial America.

The painting, *Tree of Life* by Ignacio Ries (left of the altar), shows hedonistic mortals dancing atop the Tree of Life. As a skeletal Grim Reaper prepares to receive them into Hell (by literally chopping down the tree...timberrrr), Jesus rings a bell imploring them to wake up before it's too late. The center statue is Mary of the Apocalypse (as described in Revelations, standing on a devil and half moon, which looks like bull's horns). Mary's pregnant and the devil licks his evil chops, waiting to devour the baby Messiah.

Opposite, a fine door (which leads into the cloister) is crowned by a painted Flamboyant Gothic *pietà* in its tympanum (the statue of Jesus with a skirt, on the left, is a reminder of how prudishness from the past looks silly in the present).

The **cloister** holds a fine little one-room museum containing French tapestries, paintings, and silver reliquaries. A glass case holds keys to the 17th-century private chapel gates. The gilded chapter room is draped with precious Flemish tapestries. Notice the gilded wagon. The Holy Communion wafer is placed in the top of this temple-like cart and paraded through town each year during the Corpus Christi festival. From the cloister courtyard, you can see the Renaissance dome rising above the otherwise Gothic rooftop (€2, free on Sun 9:30–13:00, daily April–Sept 9:30–18:30, Oct–March 9:00–17:30).

▲**Alcázar**—In the Middle Ages, this fortified palace was one of the favorite residences of the monarchs of Castile, a key fortress for controlling the region. The Alcázar grew through the ages, and its function changed many times: After its stint as a palace, it was a prison for 200 years, and then a Royal Artillery School. It burned in 1862. Since the fire, it's basically been a museum. You'll enjoy a one-way route through 11 rooms, including a fine view terrace. The visit ends at the tower (€1.50 extra); its 152 steps up a tight spiral staircase reward you with the only 360-degree city view in town. The Alcàzar's 45-minute audioguide describes each room. What you see today is rebuilt—a Disneyesque exaggeration of the original. Still, its fine Moorish decor and historic furnishings are fascinating. The sumptuous ceilings are accurately restored in Mudejar style, and the throne-room ceiling is the artistic highlight of the palace.

You'll see a big mural of Queen Isabel the Catholic being proclaimed Queen of Castile and León in Segovia's main square in 1474. The Hall of the Monarchs is lined with the busts of the 52 rulers of Castile and León who ruled during the long and ultimately successful Reconquista (711–1492): from Pelayo (the first), clockwise to Juana VII (the last). There were only seven queens during the period (the numbered ones). In this current age of Islamic extremists decapitating Christians' heads, study the painting of St. James the Moor Slayer—with Muslim heads literally rolling at his feet (poignantly...in the chapel). James is the patron saint of Spain. His name was the rallying cry in the centuries-long Christian crusade to push the Muslim Moors back into Africa.

Stepping onto the terrace (the site of the original Roman military camp, circa A.D. 100) with its vast views, marvel at the natural fortification provided by this promontory cut by the confluence of two rivers. The Alcázar marks the end (and physical low point) of the gradual downhill course of the nine-mile-long Roman aqueduct. Can you find the mountain nicknamed *Mujer Muerta*, meaning "dead woman"?

In the armory (just after the terrace), find the king's 16th-century, ornately carved ivory crossbow with the hunting scene shown in the adjacent painting. The final rooms are the Museum of Artillery, recalling the period (1764–1862) when this was the

Royal Artillery School. It shows the evolution of explosive weaponry, with old photos and prints of the Alcázar.

Cost and Hours: €3.50 for palace, €1.50 for tower, €5 for combo-ticket, free on Tue, daily April–Sept 10:00–19:00, Oct–March until 18:00. Buy your ticket at Casa de Chimia, facing the palace on your left. The audioguide costs €3. Pick up a free English leaflet. Tel. 921-460-759.

Church of San Justo—This simple yet stately old church has fascinating 12th- and 13th-century frescoes filled with Gothic symbolism, plus a storks' nest atop its tower. From the base of the aqueduct, it's a short climb uphill into the newer part of town (free, Mon–Sat 11:00–14:00 & 17:00–19:00; closed Sun and when the volunteer caretaker, Rafael, needs to run an errand; located a couple of blocks from Plaza del Azoguejo). Kind old Rafael may let you risk climbing the dangerous, claustrophobic bell tower (filled with pigeon poop) for a commanding Segovia view.

Museo de Arte Contemporáneo Esteban Vicente—A collection of local artist Esteban Vicente's abstract art is housed in two rooms of the remodeled remains of Henry IV's 1455 palace. Wilder than Rothko but more restrained than Pollock, his vibrant work influenced post-WWII American art. The temporary exhibits can be more interesting than the permanent collection (€2.40, free on Thu, roughly Tue–Sat 11:00–19:00, Sun 11:00–15:00, closed Mon).

Near Segovia

Vera Cruz Church—This 12-sided, 13th-century Romanesque church, built by the Knights Templar, once housed a piece of the "true cross" (€1.75, Tue–Sun 10:30–13:30 & 15:30–19:00, closed Mon and Nov, closes at 18:00 in winter, outside of town beyond the castle, a 25-min walk from main square, tel. 921-431-475). There's a postcard view of the city from here, and more views follow as you continue around Segovia on the small road below the castle, labeled *ruta turística panorámica*.

▲**La Granja Palace**—This "little Versailles," six miles south of Segovia, is much smaller and happier than nearby El Escorial. The palace and gardens were built by the homesick French-born King Philip V, grandson of Louis XIV. Today, it's restored to its original 18th-century splendor with its royal collection of clocks and crystal (actually made at the palace's royal crystal factory). Plumbers and gardeners imported from France and Italy made Philip a garden that rivaled Versailles'. The fanciful fountains feature mythological stories

(explained in the palace audioguide). The Bourbon Philip chose to be buried here rather than with his Hapsburg predecessors at El Escorial. His tomb is in the adjacent church, included with your ticket (€5 with Spanish-speaking guide, €4.50 without guide, April–Sept Tue–Sun 10:00–18:00, closed Mon; Oct–March Tue–Sat 10:00–13:30 & 15:00–17:00, Sun 10:00–14:00, closed Mon; tel. 921-470-019, www.patrimonionacional.es). Fourteen buses a day (fewer on weekends) make the 20-minute trip from Segovia (catch at the bus station) to San Ildefonso–La Granja. The park is free (daily 10:00–20:00, until 19:00 in winter).

SLEEPING

The best places are on or near the central Plaza Mayor. This is where the city action is: the best bars, most touristic and *típico* eateries, and the TI. During busy times—on weekends and in July and August—arrive early or call ahead.

In the Old Center, near Plaza Mayor
$$$ Hotel Los Linajes is ultra-classy, with rusticity mixed into its newly poured concrete. This poor man's parador is a few blocks beyond Plaza Mayor, with territorial views and modern, air-conditioned niceties (Sb-€73, Db-€99, big Db-€129, Tb-€118, cheaper off-season, breakfast-€9, elevator, parking-€11, Dr. Velasco 9, tel. 921-460-475, fax 921-460-479, www.loslinajes.com, hotelloslinajes@terra.es). From Plaza Mayor, take Escuderos downhill; at the five-way intersection, angle right on Dr. Velasco. Drivers, follow brown hotel signs from the aqueduct to its tight but handy garage.

Sleep Code

(€1 = about $1.20, country code: 34)
S = Single, **D** = Double/Twin, **T** = Triple, **Q** = Quad, **b** = bathroom, **s** = shower only. Unless otherwise noted, you can assume credit cards are accepted and English is spoken. Breakfast is generally not included.

To help you easily sort through these listings, I've divided the rooms into three categories, based on the price for a standard double room with bath during high season (breakfast and 7 percent IVA tax not included):

  $$$ Higher Priced—Most rooms €85 or more.
    $$ Moderately Priced—Most rooms between €30–85.
     $ Lower Priced—Most rooms €30 or less.

$$$ Hotel Infanta Isabel, right on Plaza Mayor, is the ritzi-est hotel in the old town, with 38 elegant rooms, some with plaza views (Sb-€60–77, Db-€97–114 depending on room size, less in winter, breakfast on the square-€9, elevator, valet parking-€12, tel. 921-461-300, fax 921-462-217, www.hotelinfantaisabel.com, admin@hotelinfantaisabel.com).

$ Hostal Plaza, just off Plaza Mayor, has extremely strict management, snaky corridors, and some tight squeezes. But its 28 rooms are clean and cozy (S-€22, Sb-€33, D-€30, Db-€42, Tb-€56, parking-€10, Cronista Lecea 11, tel. 92-146-0-303, fax 921-460-305, www.hostal-plaza.com, informacion@hostal-plaza.com).

$ Pensión Ferri, half a block off Plaza Mayor, is located opposite a Guinness beer sign and within the bowels of an old mansion. This quiet, unmarked, five-room place is cheaper than the youth hostel (S-€16, D-€23, shower-€2, cash only, Escuderos 10, tel. 921-460-957, no English spoken by laid-back Juan or Carmen, who are not about to invest in the place since retirement is just around the corner).

Outside of the Old Town, near the Aqueduct

$$ Hostal Don Jaime, opposite the Church of San Justo, is a friendly, family-run place with 31 basic, worn yet well-maintained rooms; seven rooms are in an annex across the street (S-€23, D-€30, Db-€43, Tb-€53, Qb-€63, parking-€7, Ochoa Ondategui 8; from TI at Plaza del Azogüejo, cross under the aqueduct, go right, angle left, then snake uphill for 2 blocks, tel. & fax 921-444-787, hostaldonjaime@hotmail.com).

$$ Hospedaje el Gato is another very clean, family-run place on a quiet nondescript square just outside the old town; its 10 rooms are modern and comfortable (Sb-€23, Db-€38, Tb-€52, air-con, bar serves breakfast and good tapas, uphill from Hostal Don Jaime and aqueduct at Plaza del Salvador 10, tel. 921-423-244, mobile 678-405-079, fax 921-438-047, elgato@tottel.com).

EATING

Look for Segovia's culinary claim to fame, roast suckling pig (*cochinillo asado:* 21 days of mother's milk, into the oven, and onto your plate—oh, Babe). It's worth a splurge here, or in Toledo or Salamanca.

For lighter fare, try *sopa castellana*—soup mixed with eggs, ham, garlic, and bread—or warm yourself up with the local *judiones de La Granja*, a popular soup made with flat white beans from the region.

Ponche segoviano, a dessert made with an almond-and-honey *mazapán* base, is heavenly after an earthy dinner or with a coffee in the afternoon (at the recommended Lima y Menta—see below).

Roast Suckling Pig

Mesón de Cándido, one of the top restaurants in Castile, is famous for its memorable dinners. Even though it's filled with tourists, it's a grand experience. Take time to wander around and survey the photos of celebs—from King Juan Carlos to Antonio Banderas and Melanie Griffith—who've suckled here (figure on spending €30, daily 13:00–16:30 & 20:00–23:00, Plaza del Azogüejo 5, air-con, under aqueduct, call 921-425-911 for reservations, www.mesondecandido.es, candido@mesondecandido.es).Three gracious generations of the Cándido family still run the show.

José María is *the* place to pig out in the old town, a block off Plaza Mayor. While it doesn't have the history or fanfare of Cándido, locals claim this high-energy place serves the best roast suckling pig in town. It thrives with a hungry mix of tourists and locals—reservations are usually necessary (€35 à la carte dinner, daily 13:00–16:00 & 20:30–23:30, air-con, Cronista Lecea 11, tel. 921-466-017, reservas@rtejosemaria.com).

Restaurante Casa Chapete, a homey little place filled with smoke, happy locals, and not a tourist in sight, serves traditional lamb and pig dishes—but only for lunch (€18 five-course meals including wine, €27 quarter *cochinillos* for 2–3 people, daily 12:00–16:00, 2 blocks beyond aqueduct, across from recommended Hostal Don Jaime at Calle Ochoa Ondategui 7, tel. 921-421-096).

The Old Center (No Pig)

Plaza Mayor, the main square, provides a great backdrop for a light lunch, dinner, or drink. Prices at the cafés are generally reasonable, and many offer a good selection of tapas and *raciones.* Grab a table at the place of your choice and savor the scene. **Café Jeyma** has a fine setting and cathedral view. **La Concepción Restaurante** is also good (€30 meals, closer to the cathedral).

Narizotas serves more imaginative and non-Castilian alternatives to the gamey traditions. You'll dine outside on a delightful square or inside with modern art under medieval timbers. For a wonderful dining experience, try their chef's choice mystery samplers, either the "Right Hand" (€34, about 10 courses, with wine and dessert) or the "Left Hand" (€30, about 6 courses, with wine and dessert). Their à la carte menu is also a treat (daily 12:30–16:00 & 20:30–24:00, midway down Calle Juan Bravo at Plaza de Medina del Campo 1, tel. 921-462-679).

Restaurante Bar San Martín, a no-frills place popular with locals, has a lively tapas bar, great outdoor seating by a fountain on the same square as the recommended Narizotas, and a smoky restaurant in the back. I'd eat here only to enjoy the setting on the square (daily 13:00–16:00 & 20:30–23:00, Plaza de San Martín 3, tel. 921-462-466).

Cueva de San Esteban serves traditional home cooking with a stress-free photo menu at the door, and hearty, big-enough-to-split plates (two blocks past Plaza Mayor on a quiet back street, Calle Valdelaguila 15, tel. 921-460-982).

Rodilla, the popular chain, offers a tasty selection of sand-wiches and salads (Mon–Fri 9:30–22:00, Sat–Sun 10:00–22:30, on Calle Juan Bravo, at intersection with Calle de la Herrería).

Breakfast: For breakfast, I like to sit on Plaza Mayor enjoying the cool air and the people scene (many choices). Or, a hundred yards down the main drag toward the aqueduct, **Café La Colonial** serves good breakfasts (with seating on a tiny square or inside, Avenida Fernandez Ladreda 19).

Nightlife: Inexpensive bars and eateries line Calle de Infanta Isabel, just off Plaza Mayor. For nightlife, the bars on Plaza Mayor, Calle de Infanta Isabel, and Calle Isabel la Católica are packed. There are a number of late-night dance clubs along the aqueduct.

Dessert: **Limon y Menta** offers a good, rich *ponche segoviano* (*mazapán*) cake by the slice for €2.50, or try the lighter honey-and-almond *crocantinos* (daily 9:30–21:30 but hours can vary, seating inside, Isabel La Católica 2, tel. 921-462-141).

Market: An outdoor produce market thrives on Plaza Mayor on Thursday (8:00–14:00). Nearby, a few stalls are open daily except Sunday on Calle del Cronista Ildefonso Rodríguez.

TRANSPORTATION CONNECTIONS

Trains go only to Madrid from Segovia's sleepy dead-end line, and riding the bus between Madrid and Segovia is better in every way than the train.

From Segovia by Bus to: La Granja Palace (14/day, 20 min), **Ávila** (5/day but only 2 on weekends, 1 hr), **Madrid** (2/hr, depar-tures on the half hour, 1.25 hrs, quicker than train, finishes at La Sepulvedana bus terminal at Metro: Príncipe Pío, Paseo de la Florida 11, tel. 915-598-955), **Salamanca** (2/day, 3 hrs, transfer in Labajos, it's smart to call ahead to reserve a seat for the Labajos–Salamanca segment—call Madrid's La Sepulvedana office at tel. 915-598-955 to book your seat); consider busing from Segovia to Ávila for a visit, then continuing to Salamanca by bus or train.

If you're riding the bus from Madrid to Segovia, about 30 minutes after leaving Madrid you'll see—breaking the horizon on the left—the dramatic concrete cross of the Valley of the Fallen. Its grand facade marks the entry to the mammoth underground memorial (described earlier in this chapter).

By Train to: Madrid (9/day, 2 hrs, €5.50, both Chamartín and Atocha stations). If day-tripping from Madrid, look for the *cercanías* (commuter train) ticket window and departure board (the trains are actually part of the *Regionales* line, but ticketing and boarding is through the *cercanías* gates). Be sure you're on the platform on time—many trains share the same tracks, and each train only has a few minutes to stop for passengers. Pick up a return schedule here or from the Segovia TI. Train info: tel. 902-240-202.

Route Tips for Drivers

From Madrid to Segovia: Leave Madrid on A6. Exit 39 gets you to Segovia via a slow, winding route over the scenic mountain. Exit at 60 (after a long €3 toll tunnel) or get there quicker by staying on the toll freeway all the way to Segovia (add €2 weekdays or €3 on weekends). At the Segovia aqueduct, follow *casco histórico* signs to the old town (on the side where the aqueduct adjoins the crenellated fortress walls).

Parking in Segovia: Free parking is available in the Alcázar's lot, but you must move your car out by 19:00, when the gates close. Or try the lot northwest of the bus station by the statue of Cándido, along the street called Paseo de Ezequiel González. Outside of the old city, there's an Acueducto Parking underground garage kitty-corner from the bus station, and there's free parking just down from the bus station. Although it can be a hard slog up the hill to the Alcázar on a hot day, it beats trying to maneuver uphill through tight bends. A huge garage is planned near the aqueduct (to be completed around 2008).

While there are generally lots of spots in the city center, if you want to park in the old town, be legal or risk an expensive ticket. Buy a ticket from the nearby machine to park in areas marked by blue stripes, and place the ticket on your dashboard (€0.30 for 30 min, 2-hr maximum, 9:00–14:00 & 16:30–20:00; free parking 20:00–9:00, Sat afternoon, and all day Sun).

Segovia to Salamanca (100 miles): Leave Segovia by driving around the town's circular road, which offers good views from below the Alcázar. Then follow signs for Ávila (road N110). Notice the fine Segovia view from the three crosses at the crest of the first hill. The Salamanca road leads around the famous Ávila walls to the right. The best wall view is from the signposted Cuatro Postes, a mile northwest of town. Salamanca (N501) is clearly marked, about an hour's drive away.

About 20 miles before Salamanca, you might want to stop at the huge bull on the left side of the road. There's a little dirt lane

leading right up to it. As you get closer, it becomes more and more obvious it isn't real. Bad boys climb it for a goofy photo. For a great photo op of Salamanca, complete with river reflection, stop at the edge of the city (at the light before the first bridge). In Salamanca, the only safe parking is in a garage; try the underground lot at Plaza Santa Eulalia, Plaza Campillo, or Lemans (closer to recommended Petit Palace Las Torres), or even easier, try one of the hotels (such as Hotel Don Juan) with valet parking for comparable fees. See the Salamanca chapter for more information.

Ávila

A popular side-trip from Madrid, Ávila is famous for its perfectly preserved medieval walls, as the birthplace of St. Teresa, and for its yummy *yema* treats. For more than 300 years, Ávila was on the battlefront between the Muslims and Christians, changing hands several times. Today, perfectly peaceful Ávila has a charming old town. With several fine churches and monasteries, it makes for an enjoyable quick stop between Segovia and Salamanca (each about an hour away by car). On a quick stop, everything that matters is within a few blocks of the cathedral (actually part of the east end of the wall).

Tourist Information

The TI has fine, free maps and information on walking tours (daily 9:00–14:00 & 17:00–20:00, July–mid-Sept 9:00–20:00, on Plaza Pedro Dávila 4, take first right when entering through Puerta del Rastro, tel. 920-211-387). Another TI is located outside the wall, opposite the Basilica of San Vicente (daily April–Oct 9:00–20:00, Nov–March 9:00–18:00).

A clunky **tourist train** departs every 30 minutes from outside the wall by Puerta de San Vicente, but fails to stop at the worthwhile Cuatro Postes viewpoint. It exits at the westernmost gate, loops by the Monasterio de la Encarnación (where St. Teresa lived), and then shudders along back to the north wall (€3, daily 9:00–18:00, narration in Spanish only, mobile 630-945-021).

Arrival in Ávila

Approaching by bus, train, or car, you'll need to make your way through the nondescript modern part of town to find the walled

Ávila

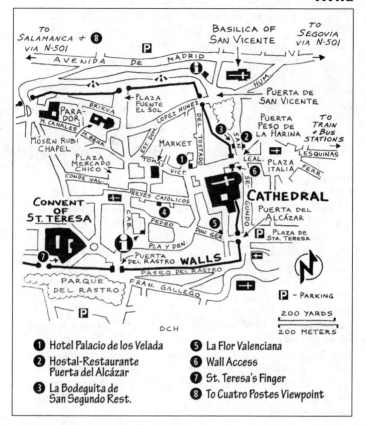

① Hotel Palacio de los Velada
② Hostal-Restaurante Puerta del Alcázar
③ La Bodeguita de San Segundo Rest.
⑤ La Flor Valenciana
⑥ Wall Access
⑦ St. Teresa's Finger
⑧ To Cuatro Postes Viewpoint

old town. The bus station is 10 minutes away, while the train station is a 15-minute walk from the cathedral and wall. By car, park at public parking east of Puerta del Alcázar, just south of the cathedral, or at Parking Dornier (€1.25/hour).

SIGHTS

▲**The Wall**—Built from around 1100 on even more ancient remains, Ávila's fortified wall is the oldest, most complete, and best preserved in Spain. It has a single access point—at the gate closest to the cathedral—where you can buy tickets. Look for the door marked *subida a la muralla*. Only a small section of the northwest segment is open for strolling (April–mid-Oct Tue–Sun 10:00–20:00, mid-Oct–March 11:00–18:00, closed Mon except July–Aug, last entry 45 minutes before closing). A night visit gives you the same walk, with the wall beautifully lit (€3.50, mid-June–mid-Sept Sun–Wed 22:00–24:00).

There's an interesting paseo scene along the wall each night—make your way along the southern wall (Paseo del Rastro) to Plaza de Santa Teresa for spectacular vistas across the plains. The best

views of the wall itself are actually from street level (especially along the north side, which drivers will see as they circle to the right from Puerta de San Vicente to catch the highway to Salamanca). The best overall view of the walled town is about a mile away on the Salamanca road (N501) at a clearly marked turn-out for the Cuatro Postes (four posts).

Cathedral—While it started as Romanesque, Ávila's cathedral, finished in the 16th century, is considered the first Gothic cathedral in Spain. Its position—with its granite apse actually part of the fortified wall—underlines the "medieval alliance between cross and sword." You can view part of the nave at the entrance for free or pay €4 to tour its sacristy, cloister, and museum—which includes an El Greco painting (Mon–Sat 10:00–20:00, Sun 12:00–19:00, off-season Mon–Sat 10:00–17:00, Sun 12:00–18:00, hours vary according to season).

Convent of St. Teresa—Built in the 17th century on the spot where the saint was born, this convent is a big hit with pilgrims (10-min walk from cathedral). A lavishly gilded side chapel marks the actual place of her birth (left of main altar, door may be closed). A separate room of relics (outside, facing the church on your right, Sala de Reliquias) houses a shop that shows off Teresa's finger, complete with a fancy emerald ring, along with one of her sandals and the bones of St. John of the Cross (free, no photos of finger allowed, daily 9:30–13:30 & 15:30–19:30). A museum in the crypt at the side entrance dedicated to the saint is worth a visit for devotees (€2, daily April–Oct 10:00–14:00 & 16:00–19:00, Nov–March 10:00–13:30 & 15:30–17:30, last entry 30 minutes before closing).

St. Teresa (1515–1582)—reforming nun, mystic, and writer—bought a house in Ávila and converted it into a convent with more stringent rules than the one she belonged to. She faced opposition in her hometown from rival nuns and those convinced her visions of Heaven were the work of the Devil. However, with her mentor and fellow mystic, St. John of the Cross, she established convents of Discalced (shoeless) Carmelites throughout Spain, and her visions and writings led her to sainthood (canonized 1622).

Yemas—These pastries, made by local nuns, are like a soft-boiled egg yolk that has been cooled and sugared. They're sold all over town. The shop Las Delicias del Convento is actually a retail outlet

for the cooks of the convent (€4.50/small box, Thu–Tue 10:30–
14:00 & 17:00–20:30, closed Wed, a block from TI, at Calle Reyes
Católicos 12, tel. 920-220-293).

SLEEPING

(€1 = about $1.20, country code: 34)
The first hotel is antique and classy, facing the cathedral. The
second is simpler and faces the wall's entrance that leads to the
cathedral. Ávila is cold in fall, winter, and early spring; both hotels
have heating.

$$$ Hotel Palacio de los Velada is a five-centuries-old palace
with 145 elegant rooms surrounding a huge and inviting arcaded
courtyard (Sb-€115, Db-€140, Tb-€170, air-con, elevator, Plaza de
la Catedral 10, tel. 920-255-100, fax 920-254-900, reserves.avila
@veladahoteles.com).

$$ Hostal-Restaurante Puerta del Alcázar has 27 basic yet
spacious rooms right next to the Puerta del Peso de la Harina just
outside the wall (Sb-€43, Db-€55, Tb-€77, Qb-€99, includes tax
and breakfast, no air-con, san Segundo 38, tel. 920-211-074, fax
920-211-075, www.puertadelalcazar.com). Also see "Eating," below.

EATING

La Bodeguita de San Segundo is a good bet for a classy light
lunch. Owned by a locally famous wine connoisseur, it serves
fine wine by the glass with gourmet tapas, including smoked-
cod salad and wild-mushroom scrambled eggs (closed Wed,
along the outside of wall near cathedral at San Segundo 19, tel.
920-257-309).

Hostal-Restaurante Puerta del Alcázar, filled with more
locals than hotel guests, serves elaborate salads, fixed-price meals
(€12/€19), and more. You can sit indoors, or even better, outdoors
with cathedral views (daily 13:00–16:00 & 21:00–23:30, San
Segundo 38, tel. 920-211-074).

On warm days, locals beat the heat at **La Flor Valenciana**
with an ice cream or a *granizado* (slushee) with some unique flavors
(daily 10:00–23:00, by Puerta del Alcázar on Calle Don Gerónimo
13, tel. 920-212-254).

TRANSPORTATION CONNECTIONS

There are lockers at Ávila's bus and train stations. The bus terminal
is closed on Sundays, but you can purchase tickets when boarding
the bus.

From Ávila to: Segovia (5 buses/day weekdays, 2 on weekends, 75 min), **Madrid** (1 train/hr until 20:00, 90 min, TALGO trains only 75 min, more frequent connections with Chamartín station than Atocha; 8 buses/day, 4 on weekends, 1.5 hrs; Estación Sur de Autobuses in Madrid, tel. 914-684-200), **Salamanca** (6 trains/day, 65 min; 4 buses/day, 2 on weekends, 90 min). Train info: tel. 902-240-202.

TOLEDO

An hour south of Madrid, Toledo teems with tourists, souvenirs, and great art by day, and delicious dinners, echoes of El Greco, and medieval magic by night. Incredibly well-preserved and full of cultural wonder, the entire city has been declared a national monument.

Spain's former capital crowds 2,500 years of tangled history—Roman, Jewish, Visigothic, Moorish, and Christian—onto a high, rocky perch protected on three sides by the Tajo (Tagus) River. It's so well-preserved that the Spanish government has forbidden any modern exteriors. The rich mix of Jewish, Moorish, and Christian heritages makes it one of Europe's artistic highlights.

Today, Toledo thrives as a provincial capital and a busy tourist attraction. This decade has been and will be an eventful one for Toledo. The advent of the new high-speed AVE train connection makes Toledo a quick 30-minute ride from Madrid. While locals worried that this link would turn their town into a bedroom community for wealthy Madrileños, the already high real-estate prices minimized the impact. The city is also undergoing a major construction project: the building of a new convention center, complete with a huge escalator that will take visitors from the bus station nearly to the main square, Plaza Zocódover. When this addition is complete (likely in 2009), the city will become largely traffic-free (except for city residents' cars, public transit, and service vehicles).

Toledo remains the historic, artistic, and spiritual center of Spain. Despite tremendous tourist crowds, Toledo sits enthroned on its history, much as it was when Europe's most powerful king and its most famous resident artist, El Greco, called it home.

Toledo

Planning Your Time

To properly see Toledo's sights—including its museums (great El Greco) and cathedral (best in Spain)—and to experience its medieval atmosphere (wonderful after dark), you'll need two nights and a day. Plan carefully for lunch closings, and for Toledo's notorious midday heat in summer. Get an early start and stay out late...but take a rest during the unbearable summer afternoons. Note that a few sights are closed on Monday (including Museo El Greco and Sinagoga del Tránsito).

ORIENTATION

Toledo sits atop a circular hill, with the cathedral roughly at dead center. Lassoed into a tight tangle of streets by the sharp bend of the Tajo River (called the Tejo in Portugal, where it hits the

Atlantic at Lisbon), Toledo has Spain's most confusing medieval street plan. But it's a small town within its walls, with only 10,000 inhabitants (80,000 total live in greater Toledo, including its modern suburbs). The major sights are well-signposted, and most locals will politely point you in the right direction if you ask.

The top sights stretch from the main square, Plaza Zocódover (zoh-KOH-doh-ver), southwest along Calle Comercio (a.k.a. Calle Ancha, "wide street") to the cathedral, and beyond to Santo Tomé and more. The visitor's city lies basically along this small but central street, and most tourists never stray from this axis. Make a point to get lost. The town is small, and bounded on three sides by the river. When it's time to return to someplace familiar, pull out the map or ask, "*¿Para Plaza Zocódover?*" From the far end of town, handy bus #12 circles back to Plaza Zocódover (take "Bus #12's Self-Guided Tour," page 315).

Keep in mind that sights appear closer on maps than they really are, because local maps don't factor into account the slope of the hill. In Toledo they say everything's uphill—it certainly feels that way.

Tourist Information

Toledo has three TIs: The TI just outside **Bisagra Gate**—in a free-standing brick building—is nearest to the bus and train stations (Mon–Fri 9:00–18:00, Sat 9:00–19:00, Sun 9:00–15:00, longer hours in summer, tel. 925-220-843). Another TI is on Plaza del Ayuntamiento, near the **cathedral** (Mon 10:30–14:30, Tue–Sun 10:30–14:30 & 16:30–19:00, tel. 925-254-030). A third, in a shop a block off of **Plaza Zocódover,** is more of a gimmicky business than a real TI (daily 10:00–14:00 & 15:00–18:30, incompetent staff, air-con, handy WC, Calle de la Sillería 14, tel. 925-220-300).

Consider the readable local guidebook, *Toledo: Its Art and Its History* (small version for €5, sold all over town). It explains all of the sights (which generally provide no on-site information), and gives you a photo to point at and say, "*¿Dónde está...?*"

Internet Access: Miradero Sicra Internet Locutorio is a good central standby for e-mail, with seven fast terminals. From Plaza Zocódover, walk a long block down the big street, Calle de las Armas, which becomes Calle de Venancio González (€2/hr, daily 10:00–23:00).

Toledo's History

Perched strategically in the center of Iberia, Toledo was a Roman transportation hub with a thriving Jewish population for centuries. After Rome fell, the city became a Visigothic capital (A.D. 554). In 711, the Moors (Muslims) made it a regional center. In 1085, the city was reconquered by Christians, but many Moors remained in Toledo, tolerated and respected as scholars and craftsmen.

While Jews were commonly persecuted elsewhere in Europe, Toledo's Jewish community—educated, wealthy, and cosmopolitan—thrived from the city's earliest times. Jews of Spanish origin are called Sephardic Jews. The American expression "Holy Toledo" likely originated from the Sephardic Jews who eventually immigrated to America. To them, Toledo was the most holy Jewish city in Europe...Holy Toledo!

During its medieval heyday (c. 1350), Toledo was a city of the humanities, where God was known by many names. In this haven of cultural diversity, people of different faiths lived together in harmony.

Toledo remained Spain's political capital until 1561, when Philip II moved to more-spacious Madrid. Historians fail to agree why the move was made; some say that Madrid was the logical place for a capital in the geographic center of newly formed *España,* while others say that Philip wanted to separate politics from religion. Whatever the reason, Toledo was mothballed only to be rediscovered by 19th-century Romantic travelers. They wrote of it as a mystical place...which it still is today.

Arrival in Toledo

"Arriving" in Toledo means getting uphill to Plaza Zocódover.

By Train: From the train station, it's an ugly, streetside 30-minute hike, a €4 taxi ride, or an easy bus ride on the #5 or #6 to Plaza Zocódover (€1, pay on bus, confirm by asking, "*¿Para Plaza Zocódover?*"). You can stow extra baggage at the station. Consider buying a city map at the kiosk; it's better than the free one at the TI. If you're walking into town: Turn right leaving the station, cross the bridge with the mighty Alcázar on your left, pass the bus station (on right), go straight through the roundabout, and continue uphill to Bisagra Gate (TI), into the old town to Plaza Zocódover.

By Bus: If you arrive by bus, go upstairs to the station lobby. You'll find luggage storage and a small bus-information office opposite the cafeteria. Confirm your departure time (probably every half hour on the hour to Madrid). You can put off buying a return ticket until just minutes before you leave Toledo. Specify you'd like a *directo* bus, because the *ruta* trip takes longer (60 min vs. 90 min). If you miss the *directo* bus (or if it's sold out), the *ruta* option offers a peek of off-the-beaten-path Madrid suburbia; you'll arrive at the same time as taking the next *directo* bus. From the bus station, Plaza Zocódover is a 15-minute walk (see directions from train station, above), a €3 taxi ride, or a short bus ride (catch #5 downstairs—underneath the lobby, €1, pay on bus).

By Car: If you're arriving by car, you can enjoy a scenic big-picture orientation by following the *Ronda de Toledo* signs on a big circular drive around the city. You'll view the city from many angles along the Circunvalación road across the Tajo Gorge. (Without a car, you can still see the city by a tourist train—see below.) Stop at a streetside viewpoint or drive to Parador de Toledo, located just south of town for the view (from the balcony) that El Greco made famous in his portrait of Toledo. The best time for this trip is the magic hour before sunset, when the top viewpoints are busy with tired old folks and frisky young lovers.

Upon arrival in Toledo, you can park in the streets at the base of the escalators for free, or for a fee (€15/day) in the parking lot across from them. If you don't park near the escalators, you can drive into town and park in Garage Alcázar (opposite the Alcázar in the old town—€1.50/hr, €15/day).

A car is useless within Toledo's city walls, and the city is no fun to drive in. Ideally, see the old town outside of car-rental time; pick up or drop off your car here. **Avis** is at the train station (Mon–Fri 9:30–13:30 & 16:30–19:30, Sat 9:30–13:30, closed Sun, tel. 925-214-535).

By Escalator into Town: A series of escalators runs outdoors past Bisagra Gate, giving you a free ride up, up, up into town (daily 8:00–22:00). You'll end up near San Ildefonso and far from Plaza Zocódover, but it's worth it for the novelty. (By 2009, Toledo expects to have a more practical escalator in place, taking visitors directly and easily from the bus station nearly to Plaza Zocódover.)

TOURS

▲**Tourist Train**—For great city views, hop on the cheesy Tren Imperial Tourist Tram. Crass as it feels, you get a 50-minute putt-putt through Toledo and around the Tajo River Gorge. It's a fine way to get a general city overview, and for non-drivers to enjoy views of the city from across the Tajo Gorge (€4, buy ticket from TI at Calle de la Sillería 14, daily from 11:00, leaves Plaza Zocódover on the hour, tape-recorded English/Spanish commentary, no photo stops, but it goes slow; for the best views of Toledo across the gorge,

Toledo at a Glance

▲▲▲**Cathedral** One of Europe's best, with a marvelously vast interior and great art. **Hours:** Mon–Sat 10:00–18:30, Sun 14:00–18:30.

▲▲**Santa Cruz Museum** Renaissance building housing wonderful artwork, including 15 El Grecos. **Hours:** Mon–Sat 10:00–18:30, Sun 10:00–14:00.

▲**Alcázar** Imposing former imperial residence that dominates Toledo's skyline. **Hours:** Interior currently closed for installation of a national military museum.

▲**Santo Tomé** Simple chapel with El Greco's masterpiece, *The Burial of the Count of Orgaz.* **Hours:** Daily 10:00–18:45, until 18:00 in winter.

▲**Tourist Train** Tacky but fun 50-minute trip through Toledo's highlights with great Tajo Gorge views. **Hours:** Daily at top of the hour from 11:00 until into the evening.

Museo El Greco in "El Greco's House" Museum that holds 20 works by the painter. **Hours:** Tue–Sat 10:00–14:00 & 16:00–21:00, until 18:00 in winter, Sun 10:00–13:45, closed Mon.

Sinagoga del Tránsito Museum of Toledo's Jewish past. **Hours:** Tue–Sat 10:00–14:00 & 16:00–18:00, Sun 10:00–14:00, closed Mon.

Sinagoga de Santa María la Blanca Synagogue that harmoniously combines Toledo's three religious influences: Jewish, Christian, and Moorish. **Hours:** Daily April–Sept 10:00–18:45, Oct–March 10:00–17:45.

Museo Victorio Macho Collection of the 20th-century Toledo sculptor's works, with expansive river-gorge view. **Hours:** Mon–Sat 10:00–19:00, Sun 10:00–15:00.

San Juan de los Reyes Monasterio Church/monastery that was to be the final resting place of Isabel and Ferdinand. **Hours:** Daily 10:00–18:45, until 17:45 in winter.

Central Toledo

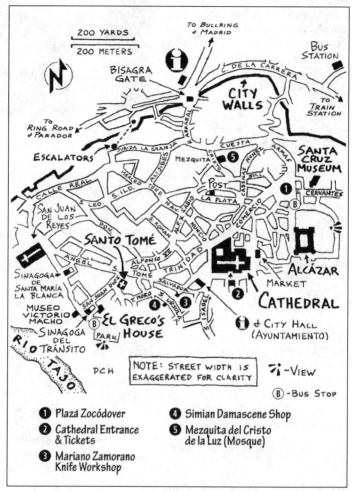

- **1** Plaza Zocódover
- **2** Cathedral Entrance & Tickets
- **3** Mariano Zamorano Knife Workshop
- **4** Simian Damascene Shop
- **5** Mezquita del Cristo de la Luz (Mosque)

sit on right side, not behind driver; tel. 925-220-300).

Local Guide—Juan José Espadas, a.k.a. Juanjo, is a good local guide who enjoys sharing his hometown in English (€130/3 hrs for individuals or groups, mobile 667-780-475, juanjoespadas @tiscali.es).

SIGHTS

Cathedral

Holy Toledo! Spain's leading Catholic city has a magnificent cathedral, worth ▲▲▲. Shoehorned into the old center (in the spot where a mosque once stood), it has an exterior that's hard to appreciate. But the interior is so lofty, rich, and vast that it'll have you wandering around like a Pez dispenser stuck open, whispering "Wow."

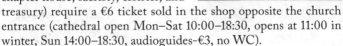

Cost and Hours: The cathedral and associated sights (choir, chapter house, sacristy, cloister, and treasury) require a €6 ticket sold in the shop opposite the church entrance (cathedral open Mon–Sat 10:00–18:30, opens at 11:00 in winter, Sun 14:00–18:30, audioguides-€3, no WC).

◑ Self-Guided Tour: Wander among all the pillars, thick and sturdy as a redwood forest. Sit under one and imagine a time when the light bulbs were candles and the tourists were pilgrims—before the *No Photo* signs, when every window provided spiritual as well as physical light. The cathedral is primarily Gothic. But since it took more than 250 years to build (1226–1495)—with continuous embellishments after that (every archbishop wanted to leave his imprint)—it's a mix of styles, including Gothic, Renaissance, Baroque, and Neoclassical. Enjoy the elaborate wrought-iron work, lavish wood carvings, window after colorful window of 500-year-old stained glass, and a sacristy with a collection of paintings that would put any museum on the map.

This confusing collage of great Spanish art deserves a close look. Hire a private guide, discreetly freeload on a tour (they come by every few minutes during peak season), rent the audioguide, or follow this quick tour. Here's a framework for your visit:

1. High Altar: First, walk to the high altar to marvel through the iron grille at one of the most stunning altars in Spain. Real

gold on wood, by Flemish, French, and local artists, it's one of the country's best pieces of Gothic art. Don't miss the finely worked gold-plated iron grille itself—considered to be the best from the 16th century in Spain. About-face to the...

2. Choir: Facing the high altar, the choir is famous for its fine carving. The rich symbolism of the carving centers on the archbishop's throne in the center. First, look carefully at the fine alabaster relief above the throne: It shows a seventh-century Visigothic miracle, when Mary came down to give the local bishop the holy robe, legitimizing Toledo as the spiritual capital (and therefore political capital) of Spain.

Toledo's Cathedral

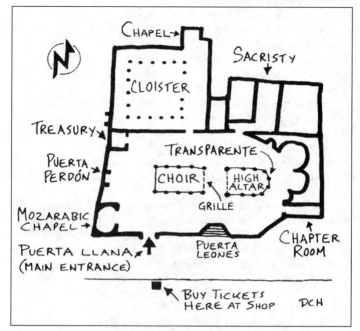

Because of its primacy in Iberia, Toledo was the first city in the crosshairs of the Reconquista Christian forces. They recaptured the city in 1085 (over 400 years before they did the same in Granada). A local saying goes, "A carpet frays from the edges, but the carpet of Al-Andalus (Muslim Spain) frayed from the very center" (meaning Toledo). The fall of Toledo marked the beginning of the end of the Muslim domination of Iberia.

The lower wooden stalls are decorated with scenes showing the finale of the one-city-at-a-time Christian victory, when Muslims were slowly pushed back into Africa. Set in the last decade of the Reconquista, these images celebrate the retaking of the towns around Granada: Each idealized castle has the reconquered town's name on it, culminating in the final victory at Granada in 1492 (the reliefs flank the archbishop's throne). While the castles are romanticized, the carvings of the clothing, armor, and weaponry are so detailed and accurate that historians have studied them to learn the evolution of weaponry.

The upper stalls feature Old Testament figures—an alabaster genealogy of the church—starting with Adam and Eve, working clockwise to Joseph and "S.M. Virgo Mater" (St. Mary the Virgin Mother). All this imagery is to remind viewers of the legitimacy of the bishop's claims to religious power. Check out the seat backs, made of carved walnut and featuring New Testament figures—with Peter (key) and Paul (sword)—alongside the archbishop himself.

And, as is typical of choir decoration, the carvings on the misericords (the tiny seats that allowed tired worshippers to lean while they "stand") feature the frisky, folksy, sexy, profane art of the day. Apparently, since you sat on it, it could never be sacred anyway.

Take a moment to absorb the marvelous complexity, harmony, and cohesiveness of the art around you. Look up. There are two fine pipe organs: one early 18th-century Baroque and the other late 18th-century Neoclassical. As you leave the choir, note the serene beauty of the 13th-century Madonna and child at the front, thought to be a gift from the French king to Spain. Its naturalism and intimacy was radical in its day.

The iron grille of the choir is notable for the dedication of the man who built it. Domingo de Céspedes, a Toledo ironworker, accepted the commission to build the grille for 6,000 ducats. The project, which took from 1541 to 1548, was far more costly than he anticipated. The medieval Church didn't accept cost overruns, so to finish it, he sold everything he owned and went into debt. He died a poor—but honorable—man. (It's a charming story, but the artistic iron gate before the altar is the true treasure.)

3. Chapter House: Face the altar, and go around it to your right to the chapter house *(sala capitular)*. Under its lavish ceiling, this fresco celebrates the humanism of the Italian Renaissance. There's a crucifixion, a *pietà,* and a resurrection on the front wall; they face a fascinating Last Judgment, where the seven sins are actually spelled out in the gang going to hell: arrogance (the guy striking a pose), avarice (holding his bag of coins), lust (the easy woman with the fiery crotch and lovely hair), anger, gluttony (fat guy), envy, and laziness. Imagine how instructive this was in 1600.

Below the fresco, a pictorial review of 1,900 years of Toledo archbishops circles the room. The upper row of portraits dates from the 16th century. Except for the last two, these were not painted from life. The lower portraits were added one at a time from 1515 on, and are therefore of more historic than artistic interest. Imagine sitting down to church business surrounded by all this tradition and theology. As you leave, notice the iron-pumping cupids carved into the pear-tree panels lining the walls.

4. Transparente: The *transparente,* behind the high altar, is a unique feature of the cathedral. In the 1700s, a hole was cut into the ceiling to let a sunbeam brighten Mass. Melding this big hole with the Gothic church presented a challenge, and the result was a Baroque masterpiece. Gape up at this riot of angels doing flip-flops, babies breathing thin air, bottoms of feet, and gilded sunbursts. Study the altar, which looks chaotic, but is actually

structured thoughtfully: The good news of salvation springs from baby Jesus, up past the archangels (including one who knows how to hold a big fish correctly) to the *Last Supper* high above, and beyond into the light-filled dome. I like it, as did (I guess) the two long-dead cardinals whose faded red hats hang from the edge of the hole. (A perk that only a cardinal enjoys is to choose a burial place in the cathedral, and hang his hat over that spot until the hat rots.)

5. Sacristy: The cathedral's sacristy is a mini-Prado, with 18 El Grecos and masterpieces by Francisco de Goya, Titian, Peter Paul Rubens, Diego Velázquez, Caravaggio, and Giovanni Bellini. First, notice the fine perspective work on the ceiling (frescoed by Lucca Giordano from Naples, c. 1690). Then walk to the end of the room for the most important painting in the collection, El Greco's *The Spoliation* (a.k.a. *Christ Stripped of His Garments*).

Spain's original great painter was Greek, and this is his first masterpiece after arriving in Toledo. El Greco's painting from 1579 hangs exactly where he intended it to—in the room where priests prepared themselves for Mass. It shows Jesus surrounded by a sinister mob, and suffering the humiliation of being stripped in public before his execution.

The scarlet robe is about to be yanked off, and the women (lower left) avert their eyes, turning to watch a carpenter at work (lower right) who bores the holes for nailing Jesus to the cross. While the carpenter bears down, Jesus—the other carpenter—looks up to heaven. The contrast between the motley crowd gambling for his clothes and Jesus' noble face underscores the quiet dignity with which he endures this ignoble treatment. Jesus' delicate white hand stands out from the flaming red tunic with an odd gesture that's common in El Greco's paintings. Some say this was the way Christians of the day swore they were true believers, not merely Christians-in-name-only, such as former Muslims or Jews who converted to survive.

On the right is a rare religious painting by Goya, the *Betrayal of Christ*, which shows Judas preparing to kiss Jesus, thus identifying him to the Roman soldiers. Enjoy the many other El Grecos. A small-but-lifelike 17th-century carving of St. Francis by Pedro de Mena is just to the right of the Goya.

6. The Cloister: Take a peaceful detour to a funerary chapel located at the far side of the cloister from the entrance. The ceiling over the marble tomb of a bishop was frescoed by a student of Giotto (a 14th-century Italian Renaissance master).

7. Treasury: The *tesoro* is tiny, but radiant with riches. The highlight is the 10-foot-high, 430-pound monstrance—the tower designed to hold the Holy Communion bread (the Host) during the festival of Corpus Christi ("body of Christ") as it parades through the city. Built in 1517 by Enrique de Arfe, it's made of 5,000 individual pieces held together by 12,500 screws. There are diamonds, emeralds, rubies, and 400 pounds of gold-plated silver. The inner part is 35 pounds of solid gold. Yeow. The base is a later addition from the Baroque period.

To the right of the monstrance is a beautiful red coral cross given by the Philippines. To the right of that is a gift from St. Louis, the 13th-century king of France: a 700-year-old Bible printed and beautifully illustrated by French monks. (It's actually a copy, and the precious original is stored elsewhere.) Imagine looking on these lavish illustrations with medieval eyes—an exquisite experience. The finely painted small crucifix on the opposite side in the corner—by the great Gothic Florentine painter Fra Angelico—depicts Jesus alive on the back and dead on the front. This was a gift from Mussolini to Franco. Underneath, you'll find the rather plain sword of Franco. Hmmm. There's even a gift in this room from Toledo's sister city, Toledo, Ohio.

If you're at the cathedral between 9:00 and 9:15, you can peek into the otherwise-locked **Mozarabic Chapel** (Capilla Mozárabe). The Visigothic Mass (in Latin), the oldest surviving Christian ritual in Western Europe, starts at 9:15 (9:45 on Sun). You're welcome to partake in this stirring example of peaceful coexistence of faiths—but once the door closes, you're a Visigoth for 30 minutes. Toledo's proud Mozarabic community of 1,500 people traces its roots back to Visigothic times.

In Central Toledo

Plaza Zocódover—The main square is Toledo's center, and your gateway to the old town. The word "zocódover" derives from the Arabic for "souk (marketplace) of the beasts" (mostly donkeys and horses).

Because Toledo is the state capital of Castile-La Mancha, the regional government administration building overlooks Plaza Zocódover. Look for the three flags: one for Europe, one for Spain, and one for Castile-La Mancha. And speaking of universal symbols—find the low-key McDonald's. A source of controversy, it was finally allowed...with only one small golden arch.

The square is a big local hangout and city hub: Old people arrive in the morning, and young people come in the evening. A goofy, white tourist train leaves from here (see above), as do buses #5 and #6, which lumber to the bus and train station. Just uphill is the stop for #41 and #42 (heading to Plaza de Toros), as well as the circular route #12, which travels around the old town to Santo Tomé.

▲▲**Santa Cruz Museum**—For years, this museum has been in a confused state of renovation—not really open, not really closed. During renovation, the museum's cloister and a room full of its best art are open and free. If the core of the building is filled with a temporary exhibit, you can generally wander in for a free look.

This stately Renaissance building was an orphanage and hospital, built from money left by the humanist and diplomat Cardinal Mendoza when he died in 1495. The cardinal, confirmed as Chancellor of Castile by Queen Isabel, was so influential that he was called "the third king."

Your visit has three parts: the main building (with temporary exhibit), the fine cloister, and the museum rooms off the cloister.

The building (especially its facade, cloister arches, and stairway leading to the upper cloister) is a fine example of the Plateresque style. This ornate strain of Spanish Renaissance is named for the fancy work of silversmiths of the 16th century. During this time (c. 1500–1550), the royal court moved from Toledo to Madrid—when Madrid was a village, and Toledo was a world power. (You'll see no Plateresque work in Madrid.) Note the Renaissance-era mathematics, ideal proportions, round arches, square squares, and classic columns.

The main building is in the form of a Greek cross. As 1500 was a time of transition, the fine ceiling is an impressive mix of two styles: indigenous Moorish and Italian Renaissance, which was in vogue at the time. After renovation, the wings of the building will be filled with 16th-century art, tapestries, furniture, armor, and documents.

Enjoy the peaceful cloister. In the corner stands an ignored well (now capped), bearing an Arabic inscription and grooves made by generations of Muslims pulling their buckets up by rope. The well was once in the courtyard of an 11th-century mosque which stood where the cathedral does today.

The museum section features a collection of 15 El Grecos. The highlight: the impressive *Assumption of Mary*, a spiritual poem on canvas. This altarpiece, finished one year before El Greco's death in 1614, is the culmination of his unique style, combining all of his techniques to express an otherworldly event.

Study the *Assumption* (which some believe is misnamed, and actually shows the Immaculate Conception). While on earth, the city of Toledo sleeps, but a vision is taking place overhead. An angel in a billowing robe spreads his wings and flies up, supporting Mary, the mother of Christ. She floats up through warped space, to be serenaded by angels and wrapped in the radiant light of the Holy Spirit. Mary flickers and ripples, charged from within by her spiritual ecstasy, caught up in a vision that takes her breath away. No painter before or since has captured the supernatural world better than El Greco.

Find the lavish but faded Astrolabe Tapestry (c. 1480, Belgian), which shows a new view of the cosmos at the dawn of the Renaissance and the Age of Discovery: God (far left) oversees all, as Atlas (with the help of two women and a crank handle) spins the universe, containing the circular Earth. The wisdom gang (far right) heralds the wonders of the coming era. Rather than a map of earth, this is a chart showing the cosmic order of things as the constellations spin around the stationary North Star (center).

Upstairs is a wonderful exhibit for tile- and ceramic-lovers. The private collection of the Carranza family has been "on loan" to the museum for the past 20 years. They began collecting tile and assorted ceramics that date from the end of the Reconquista (1492). Each piece is categorized by the Spanish region where it was made and professionally displayed. In spite of the lack of English explanations, this is the only place in Spain where you can compare regional differences in tile work and pottery (Mon–Sat 10:00–18:30, Sun 10:00–14:00; from Plaza Zocódover, go through arch to Cervantes 3).

▲**Alcázar**—This huge former imperial residence—built on the site of Roman, Visigothic, and Moorish  fortresses—dominates the Toledo skyline. Currently closed for renovation, it will be the National Military Museum when it reopens (likely in 2008). The Alcázar became a kind of right-wing Alamo during Spain's civil war, when Franco's Nationalists (and hundreds of hostages) were besieged for two months in 1936. Finally, after many fierce but futile Republican attacks that destroyed much of the Alcázar, Franco sent in an army that took Toledo. The place was rebuilt and glorified under Franco.

Mezquita del Cristo de la Luz—Of Muslim Toledo's 10 mosques, only this barren little building survives, built in 1000. Looking up, you'll notice the Moorish fascination with geometry—each of the domes is a unique design. The lovely keyhole arch faces Mecca. In

1187, after the Reconquista, the mosque was changed to a church, the Christian apse was added, and the former mosque got its current name. The fine garden with its fountains is a reminder of the Quranic image of heaven (€2, daily 10:00–18:45, winter until 18:00).

Southwest Toledo

▲**Santo Tomé**—A simple chapel holds El Greco's most-loved painting. *The Burial of the Count of Orgaz* couples heaven and earth in a way only The Greek could. It feels so right to see a painting left *in situ* where the artist placed it 400 years ago. Take this slow. Stay a while—let it perform.

The year is 1323. You're at the burial of the good count, who's being laid to rest right here in this chapel. He was so holy, even saints Augustine and Stephen have come down from heaven to lower his body into the grave. (The painting's subtitle is "Such is the reward for those who serve God and his saints.")

More than 250 years later, in 1586, a local priest hired El Greco to make a painting of the burial to hang over the count's tomb. The funeral is attended by Toledo's most distinguished citizens. (El Greco used local nobles as models.) The painting is divided in two by a serene line of noble faces—heaven above and earth below. Above the faces, the count's soul, symbolized by a little baby, rises up through a mystical birth canal to be reborn in heaven, where he's greeted by Jesus, Mary, and all the saints. A spiritual wind blows through as colors change and shapes stretch. This is Counter-Reformation propaganda—notice Jesus pointing to St. Peter, the symbol of the pope in Rome, who controls the keys to the Pearly Gates. Each face is a detailed portrait. El Greco himself (eyeballing you, seventh figure in from the left) is the only one not involved in the burial. The boy in the foreground—pointing to the two saints as if to say, "One's from the first century, the other's from the fourth...it's a miracle!"—is El Greco's son. On the handkerchief in the boy's pocket is El Greco's signature, written in Greek (€1.90, daily 10:00–18:45, until 17:45 mid-Oct–March, audioguide-€1, tel. 925-256-098). Go early or late to avoid long lines of tour groups.

Museo El Greco in "El Greco's House"—Really a small art gallery in a house built upon the spot where El Greco lived, this place has no hint of "home." Instead, you'll see about 20 El Greco paintings, including his masterful *View of Toledo* and portraits of the apostles

El Greco
(1541–1614)

Born on Crete and trained in Venice, Doménikos Theo-tokópoulos (tongue-tied friends just called him "The Greek") came to Spain to get a job decorating El Escorial. He failed there, but succeeded in Toledo, where he spent the last 37 years of his life. He mixed all three regional influences into his palette. From his Greek homeland, he absorbed the solemn, abstract style of icons. In Italy, he learned the bold use of color, elongated figures, twisting poses, and dramatic style of the later Renaissance. These elements were then fused in the fires of fanatic Spanish-Catholic devotion.

Not bound by the realism so important to his fellow artists, El Greco painted dramatic visions of striking colors and figures—bodies unnatural and lengthened as though stretched between heaven and earth. He painted souls, not faces. His work is on display at nearly every sight in Toledo. Thoroughly modern in his disregard of realism, he didn't impress the austere Philip II. But his art seems as fresh as contemporary art does today.

(€2.40, free Sat afternoon from 14:30 and all day Sun, Tue–Sat 10:00–14:00 & 16:00–21:00, until 18:00 in winter, Sun 10:00–13:45, closed Mon, air-con, Samuel Levi 3).

In the famous painting of Toledo, beautifully displayed here, Mary descends to bless the city (which has changed little since 1600). Find the Alcázar, Bisagra Gate, and the cathedral bell tower. The allegory of Tajo River comes with a cornucopia, which brings the city fertility and abundance. The boy presents a detailed city map with the major sights faintly listed on the left—familiar to anyone today who uses tourist maps.

Sinagoga del Tránsito (Museo Sefardí)—Built in 1361, this is the best surviving slice of Toledo's Jewish past. Serving as Spain's national Jewish museum, it displays Jewish artifacts, including costumes, menorahs, and books. The synagogue's interior decor looks more Muslim than Jewish. After Christians reconquered the city in 1085, many Moorish workmen stayed on, beautifying the city with their unique style called Mudejar. The synagogue's intricate, geometrical carving in stucco features leaves, vines, and flowers; there are no human shapes, which are forbidden, because

---

Toledo's Muslim Legacy

You can see the Moorish influence in the:
- Mezquita del Cristo de la Luz, the last of the town's mosques
- Sinagoga del Tránsito's Mudejar plasterwork
- Sinagoga de Santa María la Blanca's mosque-like horse-shoe arches and pinecone capitals
- Puerta de Sol (Gate of the Sun) and other surviving gates (with horseshoe arches) along the medieval wall
- The city's labyrinthine, medina-like streets

---

the Quran does not allow "graven images." In the frieze (running along the upper wall, just below the ceiling), the Arabic-looking script is actually Hebrew, quoting psalms from the Bible. The side-wall balcony is the traditional separate worship area for women. Scale models of the development of the Jewish quarter (on the ground floor) and video displays (upstairs) give a fuller picture of Jewish life in medieval Toledo.

This 14th-century synagogue was built at the peak of Toledo's enlightened tolerance—constructed for Jews with Christian approval by Muslim (Moorish) craftsmen. Nowhere else in the city does Toledo's three-culture legacy shine brighter than at this synagogue. But in 1391, just a few decades after it was built, the Church and the Spanish kings began a violent campaign to unite Spain as a Christian nation, forcing Jews and Muslims to convert or leave. In 1492, Ferdinand and Isabel exiled Spain's remaining Jews. It's estimated that, in the 15th century, a third of Spain's Jews were killed, a third survived by converting to Christianity, and a third moved elsewhere (€2.40, free Sat afternoon from 14:30 and all day Sun, Tue–Sat 10:00–14:00 & 16:00–18:00, Sun 10:00–14:00, closed Mon, audioguide-€3, near Museo El Greco on Calle de los Reyes Católicos).

Sinagoga de Santa María la Blanca—This synagogue-turned-church has Moorish horseshoe arches and wall carvings. It's an  eclectic but harmonious gem, and a vivid reminder of the religious cultures that shared this city. While it looks like a mosque, it never was one. Built by Moors around 1200, it was originally a synagogue, then a church—hence the mix-and-match name. (It's still owned by the Church, and has a Christian altar.) After being used as horse stables by Napoleonic troops, it was further ruined in the 19th century. Today, it's an evocative space, beautiful in its simplicity (€1.90, daily April–Sept 10:00–18:45, Oct–March until 17:45, no photos allowed, Calle de los Reyes Católicos 2/4).

Museo Victorio Macho—After *mucho* El Greco, try Macho. Overlooking the gorge and Tajo River, this small, attractive museum—once the home and workshop of the early-20th-century sculptor Victorio Macho—offers several rooms of his bold work interspersed with view terraces. Recognized as Spain's first modern sculptor, Macho's work is heavily influenced by Art Deco. The highlight is *La Madre,* Macho's life-size sculpture of his mother sitting in a chair. It's so lifelike and gentle that it could easily be anyone's mom. But the big draw for many is the air-conditioned theater, featuring a fast-moving nine-minute video that sweeps through Toledo's history (€3, half-price for young and old, Mon–Sat 10:00–19:00, Sun 10:00–15:00, request video showing in English, longer 29-minute history video available upon request, Plaza de Victorio Macho 2, between the two *sinagogas* listed above, tel. 925-284-225).

The **river-gorge view** from the Museo Vitorio Macho terrace (or free terraces nearby) clearly shows how the River Tajo served as a formidable moat protecting the city. Imagine trying to attack from this side. The 14th-century bridge on the right, and the remains of a bridge on the left, connected the town with the region's *cigarrales*—mansions of wealthy families with orchards of figs and apricots that dot the hillside even today.

San Juan de los Reyes Monasterio—St. John of the Monarchs is a grand monastery, impressive church, and delightful cloistered courtyard. The style is Isabeline, contemporaneous with Portugal's Manueline (c. 1500) and Flamboyant Gothic elsewhere in Europe. It was the intended burial site of the Catholic Monarchs (Isabel and Ferdinand). But after the Moors were expelled in 1492 from Granada, their royal bodies were planted there (further south) to show Spain's commitment to maintaining a Moor-free peninsula. In the chapel—the planned site of the tombs—the big coats of arms are repeated obsessively, à la Moorish decor. Had this been used as the burial site, these would have looked down on the most important tombs in Spain.

Napoleon's troops are mostly to blame for the destruction of the church, a result of Napoleon's view that monastic power in Europe was a menace. While Napoleon's biggest error was to invade Russia, his second dumbest move was to alienate the Catholic faithful by destroying monasteries such as this one. This important strategic mistake eroded popular support from people who might have seen Napoleon as a good alternative to the tyranny of kings and the Church, but instead were not inclined to support the French Emperor (€1.90, daily 10:00–18:45, until 17:45 in winter, San Juan de los Reyes 2, tel. 925-223-802).

▲**Bus #12's Self-Guided Tour with a Sweat-Free Santo Tomé-to-Plaza Zocódover Return Trip**—When you're finished with the sights at the Santo Tomé end of town, you can hike all the way back (not fun)—or simply catch bus #12 from in front of Santo Tomé (fun!). Santo Tomé is the bus terminus; buses wait to depart from here twice hourly (at :25 and :55), heading to Plaza Zocódover. The bus offers tired sightseers a quick, interesting look at the town walls. Here's what you'll see on your way from Santo Tomé:

Leaving Santo Tomé, you'll first ride through Toledo's Jewish section. On the right, you'll pass Museo El Greco in "El Greco's House," Sinagoga del Tránsito, and Sinagoga de Santa María la Blanca, followed by—on your left—the ornate Flamboyant Gothic facade of San Juan de los Reyes Monasterio. After squeezing through the 16th-century city gate, the bus follows along the mighty 10th-century wall. (Toledo was never conquered by force... only by siege.)

Just past the big escalator (which brings people from parking lots up into the city), the wall gets fancier, as demonstrated by the little Old Bisagra Gate. Soon after, you see the big New Bisagra Gate, the main entry into the old town. While the city walls date from the 10th century, this gate was built as an arch of triumph in the 16th century.

The TI is just outside the big gate, at the edge of a well-maintained and shaded park—a picnic-perfect spot, and one of Toledo's few green areas. After a detour to the bus-station basement to pick up people coming from Madrid, you swing back around Bisagra Gate and climb into the old town, passing the fine Moorish (14th-century) Sun Gate, and then arrive at the main square, Plaza Zocódover. Push the button to indicate that you'd like to get off at the square (the bus will not automatically stop at Zocódover).

SHOPPING

Toledo probably sells more souvenirs than any city in Spain. This is *the* place to buy medieval-looking swords, armor, maces, three-legged stools, lethal-looking letter-openers, and other nouveau antiques. It's also Spain's damascene center, where, for centuries, craftspeople have inlaid black steel with gold, silver, and copper wire. Spain's top bullfighters wouldn't have their swords made anywhere else.

Knives: At the workshop of English-speaking **Mariano Zamorano,** you can see swords and knives being made. Judging by what's left of Mariano's hand, his knives are among the sharpest (Mon–Sat 10:00–14:00 & 16:00–19:00, closed Sat afternoon and Sun, behind Ayuntamiento/city hall at Calle Ciudad 19, tel. 925-222-634, www.marianozamorano.com).

Damascene: Shops selling the shiny inlaid plates and decorative wares are all over town. The damascene is a real tourist racket, but it's fun to pop into a shop and see the intricate handwork in action. The **Simian** shop (just below the cathedral) offers good-quality items and a great chance to see the work (daily 9:00–20:00, Santa Ursula 6, tel. 925-250-546).

El Martes, Toledo's colorful outdoor market and a lively local scene, bustles on Paseo de Merchan, better known to locals as "La Vega" (Tue only 9:00–14:00, outside Bisagra Gate near TI).

SLEEPING

Madrid day-trippers darken the sunlit cobbles, but few stay to see Toledo's medieval moonrise. Spend the night. Spring and fall are high season; November through March and July and August are less busy.

Near Plaza Zocódover

$$ Hotel Las Conchas, a three-star hotel, gleams with marble. It's so sleek and slick it almost feels more like a hospital than a hotel. Its 35 rooms are plenty comfortable (Sb-€55, Db-€75, Db with terrace-€82, breakfast-€5, includes tax, 5 percent discount in 2007 with this book, air-con, near the Alcázar at Juan Labrador 8, tel.

Sleep Code

(€1 = about $1.20, country code: 34)
S = Single, **D** = Double/Twin, **T** = Triple, **Q** = Quad, **b** = bathroom, **s** = shower only. Unless otherwise noted, credit cards are accepted and English is spoken.

To help you easily sort through these listings, I've divided the rooms into three categories, based on the price for a standard double room with bath during high season:

$$$ Higher Priced—Most rooms €90 or more.
$$ Moderately Priced—Most rooms between €60–90.
$ Lower Priced—Most rooms €60 or less.

Near Plaza Zocódover

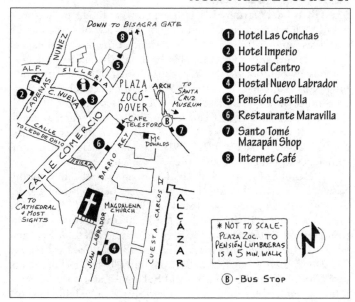

DOWN TO BISAGRA GATE

PLAZA ZOCÓDOVER

ARCH — TO SANTA CRUZ MUSEUM

CAFE TELESFORO

MC DONALDS

CALLE COMERCIO

BARRIO REY

CALLE TOLEDO DE OHIO

CALLE C. NUEVA

CADENAS

NUNEN

SILLERIA

AL.F.

FIERRE

TO CATHEDRAL & MOST SIGHTS

JUAN LABRADOR

MAGDALENA CHURCH

CUESTA CARLOS V

ALCÁZAR

❶ Hotel Las Conchas
❷ Hotel Imperio
❸ Hostal Centro
❹ Hostal Nuevo Labrador
❺ Pensión Castilla
❻ Restaurante Maravilla
❼ Santo Tomé Mazapán Shop
❽ Internet Café

* NOT TO SCALE-
PLAZA ZOC. TO
PENSIÓN LUMBRERAS
IS A 5 MIN. WALK

Ⓑ —BUS STOP

925-210-760, fax 925-224-271, www.lasconchas.com, lasconchas @ctv.es, Pablo and Yuki).

$ Hotel Imperio—well run, offering 21 basic, air-conditioned rooms with marginal beds in a handy old-town location—is your best budget bet in town. Weekends can be noisy; ask for a *tranquilo* room (Sb-€28, Db-€43, Tb-€58, includes tax, 5 percent discount in 2007 with this book, elevator, cheery café; from Calle Comercio, at #38 go a block uphill to Calle Cadenas 5; tel. 925-227-650, fax 925-253-183, www.terra.es/personal/himperio, himperio@teleline .es, friendly Pablo and Esther).

$ Hostal Centro rents 28 modern, clean, and comfy rooms (Sb-€30, Db-€48, Tb-€65, inviting roof terrace; 50 yards off Plaza Zocódover, first right off Calle Comercio at Calle Nueva 13; tel. 925-257-091, fax 925-257-848, www.hostalcentro.com, hostalcentro@telefonica.net, Asun or David).

$ Hostal Nuevo Labrador, with 12 clean, shiny, and spacious rooms, is quiet and modern—another good value (Sb-€30, Db-€45, bigger Db-€50, Tb-€65, Qb-€80, includes tax, no breakfast, air-con, elevator, Juan Labrador 10, tel. 925-222-620, fax 925-229-399, www.nuevolabrador.com, nuevolabrador@telefonica.net, Ángel).

$ Pensión Castilla, a family-run cheapie, has seven basic rooms (S-€17, Db-€27, extra bed possible, cash only, fans, Calle Recoletos 6, tel. 925-256-318, Teresa doesn't speak English).

Near the Bisagra Gate

$$$ Hostal del Cardenal, a 17th-century cardinal's palace built into Toledo's wall, is quiet and elegant, with a cool garden and a stuffy restaurant. This poor-man's parador, at the dusty old gate of Toledo, is closest to the station, but below all the old-town action. The nearby outdoor escalators take the sweat out of getting into town (Sb-€70, Db-€112, extra bed-€20, 20 percent cheaper mid-Dec–mid-March, breakfast-€8, 5 percent discount in 2007 with this book, air-con, some free parking, *serioso* staff, enter through town wall 100 yards below Bisagra Gate, Paseo de Recaredo 24, tel. 925-224-900, fax 925-222-991, www.hostaldelcardenal.com, cardenal@hostaldelcardenal.com).

$ Hotel Sol, with 15 newly decorated, pastel, no-smoking rooms, is a good value. It's on a quiet street between the Bisagra Gate and Plaza Zocódover (Sb-€43, Db-€58, Tb-€71, includes tax, breakfast-€4, 10 percent discount in 2007 with this book, air-con, parking-€10/day, leave the busy main drag at Hotel Real and head 50 yards down the lane to Azacanes 8, tel. 925-213-650, fax 925-216-159, www.hotelyhostalsol.com, info@hotelyhostalsol.com, José Carlos). Their 11-room **Hostal Sol** annex across the street is just as comfortable, and a bit cheaper (Sb-€35, Db-€48, Tb-€58, Qb-€71, includes tax, no breakfast, 10 percent discount in 2007 with this book, same contact info as above).

$ Hostal Hospedería de los Reyes has 15 colorful and thoughtfully appointed rooms in a new, attractive, yellow building 100 yards north of the Bisagra Gate, outside the wall (Sb-€41, Db-€50–60, includes breakfast, air-con, Perala 37, tel. 925-283-667, fax 925-283-668, www.hospederiadelosreyes.com).

Deep in Toledo

$$$ Hotel Pintor El Greco, at the far end of the old town, has 33 plush and rustic-feeling rooms with all the comforts, yet it's in a historic 17th-century building (Sb-€88, Db-€110, Tb-€130, Qb-€145, manager José promises 15 percent discount if you show this book and book direct in 2007, air-con, elevator, a block from Santo Tomé at Alamillos del Tránsito 13, tel. 925-285-191, fax 925-215-819, www.hotel-pintorelgreco.com, info@hotel-pintorelgreco.com). With a reasonably priced garage (€12/day) immediately opposite, this hotel is a good bet for drivers.

$$ La Posada de Manolo rents 14 thoughtfully furnished rooms across from the downhill corner of the cathedral. Manolo Junior recently opened this fine hostel according to his father's vision: a comfortable place with each of its three floors themed differently—Moorish, Jewish, and Christian (Sb-€42, Db-€72, big Db-€84, includes buffet breakfast, 10 percent discount in 2007 when reserved directly with this book, air-con, no elevator, two nice view

Toledo Hotels and Restaurants

NOTE: STREET WIDTH IS EXAGGERATED FOR CLARITY

DCH

1 Hostal & Rest. del Cardenal

2 Hotel Sol & Hostal Sol Annex

3 Hotel Pintor El Greco

4 La Posada de Manolo

5 Hotel Santa Isabel

6 To Hostal Gavilánes II,
Hostal Madrid &
Hotel María Cristina

7 To Albergue Juvenil
San Servando (Hostel)

8 To Parador de Toledo & Hotel
Residencia La Almazara

9 Los Cuatro Tiempos Rest.

10 Casa Aurelio I

11 Casa Aurelio II & III (on Sinagoga)
& Pizzeria Pastucci

12 Rest. Casón López de Toledo

13 La Perdiz Restaurante

14 Restaurante-Mesón Palacios

15 Adolfo Vinoteca

16 Taverna de Amboades

17 Mercado Municipal (Market)

18 To Hostal Hospedería de los Reyes

terraces, Calle Sixto Ramón Parro 8, tel. 925-282-250, fax 925-282-251, www.laposadademanolo.com, toledo@laposadademanolo.com).

$ Hotel Santa Isabel, in a 15th-century building two blocks from the cathedral, has 42 clean, modern, and comfortable rooms and squeaky tile hallways (Sb-€33, Db-€49, Tb-€66, includes tax, breakfast-€4, air-con, elevator, scenic roof terrace, parking-€7/day, buried deep in old town—take a taxi instead of the bus, drivers enter from Calle Pozo Amargo, Calle Santa Isabel 24, tel. 925-253-120, fax 925-253-136, www.santa-isabel.com, santa-isabel arrakis.es, Andres).

Outside of Town, near the Bullring

These next three places are on a modern street next to the bullring (Plaza de Toros, bullfights only on holidays), just beyond Bisagra Gate. In this area, parking is free on the street. The bus station is a five-minute walk away, and city buses lumber by every few minutes (all go directly to Plaza Zocódover). There are many similar, nondescript, comfy, and cheap places in this neighborhood.

$$$ Hotel María Cristina, a sprawling 74-room hotel, has all the comforts under a thin layer of prefab tradition (Sb-€62, Db-€99, Tb-€130, €159 suites available, tax not included, breakfast-€7, air-con, elevator, attached restaurant, parking-€9.50/day, Marqués de Mendigorría 1, tel. 925-213-202, fax 925-212-650, www.hotelesmayoral.com, informacion@hotelmayoral.com).

The next two listings are good budget bets, but have office-building charm and no English-language skills: **$ Hostal Gavilánes II** has 18 renovated rooms (Sb-€42, Db-€49, Db suite-€91, Tb-€63, Qb-€72, includes taxes, breakfast-€2.50, air-con, parking-€6/day, Marqués de Mendigorría 14, tel. & fax 925-211-628, www.gavilanes.to, hostallosgavilanes2@hotmail.com). **$ Hostal Madrid** has 20 rooms and a café next door (Sb-€28, Db-€40, Tb-€55, includes tax, air-con, parking-€6/day, Marqués de Mendigorría 7, tel. 925-221-114, fax 925-228-113).

$ *Hostel:* The 96-bed **Albergue Juvenil San Servando** youth hostel is lavish and newly renovated but cheap, with small rooms for two, three, or four people (€10 per bed, non-members pay €3.50/night extra, swimming pool, views, cafeteria, good management, located in 10th-century Arab castle of San Servando, 10-min walk from train station, 15-min hike from town center, over Puente Viejo outside town, tel. 925-224-554, reservations tel. 925-221-676, alberguesclm@jccm.es, no English spoken).

Outside of Town with the Grand Toledo View

$$$ Parador de Toledo, with 76 rooms, is one of Spain's best-known inns. Its guests enjoy the same Toledo view El Greco made famous from across the Tajo Gorge (Sb-€130, Db-€150, Db with view-€173, Tb with view-€202, tax not included, breakfast-€13, €28 fixed-price meals in their fine restaurant overlooking Toledo, 2 windy miles from town at Cerro del Emperador, tel. 925-221-850, fax 925-225-166, www.parador.es, toledo@parador.es).

$ Hotel Residencia La Almazara was the summer residence of a 16th-century archbishop of Toledo. A friend of the archbishop and fond of this location's classic Toledo view, El Greco hung out here for inspiration. A lumbering old place with cushy public rooms and 28 simple bedrooms, it's truly in the country, but just 1.5 miles out of Toledo (Sb-€33, Db-€47, Db with view-€59, Tb-€70, 10 rooms have view, air-con, Ctra. de Arges 47, follow signs from circular Ronda de Toledo road, tel. 925-223-866, fax 925-250-562, www.hotelalmazara.com, reservas@hotelalmazara.com).

EATING

Dining in Traditional Elegance

A day full of El Greco and the romance of Toledo after dark puts me in the mood for game meats. Typical Toledo dishes include partridge *(perdiz)*, venison *(venado)*, wild boar *(jabalí)*, roast suckling pig *(cochinillo asado)*, or baby lamb *(cordero)* similarly roasted after a few weeks of mother's milk. After dinner, find a mazapán place (such as the Santo Tomé shops) for dessert.

Los Cuatro Tiempos Restaurante specializes in local game and roasts, proficiently served in a tasteful and elegant setting. They have an extensive and inviting Spanish wine list (€19 three-course lunches, €30 à la carte dinners, daily 13:00–16:30 & 20:30–23:30, at downhill corner of cathedral at Sixto Ramón Parro 5, tel. 925-223-782).

Toledo's three **Casa Aurelio** restaurants all offer traditional cooking (game, roast suckling pig, traditional soup, €30 dinners) with a classy atmosphere more memorable than the meals (13:00–16:30 & 20:00–23:30, air-con). None have outdoor seating, and all are within three blocks of the cathedral: **Plaza del Ayuntamiento 4** is festive (tel. 925-227-716), **Sinagoga 6** is most *típico* (tel. 925-222-097), and **Sinagoga 1,** popular with Toledo's political class, is the newest and dressiest, with a wine cellar and more modern cuisine (tel. 925-221-392).

Restaurante Casón López de Toledo, a fancy restaurant located in an old noble palace, specializes in Castilian food, particularly venison and partridge. While the €11 lunch special in the more casual ground-floor bar is a swinging deal, its character unfolds upstairs in the formal restaurant (€50 dinners, Tue–Sat 13:30–16:00 & 20:30–23:30, closed Sun–Mon, reservations smart, near Plaza Zocódover at Calle de la Sillería 3, tel. 925-254-774).

Hostal del Cardenal Restaurante, a classic hotel restaurant near Bisagra Gate at the bottom of town, is understandably popular with tourists for its decent traditional roast dishes and lush patio (daily 13:00–16:00 & 20:30–23:30, Puerto de Recaredo 24, tel. 925-220-862). This place is too traditional for some, but the dining in the elegant garden ambience can't be beat.

La Perdiz is *the* place for a splurge near the Santa Tomé sights. This classy spot offers partridge (as the restaurant's name suggests), venison, suckling pig, fish, and in-house pastry-chef *mazapán* desserts that are hard to forget (Tue–Sat 13:00–16:00 & 20:00–23:00, closed Sun-Mon and first half of Aug, Calle de los Reyes Católicos 7, tel. 925-252-919).

Adolfo Vinoteca is the wine bar of the highly respected local chef Adolfo, who also runs a fine restaurant across the street. His hope is to introduce the younger generation to the culture of fine food and wine. The place offers plenty of style...without pretension. You can't go wrong with their short list of gourmet appetizers (€5 each) and fine local wines (€2–3 per glass). I'd just throw myself at the mercy of Jonathan, and enjoy the feeling of gourmet slaves in the kitchen bringing you your wildest edible fancies. If the Starship *Enterprise* had a Spanish wine and tapas bar, this would be it. Wine is sold at shop prices with a €6 cork fee (daily 12:00–24:00, across from cathedral at Calle Nuncio Viejo 1, tel. 925-224-244).

Eating Simply, but Well

For locations, see maps on pages 317 and 319.

Restaurante-Mesón Palacios is a simple diner, serving good regional food at reasonable prices in a warm and friendly atmosphere. Their bean soup with partridge *(judías con perdiz)* and roast suckling lamb and pig (€12) are good (Mon–Sat from 12:00 and from 19:00, closed Sun, near Plaza de San Vicente at Alfonso X 3, tel. 925-215-972, you've got a friend in Jesús).

Restaurante Maravilla, plain and forgettable, serves a good €11 fixed-price meal. Just half a block off Plaza Zocódover, it has cool air-conditioning and good service (open daily, lunch from 13:00, dinner from 20:00, Plaza Barrio Rey 7, tel. 925-228-582).

Plaza Zocódover is lined by bars and cafés. It has edible food at reasonable prices, considering the wonderful people-watching scene.

At **Taverna de Amboades,** a humble but earnest wine-and-tapas bar near the Bisagra Gate, Miguel Ángel enjoys explaining the differences between Spanish wines. To try some really good wines with quality local cheese and meat (combo-plate €8), drop by and let Miguel impress you (Tue–Sun 19:30–24:00, also Fri–Sun 13:00–16:00, closed Mon, Alfonso VI 5, mobile 678-483-749).

Pizzeria Pastucci, while nondescript, is a local favorite for pizza and pasta (€11 feeds two, Tue–Sun 12:00–16:00 & 19:00–24:00, closed Mon, near cathedral at Calle de la Sinagoga 10).

Mercado Municipal: Picnics are best assembled at the city market on Plaza Mayor (on the Alcázar side of cathedral, with a supermarket inside open Mon–Sat 9:00–20:00 and stalls open mostly in the mornings until 14:00, closed Sun). This is a fun market to prowl, even if you don't need food. If you feel like munching a paper-plate-size Communion wafer, one of the stalls sells crispy bags of *obleas*—a great gift for your favorite pastor. For a picnic with people-watching, consider Plaza Zocódover or Plaza del Ayuntamiento.

And for Dessert: Mazapán

Toledo's famous almond-fruity-sweet *mazapán* is sold all over town. Locals say the best is made by **Santo Tomé** (several outlets, including a handy one on Plaza Zocódover, daily 9:00–22:00). Browse their tempting window displays. They sell *mazapán* goodies individually (two for about €1, *sin relleno*—without filling—is for purists, *de piñon* has pine nuts, *imperiales* is with almonds, others have fruit fillings). Boxes are good for gifts, but sampling is much cheaper when buying by the piece. Their *Toledana* is a nutty, crumbly, not-too-sweet cookie with a subtle thread of squash filling (€1 each).

For a sweet and romantic evening moment, pick up a few pastries and head down to the cathedral. Sit on the Plaza del Ayuntamiento's benches (or stretch out on the stone wall to the right of the TI). The fountain is on your right, Spain's best-looking city hall is behind you, and there before you: her top cathedral, built back when Toledo was Spain's capital, shining brightly against the black night sky.

TRANSPORTATION CONNECTIONS

While the new AVE bullet train makes the trip in half the time (nearly hourly, 30 minutes), buses depart twice as frequently. Either way, Madrid and Toledo are very easily connected.

From Toledo to Madrid: by bus (2/hr, 60–90 min, €4 one-way, *directo* is faster than *ruta*, Madrid's Estación sur Autobuses, Metro: Mendez Álvaro, Continental Auto bus company, tel. 925-223-641), **by train** (almost hourly, 30 min, €8, AVE fast train zips to Madrid's Atocha station), **by car** (40 miles, 1 hr). Toledo bus info: tel. 925-215-850; train info: tel. 902-240-202.

From Toledo to Other Points: To get to Granada and elsewhere in Spain from Toledo, assume you'll have to transfer in Madrid. See Madrid's "Transportation Connections" for information on reaching various destinations.

Route Tips for Drivers

Granada to Toledo (250 miles, 5 hrs): The Granada–Toledo drive is long, hot, and boring. Start early to minimize the heat and make the best time you can. Follow signs for *Madrid/Jaén/N323* into what some call "the Spanish Nebraska"—La Mancha (see below). After Puerto Lapice, you'll see the Toledo exit.

Toledo to Madrid (40 miles, 1 hr): It's a speedy *autovía* north, past one last bullboard to Madrid (on N401). The highways converge into M30, which circles Madrid. Follow it to the left (*Nor* or *Oeste*) and take the Plaza de España exit to get back to Gran Vía. If you're airport-bound, keep heading into Madrid until you see the airplane symbol (N-II).

To drive to Atocha Station in Madrid, take the exit off M30 for Plaza de Legazpi, then take Delicias (second on your right off the square). Parking for car return is on the north side of the train station.

La Mancha

La Mancha, which is worth a visit if you're driving between Toledo and Granada, shows a side of Spain that you'll see nowhere else—vast and flat. Named for the Arabic word for "parched earth," it makes you feel small—lost in rough seas of olive-green polka dots. Random buildings look like houses and hotels hurled off some heavenly Monopoly board.

This is the setting of Miguel de Cervantes' *Don Quixote,* published in the early 17th century, after England sank the Armada and the Spanish Empire began its decline. Cervantes' star character fights doggedly for good, for justice, and against the fall of Spain and its traditional old-regime ideals. Ignoring reality, Don Quixote is a hero fighting a hopeless battle. Stark La Mancha is the perfect stage.

The epitome of *Don Quixote* country, the town of **Consuegra** (TI tel. 925-475-731) must be the La Mancha Cervantes had in

mind. Drive up to the ruined 12th-century castle and joust with a windmill. It's hot and buggy here, but the powerful view overlooking the village, with its sun-bleached, light-red roofs; modern concrete reality; and harsh, windy silence makes for a profound picnic (a 1-hour drive south of Toledo). The castle belonged to the Knights of St. John (12th and 13th centuries) and is associated with their trip to Jerusalem during the Crusades. Originally built from the ruins of a nearby Roman circus, it has been newly restored (€1.50). Sorry, the windmills are post-Cervantes, only 200 to 300 years old.

If you've seen windmills, the next castle north (above Almonacid, 8 miles from Toledo) is free and more interesting than the Consuegra castle. Follow the ruined lane past the ruined church up to the ruined castle. The jovial locals hike up with kids and kites.

GRANADA

For a time, Granada was the grandest city in Spain. But in the end, with the tumult that came with the change from Moorish to Christian rule, it eventually lost its power and settled into a long slumber. Today, Granada seems to specialize in evocative history and good living. We'll keep things fun and simple, settling down in the old center and exploring monuments of the Moorish civilization and its conquest. And we'll taste the treats of a North African–flavored culture that survives here today.

Granada's magnificent Alhambra fortress was the last stronghold of the Moorish kingdom in Spain. The city's exotically tangled Moorish quarter bustles under the grand Alhambra, which glows red in the evening while locals stroll, enjoying the city's cool, late-night charms.

There is an old saying: "Give him a coin, woman, for there is nothing worse in this life than to be blind in Granada." This city has much to see, yet it reveals itself in unpredictable ways. It takes a poet to sort through and assemble the jumbled shards of Granada. Peer through the intricate lattice of a Moorish window. Hear water burbling unseen among the labyrinthine hedges of the Generalife Gardens. Listen to a flute trilling deep in the swirl of alleys around the cathedral. Don't be blind in Granada—open your senses.

Planning Your Time

Granada is worth one day and two nights at a minimum. The Costa del Sol's best beach town, Nerja, is just two hours away (by bus), white hill towns such as Ronda are three hours away (bus or train), and Sevilla is an easy three-hour train ride. To use your time efficiently in Granada, reserve in advance for the Alhambra (see sidebar on page 334). The Madrid–Granada train service is slow (6 hours), but passes through beautiful countryside.

Here's the best one-day plan: In the morning, tour the cathedral and Royal Chapel (both closed roughly 13:00–16:00) and stroll the pedestrian-zone shopping scene. Do the Alhambra in the late afternoon. At sunset, be at the San Nicolás viewpoint in the Moorish quarter (the Albayzín), then find the right place for a suitably late dinner.

ORIENTATION

While modern Granada sprawls (300,000 people), its sights are all within a 20-minute walk of Plaza Nueva, where dogs wag their  tails to the rhythm of modern hippies and street musicians. All of my recommended hotels are within a few blocks of Plaza Nueva. Make this the hub of your Granada visit.

Plaza Nueva was a main square back when kings called Granada home. This historic center is in the Darro River Valley, which separates two hills (the river now flows under the square). On one hill is the great Moorish palace, the Alhambra, and on the other is the best-preserved Moorish quarter in Spain, the Albayzín. To the southeast are the cathedral, Royal Chapel, and Alcaicería (Moorish market), where the city's two main drags—Gran Vía de Colón (often just called "Gran Vía" by locals) and Calle Reyes Católicos—lead away into the modern city.

Tourist Information

The main TI is tucked away just above Plaza Nueva on Santa Ana street (above the church, Mon–Fri 9:00–19:30, Sat 10:00–19:00, Sun 10:00–14:00, tel. 958-221-002). Another TI is at the entrance of the Alhambra (daily 8:00–19:00, tel. 958-229-575). Both cover Granada as well as all Andalucía. At either TI, get a free city map and the *Viva Granada* magazine in English, and verify your Alhambra plans. To save yourself a trip to the train or bus stations, get schedule information from either TI (they list all departures on the wall). During peak season (April–Oct), TI kiosks sometimes pop up in Plaza Nueva and Plaza de Bib-Rambla.

Arrival in Granada

By Train: Granada's train station is connected to the center by frequent buses, a €4 taxi ride, or a 30-minute walk down Avenida

Greater Granada

de la Constitución and Gran Vía. The train station has luggage storage (€3/small locker, €4.50/large locker). Reserve your train out upon arrival.

Exiting the train station, walk straight ahead down the tree-lined road. At the first major intersection (Avenida de la Constitución), you'll see the bus stop on your right. Buses #3 through #9 (and most other buses—check the easy-to-read map at bus stop) go to the cathedral, the nearest stop to Plaza Nueva—confirm by asking the driver, "*¿Catedral?*" (kah-tay-DRAHL). Buy a €1 ticket from the driver. Get off when you see the fountain of Plaza Isabel La Católica in front of the bus at the stop near the cathedral; cross the busy Gran Vía and walk three short blocks to Plaza Nueva.

By Bus: Granada's bus station (Estación de Autobuses, with a good and cheap cafeteria, ATMs, luggage storage, and info office, tel. 958-185-480; or tel. 902-422-242 for the Alsa company, which serves Barcelona and east-coast destinations) is located on the outskirts of the city. To get to the center, either take a taxi (€6) or buses #3 or #33 (€1, pay driver). It's about a 20-minute bus ride; nearing the center, the bus goes up Gran Vía. For Plaza Nueva, get off at the stop for the cathedral (cathedral not visible from bus), a half block before the grand square, Plaza Isabel La Católica (a three-block walk from Plaza Nueva).

By Car: Driving in Granada's historic center is restricted to buses, taxis, and tourists with hotel reservations. Signs are posted to this effect, and entrance is strictly controlled—but generally not by an officer. Two hidden cameras snap a photo of your license plate as soon as you enter (one on Calle Recogidas and another after Puerta Real). Be sure to give your license plate number to your hotel so that they can contact the local police department (and prevent a nasty surprise when you return your rental car). Getting into the old center and finding your hotel or a parking garage is a major frustration because of the strict controls and one-way streets. Consider parking nearby, then hiring a taxi to lead you to your destination. The *autovía* (freeway) circles the city with a *circumvalación* road (Ronda Sur). If you're heading for Plaza Nueva (recommended hotels), take exit #129, direction *Centro, Recogidas.* Calle Recogidas becomes Calle Reyes Católicos and leads directly into the heart of town. There will probably be a police block at Puerta Real (Victoria Hotel). You can pull into Plaza Nueva if you have a hotel reservation: There are posts with hotel buzzers on Calle Reyes Católicos. You press a button on the pillar for your hotel; the hotel buzzes back, releasing the roadblock to allow you through. Granada has several parking garages. One is at Puerta Real (€10/day; as you enter the city on Calle Recogidas, turn right on Acera del Darro). Parking San Agustín—near the cathedral, just off Gran Vía—costs much more than the others, but is the only lot that's an easy walk to all my recommended hotels (€25/day; as you approach Plaza Isabel La Católica on Gran Vía, follow blue *Parking* sign).

By Plane: Granada's airport (code: GRX) is about 10 miles west of the city center. To get between the airport and downtown, you can take a taxi (€20–22) or, much cheaper, the airport bus, timed to leave when flights arrive and depart (€3, 6/day, 30 min). Use the bus stop at Gran Vía del Colón, nearly across from the cathedral. Airport info: tel. 958-245-223.

Helpful Hints

Theft Alert: If aggressive, obnoxious Gypsy women force sprigs of rosemary on you, avoid them. While they are mostly harmless, petty pickpockets are plentiful in Granada. In general, be on guard, especially late at night in the Albayzín. Your biggest threat is being conned while enjoying drinks and music in Sacromonte.

City Pass: The **Bono Turístico** city pass covers the Alhambra, cathedral, Royal Chapel, Carthusian Monastery, sightseeing bus, and nine free public-bus trips, plus minor sights and discounts on more (€23, valid for a week). When you buy your pass, the vendor schedules a time for your Alhambra visit. Passes are sold at the Royal Chapel, Alhambra, and Caja Granada bank on Plaza Isabel La Católica. You can save time by calling ahead to purchase your pass by credit card, and it will be ready for you when you arrive at the vendor (12 percent commission, tel. 902-100-095). During the peak-season time of spring through fall, it's worth ordering the pass in advance (rather than waiting to buy it in person) to avoid the small risk of not getting into the Alhambra—particularly if you'll only be in town for one day and haven't already made a reservation. Note that some of the fancier hotels provide one free pass per room for stays of two or more nights during peak season.

Festivals: From late June to early July, the International Festival of Music and Dance offers classical music, ballet, flamenco, and zarzuela (light opera) nightly in the Alhambra at reasonable prices. The ticket office is located in the Corral de Carbón (open mid-April–Oct). Beginning in February, you can also book tickets online at www.granadafestival.org. This festival is one of the most respected and popular in Spain, and tickets for major performers typically sell out months in advance. During the festival, flamenco is free every night at midnight; ask the ticket office or TI for the venue.

Internet Access: There are many Internet points scattered throughout Granada. **Navegaweb,** a chain that sells tickets useable in other locations (including Madrid and Barcelona), has 96 computers (daily 10:00–23:00, 100 yards off Plaza Nueva at Calle Reyes Católicos 55, tel. 958-210-528). **Madar Internet,** with 20 computers, is in the midst of tea shops at Calle Calderería Nueva 11 (Mon–Fri 10:00–24:00, Sat–Sun 12:00–24:00, 2 long blocks off Plaza Nueva).

Post Office: It's on Puerta Real (Mon–Fri 8:30–20:30, Sat 9:30–14:00, closed Sun, tel. 958-221-138).

Travel Agencies: All travel agencies book flights, and many also sell long-distance bus and train tickets. **Viajes Bonanza** sells it all, slow but convenient at Calle Reyes Católicos 30 (Mon–Fri 9:00–13:30 & 17:00–20:00, Sat 10:00–13:30, closed Sun, tel. 958-223-578). **Megachain El Corte Inglés** sells plane and train tickets, but doesn't handle bus travel (Mon–Sat 10:00–21:00, closed Sun, Acera del Darro, floor 2).

American Express: The AmEx office, at Calle Reyes Católicos 31, only offers banking services (Mon–Fri 9:30–13:30 & 16:30–19:30, Sat 10:00–13:00, closed Sun, tel. 958-224-512).

Getting Around Granada

With cheap taxis, efficient minibuses (described below), good city buses, and nearly all points of interest an easy walk from Plaza Nueva, you'll get around Granada easily.

Bus tickets for the minibuses and city buses cost €1 per ride (buy from driver). Bonobus tickets for nine trips (€5.45) or 20 trips (€10.80) save you money if you'll be riding often, or if you're part of a group (they're sharable; buy from driver, valid on minibuses and city buses, you don't need to pay for connecting bus if you transfer within 45 min).

The handy little red **minibuses,** which cover the city center, depart every few minutes from Plaza Nueva until late in evening (about 22:00). There are two stops, on either side of Cuesta de Gomérez (see stops located on map on page 349). Bus #30 goes up to the Alhambra and back; bus #31 does the Albayzín loop (a few go through Sacromonte); and bus #32 connects the Alhambra and Albayzín (from Plaza Nueva, the bus goes up to the Alhambra, returns to Plaza Nueva, then loops through the Albayzín and back to Plaza Nueva). The rare bus #34 goes up into Sacromonte.

City buses are handy if you're visiting the Carthusian Monastery (#8) or going to the bus station (#3 or #33) or train station (#3–#9).

TOURS

Walking Tours—Cicerone, run by María, Rosa, and Cristina, offers informative, 2.5-hour tours from the City Hall—labeled *Ayuntamiento*—on Plaza del Carmen (€10, kids under 14 free, daily May–Oct at 10:30 and 20:00, Nov–April 11:00 and 17:00, small groups, show up or call mobile 670-541-669 or 600-412-051, www .ciceronegranada.com, info@ciceronegranada.com). Each guide is excellent, and they describe the fitful and fascinating changes the city underwent as it morphed from a Moorish capital to a Christian one 500 years ago. The tour doesn't go inside any sights, but you'll weave together bits of the Moorish heritage that survive around the cathedral and the Albayzín. Tours finish on Plaza Nueva. Visits are generally in both English and Spanish, giving you time to take photos when the language switches.

Private Guides—Margarita Ortiz de Landázuri, a local English-speaking guide, knows how to teach and has good rates (tel. 958-221-406, www.alhambratours.com, info@alhambratours.com). If Margarita is busy, her partner, Miguel Ángel, is also very good. The guides of Cicerone (see above) are also available for private tours.

Granada at a Glance

▲▲▲**The Alhambra** The last and greatest Moorish palace, high-lighting the splendor of Moorish civilization in the 13th and 14th centuries. Reservations recommended. **Hours:** The entire complex is open daily March–Oct 8:30–20:00, Nov–Feb 8:30–18:00. The Palacios Nazaries is open for nighttime visits March–Oct Tue–Sat 22:00–23:30, closed Sun–Mon; Nov–Feb only Fri–Sat 20:00–21:30, closed Sun–Thu.

▲▲**Royal Chapel** Lavish 16th-century Plateresque Gothic chapel with the tombs of Queen Isabel and King Ferdinand. **Hours:** April–Oct Mon–Sat 10:30–13:00 & 16:00–19:00, opens Sun at 11:00; Nov–March Mon–Sat 10:30–13:00 & 15:30–18:30, opens Sun at 11:00.

▲▲**San Nicolás Viewpoint** Breathtaking vista over the Alhambra and the Albayzín. **Hours:** Always open; best at sunset.

Cathedral The second-largest cathedral in Spain, unusual for its bright, Renaissance design. **Hours:** April–Oct Mon–Sat 10:30–13:30 & 16:00–20:00, Sun 16:00–20:00; Nov–March Mon–Sat 10:45–13:30 & 16:00–19:00, Sun 16:00–19:00.

Alcaicería Tiny shopping lanes filled with a silk and jewelry market. **Hours:** Always open, with shops open long hours.

Corral del Carbón Granada's only surviving caravanserai (inn for traveling merchants), with impressive Moorish door. **Hours:** Always viewable.

SELF-GUIDED TOUR

The Alhambra

A ▲▲▲ sight, this last and greatest Moorish palace is one of Europe's top sights. Attracting up to 8,000 visitors a day, it's the reason most tourists come to Granada. Nowhere else does the splendor of Moorish civilization shine so beautifully.

The last Moorish stronghold in Europe is, with all due respect, really a symbol of retreat. Granada was only a regional capital for

Paseo de los Tristes A prime strolling strip along the Darro River lined with eateries and peppered with Moorish history. **Hours:** Always open; best in the evenings.

 Hammam El Bañuelo Eleventh-century ruins of Moorish baths. **Hours:** Tue–Sat 10:00–14:00, closed Sun–Mon.

Hammam Baños Árabes Tranquil spot for soaks and massages in Arab baths. **Hours:** Daily 10:00–24:00.

Great Mosque of Granada Brand-new Islamic house of worship featuring a minaret with a live call to prayer, an information center for the Muslim perspective on Granada history, and a courtyard with commanding views. **Hours:** Daily 11:00–14:00 & 18:00–21:00.

Zambra **Dance** Flamenco-like dance performance in Sacromonte district. **Hours:** May–Oct generally 22:00 and 23:00, fewer off-season.

Center for the Interpretation of Sacromonte Digs into geology and cave building, as well as Roma (Gypsy) crafts, food, and music. **Hours:** April–Oct Tue–Fri 10:00–14:00 & 17:00–21:00, Sat–Sun 11:00–21:00, closed Mon; Nov–March Tue–Fri 10:00–14:00 & 16:00–19:00, Sat–Sun 11:00–19:00, closed Mon.

Carthusian Monastery Lavish Baroque monastery on the outskirts of town. **Hours:** Daily April–Oct 10:00–13:00 & 15:30–20:00, Nov–March closes at 18:00.

centuries. Gradually the Christian Reconquista moved south, taking Córdoba (1237) and Sevilla (1248). The Nazarids, one of the many diverse ethnic groups of Spanish Muslims, held Granada until 1492. As you tour their grand palace, remember that while Europe slumbered through the Dark Ages, Moorish magnificence blossomed—busy stucco, plaster "stalactites," colors galore, scalloped windows framing Granada views, exuberant gardens, and water, water everywhere. Water—so rare and precious in most of the Islamic world—was the purest symbol of life to the Moors. The Alhambra is decorated with water: standing still, cascading, masking secret conversations, and drip-dropping playfully.

Orientation: The Alhambra, not nearly as confusing as it might seem, consists of four sights clustered together atop a hill:

Getting a Reservation for the Alhambra

Many tourists never get to see the Alhambra, because tickets sell out. Make a reservation as soon as you're ready to commit to a time (especially during Holy Week, on weekends, or on major holidays). Off-season (July–Aug and winter), you might be able to just walk right in. While things are getting easier, the crowds are unpredictable, and getting a reservation is quite easy.

The Alhambra's top sight is the Moorish palace—Palacios Nazaries. Only 350 visitors per half hour are allowed inside. Your 30-minute time span is printed on your ticket (you can request a particular half hour). While you must enter Palacios Nazaries within this time, once inside you may linger as long as you like. If your entry time to Palacios Nazaries is before 14:00, you can stroll the Alhambra grounds anytime in the morning, see the palace at your appointed time, and leave the Alhambra by 14:00 (although you can get away with staying longer in the fort, gardens, or palace, you won't be allowed to *enter* any of these sites after 14:00). If your ticket is stamped for 14:00 or later, you can go inside the Alhambra no earlier than 14:00. For instance, if you have a reservation to visit Palacios Nazaries between 16:30 and 17:00, you can enter the Alhambra grounds as early as 14:00 and see the fort and Generalife Gardens before the palace. (Because of the time restriction on afternoon visits, morning times sell out the quickest. But for most travelers, an afternoon is ample time to see the site.)

Reserving in Advance: There are four possibilities. Each comes with a (worth it) €1 surcharge. With any of these options, bring photo identification and arrive at the Alhambra about an hour before your palace appointment (the line to pick up the ticket can be up to 20 minutes long, and walking from the ticket office to the palace takes 15 minutes).

1. Order online at www.alhambratickets.com. This is easy and just takes a few minutes.

2. Order by phone. Within Spain, dial 902-224-460. Internationally, dial the international access code first (00 from a European country, 011 from the US or Canada), then 34-915-379-178 (daily 8:30–16:00, can reserve between one day and a year in advance). Pay with a credit card (Visa or MasterCard only). You'll get a reference number to tell the ticket-window clerk at the Alhambra to get your ticket.

3. Drop by any BBVA (Banco Bilbao Vizcaya Argentaria) bank in Spain and make a reservation (Mon–Fri 8:30–14:15, closed Sat–Sun). This is your most problematic option—in practice, there's just a lot of frustration.

4. If you plan to stay at one of the fancier hotels, ask—when you book your hotel room—if the hotelier can book a reservation for you to visit the Alhambra the day after your arrival.

If You're in Granada Without a Reservation: You have a number of alternatives, the least appealing of which involves getting up unnaturally early (#3).

1. Your hotel may be willing to book a reservation for you on short notice. The Alhambra sets aside 400 tickets daily for hotel guests.

2. Make a reservation at a BBVA bank in Granada (possible for a following day, usually not the same day). You'll find a branch near Plaza Nueva at Plaza del Carmen.

3. Stand in line at the Alhambra. The Alhambra admits 7,800 visitors a day. Six thousand tickets are sold in advance. The rest—1,800—are sold each day at the Alhambra ticket window (near Generalife Gardens and parking lot). On busy days in peak season, tickets can sell out as early as 10:00. The ticket office opens at 8:00. People start lining up at about 7:30, but generally if you're in line by 8:15, you'll get an entry time. On a slow day, you'll get in right away. During busy times, you'll have an appointment for later that day.

4. Consider getting Granada's Bono Turístico city pass if you'll be staying at least two days (see "Helpful Hints," page 329). It costs €23, covers admission to the Alhambra and Granada's other top sights, and includes a reservation for the Alhambra (scheduled when you buy the pass). But there are no guarantees that a time slot will be available (especially during April–June and Sept–Oct). This pass is easy to buy near the Royal Chapel and the Alhambra entrances.

5. Take a tour of the Alhambra. The pricier hotels can book you on a €38 GranaVisión tour that includes transportation to the Alhambra and a guided tour of the Palacios Nazaries. The same company also offers tours of the city and province (tel. 958-535-875).

6. Easiest of all, simply go at night (Palacios Nazaries only; see "The Alhambra by Moonlight," page 336).

▲▲▲**Palacios Nazaries**—Exquisite Moorish palace, the one must-see sight.

▲**Generalife Gardens**—Fancy, manicured gardens with small summer palace.

▲**Charles V's Palace**—Christian Renaissance palace plopped on top of the Alhambra after the Reconquista (free entry).

Alcazaba—Empty old fort with tower and views.

These sights are described in more detail in "The Alhambra in Four Parts," on page 339.

Cost: The Alcazaba fort, Palacios Nazaries (Moorish palace), and Generalife Gardens require a €10 combo-ticket. If the Palacios

Nazaries is booked up during the day, consider getting the €5 ticket that covers only the Generalife and Alcazaba, viewing the garden and fort during the day, and then visiting the palace at night (see "The Alhambra by Moonlight," below). Only Charles V's Palace is free. A good map is included with your ticket if you ask for it at the ticket window.

Hours: The Alhambra is open daily March–Oct 8:30–20:00, Nov–Feb 8:30–18:00 (ticket office opens at 8:00, last entry one hour before closing time, tel. 902-441-221). The Palacios Nazaries is also open most evenings (see below for information).

The Alhambra by Moonlight: If you're frustrated by the reservation system, or just prefer doing things after dark, late-night

visits to the Alhambra are easy (you never need a reservation—just buy your ticket upon arrival) and magical (less crowded and beautifully lit). The night visits only include the Palacios Nazaries (not the Alcazaba fort or the Generalife Gardens)—but,

hey, the palace is 80 percent of the Alhambra's thrills anyway. It's open March–Oct Tue–Sat 22:00–23:30 (ticket office open 21:30–22:30), closed Sun–Mon; and Nov–Feb only Fri–Sat 20:00–21:30 (ticket office open 19:30–20:30), closed Sun–Thu.

Getting to the Alhambra: There are three ways to get to the Alhambra:

1. From Plaza Nueva, hike 30 minutes up the street Cuesta de Gomérez. Keep going straight, with the Alhambra high on your left. The ticket pavilion is on the far side of the Alhambra, near the

The Alhambra

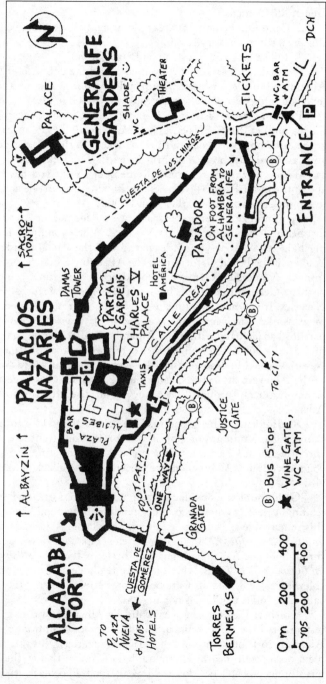

Generalife Gardens.

2. From Plaza Nueva, catch a red minibus #30 or #32, marked *Alhambra* (€1, runs every 15 min).

3. Take a taxi (€3, taxi stand on Plaza Nueva).

Don't drive. Parking is convenient, near the entrance of the Alhambra (€6.50/4 hrs), but when you leave, one-way streets will send you into the traffic-clogged center of New Granada.

Planning Your Visit: It's a 15-minute walk from the entry (at the top end) to Palacios Nazaries at the other end. Be sure to arrive at the Alhambra with enough time to make it to the palace before your allotted half-hour appointment ends. The ticket-checkers at Palacios Nazaries are strict. (Remember that if you have an appointment for Palacios Nazaries after 14:00, you can't be admitted to the Alhambra any earlier than 14:00.)

To minimize walking, see Charles V's Palace and the Alcazaba fort before your visit to Palacios Nazaries. When you finish touring Palacios Nazaries, you'll leave through the Partal Gardens. You'll exit the Partal Gardens near the Alhambra entrance, not far from the Generalife Gardens. Depending on your time, you can visit the Generalife Gardens before or after your visit to Palacios Nazaries. If you have any time to kill before your palace appointment, you can do it luxuriously on the breezy view terrace of the parador bar (actually within the Alhambra walls). While you can find drinks, WCs, and guidebooks near the entrance of Palacios Nazaries, you'll find none inside the actual palace. If you're going to the Albayzín afterwards, catch bus #32, which goes from the Alhambra back through Plaza Nueva and directly up into the Albayzín.

Audioguide: The €3 audioguide brings the palace to life, providing 105 minutes of description for 48 stops (rent it at the entrance and at Charles V's Palace; you'll need to return it where you picked it up). Audioguides are currently not available for night visits.

Guidebooks: Consider getting a guidebook in town and reading it the night before to understand the layout and history of this remarkable sight before entering. The classic is *The Alhambra and the Generalife* (€7.50, includes great map, sold in town and throughout the Alhambra), but even better is the slick *Alhambra and Generalife in Focus*, which is more readable and has vibrant color photos (€8, sold at many bookstores around town). The one called the "official guide" is not as good.

Cuisine: The only eateries within the Alhambra walls are the restaurant at the parador and a small bar/café kiosk in front of the Alcazaba fort (near entrance of Palacios Nazaries). But there are plenty of options nearby. Restaurante la Mimbre (below the top bus stop) is probably best for a real meal. You'll find snack vending machines at the entrance and the Charles V Palace (at WCs). You're welcome to bring in a picnic as long as you eat it in a public area.

The Alhambra in Four Parts

I've listed these sights in the order you're likely to visit them. Note that there are other sights you can visit for free on the Alhambra grounds (see sidebar).

Charles V's Palace

It's only natural for a conquering king to build his own palace over his foe's palace, and that's exactly what the Christian king Charles V did. The Palacios Nazaries

wasn't good enough for Charles, so he built this new home, worth ▲, which was financed by a salt-in-the-wound tax on Granada's defeated Muslim population. With a unique circle within a square design by Pedro Machuca, a devotee of Michelangelo and Raphael, this is Spain's most impressive Renaissance building. Stand in the circular courtyard, then climb the stairs. Charles' palace was designed to have a dome, but it was never finished—his son, Philip II, abandoned it to build his own palace, El Escorial. Inside are two not-so-interesting museums (both free to enter, as is the palace itself): Museo de Bellas Artes (upstairs) and the better Museo de la Alhambra, showing off some of the Alhambra's best surviving Moorish art (Tue–Sat 9:00–14:30, closed Sun–Mon, on ground floor).

Alcazaba

The fort—the original "red castle" or "Alhambra"—is the oldest and most ruined part of the complex, offering exercise and fine

city views. What you see is from the mid-13th century, but there was probably a fort here in Roman times. Once upon a time, this tower defended a town (or medina) of 2,000 Muslims living within the Alhambra walls. From the top (looking north), find Plaza Nueva and the San Nicolás viewpoint (in the Albayzín). To the south are the mountains. Is anybody skiing today?

Think of that day in 1492 when the Christian cross and the flags of Aragon and Castile were raised on this tower, and the

The Alhambra Grounds

While the Palacios Nazaries, Alcazaba fort, and Generalife Gardens are all secured with turnstiles, there's a big public zone in the middle of the former fortified city that anyone can visit without a ticket. Attractions in this area that are free and open to the public include Charles V's Palace (see sight listing); a line of shops showing off traditional woodworking techniques; the fancy Alhambra Parador (Parador Nacional San Francisco, listed under "Sleeping," below); and the foundations of baths, homes, and gardens now being excavated.

It's especially fun to snoop around the historic **parador,** which—as a national monument—must technically be open to the public. Once a Moorish palace within the Alhambra, then a Franciscan monastery, the monastery has a historic claim to fame because its church is where the Catholic Monarchs (Ferdinand and Isabel) chose to be buried. For a peek, step in and ask politely at the reception desk to see the tomb. (It's just past this desk, in the open-air ruins of the church.) The slab on the ground near the altar (and a surviving bit of the mosque that was here before the church) marks the place where the greatest king and queen of Spain were buried until 1521 (when they were moved to the Royal Chapel—see page 348). The next room is a delightful former cloister—today a comfy, inviting lounge. Downstairs (back past the reception desk and to the right) is a fine restaurant terrace for a drink or snack.

Remember as you wander these grounds that the Alhambra was a fortified city of 2,000 people. This open zone was a medina, a town with a general urban scene. The main road dead-ended at the **Wine Gate** (Puerta del Vino), which protected the fortress. When you pass through the Wine Gate, you enter a courtyard that was originally a moat, then a reservoir (in Christian times). The well—now encased in a bar/kiosk—is still a place for cold drinks. If you're done with your Alhambra visit, you can exit down to the city from the Wine Gate.

fleeing Moorish king Boabdil (Abu Abdullah in Arabic) looked back from those mountains and wept. His mom chewed him out, saying, "Weep like a woman for what you couldn't defend like a man." With this defeat, over seven centuries of Muslim rule in Spain came to an end. Much later, Napoleon stationed his troops at the Alhambra, contributing substantially to its ruin when he left.

To get to Palacios Nazaries, follow the signs down and around to the palace. If you're early, duck into the exhibit across from the palace entry. It's in Spanish, but the models of the Alhambra upstairs are easy to appreciate.

Palacios Nazaries

During the 30-minute window of time stamped on your ticket, enter the jewel of the Alhambra: the Moorish royal palace, worth

▲▲▲. Once you're in, you can relax—there are no more time constraints. You'll walk through three basic sections: royal offices, ceremonial rooms, and private quarters. Built mostly in the 14th century, this palace offers your best possible look at the refined, elegant Moorish civilization of Al-Andalus (Arabic for the Iberian Peninsula).

You'll visit rooms decorated from top to bottom with carved wood ceilings, stucco "stalactites," ceramic tiles, molded-plaster walls, and filigree windows. Open-air courtyards in the palace feature fountains with bubbling water like a desert oasis, the Quran's symbol of heaven. The palace is well-preserved, but the trick is to imagine it furnished and filled with Moorish life...sultans with hookah pipes lounging on pillows on Persian carpets, tapestries on the walls, heavy curtains on the windows, and ivory-studded wooden furniture. The whole place was painted with bright colors, many suggested by the Quran—red (blood), blue (heaven), green (oasis), and gold (wealth). And throughout the palace, walls, ceilings, vases, carpets, and tiles were covered with decorative patterns, mostly calligraphy writing out verses of praise from the Quran.

As tempting as it might be to touch, stucco is very susceptible to the oils on your hand. If everyone that went through the Alhambra touched a wall, there would be no decoration left for the next generation to treasure.

As you wander, keep the palace themes in mind: water, no images, "stalactite" ceilings—and few signs telling you where you are. Even today, the route constantly changes. Use the map in this chapter to locate the essential stops listed below.

The Alhambra's Palacios Nazaries

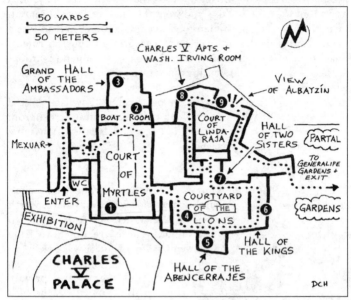

• *Begin by walking through a few administrative rooms (the* mexuar*) and a small courtyard until you hit the big rectangular courtyard with a fish pond lined by a myrtle-bush hedge.*

❶ Court of Myrtles

Moors loved their patios—with a garden and water, under the sky. Women, who rarely went out, stayed in touch with nature here, in the Court of Myrtles (Patio de los Arrayanes). One exotic theory about the function of this complex is that the living quarters for the women (harem) were upstairs—the Quran let a man have "all the women you can maintain with dignity." Notice the wooden screens (erected by jealous husbands) that allowed the cloistered women to look out without being clearly seen. The less interesting, but more likely, theory is that the upstairs was for winter use, and the cooler ground level was for the hotter summer.

• *Head left from the entry into the long, narrow antechamber to the throne room, called the...*

❷ Boat Room

It's understandable that many think the Boat Room (Sala de la Barca) is named for the upside-down-hull shape of its fine cedar ceiling. But the name is actually derived from the Arab word *baraka*, meaning "divine blessing and luck" (which was corrupted to *barca*, similar to the Spanish word for "boat," *barco*.) As you

Islamic Art

Rather than making paintings and statues, Islamic artists expressed themselves with beautiful but functional objects.

Ceramics (often blue and white, or green and white), carpets, glazed tile, stucco-work ceilings, and glass tableware are covered everywhere with complex patterns. The intricate interweaving, repetition, and unending lines suggest the complex, infinite nature of God, known to Muslims as Allah.

You'll see only a few pictures of humans or animals, since the Islamic religion was wary of any "graven images" or idols forbidden by God. However, secular art by Muslims for their homes and palaces was not bound by this restriction; you'll get an occasional glimpse of realistic art of men and women enjoying a garden paradise, a symbol of the Muslim heaven.

Look for floral patterns (twining vines, flowers, and arabesques) and geometric designs (stars and diamonds). The most common pattern is calligraphy—elaborate lettering of an inscription in Arabic, the language of the Quran (and the lettering used even in non-Arabic languages). A quote from the Quran on a vase or lamp combines the power of the message with the beauty of the calligraphy.

passed through this room, blessings and luck are exactly what you'd need—because in the next room, you'd be face-to-face with the sultan.

• *Oh, it's your turn now...*

❸ Grand Hall of the Ambassadors

The palace's largest room, the Gran Salón de los Embajadores, functioned as the throne room. It was here that the sultan, seated on a throne opposite the entrance, received foreign emissaries. Ogle the room—a perfect cube—from top to bottom. The star-studded, domed ceiling, made of cedar of Lebanon (8,000 inlaid pieces like a giant jigsaw puzzle), suggests the complexity of Allah's infinite universe. Plaster "stalactites" form the cornice, made by troweling on layers of plaster several inches thick, then carving into it. The stucco walls, even without their original paint and gilding, are still glorious, decorated with ornamental flowers made by pressing a mold into the wet plaster. The filigree windows once held stained glass, and had heavy drapes to block out the heat. Some original 14th-century tiles survive in the center of the floor.

A visitor here would have stepped from the glaring Court of Myrtles into this dim, cool, incense-filled world, to meet the silhouetted sultan. Imagine the alcoves functioning busily as work stations, and the light at sunrise or sunset, rich and warm, filling the room.

Note the finely carved Arabic script. Muslims avoided making images of living creatures—that was God's work. But they could carve decorative religious messages. One phrase—"only Allah is victorious"—is repeated 9,000 times throughout the palace. Find the character for "Allah"—it looks like a cursive W with a nose on its left side. The swoopy toboggan blades underneath are a kind of artistic punctuation setting off one phrase.

In 1492, two historic events likely took place in this room. Culminating a 700-year-long battle, the Reconquista was completed here as the last Moorish king, Boabdil, signed the terms of his surrender before eventually leaving for Africa.

And it was here that Columbus made his pitch to Isabel and Ferdinand to finance a sea voyage to the Orient. Imagine the scene: The king, the queen, and the greatest minds from the University of Salamanca gathered here while Columbus produced maps and pie charts to make his case that he could sail west to reach the East. Ferdinand and the professors laughed and called Columbus mad—not because they thought the world was flat (most educated people knew otherwise), but because they thought Columbus had underestimated the size of the globe, and thus the length and cost of the journey.

But Isabel said *"Sí, señor."* Columbus fell to his knees (promising to pack light, wear a money belt, and use the most current guidebook available), and she gave him an ATM card with a wad of traveler's checks as a backup.

• *Continue deeper into the palace, to a court where, 600 years ago, only the royal family and their servants could enter. It's the much-photographed...*

❹ Courtyard of the Lions

This patio, the Patio de los Leones, features a fountain with 12 lions. Why 12? Since the fountain was a gift from a Jewish leader celebrating good relations with the sultan (Granada had a big Jewish community), the lions probably represent the 12 tribes of Israel. During Moorish times, the fountain functioned as a clock, with a different lion spouting water each hour. (Conquering Christians disassembled the fountain to see how it worked, and it's never worked since.) From the center, four streams went out—

figuratively to the corners of the earth and literally to various apartments of the royal family. Notice how the court, with its 124 columns, resembles the cloister of a Catholic monastery. The craftsmanship is first-class. For example, the lead fittings between the pre-cut sections of the columns allow things to flex with an earthquake (which it has, preventing destruction during shakes).

Six hundred years ago, the Muslim Moors could read the Quranic poetry that ornaments this court, and they could understand the symbolism of this lush, enclosed garden, considered the embodiment of paradise or truth. ("How beautiful is this garden / where the flowers of Earth rival the stars of Heaven. / What can compare with this alabaster fountain, gushing crystal-clear water? / Nothing except the fullest moon, pouring light from an unclouded sky.") Imagine—they appreciated this part of the palace even more than we do today.

• *On the right, off the courtyard, is a square room called the...*

❺ Hall of the Abencerrajes

According to legend, the father of Boabdil took a new wife and wanted to disinherit the children of his first marriage—one of whom was Boabdil. In order to deny power to Boabdil and his siblings, the sultan killed nearly the entire pro-Boabdil Abencerraje family. He thought this would pave the way for the son of his new wife to be the next sultan. He happily stacked 36 Abencerraje heads in the pool under this sumptuous honeycombed stucco ceiling in this hall, called the Sala de los Abencerrajes. But his scheme failed, and Boabdil ultimately assumed the throne. Bloody power struggles like this were the norm here in the Alhambra.

• *At the end of the court opposite where you entered is the...*

❻ Hall of the Kings

Notice the ceilings of the three chambers branching off this gallery, the Hall of the Kings (Sala de los Reyes). Breaking from the tradition of imageless art, paintings on the goat-leather ceiling depict scenes of the sultan and his family. The center room shows a group portrait of the first 10 of the Alhambra's 22 sultans. The scene is a fantasy, since these people lived over a span of many generations. The two end rooms show scenes of princely pastimes, such as hunting and shooting skeet. In a palace otherwise devoid of figures, these offer a rare look at royal life in the palace.

• *The next room is the...*

❼ Hall of Two Sisters

This room (Sala de Dos Hermanas) has another oh-wow stucco ceiling lit from below by clerestory windows. The room features geometric patterns and stylized Arabic script quoting verses from the Quran, but no figures. If the inlaid color tiles look "Escher-esque," you've got it backwards: Escher is Alhambra-esque. M. C. Escher was inspired by these very patterns on his visit. Study the patterns—they remind us of the Moorish expertise in math.

• *That's about it for the palace. From here, you wander past the star-domed roofs of the old baths down a hallway to a pair of rooms decorated with a mahogany ceiling. Marked with a large plaque is the...*

❽ Washington Irving Room

This is where Washington Irving wrote *Tales of the Alhambra*. While serving as the US ambassador to Spain in 1829, Irving lived in the Alhambra. It was a romantic time, when the palace was home to Gypsies and donkeys. His "tales" kindled interest in the Alhambra, causing it to become recognized as a national treasure. A plaque on the wall from 1914 thanks him. Here's a quote from Irving's "The Alhambra by Moonlight": "On such heavenly nights I would sit for hours at my window inhaling the sweetness of the garden, and musing on the checkered fortunes of those whose history was dimly shadowed out in the elegant memorials around."

• *As you leave, stop at the open-air...*

❾ Hallway with a View

Here you'll enjoy the best-in-the-palace view of the labyrinthine Albayzín—the old Moorish town on the opposite hillside. Find the famous San Nicolás viewpoint (below where the white San Nicolás church tower breaks the horizon). Creeping into the mountains on the right are the Roma (Gypsy) neighborhoods of Sacromonte. Still circling old Granada is the Moorish wall (built in the 1400s to protect the city's population, swollen by Muslim refugees driven south by the Reconquista). For more on Albayzín sights, see page 355.

• *Leaving the Palacios Nazaríes, play with the acoustics in the "Secrets Room" (whisper into a corner and your friend—with an ear to the wall—hears you in the opposite corner). Then look for signs to the Partal Gardens (where you can enjoy the reflecting pond of the Partal Palace), continue through the gardens, and follow signs directing you left to the*

Generalife Gardens or right to the exit. If you're interested in poking around the Alhambra grounds (see sidebar on page 340), do it before you enter the Generalife (because you can't easily backtrack into the Alhambra grounds after leaving the Palacios Nazaries).

Generalife Gardens

The sultan's vegetable and fruit garden and summer palace, called the Generalife (hen-ne-raw-LEEF-ay, worth ▲), are a short hike

uphill past the ticket office. The 2,000 residents of the Alhambra enjoyed the fresh fruit and veggies grown here. But most importantly, the sultan enjoyed a quiet and handy escape from things in the summer: his Generalife Palace.

Walk through the sprawling gardens (planted only in the 1930s—in Moorish times, there were no cypress trees here). At the small palace, pass through the dismounting room (imagine dismounting onto the helpful stone ledge, and letting your horse drink in the trough here). Step past the guarded entry into the most perfect Arabian garden in Andalucía.

This summer home of the Moorish kings, the closest thing on earth to the Quran's description of heaven, was planted more than 600 years ago—remarkable longevity for a European garden. Five-hundred-year-old paintings show it looking essentially as it does today. The flowers, herbs, aromas, and water are exquisite... even for a sultan. Up the Darro River, the royal aqueduct diverted a life-giving stream of water into the Alhambra. It was channeled through this decorative fountain to irrigate the bigger garden outside, then along an aqueduct into the Alhambra for its 2,000 thirsty residents.

At the end of the pond, you enter the sultan's tiny, three-room summer palace. From the end, climb 10 steps into the Christian Renaissance gardens. The ancient, decrepit tree rising over the pond inspired Washington Irving, who wrote that this must be the "only surviving witness to the wonders of that age of Al-Andalus." From here, climb up and out (pausing for a view back down into the palace garden), following *salida* signs as you circle back to where you entered the Generalife. If you have a long wait before your entry to the Palacios, tour these gardens first, then the Alcazaba fort and Charles V's Palace.

Your visit to the Alhambra is complete, and you've earned your reward. "Surely Allah will make those who believe and do good deeds enter gardens beneath which rivers flow; they shall be adorned therein with bracelets of gold and pearls, and their garments therein shall be of silk" (Quran 22.23).

SIGHTS

Central Granada

Plaza Nueva—Along the main square of the city, Plaza Nueva is dominated by the Palace of Justice, hippies, Roma (Gypsies), and a Moroccan ambience. The fountain is capped by a stylized pomegranate—the symbol of the city: always open and fertile. The main action here is the comings and goings of the busy little shuttle buses serving the Alhambra and Albayzín. The local hippie community, nicknamed the *pies negros* (black feet) for obvious reasons, hangs out here and on Calle Elvira. They squat in abandoned caves above those the Roma occupy in Sacromonte. Many are the children of rich Spanish families from the north, hell-bent on disappointing their high-achieving parents.

Plaza Isabel La Católica—Granada's two grand boulevards, Gran Vía and Calle Reyes Católicos, meet a block off Plaza Nueva at Plaza Isabel La Católica. Above the fountain, a fine statue of Columbus unfurls a long contract with Isabel. It lists the terms of Columbus' MCDXCII voyage: ("Forasmuch as you, Columbus, are going by our command to discover and subdue some Islands and Continents in the ocean....")

Isabel was driven by her desire to spread Catholicism. Columbus was driven by his desire for money. For adding territory to Spain's Catholic empire, Isabel promised Columbus the ranks of Admiral of the Oceans and Governor of the New World. To sweeten the pie, she tossed in one-eighth of all the riches he brought home. Isabel died thinking that Columbus had found India or China. Columbus died poor and disillusioned.

Calle Reyes Católicos leads from this square to the busy intersection of Puerta Real. From there, Acera del Darro takes you through modern Granada to the river via the huge El Corte Inglés department store and lots of modern commerce. This area erupts with locals out strolling each night. For the best Granada paseo, be here around 19:00.

▲▲Royal Chapel (Capilla Real)—Without a doubt Granada's top Christian sight, this lavish chapel holds the dreams—and bodies—of Queen Isabel and King Ferdinand. The "Catholic Monarchs" were all about the Reconquista. Their marriage united the Aragon

Central Granada

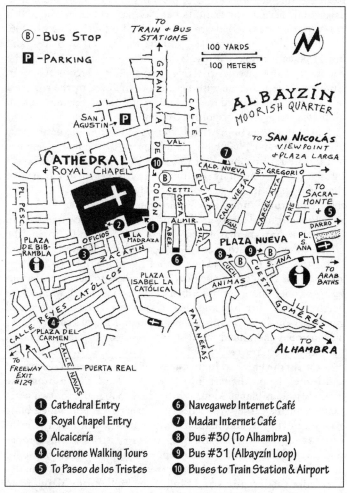

B - Bus Stop
P - Parking

1. Cathedral Entry
2. Royal Chapel Entry
3. Alcaicería
4. Cicerone Walking Tours
5. To Paseo de los Tristes
6. Navegaweb Internet Café
7. Madar Internet Café
8. Bus #30 (To Alhambra)
9. Bus #31 (Albayzín Loop)
10. Buses to Train Station & Airport

and Castile kingdoms, allowing an acceleration of the Christian and Spanish push south. In its last 10 years, the Reconquista snowballed. This last Moorish capital—symbolic of their victory—was their chosen burial place.

In the lobby, before you enter the chapel, notice the **painting of Boabdil** (on the black horse) giving the key of Granada to the conquering King Ferdinand. Boabdil wanted to fall to his knees, but the Spanish king, who had great respect for his Moorish foe, embraced him instead. They fought a long and noble war (for instance, respectfully returning the bodies of dead soldiers). Ferdinand is in red, and Isabel is behind him wearing a crown. The painting is flanked by two large portraits of Ferdinand and Isabel. Two small permanent exhibits behind glass celebrate the 500th anniversaries of Isabel's death in 2005 and Philip the Fair in 2006.

Isabel decided to make Granada the capital of Spain (and burial place for Spanish royalty) for three reasons: 1) With the conquest of this city, Christianity had finally overcome Islam in Europe; 2) her marriage with Ferdinand, followed by the conquest of Granada, had marked the beginning of a united Spain; and 3) in Granada, she agreed to sponsor Columbus.

Step into the **chapel.** It's Plateresque Gothic—light and lacy silver-filigree-style, named for and inspired by the fine silverwork of the Moors. Five hundred years ago, this was the most lavish interior money could buy. Ferdinand and Isabel spent a fourth of their wealth on it. Because of its speedy completion (1506–1521), the architecture is unusually harmonious.

The four royal tombs are Renaissance-style. Carved in Italy in 1521 out of Carrara marble, they were sent by ship to Spain. The faces—based on death masks—are considered accurate. If you're facing the altar, **Ferdinand** and **Isabel** are on the right. (Isabel fans attribute the bigger dent she puts in the pillow to her larger brain.) Isabel's contemporaries described the queen as being of medium height, with auburn hair and blue eyes, with a serious, modest, and gentle personality. (Compare Ferdinand and Isabel's tomb statues with painted and gilded wood statues of them kneeling in prayer, flanking the altarpiece.)

Philip the Fair and **Juana the Mad** (who succeeded Ferdinand and Isabel) lie on the left. Philip was so "Fair" that it drove the insanely jealous Juana "Mad." Philip died young, and for two years Juana kept his casket at her bedside, kissing his embalmed body goodnight. Philip and Juana's son, Charles V (known as Carlos I in Spain), was a key figure in European history, as his coronation merged the Holy Roman Empire (Philip the Fair's Hapsburg domain) with Juana's Spanish empire. Europe's top king, Charles V ruled a vast empire stretching from Holland to Sicily, from Bohemia to Bolivia (1519–1556, see sight listing for his palace within the Alhambra, page 339).

When Philip II, the son of Charles V, decided to build El Escorial and establish Madrid as the single capital of a single Spain, Granada lost power and importance. More importantly, Spain declined. After the reign of Charles V, Spain squandered her awesome wealth trying to maintain this impossibly huge empire. Spain's rulers did it not only for material riches, but to defend the romantic, quixotic dream of a Catholic empire—ruled by one divinely ordained Catholic monarch—against an irrepressible tide of nationalism and Protestantism that was sweeping across the vast Hapsburg holdings in Central and Eastern Europe.

Spain's relatively poor modern history can be blamed, in part, on its people's stubborn unwillingness to accept the end of this old-regime notion. Today's Spaniards reflect on how this expansion through marriage sucked their country into centuries of European squabbling, eventually impoverishing their country.

Look at the fine carving on the tombs (unfortunately vandalized by Napoleon's troops). It's a humanistic statement, with these healthy, organic, realistic figures rising out of the Gothic age.

From the feet of the marble tombs, step downstairs to see the actual **coffins.** They are plain. Ferdinand and Isabel were originally buried in the Franciscan monastery (in what is today the parador at the Alhambra). You're standing in front of the two people who created Spain. The fifth coffin (on right, marked *PM*) is that of a young Prince Michael, who would have been king of a united Spain and Portugal. (A sad—but too long—story...)

The **high altar** is one of the finest Renaissance works in Spain. It's dedicated to two Johns: the Baptist and the Evangelist. In the center, you can see the Baptist and the Evangelist chatting as if over tapas—an appropriately humanistic scene. Scenes from the Baptist's life are on the left: John beheaded after Salomé's fine dancing, and (below) John baptizing Jesus. Scenes from the Evangelist's life are on the right: John's martyrdom (a failed attempt to boil him alive in oil), and John on Patmos (where he wrote the last book of the Bible, Revelation). John is talking to the eagle that flew him to heaven, according to tradition.

The Plateresque arch leads to a small glass pyramid in the **treasury.** This holds Queen Isabel's silver crown, ringed with pomegranates (symbolizing Granada), her scepter, and King Ferdinand's sword. Beside the entry arch you'll see the devout Isabel's prayer book, in which she followed the Mass. The book and its sturdy box date from 1496. The fancy box on the other side of the door is supposedly the one that Isabel (cash-poor because of her military expenses) filled with jewels and gave to Columbus. Columbus sold these to finance his journey. Next, in the corner (and also behind glass), is the cross that Cardinal Mendoza, staunch supporter of Queen Isabel, carried into the Alhambra on that historic day in 1492. Next, the big silk, silver, and gold tapestry is the altar banner for the mobile campaign chapel of Ferdinand and Isabel, who always traveled with their army. In the next case, you'll see the original Christian army flags raised over the Alhambra in 1492.

The room holds the first great art collection ever established by a woman. Queen Isabel amassed more than 200 important paintings. After Napoleon's visit, only 30 remained. Even so, this is a fine collection, all on wood, featuring works by Sandro Botticelli, Pietro Perugino, the Flemish master Hans Memling, and less-famous Spanish masters.

Finally, at the end of the room, the two carved sculptures of Ferdinand and Isabel were the originals from the high altar. Charles V considered these primitive and replaced them with the ones you saw earlier.

Cost, Hours, Location: €3; April–Oct Mon–Sat 10:30–13:00 & 16:00–19:00, opens Sun at 11:00; Nov–March Mon–Sat 10:30–13:00 & 15:30–18:30, opens Sun at 11:00; no photos; entrance on Calle Oficios, just off Gran Vía—go through iron gate; tel. 958-227-848.

Exit behind Isabel, out through one iron gate and then immediately through the neighboring iron gate for the...

Cathedral—One of only two Renaissance churches in Spain (the other is in Córdoba), Granada's cathedral is the second-largest in Spain after Sevilla's.

The cathedral's cool, spacious, bright interior is a refreshing break from the dark Gothic and gilded-lily Baroque of so many Spanish churches. In a modern move back in the 18th century,

the choir walls were taken out so that people could be involved in the worship. At about the same time, a bishop ordered the interior painted with lime (for hygienic reasons, during a time of disease). The people liked it, and it stayed white. As you explore, remember that the abundance of Marys is all part of the Counter-Reformation. A fine series of paintings by Granada's own Alonso Cano (1601–1667), moved from niches 25 yards above, now circles the altar. The distortion was intentional, since the paintings were designed to look natural when viewed from floor level. Most of the side chapels are decorated in Baroque style. On the far wall (to the right of the high altar) is St. James the Moor Slayer, with his sword raised high and an armored Moor under his horse's hooves.

As the main altar comes into view, wander through the pews toward the gigantic main doors. A small sacristy museum is tucked away in the right corner (as you face the doors). There may be no detailed descriptions for any of the items, but a beautiful bust of St. Peter by Alonso Cano is worth seeking out. Also on display is the confusing accounting book for the cathedral's construction. The music sheets behind the main altar are mostly 16th-century Gregorian chants. Notice the sliding C clef. Rather than a fixed G or F clef, the monks knew that this clef—which could be located wherever worked best on the staff—marked middle C, and they chanted to notes relative to that. Go ahead—try singing a few verses of the Latin.

Cost, Hours, Location: €3; April–Oct Mon–Sat 10:30–13:30 & 16:00–20:00, Sun 16:00–20:00; Nov–March Mon–Sat 10:45–13:30 & 16:00–19:00, Sun 16:00–19:00; audioguide-€3, entrance off Gran Vía through iron gateway, tel. 958-222-959.

Alcaicería—Originally a Moorish silk market with seven gates and 200 shops, the Alcaicería (al-kai-thay-REE-ah) neighborhood around the cathedral still functions as a silk and jewelry market. Silk was a huge industry in Moorish times (silkworm-friendly mulberry trees flourished in the countryside), a product so important that the sultans controlled and guarded it by constructing this fine market. After the Reconquista, the Christians didn't mess with it. But a terrible fire in 1850 destroyed the place. Today's Alcaicería was rebuilt in the late 1800s as a tourist souvenir souk (marketplace) to compliment the romantic image of Granada created by the writings of Washington Irving.

Explore the mesh of tiny shopping lanes between the cathedral and Calle Reyes Católicos. Go on a photo and sound safari: popcorn machines popping, men selling balloons, leather goods spread out on streets, kids playing soccer, barking dogs, dogged shoeshine boys, and the whirring grind of bicycle-powered knife sharpeners.

Roma (Gypsy) women will probably accost you with sprigs of rosemary. The twig is free...and then they grab your hand and read your fortune for a tip. Coins are bad luck, so the minimum payment they'll accept is €5. Don't make eye contact, and say firmly but politely, *"No, gracias."* While aggressive (and even more so in the morning), these Spanish Roma are harmless. Roma from Romania (new arrivals who locals identify by their gold teeth) are more likely to be pickpockets. (See "Helpful Hints," page 329.)

Corral del Carbón—A caravanserai (of silk road fame) is a protected place for merchants to rest their camels, spend the night, get a bite to eat, and spin yarns. The only surviving caravanserai of Granada's original 14 is, logically, just a block away from the silk market. This plain-yet-elegant structure is evocative of times when traders would gather here with exotic good and tales from across Arabia. After the Reconquista, it was a coal storage facility (hence the name "Carbón"). Notice the fine Moorish door (free, across Calle Reyes Católicos from Alcaicería).

Plaza de Bib-Rambla—The exuberant square two blocks behind the cathedral is Plaza de Bib-Rambla. While today it's fine for coffee or a meal amidst the color and fragrance of flower stalls, in Moorish times this was a place of public execution. It remains a multi-generational hang-out where, it seems, everyone is enjoying a peaceful retirement. A block away, the square Pescadería is a smaller, similarly lively version of Bib-Rambla.

Paseo de los Tristes—In the cool of the early evening, consider strolling the street called Paseo de los Tristes, which runs east from Plaza Nueva along the Darro River. (If you're tired, note that buses #31 and #32 stop here.) This "Walk of the Sad Ones" was once the route of funeral processions to the cemetery at the edge of town.

Start at Plaza Nueva. The Church of Santa Ana, at the far end of the square, was originally a mosque—the church tower replaced the minaret. Notice the ceramic brickwork. This is Mudejar art, a technique of Moorish craftsmen later employed by Christians. Inside you'll see a fine Alhambra-style cedar ceiling.

Follow Carrera del Darro along the River Darro at the base of the Alhambra. (Six miles upstream, part of the Darro is diverted to provide water for the Alhambra's many fountains.) Past the church on your right is the turn-off bridge for the Hammam Bãnos Árabes (Arab baths, described below), along with lots of feral cats. On the left is Santa Catalina de Zafra, a convent of cloistered nuns (they worship behind a screen that divides the church's rich interior in half).

Farther ahead is the evocative brick facade of a Moorish bath, the Hammam El Bañuelo (across from the #31/#34 bus stop, baths described below). Across from the remains is the broken nub of a once-grand, 11th-century bridge over the river, leading to the Alhambra. Notice two slits in the column: one for a iron portcullis (to keep bad guys from entering the town via the river), and a second for a solid door that was lowered to build up water that could then be released to flush out the riverbed and keep it clean.

After the baths and broken bridge on the right (across from the Archaeological Museum) is the Church of San Pedro, the parish church of Sacromonte's Roma (Gypsy) community. Within its rich interior is an ornate oxcart used to carry the Host on the annual pilgrimage to Rocio near the Portugal border.

Finally, you reach the Paseo de los Tristes, with restaurant tables spilling out under the floodlit Alhambra. From here the road arcs up into Sacromonte. Also from here, a lane (called Cuesta de los Chinos or Carretera del Rey Chico) leads up to the Alhambra "through the back door."

Hammam El Bañuelo (Moorish Baths)—In Moorish times, hammams (public baths) were a big part of the community (private homes didn't have bathrooms). Baths were strictly segregated (as today) and functioned as more than a place to wash: Business was done here, and it was a social meeting point. In Christian times, it was assumed that conspiracies brewed in these baths—therefore, few of them survive. This place gives you the chance to explore the stark but evocative ruins of an 11th-century Moorish public bath.

Entering the baths, you pass the house of the keeper and the foyer into the cold room, the warm room (where services like a massage were offered), and finally the hot or steam room (where you wore special shoes to protect your feet from the heat). Beyond that, you can see the oven that generated the heat that flowed under the hypocaust-style floor tiles (getting less hot with distance). The romantic little holes in the ceiling once had glass louvers, which attendants opened and closed with sticks to regulate the heat and steaminess. People weren't totally immersed, but rather scooped and splashed water over themselves (free, Tue–Sat 10:00–14:00, closed Sun–Mon, along the Paseo de los Tristes—see above, at first bus stop and big broken bridge, two bridges upstream from Plaza Nueva on Carrera del Darro).

Hammam Baños Árabes (Arab Baths)—Consider a visit to these Arab baths for an intimate and subdued experience, with a maximum of 16 people allowed in the baths at one time. The 90-minute soak and a 15-minute massage cost €22; for a 90-minute bath only, it's €14 (daily 10:00–24:00, appointment times scheduled every even-numbered hour, coed with mandatory swimsuits, quiet atmosphere encouraged, free lockers available, just off Plaza Nueva at Santa Ana 16; from Plaza Nueva, it's the first right—over a bridge—past the church; 50 percent paid reservation necessary—credit card OK, tel. 958-229-978, www.hammamspain .com/granada).

The Albayzín

Explore Spain's best old Moorish quarter, with countless colorful corners, flowery patios, and shady lanes. Climb high to the San Nicolás church for the best view of the Alhambra. Then wander through the mysterious backstreets. (I've listed these sights roughly in order from the San Nicolás viewpoint.) Warning: Thefts have increased after dark in the Albayzín; take the bus or a taxi back to your hotel if you linger here for a late-night dinner.

Getting to the Albayzín: A handy city **minibus** threads its way around the Albayzín from Plaza Nueva (see "Albayzín Circular Bus Tour," below), getting you scenically and sweatlessly to the San Nicolás viewpoint (see below). You can also **taxi** to the San Nicolás church and explore from there. Consider having your cabbie take you on a Sacromonte detour en route.

If **walking** up, leave the west end of Plaza Nueva on Calle Elvira. After about 200 yards, turn right on Calle Calderería Nueva. Follow this stepped street past tapas bars and *teterías* (see

Albayzín Neighborhood

NOTE: NOT TO SCALE
PLAZA NUEVA to SAN NICOLÁS
IS A 20 MIN WALK UPHILL

❶ Calle Calderería Nueva (Tapas & Tea)

❷ Casa Torcuato

❸ Restaurante El Ladrillo

❹ Bar Kiki

❺ Carmen Mirador de Morayma

❻ Carmen de las Tomasas

❼ Great Mosque of Granada

❽ Hammam El Bañuelo (Moorish Baths)

❾ Hammam Baños Arabes (Arab Baths)

❿ To Center for the Interpretation of Sacromonte, Roma Caves & Zambra Dance Clubs

page 366) as it goes left around the church, slants, winds, and zig-zags up, heading basically straight uphill. Pass the peach-colored building on your left (resisting the temptation to turn left on Muladar Sancha). When you reach a T-intersection, go left on Calle del Almirante. Near the crest, turn right on Camino Nuevo de San Nicolás, then walk several blocks to the street that curves up left (look for brown sign *Mirador de San Nicolás*, where a street sign would normally be). Soon you'll see steps leading up to the church's viewpoint.

Albayzín Circular Bus Tour—The handy Albayzín bus #31 gallops the 15-minute loop as if in a race, departing from Plaza Nueva about every 15 minutes (pay driver €1, bus #32 does the same loop but—depending on where you catch it—goes to the Alhambra first). While good for a lift to the top of the Albayzín (buzz when you want to get off), I'd stay on for an entire circle (and return to the Albayzín later for dinner—either on foot or by bus again).

Here's the route: You'll go along the river, past the ruins of a bridge and gate and the newly constructed Paseo de los Tristes square. Turning uphill, you pass Sacromonte on the right (entrance to the neighborhood marked by a statue of a popular Roma guide). Then, turning left, you enter the actual Albayzín. After stopping at the church of San Salvador, you plunge into the thick of it, with stops below the San Nicolás church (famous viewpoint, and the jumping-off point for my suggested "Exploring the Albayzín" stroll—see below) and Plaza San Miguel Bajo (cute square with recommended eateries and another viewpoint). Then you descend, enjoying a commanding view of Granada on the left as you swing through the modern city. Hitting the city's main drag, Gran Vía, you make a U-turn at the Garden of the Triumph, celebrating the Immaculate Conception of the Virgin Mary (notice her statue atop a column). Behind Mary stands the old Royal Hospital—built in the 16th century for Granada's poor by the Catholic kings after the Reconquista, in hopes of winning the favor of Granada's conquered residents. From here, you zip past the cathedral and home to Plaza Nueva.

▲▲San Nicolás Viewpoint (Mirador de San Nicolás)—For one

of Europe's most romantic viewpoints, be here at sunset, when the Alhambra glows red and the Albayzín widows share the benches with local lovers and tourists (free, always open). In 1997, President Clinton made a point to bring his family here—a favorite spot from a trip he made as a student. For a drink with the same view, step into the Juan Ranas Bar (just below and left, at Calle de Atarazana 8).

Great Mosque of Granada—A striking and inviting new mosque is just next to the San Nicolás viewpoint (to your left as you face the Alhambra). Local Muslims write, "The Great Mosque of Granada signals, after a hiatus of 500 years, the restoration of a missing link with a rich and fecund Islamic contribution to all spheres of human enterprise and activity." Built in 2003 (with money from the local community and Islamic Arab nations), it has a peaceful

Granada's Roma (Gypsies)

Both the English word "Gypsy" and its Spanish counterpart, *gitano,* come from the word "Egypt"—where Europeans used to think these nomadic people originated. Today, as we've come to understand that "Gypsies" actually came from India—and as the term "Gypsy" has acquired negative connotations—the preferred term is "Roma." (I've used both terms throughout this book.) After migrating from India in the 14th century, the Roma people settled mostly in the Muslim-occupied lands in the south (such as the Balkan Peninsula, then controlled by the Ottoman Turks). Under the Muslims, the Roma enjoyed relative tolerance. They were traditionally good with crafts and animals.

The first Roma arrived in Granada in the 15th century—and they've remained tight-knit ever since. Today 50,000 Roma call Granada home, many of them in the district called Sacromonte. In most of Spain, Roma are more assimilated into the general population, but Sacromonte is a large, distinct Roma community. (After the difficult Civil War era, they were joined by many farmers who, like the Roma, appreciated Sacromonte's affordable, practical cave dwellings—warm in the winter and cool in the summer.)

Spaniards, who consider themselves accepting and not racist, claim that in maintaining such a tight community, the Roma segregate themselves. The Roma call Spaniards *payos* ("whites"). Recent mixing of Roma and *payos* has given birth to the term *gallipavo* (rooster-duck), although who's who depends upon whom you ask.

Are Roma thieves? Sure, a lot of them are. But others are honest citizens, trying to make their way in the world just like anyone else. It's wise to be cautious when dealing with a Roma person—but it's also important to keep an open mind.

view courtyard and a minaret that comes with a live call to prayer five times a day (including at sunset). It's stirring to see the muezzin holler "God is Great" from the minaret without amplification (two explanations: Muslims wanted it to be authentic—as in the old days—or locals didn't want it amplified). Visitors are welcome in the courtyard, which offers Alhambra views without the hedonistic ambience of the more famous San Nicolás viewpoint (free, daily 11:00–14:00 & 18:00–21:00).

While tourists come to Granada to learn about the expulsion of the Moors in 1492, local Muslims are frustrated by the "errors, nonsense, and lies local guides perpetuate without knowledge nor shame which flocks of passive tourists accept without questioning." A flier at the mosque tries to set things straight, claiming a few things: Muslims were not foreign invaders of Spain—the Muslims of Granada and Andalucía were as Iberian as the modern Spaniards of today. Islam is not a religion of immigrants. Islam is a not a culture of the Orient and Arabs. Muslims and Arabs are different. The Muslims of Al-Andalus were not hedonistic. The Reconquista did not liberate Spain. Harems were not just full of sexy women. (For more on the Muslim perspective, visit the info desk at the mosque.)

The European Union sees Granada as a center for Muslim-Christian integration. The city hosts the headquarters of several organizations designed to help the communities live peacefully together. To Muslims, the city is a symbol of the "holocaust" of the Reconquista, when 135,000 were brutally expelled and many more suffered "forced conversion" in the 16th century. Today there are about 700,000 Muslims in Spain (and about 5 million in France).

Exploring the Albayzín—From the San Nicolás viewpoint and the Great Mosque, you're at the edge of a hilltop neighborhood even the people of Granada recognize as a world apart. Each of the district's 20 churches sits on a spot once occupied by a mosque. When the Reconquista arrived in Granada, the Christians attempted to coexist with the Muslims. But after seven years, this idealistic attempt ended in failure, and the Christians forced the Muslims to convert. In 1567, Muslims were expelled, leading to 200 years of economic depression for the city.

From the viewpoint, turn your back to the Alhambra and walk north (passing the church on your right and the Biblioteca Municipal on your left). A lane leads past a white stone arch (on your right)—now a chapel built into the old Moorish wall. You're walking through the scant remains of the pre-Alhambra fortress of Granada. At the end of the lane, step down to the right through the 11th-century "New Gate" (Puerta Nueva—older than the Alhambra) and into **Plaza Larga.** In medieval times, this tiny square (called "long," because back then it was) was the local marketplace. It still is a busy market each morning. Casa Pasteles, at the near end of the square, serves good coffee and cakes.

Leave Plaza Larga on **Calle Agua de Albayzín** (as you face Casa Pasteles, it's to your right). The street, named for the public baths that used to line it, shows evidence of the Moorish plumbing system: gutters. Back when Europe's streets were filled with muck, Granada actually had Roman Empire–style gutters with drains leading to clay and lead pipes.

This road leads past the recommended Casa Torcuato restaurant (see page 366) to a T-intersection. Or just explore. You're in the heart of the Albayzín. Poke into an old church. They're plain by design—to go easy on the Muslim converts, who weren't used to being surrounded by images as they worshipped. You'll see lots of real Muslim culture living in the streets, including many recent Spanish converts.

Sacromonte

The Sacromonte district is home to Granada's thriving Roma community (see sidebar). Marking the entrance to Sacromonte is a statue of Chorrohumo (literally, "Exudes Smoke," and a play on the slang word for "thief"...*chorro*). He was a Roma from Granada, popular in the 1950s for guiding people around the city.

Sacromonte has one main street: Camino del Sacromonte is lined with caves primed for tourists and restaurants ready to fight over the bill. (Don't come here expecting to get a deal on anything.) Intriguing lanes run above and below this main drag.

***Zambra* Dance**—A long flamenco tradition exists in Granada. Sacromonte is a good place to see *zambra,* a flamenco variation with a more Oriental feel in which the singer also dances. Two popular—or at least well-established—*zambra* venues are Zambra Cueva del Rocío (€23, includes a drink, 22:00 show, 90 min, your hotel may be able to arrange a hotel pick-up, Camino del Sacromonte 70, tel. 958-227-129) and María la Canastera (€22, includes a drink and transportation from hotel, €15 without transport, May–Oct daily shows at 22:00 and 23:00, fewer off-season, Camino del Sacromonte 89, tel. 958-121-183). I'd just go and explore late at night (with no wallet and €30 in my pocket) rather than booking an evening through my hotel (they'll likely offer to reserve for you).

Center for the Interpretation of Sacromonte (Centro de Interpretación del Sacromonte)—This facility is a kind of Roma open-air folk museum, offering an insight into Sacromonte's geology and environment, cave building, and Roma crafts, food, and musical traditions (with English  explanations). There are also great views over Granada and the Alhambra. As you wander, imagine this in the 1950s, when it was still a bustling community of Roma cave-dwellers. Today, higher up, hippies squat in abandoned caves. The center also features €12 flamenco shows and classical guitar concerts in its wonderfully scenic setting (details at TI). You'll find it 300 yards up the steep hill from the Venta El Gallo restaurant on the main Sacromonte lane (€4; April–Oct Tue–Fri 10:00–14:00 & 17:00–21:00, Sat–Sun 11:00–21:00, closed Mon; Nov–March Tue–Fri 10:00–14:00 & 16:00–19:00, Sat–Sun 11:00–19:00, closed Mon; Barranco de los Negros, tel. 958-215-120, www.sacromontegranada.com). The closest a taxi can get you is the Venta El Gallo restaurant. From there, you climb on foot, following the signs.

Near Granada

Carthusian Monastery (La Cartuja)—A church with an interior that looks as if it squirted out of a can of whipped cream, La Cartuja is nicknamed the "Christian Alhambra" for its elaborate white Baroque stucco work. In the rooms just off the cloister, notice the gruesome paintings of martyrs placidly meeting their grisly fates (€3, daily April–Oct 10:00–13:00 & 15:30–20:00, Nov–March closes at 18:00, tel. 958-161-932). It's a mile north of town on the way to Madrid. Drive north on Gran Vía de Colón and follow the signs, or take bus #8 from Gran Vía.

SLEEPING

In July and August, when the streets are littered with sunstroke victims, rooms are plentiful. Crowded months are April, May, June, September, and October. Except for the hotels near the Alhambra, all my listings are within a five-minute walk of Plaza Nueva (see map on page 363).

Given all the restrictions, it is difficult to drive into Granada even when you know the system (see "Arrival in Granada," page 327). While few of the hotels have parking facilities, any of them can direct you to a garage (such as Parking San Agustín, just off Gran Vía, €25/day).

On or near Plaza Nueva

Each of these is big, professional, plenty comfortable, and perfectly located. Prices vary with the demand.

$$$ Hotel Inglaterra, a chain hotel, is modern and peaceful, with 36 rooms offering all the comforts (Sb-€77–120, Db-€79–120, extra bed-€31–48, buffet breakfast-€11, air-con, elevator to third floor only, 20 parking spaces at €12/day, Cetti Merien 4, tel. 958-221-559, fax 958-227-100, www.nh-hotels.com, nhinglaterra @nh-hotels.com).

$$ Hotel Maciá Plaza, right on the colorful Plaza Nueva, has 44 clean, modern, and classy rooms. Choose between an on-the-square view or a quieter interior room (Sb-€55, Db-€80, Tb-€91, 10 percent discount in 2007 when you show this book at check-in or reserve directly through their Web site, good buffet breakfast-€5.50, air-con, elevator, Plaza Nueva 4, tel. 958-227-536, fax 958-227-533, www.maciahoteles.com, maciaplaza@maciahoteles.com).

$$ Hotel Anacapri is a bright, cool marble oasis with 49 modern rooms, a quiet lounge, and three spacious, loft-style junior

---

Sleep Code

(€1 = about $1.20, country code: 34)
S = Single, **D** = Double/Twin, **T** = Triple, **Q** = Quad, **b** = bathroom,
s = shower only. Unless otherwise noted, credit cards are accepted and English is spoken. Breakfast and the 7 percent IVA tax are usually not included.

To help you easily sort through these listings, I've divided the rooms into three categories based on the price for a standard double room with bath during high season:

$$$ **Higher Priced**—Most rooms €100 or more.
$$ **Moderately Priced**—Most rooms between €50–100.
$ **Lower Priced**—Most rooms €50 or less.

---

suites (Sb-€54–61, Db-€72–90, extra bed-€20, breakfast free with direct bookings in 2007, air-con, elevator, 2 blocks toward Gran Vía from Plaza Nueva at Calle Joaquín Costa 7, just a block from cathedral bus stop, tel. 958-227-477, fax 958-228-909, www .hotelanacapri.com, reservas@hotelanacapri.com, helpful Kathy speaks Iowan).

$$ Hotel Maciá Gran Vía, right on Granada's main drag, has a stately lobby with Euro-modern business-class rooms (Sb-€63, Db-€93, Tb-€110, show this book for a 10 percent discount on these prices in 2007, air-con, elevator, parking-€13/day, 5-min walk from Plaza Nueva, Gran Vía 25—but enter on side street called Veluti, tel. 958-285-464, fax 958-285-591, www.maciahoteles.com, granvia@maciahoteles.com).

$$ Casa del Capitel Nazarí, just off the north (church) end of Plaza Nueva, is a restored 16th-century Renaissance palace transformed into 17 small but tastefully decorated rooms facing a courtyard (Db-€95, extra bed-€36, breakfast-€12.50, air-con, parking-€10/day, Cuesta Aceituneros 6, tel. 958-215-260, fax 958-215-806, www.hotelcasacapitel.com, info@hotelcasacapitel.com).

Cheaper Accommodations on Cuesta de Gomérez

These are cheap and ramshackle lodgings on the street leading from Plaza Nueva up to the Alhambra.

$ Pensión Landazuri is run by friendly, English-speaking Matilda Landazuri and her son, Manolo. Some of their 18 rooms are well-worn, while others are newly renovated. It boasts hard-working, helpful management and a great roof garden with an Alhambra view (S-€20, Sb-€28, D-€28, Db-€36–40, Tb-€54, includes tax, cheap breakfast, cash only, fans available on request,

Granada Hotels and Restaurants

1. Hotel Inglaterra
2. Hotel Maciá Plaza
3. Hotel Anacapri
4. Hotel Maciá Gran Vía
5. Casa del Capitel Nazarí
6. Pensión Landazuri
7. Hostal Residencia Britz
8. Hostal Gomérez
9. Hostal Viena & Hotel Austria
10. To Hotel Navas; Los Diamantes & Bar Las Copas Fish Bars
11. Hotel Residencia Lisboa
12. Hotel Los Tilos
13. To Hotel Reina Cristina
14. Bodegas Castañeda
15. Restaurante Sevilla
16. Vinoteca Salinas II
17. Naturi Albayzín Veggie Rest. & Kasbah Tea Shop
18. Los Italianos Ice Cream
19. To Paseo de los Tristes Eateries

parking–€10/day, Cuesta de Gomérez 24, tel. & fax 958-221-406).
The Landazuris also run a good, cheap café.

$ Hostal Residencia Britz, overlooking Plaza Nueva, is
simple and no-nonsense. All of its 22 basic rooms are streetside—
bring earplugs (S-€22, D-€34, Db-€44, includes tax, no breakfast,
elevator, Plaza Nueva y Gomérez 1, tel. & fax 958-223-652).

$ Hostal Gomérez is run by English-speaking Sigfrido
Sanchez de León de Torres (who'll explain to you how Spanish
surnames work if you have the time). This basic nine-room *hostal*,
listed in nearly every country's student-travel guidebook, is another
fine cheapie. Quieter rooms are in the back (S-€18, D-€30, T-€40,
Q-€45, includes tax, no breakfast, cash only, Cuesta de Gomérez
10, 1 floor up, tel. & fax 958-223-022).

$ Hostal Viena, run by English-speaking Austrian Irene (ee-
RAY-nay), is on a quiet side street, with 32 basic backpacker-type
rooms (S-€25, D-€35, Db-€45, T-€56, Tb-€65, family rooms,
includes tax, no breakfast, air-con, next-door bar noisy on weekends, Hospital de Santa Ana 2, 10 yards off Cuesta de Gomérez,
tel. & fax 958-221-859, www.hostalviena.com). Some of these
rooms are in nearby and similar **Hotel Austria,** also run by Irene.

Near Plaza del Carmen

The pleasant Plaza del Carmen and the beginning of Calle Navas
is a pedestrian street offering a couple of good values (and two
deep-fried fish bars: Los Diamantes and Bar Las Copas, both close
to Hotel Navas, below, and very popular with locals).

$$$ Hotel Navas, a block down Calle Navas, is a modern,
well-run, tour-friendly, business-class hotel with 49 spacious rooms
and no character (Sb-€77, Db-€102, Tb-€120, breakfast buffet-€8,
includes tax, air-con, elevator, Calle Navas 24, tel. 958-225-959, fax
958-227-523, www.hotelesporcel.com, navas@hotelesporcel.com).

$ Hotel Residencia Lisboa, which overlooks Plaza del
Carmen opposite Granada's city hall, offers 28 simple but well-
maintained rooms with friendly owners (S-€21, Sb-€33, D-€31,
Db-€47, T-€41, Tb-€63, includes tax, no breakfast, elevator, Plaza
del Carmen 27, tel. 958-221-413, fax 958-221-487, www.lisboaweb
.com, Mary and Juan José).

Near the Cathedral

$$ Hotel Los Tilos offers 30 comfortable rooms (some with balconies) on the charming, traffic-free Plaza de Bib-Rambla behind
the cathedral. All clients are welcome to use the fourth-floor view
terrace overlooking the great café, shopping, and people-watching
neighborhood (Sb-€41, Db-€65, Tb-€92, 20 percent discount with
this book and cash in 2007, includes tax, breakfast buffet-€7, air-
con, parking–€14/day, Plaza de Bib-Rambla 4, tel. 958-266-712,

fax 958-266-801, www.hotellostilos.com, clientes@hotellostilos
.com, friendly José María).

$$ Hotel Reina Cristina has 50 quiet, elegant rooms a
few steps off Plaza Trinidad, a park-like square, near the lively
Pescadería and Bib-Rambla squares. Check out the great Mudejar
ceiling and the painting at the entrance of this house, where the
famous Spanish poet Federico García Lorca hid until he was
captured and executed by the Guardia Civil (Sb-€65, Db-€98,
Tb-€114, breakfast not included, air-con, elevator, on Plaza de
la Trinidad at Tablas 4, tel. 958-253-211, fax 958-255-728, www
.hotelreinacristina.com, clientes@hotelreinacristina.com).

In or near the Alhambra

If you want to stay on the Alhambra grounds, there are two popu-
lar options—famous, overpriced, and generally booked up long in
advance. These are a half mile up the hill from Plaza Nueva.

$$$ Parador Nacional San Francisco offers 36 air-con-
ditioned rooms in a former Moorish palace converted into a
15th-century Franciscan monastery. It's called Spain's premier
parador (Db-€250, breakfast-€15, free parking, Calle Real de la
Alhambra, tel. 958-221-440, fax 958-222-264, granada@parador
.es). You must book months ahead to spend the night in this lavishly located, stodgy, and historic palace. Any peasant, however,
can drop in for a coffee, drink, snack, or meal (daily 13:00–16:00
& 20:30–23:00). For details about the history of the building, see
sidebar on page 340.

$$$ Hotel América, renting 17 rooms next to the parador, is
classy and cozy (Ss-€70, Db-€110, includes tax, closed Dec–Feb,
Calle Real de la Alhambra 53, tel. 958-227-471, fax 958-227-470,
www.hotelamericagranada.com, reservas@hotelamericagranada
.com). Book three months ahead in high season.

EATING

Granada bars still serve a small tapas plate free with any beer or
wine ordered—a generous tradition that's dying out elsewhere in

Spain. A series of small drinks
(in one or several bars) can actu-
ally end up being a light meal. In
search of an edible memory? A
local specialty, *tortilla Sacromonte*,
is a spicy omelet with pig's brain
and other organs. *Berenjenas fri-
tas* (fried eggplant) and *habas con
jamón* (small green fava beans
cooked with cured ham) are worth

seeking out. *Tinto de verano*—a red-wine spritzer—is refreshing on a hot evening with lemon and ice. For tips on eating near the Alhambra, see "Cuisine" on page 338.

In the Albayzín

The most interesting meals hide out deep in the Albayzín (Moorish quarter). The easy way to get there is by taking bus #31 or #32 from Plaza Nueva. To find a particular square, ask any local, or follow my directions and the map on page 356. If dining late, take the bus or a taxi back to your hotel, as Albayzín back streets can be dangerous because of pickpockets.

Casa Torcuato is a hardworking eatery serving straight-forward yet creative food in a smart upstairs dining room. They serve a good €8 fixed-price meal. Plates of fresh fish run €8–12. Their tropical salad includes a Tahitian wonderland of fruits (Mon–Sat 13:00–16:00 & 20:00–24:00, closed Sun, 2 blocks beyond Plaza Larga at Calle Aqua 20, tel. 958-202-039).

Restaurante El Ladrillo, with outdoor tables on a peaceful square, is *the* place for piles of fish. Their popular *barco* (€9 "boat-load" of mixed fried fish) is a fishy feast that stuffs two to the gills. The smaller *medio-barco*, for €7, fills one person adequately, or, when combined with a salad, can feed two (daily 12:00–24:00, on Plaza Fátima, just off Calle Pages).

Near the San Nicolás Viewpoint: The **Bar Kiki** is a laid-back and popular bar/restaurant serving simple tapas on an unpreten-tious square (try their tasty fried eggplant; just behind viewpoint at Plaza de San Nicolás 9).

On Plaza San Miguel el Bajo: While it's the farthest hike into the Albayzín, this neighborhood square boasts my favorite funky, local scene—with kids kicking soccer balls, old-timers warm-ing benches, and women gossiping under the facade of a humble church. Tables from four bars (serious tapas) and a good little res-taurant (€10 fixed-price meal) spill onto the square. This is a fine spot to end your Albayzín visit, as there's a viewpoint overlooking the modern city a block away. Buses #31 and #32 rumble by every few minutes, ready to zip you back to Plaza Nueva.

Carmens: For a more memorable but expensive experience, consider fine dining with Alhambra views in a *carmen*, a typical Albayzín house with a garden (buzz to get in). **Carmen Mirador de Morayma** boasts great atmosphere and fine rustic cuisine. This is where famous visitors from local celebrities to President Clinton dine to the sounds of classical guitar. For seating, choose between outdoor (on one of three dreamy garden terraces) or inside the noble mansion (with an intimate, garden-view ambience). With one night in Granada, I'd eat here. Reservations are smart (€30 meals, daily 13:30–15:30 & 20:30–23:30, July–Aug closed Sun, read the romantic history on the card, Calle Pianista García Carrillo 2, tel. 958-228-290). **Carmen de las Tomasas** serves gourmet traditional Andalusian cuisine with killer views in a dressy/stuffy atmosphere (€40 meals, Mon–Sat 21:00–24:00, closed Sun, reservations required, Carril de San Agustín, tel. 958-224-108, Cristina).

Near Plaza Nueva

For people-watching, consider the many restaurants on Plaza Nueva or Bib-Rambla (south of cathedral). For a happening-if-seedy hippie scene, check out the bars along Calle Elvira.

Bodegas Castañeda is the best mix of lively, central, untouristy, and good-value among the tapas bars I visited. Cheap and easy, it's just a block off Plaza Nueva. It's self-service: When it's crowded, you need to power your way to the bar to order; when it's quiet, you can order at the bar and grab a little table (same cheap prices). Consider their *tablas combinadas*—variety plates of cheese, meat, and *ahumados* (four different varieties of smoked fish). The big kegs tempt you with different local sherries (daily 11:30–16:30 & 17:00–24:00, Calle Almireceros 1, tel. 958-215-464). Don't be confused by a different "Castaneda" restaurant nearby (unless you're hankering for stuffed potatoes).

Restaurante Sevilla, with its tight and charming little dining room, has been a favorite of natives for 75 years. Specialties include paella, other rice dishes, soups, and salads. You'll eat among locals in suits, surrounded by old photos of local big shots who've dined here. On hot nights, tables spill out onto the little square facing the Royal Chapel. It's a local-feeling, elegant, urban scene (€15 plates, Mon–Sat 13:00–16:30 & 20:00–24:00, closed Sun, across from Royal Chapel at Calle Oficios 12, tel. 958-221-223).

Vinoteca Salinas II is mod rather than traditional, serving tapas and wines a cut above the other bars. You'll sit on a stool enjoying a good selection of sophisticated *montaditos* (open-face sandwiches), tapas, and the best selection of fine wine by the glass in town—a little pricier, but still reasonable (daily 12:30–24:00, Calle Almireceros).

Hippie Options on Calle Calderería Nueva: From Plaza Nueva, walk two long blocks down Calle Elvira and turn right onto the wonderfully hip and Arabic-feeling Calle Calderería Nueva, which leads uphill into the Albayzín. The street is lined with trendy *teterías*. These small tea shops, open all day, are good places to linger, chat, and imagine you're in Morocco. Some are conservative and unmemorable, and others are achingly romantic, filled with incense, beaded cushions, live African music, and effervescent young hippies. They sell light meals and a worldwide range of teas, all marinated in a candlelit snakecharm. The plush **Kasbah,** with good (canned) music and Moorish dishes, desserts, and teas, is a hit with local Muslims. Here's your chance to smoke perfumed tobacco in an opium pipe-like *narguile*.

Vegetarian: **Naturi Albayzín** is a mellow and intimate little vegetarian eatery with €7.95 rotating three-course meals, typically featuring classy couscous (Sat–Thu 13:00–16:00 & 19:00–23:00, Fri 19:00–23:00 only, reserve for evenings and weekends, Calle Calderería Nueva 10, tel. 958-227-383).

Dessert: **Los Italianos,** teeming with locals, is popular for its ice cream, *horchata* (*chufa*-nut drink), and shakes (March–mid-Oct daily 8:00–24:00, closed mid-Oct–Feb, Gran Vía 4, across the street from cathedral and Royal Chapel, tel. 958-224-034).

Markets: Though heavy on meat, the **Mercado San Agustín** also sells fruits and veggies. If nothing else, it's as refreshingly cool as a meat locker (Mon–Sat 8:00–15:30, closed Sun, has small café/bar, Calle Cristo San Agustín, a block north of cathedral, half block off Gran Vía). The Pescadaría square, a block from Plaza de Bib-Rambla, usually has some fruit stalls on its northern end, along with inviting restaurants on the square itself.

TRANSPORTATION CONNECTIONS

From Granada by Train to: Barcelona (2/day, depart at 8:40 and 21:25, 12 hrs, handy night train), **Madrid** (2/day, 6 hrs, depart

Granada at 8:00 and 17:10, confirm time at station), **Toledo** (4/day, required transfer—most likely in Madrid, leave Granada at 7:55 or 8:20 for quickest trip, confirm times at station, allow 9–10 hours total, longer on weekends), **Algeciras** (3/day, 4.5 hrs), **Ronda** (3/day, 2.5 hrs), **Sevilla** (4/day, 3 hrs), **Córdoba** (2/day, 4–6.5 hrs, transfer in Bobadilla), **Málaga** (3/day, 3.25 hrs, transfer in Bobadilla). Train info: tel. 902-240-202. Many of these connections have a more frequent (and sometimes much faster) bus option—see below.

By Bus to: Nerja (4/day, 2.5 hrs, more with transfer in Motril), **Sevilla** (10/day, 7 direct—3 hrs *directo*, 4 hrs *ruta*), **Córdoba** (8/day, 1.5–3 hrs), **Málaga** (8/day, 2 hrs), **Algeciras** (4/day, 4–5 hrs, some are *directo*, others are the slow *ruta*), **La Línea/Gibraltar** (5/day, 5 hrs), **Jerez** (1/day, 4.5 hrs). All of these buses are run by the Alsina Graells company (tel. 958-185-480, www.alsinagraells.es).

To better handle the winding roads, some tourists like to reserve a seat at the front of the bus (generally seats 1–20, request when you book). You (or your hotel or travel agency) can call the station to book a seat—they'll hold it until 40 minutes before departure (tel. 958-185-480; or 902-422-242 for Alsa, serving Barcelona or east-coast destinations, www.alsa.es). Or, if you don't want to show up early to claim your seat, you can buy your ticket in advance with a credit card (tel. 902-330-400). During peak season, the bus to Nerja can fill up; purchase tickets as far in advance as possible to snare a spot.

By Car: To drive to Nerja (1.5 hours away), take the exit for the coastal town of Motril. You'll wind through 50 scenic miles south of Granada, then follow signs for Málaga.

SEVILLA

Sevilla is the flamboyant city of Carmen and Don Juan, where bullfighting is still politically correct and where little girls still dream of growing up to become flamenco dancers. While Granada has the great Alhambra and Córdoba has the remarkable Mezquita, Sevilla has a soul. It's a wonderful-to-be-alive-in kind of place.

The gateway to the New World in the 16th century, Sevilla boomed when Spain did. The explorers Amerigo Vespucci and Ferdinand Magellan sailed from its great river harbor, discovering new routes and sources of gold, silver, cocoa, and tobacco. In the 17th century, Sevilla was Spain's largest and richest city. Local artists Diego Velázquez, Bartolomé Murillo, and Francisco de Zurbarán made it a cultural center. Sevilla's Golden Age—and its New World riches—ended when the harbor silted up and the Spanish empire crumbled.

In the 19th century, Sevilla was a big stop on the Romantic "Grand Tour" of Europe. To build on this tourism and promote trade among Spanish-speaking nations, Sevilla planned a grand exposition in 1929. Bad year. The expo crashed along with the stock market. In 1992, Sevilla got a second chance at a World's Fair. This expo was a success, leaving the city with an impressive infrastructure: a new airport, train station, sleek bridges, and the super AVE bullet train (making Sevilla a 2.5-hour side-trip from Madrid).

Today, Spain's fourth-largest city (pop. 700,000) is Andalucía's leading destination, buzzing with festivals, orange and jacaranda trees, sizzling summer heat, color, guitars, and castanets. James Michener wrote, "Sevilla doesn't *have* ambience, it *is* ambience."

Greater Sevilla

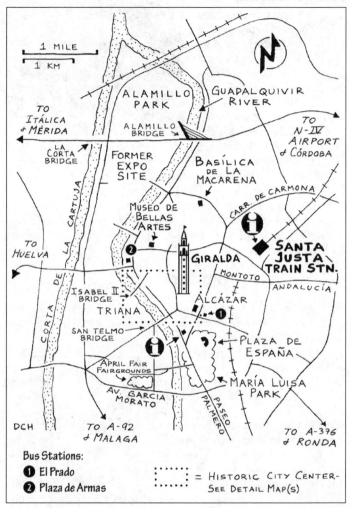

1 MILE
1 KM

TO
ITÁLICA
& MÉRIDA

ALAMILLO
PARK

GUADALQUIVIR
RIVER

ALAMILLO
BRIDGE

TO
N-IV
AIRPORT
& CÓRDOBA

LA
CORTA
BRIDGE

FORMER
EXPO
SITE

BASÍLICA
DE LA
MACARENA

CARR. DE CARMONA

LA CARTUJA

MUSEO DE
BELLAS
ARTES

SANTA
JUSTA
TRAIN STN.

TO
HUELVA

GIRALDA

MONTOTO

ANDALUCÍA

CORTA DE

ISABEL II
BRIDGE

ALCÁZAR

TRIANA

SAN TELMO
BRIDGE

PLAZA DE
ESPAÑA

APRIL FAIR
FAIRGROUNDS

MARÍA LUISA
PARK

AV. GARCÍA
MORATO

PASEO
PALMERO

DCH

TO A-92
& MÁLAGA

TO A-376
& RONDA

Bus Stations:
1 El Prado
2 Plaza de Armas

•••••• = HISTORIC CITY CENTER-
SEE DETAIL MAP(S)

Sevilla has its share of impressive sights, but the real magic is the city itself, with its tangled Jewish Quarter, riveting flamenco shows, thriving bars, and teeming evening paseo.

Planning Your Time

If ever there was a big Spanish city to linger in, it's Sevilla. On a three-week trip, spend two nights and two days here. On a shorter trip, zip here on the slick AVE train for a day trip from Madrid.

The major sights are few and simple for a city of this size; the cathedral and the Alcázar are worth about three hours, and

a wander through the Santa
Cruz district takes about one
hour. You could spend half a
day touring its other sights.
Stroll along the bank of the
Guadalquivir River and cross
the Bridge of Triana for a
view of the cathedral and
Golden Tower. An evening
is essential for the paseo and

a flamenco show. Bullfights take place on most Sundays from April
through October. Sevilla's Alcázar and Museo de Bellas Artes
are closed on Monday, while the Museo Palacio de la Condesa
de Lebrija is closed on Sunday. Tour groups clog the Alcázar and
cathedral in the morning; go late in the day to avoid the lines.

Córdoba (see next chapter) is a convenient and worthwhile
side-trip from Sevilla, or a handy stopover if you're taking the
AVE to or from Madrid.

ORIENTATION

For the tourist, this big city is small. Sevilla's major sights—including the lively Santa Cruz district and the Alcázar—surround the

cathedral. The central north–south
boulevard, Avenida de la Constitución
(with TI, banks, and a post office),
zips right past the cathedral to Plaza
Nueva (gateway to the shopping district). Nearly everything is within
easy walking distance. The bullring
is a few blocks west of the cathedral,
and Plaza de España is a few blocks
south. The area on the west bank of
the Guadalquivir River is working-

class and colorful, but lacks tourist sights. With taxis so friendly,
easy, and reasonable (€3 for a short ride), I rarely bother with the
bus—though a bus pass can be worthwhile for those on a tight
budget.

Expect a little confusion for 2007. Metro construction is stop-
and-go after finding archaeological remains underneath Avenida
de la Constitución. The entire street is blocked off to traffic, but
there are pedestrian crosswalks at regular intervals.

Tourist Information

Sevilla has many handy tourist offices: The **central** office is a block
toward the river from the cathedral (Mon–Fri 9:00–19:00, Sat

10:00–14:00 & 15:00–19:00, Sun and festivals 10:00–14:00, Avenida de la Constitución 21, tel. 954-221-404). There's a less-crowded county/city TI at **Plaza del Triunfo,** across from the cathedral (Mon–Fri 10:30–20:45, closed Sat–Sun, tel. 954-501-001). Another TI is on **Plaza San Francisco,** near the start of the shopping walk described on page 401 (Mon–Fri 8:00–20:00, closed Sat–Sun, tel. 954-595-288, free Internet access for 1 hour—see below). There are also TIs at the **train station** (Mon–Fri 9:00–20:00, Sat–Sun 10:00–14:00, overlooks track 6, tel. 954-537-626) and at the **airport** (Mon–Fri 9:00–21:00, Sat–Sun 11:00–15:00, tel. 954-449-128).

At any TI, ask for the city map (far better than the one in the promo city magazine); the English-language magazines *Welcome Olé* and *The Tourist*; a current listing of sights, hours, and prices; and a schedule of bullfights. The free monthly events guide—*El Giraldillo*, written in Spanish basic enough to be understood by travelers—covers cultural events throughout Andalucía, with a focus on Sevilla. If heading south, ask for the free *Route of the White Towns* brochure and a Jerez map. Helpful Web sites are www.turismo.sevilla.org and www.andalucia.org.

Sevilla Card: This card, sold at any TI, covers admission to most of Sevilla's sights (cathedral, Alcázar, Flamenco Dance Museum, Museo Palacio de la Condesa de Lebrija, Basílica de la Macarena, Bullfight Museum). There are many confusing options for this card—choose the *Cultura* one. You'll also get a 15 percent discount at the recommended Los Gallos flamenco bar. If you're doing a lot of sightseeing in Sevilla, the card can be a money-saver (€28/1 day, €32/2 days, €36/3 days, www.sevillacard.es).

Arrival in Sevilla

By Train: Trains arrive at the sublime Santa Justa station (banks, ATMs, TI, luggage storage). The town center is marked by the ornate Giralda bell tower, visible from the front of the station—using an imaginary clock as a compass, it's at 1 o'clock. It's a flat and boring 30-minute walk, a €5 taxi ride, or a short bus ride away. The bus is the least convenient option, with no service from the train station to the recommended hotels in the Santa Cruz district. However, bus #C1 runs from the train station to a stop near the El Prado bus station (see below), which is only a 15-minute walk from the Santa Cruz district (€1, pay driver). If you don't have a hotel room reserved, the room-finding booth above track 11 can help (daily 8:00–22:00).

By Bus: Sevilla's two major bus stations both have information offices, cafés, and luggage storage. The **El Prado station** covers most of Andalucía (Mon–Fri 7:30–22:00, Sat–Sun 9:00–21:00, information tel. 954-417-111, no English spoken; luggage storage at back of station, €2/day, Mon–Fri 7:30–22:00, Sat–Sun 9:00–21:00).

To get downtown from the station, it's a 10-minute walk: turn right on the major street, San Fernando, then right again on Avenida de la Constitución. The Santa Cruz hotel neighborhood is five minutes farther (behind the cathedral and Alcázar).

The **Plaza de Armas station** (near the river, opposite Expo '92 site) serves long-distance destinations like Madrid, Barcelona, and Lisbon. Luggage lockers are across from the ticket counters (€3/day). As you exit onto the main road (Calle Arjona), the bus stop is to the left, in front of the taxi stand. Look for bus #C4, which goes downtown (€1, pay driver, get off at Puerta de Jerez near main TI). Taxis to downtown cost around €5.

By Car: To drive into Sevilla, follow *Centro Ciudad* (city center) signs and stay along the river. For short-term parking on the street, the riverside Paseo de Cristóbal Colón has two-hour meters and hardworking thieves. Ignore the bogus traffic wardens who direct you to an illegal spot, take a tip, and disappear later when your car gets towed. Consider hiring a taxi to lead you to your hotel, where you can get parking advice.

Driving in Sevilla is difficult, and many cars are broken into. I'd pay to park in a garage—try the big one under the bus station at Plaza de Armas (€10/day), the Cristóbal Colón garage (by the bullring and river, €1.15/hr, €13/day), or at Avenida Roma/Puerta de Jerez (€17/24 hrs, cash only). For hotels in the Santa Cruz area, the handiest parking is the Cano y Cueto garage near the corner of Calle Santa María la Blanca and Menéndez Pelayo (€14/day, open 24/7, at edge of big park, unsigned and underground).

By Plane: The Especial Aeropuerto (EA) bus connects the airport with the train station and town center (€2.50, 30 min, 2/hr, departs at top and bottom of each hour, buy ticket from driver; if going from Sevilla to the airport, catch the bus at Avenida Roma—across from Hotel Alfonso XIII). Taxis have a fixed €20 rate between the airport and town center (but confirm price anyway). Flight info tel. 954-449-000.

Getting Around Sevilla

On a hot day, buses in Sevilla can be a blessing. A single trip costs €1 (pay driver) or you can buy a Bonobus pass, which gives you 10 trips for €5 (sharable, sold at kiosks). The various #C buses make a circular loop that covers María Luisa Park and Basílica de la Macarena. The #C3 stops in Murillo Gardens, Triana (district south of the river), then Macarena. The #C4 goes the opposite direction without entering Triana.

Helpful Hints

Festivals: Sevilla's peak season is April and May. And it has two one-week festival periods when the city is packed. While

Holy Week *(Semana Santa)* is big all over Spain, it's biggest in Sevilla. It's held the week between Palm Sunday and Easter Sunday (April 1–8 in 2007). Then, two weeks after Easter, after taking enough time off to catch its communal breath, Sevilla holds its **April Fair** (April 16–22 in 2007, described on page 400). This is a celebration of all that's Andalusian, with plenty of eating, drinking, singing, and merrymaking (though most of the revelry takes place in private parties at a large fairground). Book rooms well in advance for festival times. Warning: Prices can go sky-high, and many hotels have four-night minimums.

Internet Access: Sevilla has plenty of places to get online, including **Internet Workcenter** (daily 7:00–23:00, on river side of Alcázar at San Fernando 1, tel. 954-212-074). The **TI** on Plaza San Francisco offers up to one hour of free Internet access from eight terminals (Mon–Fri 10:00–14:00 & 17:00–20:00—most likely available in morning, closed Sat–Sun).

Post Office: The post office is at Avenida de la Constitución 32, across from the cathedral (Mon–Fri 8:30–20:30, Sat 9:30–14:00, closed Sun).

Laundry: Lavanderia Roma offers quick and economical drop-off service (€6/load wash and dry, Mon–Fri 9:30–13:30 & 17:00–20:30, Sat 9:00–15:00, closed Sun, Castelar 2, tel. 954-210-535). Near the Santa Cruz hotels, the handy **Lavanderia** offers self-serve and full-serve with a big smile (full-service in 3 hours—wash, dry, and fold for €7.20; Mon–Fri 10:00–20:30, Sat 10:00–14:00, closed Sun, near Plaza de la Alfalfa at Calle Candilejo 10, tel. 649-544-869, Cindy).

Train and Plane Tickets: The RENFE offices give out train schedules and sell train tickets. There's a RENFE Travel Center at the **train station** (daily 8:00–22:00, take a number and wait, tel. 902-240-202 for reservations and info) and one near **Plaza Nueva** in the center (Mon–Fri 9:30–14:00 & 17:30–20:00, closed Sat–Sun, Calle Zaragoza 29, tel. 954-211-455). Many travel agencies sell train tickets for the same price as the train station (look for train sticker in agency window).

TOURS

Guided City Walks—Concepción Delgado, an enthusiastic teacher and a joy to listen to, takes small groups on English-language-only walks. Using me as her guinea pig, Concepción designed a fine two-hour introduction to the city, sharing important insights the average visitor misses. Her cultural show-and-tell is worthwhile, even on a one-day visit (€12/person, daily except Sun at 10:30, starting from statue in Plaza Nueva). For those wanting

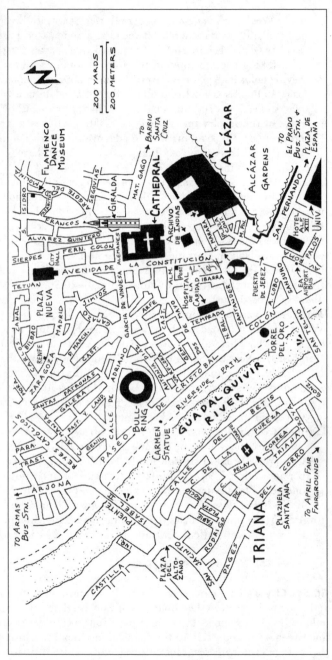

to really understand the city's two most important sights—which are tough to fully appreciate, she also offers in-depth tours of the cathedral and the Alcázar. Tours last 75 minutes, cost €6, and meet at 13:00 at the statue in Plaza del Triunfo (cathedral tours—Mon, Wed, and Fri; Alcázar tours—Tue, Thu, and Sat). While you can just show up for tours, it's smart to confirm the departure and reserve a place (tel. 902-158-226, mobile 616-501-100, www.sevillawalkingtours.com, info@sevillawalkingtours.com).

Hop-on, Hop-off Bus Tours—Two competing city bus tours leave from the curb near the riverside Golden Tower. You'll see the buses parked with salespeople handing out fliers. Each does about an hour-long swing through the city with a tape-recorded narration (green route slightly better because it includes María Luisa Park). The tours, which allow hopping on and off at four stops, are heavy on Expo '29 and Expo '92 neighborhoods of little interest in '07. While the narration does its best, Sevilla is most interesting where buses can't go (€11, daily 10:00–21:00).

Horse and Buggy Tours—A carriage ride is a classic, popular way to survey the city and a relaxing way to enjoy María Luisa Park

(about €40 for a 45-min clip-clop, if shared by 2 couples the ride is actually quite inexpensive, find a likable English-speaking driver for better narration). Look for rigs at Plaza América, Plaza del Triunfo, Golden Tower, Alfonso XIII hotel, and Avenida Isabel la Católica.

Boat Cruises—Boring one-hour panoramic tours leave every 30 minutes from the dock behind Torre de Oro. The low-energy recorded narration is hard to follow, but there's little to see anyway (overpriced at €12, tel. 954-561-692).

Andalusian Minibus Tours—Aussie Paul McGrath, who's lived in Sevilla for eight years, takes small groups on all-day tours in his nine-seat minivan. You'll head to the villages south of Sevilla, which are difficult to reach without a car. Paul doesn't really provide tours, just an efficient, economic way to explore the great whitewashed towns along the "Route of the Pueblos Blancos." You'll leave in the morning and visit Olvera, Zahara, Grazalema, and Setenil de las Bodegas; the tour also includes a stop at the

Sevilla at a Glance

▲▲▲**Flamenco** Flamboyant, riveting music-and-dance performances, offered at clubs throughout town. **Hours:** Shows start as early as 19:30.

▲▲**Flamenco Dance Museum** Brand-new, high-tech museum explaining the history of Sevilla's favorite dance. **Hours:** Daily 9:00–19:00.   *9–9pm*

▲▲**Cathedral and Giralda Bell Tower** The world's largest Gothic church, with Columbus' tomb, a treasury, and climbable tower. **Hours:** June–mid-Sept Mon–Sat 9:30–15:30, free on Sun 14:30–18:00, mid-Sept–May Mon–Sat 11:00–17:00, free on Sun 14:30–19:00.

▲▲**Basílica de la Macarena** Church and museum with the much-venerated Weeping Virgin statue and two significant floats from Sevilla's Holy Week celebrations. **Hours:** Daily 9:30–14:00 & 17:00–20:00.

▲▲**Evening Paseo** Locals strolling in the cool of the evening, mainly through Barrio Santa Cruz, the Calle Sierpes and Tetuán shopping pedestrian zone, and along the Guadalquivir River. **Hours:** Spring through fall, until very late in summer.

▲▲**Bullfight Museum** Guided tour of the bullring and its museum. **Hours:** Daily 9:30–19:00, fight days until 15:00.

▲▲**Alcázar** Palace built by the Moors in the 10th century, revamped in the 14th century, and still serving as royal digs. **Hours:** Tue–Sat 9:30–19:00, Sun 9:30–17:00, off-season Tue–Sat 9:30–17:00, Sun 10:30–13:30, closed Mon.

▲**Bullfights** Some of Spain's best bullfighting, held at Sevilla's arena. **Hours:** Most Sun, Easter through October at 18:30 or 19:30.

▲**Museo de Bellas Artes** Andalucía's top collection of paintings, including Spanish masters such as Murillo and Zurbarán. **Hours:** Tue 14:30–20:30, Wed–Sat 9:00–20:30, Sun 9:00–14:30, closed Mon.

▲**Museo Palacio de la Condesa de Lebrija** A fascinating 18th-century aristocratic mansion. **Hours:** June–Sept Mon–Fri 10:30–13:30 & 17:00–20:00, Sat 10:00–14:00, closed Sun; Oct–May Mon–Fri 10:30–13:30 & 16:30–19:30, Sat 10:00–14:00, closed Sun.

Moorish castle Aguzaderas, an olive-oil mill, and a swimming-stop option in the summer (€48, leaves daily from Torre de Oro at 9:30, returns about 19:30, call or e-mail to reserve, tel. 657-889-875, www.theotherspain.galeon.com, the-other-spain@hotmail.com).
More Tours—**Visitours,** a typical, big bus-tour company, does €70 all-day trips to Córdoba daily except Sunday (tel. 954-460-985, mobile 686-413-413, www.visitours.es.mn, visitours@terra.es). American expat **Daniel O'Beirne** organizes excursions for visitors (mobile 615-291-736, www.magicalspain.com). For other guides, contact the **Guides Association of Sevilla** (tel. 954-210-037, www.apitsevilla.com, visitas@apitsevilla.com).

SELF-GUIDED WALK

Barrio Santa Cruz

Of Sevilla's once-thriving Jewish Quarter, only the tangled street plan and a wistful Old World ambience survives. This classy maze of lanes (too narrow for cars), small plazas, tile-covered patios, and whitewashed houses with wrought-iron latticework draped with flowers is a great refuge from the summer heat and bustle of Sevilla. The narrow streets—some with buildings so close they're called "kissing lanes"—were actually designed to maximize shade.

Even today, locals claim the Barrio Santa Cruz is three degrees cooler than the rest of the city.

Orange trees abound. Since they never lose their leaves, they provide constant shade. But forget about eating any of the oranges. They're bitter and used only to make vitamins, perfume, cat food, and that marmalade you can't avoid in British B&Bs.

The Barrio is made for wandering. Getting lost is easy, and I recommend doing just that. But to get started, here's a plaza-to-plaza walk that loops you through the *corazón* (heart) of the neighborhood and back out again. Ideally, don't do the walk in the morning, when the Barrio's charm is trampled by tour groups. Early evening (around 18:00) is ideal.

Start at the cathedral and head toward the Alcázar (both described below) through **Plaza del Triunfo**—the "Plaza of Triumph," named for the 1755 earthquake that destroyed Lisbon, but didn't rock Sevilla or its tower—with its statue thanking the Virgin. Pass through an opening in the Alcázar wall under the arch. You'll emerge in a courtyard called the **Patio de Banderas.**

Barrio Santa Cruz Self-Guided Walk

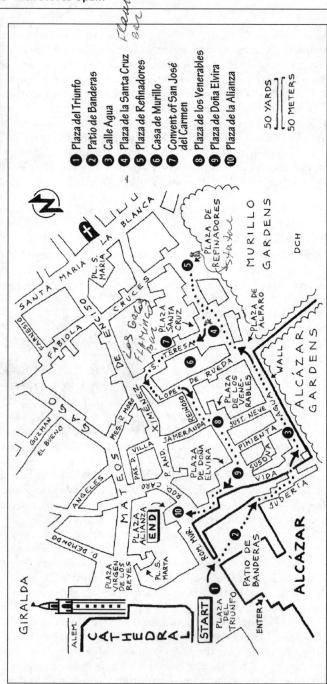

1. Plaza del Triunfo
2. Patio de Banderas
3. Calle Agua
4. Plaza de la Santa Cruz
5. Plaza de Refinadores
6. Casa de Murillo
7. Convent of San José del Carmen
8. Plaza de los Venerables
9. Plaza de Doña Elvira
10. Plaza de la Alianza

50 YARDS
50 METERS

Bartolomé Murillo
(1617–1682)

The son of a barber of Seville, Bartolomé Murillo got his start selling paintings meant for export to the frontier churches of the Americas. In his 20s, he became famous after he painted a series of saints for Sevilla's Franciscan monastery. By about 1650, Murillo's sugary, simple, and accessible religious style was spreading through Spain and beyond.

He painted street kids with cute smiles and grimy faces, and radiant young Marías with Ivory-soap complexions and rapturous poses (Immaculate Conceptions). Murillo's paintings view the world through a soft-focus lens, wrapping everything in warm colors and soft light, with a touch (too much, for some) of sentimentality.

Murillo became rich, popular, a family man, and the toast of Sevilla's high society. In 1664, his wife died, leaving him heartbroken, but his last 20 years were his most prolific. At age 65, Murillo died painting, falling off a scaffold. His tomb is lost somewhere under the bricks of Plaza de la Santa Cruz.

Named for "flags," not Antonio, the Banderas Courtyard offers a postcard view of the Giralda bell tower.

Exit the courtyard at the far corner, through the Judería arch. Walking alongside the Alcázar wall, take the first left, then right, and follow the narrow alleyway called **Calle Agua**. It's named for the water pipes in the wall that flowed into the Alcázar (you can see them at the end of the lane—they follow the wall of the Alcázar gardens). On the left, peek through iron gates for the occasional glimpse of the flower-smothered patios of exclusive private residences. The patio at #2 is a delight—ringed with columns, filled with flowers, and colored with glazed tiles. The tiles are not only decorative; they keep buildings cooler in the summer heat. At the end of the street is an entrance into the pleasant Murillo Gardens (to the right), formerly the fruit-and-vegetable gardens for the Alcázar.

Don't enter the gardens now, but instead cross the square and continue 20 yards down a lane to **Plaza de la Santa Cruz,** arguably the heart of the Barrio. This was once the site of a synagogue (there were three, now there are none), which Christians destroyed. They replaced the synagogue with a church, which the French (under Napoleon) then demolished. It's a bit of history that locals remember when they see the red, white, and blue French flag marking the French consulate, now overlooking this peaceful square. The painter Murillo, buried in the church, now lies somewhere below you. On the square you'll find the recommended Los Gallos flamenco bar (described on page 403).

Follow Calle Mezquita farther east to the nearby **Plaza de Refinadores.** Sevilla's most famous (if fictional) 17th-century citizen is honored here with a statue. Don Juan Tenorio—the original Don Juan—was a notorious sex addict and atheist who thumbed his nose at the stifling, Church-driven morals of his day.

Backtrack to Plaza de la Santa Cruz and turn right (north) on Calle Santa Teresa. At #8 is **Casa de Murillo.** One of Sevilla's famous painters lived here, soaking in the ambience of street life and reproducing it in his paintings of cute beggar children.

Directly across from Casa Murillo, the **Convent of San José del Carmen** is where Saint Teresa stayed when she visited from her hometown of Ávila. The convent (closed to the public) keeps relics of the mystic nun, such as the manuscript of her treatise *Las Moradas* ("The Interior Castle," "where truth dwells").

Continue north on Calle Santa Teresa, then left (west) on Calle Lope de Rueda, then right on Calle Reinoso. This street—so narrow that the buildings almost touch—is one of the Barrio's "kissing lanes."

The street spills into **Plaza de los Venerables,** another candidate for heart of the Barrio. The streets branching off it ooze local ambience. The large, harmonious, Baroque-style Hospital of the Venerables (1675), once an old priests' home (the "venerables"), is now a museum. The highlight is the church and courtyard, featuring a round, sunken fountain. Frescoes by Valdes Leal and his son decorate the hospital's church (1698). The complex now houses temporary art exhibits (€4.75, daily 10:00–14:00 & 16:00–20:00, last entry 30 min before closing).

Continuing west on Calle Gloria, you soon reach **Plaza de Doña Elvira.** This small square—with orange trees, tile benches, and a stone fountain—sums up our Barrio walk. Shops sell work by local artisans, such as ceramics, embroidery, and fans.

Cross the Plaza and head north along Calle Rodrigo Caro into **Plaza de la Alianza.** Ever consider a career change? Gain inspiration at the John Fulton Studio, a former art gallery featuring the work of the American who pursued two dreams. Though born in Philadelphia, Fulton got hooked on bullfighting. He trained in the tacky bullrings of Mexico, then in 1956 he moved to Sevilla, the world capital of the sport. His career as matador was not top-notch, and the Spaniards were slow to warm to the Yankee, but

Sevilla's Jews

In the summer of 1391, smoldering anti-Jewish sentiment flared up in Sevilla. On June 6, the city's Jewish Quarter (Judería) was ransacked by Christian mobs. Four thousand Jews were killed, 5,000 Jewish families driven from their homes, synagogues were stripped and transformed into churches, the Star of David came down, and the former Judería eventually became the neighborhood of the Holy Cross—Barrio Santa Cruz. Sevilla's uprising spread through Spain (and Europe), the first of many nasty pogroms during the next century.

Before the pogrom, Jews had lived in Sevilla for centuries as the city's respected merchants, doctors, and bankers. They flourished under the Muslim Moors. When Sevilla was "liberated" by King Ferdinand (1248), Jews were given protection by Spain's kings and allowed a measure of self-government, though they were confined to the Jewish neighborhood.

But by the 14th century, Jews were increasingly accused of everything from poisoning wells to ritually sacrificing Christian babies. Mobs killed suspected Jews, some of Sevilla's most respected Jewish citizens had their fortunes confiscated, and Jewish kids were mocked and bullied on the playground.

After 1391, Jews faced a choice: Be persecuted (even killed), relocate, or convert to Christianity. Those who converted—called *conversos*, New Christians, or *marranos* ("swine")—were always under suspicion of practicing their old faith in private, undermining true Christianity. Fanning the suspicion was the fact that Old Christians were threatened by this new social class of converted Jews who now had equal status.

To root out the perceived problem of underground Judaism, the "Catholic Monarchs" Ferdinand and Isabel established the Inquisition in Spain (1478). Under the direction of Grand Inquisitor Tomás de Torquemada, these religious courts arrested and interrogated *conversos* suspected of practicing Judaism. Using long solitary confinement and torture, they extracted confessions.

On February 6, 1481, Sevilla hosted Spain's first *auto da fe* ("act of faith"), a public confession and punishment for heresy. Six accused *conversos* were paraded barefoot into the cathedral, made to publicly confess their sins, then were burned at the stake. Over the next three decades, thousands of *conversos* (some historians say hundreds, some say tens of thousands) were tried and killed in Spain.

In 1492, the same year the last Moors were driven from Spain, Ferdinand and Isabel decreed that all remaining Jews convert or be expelled (to Portugal and ultimately to Holland). Spain emerged as a nation unified under the banner of Christianity.

his courage and persistence earned their grudging respect. After retirement, he put down the cape and picked up a brush, making the colorful paintings in this studio.

From Plaza de la Alianza, you can return to the cathedral by turning left (west) on Calle Romero Murube (along the wall). Or head east/northeast on Callejón de Rodrigo Caro, which intersects with Calle Mateos Gago, a street lined with atmospheric tapas bars.

SIGHTS

Cathedral and the Giralda Bell Tower

A ▲▲ sight, this is the third-largest church in Europe (after St. Peter's at the Vatican and St. Paul's in London), and the largest Gothic church anywhere. When they ripped down a mosque of brick on this site in 1401, the Reconquista Christians bragged, "We'll build a cathedral so huge that anyone who sees it will take us for madmen." They built for 120 years. Even today, the descendants of those madmen proudly display an enlarged photocopy of their *Guinness Book of Records* letter certifying, "The cathedral with the largest area is: Santa María de la Sede in Sevilla, 126 meters long, 82 meters wide, and 30 meters high"

Cost, Hours, Tours: (€7.50, covered by Sevilla Card; June–mid-Sept Mon–Sat 9:30–15:30, free on Sun 14:30–18:00; mid-Sept–May Mon–Sat 11:00–17:00, free on Sun 14:30–19:00; last entry 1 hour before closing, WC and drinking fountain inside near entrance and in courtyard near exit, tel. 954-214-971). The €3 audioguide explains each side chapel for anyone interested in all the old paintings and dry details (consider Concepción Delgado's tour instead, described on page 375).

⊙ Self-Guided Tour: Enter the cathedral at the south end (closest to the Alcázar, with a copy of the Giralda's weathervane statue in the patio).

• *First, head to the...*

Art Pavilion and Restoration: Just past the turnstile, you step into a pavilion of paintings that once hung in the church, including works by Sevilla's two 17th-century masters—Bartolomé Murillo *(St. Ferdinand)* and Francisco de Zurbarán *(St. John the Baptist in the Desert)*. Walking past a rack of church maps and a WC, enter the actual church. The first things you'll see are the restoration braces supporting huge pillars. These help keep the building from

Sevilla's Cathedral

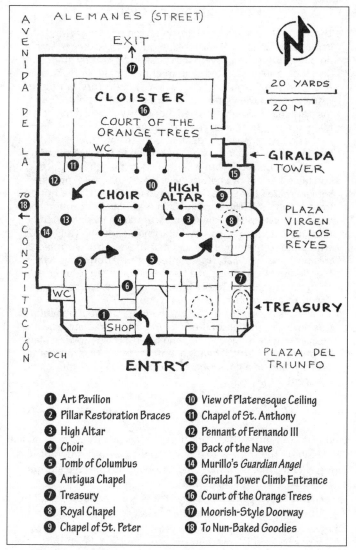

ALEMANES (STREET)

EXIT

⑰

AVENIDA DE LA

CLOISTER

⑯

COURT OF THE ORANGE TREES

WC

⑪

⑫

TO ⑱

C O N S T I T U C I Ó N

CHOIR

⑩

HIGH ALTAR

⑨

⑬

④

③

⑧

⑭

②

⑤

WC

⑥

⑦

①

SHOP

DCH

ENTRY

GIRALDA TOWER

⑮

PLAZA VIRGEN DE LOS REYES

◄ **TREASURY**

PLAZA DEL TRIUNFO

20 YARDS

20 M

- ❶ Art Pavilion
- ❷ Pillar Restoration Braces
- ❸ High Altar
- ❹ Choir
- ❺ Tomb of Columbus
- ❻ Antigua Chapel
- ❼ Treasury
- ❽ Royal Chapel
- ❾ Chapel of St. Peter
- ❿ View of Plateresque Ceiling
- ⓫ Chapel of St. Anthony
- ⓬ Pennant of Fernando III
- ⓭ Back of the Nave
- ⓮ Murillo's *Guardian Angel*
- ⓯ Giralda Tower Climb Entrance
- ⓰ Court of the Orange Trees
- ⓱ Moorish-Style Doorway
- ⓲ To Nun-Baked Goodies

collapsing as people search for an answer to the problem of the pillars' cracking.

• *In the center of the church, sit down in front of the...*

High Altar: Look through the wrought-iron Renaissance grill at what's called the largest altarpiece *(retablo mayor)* ever made—65 feet tall, with 44 scenes from the life of Jesus carved out of walnut and chestnut, blanketed by a staggering amount of

Immaculate Conception

Throughout Sevilla and Spain, you'll see paintings titled *The Immaculate Conception,* all looking quite similar (see example on page 381). Young, lovely, and beaming radiantly, these virgins look pure, untainted...you might even say "immaculate." According to Catholic doctrine, Mary, the future mother of Jesus, entered the world free from the original sin that other mortals share. When she died, her purity allowed her to be taken up directly to heaven (the Assumption).

The doctrine of Immaculate Conception can be confusing, even to Catholics. It does not mean that the Virgin Mary herself was born of a virgin. Rather, Mary's mother and father conceived her in the natural way. But at the moment Mary's soul animated her flesh, God granted her a special exemption from original sin. The doctrine of Immaculate Conception had been popular since medieval times, though it was not codified until 1854. It was Sevilla's own Bartolomé Murillo (1617–1682) who painted the model that so many lesser artists copied of this goddess-like Mary. In Counter-Reformation times (when Murillo lived), paintings of a fresh-faced, ecstatic Mary made abstract doctrines like the Immaculate Conception and the Assumption tangible and accessible to all.

An easy way to recognize an image of the Immaculate Conception is to look for the following clues: a radiant crown, a crescent moon at Mary's feet, and often a pose showing Mary stepping on cherubs' heads. Paintings by Murillo frequently portray Mary in a blue robe with long, wavy hair—young and innocent.

---

gold leaf (and dust). The work took three generations to complete (1481–1564). The story is told left to right, bottom (birth of Jesus) to top (Pentecost), with the Crucifixion at the dizzying summit.

• *Turn around and check out the...*

Choir: Facing the high altar, the choir features an organ of 7,000 pipes (played at the 10:00 Mass, free for worshippers). A choir area like this (an enclosure within the cathedral for more intimate services) is common in Spain and England, but rare in churches elsewhere. The big spinnable book holder in the middle of the room held giant hymnals—large enough for all to chant from in a pre-Xerox age when there weren't enough books for everyone.

• *Now turn 90 degrees to the left and march to find the...*

Tomb of Columbus: In front of the cathedral's entrance for pilgrims are four kings who carry the tomb of Christopher Columbus. His pallbearers represent Castile, Aragon, León, and Navarre (identify them by their team shirts). Columbus even traveled a lot posthumously. He was buried first in Spain, then in Santo Domingo in the Dominican Republic, then Cuba, and—when Cuba gained independence from Spain, around 1900—he sailed home again to Sevilla. Are the remains actually his? Sevillans like to think so. High above on the left is a mural of St. Christopher—patron saint of travelers—from 1584. The clock above has been ticking since 1788.

• *Head to the next chapel on the right to find the...*

Antigua Chapel: Within this chapel is the gilded fresco of the Virgin Antigua, the oldest art in the church. It was actually painted onto the horseshoe-shaped prayer niche of the former mosque which, when conquered in 1248, served as a church for about 120 years—until it was torn down to be replaced by this huge church. Rebuilders, captivated by the beauty of the Virgin holding the rose and the Christ child holding the bird, decided to save it.

• *Exiting the chapel, we'll tour the cathedral counterclockwise. As you explore, note that its many chapels are described in English, and many of the windows have their dates worked into the design. Step into the...*

Treasury: The *tesoro* fills several rooms in the corner of the church. Start by marveling at the ornate, 16th-century Plateresque dome of the main room, a grand souvenir from Sevilla's Golden Age. The intricate masonry resembles lacy silverwork (from *plata*—silver). God is way up in the cupola. The three layers of figures below him show the heavenly host; relatives in purgatory—hands folded—looking to heaven and hoping you do them well; and the wretched in hell, including a topless sinner engulfed in flames and teased cruelly by pitchfork-wielding monsters. Locals use the 110-pound silver monstrance, which dominates this room, to parade the holy host (communion bread) through town during Corpus Christi festivities.

Wander deeper into the treasury to find a unique oval dome. It's in the 16th-century chapter room (Sala Capitular), where monthly meetings take place with the bishop (see his throne). The paintings here are by Murillo: a fine *Immaculate Conception* (1668, above the bishop's throne) and portraits of saints important to Sevillans.

The wood-paneled "room of ornaments" shows off gold and silver reliquaries, which hold hundreds of holy body parts, as well as Spain's most valuable crown. The Corona de la Virgen de los Reyes sparkles with 11,000 precious stones and the world's largest pearl—

used as the torso of an angel. Opposite the crown is a reliquary featuring "a piece of the true cross."

Cross the church, passing the closed-to-tourists Royal Chapel, the burial place of several of the kings of Castile (open for worship—access from outside), and the Chapel of St. Peter, which is dark but filled with paintings by Francisco de Zurbarán (showing scenes from the life of St. Peter). At the far corner—past the glass case displaying the *Guinness* certificate declaring that this is indeed the world's largest church in area—is the entry to the Giralda bell tower. You'll finish your visit here. But for now, continue your counterclockwise circuit. Near the middle (and high) altar, crane your neck skyward to admire the Plateresque tracery on the ceiling.

The **Chapel of St. Anthony** (Capilla de San Antonio), the last chapel on the right, is used for baptisms. The Renaissance baptismal font has delightful carved angels dancing along its base. In Murillo's painting, *Vision of St. Anthony* (1656), the saint kneels in wonder as a baby Jesus comes down surrounded by a choir of angels. Anthony is one of Iberia's most popular saints. As the patron saint of lost things, people come here to pray for Anthony's help in finding

jobs, car keys, and life partners. Above that is the *Baptism of Christ,* also by Murillo. You don't need to be an art historian to know that the stained glass dates from 1685.

Nearby, a glass case displays the **pennant of Fernando III,** which was raised over the minaret of the mosque on November 23, 1248, as Christian forces finally expelled the Moors from Sevilla. For centuries, it was paraded through the city on special days.

Continuing on, stand at the **back of the nave** (behind the choir) and appreciate the ornate immensity of the church. Can you see the angels trumpeting on their Cuban mahogany? Any birds?

Turn around. The massive candlestick holder dates from 1560. To the left is a niche with Murillo's *Guardian Angel* pointing to the light, and showing an astonished child the way.

• *Backtrack the length of the church toward the Giralda bell tower, and notice the back of the choir's Baroque pipe organ. The* exit *sign leads to the Court of the Orange Trees and the exit. But first, some exercise...*

Giralda Tower Climb: Your church admission includes entry to the bell tower. Notice the beautiful Moorish simplicity as you climb to its top, 330 feet up, for a grand city view. The spiraling ramp was designed to accommodate riders on horseback, who galloped up five times a day to give the Muslim call to prayer.

Christopher Columbus
(1451–1506)

This Italian wool-weaver ran off to sea, was shipwrecked in Portugal, married a captain's daughter, learned Portuguese and Spanish, and convinced Spain's monarchs to finance his bold scheme to trade with the East by sailing west. On August 3, 1492, Columbus set sail from Palos (near Huelva, 60 miles west of Sevilla) with three ships and 90 men, hoping to land in Asia, which Columbus estimated was 3,000 miles away. Three thousand miles later—with the superstitious crew ready to mutiny, having seen evil omens like a falling meteor and a jittery compass—Columbus landed on an island in the Bahamas (October 12, 1492), convinced he'd reached Asia. They traded with the "Indians" and returned home to Palos harbor, where they were received as heroes.

Columbus made three more voyages to the New World and became rich with gold. He gained a bad reputation among the colonists, was arrested, and returned to Spain in chains. Though pardoned, Columbus fell out of favor with the court. On May 20, 1506, he died in Valladolid. His son said he was felled by "gout and by grief at seeing himself fallen from his high estate," but historians speculate that diabetes or syphilis may have contributed. Columbus died thinking he'd visited Asia, unaware he'd opened up Europe to a New World.

• *Go back down the stairs and visit the...*

Court of the Orange Trees: Today's cloister was once the mosque's Court of the Orange Trees (Patio de los Naranjos). Twelfth-century Muslims stopped at the fountain in the middle to wash their hands, face, and feet before praying. The ankle-breaking lanes between the bricks were once irrigation streams—a reminder that the Moors introduced irrigation to Iberia. The mosque was  made of bricks; the church is built of stone. The only remnants of the mosque today are the Court of the Orange Trees, the Giralda bell tower, and the site itself.

As you exit the Court of the Orange Trees (and the cathedral), notice the arch over the **Moorish-style doorway.** As with much of the Moorish-looking art in town, it's actually Christian—the two coats of arms are a giveaway. The relief above the door (looking in from outside) shows the Bible story of Jesus ridding the temple of the merchants...a reminder to contemporary merchants that there will be no retail activity in the church. The plaque on the right is one of many scattered throughout town showing a place mentioned in the books of Miguel de Cervantes, the great 16th-century Spanish writer. (In this case, the topic was pickpockets.) The huge green doors predate the church. They are a bit of the surviving

pre-1248 mosque—wood covered with bronze. Study the fine workmanship.

Giralda Tower Exterior: Step across the street from the exit gate and look at the bell tower. Formerly a Moorish minaret from which Muslims were called to prayer, it became the cathedral's bell tower after the Reconquista. It's crowned by a 4,500-pound bronze statue symbolizing the Triumph of Faith (specifically, the Christian faith over the Muslim one) that caps it and serves as a weathervane (*giraldillo* in Spanish). In 1356, the original top of the tower fell. You're looking at a 16th-century Christian-built top with a ribbon of letters proclaiming, "The strongest tower is the name of God" (you can see *Fortísima*—"strongest"—from this vantage point).

Needing more strength than their bricks could provide for the lowest section of the tower, the Moors used Roman-cut stones. Now circle around for a close look at the corner of the tower at ground level; you can actually read the Latin chiseled onto one of the stones 2,000 years ago. The tower offers a brief recap of the city's history—sitting on a Roman foundation, a long Moorish period capped by our Christian age. Today, by law, no building can be higher than the statue atop the tower.

Nun-Baked Goodies: Stop by the "El Torno" Pasteleria de Conventos, a co-op where the various orders of cloistered nuns sell their handicrafts (such as baby's baptismal dresses) and baked goods. "El Torno" is the lazy Susan that the cloistered nuns spin to sell their cakes and cookies without being seen. This is a humble little hole-in-the-wall, but it's worth a peek (Sept–July Mon–Fri 10:00–13:30 & 17:00–19:30, Sat–Sun 10:30–14:00, closed Aug, across Avenida de la Constitución, immediately in front of the cathedral's biggest door, follow *dulces de convento* sign down a little covered lane to Plaza Cabildo 21).

Alcázar and Nearby

▲▲**Alcázar**—Originally a 10th-century palace built for the governors of the local Moorish state, this still functions as a royal

palace...the oldest still in use in Europe. What you see today is an extensive 14th-century rebuild, done by Moorish workmen (Mudejar) for the Christian king Pedro I. Pedro was nicknamed either "the Cruel" or "the Just," depending on which end of his sword you were on.

Cost, Hours, Tours: €7, covered by Sevilla Card (must get free ticket—no jumping ahead of the line); peak season Tue–Sat 9:30–19:00, Sun 9:30–17:00, closed Mon; off-season Tue–Sat 9:30–17:00, Sun 10:30–13:30, closed Mon; tel. 954-502-323. The fast-moving, easy-to-use €3 audioguide gives you an hour of information as you wander—if you want that much (drop it off at the exit). Tour groups clog the palace and rob it of any mystery in the morning (especially on Tue); come as late as possible. Again, you could consider Concepción's Alcázar tour, described on page 375.

● Self-Guided Tour: The Alcázar is a thought-provoking glimpse of a graceful Al-Andalus (Moorish) world that might have survived its Castilian conquerors...but didn't. The floor plan is intentionally confusing, part of the style designed to make experiencing the place more exciting and surprising. While Granada's Alhambra was built by Moors for Moorish rulers, what you see here is essentially a Christian ruler's palace, built in the Moorish style.

Just past the turnstiles, walk through the Patio of the Lions and stop under the arch of the wall to orient yourself. Facing the Patio de la Montería, you see the palace's three wings: the wing on the right is the 16th-century Admiral's Apartments; straight ahead is King Pedro the Cruel's Palace; and on the left is the 13th-century Gothic wing. You'll tour them in that order (entering the Gothic wing from within Pedro's palace).

• *Start by heading to the...*

Admiral's Apartments: When Queen Isabel debriefed Columbus here after his New World discoveries, she realized this could be big business. In 1503, she created this wing to administer Spain's New World ventures. Step inside.

Straight ahead, through the main hall, you'll find the Admirals' Lounge with a chapel featuring a painting of Santa María de los Buenos Aires Chapel (St. Mary of the Fair Winds—or, as many Spanish boys would say, "of the Good Farts"). The Virgin of the

Fair Winds was the patron saint of navigators and a favorite of Columbus. The fine Virgin of the Navigators altarpiece (painted by Alejo Fernández in the 1530s) is said to have the only portrait of Ferdinand (on left, with gold cape) with Columbus. Columbus is the blond guy on the right; his son said of his dad: "In his youth his hair was blond, but when he reached 30, it all turned white." As it's the earliest known portrait of Columbus, it's considered the most accurate. Notice how the Virgin's cape seems to protect everyone under it—even the Native Americans in the dark background (the first time "Indians" were painted in Europe). Left of the painting is a model of Columbus' *Santa María*, his flagship and the only one of his three ships not to survive the 1492 voyage. Columbus complained that the *Santa María*—a big cargo ship, different from the sleek *Niña* and *Pinta* caravels—was too slow. On Christmas Day, it ran aground and tore a hole in its keel. The ship was dismantled to build the first permanent structure in America, a fort for 39 colonists. (After Columbus left, the natives burned the fort and killed the colonists.) Opposite the altarpiece (in the center of the back wall) is the family coat of arms of Columbus' descendants, who now live in Spain and Puerto Rico. Using Columbus' Spanish name, it reads: "To Castile and to León, Colón gave a new world."

Before leaving, pop into the room beyond the grand piano in the still-used reception room for a look at ornate fans (mostly foreign, described in English) and a long painting showing 17th-century Sevilla during Holy Week. Follow the procession, which is much like today's procession of traditional floats, carried by teams of 24 to 48 men and followed by a parade of KKK-looking penitents.

• *Return to the main courtyard. You'll notice a desk selling tickets to the lived-in royal apartments upstairs; they're similar to what you'll see downstairs, but with furniture (€3 for 25-min Spanish tours with a little English). From the main courtyard, enter the middle wing, and walk to the left through the vestibule until you hit the big courtyard called the Court of the Maidens.*

King Pedro the Cruel's Palace: This 14th-century nucleus of the complex—the real Alcázar—is centered around the elegantly proportioned Court of the Maidens (Patio de las Doncellas), decorated in 14th-century Moorish style below and a 16th-century Renaissance style above.

As you explore this wing, circulate counterclockwise (watching out for the tiny but jolting steps) and imagine day-to-day life in the palace. King Pedro (1334–1369) cruelly abandoned his wife and moved into the Alcázar with his mistress. He hired Muslim workers from Granada to recreate the romance of that city's Alhambra in the stark Alcázar. The designers created a microclimate engineered for coolness: water, plants, pottery, thick walls, and darkness. Even with the inevitable hodgepodge of style that comes with 600 years of renovation, it's considered Spain's best example of the Mudejar style. Notice the sumptuous ceilings; you'll see peacocks, castles, and kings that you wouldn't find in religious Muslim decor, which avoids images. The stylized Arabic script survives, creating a visual chant of verses from the Quran seen in Moorish buildings (including the Alhambra). The artisans added propagandist phrases such as "dedicated to the magnificent Sultan Pedro—thanks to God!"

The second courtyard, the smaller and more delicate Dolls' Court (Patio de las Muñecas), was for the king's private and family life. Originally, the center of the courtyard had a pool, cooling the residents and reflecting the decorative patterns once brightly painted on the walls.

• *Leave this wing from the big courtyard. Head to the staircase opposite from where you entered, and climb up into the...*

Gothic Wing: This wing of the palace shows fine tapestries from Brussels (1554). Find the hall with the six biggest tapestries. These celebrate Emperor Charles V's 1535 victory in Tunis over the Turks (described both in Spanish along the top and in Latin along the bottom). The map tapestry comes with an unusual perspective—with Africa at the top (it's supposed to be from a Barcelona aerial perspective). Find the big fortified city in the middle (Barcelona, just above eye level), Lisboa (Lisbon), Gibraltar, the west edge of Italy, Rome, Sicily, and the Mediterranean islands. The artist paints himself holding the legend—with a scale in both leagues and miles. This is an 18th-century copy of the original.

• *Head outside to...*

The Garden: The best-tended and safest in town, it's full of tropical flowers, wild cats, cool fountains, and hot tourists. The intimate geometric zone nearest the palace is the Moorish garden. The far-flung garden beyond that was the backyard of the Christian ruler.

Archivo de Indias—The Lonja Palace (across street from Alcázar) was designed by the same person who did El Escorial. Originally a market, it's the top building in Sevilla from its 16th-century glory days. Today, it houses the archive of documents from the discovery and conquest of the New World. This could be fascinating, but little of importance is on display (old maps of Havana) and there's barely a word of English (free, Mon–Sat 10:00–16:00, Sun 10:00–14:30).

Between the River and the Cathedral

Hospital de la Caridad—This Charity Hospital was founded by a nobleman in the 17th century. Peek into the fine courtyard. On the left, the chapel has some gruesome art (above both doors) illustrating that death is the great equalizer, and an altar so sweet only a Spaniard could enjoy it. The Dutch tiles depicting scenes of the Old and New Testament are a reminder of the time when the Netherlands were under Spanish rule in the mid-16th century (€3, Mon–Sat 9:00–13:30 & 15:30–19:30, Sun 9:00–18:00, tel. 954-223-232).

Golden Tower (Torre del Oro) and Naval Museum—Sevilla's historic riverside Golden Tower was the starting point and ending point for all shipping to the New World. It's named for the golden tiles that once covered it—not for all the New World booty that landed here. Since the Moors built it in the 13th century, it has been part of the city's fortifications, with a heavy chain draped across the river to protect the harbor. Today it houses a dreary little naval museum. Looking past the dried fish and charts of knots, find the mural showing the world-spanning journeys of Vasco da Gama, the model of Columbus's *Santa María* (the first ship to have landed in the New World), and an interesting mural of Sevilla in 1740. Enjoy the view from the balconies upstairs. The Guadalquivir River is now just a trickle of its former self, after canals built in the 1920s siphoned off most of its water to feed ports downstream (€1, free Tue, open Sept–July Tue–Fri 10:00–14:00, Sat–Sun 11:00–14:00, closed Mon and Aug, tel. 954-222-419).

North of the Cathedral, near Plaza Nueva

▲▲**Flamenco Dance Museum (Museo del Baile Flamenco)**— Whether you feel the need to strut your stuff, or just want to understand more about the dance that embodies the spirit of southern Spain, this newly built, high-tech museum does the trick. The grand dame of flamenco, Cristina Hoyos, has put together a project that was desperately needed in Sevilla. She combined a museum exhibit with the opportunity to take classes at any level.

The museum is housed in a restored mansion, with a performance stage underneath the patio (check the schedule for events). Interactive panels explain the basics of flamenco in multiple languages. Monitors and projection screens focus on different aspects of dance, dress, song, percussion, and guitar (€10, covered by Sevilla Card, daily 9:00–19:00, last entry 30 min before closing, tricky to find on Calle Manuel Rojas Marcos 3, about 3 blocks east of Plaza Nueva, tel. 954-340-311, www.museoflamenco.com).

Classes: If you plan to stay in Sevilla for a few days, consider scheduling a flamenco dance or guitar class in advance.

Scheduling is extremely flexible, classes of all levels and styles are available almost daily, and the teachers are superb. Average prices range from €50–80 per week (same contact information as above). Private, one-time instruction is also available. And now you have an excuse to buy a flamenco dress on Calle Sierpes.

▲**Museo Palacio de la Condesa de Lebrija**—This aristocratic mansion takes you back into the 18th century like no other place in town. The Countess of Lebrija was a passionate collector of antiquities. Her home's ground floor is paved with Roman mosaics (that you actually walk on) and lined with musty old cases of Phoenician, Greek, Roman, and Moorish artifacts—mostly pottery. To see a plush world from a time when the nobility had a private priest and their own chapel, take a quickie tour of the upstairs, which shows the palace as the countess left it when she died in 1938 (€4 for ground floor unescorted, covered by Sevilla Card, €8 includes 20-minute tour of "lived-in" upstairs—2 departures/hr; open June–Sept Mon–Fri 10:30–13:30 & 17:00–20:00, Sat 10:00–14:00, closed Sun; Oct–May Mon–Fri 10:30–13:30 & 16:30–19:30, Sat 10:00–14:00, closed Sun; Calle Cuna 8, tel. 954-227-802).

South of the Cathedral, near Plaza de España

University—Today's university was yesterday's *fábrica de tabacos* (tobacco factory), which employed 10,000 young female *cigareras*—including the saucy femme fatale of Bizet's opera *Carmen*. In the 18th century, it was the second-largest building in Spain, after El Escorial. Wander through its halls as you walk to Plaza de España. The university's bustling café is a good place for cheap tapas, beer, wine, and conversation (Mon–Fri 8:00–21:00, Sat 9:00–13:00, closed Sun).

Plaza de España—The square, the surrounding buildings, and the nearby María Luisa Park are the remains of the 1929 inter-

national fair—where for a year the Spanish-speaking countries of the world enjoyed a mutual admiration fiesta. When they finish the construction work here (it's taking years), this delightful area, the epitome of World's Fair–style building, will once again be great for people-watching (especially during the 19:00–20:00 peak paseo hour). The park's highlight is what was once the Spanish Pavilion. Its tiles (a trademark of Sevilla) show historic scenes and maps from every province of Spain (arranged in alphabetical order from Álava to Zaragoza). Climb to one of the balconies for a fine view. Beware: This is a classic haunt of thieves and con artists. Believe no one here. Thieves, posing as lost tourists, will come at you with a map unfolded to hide their speedy, greedy fingers.

Away from the Center

▲**Museo de Bellas Artes**—Sevilla's passion for religious art is preserved and displayed in its Museum of Fine Art. While most

Americans go for El Greco, Goya, and Velázquez (not a forte of this collection), this museum gives a fine look at the other, less-appreciated Spanish masters—Zurbarán and Murillo. Rather than exhausting, the museum is pleasantly enjoyable.

Cost, Hours, Location: Free, Tue 14:30–20:30, Wed–Sat 9:00–20:30, Sun 9:00–14:30, closed Mon, 15-min walk from the cathedral, Plaza Museo 9, tel. 954-220-790. Pick up the English-language floor plan, which explains the theme of each room.

Background: Several of Spain's top artists—Zurbarán, Murillo, and Velázquez—lived in Sevilla. This was Spain's wealthy commercial capital—like New York City—while Madrid was a newly built center of government, like Washington D.C. In the early 1800s, Spain's liberal government was disbanding convents and monasteries, and secular fanatics were looting churches. Thankfully, the region's religious art was rescued and hung safely here in this convent-turned-museum.

Spain's economic Golden Age—the 1500s—blossomed into the golden age of Spanish painting—the 1600s. Artists such as Zurbarán combined realism with mysticism. He painted balding saints and monks with wrinkled faces and sunburned hands. The style suited Spain's spiritual climate, as the Catholic Church used this art in its Counter-Reformation battle against the Protestant rebellion.

❸ Self-Guided Tour: The core of the collection is in Rooms 3 through 10. Most of the major works are displayed in Room 5, the convent's former chapel. It's difficult not to say "Wow!" when entering. Tour the collection starting upstairs in Room 10. Then, after exploring the first floor according to your interests, finish in the big former church (Room 5).

Francisco de Zurbarán (thoor-bar-AHN, 1598–1664) paints saints and monks, and the miraculous things they experience, presented with unblinking, crystal-clear, brightly lit, highly detailed realism. Monks and nuns could meditate upon Zurbarán's meticulous paintings (Room 10 and the room leading to 10) for hours, finding God in the details.

Zurbarán shines a harsh spotlight on his subject, creating strong shadows. Like the secluded monks themselves, Zurbarán's people stand starkly isolated against a dark, single-color background. He was the ideal painter of the austere religion of 17th-century Spain.

In Zurbarán's *St. Hugo visiting the Cartugian Monks at Supper* (Room 10), white-robed monks gather together for their

simple meal in the communal dining hall. Above them hangs a painting of Mary, baby Jesus, and John the Baptist. Zurbarán created paintings for monks' dining halls like this. His audience: celibate men and women who lived in isolation, as in this former convent, devoting their time (much of it in peaceful cloistered courtyards as you'll see in this building) to quiet meditation, prayer, and Bible study.

The *Apotheosis of St. Thomas Aquinas* (ground level, Room 5) is considered Zurbarán's most important work. It was done at the height of his career, when stark realism was all the rage. Here again Zurbarán presents the miraculous moment (when the saint gets his spiritual awakening) in a believable, down-to-earth way.

Bartolomé Murillo (mur-EE-oh, 1617–1682) was another hometown boy (see page 381). In Room 5, his *Madonna and Child* (*La Servilletta*, 1665; facing the front of the room, it's in a small room around the corner on the right) shows the warmth and appeal of his work. By about 1650, Murillo's easy-to-appreciate style had replaced Zurbarán's harsh realism.

The Immaculate Conception (several versions in the museum, ground floor, Room 5) was Murillo's favorite subject. To many Spaniards, Mary is their main connection to heaven. They pray directly to her, asking her to intercede for them with God. Murillo's *Mary*s are always receptive and ready to help.

▲▲**Basílica de la Macarena**—Sevilla's Holy Week (Semana Santa) celebrations are Spain's grandest. During the week leading up to Easter, the city is packed with pilgrims witnessing 50 processions carrying about 100 religious floats. Get a feel for this event by visiting Basílica de la Macarena (built in 1947) to see the two most impressive floats and the darling of Holy Week, the Weeping Virgin (Virgen de la Macarena, or La Esperanza; church free,

museum-€3, buy ticket at shop by entrance, covered by Sevilla Card, daily 9:30–14:00 & 17:00–20:00, taxi to Puerta Macarena or bus #C3 or #C4 from Puerta de Jerez, tel. 954-901-800).

Grab a pew and study Mary, complete with crystal teardrops. She's like a 17th-century doll with human hair and articulated arms, and even dressed with underclothes. Her beautiful expression—halfway between smiling and crying—is moving, in a Baroque way. Her weeping can be contagious—look around you. Filling a side chapel (on left) is the Christ of the Sentence (from 1654), showing Jesus the day he was condemned.

The two most important floats of the Holy Week parades—the floats that Jesus and Mary ride every Good Friday—are parked behind the altar (through the door left of the altar, show ticket).

The three-ton float that carries Jesus is slathered in gold leaf, and shows a commotion of figures acting out the sentencing of Christ (who's placed in the front of this crowd). Pontius Pilate is about to wash his hands. Pilate's wife cries as a man reads the death sentence. While pious Sevillan women wail in the streets, relays of 48 men carry this on the backs of their necks—only their feet showing under the drapes—as they shuffle through the streets from midnight to 14:00 every Good Friday. Shuffle upstairs for another perspective.

La Esperanza follows the Sentencing of Christ in the procession. Mary's smaller (1.5-ton) float, in the next room, seems all silver and candles—"strong enough to support the roof but tender enough to quiver in the soft night breeze." Mary has a wardrobe of three huge mantles (each displayed here) worn in successive years. The big, green one is from 1900. Her six-pound gold crown/halo (in a glass case in the wall) is from 1913. This float has a mesmerizing effect on the local crowds. They line up for hours, clapping, weeping, and throwing roses as it slowly works its way through the city. My Sevillan friend explained, "She knows all the problems of Sevilla and its people. We've been confiding in her for centuries. To us, she is hope. That's her name—Esperanza."

Before leaving, find the case of matador outfits (also upstairs) given to the church by bullfighters over the years. They are a form of thanks for the protection they feel they received from La Macarena. Considered the protector of bullfighters, she's big in bullring chapels. In 1912, the bullfighter José Ortega, hoping for protection, gave her the five emerald brooches she wears. It worked for eight years...until he was gored to death in the ring.

Outside, notice the best surviving bit of Sevilla's old walls. Originally Roman, what remains today is 12th-century Moorish, a reminder that for centuries Sevilla was the capital of the Islamic kingdom in Iberia.

And yes, it's from this city that a local dance band (Los del Río) changed the world by giving us "The Macarena."

Near Sevilla

Itálica—One of Spain's most impressive Roman ruins is found outside the sleepy town of Santiponce, about six miles northwest of Sevilla. Founded in 206 B.C. for wounded soldiers recuperating from the Second Punic War, Itálica became a thriving town of great agricultural and military importance. It was the birthplace of famous Roman emperors Trajan and Hadrian. Today its best-preserved ruin is its amphitheater—one of the largest in the Roman Empire—with a capacity for 30,000 spectators. Other highlights include beautiful floor mosaics, such as the one in Casa de los Pájaros (birds) that shows more than 30 species of birds. To avoid the midday heat, plan your visit to arrive early or late, and definitely bring water (€1.50; April–Sept Tue–Sat 8:30–20:30, Sun 9:00–15:00, closed Mon; Oct–March 9:00–17:30, Sun 10:00–16:00, closed Mon; tel. 955-997-376).

You can get to Itálica by bus (30-min trip, frequent departures from Sevilla's Plaza de Armas station). Drivers: Leave Sevilla heading west in the direction of Huelva; after you cross the second branch of the river, turn north on N630, and after a few miles, get off at Santiponce. Drive past pottery warehouses and through the town to the ruins at the far (west) end.

EXPERIENCES

Bullfighting

▲**Bullfights**—Some of Spain's best bullfighting is done in Sevilla's 14,000-seat bullring, the Plaza de Toros (fights on most Sundays, Easter–Oct, 18:30 or 19:30). Serious fights with adult matadors—called *corrida de toros*—are in April and October (and often sell out in advance). Summer fights are usually *novillada*, with teenage novices doing the killing. *Corrida de toros* seats range from €20 for high seats  looking into the sun to €100 for the first three rows in the shade under the royal box; *novillada* seats are half that—and easy to buy

at the arena a few minutes before show time (ignore scalpers outside; get information at TI, your hotel, or call 954-210-315.)

▲▲**Bullfight Museum**—Follow a two-language (Spanish and English), 20-minute guided tour through the bullring's strangely quiet and empty arena, its museum, the first-aid room where injured fighters are rushed, and the chapel where the matador prays before the fight. (Today, thanks to readily available blood transfusions, there have been no deaths in 28 years.) The two most revered figures of Sevilla, the Virgin of Macarena and the Christ of Gran Poder (All Power), are represented in the chapel. In the museum, you'll see great classic scenes and the heads of a few bulls—awarded the bovine equivalent of an Oscar for a particularly good fight. They were so appalled when the famous matador Manolete was killed in 1947 that they even destroyed the mother of the bull who gored him. Matadors—dressed to kill—are heartthrobs in their "suits of light." Many girls have their bedrooms wallpapered with posters of cute bullfighters. See the appendix for more on the "art" of bullfighting (€4, entrance with escorted tour only, covered by Sevilla Card, 3/hr, daily 9:30–19:00, until 15:00 on fight days, when chapel and horse room are closed).

The April Fair

For seven days each April (April 16–22 in 2007), much of Sevilla is packed into its vast fairgrounds for a grand party. The fair, seeming to bring all that's Andalusian together, feels friendly, spontaneous, and very real. The local passion for horses, flamenco, and sherry is clear—riders are ramrod straight, colorfully clad girls ride sidesaddle, and everyone's drinking sherry spritzers. Women sport outlandish dresses that would look clownish all alone but are somehow brilliant here en masse. Horses clog  the streets in an endless parade until about 20:00, when they clear out and the streets fill with exuberant locals. The party goes for literally 24 hours a day for the entire week.

Countless private party tents, or *casetas*, line the lanes. Each tent is the private party zone of a family, club, or association. You need to know someone in the group—or make friends quickly—to get in. Because of the exclusivity, it has a real family-affair feeling. In each *caseta*, everyone knows everyone. It seems like a thousand wedding parties being celebrated at the same time.

Any tourist can have a fun and memorable evening by simply crashing the party. The city's entire fleet of taxis (who'll try to charge double) and buses seems dedicated to shuttling people from downtown to the fairgrounds. With the traffic jams, you may be better off hiking: From the Golden Tower, cross the San Telmo bridge to Plaza de Cuba and hike down Calle Asunción. You'll see the towering gate to the fairgrounds in the distance. Just follow the crowds (there's no admission charge). Arrive before 20:00 to see the horses, but stay later, as the ambience improves after they giddy-up on out. Some of the larger tents are sponsored by the city and open to the public, but the best action is in the streets, where party-goers from the livelier *casetas* spill out. While private tents have bouncers, everyone is so happy, it's not tough to strike up an impromptu friendship, become a "special guest," and be invited in. The drink flows freely and the food is fun and cheap.

SHOPPING

For the best local shopping experience, follow my shopping stroll (see below). The popular pedestrian streets Sierpes, Tetuán, and Velázquez—as well as the sur-rounding lanes near Plaza Nueva—are packed with people and shops. While small shops close between 13:30 and 16:00 or 17:00, big ones such as El Corte Inglés stay open (and air-conditioned) right through the siesta. It has a super-market downstairs and a good but expensive restaurant (Mon–Sat

10:00–22:00, closed Sun). Popular souvenir items include ladies' fans, ceramics, and items from flamenco (castanets, guitars, cos-tumes) and bullfighting (posters).

Flea markets hop on Sunday: stamps and coins at Plaza del Cabildo (near the cathedral) and animals at Plaza de la Alfalfa. El Jueves ("Thursday"), held on Thursday on Calle Feria, is the oldest market in Sevilla (dating from the Moors), offering an assortment of odds and ends.

Shopping Paseo Tour

While many tourists never get beyond the cathedral and the Santa Cruz neighborhood, it's important to wander west into the lively pedestrian shopping center of town (a ▲▲ sight). These streets—on Calle Tetuán, Calle Sierpes, and Calle Cuna—also happen to be part of the oldest section of Sevilla. A walk here is a chance to join in one of Spain's liveliest paseos—that bustling celebration of life that takes place before dinner each evening, when everyone is out strolling. Locals stroll to show off their fancy shoes and make the scene. This walk (if done between 18:00 and 20:00) gives you a look at the paseo scene and the town's most popular shops. You'll pass windows displaying the best in both traditional and trendy fashion. The walk ends at a plush mansion of a local countess (open to the public).

Start on **Plaza Nueva,** a 19th-century square facing the ornate city hall, which features a statue of Ferdinand III, a local favorite because he freed Sevilla from the Moors in 1248. From here, wander the length of Calle Tetuán (notice the latest in fancy shoes—Paris Hilton would not be all that outrageous in Sevilla). Calle Tetuán becomes Velázquez, and ends at La Campana (a big intersection and popular meeting point, with the super department store, El Corte Inglés, just beyond). From La Campana, take two rights—stopping to tempt yourself with sweets at the venerable Confitería La Campana—to get to Calle Sierpes, great for shopping and strolling. Calle Sierpes is the main street of the Holy Week processions—imagine it packed with celebrants and with balconies bulging with spectators. At the corner of Sierpes and Jovellanos/Sagasta, you're near several fine shops featuring Andalusian accessories. Drop in to see how serious local women are about their fans, combs, shawls, and *mantillas* (ornate head scarves).

Andalusian women have various fans to match different dresses. The *mantilla* comes in black (worn only on Good Friday and by the mother of the groom at weddings) and white (worn at bullfights during the April Fair).

From here, turn left down Calle Sagasta. Notice that the street has two names—the modern version and a medieval one: Antigua Calle de Gallegos ("Ancient Street of the Galicians"). With the Christian victory in 1248, the Muslims were given one month to evacuate. To consolidate Christian control, settlers from the north were planted here. This street was home to the Galicians.

Finally, backtrack left along Calle Cuna, famous for its exuberant flamenco dresses and classic wedding dresses. If all this shopping makes you feel like a countess, Calle Cuna leads to the Museo Palacio de la Condesa de Lebrija (see listing on page 395).

NIGHTLIFE

▲▲**Evening Paseo**—Sevilla is meant for strolling. The areas along either side of the river between the San Telmo and Isabel II bridges (Paseo de Cristóbal Colón and Triana district; see "Eating," page 410), around Plaza Nueva, at Plaza de España, and throughout the Barrio Santa Cruz thrive every non-winter evening. On hot summer nights, even families with toddlers are out and about past midnight. Spend some time rafting through this sea of humanity. Savor the view of floodlit Sevilla by night from the far side of the river—perhaps over dinner (but the seedy Alameda de Hercules district is best avoided).

▲▲▲**Flamenco**—This music-and-dance art form has its roots in the Roma (Gypsy) and Moorish cultures. Even at a packaged "Flamenco Evening," sparks fly. The men do most of the flamboyant machine-gun footwork. The women concentrate on graceful turns and a smooth, shuffling step. Watch the musicians. Flamenco guitarists, with their lightning-fast finger-roll strums, are among the best in the world.

The intricate rhythms are set by castanets or the hand-clapping (called *palmas*) of those who aren't dancing at the moment. In the raspy-voiced wails of the singers, you'll hear echoes of the Muslim call to prayer.

Like jazz, flamenco thrives on improvisation. Also like jazz, good flamenco is more than just technical proficiency. A singer or dancer with "soul" is said to have *duende*. Flamenco is a happening, with bystanders clapping along and egging on the dancers with whoops and shouts. Get into it. For a tourist-oriented flamenco show, your hotel can get you nightclub show tickets (happily, since they snare a hefty commission for each sale). But it's easy to book a place on your own.

Casa de la Memoria de Al-Andalus ("House of the Memory of Al-Andalus"), run by Andalusian-culture devotees Sebastián and Rosana, offers more of an intimate concert with a smaller cast and more classic solos. Other, touristy flamenco shows give you all the clichés, and they can feel crass; here, you'll enjoy an elegant and classy musical experience. In an alcohol-free atmosphere, tourists sit on folding chairs circling a small stage for shows featuring flamenco, Sephardic, or other Andalusian music. Their exhibits on Sephardic and Muslim art and musical instruments are a fresh change in a city full of Baroque and Christian icons. It's also a perfect place to practice your Spanish fan *(abanico)* skills on warm nights. Summer concerts are nightly at 21:00 and 22:30 (off-season at 21:00). Wednesday concerts are Sephardic, rather than flamenco (€12, 1-hour shows vary, reservations welcome, arrive 45 min early for best seats, in Barrio Santa Cruz, adjacent to Hotel Alcántara at Ximénez de Enciso 28, tel. 954-560-670, memoria@terra.es).

Los Gallos gives nightly two-hour shows at 20:00 and 22:30

(€27 ticket includes a drink, 15 percent discount with Sevilla Card, arrive 30 min early for better seats without obstructed views, noisy bar, Plaza de la Santa Cruz 11, tel. 954-216-981, manager Nuria promises goosebumps). **El Arenal** has arguably more professional performers and a classier setting for its show (€33 including a drink, €64 with dinner, shows at 20:30 and 22:30, near bullring at Calle Rodó 7, tel. 954-216-492). **El Patio Sevillano** is more of a variety show (€32 including a drink, 15 percent discount with Sevilla Card, shows at 19:30 and 22:00, next to bullring at Paseo de Cristóbal Colón, tel. 954-214-120). These packaged shows can be a bit sterile, and an audience of tourists doesn't help. But I find both Los Gallos and El Arenal entertaining and riveting. While El Arenal may have a slight edge on talent, Los Gallos has a cozier setting, with cushy rather than hard chairs—and it's a bit cheaper.

Impromptu flamenco still erupts spontaneously in bars throughout the old town after midnight. Just follow your ears as you wander down Calle Betis, leading off Plaza de Cuba across the bridge. The **Lo Nuestro** and **Rejoneo** bars are local favorites (at Calle Betis 30 and 32).

For flamenco music without dancing, consider **La Carbonería Bar.** The sangria equivalent of a beer garden, it's a sprawling place with a variety of rooms leading to a big, open, tented area filled with young locals, casual guitar strummers, and nearly nightly flamenco music after midnight. Located just a few blocks from most of my recommended hotels, this is worth finding if you're not quite ready to end the day (no cover, €2 sangria, daily 20:00–3:00 in the morning; near Plaza Santa María: find Hotel Fernando III, the side alley Céspedes dead-ends at Levies, head left to Levies 18, unsigned door; for location, see map on page 406).

SLEEPING

All of my listings are centrally located, mostly within a five-minute walk of the cathedral. The first are near the charming but touristy Santa Cruz neighborhood. The last group is just as central but closer to the river, across the boulevard in a more workaday, less touristy zone.

Room rates as much as double during the two Sevilla fiestas (Holy Week—April 1–8 in 2007; and the weeklong April Fair, held 2 weeks after Easter—April 23–29 in 2007). In general, the busiest and most expensive months are April, May, September, and October. Hotels put rooms on the discounted push list in July and August—when people with any sense avoid this furnace—and from November through February. Prices rarely include the 7 percent IVA tax. A price range indicates low- to high-season prices (but I have not listed festival prices). Ground-floor rooms come

Sleep Code

(€1 = about $1.20, country code: 34)
S = Single, **D** = Double/Twin, **T** = Triple, **Q** = Quad, **b** = bathroom, **s** = shower only. Unless otherwise noted, credit cards are accepted, hoteliers speak enough English, and breakfast generally costs extra.

To help you easily sort through these listings, I've divided the rooms into three categories, based on the price for a standard double room with bath during high season:

$$$ **Higher Priced**—Most rooms €100 or more.
$$ **Moderately Priced**—Most rooms between €60–100.
$ **Lower Priced**—Most rooms €60 or less.

with more noise. Ask for upper floors *(piso alto)*. Always telephone to reconfirm what you think is a reservation. If you do visit in July or August, the best values are central business-class places. They offer summer discounts and provide a necessary cool, air-conditioned refuge.

Santa Cruz Neighborhood

These places are off Calle Santa María la Blanca and Plaza Santa María. The most convenient parking lot is the Cano y Cueto garage near the corner of Calle Santa María la Blanca and Menéndez Pelayo (€14/day, open 24/7, at edge of big park—unsigned and underground).

$$$ **Hotel Las Casas de la Judería** has quiet, elegant rooms and suites tastefully decorated with hardwood floors and a Spanish flair. The rooms surround a series of peaceful courtyards. This is a romantic splurge and a fine value (Sb-€90–100, Db-€135–168, extra bed-€40; low-season prices—July, Aug, late-Nov–Feb—are discounted a further 10 percent to those with this book who ask in 2007; expensive but great buffet breakfast-€16, air-con, elevator, valet parking-€16/day, on small traffic-free lane off Plaza Santa María, Callejón de Dos Hermanas 7, tel. 954-415-150, fax 954-422-170, www.casasypalacios.com, juderia@casasypalacios.com).

$$ **Hotel Amadeus** is a little gem that music-lovers will appreciate (it even has a couple of soundproofed rooms with pianos—something I've never seen anywhere else in Europe). It's lovingly decorated with a music motif around a little courtyard and a modern glass elevator that takes you to a roof terrace. While small, this 14-room place is classy and comfortable, with welcoming public spaces and a charming staff (Db-€85, big Db-€99, 2 suites-€110 and €130, air-con, elevator, parking-€14; the €7 breakfast comes on a trolley—

Santa Cruz Hotels and Restaurants

1 Hotel Las Casas de la Judería
2 Hotel Amadeus, La Música de Sevilla, Hostal Córdoba & Hostal Buen Dormir
3 Hotel Alcántara & Casa de la Memoria de Al-Andalus (Flamenco, Music)
4 Hostal San Benito
5 Corral del Agua Restaurante
6 Restaurante La Albahaca
7 Restaurante Modesto
8 Freiduría Puerta de la Carne
9 Bar Restaurante El 3 de Oro
10 Restaurante San Marco
11 Cervecería Giralda
12 Bodega Santa Cruz
13 Las Teresas Bar
14 Los Gallos Flamenco
15 To La Carbonería Bar

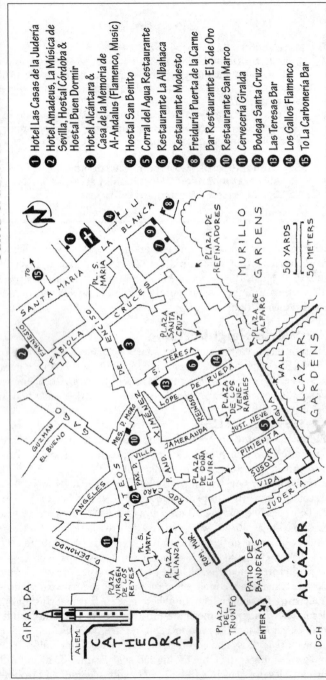

enjoy it in your room, in the lounge, or on the delightful roof garden; Calle Farnesio 6, tel. 954-501-443, fax 954-500-019, www
.hotelamadeussevilla.com, reservas@hotelamadeussevilla.com,
wonderfully run by María Luisa and her staff—Zaida and
Cristina). The owners recently opened another hotel next door,
$$ La Música de Sevilla, offering six additional, beautifully
appointed rooms; three rooms face the interior patio, and three are
streetside with small balconies (patio Db-€99, exterior Db-€125,
reserve and check in at Hotel Amadeus).

$$ Hotel Alcántara offers more comfort than character.
Well-located but strangely out of place in the midst of the Santa
Cruz jumble, it rents 21 slick rooms at a good price (Sb-€66, small
Db-€78, bigger Db twin-€87, fancy Db-€110, breakfast-€5, 10
percent cash discount with this book in 2007, air-con, elevator,
Ximénez de Enciso 28, tel. 954-500-595, fax 954-500-604, www
.hotelalcantara.net, info@hotelalcantara.net). The hotel is adjacent
to Casa de la Memoria de Al-Andalus, which offers concerts (see
page 403).

$ Hostal Córdoba, a homier and cheaper option, has 12
tidy, quiet, air-conditioned rooms, solid modern furniture, and a
showpiece plant-filled courtyard (S-€30, Sb-€35, D-€40, Db-€50,
cheaper Nov–March, includes tax, no breakfast, cash only, a tiny
lane off Calle Santa María la Blanca, Farnesio 12, tel. 954-227-498,
hostalcordoba@mixmail.com, Ana and María).

$ Hostal Buen Dormir ("Good Sleep") is a funky little fam-
ily-run place with turtles and children in the blue-tinted courtyard.
They rent 17 cheap, clean, basic rooms on a very quiet, traffic-free
lane (S-€20, D-€30, Ds-€35, Db-€40, Ts-€50, Tb-€55, air-con,
Farnesio 8, tel. 954-217-492, Miriam and Rene).

$ Hostal San Benito, with eight humble rooms, faces a tra-
ditional Sevilla courtyard buried at the end of a dead-end lane just
off Plaza Santa María. The rooms are dark, with windows that
open onto an inner courtyard. The hardworking owners don't speak
English, but offer some of the best cheap rooms in town (S-€18,
D-€36, Db-€40, Tb-€54, no breakfast, a tiny lane next to Cano y
Cueto at Calle Canarios 4, tel. 954-415-255, www.hostalsanbenito
.com, burlon11@hotmail.com, the woman of the house—Charo—
has that coo-chee-coo Charo attitude).

Near the Cathedral
$$$ Hotel Husa Los Seises, a modern, 42-room, business-class
place spliced tastefully into the tangled old town, offers a fresh
and spacious reprieve for anyone ready for good old contemporary
luxury. You'll eat breakfast amid Roman ruins. Its rooftop garden
includes a pool and a great cathedral view (Db-€158–198, Tb-
€190–222, breakfast-€15, lower prices in July–Aug and Dec–Feb,

Sevilla Hotels

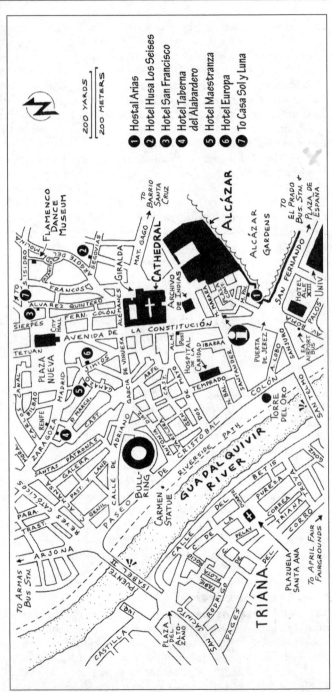

200 YARDS
200 METERS

1. Hostal Arias
2. Hotel Husa Los Seises
3. Hotel San Francisco
4. Hotel Taberna del Alabardero
5. Hotel Maestranza
6. Hotel Europa
7. To Casa Sol y Luna

air-con, elevator, valet parking-€18/day, 2 blocks northwest of cathedral at Segovias 6, tel. 954-229-495, fax 954-224-334, www .hotellosseises.com, info@hotellosseises.com).

$$ Hotel San Francisco, with a classy facade but little character, offers 16 rooms with metal doors, and a central location (Sb-€40–55, Db-€50–68, Tb-€62–80, no breakfast, air-con, elevator, small rooftop terrace, located on quiet pedestrian street at Álvarez Quintero 38, tel. 954-501-541, www.sanfranciscoh.com, info @sanfranciscoh.com, Carlos).

$ Hostal Arias is low-service and no-nonsense. Its 14 basic rooms come equipped with medieval disco balls. This funky hotel gets mixed reviews from readers, but it's cheap, central, clean, air-conditioned, and relatively quiet (big Sb-€45, Db-€58, Tb-€78, Qb-€85, Quint/b-€100, nearby parking-€14/day, elevator, between the Alcázar and Avenida de la Constitución at Calle Mariana de Pineda 9, tel. 954-226-840, fax 954-211-649, www.hostalarias.com, reservas@hostalarias.com, manager Manuel Reina speaks English, but rest of staff doesn't).

West of Avenida de la Constitución

$$$ Hotel Taberna del Alabardero is a unique hotel with only seven rooms, taking the top floor of a poet's mansion (above a classy restaurant, Taberna del Alabardero, listed in "Eating," below). It's nicely located and a great value, but often booked in advance. The ambience is perfectly 1900, and cooking classes are sometimes available (Db-€130–160, Db suite-€150–190, includes breakfast, air-con, elevator, closed in Aug, Zaragoza 20, tel. 954-502-721, fax 954-563-666, www.tabernadelalabardero.com, hotel .alabardero@esh.es).

$$ Hotel Maestranza, sparkling with loving care and charm, has 18 small, clean, simple rooms well-located on a peaceful street just off Plaza Nueva (Sb-€53, Db-€65 most of the year, Db-€80 April–May, extra bed-€20, 5 percent cash discount, family suite, no breakfast, air-con, elevator, free Internet access, Gamazo 12, tel. 954-561-070, fax 954-214-404, www.hotelmaestranza.es, sevilla @hotelmaestranza.es, Antonio).

$$ Hotel Europa is a somber and sturdy place renting 16 rooms around an elegant wicker furniture courtyard in what was a traditional old mansion (Db-€67–89, 20 percent less for Sb, 40 percent more for Tb, 10 percent discount with cash and this book in 2007, air-con, elevator, parking-€13/day, 200 yards from cathedral and Plaza Nueva on a tranquil street, Calle Jimios 5, tel. 954-500-443, fax 954-210-016, www.hoteleuropasevilla.com, info @hoteleuropasevilla.com, Claudio).

North of Plaza Nueva, Between
Plaza de la Encarnación and Plaza de la Alfalfa

$ **Casa Sol y Luna,** run by an Englishman named Geno and his Spanish wife Esther, is inexpensive, but a bit farther from the cathedral (S-€22, D-€38, Db-€45, a 10-minute walk from the cathedral at Calle Pérez Galdós 1A, tel. 954-210-682, www .casasolyluna1.com, info@casasolyluna1.com).

EATING

A popular Andalusian meal is fried fish, particularly marinated *adobo.* The soups, such as *salmorejo* (Córdoba-style super-thick gazpacho) and *ajo blanco* (almond-based with garlic), are tasty.

If you're hungry for dinner before the Spaniards are, do the tapas tango, using the tapas tips on page 34. Wash down your tapas with *fino* (chilled dry sherry) or the more refreshing *tinto de verano* ("summer red wine"), an Andalusian red wine with soda, like a mild sangria. A good light white wine is *barbadillo.*

Eating in Triana, Across the River

The colorful Triana district—south of the river, between the San Telmo and Isabel II bridges—is filled with rustic and fun eateries.

Tapas: Bars along the riverside street, Calle Betis, and the parallel street one block inland are good for tapas. Before sitting down, walk to the Santa Ana church (midway between the bridges, 2 blocks off the river), where tables spill into the square in the shadow of the floodlit church spire. It feels like the whole neighborhood is out celebrating. On Plazuela Santa Ana, two restaurants feed the neighborhood: **Taberna La Plazuela** is self-service, doing simpler fare with enticing €9 *tostones* (giant, fancy Andalusian bruschetta, good for 3–4 people) and €1.80 *montaditos* (little sandwiches). Get what you want and grab a table on the leafy square. **Restaurante Bistec,** with most of the square's tables, does grilled fish with enthusiasm. I liked *taquitos de merluza* (hake fish), but for a mix of fish, ask for *frito variado* (daily 11:30–16:00 & 20:00–24:00, Plazuela de Santa Ana, tel. 954-274-759).

For tapas in a rougher bull bar, head a block down the street, where **Bar Santa Ana,** draped in bullfighting and Weeping Virgin memorabilia, is busy filling locals from a fun list of tapas like *delicia de solomillo*—tenderloin (long hours, closed Sun, Pureza 82, tel. 954-272-102).

Riverside Dinners: For a restaurant dinner (with properly attired waiters and full menus, as opposed to tapas), consider these neighbors on Calle Betis, next to the San Telmo bridge. **Río Grande** is your candlelight-fancy option (€35 dinners, daily 13:00–16:00 & 20:00–24:00, tel. 954-273-956); its terrace is less expensive, more

Restaurants and Flamenco in Sevilla

1. Taberna La Plazuela & Restaurante Bistec
2. Bar Santa Ana
3. El Faro de Triana & La Taberna del Pescador
4. Río Grande & Restaurante La Primera del Puente
5. Horno San Buenaventura Café
6. Bodega Morales & Freiduría La Isla
7. El Buzo Restaurant
8. Cafetería Mesón Serranito
9. Bodega Paco Góngora
10. Restaurante Enrique Becerra
11. Mercado del Arenal (Market)
12. Taberna del Alabardero
13. El Arenal (Flamenco)
14. El Patio Sevillano (Flamenco)
15. Lo Nuestro & Rejoneo Bars
16. 5J Bar

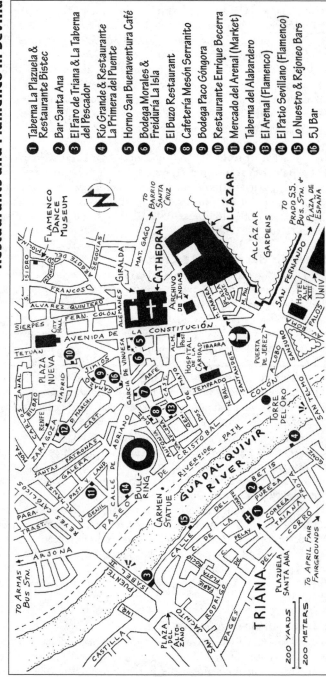

casual, and a better value. Next door, the simpler **Restaurante La Primera del Puente** serves about the same thing with nearly the same view for half the price (Thu–Tue 11:30–17:00 & 20:00–24:00, closed Wed and the last half of Aug, tel. 954-276-918).

At the Isabel II bridge, in the yellow bridge tower, **El Faro de Triana** offers inexpensive tapas, a €6 fixed-price lunch, €15 à la carte dinners, and the best views over the river from the top floor (Thu–Tue 8:00–24:00, closed Wed, tel. 954-336-192). While they have four eating zones, the rooftop and outside riverside tables are best.

Nearby, in tippy tables lined up along the riverbank, **La Taberna del Pescador** (along with a couple other places) serves from a bigger menu (more salads). Locals order *pescados fritos* (fried fish) *raciones* for €8—maximum romance at a minimum price (Wed–Mon 12:00–16:00 & 20:00–23:00, closed Tue, Puente de Isabel II, tel. 954-330-069).

Tapas in Barrio Santa Cruz

For tapas, the Barrio Santa Cruz is trendy and *romántico*. Plenty of atmospheric-but-touristy restaurants fill the neighborhood near the cathedral and along Calle Santa María la Blanca.

From the cathedral, walk up Mateos Gago, where several classic old bars—with the day's tapas scrawled on chalkboards—keep tourists and locals well fed and watered. (Turn right at Mesón del Moro for several more.)

Cervecería Giralda is a long-established meeting place for locals. It's famous for its fine tapas (confirm prices, stick with straight items on menu rather than expensive trick specials proposed by waiters; long hours, no food 16:00–20:00, at Mateos Gago 1).

A block farther, you'll find **Bodega Santa Cruz** (a.k.a. **Las Columnas**), a popular standby with good cheap tapas and *montaditos* (€2 sandwiches listed on chalkboards). You can keep an eye on the busy kitchen from the bar or hang out like a cowboy at the tiny stand-up tables out front.

At the next intersection, turn right off Mateos Gago onto Calle Mesón del Moro, which leads past the recommended San Marco pizzeria to **Las Teresas,** a fine and characteristic small bar draped in fun photos. It serves good tapas from a tight little user-friendly menu (daily, Calle Santa Teresa 2, tel. 954-213-069). Prices at the bar and outside tables (for fun tourist-watching) are the same.

Dining in Barrio Santa Cruz

Corral del Agua Restaurante, a romantic pink-tablecloth place with classy indoor and charming courtyard seating, serves fine Andalusian cuisine deep in the Barrio Santa Cruz (plan on €16 entrées, Mon–Sat 12:00–16:00 & 20:00–24:00, closed Sun, arrive early or reserve, Calle Agua 6, tel. 954-224-841).

Restaurante La Albahaca fills a luxurious mansion, with tables spilling onto a quaint Santa Cruz square, offering French Basque and Spanish food in a convenient location next to the Los Gallos flamenco club (fixed-price meal–€29, plates–€18, Mon–Sat 13:00–16:00 & 20:30–24:00, closed Sun, air-con, Plaza de la Santa Cruz 12, tel. 954-220-714).

Restaurante Modesto is a bustling local favorite serving pricey but top-notch Andalusian fare—especially fish—with atmospheric outdoor seating and forgettable indoor seating. They offer creative, fun meals—look around before ordering—and a good €17 daily fixed-price meal with energetic, often-pushy waiters. Their mixed salad is a meal (daily 12:00–17:00 & 20:00–24:00, just off Santa Cruz near Santa María la Blanca at Cano y Cueto 5, tel. 954-416-811).

Eating Cheap in Barrio Santa Cruz

Freiduría Puerta de la Carne and Bar Restaurante El 3 de Oro is a fried-fish-to-go place, with great outdoor seating and a restaurant across the street that serves fine wine or beer. You can order a cheap cone of your choice of tasty fish and sip a nice drink (served by a waiter from the restaurant), almost dining for the cost of a picnic. Stand in line and study the photos of the various kinds of seafood available—*un quarto* (250 grams for about €5) serves one (daily until 24:00, Santa María la Blanca 34, tel. 954-426-820).

Restaurante San Marco offers cheap pizza and fun, basic Italian cuisine under the arches of what was an Arab bath in the Middle Ages (and a disco in the 1990s). The atmosphere is air-conditioned and easygoing (good salads, pizza, and pasta for €8, daily 13:15–16:30 & 20:15–24:00, Calle Mesón del Moro 6, tel. 954-564-390).

Eating with Atmosphere Along Calle García de Vinuesa

I don't like the restaurants surrounding the cathedral, but many good places are just across Avenida de la Constitución. Calle García de Vinuesa leads past several colorful and cheap tapas places to a busy corner surrounded with happy eateries.

Horno San Buenaventura, across from the cathedral, is slick, chrome-filled, spacious, and handy for tapas, coffee, pastries, and ice cream (open daily, light meals are posted by the door, good quiet seating upstairs).

Bodega Morales is farther up Calle García de Vinuesa, at #11. While the front area is more of a drinking bar, go in the back section (around the corner) to munch tiny sandwiches *(montaditos)* and tapas, and sip wine among huge kegs. Everything is the same price (*montaditos*-€1.80, tapas-€1.80, half-*raciones* €6—order at the bar), with the selections chalked onto giant adobe jugs. Request their English menu at the bar (Mon–Sat 12:00–16:00 & 20:00–24:00, closed Sun, tel. 954-22-1242).

Freiduría La Isla, next door, has been frying fish since 1938 (they just renovated and changed the oil). Along with *pescado frito*, they also sell wonderful homemade potato chips and fried almonds. Try their €5 *adobo* (marinated shark) or *frito variado* for a fish sampler. Their €1.20 gazpacho is a great starter (Mon 20:00–23:30, Tue–Sat 13:00–15:30 & 20:00–23:30, closed Sun).

At the end of Calle García de Vinuesa, angle right and you'll find several good places. The **"5J" Bar** on the corner is a mod alternative to all the traditional bars—popular with locals for its ham.

The **El Buzo** restaurant is a busy neighborhood place on a lively street corner, with good outdoor seating and homey indoor seating, frisky service, and great fish and seafood (€15 meals, more with seafood, be careful—appetizers are priced per person and they push expensive options, daily 12:00–24:00, Calle Antonia Díaz 5, tel. 954-210-231). Just down the street, **Cafetería Mesón Serranito** is full of bull lore and locals consuming €7 *platos combinados* (Antonia Díaz 4, tel. 954-211-243).

Near Plaza Nueva

Restaurante Enrique Becerra is a fancy little 10-table place popular with local foodies. It's well-known for its gourmet Andalusian cuisine and fine wine (€40 dinners, Mon–Sat 13:00–16:30 & 20:00–24:00, closed Sun, reservations essentially required, Gamazo 2, tel. 954-213-049). Drop in to their tapas bar for fine snacks and wine by the glass if you have a tighter budget.

Bodega Paco Góngora is colorful and a bit classier than a tapas bar, with a tight dining area and a popular tapas counter that specializes in fish (tapas at the bar only). Its sit-down meals are well-presented and reasonable (daily 12:00–16:00 & 20:00–24:00, ask for the English menu, off Plaza Nueva at Calle Padre Marchena 1, tel. 954-214-139).

Mercado del Arenal, the covered fish-and-produce market, is perfect for hungry photographers (with a small café/bar for breakfast inside, Mon–Sat 9:00–14:30, closed Sun, not lively on Mon, on Calle Pastor y Landero at Calle Arenal, just beyond bullring). A more bustling market recently opened, just across the Isabel II bridge in Triana.

Dining Between the Cathedral and Plaza Nueva

Taberna del Alabardero, one of Sevilla's finest restaurants, serves refined Spanish cuisine in chandeliered elegance just a couple of blocks from the cathedral. If you order à la carte it will add up to about €45 a meal, but for €50 you can have a fun, seven-course fixed-price meal with lots of little surprises from the chef. Or consider their €15 starter sampler, followed by an entrée (daily 13:00–16:00 & 20:00–24:00, closed Aug, air-con, reservations smart, Zaragoza 20, tel. 954-502-721). The service in the fancy upstairs dining rooms gets mixed reviews (carefully read and understand your bill)...but the setting is stunning.

Taberna del Alabardero Student-Served Lunch: Their ground-floor dining rooms (elegant but nothing like upstairs) are popular with local office workers for their great-value, student-chef fixed-price sampler (daily 13:00–16:30, €12 for three delightful courses Mon–Fri, €17 Sat-Sun). To avoid a wait, arrive before 13:30.

TRANSPORTATION CONNECTIONS

Note that many destinations are served by both trains and buses.

From Sevilla by Train to: Madrid (2.5 hrs by AVE express train, departures 7:00–23:00 on the hour, €10 reservation fee with railpass, see page 264 for more on the Sevilla–Madrid train route), **Córdoba** (hourly, 1.5 hrs for €6; 45 min by speedy AVE for €22), **Málaga** (7/day, 2.5 hrs), **Ronda** (6/day, 4 hrs, change at Bobadilla), **Granada** (4/day, 3 hrs), **Jerez** (12/day, 1.25 hrs), **Barcelona** (3/day, 8.5–11 hrs), **Algeciras** (3/day, 5 hrs, change at Bobadilla). Trains run to **Lisbon,** Portugal, but it's the slowest option (take AVE to Madrid and then the pricey night train to Lisbon)—much better is the bus (see below). Train info: tel. 902-240-202, www.renfe.es.

By Bus to: Madrid (13/day, €17), **Córdoba** (9/day, 2 hrs), **Málaga** (10/day, 7 direct, 2.5 hrs, connects to Nerja), **Ronda** (6/day, 2.5 hrs, less on weekends), **Tarifa** (4/day, 3 hrs), **La Línea/Gibraltar** (4/day, 4 hrs), **Granada** (10/day, 7 direct—3 hrs *directo*, 4 hrs *ruta*), **Arcos** (2/day, 2 hrs, more departures with a change in Jerez), **Jerez** (7/day, 1.5 hrs), **Barcelona** (2/day), **Algeciras** (4/day, 3.5 hrs). Bus info: tel. 954-908-040 but rarely answered, go to TI for latest schedule info.

The best way to get to **Lisbon,** Portugal, is by bus (Alsa offers 2/day, 7 hrs, €39 by way of Faro, departs Plaza de Armas station). **Lagos,** Portugal has a direct bus (€18, 2/day, about 7 hrs, buy ticket a day or two in advance May–Oct, schedule from **Sevilla to Lagos:** Mon-Fri at 7:30 & 16:30, runs year-round, confirm schedule, tel. 954-908-040 or 954-901-160). The bus departs from Sevilla's Plaza de Armas bus station and arrives at the Lagos bus station. If you'd like to visit Tavira on the way to Lagos, purchase a bus ticket to Tavira, have lunch there, then take the train to Lagos.

CÓRDOBA

Straddling a sharp bend of the Guadalqivir River, Córdoba has a glorious Roman and Moorish past, once serving as a regional capital for both empires. It's home to Europe's best Islamic sight after Granada's Alhambra: the Mezquita, a mosque that dates from A.D. 784. When you step inside the mosque—magical in its grandeur—you can imagine Córdoba as the center of a thriving and sophisticated culture. During the Dark Ages, when much of Europe turned inward, Córdoba was known for religious tolerance, artistic expression, and dedication to philosophy and the sciences.

Planning Your Time

Córdoba is worth an overnight stop. See the sights in town during the day, take the bus to Madinat al-Zahra (Moorish palace ruins) the next morning, return to Córdoba in the afternoon, and then move on to your next destination. If you're only in town for the day, go straight to the Mezquita.

ORIENTATION

Córdoba's big draw is the mosque-turned-cathedral called the Mezquita. Most of the town's major sights are nearby, including the Alcázar, a former royal castle. A surviving Roman bridge spans the marshy Guadalqivir River (a prime bird-watching area). North of the mosque are the main shopping areas and the Art Deco–filled Plaza de las Tendillas. A bit farther north, Art Nouveau buildings line Avenida del Gran Capitán, which intersects with Avenida de América, where the train station is located.

Tourist Information

Córdoba has four friendly tourist offices. The TI in the **train station**—convenient for those arriving by AVE train or bus—has a lot of information and a room-finding service (Mon–Fri 9:30–14:00 & 16:30–19:30, Sat–Sun 9:30–14:30 & 16:30–19:30, tel. 957-201-774). A small kiosk is set up in **Plaza de las Tendillas** (daily 10:00–13:30 & 18:00–22:00). Two more TIs are close to the major sights; one is across from the **Mezquita** (Mon–Fri 9:30–14:00 & 16:30–19:30, Sat–Sun 9:30–14:30 & 16:30–19:00, tel. 957-201-774), and another is opposite the **Alcázar** (daily 9:30–14:30 & 16:30–19:00). The TIs have shorter, erratic hours in winter (for specifics, check the TI's official Web site, www.turismodecordoba.org).

Córdoba Card: This card, sold at any TI, gives you free admission to all of the city's major sights (including all the sights I list below); a few minor discounts on restaurants and shopping; and a free bus ride to Madinat al-Zahra (you must make arrangements in advance at the TI). The card also includes a free town walk with a local guide; make a reservation at the TI—they'll give you a slip of paper with your tour's scheduled time. You can buy the card only at Córdoba's TIs, not at participating sights. If you plan to see the top four attractions—Mezquita, Alcázar, Synagogue, and Madinat al-Zahra—the card pays for itself. The card is valid for 24 hours from the time you visit the first sight or go on the walking tour, but you can visit Madinat al-Zahra on the day after your card expires. A one-day card is the best value (€17/1 day, www.cordobacard.com).

Arrival in Córdoba

By Train or Bus: Córdoba's train station is located on Avenida de América, just northwest of the old town. The bus station is across the street from the train station on Avenida Vía Augusta (to the north). It's about a 25-minute walk from either station to the old town. You'll have better luck storing luggage at the bus station (at the back) than at the train station.

At the modern train station, built in 1991 to accommodate the high-speed AVE train line, there are ATMs, restaurants, a variety of shops, a TI booth, an information counter, and a small lounge for first-class AVE passengers. Taxis and local buses are just outside (follow signs to bus station); a taxi ride to the Mezquita costs about €5.

The only local bus from the train station to the old town (#3) does a long, slow loop through most of Córdoba (eventually stopping one block from the Mezquita); a better option is to ride it only to Plaza de las Tendillas and walk 15 minutes from there. Because the bus does a one-way loop, if you take the #3 from the old town back to the bus and train stations, it's much quicker.

Córdoba

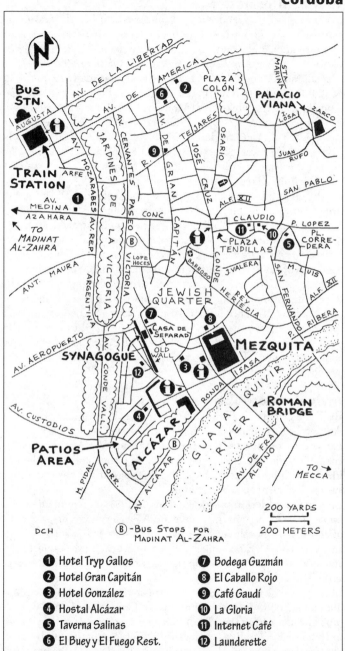

B-Bus Stops for Madinat Al-Zahra

200 YARDS
200 METERS

DCH

1 Hotel Tryp Gallos
2 Hotel Gran Capitán
3 Hotel González
4 Hostal Alcázar
5 Taverna Salinas
6 El Buey y El Fuego Rest.
7 Bodega Guzmán
8 El Caballo Rojo
9 Café Gaudí
10 La Gloria
11 Internet Café
12 Launderette

To walk from the train station to the Mezquita, make a left on Avenida de América and a right on Avenida del Gran Capitán, which becomes a pedestrian zone; when it ends, ask someone "*¿Dónde está la Mezquita?*" You'll be directed downhill, through the whitewashed old Jewish Quarter.

Helpful Hints

Closed Days: Many sights—the Synagogue, the Alcázar, and Madinat al-Zahra—are closed on Monday, while the Palacio de Viana is closed Sunday. The Mezquita is open daily, but closes for Sunday Mass.

Festival: During the first half of May, Córdoba hosts the Concurso Popular de Patios Cordobeses—a patio contest (also see "Patios," page 425).

Internet Access: Córdoba has very few places to check e-mail. **La Emp** is the most centrally located, just down from Plaza de las Tendillas at Calle Claudio Marcelo 14 (Mon–Fri 10:00–14:00 & 17:30–21:30, Sat 10:00–14:00, closed Sun).

Laundry: The helpful staff at **Sol y Mar** will quickly wash, dry, and fold your laundry. They'll usually have it ready for pickup on the same day (€11/load, cheaper for self-service, Mon–Fri 9:00–13:30 & 17:00–20:30, Sat 9:30–13:30, closed Sun, Doctor Fleming 8).

SIGHTS

The Mezquita

Córdoba's Mezquita, worth ▲▲▲, was built on a ruined cathedral, served as a mosque, and is now a cathedral again. The massive former mosque—now with a 16th-century church rising up from the middle—was once the center of Western Islam and the wonder of the medieval world. It's remarkably well-preserved, giving today's visitors a chance to soak up the ambience of Islamic Córdoba in its 10th-century prime. Avoid the congestion of midday crowds by coming early or late (€8, covered by Córdoba Card, free entry until 10:00 Mon–Sat; Mon–Sat 8:30–19:30, Sun 8:30–10:15 & 14:00–19:30; tel. 957-470-512).

➲ Self-Guided Tour: The mosque reveals itself bit by bit. You enter through the **Patio de Naranjas.** When this was a mosque, the Muslim faithful would gather in this courtyard in the shade of orange trees to ritually wash themselves before entering. Gaze up through the trees for magnificent views of the Baroque bell tower, which encases the original minaret—the tower where a muezzin would call out five times a day to alert Muslims to face Mecca and pray.

Interior: Entering the church from the Patio, you pass from an orchard of orange trees into a forest of columns. The 850 red  and blue columns are topped with double arches—one horseshoe arch atop another—made from alternating red brick and white stone. Many of the columns and capitals (of marble, porphyry, jasper, and onyx) were recycled from ancient Roman ruins and conquered Visigoth churches. As the columns seem to recede to infinity, they may have been intended to reflect the immensity and complexity of Allah's creation. To achieve this effect, the solution was to build further upward from the original structure. Supporting such a tall ceiling with thin columns required extra bracing with the double arches you see—a beautiful way to invent a practical solution.

At 85,000 square feet (including the Patio), the Mezquita is nearly as big as St. Peter's Basilica in Rome, but the low ceilings and dense columns create a different atmosphere than many religious buildings, whether churches or mosques. Unfortunately, the Mezquita is dimmer today than intended, because entrances to the Patio and the street were later closed up by Christians.

• *From the entrance, find the* **Roman mosaic** *nearby from a Temple of Janus that stood here long before the mosque. Roman Corduba was the main city of central Spain. Walk in the same direction as the rows of arches (chapels on right, back of cathedral choir on left) to locate the mihrab—the ornately decorated Muslim prayer niche—in the far south wall.*

Mihrab: This was the focus of the original mosque and the highlight of the Mezquita today. Picture 7,000 men kneeling in prayer, facing the mihrab, rocking forward to touch their heads to the ground, and saying, *"Allahu Akbar, La illa a il Allah, Muhammad razul Allah"*—"Allah is great, there is no god but Allah, and Muhammad is his prophet."

• *Approach the mihrab at the far south wall—bypassing, for now, the cathedral rising from the center of the Mezquita.*

The mihrab, a feature found in all mosques, is a decorated "niche"—in this case, more like a small room with a golden-arch entrance—that served as the focal point of the mosque. In a service, the imam (prayer leader) stood here to read scripture and give sermons. The mihrab sits in a screened-off room (*maqsura*, or prayer hall) reserved for the emirs and caliphs who ruled the surrounding state of Al-Andalus. Built (962–965) by Al-Hakam II, the room reflects the wealth of Córdoba in its prime. Three thousand pounds of multicolored glass-and-enamel cubes panel the walls and domes in mosaics designed by Byzantine craftsmen, depicting flowers and quotes from the Quran. Overhead rises a colorful, starry dome with skylights and interlocking lobe-shaped arches.

In most Muslim mosques, the mihrab indicates the direction the faithful should face during prayer, namely toward the holy city of Mecca. This is where Muhammad first received his call, but contrary to popular belief, Muslims face Mecca not for that reason but because it's the city of the prophet Abraham. Mecca (in modern Saudi Arabia) is east of Córdoba, but get out your compass, and you'll see that this mihrab actually faces roughly south, towards Kenya, Africa. One theory is that Abd Al-Rahman and his (homesick?) Umayyad descendents built the mosque facing the direction Mecca is from their ancestral hometown of Damascus.

Visigoth Ruins, Villaviciosa Chapel, and Royal Chapel: On display in the corner to the right of the mihrab are some of the **Visigoth ruins** of the fifth-century Christian church of San Vicente that preceded the mosque. Abd Al-Rahman I bought the church/monastery from his Christian subjects before leveling it to build the mosque.

In 1236, Saint-King Ferdinand III conquered the city and turned the mosque into a church. Still, the locals continued to call it La Mezquita, and left the structure virtually unchanged. The exceptions are the **Villaviciosa Chapel** and **Royal Chapel** (Capilla Real), built for Christian worship, but lavishly decorated in the 1370s in Mudejar style—*azulejos* (tiles), lobed arches, and stucco-work—by Muslims still living in the city. These days the Villaviciosa Chapel has two sides with non-uniform arches. The Royal Chapel is completely closed off, but the tall, decorative walls and dome are easily visible.

• *Circle back to the left of the mihrab/maqsura to find the Baroque* ***Treasury*** *(Tesoro), with display cases of religious artifacts and the enormous monstrance used during Holy Week.*

From here, it's fairly apparent from the general outlines of the building how this great mosque was built in stages, over two centuries, by four different rulers:

1) The original mosque—the area near the entrance, north of the cathedral—was built by Abd Al-Rahman I (784–786).

2) As Córdoba itself grew, the mosque was expanded southward—where the cathedral now stands—by Abd Al-Rahman II (833–852).

3) At the city's peak, Al-Hakam II built the extension south

Islamic Córdoba (756–1236): Medieval Europe's Cultural Capital

After his family was slaughtered by political rivals (A.D. 750), 20-year-old Prince Abd Al-Rahman fled the royal palace at Damascus, headed west across North Africa, and went undercover among the Berber tribesmen of Morocco. For six years he avoided assassination while building a power base among his fellow Arab expatriates and the local Muslim Berbers. As an heir to the title of "caliph," or ruler of Islam, he sailed north and claimed Moorish Spain as his own, confirming his power by decapitating his enemies and sending their salted heads to the rival caliph in Baghdad. This split in Islam parallels the divide in Christianity between Protestants and Catholics.

Thus began an Islamic flowering in southern Spain under Abd Al-Rahman's family, the Umayyads. They dominated Sevilla and Granada, ruling the independent state of "Al-Andalus," with their capital at Córdoba.

By the year 950—when the rest of Europe was mired in poverty, ignorance, and superstition—Córdoba was Europe's greatest city, rivaling Constantinople and Baghdad. It had more than 100,000 people (Paris had a third that many), with hundreds of mosques, palaces, and public baths. The streets were paved and lighted at night with oil lamps, and running water was piped in from the outskirts of the city. Medieval visitors marveled at the size and luxury of the Mezquita mosque, a symbol that the

of the cathedral, including the lavish mihrab (961–976).

4) Finally, Al-Mansur added the massive (and brighter) expansion to the east, turning the rectangular mosque into a square (987).

Remarkably, each ruler kept to Abd Al-Rahman I's original vision—of rows and rows of multicolored columns topped by double arches. Then came the...

Cathedral: Rising up in the middle of the forest of columns is the cathedral, oriented in the Christian tradition facing the altar at the east end. It's easy to look at the rich decoration and forget that you were in a former mosque just seconds ago.

In 1523, Córdoba's bishop proposed building this church in the Mezquita's center. The town council opposed it, but King Charles V ordered it done. However, when he saw the final product, he declared that they'd destroyed something unique to build something ordinary.

The basic structure is late Gothic with obvious Manueline/Plateresque columns. The Baroque-era choir stalls (1750) are made of New World mahogany, and the twin pulpits feature a marble

Umayyads of Spain were the equal of the caliphs of Baghdad.

This Golden Age was marked by a remarkable spirit of tolerance and cooperation among the three great monotheistic religions: Islam, Judaism, and Christianity. The university rang with voices in Arabic, Hebrew, and Latin, sharing their knowledge of *al-jibra* (algebra), medicine, law, and literature. The city fell under the enlightened spell of the ancient Greeks, and Córdoba's 70 libraries bulged with translated manuscripts of Plato and Aristotle, works that would later inspire medieval Christians.

Ruling over the Golden Age were two energetic leaders—Abd Al-Rahman III (912–961) and Al-Hakam II (961–976)—who conquered territory, expanded the Mezquita, and boldly proclaimed themselves caliphs.

Córdoba's Y1K crisis brought civil wars that toppled the caliph (1031), splintering Al-Andalus into several kingdoms. Córdoba came under the control of the Almoravids (Berbers from North Africa), who were less sophisticated than the Arab-based Umayyads. Then a wave of even stricter Islam swept through Spain, bringing the Almohads to power (1147) and driving Córdoba's best and brightest into exile. The city's glory days were over, and it was replaced by Sevilla and Granada as the centers of Spanish Islam. In 1236, Christians conquered the city, it declined in importance, and "Ave Marias" soon echoed through the columns of the mosque.

bull, lion, and eagle. The nave's towering Renaissance arches and dome emphasize the triumph of Christianity over Islam in Córdoba.

Synagogue (Sinagoga)

Rich Mudejar decorations—of intertwined flowers, arabesques, and Stars of David—plaster the inside walls of this small Jewish synagogue (€0.30, covered by Córdoba Card, Tue–Sat 9:30–14:00 & 15:30–17:30, Sun 9:30–13:30, closed Mon, Calle de los Judíos 20, tel. 957-202-928). What appear to be quotes from the Quran in Arabic are actually quotes from the Bible in Hebrew. On the east wall (the symbolic direction of Jerusalem), find the niche for the Ark, where they kept the scrolls of the Torah (the Jewish scriptures, including the first five books of the Christian Bible). The upstairs gallery was reserved for women.

The synagogue was built in 1315, under Christian rule, but the Islamic decoration has roots way back to Abd Al-Rahman I (see sidebar). During Muslim times, Córdoba's sizable Jewish community was welcomed, though they paid substantial taxes to the city—money that enlarged the Mezquita and generated good will. That good will came in handy when Córdoba's era of prosperity and mutual respect came to an end with the arrival of the intolerant Almohad Berbers. Christians and Jews were repressed, and brilliant minds—such as the rabbi and philosopher Maimonides (see below)—left for safer climates.

The Christian Reconquista of Córdoba (1236) brought another brief period of religious tolerance, and this synagogue was built, a joint effort by Christians, Jews, and Muslim (Mudejar) craftsmen. By the end of the 14th century, Spain's Jews were again persecuted, then were finally expelled or forced to convert in 1492. This is only one of three surviving synagogues in Spain built before the completion of the Reconquista, and it's preserved largely unaltered.

Near the synagogue, you'll find...

Statues of Maimonides and Averroes: Statues honor two of Córdoba's deepest-thinking homeboys—one Jewish, one Muslim—who both fell victim to the wave of Islamic intolerance after the fall of the Umayyad caliphate. (Find Maimonides just south of the synagogue. Averroes is northwest of the synagogue, outside the Puerta de Almodovar gate.)

Maimonides (1135–1204) was born in Córdoba and raised on both Jewish scripture and Aristotle's philosophy.  Like many tolerant Córdobans, he saw no conflict between the two. Maimonides—sometimes called the "Jewish Aquinas"—wrote the *Guide of the Perplexed* (in Arabic), in which he asserted (as the Christian philosopher St. Thomas Aquinas later would) that secular knowledge and religious faith could go hand-in-hand.

Córdoba changed in 1147, when the fundamentalist Almohads assumed power. Maimonides was driven out, eventually finding work in Cairo as the sultan's doctor. Today tourists, Talmudic scholars, and fans of Aquinas rub the statue's foot for good luck.

The story of **Averroes** (1126–1198) is a mirror image of Maimonides', except that Averroes was a Muslim lawyer, not a Jewish doctor. He became the medieval world's number one authority on Aristotle, influencing Aquinas. Averroes' biting tract *The Incoherence of the Incoherence* attacked narrow-mindedness, asserting that secular philosophy (for the elite) and religious

Patios

In Córdoba, patios are taken very seriously, as shown by the fiercely fought contest that takes place the first half of every May to pick the city's most  picturesque. Patios, a common feature of houses throughout Andalucía, have a long history here. The Romans used them to cool off, and the Moors added lush, decorative touches. The patio functioned as a quiet outdoor living room, an oasis from the heat. Inside elaborate ironwork gates, roses, geraniums, and jasmine spill down whitewashed walls, while fountains play and caged birds sing. Some patios are owned by individuals, some are communal courtyards for several homes, and some grace public buildings like museums or convents.

Today, homeowners take pride in these mini-paradises, and have no problem sharing them with tourists. Keep an eye out for square metal signs that indicate historic homes. As you wander Córdoba's backstreets, pop your head into any wooden door that's open. The owners won't mind (they keep inner gates locked), and you may be treated to a view of a picture-perfect patio. A concentration of previous patio-contest award-winners runs along Calle San Basilio and Calle Martín Roa, just across from the Alcázar gardens.

faith (for the masses) both led to truth. The Almohads banished him from the city and burned his books, ending four centuries of Córdoban enlightenment.

More Sights in Córdoba

Casa de Sefarad—Set inside a restored 14th-century home directly across from the synagogue, this interpretive museum brings to life Córdoba's rich Jewish past. Five rooms around a central patio are themed to help you understand different aspects of daily life for Spain's former Jewish community. The basement contains kitchen pots, dishes, and utensils, along with objects used in celebrations. The rooms upstairs focus on contributions from women in the fine arts and sciences; Jewish holidays; and musical traditions. Most displays have English descriptions (€4, Mon–Sat 11:00–19:00, Sun 11:00–14:00, guided tours in English available for small groups, at the corner of Calle Judíos and Calle Averroes, tel. 957-421-404, www.casadesefarad.com). Weekly **concerts** in the patio happen most Fridays at 20:00—reservations are smart.

Alcázar de los Reyes Cristianos—Literally the "Castle of the Christian Monarchs," this fortress sits strategically on the Guadalqivir River. Constant reuse and recycling of the building has left very little of the original Visigothic structure, which was built along the Roman walls. The castle was rebuilt and expanded by the Moors, who added gardens and an enormous library. Ferdinand and Isabel donated the castle to the Inquisition in 1482, and it became an administrative and ecclesiastical center. It was central in the church's effort to discover "false converts to Christianity"—mostly Jews who had decided not to flee Spain in 1492. The interior is currently threadbare, with the exception of large Roman mosaics uncovered in the Plaza de Corredera. Medusa could use a comb, but don't stare too long (€4, covered by Córdoba Card; May–mid-June Tue–Sun 10:00–14:00 & 17:30–19:30, closed Mon; mid-June–mid-Sept Tue–Sun 8:30–14:30, closed Mon; erratic hours in winter—check with TI).

Palacio de Viana—Decidedly off the beaten path, this former palatial estate is a 20-minute walk northeast from the cluster of sights near the Mezquita. With a guided tour, you'll be whisked through each room of an exuberant 16th-century estate. An English handout drudges through the dates and origin of each important piece, but the house is best enjoyed by ignoring the guide and gasping at the massive collection of—for lack of a better word—stuff. Decorative-art fans will have a field day. The sight is known as the "patio museum" for its 12 connecting patios, each with a different theme (house-€6, patios only-€3, covered by Córdoba Card; Aug and Oct–May  Mon–Fri 10:00–13:00 & 16:00–18:00, closed Sun; June–July and Sept Mon–Fri 9:00–14:00, Sat 10:00–13:00, closed Sun; confirm hours at TI, no photos inside, Plaza Don Gome 2, tel. 957-496-741).

Away from the Center

Madinat al-Zahra (Medina Azahara)—The ruins of a once-fabulous palace of the caliph, five miles northwest of Córdoba, were completely forgotten until excavations began in the early 20th century. This site was a power center built in A.D. 929 to replace Córdoba. Legend has it that Abd Al-Rahman III erected it on a whim to please his favorite concubine, but recent investigations have discovered that it was much more important than a love token. Madinat al-Zahra was both a palace and an entirely new capital city—the "City of the Flower"—covering nearly half a square mile (only about 10 percent has been uncovered). Extensively planned with an orderly design, Madinat al-Zahra was meant to symbolize and project a new discipline on an increasingly unstable Moorish empire in Spain. It didn't work. Only 75 years later, the city was looted and

destroyed. No wonder it was forgotten for so long.

What remains is more like a jigsaw puzzle that is being slowly reconstructed. Throughout the site are millions of bits and pieces waiting for reassembly by patient archaeologists. Upper terrace excavations have uncovered stables and servants' quarters. (The terraced location shows off the surrounding countryside well.) Farther downhill, the house of a high-ranking official has been partially reconstructed. Continuing around to reach the lowest level, you'll come to the remains of the mosque—placed at a diago-

nal, facing true east. The highlight of the visit is an elaborate reconstruction of the caliph's throne room, capturing a moody world of horseshoe arches and delicate stucco. Accounts by contemporaries (which border on legend) say the palace featured waterfall walls, lions in cages, and—in the center of the throne room—a basin filled with mercury, reflecting the colorful walls. The effect likely humbled anyone fortunate enough to see the caliph.

Cost and Hours: €1.50, covered by Córdoba Card, Tue–Sat 10:00–20:30, Sun 10:00–14:00, closed Mon.

Getting There: Madinat al-Zahra is located on a back road five miles from Córdoba. By **car,** head to Avenida de Medina Azahara (one block south of the train station), following signs for Highway A431. Go through Plaza del Poeta ibn Zaydun and turn onto Calle Periodista Quesada Chacón, still following A431. It curves to the right and becomes Carretera a Palma del Río. Turn right at signposted CV119, and continue on to the site.

No regular public transportation goes to the ruins, but you can get there via a tourist **bus**—set up by the TI—that leaves in the morning and returns two hours later (€5, free with Córdoba Card, bus ticket includes informative English booklet, runs year-round, Tue–Fri at 11:00, Sat–Sun at 10:00 and 11:00, sight closed Mon). Catch the bus either at Avenida Alcázar, along the river, or on Paseo de la Victoria, downhill from Plaza de las Tendillas and the Roman Mausoleum.

SLEEPING

My first two listings—comfortable, air-conditioned, expensive business-class hotels—are located within a 10-minute walk of the bus and train stations. The last two are cheaper and located near the Mezquita, about a 25-minute walk (or a bus ride) from the stations.

$$$ Hotel Tryp Gallos has all the modern conveniences in its 115 rooms (Sb-€87, Db-€102, extra bed-€25; less July–Aug and Nov–Feb: Sb-€59, Db-€85; includes tax, breakfast-€10, elevator, Avenida de Medina Azahara 7, tel. 957-235-500, fax 957-231-636, www.trypgallos.solmelia.com, tryp.gallos@solmelia.com).

$$ Hotel Gran Capitán, farther from the train station, offers 96 big, spacious, cavernous rooms with little personality or charm, but with excellent air-conditioning. They list their best prices on their Web site (Sb-€80, Db-€90, breakfast-€11, parking-€12, Avenida de América 5, tel. 957-470-250, fax 957-474-643, www .occidental-hoteles.com, cordoba.ogc@oh-es.com).

$$ Hotel González, with some of its 17 basic rooms around a plant-filled patio, provides a bit of budget charm in Córdoba. Sparse but clean and quiet, the location and price make up for the lack of decor (Sb-€40, Db-€78, includes tax and breakfast, Manríquez 3, tel. 957-479-819, fax 957-486-187, www.hotelgonzalez .com).

$ Hostal Alcázar, located in the heart of an area known for prize-winning patios, has a quaint one of its own. Basic and budget-priced, this friendly place is just outside of the old

---

Sleep Code

(€1 = about $1.20, country code: 34)
S = Single, **D** = Double/Twin, **T** = Triple, **Q** = Quad, **b** = bathroom, **s** = shower only. Unless otherwise noted, credit cards are accepted, English is spoken, and breakfast generally costs extra.

To help you easily sort through these listings, I've divided the rooms into three categories, based on the price for a standard double room with bath during high season:

$$$ **Higher Priced**—Most rooms €100 or more.
$$ **Moderately Priced**—Most rooms between €60–100.
$ **Lower Priced**—Most rooms €60 or less.

city wall (D-€24–27, Db-€30–45, Tb-€45–54, Qb apartment-€60–72, breakfast-€3, Calle San Basilio 2, tel. 957-202-561, www.hostalalcazar.com, hostalalcazar@hotmail.com).

EATING

Taverna Salinas is deservedly in all the guidebooks for its winning combination of traditional cuisine and professional service. No one should leave town without trying Córdoba's version of gazpacho—*salmorejo*. It's creamier, due to the addition of extra bread and even more olive oil. *Salmorejo* is typically served with pieces of *jamón* and hard-boiled egg (Mon–Sat 12:00–16:00 & 20:00–24:00, closed Sun, Tendidores 3, tel. 957-480-135).

El Buey y El Fuego is a steak-lover's dream come true. Friendly yet professional, this restaurant serves enormous portions of anything that can be grilled. The locals who come here all seem to know each other, and they enjoy its fancy but relaxed atmosphere (€15 fixed-price lunches, €20 entrées, Mon–Sat 13:30–16:30 & 21:00–24:00, closed Sun, reservations smart for lunch and dinner, Benito Pérez Galdós 1, tel. 957-491-012). After dinner, stroll down Art Nouveau–rich Avenida del Gran Capitán to walk it off.

Bodega Guzmán, which proudly displays the heads of brave-but-unlucky bulls, serves tapas to delighted locals who burst into song when they feel the flamenco groove. Belly up to the bar and try a sherry from the nearby Montilla-Moriles region; the *finos* are slightly less dry but more aromatic than those produced in Jerez de la Frontera (daily 10:00–24:00, Calle de los Judíos 7).

El Caballo Rojo, located next to the Mezquita, has been making tourists happy with regional cuisine for 45 years. Head downstairs to the bar if you want a lighter meal of tapas and drinks (€5–10 *raciones*), or try the boisterous restaurant upstairs for a pricey but well-worth-it meal (€30 fixed-price meal, lunch from 13:00, dinner from 20:00, Cardenal Herrero 28, tel. 957-475-375).

Café Gaudí may not have been designed by Catalunya's top architect, but it does boast a rich Modernista interior. The terrace is great for people-watching. A variety of on-tap beer hits the spot on a warm day. But most locals come here for a typical Andalusian breakfast; join them, and get your morning off to a great start with a *media tostada de aceite y tomate*—olive oil and tomato puree with a hint of garlic on a toasted baguette (Mon–Sat 8:00–23:00, Sun 10:00–22:00, Avenida del Gran Capitán 22, tel. 957-471-736).

La Gloria provides an earthy Art Nouveau experience. Located just down the street from Plaza de las Tendillas, it has an unassuming entrance, but a sumptuous interior. Carved floral designs wind around the bar and mix with *feria* posters and bullfighting memories. Pop in for a quick beer or coffee (Mon–Sat from 8:30, closed Sun, quiet after lunch crowd clears out, Calle Claudio Marcelo 20).

TRANSPORTATION CONNECTIONS

From Córdoba by Train: Córdoba is on the slick AVE train line, making it an easy stopover between **Madrid** (30/day, 2 hrs, reservations required on AVE trains) and **Sevilla** (hourly, 1.5 hrs, 45 min by speedy AVE, reservations mandatory). Other trains go to **Ronda** (4/day, 2.5 hrs direct, 3.5 hrs with transfer in Bobadilla), **Málaga** (10/day, 2–3 hrs), and **Granada** (2/day, 4–6.5 hrs, transfer in Bobadilla). Train info: tel. 902-240-202.

By Bus to: Granada (8/day, 1.5–3 hrs), **Sevilla** (9/day, 2 hrs), **Madrid** (6/day, 5 hrs), **Málaga** (5/day, 2.75 hrs *directo*), **Barcelona** (2/day, 10 hrs). No luggage storage is available at the bus station, but train station lockers are directly across the street. The efficient staff at the information desk prints bus schedules for you. Bus info: tel. 957-404-040.

ANDALUCÍA'S WHITE HILL TOWNS

(Los Pueblos Blancos)

Just as the American image of Germany is Bavaria, the Yankee dream of Spain is Andalucía. This is the home of bullfights, flamenco, gazpacho, pristine-if-dusty whitewashed hill towns, and glamorous Mediterranean resorts. The big cities of Andalucía (Granada, Sevilla, and Córdoba) and the South Coast (Costa del Sol) are covered in separate chapters. This chapter explores its hill-town highlights.

The Route of the White Towns (Ruta de los Pueblos Blancos), Andalucía's charm bracelet of cute towns perched in the sierras, gives you wonderfully untouched Spanish culture. Spend a night in the romantic queen of the white towns, Arcos de la Frontera. Towns with "de la Frontera" in their names were established on the front line of the centuries-long fight to recapture Spain from the Muslims, who were slowly pushed back into Africa. The hill towns—no longer strategic, no longer on any frontier—are now just passing time peacefully. Join them. Nearby, the city of Jerez is worth a peek for its famous horses and a glass of sherry.

To study ahead, visit www.andalucia.com for information on hotels, festivals, museums, nightlife, and sports in the region.

Planning Your Time

On a three-week vacation in Spain, the region is worth two nights and up to two days sandwiched between Sevilla and Tarifa. Arcos makes the best home base, though the towns can be (and often are) accessed from the Costa del Sol resorts via Ronda. Arcos, near Jerez and close to interesting smaller towns, is conveniently situated halfway between Sevilla and Tarifa.

See Jerez on your way in or out, spend a day hopping from town to town (Grazalema and Zahara, at a minimum) in the more remote interior, and enjoy Arcos early and late in the day.

Without a car you might keep things simple and focus only on Arcos and Jerez (both well-served by public buses). If you're staying in Sevilla, another option is using Andalusian Minibus Tours to get you to Olvera, Zahara, Grazalema, and Setenil de las Bodegas on an all-day excursion (see page 377).

Spring and fall are high season throughout this area. In summer you'll find intense heat, but empty hotels and no crowds.

Arcos de la Frontera

Arcos smothers its long, narrow hilltop and tumbles down the back of the ridge like the train of a wedding dress. It's larger than most other Andalusian hill towns,

but equally atmospheric. Arcos consists of two towns: the fairy-tale old town on top of the hill and the fun-loving lower, or new, town. The old center is a labyrinthine wonderland, a photographer's feast. Viewpoint-hop through town. Feel the wind funnel through the narrow streets as cars inch around tight corners. Join the kids' soccer game on the churchyard patio. Enjoy the moonlit view from the main square.

Though it tries, Arcos doesn't have much to offer other than its basic whitewashed self. The locally produced English guidebook on Arcos waxes poetic and at length about very little. You can arrive late and leave early and still see it all.

ORIENTATION

Tourist Information

The TI, on the main square across from the parador, is helpful and loaded with information, including bus schedules (March–Sept Mon–Sat 10:00–14:00 & 16:00–20:00, Sun 10:00–14:00; Oct–Feb Mon–Sat 10:00–14:00 & 15:30–19:30, Sun 10:00–14:00; Plaza del Cabildo, tel. 956-702-264, www.ayuntamientoarcos.org).

The TI organizes one-hour **walking tours** of the old town and of the patios of Arcos. They cost €5, leave from the main square, and are given in Spanish and/or English. The Old Town walk describes the church and the town's history (Mon–Sat at 10:30).

Southern Spain

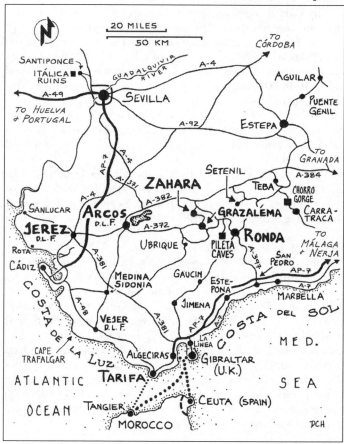

The Patios walk gets you into private courtyards and covers lifestyles, Moorish influences, and the two main churches (Mon–Sat at 12:00). A third walk, which takes place in the evening, focuses on whatever the guide wants to show you (Mon–Sat at 18:00). You need to reserve ahead for the Saturday and evening walks (call or drop by the TI to book).

Arrival in Arcos

By Bus: The bus station is on Calle Corregidores, at the foot of the hill. To get up to the old town, catch the shuttle bus marked *Centro* (€1, 2/hr, runs 8:15–21:15 but not on Sun), hop a taxi (€5 fixed rate), or take a 20-minute uphill walk: As you leave the station, turn left on Corregidores, angle left uphill, cross the four-way intersection, angle right uphill, and take Muñoz Vázquez up into town. Go up the stairs by the church to the main square and TI.

By Car: Avoid entering the old town with a larger car—narrow, one-way streets and difficult turns invite frustration. Small cars can park in the main square of the old town at the top of the hill (Plaza del Cabildo, ticket from machine €0.70/hr, 2 hours maximum, only necessary Mon–Fri 9:00–14:00 & 17:00–21:00 and Sat 9:00–14:00—confirm times on machine, can get €3 all-day ticket from old-town hotels, free Sat afternoon and all day Sun). If arriving to check in at a hotel, tell the uniformed parking man the name of your hotel. If there's no spot, wait until one opens up (he'll help). Once you grab a spot, tell him you'll be back from your hotel with a ticket.

Plenty of parking is available in the new town, including the underground lot at Plaza de España. From this lot, catch a taxi or the shuttle bus up to the old town (2/hr; as you're looking uphill, the bus stop is to the right of the traffic circle).

Getting Around Arcos

The old town is easily walkable, but it's fun and relaxing to take a circular **minibus** joyride. The little shuttle bus constantly circles through the town's one-way system and around the valley (€1, 2/hr, daily 8:15–21:15 except Sun). For a 30-minute tour, hop on. You can catch it just below the main church in the old town (near mystical stone circle, described below). Note that its route may be changed a bit because of roadwork in 2007, but it'll still do a loop trip. As you wind through the old town, sit in the front seat for the best view of the tight squeezes and the schoolkids hanging out in the plazas. Passing under a Moorish gate, you enter a modern residential neighborhood, circle under the eroding cliff, and return to the old town by way of Plaza de España.

Helpful Hints

Internet Access: Try the single computer at the TI or **Arcomputer** on Paseo de Andalucía.

Post Office: It's in the old town at Paseo de los Boliches 24, a few doors up from Hotel Los Olivos (Mon–Fri 8:30–14:30, Sat 9:30–13:00, closed Sun).

Laundry: Pressto is full-service and reliable (€10–16, Mon–Fri 9:30–13:30 & 17:00–20:30, Sat 9:30–13:30, closed Sun, in new town, across from recommended Hotel La Fonda on Calle Debajo del Corral 6, tel. 956-700-555).

Viewpoint: For drivers, the best town overview is from a tiny park just beyond the new bridge on the El Bosque road.

SELF-GUIDED TOUR

Welcome to Arcos' Old Town

• *Start at the top of the hill, in the main square dominated by the church. (Avoid this walk during the hot midday siesta.)*

Plaza del Cabildo: Stand at the viewpoint opposite the church on the town's main square. Survey the square, which in the old days doubled as a bullring. On your right is the parador, a former palace of the governor. On your left is the city hall and the TI, below the 11th-century Moorish castle where Ferdinand and Isabel held Reconquista strategy meetings (castle privately owned and closed to the public). Directly in front is the Church of Santa María. Notice the church's fine but chopped-off bell tower. The old one fell in the earthquake of 1755 (famous for destroying Lisbon). The new replacement was intended to be the

tallest in Andalucía after Sevilla's—but money ran out. It looks like someone lives on an upper floor. Someone does. The church guardian lives there in a room strewn with bell-ringing ropes.

Enjoy the square's viewpoint. Belly up to the railing and look down. The people of Arcos boast that only they see the backs of the birds as they fly. Ponder the parador's erosion concerns (it lost part of its lounge in the 1990s—it dropped right off), orderly orange groves, and fine views toward Morocco. The city council considered building an underground parking lot to clear up the square, but nixed it because of the land's fragility. You're 330 feet above the Guadalete River. This is the town's suicide departure point for men (women jump from the other side).

• *Enter the square's big church.*

Inside the Church of Santa María: After Arcos was retaken from the Moors in the 13th century, this church was built atop a mosque. Buy a ticket (€1.50, March–Dec Mon–Fri 10:00–13:00 & 16:00–19:00, Sat 10:00–14:00, closed Sun and Jan–Feb), and step into the center, where you can see the finely carved choir. The organ was built in 1789 with that many pipes. The fine Renaissance high altar—carved in wood—covers up a Muslim prayer niche that survived from the older mosque. The altar shows God with a globe in his hand (on top), and scenes from the life of Jesus (on the right) and Mary (left). Circle the church counterclockwise and notice the elaborate chapels. While most of the architecture is Gothic, the chapels are decorated in Baroque and Rococo styles. The ornate statues are used in Holy Week processions. Sniff out the

Arcos de la Frontera

1. Parador de Arcos de la Frontera
2. Hotel El Convento
3. La Casa Grande
4. Hostal & Rest. San Marcos
5. Hostal Callejón de las Monjas
6. Hotel Los Olivos (Upper Map)
7. Hotel La Fonda (Upper Map)
8. Hostal Málaga (Upper Map)
9. Restaurante El Convento
10. Alcaraván Restaurant
11. Las Doce Campañas Bakery
12. Plaza Boticas, Cloistered Nuns & Rest. Don Fernando

"incorruptible body" (miraculously never rotting) of St. Felix—a third-century martyr. Felix may be nicknamed "the incorruptible," but take a close look at his knee. He's no longer skin and bones... just bones and the fine silver mesh that once covered his skin. Rome sent his body here in 1764, after recognizing this church as the most important in Arcos. In the back of the church, under a huge fresco of St. Christopher (carrying his staff and baby Jesus), is a gnarly Easter candle from 1767.

• *Back outside, examine the...*

Church Exterior: Circle clockwise around the church, down four steps, to find the third-century Roman votive altar with a carving of the palm tree of life. While the Romans didn't build this high in the mountains, they did have a town and temple at the foot of Arcos. This carved stone was found in the foundation of the original Moorish mosque, which stood here before the first church was built.

Head down a few more steps and come to the main entrance (west portal) of the church (open for worship on Sun and every evening at 20:00, 19:00 in winter). This is a fine example of Plateresque Gothic—Spain's last and most ornate kind of Gothic. In the pavement, notice the 15th-century magic circle with 12 red and 12 white stones—the white ones have various "constellations" marked (though they don't resemble any of today's star charts). When a child would come to the church to be baptized, the parents would stop here first for a good Christian exorcism. The exorcist would stand inside the protective circle and cleanse the baby of any evil spirits. While locals no longer do this (and a modern rain drain now marks the center), Sufis, a sect of Islam, still come here in a kind of magical pilgrimage every November. (Down a few more steps and 10 yards to the left, you can catch the public bus for a circular minibus joyride through Arcos; see "Getting Around Arcos," page 434.)

Continue around the church to the intersection below the flying buttresses. These buttresses were built to shore up the church when it was damaged by an earthquake in 1699. Thanks to these supports, the church survived the bigger earthquake of 1755. The spiky security grille (over the window above) protected cloistered nuns when this building was a convent. Look at the arches that prop up the houses downhill on the left; all over town, arches support earthquake-damaged structures—the reason why the town was named "Arcos."

At the corner, Sr. González Oca's tiny barbershop has some exciting posters of bulls running Pamplona-style through the streets of Arcos during Holy Week—an American from the nearby Navy base at Rota was killed here by a bull in 1994. (Sr. González Oca is happy to show off his posters; drop in and say, *"Hola."* Need a haircut? €7.) Downstairs in Sr. González Oca's bar, you can see a framed collection of all the euro coins of each of the 12 participating nations. Continuing along under the buttresses, notice the scratches of innumerable car mirrors on each wall (and be glad you're walking).

• *We'll now make our way...*

From the Church to the Market: Completing your circle around the church, turn left under more arches built to repair earthquake damage and walk east down the bright, white Calle Escribanos. From now to the end of this walk, you'll basically go straight until you come to the town's second big church (St. Peter's). After a block, you hit Plaza Boticas. At the end of the street on your left is a fine restaurant, El Convento (see "Eating," page 442). On your right is the last remaining convent in Arcos. Notice the no-nunsense window grilles high above, with tiny peepholes in the latticework for the cloistered nuns to see through. Step into the lobby under the fine portico to find their one-way mirror and a spinning cupboard that hides the nuns from view. Push the buzzer, and one of the eight sisters (several are from Kenya and speak English well) will spin out some €5 boxes of excellent, freshly baked pine-nut cookies for you to consider buying. (Be careful, if you stand big and tall to block out the light, you can actually see the sister through the glass.) If you ask for *magdalenas,* bags of cupcakes will swing around (€1.50). These are traditional goodies made from natural ingredients (open daily but not reliably 8:30–14:30 & 17:00–19:00). Buy some cupcakes to support their church work, and give them to kids as you complete your walk.

The covered market *(mercado)* at the bottom of the plaza (down from the convent) resides in an unfinished church. At the entry, notice what is half of a church wall. The church was being built for the Jesuits, but construction stopped in 1767 when King Charles III, tired of the Jesuit appetite for politics, expelled the order from Spain. The market is closed on Sunday and on Monday—since they rest on Sunday, there's no produce, fish, or meat ready for Monday. Poke inside. It's tiny but has everything you need. Pop into the *servicio público* (public WC)—no gender bias here.

• *Continue straight down Calle Boticas...*

From the Market to the Church of St. Peter: As you walk, peek discreetly into private patios. These wonderful, cool-tiled courtyards filled with plants, pools, furniture, and happy family activities are typical of Arcos (and featured on the TI's Patios walks). Except in the mansions, these patios are generally shared by several families. Originally, each courtyard served as a catchment system, funneling rainwater to a drain in the middle, which filled the well. You can still see tiny wells in wall niches with now-decorative pulleys for the bucket.

Look for Las Doce Campañas bakery, which sells traditional and delicious *sultana* cookies (€1 each). These big, dry macaroons (named for the wives of sultans) go back to Moorish times. At the next corner, squint back above the bakery to the corner of the tiled rooftop. The tiny and very eroded mask was placed here to scare evil spirits from the house. This is Arcos' last surviving mask from a tradition that lasted until the mid-19th century.

Also notice the ancient columns on each corner. All over town, these columns—many actually Roman, appropriated from their ancient settlement at the foot of the hill—were put up to protect buildings from reckless donkey carts. These days, cars are the biggest danger.

As you continue straight, notice that the walls are scooped out on either side of the windows. These are a reminder of the days when women stayed inside but wanted the best possible view of any people-action in the streets. These "window ears" also enabled boys in a more modest age to lean inconspicuously against the wall to chat up eligible young ladies.

Opposite the old facade ahead, find the Association of San Miguel. Duck right, past a bar, into the oldest courtyards in town—you can still see the graceful neo-Gothic lines of this noble home from 1850. The bar is a club for retired men—always busy when a bullfight's on TV or during card games. The guys are friendly. Drinks are cheap (a stiff Cuba Libre costs €1.50). You're welcome to flip on the light and explore the old-town photos in the back room.

Just beyond (facing the elegant front door of that noble house) is Arcos' second church, St. Peter's. You know it's St. Peter's because St. Peter, mother of God, is the centerpiece of the facade. Let me explain. It really is the second church, having had an extended battle with Santa María for papal recognition as the leading church in Arcos. When the pope finally favored Santa María, St. Peter's parishioners even changed their prayers. Rather than honoring "María," they wouldn't even say her name. They prayed "St. Peter, mother of God."

In the cool of the evening, the tiny square in front of the church—about the only flat piece of pavement around—serves as the old-town soccer field for neighborhood kids. Until a few years ago, this church also had a resident bellman—notice the cozy balcony halfway up. He was a basket maker and a colorful character, famous for bringing a donkey into his quarters, which grew too big to get back out. Finally, he had no choice but to kill and eat the donkey (€1 donation, church open Mon–Fri 10:30–14:00, Sat–Sun sporadically in the afternoon).

Twenty yards beyond the church, step into the fine Galería de Arte San Pedro, featuring artisans in action and their reasonably priced paintings and pottery. Walk inside. Find the water drain and the well.

Across the street, a sign directs you to *Mirador*—a tiny square 100 yards away that affords a commanding view of Arcos. The reservoir is used for water sports in the summertime, and forms part of a power plant that local residents protested based on environmental issues but to no avail.

From the Church of St. Peter, circle down and around back to the main square, wandering the tiny neighborhood lanes (the delightful Higinio Capote is particularly picturesque with its many geraniums), peeking into patios, kicking a few soccer balls, and savoring the views.

NIGHTLIFE

Evening Action in the New Town—The newer part of Arcos has a modern charm. In the cool of the evening, all generations enjoy life out around Plaza de España (10-min walk from the old town). Several fine tapas bars border the square.

The big park (Recinto Ferial) below Plaza de España is the late-night fun zone in the summer (June–Sept) when *carpas* (restaurant tents) fill with merrymakers, especially on weekends. The scene includes open-air tapas bars, disco music, and dancing. Throughout the summer, there are free live concerts here on Friday evenings, and free open-air cinema on Sunday evenings.

Flamenco—On Plaza del Cananeo in the old town and three other venues (check TI), amateur flamenco sizzles on Thursday and Saturday evenings (free, from 22:00 July–Aug).

SLEEPING

Note that some hotels double their rates during the motorbike races in nearby Jerez (early May) and Holy Week (April 1–8 in 2007); I have not listed these spikes in the prices below.

In the Old Town

$$$ Parador de Arcos de la Frontera is royally located, elegant, recently refurbished, and reasonably priced, with 24 rooms (8 with balconies). If you're going to experience a parador, this is a good one (Sb-€108, Db-€135, Db with terrace-€162, breakfast-€12, air-con, elevator, minibars, free parking, Plaza del Cabildo, tel. 956-700-500, fax 956-701-116, www.parador .es, arcos@parador.es).

$$ Hotel El Convento, deep in the old town just beyond the parador, is the best value in town. Run by a hardworking family, this cozy hotel offers 13 fine rooms—all with great views, most with balconies. In 1998, I enjoyed a big party with most of Arcos' big shots as they dedicated a fine room with a grand-view balcony to "Rick Steves, Periodista Turístico"—a hint to where I sleep when in Arcos (Sb-€40–55, Db-€55–70, Db with terrace-€65–85, third person-€18 extra, includes tax; 10 percent discount in 2007 when you book direct, pay in cash, and show this year's book; parking on

Plaza del Cabildo-€3, Maldonado 2, tel. 956-702-333, fax 956-704-128, www.webdearcos.com/elconvento, reservas@hotelelconvento.es). Over an à la carte breakfast, bird-watch on their view terrace, with all of Andalucía spreading beyond your *café con leche*.

$$ La Casa Grande is a lovingly appointed *Better Homes and Moroccan Tiles* kind of place that rents eight rooms with grand-view windows. Like in a lavish B&B, you're free to enjoy its fine view terrace, homey library, and classy courtyard, where you'll be served a traditional breakfast (Db-€65–70, Db suite-€77–82, Tb-€115, Qb suite-€130, Maldonado 10, tel. 956-703-930, fax 956-717-095, www.lacasagrande.net, info@lacasagrande.net, Elena).

$ Hostal San Marcos, in the heart of the old town, offers four air-conditioned rooms and a great sun terrace with views of the reservoir above a neat little bar (Sb-€25, Db-€35, Tb-€45, includes tax, Marqués de Torresoto 6, tel. 956-700-721, sanmarcosarcos@mixmail.com, Loli speaks no English).

$ Hostal Callejón de las Monjas, with a tangled floor plan and nine simple rooms (seven with air-con), offers the best cheap beds in the old town. It's on a sometimes-noisy street behind the Church of Santa María (Sb-€20, D-€27, Db-€33, Db with terrace-€39, Tb-€44, 2 apartments-€66, includes tax, Calle Dean Espinosa 4, tel. & fax 956-702-302, padua@mesonelpatio.com, staff speak no English). Friendly Sr. González Oca runs a tiny barbershop in the foyer and a restaurant in the cellar.

In the New Town

The first two hotels are close to the old town; the third is farther away, on the highway.

$$ Hotel Los Olivos is a bright, cool, and airy place with 19 rooms, an impressive courtyard, roof garden, bar, view, friendly folks, and easy parking. The seven view rooms can be a bit noisy in the afternoon but—with double-paned windows—are usually fine at night (Sb-€45, Db-€70, Tb-€82, extra bed-€18, breakfast-€6, includes tax, 10 percent discount with this year's book in 2007, Paseo de los Boliches 30, tel. 956-700-811, fax 956-702-018, www .hotelolivosarcos.com, losolivosdelc@terra.es, Raquel and Miguel Ángel).

$ Hotel La Fonda is a great, traditional Spanish inn, with all 19 rooms off one grand hall above a tacky little lobby (Sb-€30–37, Db-€49–57, third person-€9–12, air-con, request a quiet *tranquilo* room, Calle Corredera 83, tel. 956-700-057, fax 956-703-661, hotelafonda@yahoo.es, Isabel).

$ Hostal Málaga is surprisingly nice, if for some reason you want to stay on the big, noisy road at the Jerez edge of town. Nestled on a quiet lane between truck stops on A382, it offers 18 clean, attractive rooms and a breezy two-level roof garden (Sb-€18–21, Db-€33–36, Qb apartment-€48, air-con, easy parking, Ponce de León 5, tel. & fax 956-702-010, hostalmalaga@teleline .es, Josefa speaks German if that helps). She also rents two apartments in the center of Arcos overlooking lively Plaza de España in the new town (Db-€50).

EATING

Restaurante El Convento is wonderfully atmospheric and graciously run by Señora María Moreno-Moreno and her husband, Señor José Antonio Roldan. It serves quality Andalusian cuisine in a dressy setting (generally daily 13:00–16:00 & 19:30–22:00, closed one rotating day a week—call to check, near parador at Marqués de Torresoto 7, reservations recommended, tel. 956-703-222). The hearty €26 fixed-price daily special includes a fine house red wine and a glass of sherry with dessert. This is a good opportunity to dine on game.

The **Parador** has an expensive restaurant with a cliff-edge setting. Its €27 11-course sampler menu is an interesting option. A costly drink on the million-dollar-view terrace can be worth the price (lunch and dinner daily, on main square).

To eat cheaper in the old town, try **Restaurante San Marcos**, which offers a good €8 fixed-price meal, or prowl the many tapas bars along the main drag (Calle Dean Espinosa). **Restaurante Don Fernando** has nice salads and meat dishes just across from the market on Plaza Boticas. The flower pot-lined *típico* **Alcaraván** serves barbecued pork loin *(solomillo)* under medieval vaults in what was the castle's dungeon. Look for the hibachi set up by the door (closed Mon, Calle Nueva 1).

Plaza de España, in the lower new town, is lined with tapas

bars and restaurants, including Arabic food if you're in the mood for a change.

TRANSPORTATION CONNECTIONS

From Arcos by Bus to: Jerez (hourly, 30 min), **Ronda** (3/day, 2 hrs), **Cádiz** (4/day, 75 min), **Sevilla** (2/day direct, 2 hrs, more departures with a change in Jerez). From Jerez, there are hourly connections to Sevilla. Two bus companies (Los Amarillos and Comes) share the Arcos bus station. Their Jerez offices keep longer hours and know the Arcos schedules (Jerez tel. 956-342-174 or 956-341-063—if you want to find out about the Arcos–Jerez schedule, make it clear you're coming from Arcos, or visit the Comes Web site at www.tgcomes.es). The closest train station to Arcos is Jerez.

   By Car to: Sevilla (just over an hour if you pay €5 for the toll road), **southern Portugal** (follow freeway to Sevilla, skirt the city by turning west on C30, direction Huelva, and it's a straight shot).

Ronda

With 40,000 people, Ronda is one of the largest white towns. With its gorge-straddling setting, it's also one of the most spectacular. While day-trippers from the touristy Costa del Sol clog Ronda's streets during the day, locals retake the town in the early evening, and nights are peaceful. If you liked Toledo at night, you'll love the local feeling of evenings in Ronda. Since it's served by train and bus, Ronda makes a relaxing break for nondrivers traveling between Granada, Sevilla, and Córdoba.

   Ronda's main attractions are its gorge-spanning bridges, the oldest bullring in Spain, and an interesting old town. The cliffside setting, dramatic today, was practical back in its day. For the Moors, it provided a tough bastion, taken by the Spaniards only in 1485, seven years before Granada fell. Spaniards know Ronda as the cradle of modern bullfighting and the romantic home of 19th-century *banditos*.

Ronda

1. Parador de Ronda
2. To Hotel Reina Victoria
3. Hotel San Gabriel
4. Hotel La Española &
   Rest. Tragabuches
5. Hotel & Rest. Alavera
   de los Baños
6. Hotel Don Miguel
7. Hotel En Frente Arte Ronda
8. Hotel El Tajo
9. Hotel San Francisco
10. Hotel Royal
11. Hostal Ronda Sol

12. Hostal Biarritz
13. To Hostal Andalucía
14. Restaurante Pedro Romero
15. Restaurante Santa Pola
16. Restaurante del Escudero
17. Café & Bar Faustino
18. To Casa Manolo Restaurant
19. Spar Supermarket
20. Casa del Rey Moro Garden
21. Palacio del Marqués de
    Salvatierra
22. Museo Joaquín Peinado
23. Trail to Puerta de los Molinos

ORIENTATION

Ronda's breathtaking ravine divides the town's labyrinthine Moorish quarter and its new, noisier, and more sprawling Mercadillo quarter. A massive-yet-graceful 18th-century bridge connects these two neighborhoods. Most things of touristic importance (TI, post office, hotels, bullring) are clustered within a few blocks of the bridge. The paseo (early evening stroll) happens in the new town, on Ronda's major pedestrian street, Carrera Espinel. The Alameda del Tajo park can be lively before lunch, filled with seniors taking a break from the nearby *geriatrico*.

Tourist Information: The main TI is on the main square, Plaza de España, opposite the bridge (Mon–Fri 9:00–19:30, Sat–Sun 10:00–14:00, longer hours in summer, tel. 952-871-272). Get the free Ronda map, the excellent Andalusian road map, and a listing of the latest museum hours. Consider buying cheap maps of Granada, Sevilla, or the Route of the White Towns. A second TI, located opposite the bullring at Paseo Blas Infante, rents a two-hour MP3 **audioguide** for €15 that comes with an informative map and can be shared by two people (Mon–Fri 9:30–19:30, Sat–Sun 10:00–14:00 & 15:30–18:30, tel. 952-187-119, informacion @turismoderonda.es).

Local Guide: Energetic and knowledgeable Antonio Jesús Naranjo will take you on a two-hour walking tour of the city's sights (€60 on Mon–Sat, €90 on Sun, plus €1/person, reserve early, tel. 952-879-215, mobile 639-073-763). If Antonio is busy, ask the TI for another option.

Arrival in Ronda

By Train: The train station is a 15-minute walk from the center—turn right out of the station on Avenida de Andalucía, and go through the roundabout (you'll see the bus station on your right). Continue straight down the street (now called San José), until the street dead-ends. Turn left and walk downhill past a church and the Alameda. Keep going down this street, passing the bullring, to get to the TI and the famous bridge. A **taxi** to the center costs about €4.

By Bus: To get to the center from the bus station (lockers inside, buy coin at kiosk by exit), leave the station walking to the right of the roundabout, then follow the directions for train travelers (above), heading down San José.

By Car: Drivers coming up from the coast catch A376 at San Pedro de Alcántara and climb about 20 miles into the mountains. A369 offers a much longer, winding, but scenic alternative that takes you through a series of whitewashed villages. The handiest place to park in Ronda is the underground lot at Plaza del Socorro

(1 block from bullring, €13/24 hrs).

SIGHTS

Ronda's New Town

▲▲▲The Gorge and New Bridge—The ravine, called El Tajo—360 feet down and 200 feet wide—divides Ronda into the whitewashed old Moorish town (La Ciudad) and the new town (El Mercadillo) that was built after the Christian reconquest in 1485.

Ronda's main bridge, called Puente Nuevo (New Bridge), mightily spans the gorge. A bridge was built here in 1735 but fell after six years. This one was built from 1751 to 1793. Look down...carefully. Legend has it the architect fell to his death while inspecting it, and hundreds from both sides were thrown off this bridge during Spain's brutal civil war.

You can see the foundations of the original bridge (and a super view of the New Bridge) from the park named Jardines Ciudad de Cuenca. From Plaza de España, walk down Calle Rosario, turn right on Calle Los Remedios, and then take another right at the sign for the park.

▲▲Bullfighting Ring—Ronda is the birthplace of modern bullfighting, and this ring was the first great Spanish bullring. While Philip II initiated bullfighting as war training for knights in the 16th century, it wasn't until the early 1700s that Francisco Romero established the rules of modern bullfighting and introduced the scarlet cape, held unfurled with a stick. His son Juan further developed the ritual (or art), and his grandson Pedro was one of the first great matadors (killing nearly 6,000 bulls in his career).

To see the bullring, stables, and **museum,** buy tickets from the booth at the main entrance (it's at the back of the bullring, the furthest point from the main drag). The museum is located just before the entry into the arena.

This museum—which has translations in English—is a shrine to bullfighting and the historic Romero family. You'll see stuffed heads (of bulls), photos, artwork, posters, and costumes (€5, daily April–Sept 10:00–20:00, March and Oct 10:00–19:00, Nov–Feb 10:00–18:00, on main drag in new town, 2 blocks up and on left from the New Bridge and TI, tel. 952-874-132).

Take advantage of the opportunity to walk in the actual arena, with plenty of time to play *toro,* surrounded by 5,000 empty seats. The arena was built in 1784. Notice the 176 classy Tuscan columns.

With your back to the entry, look left to see the ornamental col-umns and painted doorway where the dignitaries sit (over the gate where the bull enters). On the right is the place for the band—in the case of a small town like Ronda, a high school band.

Bullfights are scheduled only for the first weekend of September during the *feria* (fair) and occur rarely in the spring. While every other *feria* in Andalucía celebrates a patron saint, the Ronda fair glorifies legendary bullfighter Pedro Romero. For September bullfights, tickets go on sale the preceding July (ticket-sales concession changes yearly, call TI for current year's office and phone number—TI does not sell tickets). *Sol* means "sun" (cheap seats) and *sombra* means "shade" (pricier seats).

The Alameda del Tajo park, a block away, is a fine place for people-watching, a snooze in the shade, or practicing your Spanish with seniors from the old folks' home.

Parador National de Ronda—Walk around and through this newest of Spain's fabled paradors. The views from the walkway just below the outdoor terrace are magnificent. Anyone is welcome at the cafés (daily 11:00–17:00), but you have to be a guest to use the pool.

Ronda's Old Town

Santa María la Mayor Collegiate Church—This 15th-century church shares a fine park-like square with orange trees and the city hall. Its Renaissance bell tower still has parts of the old minaret. It was built on and around the remains of Moorish Ronda's main mosque (which was itself built on the site of a temple to Julius Caesar). Look for the only surviving mosque archway in the room where you purchase your ticket. Partially destroyed by an earth-quake, the reconstruction of the church resulted in the Moorish/ Gothic/Renaissance/Baroque fusion (or confusion) you see today. Enjoy the bright frescoes, elaborately carved choir and altar, and the new bronze sculpture depicting the life of the Virgin Mary. The treasury displays vestments that look curiously like matadors' brocaded outfits (€2.50, daily June–Oct 10:00–20:00, March–May 10:00–19:00, Nov–Feb 10:00–18:00, closed Sun lunch, Plaza Duquesa de Parcent in old town).

Mondragón Palace (Palacio de Mondragón)—This beautiful Moorish building was built in the 14th century, possibly as the residence of Moorish kings, and was carefully restored in the 16th century. It houses an enjoyable prehistory museum, with exhibits on Neolithic toolmaking and early metallurgy (many captions in English). Even if you have no interest in your ancestors, this is worth it for the architecture alone (€2, May–Sept Mon–Fri 10:00–19:00, Sat–Sun 10:00–15:00, Oct–April closes an hour earlier, on Plaza Mondragón in old town, tel. 952-878-450). Linger in the two small gardens, especially the shady one.

Wander left out to the nearby Plaza de María Auxiliadora for more views and a look at the two rare *pinsapo* trees (resembling firs) in the middle of the park; this is the only area of the country where these ancient trees are found. For an intense workout but a picture-perfect view, find the *Puerta de los Molinos* sign and head down, down, down. Just remember you have to walk back up, up, up. Not for the faint of heart or for the heat of the afternoon sun, this pathway leads down to the viewpoint where windmills once stood and photographers go crazy reproducing the most famous postcard view of Ronda—the entirety of the New Bridge. Wait until just before sunset for the best light and the coolest temperatures.

Museo del Bandolero—This tiny museum, while not as intriguing as it sounds, is an interesting assembly of *bandito* photos, guns, clothing, and knickknacks. The Jesse Jameses and Billy el Niños of Andalucía called this remote area home, and brief but helpful English descriptions make this a fun detour. One brand of romantic bandits were those who fought Napoleon's army—often more effectively than the regular Spanish troops (€3, daily May–Sept 10:30–20:30, Oct–April 10:30–18:00, across main street below Church of Santa María la Mayor at Calle Armiñan 65, tel. 952-877-785).

▲**Museo Joaquín Peinado**—Housed in an old palace, this fresh museum features a professional overview of the life's work of

Joaquín Peinado, a Ronda native and pal of Picasso's. His style ranges from Expressionist to Cubist and even to erotic. Some of the most famous 20th-century depictions of Don Quixote and Sancho Panza were painted by Peinado. You'll have an interesting modern-art experience without the crowds of Madrid's museums (€3, Mon–Sat 10:00–14:00 & 16:00–20:00, Sun 10:00–14:00, Plaza del Gigante, tel. 952-871-585).

Walk through Old Town—From the New Bridge, you can descend down Cuesta de Santo Domingo into a world of whitewashed houses, tiny grilled balconies, and winding lanes—the old town.

The **Casa del Rey Moro** garden may be in jeopardy if a five-star hotel opens on this site as planned. It offers access to "the Mine," an exhausting series of 365 slick, narrow stairs (like climbing down and then up a 20-story building) leading to the floor of the gorge. The Moors cut this zigzag staircase into the wall of the gorge in the 14th century, then used Spanish slaves to haul water to the thirsty town (€4, daily 10:00–19:00).

Fifty yards downhill from the garden is **Palacio del Marqués de Salvatierra** (closed to public). With the "distribution" following the Reconquista here in 1485, the Spanish king gave this fine house to the Salvatierra family. The facade is rich in colonial symbolism from Spanish America—note the pre-Columbian–looking characters flanking the balcony above the door and below the family coat of arms.

Continuing downhill you come to **Puente Viejo** (Old Bridge), built in 1616 upon the ruins of an Arab bridge. From here, look down to see the old Puente Romano, originally built by the Romans. Far to the right you can glimpse some of the surviving, highly fortified, Moorish city walls.

Before heading back to the main town, stop in to visit the **Arab Baths,** a museum located at one of the former city gates to the Moorish town. You would traditionally stop here first to wipe away the grime of traveling. For the moment, skip the cold, warm and hot rooms, and head directly to the last room. An interpretive, 10-minute video explains the entire layout using 3-D computer animation. Wait for the English version and imagine how good a massage would be right now (€2, Mon–Fri 10:00–19:00, Sat–Sun 10:00–15:00, Nov–April closes at 18:00 on weekdays).

Crossing the bridge, you'll see stairs on the right, leading scenically along the gorge back to the New Bridge via a fine viewpoint. Straight ahead bubbles the welcoming Eight Springs fountain. In Ronda, what goes down must come up, so continue climbing (veering left) on Calle Penas to reach the new Mercadillo part of town and the pedestrian strip.

Near Ronda: Pileta Caves

The Pileta Caves (Cuevas de la Pileta) are the best look a tourist can get at prehistoric cave painting in Spain. Because the famous caves at Altamira in northern Spain are closed (though you can tour a replica cave nearby, see page 150), if you want to see real Neolithic paintings in Spain, this is it. The caves, complete with stalagmites, bones, and 20,000-year-old paintings, are 14 miles from Ronda, past the town of Benaoján, at the end of the road.

Farmer José Bullón and his family live down the hill from the caves. He offers tours on the hour, leading up to 25 people through the caves, which were discovered by his grandfather. Call the night before to make sure no groups are scheduled for the time you want to visit—otherwise you'll have to wait (€8, daily 10:00–13:00 & 16:00–18:00, closes Nov-April at 17:00, closing times indicate last entrance, no reservations taken—just join the line, minimum of 12 people required for tour—expect to wait a while if not enough people are present, bring flashlight, sweater, and good shoes—it's slippery inside, tel. 952-167-343, www.cuevadelapileta.org).

Sr. Bullón is a master at hurdling the language barrier. As you walk the cool half mile, he'll spend an hour pointing out lots of black, ochre, and red drawings, which are five times as old as the Egyptian pyramids. Mostly it's just lines or patterns, but there are also crude fish, horses, and buffalo, made from a mixture of clay and fat by finger-painting prehistoric *hombres*. The 200-foot main cavern is impressive, as are some weirdly recognizable natural formations such as the Michelin man and a Christmas tree.

It's possible to get here without wheels (taking the Ronda–Benaoján bus—2/day, 8:30 & 13:00, 30 min—and then it's a 2-hour, 3-mile, uphill hike), but I wouldn't bother. You can get from Ronda to the caves by taxi (€25) and try to hitch a ride back with another tourist, or hire the taxi for a round-trip (€50). If you're driving, it's easy: Leave Ronda through the new part of town, and take A376. After a few miles, passing Cueva del Gato, exit left toward Benaoján on MA555. Go through Benaoján and follow the numerous signs to the cave. Leave nothing of value in your car. Nearby Montejaque has a great outdoor restaurant, La Casita (tel. 952-167-120).

A good base for visiting Ronda and the Pileta Caves as well as Grazalema is **El Cortijo de las Piletas.** Nestled at the edge of Sierra de Grazalema Natural Park, this spacious, family-run country estate has opportunities for swimming, hiking, horseback riding, and exploring the surrounding area. Access is easy from the main highway (Sb-€64, Db-€79, includes breakfast, tel. 605-080-295, www.cortijolaspiletas.com, info@cortijolaspiletas.com, Pablo and Elisenda). Another countryside option is **Finca La Guzmana,** run by expat Brits, Peter and Claire. Five beautifully appointed pastel rooms surround an open patio at this renovated estate house. Birdwatching, swimming, and trekking are available (Db-€75, includes tax and breakfast, tel. 600-006-305, www.laguzmana.com, info@laguzmana.com).

SLEEPING

Ronda has plenty of reasonably priced, decent-value accommodations. It's crowded only during Holy Week (the week leading up to Easter, April 1–8 in 2007) and the first week of September. Most of my recommendations are in the new town, a short walk from the New Bridge and a 10-minute walk from the train station. (The

Sleep Code

(€1 = about $1.20, country code: 34)
To help you easily sort through these listings, I've divided the rooms into three categories, based on the price for a standard double room with bath during high season:

$$$ **Higher Priced**—Most rooms €90 or more.
$$ **Moderately Priced**—Most rooms between €50–90.
$ **Lower Priced**—Most rooms €50 or less.

exceptions are Hostal Andalucía, across from the train station, and Reina Victoria, at the edge of town—and at the edge of the gorge.) In the cheaper places, ask for a room with a *ventana* (window) to avoid the few interior rooms. Breakfast and the 7 percent IVA tax are usually not included in the price.

$$$ You can't miss the striking **Parador de Ronda** on Plaza de España. It's an impressive integration of stone, glass, and marble. All 78 rooms have hardwood floors and most have fantastic view balconies (ask about family-friendly duplexes). There's also a pool overlooking the bridge (Sb-€112–120, Db-€140–150—depending on views, breakfast-€13, air-con, on-site garage-€15, Plaza de España, tel. 952-877-500, fax 952-878-188, ronda@parador.es). Consider at least a drink on the terrace.

$$$ The royal **Reina Victoria,** hanging over the gorge at the edge of town, has a marvelous view—Hemingway loved it—but you'll pay for it (89 rooms, Sb-€78–86, Db-€105–130, extra bed-€21–23, breakfast-€11, air-con, elevator, pool, free parking, 10-min walk from city center and easy to miss, look for intersection of Avenida Victoria and Calle Jerez, Jerez 25, tel. 952-871-240, fax 952-871-075, www.hotelreinavictoriaronda.com, reinavictoriaronda @husa.es).

$$$ Family-run **Hotel San Gabriel** has 16 pleasant rooms, a kind staff, public rooms filled with art books, a cozy wine cellar, and a fine garden terrace (Sb-€68, Db-€90–100, Db suite-€110, air-con, Calle Marqués de Moctezuma 19, just off Plaza Poeta Abul-Beca, tel. 952-190-392, fax 952-190-117, www.hotelsangabriel .com, info@hotelsangabriel.com, José Manuel and Ana). If you are a cinephile, kick back in the charming TV room—with seats from Ronda's old theater—then head to the breakfast room to check out photos of big movie stars that have stayed here.

$$$ **Hotel La Española** has 16 comfy rooms with air-conditioning and modern bathrooms (Sb-€60, Db-€100, Tb-€115, includes breakfast buffet, 15–20 percent less in June–July and Nov–Feb, 10 percent discount with this book in 2007, José Aparicio

3, tel. 952-871-052, fax 952-878-001, www.ronda.net/usuar /laespanola, laespanola@ronda.net).

$$ Alavera de los Baños, located next to ancient Moorish baths at the bottom of the hill, has 10 clean and colorful rooms (Sb-€60, Db-€80–95, Db with terrace-€90–95, includes tax and breakfast, closed Dec–Jan, Calle San Miguel, tel. & fax 952-879-143, www.andalucia.com/alavera, alavera@telefonica.net, personable Christian and Imma). This hotel offers a rural setting within the city, a swimming pool, a peaceful Arabic garden, and a wonderful restaurant (see page 453)—a unique combination in Ronda.

$$ Don Miguel, facing the gorge, is just left of the bridge. Of its 30 comfortable rooms, 20 have balconies and/or gorgeous views at no extra cost, but street rooms come with a little noise (Sb-€55, Db-€85, includes buffet breakfast, air-con, elevator, parking garage a block away-€9/day, Plaza de España 4, tel. 952-877-722, fax 952-878-377, reservas@dmiguel.com).

$$ Hotel en Frente Arte Ronda, relaxed and friendly, has 14 spacious rooms with dim lights, a peaceful tropical garden, views, terraces, a small swimming pool, and avant-garde decor (Sb-€66, Db-€77–99, extra bed-€35, includes buffet breakfast, lunch, and drinks, air-con, elevator, Internet access in lobby, Real 40, tel. 952-879-088, fax 952-877-217, www.enfrentearte.com, reservations @enfrentearte.com).

$$ Hotel El Tajo has 65 decent, quiet rooms once you get past the tacky, faux-stone Moorish decoration in the foyer (Sb-€35, Db-€55, parking-€10/day, air-con, Calle Cruz Verde 7, a half block off the pedestrian street, tel. 952-874-040, fax 952-875-099, www .hoteleltajo.com, reservas@hoteleltajo.com).

$$ Hotel San Francisco offers 27 small, nicely decorated rooms a block off the main pedestrian street in the town center (Sb-€40, Db-€60–70, Tb-€80, breakfast-€2, includes tax, air-con, 6 parking spaces-€6, María Cabrera 20, tel. 952-873-299, fax 952-874-688, www.hotelsanfranciscoronda.com, hotelronda@terra.es).

$ Hotel Royal has 29 clean, spacious, but boring rooms— many on a busy, noisy street, with pleasant views of treetops. If you like it quiet, ask for a *tranquilo* room in the back (Sb-€28, Db-€45, Tb-€56, air-con, Calle Virgen de la Paz 42, 3 blocks off Plaza de España, tel. 952-871-141, fax 952-878-132, www.ronda.net/usuar /hotelroyal, hroyal@ronda.net, some English spoken).

$ Hostal Ronda Sol has a homey atmosphere with 15 cheap but monkish rooms (S-€13, D-€20, cash only, parking-€10/day, Almendra 11, tel. 952-874-497, friendly María or Rafael). Next door, run by the same owner, **Hostal Biarritz** offers 21 similar rooms, some with private baths (S-€13, D-€20, Db-€28, T-€30, Tb-€42, includes tax, cash only, parking-€10/day, Almendra 7, tel. 952-872-910, no English spoken).

$ Hostal Andalucía, a plain but clean place with 11 comfortable rooms, is immediately across the street from the train station (Sb-€24, Db-€36, includes tax, air-con, easy street parking, Martínez Astein 19, tel. 952-875-450, no English spoken).

Near Ronda

Los Pastores, 2.5 miles southwest of Ronda on A-369, is a pleasant, renovated farmhouse in the countryside (Db-€50, Db apartment-€65, Tb/Qb apartment-€75, add €10 for one-night stay, breakfast-€5.50, optional dinner-€15, Apartado de Correos 167, on A-369, tel. 952-114-464, www.lospastores.com, info@lospastores.com).

EATING

Dodge the tourist traps. They say the best meal in Ronda is at the **parador** (*muy elegante,* figure €30). **Plaza del Socorro,** a block in front of the bullring, is a wonderful local scene, where families enjoy the square and its restaurants. Take a *paseo* with the locals down pedestrian-only Carrera Espinel, and choose a place with tables spilling out into the action. The best drinks and views in town are enjoyed on the terraces of the **Hotel Don Miguel** or the parador.

Restaurante Pedro Romero—assuming a shrine to bullfighting draped in *el toro* memorabilia doesn't ruin your appetite—gets good reviews but is touristy and priced to match (€16 fixed-price meals, or €30 à la carte, daily 12:30–16:00 & 19:00–23:00, air-con, across the street from bullring at Calle Virgen de la Paz 18, tel. 952-871-110). Rub elbows with the local bullfighters or dine with the likes (well, photographic likenesses) of Orson Welles, Ernest Hemingway, and Francisco Franco.

Restaurante Santa Pola offers traditional food with friendly service—and gorge views for an extra 10% (€20 fixed-price meal, €30 three-course dinners, good foie gras, oxtail stew, roasted lamb, and honey-tempura eggplant, lunch from 12:30, dinner 20:00–23:30, crossing New Bridge, take the first left downhill and you'll see the sign, Calle Santo Domingo, tel. 952-879-208).

Alavera de los Baños, located in the hotel of the same name, serves tasty Moorish specialties such as lamb and chicken *tajine,* along with vegetarian dishes, and offers great outdoor dining (open to public occasionally for dinner, reservations required, closed Jan–Feb along with hotel, Calle San Miguel, tel. 952-879-143).

Restaurante del Escudero serves tasty Spanish cuisine with a posh, modern touch on a terrace over the gorge (worth-it €15 and €30 gourmet fixed-price meals, also extensive à la carte, Mon–Sat 12:00–16:00 & 19:00–23:00, Sun 12:00–16:00, Paseo Blas Infante 1, behind bullring, tel. 952-871-367).

Trendy, spendy **Restaurante Tragabuches** serves "nouvelle cuisine Andalouse," prepared by Spain's renowned chef, Daniel García (€70 multi-course fixed-price meal—drinks not included, à la carte around €30 for main course, Tue–Sat 13:30–15:30 & 20:30–22:30, Sun 13:30–15:30, closed Mon, José Aparicio 1, tel. 952-190-291, www.tragabuches.com).

The no-frills **Café & Bar Faustino** offers the cheapest tapas in town (€1) to a lively crowd of students, blue-collar workers, and tourists (Tue–Sun 12:00–24:00, closed Mon, just off Plaza Carmen Abela, Santa Cecilia 4, tel. 952-190-307).

Simple **Casa Manolo,** a 10-minute walk from the town center, is an affordable option popular with locals, especially at lunchtime. It's a convenient stop on the way to or from the bus or train station (three-course lunch–€6, good oxtail stew, daily 12:00–16:00 & 20:30–23:00, Lauría 54, go up Carrera Espinel, left on Montejeras, then third right, tel. 952-878-050).

Supermarket: Picnic shoppers find the **Spar** supermarket convenient, at Calle Cruz Verde 18 opposite Hotel El Tajo. (Mon–Sat 9:15–21:15). A good picnic spot is the Alameda del Tajo park (with WC) near the bullring.

TRANSPORTATION CONNECTIONS

Note that some destinations are linked with Ronda by both bus and train.

From Ronda by Bus to: Algeciras (1/day, Mon–Fri only, 2.75 hrs), **Arcos** (3/day, 2 hrs), **Benaoján** (2/day, 30 min), **Jerez** (4/day, 3 hrs), **Grazalema** (2/day, 1 hr), **Zahara** (2/day, Mon–Fri only, 1 hr), **Sevilla** (6/day, 2.5 hrs, less on weekends; also see trains below), **Málaga** (10/day, 1.75 hrs direct, slower *ruta* buses, 3 hrs; access other Costa del Sol points from Málaga), **Marbella** (6/day, 75 min), **Fuengirola** (6/day, 2 hrs), **Nerja** (4 hrs, transfer in Málaga; can take train or bus from Ronda to Málaga). With no direct bus, it's easiest to train from Ronda to **Córdoba** (see below). There's no efficient way to call "the bus company" because there are four sharing the same station; one of them is at tel. 952-187-061. It's best to just drop by and compare schedules (on Plaza Concepción García Redondo, several blocks from train station).

By Train to: Algeciras (6/day, 2 hrs), **Bobadilla** (6/day, 1 hr), **Málaga** (1/day direct, 1 hr, and 6/day with transfer in Bobadilla, 2.5 hrs), **Sevilla** (6/day, 4 hrs, transfer in Bobadilla), **Granada** (3/day, 2.5 hrs), **Córdoba** (4/day, 2.75 hrs direct, 3.5 hrs with transfer in Bobadilla), **Madrid** (2/day, 5–7 hrs, 1 direct night train—23:27–8:40). Transfers are a snap and time-coordinated in Bobadilla; with four trains arriving and departing simultaneously, double-check that you're jumping on the right one. Train info: tel. 902-240-202.

More Hill Towns: Zahara and Grazalema

There are plenty of undiscovered and interesting hill towns to explore. About half of the towns I visited were memorable. Unfortunately, public transportation is frustrating, so I'd do these towns only by car. Good information on the area is rare. Fortunately, a good map, the tourist brochure (pick it up in Sevilla or Ronda), and a spirit of adventure work fine. Along with Arcos, Zahara and Grazalema are my favorite white villages.

Zahara

This tiny town in a tingly setting under a Moorish castle (worth the climb) has a spectacular view. While the big church facing the town square is considered one of the richest in the area, the smaller church has the most-loved statue. The Virgin of Dolores is Zahara's answer to Sevilla's Virgin of Macarena (and is similarly paraded through town during Holy Week). Zahara is a fine overnight stop for those who want to hear only the sounds of the wind, birds, and elderly footsteps on ancient cobbles. (**TI** open Mon–Sat 9:00–14:00 & 16:00–19:00, Sun 9:00–14:00, tel. 956-123-114.)

Andalusian Minibus Tours stops at Zahara and Grazalema on its all-day tour from Sevilla (see page 377).

SIGHTS

▲**Zahara Castle**—During Moorish times, Zahara lay within the fortified castle walls above today's town. It was considered the gateway to Granada, and a strategic stronghold for the Moors by the Christian forces of the Reconquista. Locals tell of the Spanish conquest of the Moors' castle (in 1482) as if it happened yesterday: After the Spanish failed several times to seize the castle, a clever Spanish soldier noticed that the Moorish sentinel would check if any attackers were hiding behind a particular section of the wall by tossing a rock and setting the pigeons in flight. If they flew, the sentinel figured there was no danger. One night a Spaniard

Route of the White Hill Towns

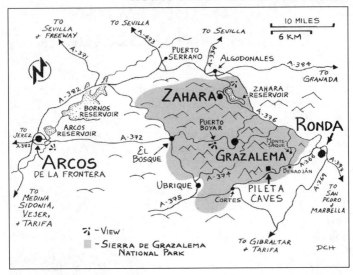

hid there with a bag of pigeons and let them fly when the sentinel tossed his rock. Seeing the birds fly, the guard assumed he was clear to enjoy a snooze. The clever Spaniard then scaled the wall and opened the door to let his troops in, and the castle was conquered. Ten years later Granada fell, the Muslims were back in Africa, and the Reconquista was complete. Today the castle is little more

than an evocative ruin (free, always open) offering a commanding view and some newly discovered Roman ruins along the way. The lake is actually a reservoir—before 1991, the valley had only a tiny stream.

El Vínculo—This family-run olive mill welcomes visitors for a look at its traditional factory, as well as a taste of some homemade sherry and the olive oil that the Urruti family has been producing on this site for centuries. Juan will treat you to a glass of sherry if you show the current edition of this book (€4.50, daily 9:30–20:00, on CA531 just outside Zahara, tel. 956-123-002, mobile 696-404-368, www.molinoelvinculo.com). Juan also rents the various houses of his estate, with access to a big swimming pool and great views surrounded by fragrant olive trees (ranges from a large house that sleeps up to 12 for €385, July–Aug €432, to a small house for €86, July–Aug €96).

SLEEPING AND EATING

(€1 = about $1.20, country code: 34)

Also see El Vínculo, above, for accommodations.

$$ Hotel Arco de la Villa—long on comfort, short on character—has 17 rooms with views just five minutes from the main square (Sb-€33, Db-€55, extra bed-€12.10, Camino Nazarí, tel. 956-123-230, fax 956-123-244, www.tugasa.com, info@tugasa.com).

$ Hostal Marqués de Zahara is the best central hotel and a good value, with 11 comfortable rooms gathered around a cool, quiet courtyard. The hostess cooks traditional specialties in the restaurant (Sb-€30, Db-€40, Db-€45 with view, less Nov–March, taxes not included, breakfast-€5, air-con, San Juan 3, tel. & fax 956-123-061, www.marquesdezahara.com, info@marquesdezahara .com, Santiago).

$ Pensión Los Tadeos is a simple, blocky place just outside of town by the municipal swimming pool *(piscina)* offering 10 remodeled rooms with great views (Db-€40, Tb-€50, basic breakfast-€1.50, Paseo de la Fuente, tel. 956-123-086, Ruíz family doesn't speak English).

Eating: Sr. Manolo Tardio runs **Mesón Los Estribos,** a fine little restaurant with fine views across from the church (Tue–Sun 13:00–16:00 & 20:00–23:00, closed Mon), and rents affordable apartments (tel. 956-123-145).

Grazalema

Another postcard-pretty hill town, Grazalema offers a royal balcony for a memorable picnic,

a square where you can watch old-timers playing cards, and plenty of quiet, whitewashed streets to explore. Graced with cork, carob, and *pinsapo* fir trees, Grazalema offers lots of scenery with greenery. Situated on a west-facing slope of the mountains, the peaks around Grazalema catch the clouds, and it's known as the rainiest place in Spain—but I've had only blue skies on every visit (**TI** open March–Sept Tue–Sun 10:00–14:00 & 18:00–20:00, Oct–Feb Tue–Sun 10:00–14:00 & 17:00–19:00, closed Mon, Plaza de España 11, tel. 956-132-225).

Plaza de Andalucía, a block off the view terrace, has several decent little bars and restaurants, and a popular candy store. Shops sell the town's beautiful handmade wool blankets.

The town makes a good home base to explore nearby Sierra de Grazalema Natural Park, famous for its spectacularly rugged limestone landscape of cliffs, caves, and gorges. For outdoor adventures, including hiking, caving, and canoeing, contact **Horizon** (off Plaza de España at Corrales Terceros 29, tel. & fax 956-132-363, www.horizonaventura.com, info@horizonaventura.com).

SLEEPING AND EATING

$$ Villa Turística de Grazalema is a big, popular, happy place for locals enjoying their national park. It has 38 apartments and 24 regular hotel rooms, opening onto the swimming-pool garden on the ground floor or onto balconies on the first floor (Sb-€33, Db-€55, extra person-€13, apartments-€65–115, extra bed-€20, includes breakfast, restaurant, half-mile outside town, tel. 956-132-136, fax 956-132-213).

$ Casa de Las Piedras has 16 comfortable rooms just a block up from the town center—ask for a room in their newer wing (Sb-€37, Db-€45, two €55 one-room and €80 two-room apartments with kitchen and fireplace, includes tax, discounts for kids, 10 percent discount with this book for stays of 2 or more nights in 2007, buffet breakfast-€6, Calle Las Piedras 32, 11610 Grazalema, tel. & fax 956-132-014, www.casadelaspiedras.net, info@casadelaspiedras .net, Katy and Rafi). Casa de las Piedras also has a good **restaurant** with a pleasant patio and local specialties, such as tasty and tender *solomillo ibérico* (Iberian pig tenderloin with eggplant) and *sopa de tomate* (bread and tomato soup with mint leaves and garlic).

Jerez

With nearly 200,000 people, Jerez is your typical big-city mix of industry, garbage, car bandits, and dusty concrete suburbs, but it has a lively old center and two claims to touristic fame: horses and sherry.

Jerez is ideal for a noontime (or midday) visit on a weekday. See the famous horses, sip some sherry, wander through the old quarter, and swagger out.

Tourist Information: The helpful **TI** on Plaza Alameda Cristina gives out free maps and info on the sights (mid-June–mid-Sept Mon–Fri 10:00–15:00 & 17:00–19:00, Sat–Sun 10:00–14:30; mid-Sept–mid-June Mon–Fri 9:30–14:30 & 16:30–18:30, Sat–Sun 9:30–14:30; tel. 956-324-747, www.turismojerez.com).

Jerez

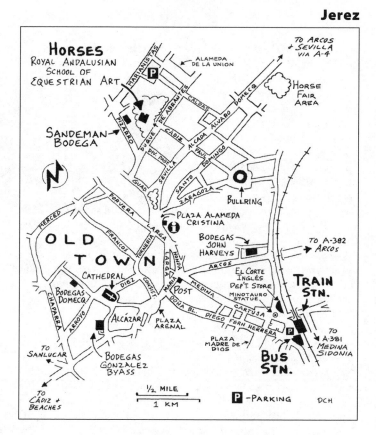

HORSES
ROYAL ANDALUSIAN
SCHOOL OF
EQUESTRIAN ART

TO ARCOS
& SEVILLA
VIA A-4

ALAMEDA
DE LA UNION

HORSE
FAIR
AREA

SANDEMAN
BODEGA

MARIANISTAS
P
PIZARRO
DQUE DE ABRANTES
CADIZ
DUQ. DIV. PATRI
GUAD
SEVILLA
SANTO
DOMINGO
ALVARO DOMECQ
ALCALDE
PAUL

N

PORVERA
MERCED
OLD
TOWN
FRANCOS
TORNERIA
LARGA

ZARAGOZA
BULLRING

PLAZA ALAMEDA
CRISTINA
i

BODEGAS
JOHN
HARVEYS

TO A-382
ARCOS

ARGA
HONDA
MARIA

ARCOS

EL CORTE
INGLES
DEP'T. STORE

TRAIN
STN.

CATHEDRAL
DIEZ
CONSIST
BODEGAS
DOMECQ
CHAPARRA
ARROYO
ALCÁZAR
PLAZA
ARENAL
POST
MEDINA
DOÑA BL.
DIEGO FERN HERRERA
CARTUJA
MINOTAURO
STATUE

TO
SANLUCAR
BODEGAS
GONZALEZ
BYASS
PLAZA
MADRE DE
DIOS

BUS
STN.

TO
A-381
MEDINA
SIDONIA

TO
CÁDIZ &
BEACHES

½ MILE
1 KM

P –PARKING

DCH

Arrival in Jerez

The bus station (by the enormous Glorieta del Minotauro head-less statue) can't store baggage, but the train station next door has 30 lockers by the train tracks; buy a €3 locker token *(ficha)* at the ticket counter (daily 7:00–22:30).

The center of town and the TI are a 20-minute walk from both the bus and train stations. Exit either, keeping the large parking lot on your left. You'll soon be greeted by the gigantic Glorieta del Minotauro statue at a traffic circle. Take the crosswalk straight over to Calle Medina and follow it faithfully. At the confusing five-way intersection, angle right on Honda, continue past a small roundabout decorated with empty sherry barrels, and go straight until you reach Plaza Alameda Cristina—the TI is tucked away on your right. There is no easy way to feel oriented in Jerez due to the complicated, medieval street plan, so ask for directions if you feel like you're heading the wrong way.

SIGHTS

▲▲**Royal Andalusian School of Equestrian Art**—If you're into horses, this is a must. Even if you're not, this is art like you've never seen. The school does its Horse Symphony show year-round at noon every Tuesday and Thursday, plus every Friday in August (€17 General seating, €23 Preference seating, 90 min, tel. 956-318-008, fax 956-318-015, can buy tickets online at www.realescuela .org). General seating is fine;

some Preference seats are too close for good overall views. The show explanations are in Spanish.

This is an equestrian ballet with choreography, purely Spanish music, and costumes from the 19th century. The stern riders and their talented, obedient steeds prance, jump, hop on their hind legs, and do-si-do in time to the music, to the delight of an arena filled with mostly tourists and local horse aficionados.

The riders, trained in dressage (dreh-SAZH), cue the horses with the slightest of commands (verbal or body movements). You'll see both purebred Spanish horses (of various colors, with long tails, calm personalities, and good jumping ability) and the larger mixed breeds (with short tails and a walking—not prancing—gait). The horses must be three years old before their three-year training begins, and most performing horses are male (stallions or geldings), since mixing the sexes brings problems.

Training sessions on non-performance days offer the public a sneak preview (€8, usually Mon, Wed, Fri 11:00–13:00, no Fri in Aug, Tue sessions added Nov–Feb). Schedules may vary, so it's wise to call ahead. Sessions can be exciting or dull, depending on what the trainers are working on. After the training session, you can take a 60-minute guided tour of the stables, horses, multimedia and carriage museums, tack room, gardens, and horse health center. Sip sherry in the arena's bar to complete this Jerez experience.

If you're driving to the horse school, follow signs from the center of Jerez to Real Escuela Andaluza del Arte Ecuestre (parking lot behind complex). From the bus or train stations to the horses, it's about a €4 taxi ride or a 40-minute walk.

▲▲**Sherry Bodega Tours**—Spain produces more than 10 million gallons per year of this fortified wine. The name "sherry" comes from English attempts to pronounce Jerez. While traditionally the drink of England's aristocracy, today it's more popular with Germans. Your tourist map of Jerez is speckled with *venencias*,

Sherry

Spanish sherry is not the sweet dessert wine sold in the States as sherry. In Spain, sherry is (most commonly) a chilled, white, very dry, fortified wine, often served with appetizers (tapas, seafood, and cured meats).

British traders invented the sherry-making process as a way of transporting wines that wouldn't go bad on a long sea voyage. Some of the most popular brands (such as Sandeman and Osbourne) were begun by Brits, and for years it was a for-eigners' drink. But today, sherry is typically Spanish.

Sherry is made by blending wines from different grapes and different vintages, all aged together. Start with a strong, acidic wine (from grapes that grow well in the hot, chalky soil around Jerez). Mature it in large vats until a yeast crust *(flor)*

forms on the surface, protecting the wine from the air. Then fortify it with distilled alcohol.

Next comes sherry-making's dis-tinct *solera* process. Pour the young, fortified wine into the top barrel of a unique contraption—a stack of oak barrels called a *criadera*. Every year, one-third of the oldest sherry (in the barrels on the ground level) is bottled. To replace it, one-third of the sherry in the barrel above is poured in, and so on, until the top barrel is one-third empty, waiting to be filled with the new year's vintage.

Fino is the most popular type of sherry (and the most dif-ferent from Americans' expectations)—white, dry, and chilled. (The best-selling commercial brand of *fino* is Tío Pepe, and *manzanilla* is a regional variation of *fino*—best from Córdoba.) Darker-colored and sometimes sweeter varieties of sherry include *amontillado* and *oloroso*. And yes, Spain also produces the thick, sweet cream sherries served as dessert wines. A good, raisin-y, syrupy sweet variety is Pedro Ximénez, made from sun-dried grapes of the same name.

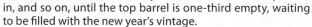

specially designed ladles to dip inside the sherry barrel, break through the yeast layer, and get to the good stuff. Each of these *venencia* symbols represents a sherry bodega that offers tours and tasting.

Sandeman Sherry: Just around the corner from the horse school is the venerable Sandeman Bodega, which has been produc-ing sherry since 1790 and is the longtime choice of English royalty. This tour is the aficionado's choice for its knowledgeable guides

and their quality explanations of the process (€5, tours Mon–Fri 10:30–17:00, last tour at 16:30, bottling finishes at 14:00, closed Sat–Sun, finale is a chance to taste three varieties, reservations not required, call 956-151-700 for English tour times, www.sandeman.com). It's efficient to see the Horse Symphony (ends at 13:30), and then walk to Sandeman's for the English tour at 14:15.

Harvey's Bristol Cream: Their English-language tours aren't substantial but include a 15-minute video, a visit to the winery, and all the sherry you like in the tasting room (€5, Mon–Fri at 10:00 and 11:30, 90-min tour, reservations recommended one day in advance, Calle Pintor Muñoz Cebrian, tel. 956-346-000, fax 956-349-427, jerez@domecq.es).

González Byass: The makers of the famous Tío Pepe offer a tourist-friendly tour, with more pretense and less actual sherry-making on display (it's done in a new, enormous plant outside of town), but it's the only bodega that offers daily tours with no reservations necessary (€7, tours run hourly at :30 past the hour, Mon–Sat 11:30–17:30, extra tour at 14:00; Sun 11:30–14:00, last tour at 14:00; Manuel María González 12, tel. 956-357-000, fax 956-357-046). This bodega is Disney-fying its tours, and schedules change frequently—call for the latest.

Alcázar—This gutted castle looks tempting, but don't bother. The €1.30 entry fee doesn't even include the Camera Obscura (€3.30 combo-ticket covers both, daily 10:00–18:00). Its underground parking is convenient for those touring the González Byass bodega (€1.10/hr).

TRANSPORTATION CONNECTIONS

Jerez's bus station is shared by six bus companies, each with its own schedules. Some specialize in certain destinations, while others share popular destinations such as Sevilla and Algeciras. The big ones serving most southern Spain destinations are Los Amarillos, Comes (www.tgcomes.es), and Linesur. Shop around for the best departure time. By car, it's a zippy 30 minutes from Jerez to Arcos.

From Jerez by Bus to: Tarifa (1/day, 2 hrs, more frequent with transfer in Cádiz), **Algeciras** (2/day, 2.5 hrs), **Arcos** (hourly, 30 min), **Ronda** (4/day, 3 hrs), **Sevilla** (7/day, 1.5 hrs), **Málaga** (1/day, 5 hrs), **Córdoba** (1/day, 3 hrs), **Granada** (1/day, 4.5 hrs), **Madrid**

(6/day, 7 hrs). Bus info: tel. 956-345-202.

By Train to: Sevilla (12/day, 1.25 hrs), **Madrid** (2/day, 4 hrs), **Barcelona** (2/day, 12 hrs). Train info: tel. 902-240-202.

Drivers: In Jerez, blue-line zones require prepaid parking tickets on your dashboard (Mon–Fri 9:00–13:30 & 17:00–20:00, Sat 9:00–14:00, Sun and July–Aug afternoons free). Otherwise, there's the handy underground parking lot near the Alcázar, at Plaza Alameda Cristina, and at Plaza Arenal (€1.10/hour).

Easy Stops for Drivers

If you're driving between Arcos and Tarifa, here are several sights to explore.

Yeguada de la Cartuja—This breeding farm, which raises Hispanic Arab horses according to traditions dating back to the 15th century, offers shows on Saturday at 11:00 (€15 for best seats in *tribuna* section, Finca Fuente del Suero, Ctra. Medina–El Portal, km 6.5, Jerez de la Frontera, tel. 956-162-809, www.yeguadacartuja .com). From Jerez, take the road to Medina Sidonia, then take a right in the direction of El Portal—you'll see a cement factory on your right. Drive for five minutes until you see the farm. A taxi from Jerez will charge about €12 one-way.

Medina Sidonia—The town is as whitewashed as can be, surrounding its church and hill, which is topped with castle ruins. Give it a quick look. Signs to *Vejer* and then *Centro Urbano* route you through the middle to Plaza de España—great for a coffee stop. Or, if it's lunchtime, consider buying a picnic, as all the necessary shops are nearby and the plaza benches afford a fine workaday view of a perfectly untouristy Andalusian town. You can drive from here up to Plaza Iglesia Mayor to find the church and **TI** (Tue–Sun 10:00–14:00 & 18:00–20:00 in summer, 10:00–14:00 & 16:00–18:00 in winter, closed Mon, tel. 956-412-404). At the church, a man will show you around for a tip. Even without a tip, you can climb yet another belfry for yet another vast Andalusian view. The castle ruins just aren't worth the trouble.

Sleeping in Medina Sidonia: **$$$ Casa La Loba,** a B&B located near Plazuela de Santiago, is run by English-speaking owner James Barr (Ds-€95–105, Calle la Loba 21, this street branches off the Plazuela, tel. 956-412-051, www.casalaloba.com, info@casalaloba.com).

Vejer de la Frontera—Vejer, south of Jerez and just 20 miles north of Tarifa, will lure all but the very jaded off the highway. Vejer's strong Moorish roots give it a distinct Moroccan (or Greek Island) flavor—you know, black-clad women whitewashing their homes, and lanes that can't decide if they're roads or stairways. Only a few years ago, women wore veils. The town has no real sights (other than its women's faces) and very little tourism, but it makes for a pleasant stop. (**TI** open June–Sept Mon–Fri 8:00–14:30 & 18:00–22:00, Sat–Sun 10:30–14:30 & 18:00–22:00; Oct–May Mon–Fri 8:00–15:00 & 17:00–20:00, closed Sat–Sun; Marqués de Tamarón 10, tel. 956-451-736.)

The coast near Vejer is lonely, with fine but windswept beaches. It's popular with windsurfers and sand flies. The Battle of Trafalgar was fought just off Cabo de Trafalgar (a nondescript lighthouse today). I drove the circle so you don't have to.

Sleeping in Vejer: A newcomer on Andalucía's tourist map, the old town of Vejer has just a few hotels. They are all at the entrance to the old town, at the top of the switchbacks past the town's lone traffic cop.

$$ Hotel La Botica de Vejer provides 13 comfortable rooms in what was once a local apothecary. Homey decor and view patios made for an afternoon beer add to the charm (Sb-€40–55, interior Db-€50–65, view Db-€60–75, junior suite-€75–95, extra bed-€15–20, includes taxes and breakfast, Canalejas 13, near Plaza de España, tel. 956-450-225, mobile 617-477-636, www.laboticadevejer.com, info@laboticadevejer.com, Josip).

$$ Convento de San Francisco is a poor-man's parador in a refurbished convent (Sb-€45, Db-€63.50, breakfast-€3.70, prices soft off-season, La Plazuela, tel. 956-451-001, fax 956-451-004, convento-san-francisco@tugasa.com). They have the rare but unnecessary Vejer town map.

$ Hostal La Posada, with 10 clean and charming rooms, is a much better value (S-€15–18, Db-€43, cheaper off-season, also 6 €72 apartments, Los Remedios 21, tel. & fax 956-450-258, no English spoken).

Route Tips for Drivers

Arcos to Tarifa (80 miles): You can drive from Arcos to Jerez in 30 minutes. If you're going to Tarifa, take the tiny C343 road at the Jerez edge of Arcos toward Paterna and Vejer. Later, you'll pick up signs to *Medina Sidonia* and then to *Vejer* and *Tarifa*.

Sevilla to Arcos: The remote hill towns of Andalucía are a joy to tour by car with Michelin map 446 or any other good map. Drivers can zip south on NIV from Sevilla along the river, following signs to *Cádiz*. Take the fast toll freeway (blue signs, E5, A4). The toll-free NIV is curvy and dangerous. About halfway to Jerez, at Las Cabezas, take CA403 to Villamartín. From there, circle scenically (and clockwise) through the thick of the Pueblos Blancos—Zahara and Grazalema—to Arcos.

It's about two hours from Sevilla to Zahara. You'll find decent but winding roads and sparse traffic. It gets worse (but very scenic) if you take the tortuous series of switchbacks over the 4,500-foot summit of Puerto de Las Palomas (Pass of the Pigeons, climb to the viewpoint) on the direct but difficult road from Zahara to Grazalema (several stops closer to Zahara offer hiking trailheads). Remember to refer to your *Ruta de los Pueblos Blancos* pamphlet.

Another scenic road option from Grazalema to Arcos is the road that goes through Puerto del Boyar (Pass of the Boyar), El Bosque, and Benamahoma. The road from Ronda to El Gastor, Setenil (cave houses and great olive oil), and Olvera is another scenic alternative.

Traffic flows through old Arcos only from west to east (coming from the east, circle south under town). The TI, my recommended hotels, and parking (Paseo Andalucía or Plaza del Cabildo) are all in the west. Driving in Arcos is like threading needles. But if your car is small and the town seems quiet enough, follow signs to the parador, where you'll find the only parking lot in the old town.

SPAIN'S SOUTH COAST

(Costa del Sol)

It's so bad, it's interesting. To northern Europeans, the sun is a drug, and this is their needle. Anything resembling a quaint fishing village has been bikini-strangled and Nivea-creamed. Oblivious to the concrete, pollution, ridiculous prices, and traffic jams, tourists lie on the beach like game hens on skewers—cooking, rolling, and sweating under the sun.

Where Europe's most popular beach isn't crowded by high-rise hotels, most of it's in a freeway choke hold. Wonderfully undeveloped beaches between Tarifa and Cádiz, and east of Almería are ignored, while human lemmings make the scene where the coastal waters are so polluted that hotels are required to provide swimming pools. It's a fascinating study in human nature.

Laugh with Ronald McDonald at the car-jammed resorts. But if you want a place to stay and play in the sun, unroll your

beach towel at **Nerja.** And don't forget that you're surprisingly close to jolly olde England. The land of tea and scones, fish-and-chips, pubs and bobbies awaits you—in **Gibraltar.** Beyond "The Rock," the whitewashed port of **Tarifa**—the least-developed piece of Spain's generally overdeveloped southern coast—provides an enjoyable springboard for a quick trip to Morocco (see next chapter). These three places alone—Nerja, Gibraltar, and Tarifa—make the Costa del Sol worth a trip.

Costa del Sol

Planning Your Time

My opinions on the "Costa del Turismo" are valid for peak season (mid-July–mid-Sept). If you're there during a quieter time and you like the ambience of a beach resort, it be a pleasant stop. Off-season it can be neutron-bomb quiet.

The whole 150 miles of coastline takes six hours by bus or three hours to drive with no traffic jams. You can resort-hop by bus across the entire Costa del Sol and reach Nerja for dinner. If you want to party on the beach, it can take as much time as Mazatlán.

To day-trip to Tangier, Morocco, you can take a tour from Tarifa (best), Algeciras, or Gibraltar (last resort).

Nerja

While cashing in on the fun-in-the-sun culture, Nerja (NEHR-hah) has actually kept much of its quiet, Old World charm. It has good

beaches, a fun evening paseo (strolling scene) that culminates in the proud Balcony of Europe terrace, enough pastry shops and nightlife, and locals who get more excited about their many festivals than the tourists do.

With cheap airfares and the completion of the expressway, real estate is booming (property values have doubled in six years). Because of "residential tourism," Nerja's population of 22,000 swells to about 90,000 in the summer. For an insight into the mostly English expat community, read the free local expat magazines. Spanish visitors complain that some restaurants have only English menus. You'll find beans on your breakfast plate and Tom Jones for Muzak. Pensioners from northern Spain also retire here—enjoying long lives thanks to low blood pressure from the diet of fish and wine. As elsewhere along the Costa del Sol, real estate, construction, and tourism motor the economy.

ORIENTATION

The tourist center of Nerja is right along the water and crowding close to its famous bluff, the "Balcony of Europe." Two fine beaches flank the bluff. The old town is just inland from the Balcony, while the more modern section slopes away from the water.

Tourist Information

The helpful, English-speaking TI has bus schedules, tips on beaches and side trips, and brochures for nearby destinations such as Málaga and Gibraltar (April–Oct Mon–Fri 10:00–14:00 & 17:00–20:00, Sat 10:00–13:00, closed Sun; Nov–March Mon–Sat 10:00–14:00 & 16:30–19:00, closed Sun; Puerta del Mar 2, just off Balcony of Europe, tel. 952-521-531, www.nerja.org, turismo @nerja.org). Ask for a free city map (or buy the more detailed version for €0.80) and the *Leisure Guide,* which has a comprehensive listing of activities. Their booklet on hiking is good, and you can reach some of the trailheads by bus.

To get a free flier with the latest theater and musical events, stop by the Villa de Nerja Cultural Center at Granada 45 (shows also take place here, tel. 952-523-863). In the third week of July, they host the music festival in the Caves of Nerja.

Arrival in Nerja

By Bus: The Nerja bus station is actually just a bus stop with an info booth on Avenida de Pescia (daily 6:00–21:00, helpful schedules posted, tel. 952-521-504).

By Car: Follow signs to *Balcón de Europa,* and then into the big underground parking lot (which deposits you 200 yards from the Balcony of Europe).

Helpful Hints

Market: The lively open-air market is colorful and fun (food on Tue 9:30–14:00, flea market on Sun 9:30–14:00, Verano Azul park, along Calle Antonio Ferrandis Chanquete, in the south-west corner of town).

Nerja

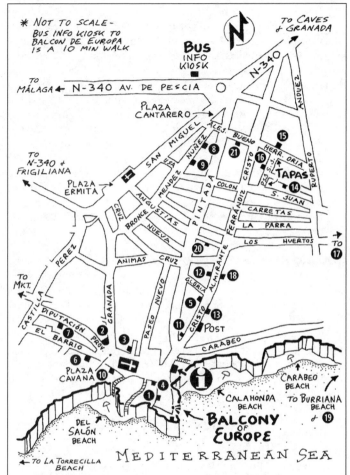

* NOT TO SCALE –
BUS INFO KIOSK TO
BALCON DE EUROPA
IS A 10 MIN WALK

1. Balcón de Europa
2. Hotel Plaza Cavana
3. Hotel Puerta del Mar
4. Hostal Marissal & Cochran's Terrace
5. Hostal Miguel
6. Hostal Residencia Mena
7. Hostal Residencia Don Peque
8. Hostal Lorca
9. Pensión El Patio
10. Casa Luque Rest.
11. Los Mariscos Rest.
12. Pinocchio Rest.
13. El Pulguilla Rest.
14. El Chispa Rest.
15. Los Cuñaos Rest.
16. La Puntilla Bar Rest.
17. To Café New Orleans
18. Haveli Restaurant
19. To Ayo's Café
20. Bar El Molino
21. Bodega Los Bilbainos

Internet Access: Two of the most scenically situated of Nerja's few Internet cafés are next door to each other, on a square overlooking Playa Torrecilla, where Calle Castilla Pérez meets Calle Málaga: **Med Web C@fé** (daily 10:00–24:00, 18 computers and cold snacks) and **Europ@Web** (daily 10:00–22:00, until 24:00 in summer, 24 computers, tel. 952-526-147).

Radio: For a taste of the British expat scene, pick up the monthly *Street Wise* magazine or tune in to Coastline Radio at 97.6 FM.

Local Guide: Cristina Burgos Flachmann is a good guide for any Costa del Sol explorations (€92/half-day is the "official rate," extra for transport fees, tel. 952-443-849, mobile 627-378-215).

Massage: Tiny yet muscular Marie, who moved here from France five years ago, runs a massage parlor out of her apartment. She does an excellent one-hour massage for €30—just give her a call (Amarilys Masaje, Calle Castilla Perez 10, mobile 667-825-828).

Getting Around Nerja

You can easily walk anywhere you need to go. A goofy little **tourist train**—nicknamed the "Wally Trolley" by Brits here—does a 30-minute loop through town every 45 minutes (€3.50, daily 10:30–22:30, until 24:00 July–Aug, departs from Plaza de Cavana, you can get off and catch a later train with the same ticket, route posted on door of train, unfortunately it doesn't go to Burriana Beach). Nerja's **taxis** charge set fees (e.g., €5 to Burriana Beach, taxi tel. 952-524-519). To clip-clop in a **horse and buggy** through town, it's €25 for about 25 minutes (hop on at Balcony of Europe).

SIGHTS AND ACTIVITIES

In Nerja

▲▲**Balcony of Europe (Balcón de Europa)**—The bluff, jutting happily into the sea, is the center of Nerja's paseo and a magnet for street performers. The mimes, music, and puppets can draw bigger crowds than the Balcony itself, which overlooks the Mediterranean, miles of coastline, and little coves and caves below. In the ninth century, a Moorish castle stood here, later partially destroyed by the English in a battle against  the French troops of Napoleon. Now it's a people-friendly view terrace.

The cute statue of King Alfonso XII reminds locals of how

Costa del History

Many Costa del Sol towns come in pairs: the famous beach town with little history, and its smaller yet much more historic partner established a few miles inland—safely out of reach of the Barbary pirate raids that plagued this coastline for centuries. Nerja is a good example of this pattern. While it has almost no history and was just an insignificant fishing village until tourism hit, its more historic sister, Frigiliana, hides out tucked away in the nearby hills. The Barbary pirate raids were a constant threat. In fact, the Spanish slang for "the coast is clear" is *"no hay moros en la costa"* (There are no Moors on the coast).

Nerja was overlooked by the tourism scene until about 1980, when the phenomenal Spanish TV hit *Verano Azul (Blue Summer)* was set here. This post-Franco hit featured the until-then off-limits topics of sexual intimacy, marital problems, adolescence, and so on in a beach-town scene. Today when any Spaniard hears the word "Nerja," they think of this *All in the Family/The O.C.*–type TV hit.

Despite the fame, development didn't really hit until about 2000, when the expressway finally and conveniently connected Nerja with the rest of Spain. Thankfully, a building code prohibits any new buildings in the old town higher than three stories.

this popular sovereign (the great-grandfather of today's King Juan Carlos) came here after a devastating earthquake in which a huge number of locals died. He mobilized the local rich to dig out the community and put things back together. Standing on this promontory, he coined its now-famous name, "Balcón de Europa."

Scan the horizon. Until recently, this was a favored landing spot (just beyond the tighter security zone near Gibraltar) for illegal immigrants and drug runners coming in from Africa. Thanks to a new high-tech satellite-scanning system, the Guardia Civil can now detect floating objects as small as makeshift rafts and intercept them before they reach land.

Walk below the Balcony for views of the scant remains (bricks and stones) of the Moorish castle. Locals claim an underground passage connected the Moorish fortress with the mosque that stood where the San Sebastián church stands today.

Promenades—Pleasant seaview promenades lead in opposite directions from the Balcony of Europe, going east to Burriana Beach and west to Torrecilla Beach. An early-morning walk along the delightful Paseo de los Carabineros from the Balcony of Europe to Burriana Beach past several coves is a great way to start your

day (10-min walk, farther to get
to Ayo's for breakfast—see page
477). In Spain, all beaches (except
the one in Rota, which is reserved
for American soldiers) are open to
the public...by law.

Beaches (Playas)—Nerja has
several good beaches. They are
well-equipped, with bars and res-
taurants, free showers, and rentable lounges and umbrellas (about
€4, same cost for 10 minutes or all day). Watch out for red flags
on the beach, which indicate that the seas are too rough for safe
swimming.

The sandiest—and most crowded—is **Del Salón Beach** (Playa
del Salón), down the walkway to the right of the Restaurante
Marissal, just off the Balcony of Europe. For the best drink-

with-a-view in town, stop
by Cochran's Terrace on the
way down (see page 477).

The pebblier **Calahonda
Beach** (Playa Calahonda) is
full of fun pathways, crags,
and crannies (head down
through the arch to the
right of the TI). The humble
Papagayo restaurant is open
all day. Antonio can be seen each morning working with his nets
and sorting through his fish. His little pre-tourism beach hut is
wonderfully photogenic.

Burriana Beach (Playa de Burriana) is Nerja's leading beach
(a 10-min walk from the Balcony of Europe along the Paseo de
los Carabineros), with paddleboats and entertainment options. It's
most fun for families. Burriana is a destination for Ayo's paella-
feast restaurant (see page 477).

Cantarriján Beach, a 15-minute drive east of Nerja, is the
nudists' choice.

Near Nerja

▲**Caves of Nerja (Cuevas de Nerja)**—These caves, 2.5 miles east
of Nerja (exit 295), have the most impressive array of stalactites
and stalagmites I've seen anywhere in Europe, their huge caverns
filled with expertly backlit formations and appropriate music. The
visit is a 30-minute unguided ramble deep into the mountain, up
and down lots of dark stairs congested with Spanish families. At
the end, you reach the Hall of the Cataclysm, where you'll circle
the world's largest stalactite column, according to the *Guinness*

Book of World Records. Someone figured out that it took one trillion drops to make the column (€5, daily 10:00–14:00 & 16:00–18:30, July–Aug until 20:00, tel. 952-529-520).

The free exhibit in the Centro de Interpretación explains the cave's history and geology (orange house next to bus parking; exhibit in Spanish, but includes free English brochure).

To get to the caves, catch a bus from the Nerja bus stop on Avenida de Pescia (€1, 13/day, 10 min). During the festival held here the third week of July, the caves provide a cool venue for hot flamenco and classical concerts (tickets sold out long in advance). The restaurant with a view offers three-course fixed-price meals for €8, but the picnic spot with pine trees, benches, and a kids' play area just up from and behind the ticket office is even better.

Frigiliana—This picture-perfect whitewashed village, only four miles inland from Nerja, is easy by car or bus (€1, 9/day, 15 min, none on Sun). It's a worthwhile detour from the beach, particularly if you don't have time for the Pueblos Blancos hill towns (www .frigiliana.com). To bring the town to life, catch the 90-minute, Frigiliana Tours town walk by David Riordan, an American who has lived here for 12 years (€7, includes guidebooklet, Mon–Fri at 11:30, call or e-mail to make a reservation, also does ghost tours, mobile 607-545-299, vaquerodave@gmail.com).

Cantarijan Beach—For a more desolate beach, those with a car can drive 12 miles east (direction Herradura) to the Cerro Gordo exit, and follow signs (paved road, just before the tunnel) to Playa Cantarijan. You'll park right on the beach, where rocks and two restaurants separate two pristine beaches—one for people with bathing suits, the other for nudists.

Hiking—Europeans visiting the region for a longer stay generally use Nerja as a base from which to hike. The TI (and your hotel) can describe a variety of hikes. One of the most popular includes a refreshing and delightful two- to three-hour walk up a river (up to your shins in water). Another, more demanding hike takes you to the 5,000-foot summit of El Cielo for the best memorable king-of-the-mountain feeling this region offers.

NIGHTLIFE

If you're out late, consider **Bar El Molino** for folk singing after 23:00; it's touristy but fun (no cover, just buy a drink, Calle San José 4). For a more colorful hole-in-the-wall, consider the **Bodega Los Bilbainos,** a favorite with local men and communists (tapas and drinks, Calle Alejandro Bueno 8). For more trendy and noisy nightlife, check out the bars and dance clubs on Antonio Millón and Plaza Tutti Frutti.

SLEEPING

The entire Costa del Sol is crowded during August and Holy Week (April 1–8 in 2007), when prices are at their highest. Reserve in advance for peak season—basically mid-July through mid-September—prime time for Spanish workers to hit the beaches. Any other time of year, you'll find that Nerja has plenty of comfy, low-rise, easygoing, resort-type hotels and rooms. Room rates are three-tiered, from low season (Nov–March) to high season (July–Sept).

Compared to the pricier hotels, the better *hostales* (Marissal, Miguel, and Lorca) are an excellent value. The Mena and Don Peque are central—within three blocks of the Balcony of Europe—but neither will stun you with warmth.

Close to the Balcony of Europe

$$$ **Balcón de Europa** is the most central place in town. It's right on the water and on the square, with the prestigious address Balcón de Europa 1. It has 110 rooms with all the modern comforts, including a pool and an elevator down to the beach. Groups love this spot, hence the stuffy management. All the suites have seaview balconies, and most regular rooms also come with views (Sb-€65/74/97, standard Db-€89/104/126, add about €26 for sea view and balcony, breakfast-€10, air-con, elevator, drivers follow signs to parking-€9/day, tel. 952-520-800, fax 952-524-490, www .hotelbalconeuropa.com, reservas@hotelbalconeuropa.com).

$$ **Hotel Plaza Cavana,** with 39 rooms, overlooks a plaza lily-padded with cafés. If you like a central location, marble floors, modern furnishings, an elevator, and a small rooftop swimming

---

Sleep Code

(€1 = about $1.20, country code: 34)
S = Single, **D** = Double/Twin, **T** = Triple, **Q** = Quad, **b** = bathroom, **s** = shower only. Unless otherwise noted, credit cards are accepted and English is spoken. Breakfast and the 7 percent IVA tax are not included (unless noted). Ayo's on Burriana Beach is a great place for breakfast (see page 477).

To help you easily sort through these listings, I've divided the rooms into three categories, based on the price for a standard double room with bath during high season:

$$$ **Higher Priced**—Most rooms €100 or more.
$$ **Moderately Priced**—Most rooms between €50–100.
$ **Lower Priced**—Most rooms €50 or less.

pool, dive in (Sb-€50–75, Db-€85–110, extra bed-€20, 10 percent discount with this book in 2007, breakfast-€6, some view rooms, air-con, second small pool in basement, parking-€10/day, 2 blocks from Balcony of Europe at Plaza de Cavana 10, tel. 952-524-000, fax 952-524-008, www.hotelplazacavana.com, info@hotelplazacavana .com).

$$ Hotel Puerta del Mar, just around the corner from Hotel Plaza Cavana and run by the same owners, offers 24 newer rooms at a better value (Sb-€35–55, Db-€50–95, Tb-€70–105, Qb-€75–120, 10 percent discount with this book in 2007, includes breakfast next door, air-con, use of Cavana pool, Calle Gómez, tel. 952-527-304, www.hotelpuertadelmar.com, info@hotelpuertadelmar.com).

$$ Hostal Marissal, next door to the fancy Balcón de Europa hotel, has an unbeatable location and 23 modern, spacious rooms— six of them with small view balconies overlooking the action on the Balcony of Europe (Db-€40/€50/€60, €5 breakfast with beans, double-paned windows, air-con, elevator, Internet in lobby, Balcón de Europa 3, reception at Marissal café, tel. 952-520-199, fax 952-526-654, www.hostalmarissal.com, reserva@hostalmarissal.com, Carlos, María, and Carmen).

$ Hostal Miguel offers nine bright and airy rooms in the heart of "Restaurant Row." Top-floor rooms have mountain views, and breakfast is served on the pretty green terrace. The owners—a young Brit expat couple, Matt and Nat—are long-time Nerja devotees, happy to provide hiking info for the more adventurous (Sb-€36, Db-€49, cash preferred, Almirante Ferrándiz 31, tel. 952-521-523, mobile 661-228-250, www.hostalmiguel.com, hostalmiguel@gmail.com).

$ Hostal Residencia Mena is erratically run but has 11 fine rooms—four with terraces and sea views—and a quiet, breezy garden (Sb-€18–26, Db-€27–39, €5 more for terrace, includes tax, street noise, El Barrio 15, tel. & fax 952-520-541, hostalmena @hotmail.com, María). You can check in only when the reception is open: daily 9:30–14:00 & 17:00–20:30.

$ Hostal Residencia Don Peque has 10 simple rooms (with older bathrooms), eight with balconies. Front rooms over the noisy street have air-conditioning (Db-€33–42, includes tax, breakfast-€3, Diputación 13, tel. & fax 952-521-318).

In a Residential Neighborhood

A quiet residential area five minutes from the center (and three blocks from the bus stop) offers the following two good options (near a small, handy grocery store and free parking lot).

$ Hostal Lorca, run by a friendly young Dutch couple, Femma and Rick, has nine modern, comfortable rooms and an inviting, compact backyard with a terrace, palm tree, and small pool. You can use the microwave and take drinks (on the honor system) from the well-stocked fridge. This quiet, homey place is a winner (Sb-€29–32, Db-€32–47, extra bed-€12, includes tax, breakfast-€4, cash only, Mendez Nuñez 20, look for yellow house, near bus stop, tel. 952-523-426, www.hostallorca.com, info@hostallorca.com).

$ Pensión El Patio has four clean, simple rooms. If you want to go local, this is worth the communication struggles (Sb-€18–36; Db-€25 most of the year, €40 in Aug; Tb-€36–48, cash only, Méndez Nuñez near bus stop, unmarked but first door left of #12, tel. 952-522-930, Angeles doesn't speak English). If no one answers, ask at #12, where the daughter lives.

EATING

There are three Nerjas: the private domain of the giant beachside hotels; the central zone, packed with fun-loving (and often tipsy) expats and tourists enjoying great food from trilingual menus; and the back streets, where local life goes on as if there were no tourists. The whole old town (around the Balcony of Europe) sizzles with lively restaurants. Wander around and see who's eating best.

Close to the Water

Drinks with a View: For drinks or a meal with a sea view, **Cochran's Terrace** does the trick (open daily anytime for drinks, 12:00–15:00 & 19:00–23:00 for meals, just behind Hostal Marissal). Its great view tables overlook the Del Salón Beach

Casa Luque is a worthwhile splurge, with a terrace in back with wicker furniture, sea views, and enough ambience to justify the price (€17 dinners, €2–5 tapas, wines can be purchased by the glass).

"Restaurant Row": You'll find lots of options on Calle Almirante Ferrándiz (which changes its name farther uphill to "Cristo"). Consider **Los Mariscos,** a traditional, family-style fish restaurant (at #17), and **Pinocchio,** a big, popular eatery serving good Spanish food at #51. **El Pulguilla,** which specializes in seafood—with clams so fresh they squirt—is a delight, with a lively tapas bar up front and a breezy and casual terrace way out back. Though not listed on the menu, half-portions (*media raciones*) are available for many items, allowing you to easily sample different dishes (€10–15 dinners, Tue–Sun 13:00–16:00 & 19:00–24:00, closed Mon, Almirante Ferrándiz 26, tel. 952-521-384).

Tapas and Colorful Holes-in-the-Wall Farther Inland

A 10-minute uphill hike takes you into the residential thick of things, where the sea views come thumbtacked to the walls, prices are lower, and locals fill the tables.

Tapas near Herrera Oria: These two eateries are within a block of each other around Herrera Oria (see map on page 469). Each specializes in seafood and is fine for a sit-down meal, or for a stop on a tapas crawl. Remember—tapas are snack-size portions; to turn them into more of a meal, ask for a *ración,* a *media* (half) *ración*—or a menu. These places maintain the wonderful tradition of serving free tapas with each drink you order at the bar. They're generally open all day for tapas and drinks; I've included just their serving hours in case you're hungry for a sit-down meal: **El Chispa** is big on seafood, with an informal terrace. Their *tomate ajo* (garlic tomato) is tasty, and their *berenjenas* (fried and salted eggplant) is also worth considering (Tue–Sun 11:00–16:00 & 19:30–24:00, closed Mon, San Pedro 12, tel. 952-523-697). **Los Cuñaos** is the most fun late in the evening, when families munch tapas, men watch soccer on TV, women chat, and kids wander around like it's home (good seafood and prices, Sun–Fri 12:00–16:00 & 19:00–23:00, closed Sat, Herrera Oria 19, tel. 952-521-107).

La Puntilla Bar Restaurante is a boisterous little place, with its rickety, plastic Coca-Cola furniture spilling out onto the cobbles on hot summer nights (cheap and good fish, tapas at bar, daily 12:00–24:00, a block in front of Los Cuñaos at Calle Bolivia 1, tel. 952-528-951).

At **Café New Orleans,** American Stephen Picchi has done a marvelous job of splicing a bit of New Orleans into Nerja. While in a blah neighborhood a five-minute walk from nowhere, this comfy one-room restaurant has a fresh, friendly ambience. Ribs and creative €9 entrée salads are a hit here, the house special "New Orleans Platter" is well worth €14, and Stephen is understandably proud of his wine list (Thu–Tue 19:00–24:00, closed Wed, Calle Los Huertos, reservations smart, tel. 952-521-941).

Haveli, run by Amit and his Swedish wife, Eva, serves good Indian food in a big and happening atmosphere. This is a hit with vacationing Brits (€10–12 plates, daily 19:00–24:00 in summer, closed Mon off-season, Cristo 42, tel. 952-524-297).

On Burriana Beach

Ayo's is famous for its characteristic owner and its beachside, €5 all-you-can-eat paella feast. For 30 years, Ayo—a lovable, pony-tailed bohemian who promises to be here until he dies—has been feeding locals. The paella fires get stoked up at about noon. Grab one of a hundred tables under the canopy next to the rustic, open-fire cooking zone, and enjoy the beach setting in the shade with a jug of sangria (daily 9:00–17:00, breakfast at 9:00—see below, not open in the evenings, Playa de Burriana, tel. 952-522-289). It's a 20-minute walk from the Balcony of Europe to the east end of

Burriana Beach—look for Ayo's orange rooftop pyramid.

Breakfast at Ayo's: Consider hiking the deserted beach early and arriving at Ayo's at 9:00 for breakfast. Locals order the *tostada con aceite de oliva* (toast with olive oil and salt—€0.40), and Ayo also serves omelets and good coffee.

TRANSPORTATION CONNECTIONS

Nerja

From Nerja by Bus to: Nerja Caves (13/day, 10 min), **Frigiliana** (9/day, 15 min, none on Sun), **Málaga** (18/day, 70–90 min), **Granada** (4/day, more frequent with transfer in Motril, 2.5 hrs), **Córdoba** (1/day, 4.5 hrs), **Sevilla** (3/day, 4 hrs).

To the Málaga Airport (about 40 miles west): Catch the bus to Málaga (€1, about 2/hr, 70–90 min) and take a shuttle from there, or pay €55 for a taxi from Nerja (airport tel. 952-048-804).

Málaga

The closest train station to Nerja is in Málaga, a 70–90-minute bus ride away (about 2/hr). Málaga's train and bus stations—a block apart—both have pickpockets and lockers (train station lockers are better). You can rent a car at the train station from Atesa or Europcar.

From Málaga by Train to: Ronda (1/day *directo*, 60 min, 6/day with transfer in Bobadilla, 2.5 hrs), **Madrid** (7/day, 4–7 hrs on TALGO train), **Córdoba** (10/day, 2–3 hrs, fastest on TALGO), **Granada** (3/day, 3.25 hrs, transfer in Bobadilla), **Sevilla** (7/day, 2.5 hrs), **Barcelona** (2/day, 14 hrs). Train info: tel. 902-240-202.

Buses: Málaga's bus station, a block from the train station, has a helpful information office with bus schedules (daily 7:00–22:00, tel. 952-350-061) and a TI (daily 11:00–19:00, Internet access, ATM, and lockers, on Paseo de los Tilos).

By Bus to: Algeciras (11/day, 2 hrs *directo*, 3 hrs *ruta*), **Nerja** (about 18/day, 70–90 min), **Ronda** (10/day, 1.75 hrs *directo*, 3 hrs *ruta*), **La Línea/Gibraltar** (4/day, 3 hrs), **Sevilla** (10/day, 2.5 hrs), **Jerez** (1/day, 5 hrs), **Granada** (8/day, 2 hrs), **Córdoba** (5/day, 2.75 hrs *directo*), **Madrid** (10/day, 6 hrs).

Between Nerja and Gibraltar

Buses take five hours to make the Nerja–Gibraltar trip. They leave nearly hourly and stop at each of these towns.

Fuengirola and Torremolinos—The most built-up part of the region, where those most determined to be envied settle down, is a bizarre world of Scandinavian package tours, flashing lights, pink flamenco, multilingual menus, and all-night happiness. Fuengirola is like a Spanish Mazatlán with a few older, less-pretentious budget hotels between the main drag and the beach. The water here is clean and the nightlife fun and easy. James Michener's idyllic Torremolinos has been strip-mauled and parking-metered.

Marbella—This is the most polished and posh town on the Costa del Sol. High-priced boutiques, immaculate streets, and beautifully landscaped squares are testimony to Marbella's arrival on the world-class-resort scene. Have a *café con leche* on the beautiful Plaza de Naranjas in the old city's pedestrian section. Wander down to new Marbella and the high-rise, beachfront apartment buildings to check out the beach scene. Marbella is an easy stop on the Algeciras–Málaga bus route (as you exit the bus station, take a left to reach the center of town).

San Pedro de Alcántara—This town's relatively undeveloped sandy beach is popular with young travelers. San Pedro's neighbor, Puerto Banús, is "where the world casts anchor." This luxurious, Monaco-esque jet-set port, complete with casino, is a strange mix of Rolls-Royces, yuppies, boutiques, rich Arabs, and budget browsers.

Gibraltar

One of the last bits of the empire upon which the sun never set, Gibraltar is a quirky mix of Anglican propriety, "God Save the Queen" tattoos, English bookstores, military memories, and tourist shops. The few British soldiers you'll see are enjoying this cushy assignment in the Mediterranean sun as a reward for enduring and surviving an assignment in another remnant of the British Empire: Northern Ireland. While things are cheaper in pounds, your euros work here, as well as your English words.

The 30,000 Gibraltarians have a mixed and interesting heritage. Spaniards call them Llanitos (yah-NEE-tohs), meaning "flat" in Spanish, though the residents live on a rock. The locals—a fun-loving and tolerant mix of British, Spanish, and Moroccan—speak a Creole-like Spanglish and call the place "Gib."

You'll need your passport to cross the border (and you may still be able to charm an official into stamping it—ask, or you'll get just a wave-through).

Planning Your Time

Make Gibraltar a day trip (or just an overnight); rooms are expensive compared to Spain.

For the best day trip to Gibraltar, consider this plan: Walk across the border, catch bus #3, and ride it to the end, following my self-guided tour (see page 484). Ride bus #3 back to the cable-car station, then catch the cable car to the top, and walk down via St. Michael's Cave and the Apes' Den. From there, either walk or take the cable car back into town. Spend your remaining free time in town before returning to Spain.

Tourists who stay overnight find Gibraltar a peaceful place in the evening, when the town can just be itself. No one is in a hurry. Families stroll, kids play, seniors window-shop, and everyone chats.

You can take a boat to Tangier, Morocco from here (see page 490), but only as a weekend trip, not a day trip. To day-trip to Tangier, leave from Tarifa or Algeciras (specifics covered in next chapter).

ORIENTATION

(tel. code: 9567 from Spain, 350 from other countries)
Gibraltar is a narrow peninsula (3 miles by 1 mile) jutting into the Mediterranean. Virtually the entire peninsula is dominated by the steep-faced Rock itself. Most tourist sights are up on the mountain. The locals live down below in the long, skinny town at the western base of the mountain (much of it on reclaimed land). Everyone must enter Gibraltar from the north. You need to travel through town to get access up the mountain (via cable car or taxi/minibus tour).

For information on all the little differences between Gibraltar and Spain—from area codes to electricity—see "Helpful Hints," below.

Tourist Information

Gibraltar's main TI is at Casemates Square, the grand square at the entrance of town (Mon–Fri 9:00–17:30, Sat 10:00–15:00, Sun 10:00–13:00, tel. 74982, www.gibraltar.gi). Another TI is in the Duke of Kent House on Cathedral Square, nearer the town center (Mon–Fri 9:00–17:30, closed Sat–Sun, bus #3 stops here, just after NatWest House, tel. 74950). There are more TIs where you cross the border (at Customs) and at the Coach Park (bus terminal), that give out free maps and can tell you about tours of caves and the WWII tunnels crisscrossing the island (€3/£2 per tour, 90 min).

Arrival in Gibraltar

By Bus: Spain's La Línea bus station is a five-minute walk from the Gibraltar border (baggage storage-€3/day, daily 6:30–22:00, purchase token, or *ficha*, from any ticket counter). From the station, exit left and go towards the Rock, crossing the border on foot (have your passport ready to flash). To get into town from

Gibraltar

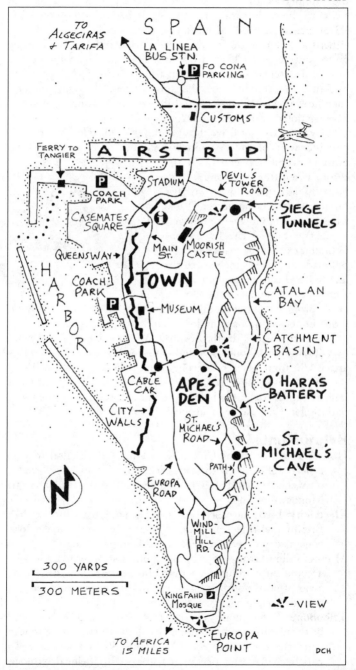

SPAIN

TO ALGECIRAS & TARIFA

LA LÍNEA BUS STN.

FO CONA PARKING

CUSTOMS

AIRSTRIP

FERRY TO TANGIER

STADIUM

DEVIL'S TOWER ROAD

SIEGE TUNNELS

COACH PARK

CASEMATES SQUARE

MAIN ST.

MOORISH CASTLE

QUEENSWAY

HARBOR

COACH PARK

TOWN

MUSEUM

CATALAN BAY

CATCHMENT BASIN

CABLE CAR

APE'S DEN

O'HARA'S BATTERY

CITY WALLS

ST. MICHAEL'S ROAD

ST. MICHAEL'S CAVE

PATH

N

EUROPA ROAD

WIND-MILL HILL RD.

300 YARDS

300 METERS

KING FAHD MOSQUE

☾ - VIEW

TO AFRICA 15 MILES

EUROPA POINT

DCH

the "frontier" (as the border is called), you can walk (30 min), take a taxi to the cable-car station (pricey at €9/£6), or hop on a bus (€1/60 pence, €2.60/£1.50 all-day pass, runs every 15 min). Catch either the #3 bus to the TI at Cathedral Square (you can also stay on to continue my self-guided tour, below) or the double-decker bus #9 to Casemates Square, which also has a TI. To get into town by foot, walk straight across the runway (look left, right, and up), then head down Winston Churchill Avenue, angling right at the Shell station on Smith Dorrien Avenue.

By Car: Do not drive into Gibraltar itself unless you're pre-pared for waits of up to 90 minutes in either direction to cross the border—worst between 16:00 and 19:00, when lines are longest. It's better to park in La Línea, walk five minutes across the border, and catch a bus or taxi into town—see above.

After taking the La Línea–Gibraltar exit off the main Costa del Sol road, continue as the road curves left (with the Rock to your right). Enter the left-hand lane at the traffic circle prior to the border and you'll end up in La Línea. The Fo Cona underground parking lot is handy (€1/hr, €6/day, on street called "20th of April" by the Spanish, "Winston Churchill Avenue" by Gibraltarians). You'll also find blue-lined parking spots in this area (€1/hr from meter, bring coins, leave ticket on dashboard).

If you insist on driving into Gibraltar, get in the right-hand lane at the traffic circle before the border. You'll find plenty of parking lots (like the huge one near the cable car).

Helpful Hints

Hours: This may be the United Kingdom, but Gibraltar follows a siesta schedule, with some businesses closing 13:00–15:00 on weekdays, and shutting up at 14:00 on Saturdays until Monday morning.

Electricity: If you have electrical gadgets, note that Gibraltar, like Britain, uses three-prong plugs. Your hotel may be able to loan you an adapter (which plugs onto a European plug).

Money: Gibraltar uses the British pound sterling (£), but also accepts euros (rough exchange rates: £1 = $1.85 = €1.50). Be aware that if you pay for something in euros, you may get pounds back in change.

Telephone: To telephone Gibraltar from Spain, dial 9567 followed by the five-digit local number. To call the Rock from European countries other than Spain, dial 00-350-local number. To call from America or Canada, dial 011-350-local number.

Spain vs. Gibraltar

Spain has been annoyed about Gibraltar ever since Great Britain snagged this prime 2.5-square-mile territory through the 18th-century Treaty of Utrecht (1713) at the end of the War of the Spanish Succession. Although Spain long ago abandoned efforts to reassert its sovereignty by force, it still tries to make Gibraltarians see the error of their British ways by messing up things like border crossings and the phone system. Still, given the choice—and they got it in referenda in 1967 and 2002—Gibraltar's residents steadfastly remain Queen Elizabeth's loyal subjects, voting overwhelmingly to continue as a self-governing British dependency.

A key British military base in World Wars I and II, Gibraltar is now a banking, shipping, and tourist magnet, connected to Spain by a sandy isthmus. Over the years, Spain has limited air and sea connections and choked traffic at the three-quarter-mile border in efforts to convince Gibraltar to give back the Rock. And then there's the phone issue. Spain refuses to recognize (or dial) a separate country code for Gibraltar, which essentially ends up making Gibraltar's phone system part of Spain's. This means that Spain can decide how many numbers Gibraltar residents get—and it's a lot less than they want. That's why when you call Gibraltar from Spain, you first dial 956 (the prefix for the Spanish province of Cádiz) plus 7; but when you call Gibraltar from anywhere else, you dial the country code 350. There have been similar problems with mobile phones. Gibraltar, a European Union member, has made its case all the way up to the European Commission, which told Spain and Britain to sort it out. Please hold...

If you plan to make calls from Gibraltar, note that phone booths take English coins or phone cards bought in Gibraltar (available at kiosks).

Internet Access: Café Cyberworld has pricey Internet access (daily 12:00–24:00, Queensway 14, in Ocean Heights Gallery, near Casemates end of town, tel. 51416).

TOURS

It's easy to visit the Rock's uppermost sights on your own at your own pace. For example, you can take bus #3 (or walk) to the cable-car lift, take the lift up, and hike down to the sights. Allow about three hours total for the trip.

Those with more money than time take a tour (covers admission to the Upper Rock Nature Reserve sights included on tour). There are two types of tours: by bus and by taxi. For the bus tours, book at a travel agency. You can catch a taxi tour at the border (or cheaper at taxi stands at squares in the center).

By Bus: Travel agencies offer approximately 90-minute tours for a set fee (about €16.50–22/£11–15). Stops include St. Michael's Cave, the Apes' Den, and Siege Tunnels. Consider Bland Travel (tours on Mon, Wed, and Fri, 220 Main Street, tel. 79068) or Parodytur (daily at 12:45, priciest, Cathedral Square, tel. 76070). If you call ahead to reserve a seat, you pay when you arrive in Gibraltar. Or just drop by any agency when you're in town (usually open Mon–Fri 9:30–18:00, closed Sat–Sun). Nearly every travel agency in town offers the tour, with only minor variations.

By Taxi: Lots of aggressive cabbies at the border would love to take you for a ride—about €24/£16 per person if the taxi is packed (at least four people). More people in a taxi means a lower cost per person, so try to buddy up with other travelers. Cabbies at taxi stands in the center of Gibraltar are more low-key and charge a bit less (though it's harder to gather a group). The basic tour consists of four stops: a Mediterranean viewpoint (called the Pillar of Hercules), St. Michael's Cave (15-minute visit), a viewpoint near the top of the Rock, and sometimes also the Siege Tunnels (15-min visit). A fifth stop—the ATM at NatWest House—is added for people who mistakenly thought they could pay for this tour with a credit card.

By Foot: Walking tours of the town center give you the essentials on the history of the Rock (€8/£5, Mon–Fri at 11:00 and 12:00, 90 min, departs from Let's Go sentry box in Casemates Square, tel. 78434).

SELF-GUIDED TOUR

The Quick, Cheap Bus #3 Orientation Tour

At the border, pick up a map at the Customs TI. Then walk straight ahead for 200 yards to the bus stop on the right. Catch bus #3 and enjoy the ride (every 15 min, pay driver €1/60p, 20 min to Europa Point and the end of the line). To save money, ask the driver for a round-trip ticket (€1.50/90p) instead of purchasing two separate fares.

You enter Gibraltar by crossing an **airstrip.** Fourteen times a week, the entry road into Gibraltar is closed to allow airplanes to land or take off. (You can fly to London for as little as $100.) The airstrip, originally a horse-racing stadium, was filled in with stones excavated from the 30 miles of military tunnels in the Rock. This airstrip was a vital lifeline in the days when Spain and Britain were quarreling over Gibraltar (especially 1970–1985) and the border was closed.

Just after the airstrip, the bus passes a road leading left (which heads clockwise around the Rock to the town of Catalan Bay, peaceful beaches, and the huge, mountainside rainwater-catchment wall). As you pass apartments on the left, find the **Moorish Castle** above (now a prison; only the tower is open to the public).

Over the bridge and on the right after the next stop, you'll see **World War memorials.** The first is the American War Memorial (a building-like structure with a gold plaque and arch), built in 1932 to commemorate American sailors based here in World War I. Farther along you'll see 18th-century cannons and a memorial to Gibraltarians who died in World War II.

The following sights come up quickly: Passing the NatWest House office tower on the left, you'll immediately see a **synagogue** (only the top peeks out above a wall; the wooden doors in the wall bear the Star of David). In the 19th century, half of Gibraltar was Jewish. The Jewish community now numbers 600.

Just after the synagogue is little **Cathedral Square,** with a playground, TI, and the Moorish-looking Anglican church (behind the playground).

Now you'll pass a lo-o-o-ong wall; most of it is the back of the Governor's Residence (also called the Convent). The bus stops before the old **Charles V wall,** built in response to a 1552 raid in which the pirate Barbarossa captured 70 Gibraltarians into slavery.

Immediately after you pass under the wall, you'll see—on your left—a green park that contains the **Trafalgar cemetery** (free, daily 9:00–19:00). Buried here are some British sailors who died defeating the French off the coast of Portugal's Cape Trafalgar in 1805.

The next stop is at the big parking lot for the **cable car** to the top of the Rock, as well as for the **botanical gardens** (free, daily 8:00–sunset) at the base of the lift. You can get off to do this now—or finish the tour, and come back here later, on the way back into town.

Heading uphill out of town, you pass the big, ugly casino and the path leading up the Rock (a 2.5-hour hike). Reaching the end of the Rock, you pass modern apartments and the mosque. The lighthouse marks windy Europa Point—the end of the line. Buses retrace the route you just traveled, departing about every 15 minutes (check schedule before exploring further).

Europa Point, up the mound from the bus stop and tourist shop (on right), is an observation post. A plaque here identifies the mountains of Morocco 15 miles across the strait. The light of the lighthouse (150 feet tall, from 1841, closed to visitors) can be seen from Morocco.

The **King Fahd Mosque,** a gift from the Saudi sultan, was completed in 1997, and Gibraltar's 900 Muslims worship here each Friday. Five times a day—as across the strait in Morocco—an imam sings the call to prayer. Visitors (without shoes) are welcome, except at prayer time.

Your tour is finished. Enjoy the views of Africa before catching a bus back into town. Get off at Trafalgar Cemetery and walk five minutes to the cable car.

SIGHTS

Gibraltar's Upper Rock Nature Reserve

The Reserve covering the Rock contains a number of sights—including St. Michael's Cave and the Apes' Den—accessible by cable car or guided tour (see "Tours," above). Note that rental cars are not allowed in the Nature Reserve.

To get to the top of the Rock and the Reserve, take the cable car from the south end of Main Street. At the cable-car station, choose between Tour A and B. Tour A covers only the round-trip ride by cable car (€13.50/£8). If you plan only to walk around up top, then Tour A is all you need. Tour B includes the round-trip cable-car ride, plus admission to all of the Upper Rock Nature Reserve sights (€26.50/£16).

I'd recommend Tour B; it saves you money if you plan to visit more than one sight on the Upper Rock. Either tour includes a free multimedia device that explains the spectacular views (pick it up at the well-marked booth when you get off the cable car at the top).

The cable car departs every 10 minutes (April–Oct daily 9:30–17:15; Nov–March Mon–Sat 9:30–17:15, closed Sun; cable car closed when it's windy, last cable car down at 17:45, brochure with necessary map included with ticket).

The entire Upper Rock Nature Reserve is open daily 9:30–19:00. Only the Apes' Den is free with your cable-car ticket.

If you're in a hurry, your best strategy is to take the cable car up, hike downhill to St. Michael's Cave and the Apes' Den, and then take the cable car down into town from the Apes' Den, skipping the other sights. Why hike at all, you ask? Because you'd miss St. Michael's Cave if you relied solely on the cable car.

If you want to see all the sights, you'll end up hiking down, rather than taking the cable-car lift back. Approximate hiking times: From the top of cable-car lift to St. Michael's Cave—25 minutes; from the cave to the Apes' Den—20 minutes; from the

Apes' Den to the Siege Tunnels—30 minutes; from the tunnels to the "City Under Siege" exhibit—five minutes; from the "City Under Siege" exhibit to the Moorish Castle—five minutes; and from the castle down to town—10 minutes. Total from top to bottom: about 90 minutes, not including sightseeing.

I've listed the following sights in the order you'll reach them as you descend from the top of the Rock.

▲▲▲**The Rock**—The real highlight of Gibraltar is the spectacular Rock itself. The limestone massif, or large rock mass, is nearly a

mile long and five football fields wide, rising 1,388 feet high with very sheer faces. In ancient legend, this was one of the "Pillars of Hercules" (paired with another mountain across the water in Africa), marking the edge of the known world. In A.D. 711, the Muslim chieftain Tarik ibn Ziyad crossed over from Africa and landed on the Rock, beginning the Moorish conquest of Spain and naming the Rock after himself—"The Rock of Tarik," or Djebel-Tarik, which became Gibraltar.

The cable car drops you at an expensive **restaurant/view terrace** (second stop) at the top of the Rock, from which you can explore old ramparts and drool at the 360-degree view of Morocco (including the Rif Mountains and Djebel Musa, the other "Pillar of Hercules"), the Strait of Gibraltar, the bay stretching west toward Algeciras, and the twinkling Costa del Sol arcing eastward. The views are especially crisp on brisk off-season days. Below you (to the east) stretches the giant catchment system that the British built to catch rainwater in the not-so-distant past, when Spain allowed neither water nor tourists to cross its disputed border. Broad sheets catch the rain, sending it through channels to reservoirs located inside the rock.

▲▲**O'Hara's Battery**—The battery is officially closed, and for many it's not worth the 20-minute hike from the top of the cable-car lift (only those seriously interested should contact the TI for a possible visit—ask nicely and they might oblige, tel. 74982). At 1,400 feet, this is the highest point on the Rock. A 100-ton, nine-inch gun sits on the summit where a Moorish lookout post once stood. It was built after World War I, and the last test shot was fired in 1974. Locals are glad it's been mothballed—during test firings, if locals didn't open their windows to allow air to move freely after the concussion, the windows would shatter. Thirty miles of tunnels, like the tiny bit near the Battery, honeycomb this strategic rock.

During World War II, an entire garrison could have survived six months with the provisions stored in this underground base.

Early in the war, when Fascist forces occupied virtually the entire European continent, US General Dwight D. Eisenhower made a damp Gibraltar cave his headquarters (November 1942) to plan the Allied invasion of North Africa, a prelude to the assault on Europe. The iron rings are anchored pulleys used to haul up guns such as the huge one at O'Hara's Battery.

▲**St. Michael's Cave**—Studded with stalagmites and stalactites, eerily lit and echoing with classical music, this cave is dramatic, corny, and slippery when wet. Considered a one-star sight since Neolithic times, these caves were alluded to in ancient Greek legends—when the caves were believed to be the Gates of Hades (or the entrance of a tunnel to Africa). In the last century, they were prepared (but never used) as a WWII hospital, and are now just another tourist sight with an auditorium for musical events. Notice the polished cross-section of a stalagmite, showing weirdly beautiful rings similar to a tree's. Spelunkers who'd enjoy a three-hour subterranean hike through the lower cave need to make arrangements three days in advance at the TI (€7.50/£5 per person, Mon–Fri from 18:00, Sat from 14:40, Sun only by appointment).

To continue to the Apes' Den, refer to your map (free with lift ticket) and take the left fork.

Apes' Den—This small zoo without bars gives you a chance at a close encounter with some of the famous (and very jaded) apes of Gibraltar. The Rock is home to about 200 apes (actually, tailless monkeys). The males are bigger, females have beards, and newborns are black. They live about 15–20 years. Legend has it that as long as the apes remain here, so will the Brits. Keep your distance from the apes and beware of their kleptomaniac tendencies; they'll  ignore the peanut in your hand and claw after the full bag in your pocket. The man at the little booth posts a record of the names of all the apes. If there's no ape action, wait for a banana-toting taxi tour to stop by and stir some up. Note that it's against the law to feed the apes, and offenders—though rarely fined—can get a £500 ticket.

The cable car stops here, so you can catch the car down to town from here (if it's too crowded with visitors descending from the top for you to get on, ask the driver to save a spot for you on the next trip down), or continue on foot to see the following sights.

▲**Siege Tunnels**—Also called the Upper Galleries, these chilly tunnels were blasted out of the rock by the Brits during the Spanish and French siege of 1779 to 1783. The clever British, safe inside the Rock, used hammers and gunpowder to carve these tunnels in order to plant four big guns on the north face and drive off the French. During World War II, 30 more miles of tunnels were blasted out. Hokey but fun dioramas help recapture a time when Brits were known more for their conquests than for crumpets. The tunnels are at the northern end of the Rock, about a mile from the Apes' Den.

Gibraltar: A City Under Siege Exhibition—A spin-off of the Siege Tunnels, this excuse for a museum gives you a look at life during the siege. It's worth a stop only if you already have a combo-ticket (just downhill from Siege Tunnels).

Moorish Castle—Actually more tower than castle, this building offers a tiny museum of Moorish remnants and carpets. It was built on top of the original castle built in A.D. 711 by the Moor Tarik ibn Ziyad, who gave his name to Gibraltar (see "The Rock" listing, page 487). The tower marks the end of the Upper Rock Nature Reserve. Head downhill to reach the lower town and Main Street.

Lower Gibraltar

The town at the base of the hill (pop. 30,000) survives on banking, tourism, and its port facilities (especially refueling). Most locals speak both English and Spanish. There's not much to the town except souvenir and cheap electronics shops, but here are a few sights:

Gibraltar Museum—Built atop a Moorish bath, this museum in Gibraltar's lower town tells the story of a rock that has been fought over for centuries. Highlights are the history film and the prehistoric remains discovered here.

On the ground floor, you can see the 15-minute film, a "teaser" prehistoric-skull display, and the empty rooms of the 14th-century Moorish baths. The first floor contains military memorabilia, a 15-foot-long model of the Rock, paintings by local artists, and, in a cave-like room off the art gallery, a collection of prehistoric remains and artifacts. The famous skull of a Neanderthal woman found in Forbes' Quarry is a copy (original in British Museum in London). This first Neanderthal skull ever discovered was found in Gibraltar in 1848, though no one realized its significance until a similar skull found years later in Germany's Neanderthal Valley was correctly identified—stealing the name, claim, and fame from Gibraltar (€3/£2, Mon–Fri 10:00–18:00, Sat 10:00–14:00, closed Sun, no photos, on Bomb House Lane just around the corner from the recommended Bristol Hotel).

▲**Catalan Bay**—Gibraltar's tiny second town originated as a settlement of Italian shipwrights whose responsibility was keeping the royal ships in good shape. Today it's just a huddle of apartments around a cute little Catholic church and the best beach on the Rock (fully equipped). Catch bus #4 from the cable car (direction: Both Worlds).

Dolphin-Watching Cruises—Numerous companies take you on two-hour cruises of the bay to look for dolphins (all companies charge about €30/£20).

Trip to Tangier, Morocco

Virtually any travel agency in Gibraltar offers weekend trips to Tangier (ask at the TI for their "Tangier Trips" list, stop by any travel agency in Gibraltar, or check with Parodytur—listed on page 516). Ferries leave Gibraltar on Friday at 19:00 and depart Tangier only on Sunday at 20:00 (Morocco time). The weekend ferry schedule was adopted so the large number of Moroccans working in Gibraltar can spend the weekend with their families (€36/£23 one-way, €64/£41 round-trip). Because Gibraltar is expensive compared to Spain, it makes sense to use your time here just to see the Rock, and day-trip to Morocco from a cheaper home base such as Tarifa (see page 496) or Algeciras.

SLEEPING

To call Gibraltar from Spain, dial 9567 plus the five-digit local number. To call from Europe, dial 00-350-local number. To call from America or Canada, dial 011-350-local number.

   $$$ O'Callaghan Eliott Hotel is four stars and then some. It boasts a rooftop pool with a view, a nice restaurant, bar, and terrace, fine sit-a-bit public spaces, and 120 modern, if sterile, settle-in rooms. If you're a jazz fan, you can enjoy their summer concerts

---

Sleep Code

(€1 = about $1.20, £1 = about $1.80, tel. code: 9567 from Spain, or 350 international)

S = Single, **D** = Double/Twin, **T** = Triple, **Q** = Quad, **b** = bathroom, **s** = shower only. Exterior rooms (with views and traffic noise) often cost more than interior rooms (quiet, without a view). All of these places accept credit cards and speak English.

   To help you easily sort through these listings, I've divided the rooms into three categories, based on the price for a standard double room with bath during high season:

  $$$ Higher Priced—Most rooms €110/£75 or more.
   $$ Moderately Priced—Most rooms between €50/£35 and €110/£75.
    $ Lower Priced—Most rooms €50/£35 or less.

Gibraltar Town

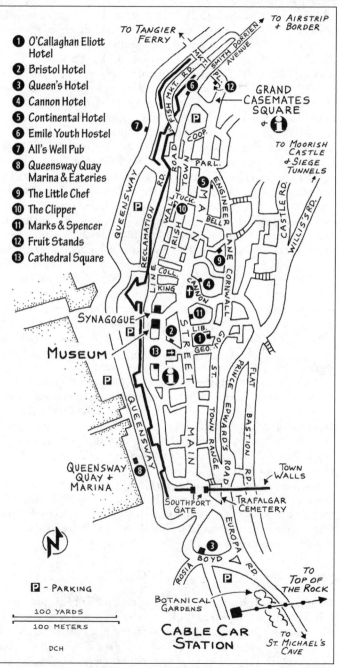

1. O'Callaghan Eliott Hotel
2. Bristol Hotel
3. Queen's Hotel
4. Cannon Hotel
5. Continental Hotel
6. Emile Youth Hostel
7. All's Well Pub
8. Queensway Quay Marina & Eateries
9. The Little Chef
10. The Clipper
11. Marks & Spencer
12. Fruit Stands
13. Cathedral Square

TO TANGIER FERRY

TO AIRSTRIP & BORDER

GRAND CASEMATES SQUARE

TO MOORISH CASTLE & SIEGE TUNNELS

SMITH DORRIEN AVENUE

FISH MKT. RD.

MKT. PL.

COOP. PARL.

ENGINEER LANE

BELL LANE

TUCK.

MAIN

TOWN

IRISH TOWN

WALL ROAD

CORNWALL

CASTLE RD.

WILLIS'S RD.

QUEENSWAY

RECLAMATION RD.

LINE WALL

KING'S COLL.

CANNON

LIB.

GOV.

ST. GEO.

PRINCE EDWARD'S ROAD

FLAT BASTION RD.

SYNAGOGUE

MUSEUM

STREET

MAIN

TOWN RANGE

QUEENSWAY

QUEENSWAY QUAY & MARINA

TOWN WALLS

SOUTHPORT GATE

TRAFALGAR CEMETERY

EUROPA RD.

BOYD

ROSIA

BOTANICAL GARDENS

TOWN TO TOP OF THE ROCK

TO ST. MICHAEL'S CAVE

CABLE CAR STATION

N

P – PARKING

100 YARDS

100 METERS

DCH

even if you're not staying here—ask at the reception desk for the schedule (Db-€278–330/£185–220, usually half off if booked online, breakfast-€20/£13, non-smoking floor, air-con, elevator, laundry service, free parking, centrally located at Governor's Parade up Library Street from main drag, tel. 70500, fax 70243, www.ocallaghanhotels.com, eliott@gibnet.gi).

$$$ Bristol Hotel offers drab, overpriced rooms in the heart of Gibraltar (Sb-€83–91/£57–62, Db-€108–115/£74–79, Tb-€123–134/£85–93, higher prices for exterior rooms, breakfast-€7.25/£5, air-con, elevator, swimming pool oddly located off breakfast room in the annex, free parking, Cathedral Square 10, tel. 76800, fax 77613, www.bristolhotel.gi, reservations@bristolhotel.gi).

$$ Queen's Hotel, near the cable-car lift, has 62 comfortable, remodeled rooms in a noisy location (Sb-€75/£50, Db-€98/£65, seaview Db-€113-143/£75-95, Tb-€128/£85, Qb-€135/£90, includes breakfast, 20 percent discount for students with ISIC cards and paying cash, elevator, free parking, at #3 bus stop, Boyd Street 1, tel. 74000, fax 40030, www.queenshotel.gi, queenshotel@gibtelecom.gi).

$$ Cannon Hotel, charming and central, is a good value, with 18 quiet rooms (most without bathroom) and a little patio. Its style is somewhere between a hotel and an upscale youth hostel (S-€37/£24.50, D-€54/£36.50, Db-€67/£45, T-€69/£46.50, Tb-€76/£52, includes full English breakfast, Cannon Lane 9, behind cathedral, tel. 51711, fax 51789, www.cannonhotel.gi, cannon@gibnet.gi). The bar downstairs is open all day.

$$ Continental Hotel isn't fancy, but it has a friendly feel. Its 18 high-ceilinged, air-conditioned rooms border an unusual elliptical atrium, and there's an inexpensive café downstairs (Sb-€78/£52, Db-€105/£70, Tb-€128/£85, Qb-€143/£95, includes continental breakfast, elevator, in pedestrian area on Main Street, a couple of blocks south of Casemates TI, Engineer Lane, tel. 76900, fax 41702, contiho@gibnet.gi).

$ Emile Youth Hostel Gibraltar is the cheapest place in town, with 44 beds (dorm bed-€20/£15, S-€30/£20, D-€50/£30, includes breakfast, lockout 10:30–17:00, on Montagu Bastion with ramped entrance on Line Wall Road, tel. & fax 51106, www.emilehostel.com).

EATING

Take a break from *jamón* and sample some English pub grub: fish-and-chips, meat pies, jacket potatoes (baked potatoes with fillings), or a hearty English breakfast of eggs, bacon, and side dishes. Anything smothered with gravy goes. English-style beers include chilled lagers and nearly-room-temperature ales, bitters,

and stouts. In general, the farther you venture away from Main Street, the cheaper and more local the places become.

Casemates Square, the big square at the entrance of Gibraltar, contains a variety of restaurants, ranging from fast food (fish-and-chips joint, Burger King, and Pizza Hut) to pubs spilling out into the square. Consider the **All's Well** pub, near the TI, with €7.50/£5 meals (burgers, fish-and-chips, and more) and pleasant tables with umbrellas under leafy trees (daily 9:30–22:00).

Queensway Quay Marina, at the cable-car end of town, is the place to be when a misty sun sets over the colorful marina and rugged mountains of Spain. The string of restaurants that line the promenade have indoor and outdoor seating, offer seafood and other dishes, and are usually open daily for lunch and dinner. One option is **Claus on the Rock Bistro** (closed Sun, colorful menu from around the world, good cigar and wine selection, tel. 48686). **Waterfront,** farther on, is less expensive, and the **Jolly Parrot** (just tapas and drinks) offers the cheapest seat on the promenade. To reach Queensway Quay, walk through Ragged Staff Gates toward the water.

For good-value meals, consider **The Little Chef,** an adventure when the one English-speaking guy is off-duty. They have tasty, cheap €5/£3.50 meals but no menu. You just ask—in Spanish if necessary—what's cooking (daily 8:00–15:00, no dinner, Cornwall's Parade 7, a few blocks from Casemates Square). **The Clipper** has filling €7.50/£5 pub meals (English breakfast €5.70/£3.95, daily 9:00–11:00, on Irish Town, at intersection with tiny Irish Place).

Groceries: **In & Out** minimarkets are on Main Street, off Cathedral Square (Mon–Fri 8:30–20:00, Sat 8:30–18:00, closed Sun). Nearby **Marks & Spencer** has an inside take-away window that serves roast chicken and fresh-baked cookies (Mon–Sat 8:30–19:00, Sun 10:00–15:00). Fruit stands bustle at the Market Place (Mon–Sat 9:00–15:00, closed Sun, outside entry to Casemates Square).

TRANSPORTATION CONNECTIONS

If you're leaving Gibraltar without a car, you must walk five minutes from Gibraltar's border into Spain to reach La Línea, the nearest bus station. The region's main transportation hub is Algeciras, with lots of train and bus connections, as well as ferries to Tangier and Ceuta. (For Algeciras connections, see page 504.) If you're traveling between La Línea and Algeciras, buy tickets on the bus;

otherwise, buy tickets inside the station.

From La Línea by Bus to: Algeciras (2/hr, 45 min), **Tarifa** (4/day, *directo*, 60 min, more often with transfer in Algeciras), **Málaga** (4/day, 3 hrs), **Granada** (5/day, 5 hrs), **Sevilla** (4/day, 4 hrs), **Jerez** (1/day, 3 hrs), **Huelva** (1/day, 6 hrs), **Madrid** (2/day, 8 hrs). Tel. 902-199-208 or 956-172-396.

Tarifa

Europe's southernmost town is a pleasant alternative to gritty, noisy Algeciras...as most Europeans have now discovered. It's a whitewashed, Arab-looking town with a lovely beach, an old castle, restaurants swimming in fresh seafood, inexpensive places to sleep, enough windsurfers to sink a ship, and best of all, hassle-free boats to Morocco.

As I stood on Tarifa's town promenade under the castle, looking out at almost-touchable Morocco across the Strait of Gibraltar, I regretted only that I didn't have this book to steer me clear of Algeciras on earlier trips. Tarifa, with daily 35-minute trips to Tangier, is the best jumping-off point for a Moroccan side-trip.

Tarifa has no blockbuster sights (and can be quiet off-season), but it's a town where you just feel good to be on vacation.

ORIENTATION

The old town, surrounded by a wall, slopes gently up from the water's edge. The modern section is farther inland.

Tourist Information: The TI is on Paseo Alameda (June–Sept daily 10:00–14:00 & 18:00–20:00; Oct–May Mon–Sat 10:00–14:00 & 16:00–18:00, closed Sun; tel. 956-680-993, turismo @aytotarifa.com).

Arrival in Tarifa

By Bus: The bus station (actually a couple of portable buildings with an outdoor sitting area) is on Batalla del Salado, about a five-minute walk from the old town. The more central TI also has bus schedules. Buy tickets directly from the driver if the ticket booth is not open (Mon–Fri 7:30–9:30 & 10:00–11:00 & 14:30–18:30, Sat–Sun 15:00–19:45, tel. 902-199-208). To reach the old town, walk away from the wind generators perched on the mountain ridge. The recommended hotels in the old town are through the

Tarifa

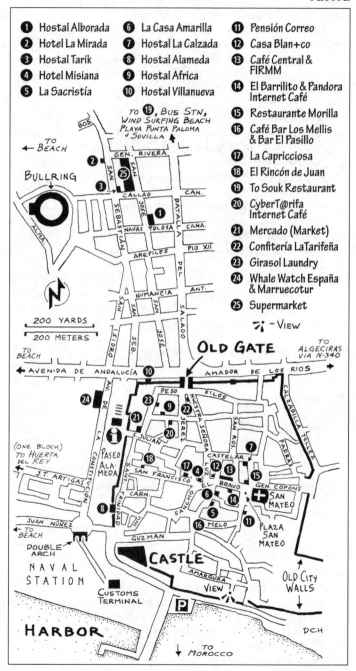

1. Hostal Alborada
2. Hotel La Mirada
3. Hostal Tarik
4. Hotel Misiana
5. La Sacristía
6. La Casa Amarilla
7. Hostal La Calzada
8. Hostal Alameda
9. Hostal Africa
10. Hostal Villanueva
11. Pensión Correo
12. Casa Blan+co
13. Café Central & FIRMM
14. El Barrilito & Pandora Internet Café
15. Restaurante Morilla
16. Café Bar Los Mellis & Bar El Pasillo
17. La Capricciosa
18. El Rincón de Juan
19. To Souk Restaurant
20. CyberT@rifa Internet Café
21. Mercado (Market)
22. Confitería LaTarifeña
23. Girasol Laundry
24. Whale Watch España & Marruecotur
25. Supermarket

7ᵢ – VIEW

horseshoe arch gate; the hotels in the newer part of town are a couple of blocks into town and to the right.

By Car: If you're staying in the center of town, follow signs for *Alameda* or *Puerto,* and continue along Avenida de Andalucía. Follow signs to make an obligatory loop to the port entrance and parking at Calle Juan Núñez. Note that Avenida de la Constitución is one-way (going away from the port).

Helpful Hints

Internet Access: Pandor@, in the heart of the old town, is across from Café Central and near the church (long hours, 15 computers). **CyberT@rifa** is near the old-town gate (Mon–Sat 10:30–14:00 & 17:00–22:00, closed Sun, María Antonia Toledo 3).

Laundry: Girasol Adventure disguises a small, drop-off laundry service; leave your load of laundry (8 pounds max), and they'll wash and dry it for €8 (Mon–Sat 10:30–13:30 & 19:30–20:00, longer hours in summer, closed Sun, Calle Colón 14, tel. 956-627-037).

Excursions: Girasol Adventure not only does your laundry, but also offers a variety of outdoor excursions—rock climbing, hiking, biking, and horseback riding—for around €25 per person. Ask Christian for details (see contact info above).

Ferry to Morocco (Marruecos)

Boats to Tangier, Morocco, sail from both Tarifa and nearby Algeciras. As recently as August 2003, the Tarifa–Tangier crossing was open only to people from EU countries, but now it's open to anyone of any nationality, whether solo or on a tour. However, the port still might close to non-Europeans at times (most likely at end of June and beginning of July, and end of July and beginning of Aug). E-mail the TI for details prior to your trip.

Note that the Spanish refer to Morocco as "Marruecos" (mar-WAY-kohs) and Tangier as "Tanger" (pronounced with a guttural "g" at the back of the throat, sounding like TAHN-hair).

Procedure: Although the only ferry from Tarifa is now a fast Nordic hydrofoil that theoretically takes 35 minutes, it often leaves late (but not always—so be there on time). If you go on your own (without a tour), Spanish officials will check your passport at the terminal before boarding, and Moroccan officials will stamp your ticket and usually your passport aboard the boat.

If you take a tour and already have your ticket, be at the terminal 15 or 20 minutes in advance. You still must have your ticket stamped by the Moroccan official on board (they won't stamp your passport; your guide should tell you this). You'll have to wear a sticker, and upon arrival in Tangier, someone will guide you to your guide.

The boat is equipped with WCs, a shop, and a snack bar. The new terminal has a cafeteria and WCs.

Tours: Ideally, get your ticket the day before you sail, when you arrive in Tarifa. Prices are roughly the same at the various travel agencies (€27 one-way, €49 round-trip, 6–8 boats daily). You can take some daylong tours for the same price as just the boat ticket (the tour company makes money off commissions if you shop, and they get a group rate for boat tickets).

FRS Iberia, which owns the ferry service, offers an economic VIP-tour option if you are traveling with others. For an additional €60, up to four people can have a private guide and vehicle, plus lunch. This is a better deal than their regular €56 tour option, which only includes the guide's fee—transportation and lunch are extra (tel. 956-681-830, at Tarifa terminal, www.frs.es).

Marruecotur in Tarifa offers a herded, one-day excursion that takes you from Tarifa to Tangier, then on a panoramic bus tour, a walking tour of old Tangier, a typical lunch in the medina, and a stroll through the bazaar (€52, no limit to size of group, tours depart Tarifa at 9:00 and 11:30, back at 15:30 and 18:30 respectively, 2-day option available for €89 per person). Marruecotur's office, across the street from the Tarifa TI, is open long hours (daily June–Sept 7:40–21:00, Oct–May 8:00–20:00, Avenida de la Constitución 5, tel. 956-681-821 or 956-681-242, fax 956-680-256, mcotur1@mcotur1.e.telefonica.net, Luís, Roberto, and Jaime). They also book flights, trains, and some long-distance buses to destinations in Spain and Portugal.

Speedlines Tours, near the town gate in the new town, books Tangier tours as well as flights, trains, car and bike rentals, and more (Batalla del Salado 10, tel. 956-627-048).

SIGHTS AND ACTIVITIES

Church of St. Matthew (Iglesia de San Mateo)—Tarifa's most important church, facing its main drag, is wonderfully decorated for being in such a small town. Most nights, it seems life squirts from the church out the front door and into the fun-loving Calle El Bravo. Wander inside (daily 9:00–13:00 & 17:30–21:00, English-language leaflets—unless they're out— are inside on the right).

Find the tiny square (about the size of a piece of copier paper) of an **ancient tombstone** in the wall just before the transept on the right side. Probably the most important historical item in town, this stone fragment proves there was a functioning church here during Visigothic times, before the Moorish conquest. The tombstone reads, in a kind of Latin Spanish, "Flaviano lived as a Christian for 50 years, a little more or less. In death he received forgiveness as a servant of God on March 30, 674. May he rest in peace." If that gets you in the mood to light a candle, switch on an electric "candle" for a coin.

Step into the side chapel at the transept. The centerpiece of the **altar** is a boy Jesus. By Andalusian tradition, he used to be naked, but these days he's clothed with outfits that vary with the Church calendar. Cherubs dance around on the pink-and-purple interior above an exquisite chandelier.

A statue of **St. James the Moor Slayer** (missing his sword) is on the right wall of the main central altar. Since the days of the Reconquista, James has been Spain's patron saint. For more on this important figure—and why he's fighting invaders that came to Spain centuries after his death—see "St. James," page 174.

The chapel to the left of the main altar harbors several **statues** that go on parade through town during Holy Week. Circling around to the left side, you'll see the **Captive Christ** (with hands bound, on left wall), which evokes the times when Christians were held captive by Moors. You'll also find a side door, the **"door of pardons."** For a long time, Tarifa was a dangerous place—on the edge of the Reconquista. To encourage people to live here, the Church offered a huge amount of forgiveness to anyone who lived in Tarifa for a year. One year and one day after moving to Tarifa, they would have the privilege of passing through this special "door of pardons," and a Mass of thanksgiving would be held in that person's honor.

Castle of Guzmán el Bueno—This castle was named after a 13th-century Christian general who gained fame in a sad show

of courage while fighting the Moors. Holding Guzmán's son hostage, the Moors demanded he surrender the castle or they'd kill the boy. Guzmán refused, even throwing his own knife down from the ramparts. It was used on his son's throat. Ultimately, the Moors withdrew to Africa, and Guzmán was a hero. *Bueno.* The castle itself is a concrete hulk in a vacant lot, interesting only for the harbor views from the ramparts (€1.20; mid-June–Sept Tue–Sat 11:00–14:00 & 18:00–20:00, Sun 11:00–14:00, closed Mon; Oct–mid-June Tue–Sat 11:00–14:00 & 17:00–19:00, Sun 11:00–14:00, closed Mon).

You'll get equally good views from the plaza just left of the town hall. Follow *ayto* signs to the ceramic frog fountain in front of the Casa Constitorial and continue left. Fun views of Africa, ferry traffic, and confused tourists are yours for free.

Bullfighting—Tarifa has a third-rate bullring where novices botch fights on occasional Saturdays through the summer. Professional bullfights take place the first week of September. The ring is a short walk from the town. You'll see posters everywhere.

▲**Whale Watching**—Daily whale- and dolphin-watching excursions are offered by several companies in Tarifa. In little more than 40 years, people in this area went from eating whales to protecting them and sharing them with 20,000 visitors a year. Talks are underway between Morocco and Spain to protect the Strait of Gibraltar by declaring it a national park.

For any of the tours, it's wise to reserve one to three days in advance, though same-day bookings are possible. You'll get a multilingual tour and a two-hour boat trip (usually no WC on board). Sightings occur more than 90 percent of the time. Dolphins and pilot whales frolic here any time of year, while sperm whales visit May through July and orcas pass through July and August. Depending on the wind and weather, boats may leave from Algeciras instead (drivers follow in a convoy, people without cars usually get rides from staff).

The best company is the Swiss nonprofit **FIRMM** (Foundation for Information and Research on Marine Mammals), which gives a 25-minute educational talk prior to departure—and if you don't see any dolphins or whales, you can go on another trip for free (€27 per person, cash only, 1–5 trips/day April–Oct, Pedro Cortés 4, around the corner from Café Central—one door inland, also offers courses, tel. 956-627-008, mobile 619-459-441, www.firmm.org, firmm98@aol.com).

Another good option is the first non-profit to launch these trips, **Whale Watch España,** part of a Whale Protection Association that runs classes and studies dolphins and whales (€30 per person, includes helpful illustrated brochure, also offers a free trip if you don't see whales or dolphins, 1–3 trips/day April–Oct, across from TI on Avenida de la Constitución 6, tel. 956-627-013, mobile 670-796-508, www.whalewatchtarifa.net, run by Lourdes). Yet another company is **Turmares** (tel. 956-680-741, mobile 696-448-349, www.turmares.com).

▲**Windsurfing**—The vast, sandy beach **Playa Punta Paloma** lies about five miles northwest of town. On windy summer days, the sea is littered with sprinting windsurfers, while the beach holds a couple hundred vans and fun-mobiles from northern Europe. Under mountain ridges lined with modern

energy-generating windmills, it's a fascinating scene. Drive down the sandy road and stroll along the beach. You'll find a cabana-type hamlet with rental gear, beachwear shops, a bar, and a hip, healthy restaurant with great lunch salads.

For drivers, it's a cinch to reach. Without a car, you're in luck July through September, when inexpensive buses do a circuit of nearby campgrounds, all on the waterfront (€1.75, Mon–Fri every 2 hours from 8:00–22:00, Sat–Sun 8:00–3:00, confirm times with TI, the stop Punta Paloma is best, look for yellow cabin of Tarifa Lines along main drag, tel. 956-627-048).

SLEEPING

Room rates vary with the season (three seasonal tiers vary, but are roughly: highest prices—mid-June-Sept; medium prices—spring and fall; and lowest prices—winter).

Outside the City Wall

These hotels are right off the main drag—Batalla del Salado—and close to the beach with easy parking in the plain, modern part of town. If arriving by bus, walk away from the mountaintop wind generators into town; these hotels are a few blocks ahead and to your right.

$$ Hostal Alborada is a squeaky-clean, family-run, 37-room place with two attractive courtyards and modern conveniences (Sb-€30/40/55, Db-€43/55/70, Tb-€65/75/90, get your price and then show this book in 2007 for a 10 percent discount *except* during high season, includes tax, air-con, 5 Internet terminals in lobby, Wi-Fi in rooms, laundry-€12, can book ferry tickets, Calle San José 40, tel. 956-681-140, fax 956-681-935, www.hotelalborada .com, alborada@cherrytel.com).

$$ Hotel La Mirada has 25 standard rooms, most of which come with sea views at no extra cost (Sb-€30/36/42, Db-€54/60/66, extra bed-€12, breakfast-€3.60, extra for American-type breakfast, includes tax, elevator, expansive views from large common terrace, Calle San Sebastián 41, tel. 956-684-427, fax 956-681-162, www .hotel-lamirada.com, reservas@hotel-lamirada.com, Antonio and Salvador). It's two blocks off the main drag and about five blocks away from the old town.

$$ The motel-style **Hostal Tarik** is a lesser value. Clean but noisy, it's a bit tattered, and the ground floor is short on windows (request an upstairs room). Of its 18 rooms, eight are newly renovated, with balconies and views (Db-€40/50/70, Tb-€55/65/85, breakfast-€2.75, Calle San Sebastián 34, tel. 956-680-648, Mario speaks some English). Surrounded by warehouses, it's one block toward the town center from Hotel La Mirada.

Sleep Code

(€1 = about $1.20, country code: 34)
S = Single, **D** = Double/Twin, **T** = Triple, **Q** = Quad, **b** = bathroom,
s = shower only. Unless otherwise noted, credit cards are
accepted and English is spoken. Breakfast and the 7 percent
IVA tax are not included (unless noted).

To help you easily sort through these listings, I've divided
the rooms into three categories, based on the price for a standard double room with bath during high season:

$$$ **Higher Priced**—Most rooms €100 or more.
 $$ **Moderately Priced**—Most rooms between €50–100.
  $ **Lower Priced**—Most rooms €50 or less.

On or Inside the City Wall

$$$ **La Sacristía,** formerly a Moorish stable, now houses travelers
who want chic surroundings. It offers 10 fine rooms, each deco-
rated differently: fancier on the first floor, Japanese-style on the
second floor (Db-€115–135, extra bed-€35, includes breakfast, fans,
massage room, roof terrace with views, very central at San Donato
8, tel. 956-681-759, fax 956-685-182, www.lasacristia.net, tarifa
@lasaristia.net, helpful Teresa).

$$$ **Casa Blan+co,** where minimal meets Moroccan, is the
newest, reasonably priced, designer hotel on the block. Each of
its seven rooms is decorated (and priced) differently, but expect
romantic amenities such as loft beds, walk-in showers, and subtle
lighting (Db-€70–150, includes tax, discounts for longer stays,
small kitchens, small roof terrace, off main square at Calle Nuestra
Señora de la Luz 2, tel. & fax 956-681-515, www.casablan-co.com,
info@casablan-co.com).

$$$ **Hotel Misiana** has 13 comfortable, newly remodeled,
spacious rooms. The top-floor suite is grand, with private eleva-
tor access, a Jacuzzi, great views, and a big terrace—worth the
splurge. The management is friendly and casual, and the restau-
rant and trendy bar on the ground floor are open late on sum-
mer weekend nights (Sb-€39/52/86, Db-€60/86/112, top-floor
Db suite-€141/185/224, includes breakfast 9:00–12:00, includes
tax, double-paned windows, elevator, a block from Café Central,
Sancho IV El Bravo 18, tel. 956-627-083, fax 956-627-055, www
.misiana.com, reservas@misiana.com).

$$ **La Casa Amarilla** ("The Yellow House") offers 10 posh
apartments plus three regular rooms with modern decor and tiny
kitchens (Db-€34–56, larger Db-€44–66, Tb-€59–88, 20 percent
deposit requested, across street from Café Central, Calle Sancho

IV El Bravo 9, entrance on alley, tel. 956-681-993, fax 956-684-029, www.lacasaamarilla.net, info@lacasaamarilla.net).

$$ Hostal La Calzada has eight airy, well-appointed rooms right in the noisy-at-night, old-town thick of things (Db-€45–80, Tb-€55–90, includes tax, closed Nov–March, Calle Justino Pertinez 7, veer left and down from the old-town gate, tel. & fax 956-680-366 or 956-681-492).

$$ Hostal Alameda, overlooking a square where the local children play, glistens with pristine marble floors and dark red decor. Its 11 bright rooms—five with views—are above its restaurant, which serves tasty gazpacho (Db-€40/50/60, Tb-€55/65/80, breakfast-€3.40, includes tax, Paseo Alameda 4, tel. & fax 956-681-181, www.hostalalameda.com, some English spoken).

$ Hostal Villanueva, with 12 remodeled rooms, is your best budget bet. It's simple, clean, and friendly, and includes an inviting terrace that overlooks the old town. It's on a busy street, and the four quiet rooms in the back come with the best views (Sb-€20–25, Db-€35–45, breakfast-€2.50, includes tax, can use credit card if you stay at least 2 nights, double-paned windows, attached restaurant, Avenida de Andalucía 11, just west of the old-town gate, with access outside the wall, tel. & fax 956-684-149, Pepe).

$ Hostal Africa, with 13 bright, newer rooms and a roof garden on a very quiet street in the center of town, has a Moorish ambience (S-€15–25, Sb-€20–35, D-€22–40, Db-€30–50, Tb-€42–75, cash only, breakfast options in the market next door, includes tax, laundry-€10, storage for boards and bikes, Calle María Antonia Toledo 12, tel. 956-680-220, mobile 606-914-294, hostal_africa@hotmail.com, Miguel and Eva).

$ Pensión Correo rents 14 simple rooms at a good value (Db-€30–50, extra bed-€15–17, reservations accepted only within 24 hours of arrival, roof garden, Coronel Moscardo 8, tel. 956-680-206, pensioncorreo@ya.com, María José and Lucca).

EATING

You'll find good tapas throughout the old town. I've loosely arranged my listings as a one-way tapas pub crawl, beginning at the landmark Café Central.

Café Central is the happening place nearly any time of day. The tapas are priced at €1.20—just go to the bar and point. They also offer great, ingenious €5 salads (study the menu) and impressively therapeutic, healthy fruit drinks (daily 9:00–24:00, off Plaza San Mateo, near church, tel. 956-680-560).

The popular **El Barrilito,** across the street, makes interesting open-face sandwiches (€1.80–2.40, daily 8:00–24:00), with a tapas option and a few tables outside.

Restaurante Morilla, a few doors down and in front of the church, serves good local-style fish—grilled or baked—on the town's prime piece of people-watching real estate (daily 13:00–16:30 & 19:30–23:00, Calle Sancho IV El Bravo, tel. 956-681-757).

From Café Central, follow the cars 100 yards to the first corner on the left to reach the simple, untouristy **Bar El Francés** ("The French"—after owner Marcial). This spot is popular for its fine tapas (generally €1–3)—especially oxtail *(rabo del toro)*, snails *(caracoles,* June–mid-July only), pork with tomato sauce *(carne con tomate)*, and pork with spice *(chicharrones)*. The outdoor terrace is a popular hangout in the early evening hours (April–Sept open long hours daily, Oct–March closes Sat–Sun nights, Calle Sancho IV El Bravo 21A).

The nearby **Café Bar Los Mellis** is family-friendly and serves a good chorizo sandwich and *patatas bravas*—potatoes with a hot tomato sauce served on a wooden board, as well as stuffed chicken (daily 12:00–16:00 & 20:00–24:00, closed Wed in winter, run by brothers José and Ramón, from Bar El Francés, cross parking lot and take Calle del Legionario Ríos Moya up 1 block). **Bar El Pasillo,** next to Los Mellis, also serves tapas (closes Mon).

From Los Mellis, you can circle around toward the church past some very gritty and colorful tapas bars. Just to the sea side of the church, you'll see the mysterious **Casino Tarifeño.** This is an old-boys' social club "for members only," but it offers a big, musty, Andalusian welcome to visiting tourists, including women. Wander through. There's a low-key bar with tapas, a TV room, a card room, and a lounge.

From the town center, walk the narrow Calle San Francisco to survey a number of good restaurants. A large expat Italian community has left its mark in Tarifa with numerous pizza and pasta joints; the best is cozy **La Capricciosa.** Sergio has his bike trophies on display above the door (daily 20:00–24:00, at the beginning of Calle San Francisco, tel. 956-685-040). **El Rincón de Juan** is the only restaurant offering outdoor seating on the street with a nice local vibe. Enjoy the great grilled local fish—*urta* and *voraz*—or tuna caught just offshore (€12 dinners, Fri–Wed 12:00–15:00 & 20:00–23:00, closed Thu, tel. 956-681-018).

The street Huerta del Rey is a family scene at night. Stop by the produce shop for fruit and veggies, the *heladería* for ice cream, or **El Tuti** for a drink (outside the old city walls, 2 blocks west; a clothing market is held here Tue 9:00–14:00).

Romantic Upscale: For a romantic dinner with a Moroccan and Thai flavor, **Souk** is a good place to spend €20, if you don't mind a 15-minute walk. Head towards Sevilla; the restaurant is off Batalla del Salado at Mar Tirreno 46 (daily 8:00–24:00, closed Tue Sept–June and Feb, tel. 956-627-065, Patricia is very friendly). It's a Moroccan-style tea house during the day.

Dessert: **Confitería La Tarifeña** serves super pastries and flan (at the top of Calle Nuestra Señora de la Luz, near the main old-town gate).

Windsurfer Bars: With a car, head to the bars at Camping Torre de la Peña to check out Tarifa's popular windsurfing scene—give **Chozo** or **Spin Out** a try.

Picnics: Stop by the *mercado municipal* (Mon–Sat 8:00–14:00, closed Sun, in old town, inside gate nearest TI), any grocery, or the **Eroski Center supermarket** (Mon–Sat 9:15–21:15, closed Sun, simple cafeteria, at Callao and San José, near the hotels in the new town).

TRANSPORTATION CONNECTIONS

Tarifa

From Tarifa by Bus to: La Línea/Gibraltar (4/day, 60 min, first departure at 10:40, last return at 20:00, most involve transfer in Algeciras), **Algeciras** (10/day, 30 min, first departure from Tarifa weekdays at 6:30, on Sat 8:00, on Sun 10:00; return from Algeciras as late as 22:15), **Jerez** (1/day, 2 hrs, more frequent with transfer in Cádiz), **Sevilla** (4/day, 3 hrs), **Huelva** (1/day, 5 hrs), and **Málaga** (2/day, 3.5 hrs). Bus info: tel. 902-199-208.

Algeciras

Algeciras is only worth leaving. It's useful to the traveler mainly as a transportation hub, offering ferries to Tangier (see Tangier chapter) and trains and buses to destinations in southern and central Spain. The **TI** is on Juan de la Cierva, a block inland from the port, and on the same street as the train station and the bus station, which runs frequent service to Tarifa and La Línea. If you need a place to stay, try **Hotel Reina Cristina** (Db-€110, free parking, easy walk to ferry dock, Paseo de la Conferencia, tel. 956-602-622).

Trains: The train station is four blocks inland, opposite Hotel Octavio (up San Bernardo, lockers on platform for €3—buy token at ticket window, tel. 956-630-202). If arriving by train, head down San Bernardo toward the sea to Juan de la Cierva for the TI and port. As an alternative, you can also purchase ferry tickets at the train-station branch of Viajes Lixus Travel (daily 9:00–18:00, tel. 956-657-311).

From Algeciras by Train to: Madrid (2/day, 6 hrs during day arriving at Atocha, 11 hrs overnight arriving at Chamartín), **Ronda** (6/day, 2 hrs), **Granada** (3/day, 4.5 hrs), **Sevilla** (3/day, 5 hrs, transfer in Bobadilla), **Córdoba** (4/day, 4.5–5 hrs, transfer in Bobadilla), **Málaga** (4/day, 4 hrs, transfer in Bobadilla). With the exception of the route to Madrid, these are particularly scenic trips; the best is the mountainous journey to Málaga via Bobadilla.

Buses: Algeciras is served by three different bus companies (Comes, Portillo, and Linesur), all located in the same terminal next to Hotel Octavio and directly across from the train station. Different companies generally serve different destinations, but there is some overlap. Compare schedules and rates to find the most convenient bus for you.

Comes (tel. 902-199-208, www.tgcomes.es) runs buses to **La Línea** (2/hr, 45 min, from 7:00–21:30), **Tarifa** (10/day, 7/day on Sun, 30 min), **Sevilla** (4/day, 3.5 hrs), **Jerez** (2/day, 2.5 hrs), **Huelva** (1/day, 6 hrs), and **Madrid** (4/day, 8 hrs).

Portillo (tel. 956-654-304) offers buses to **Málaga** (11/day, 2 hrs) and **Granada** (4/day, 4-5 hrs).

Linesur (tel. 956-667-649) runs the most frequent direct buses to **Sevilla** (9/day, 3.25 hrs) and **Jerez** (8/day, 1.25 hrs).

Route Tips for Drivers

Tarifa to Gibraltar (45 min): It's a short drive, passing a silvery-white forest of windmills, from peaceful Tarifa past Algeciras to La Línea (the Spanish town bordering Gibraltar). Passing Algeciras, continue in the direction of Estepona. At San Roque, take the La Línea–Gibraltar exit.

Gibraltar to Nerja (130 miles): Barring traffic problems, the trip along the Costa del Sol is smooth and easy by car—much of it on new highways. Just follow the coastal highway east. After Málaga, follow signs to Almería and Motril.

Nerja to Granada (80 miles, 1.5 hrs, 100 views): Drive along the coast to Motril, catching N323 north for about 40 miles to Granada. While scenic side trips may beckon, don't arrive late in Granada without a firm hotel reservation.

MOROCCO

MOROCCO

(Al-Maghrib)

A young country with an old history, Morocco is a photographer's delight and a budget traveler's dream. It's cheap, exotic, and comes with lots of hotels and decent transportation. Along with a rich culture, Morocco offers plenty of contrast—from beach resorts to bustling desert markets, from jagged mountains to sleepy, mud-brick oasis towns.

Morocco (*Marruecos* in Spanish; *Al-Maghreb* in Arabic) also provides a good dose of culture shock—both bad and good. It makes Spain and Portugal look meek and mild. You'll encounter oppressive friendliness, brutal heat, the Arabic language, the Islamic faith, ancient cities, and aggressive beggars.

While Morocco is clearly a place apart from Mediterranean Europe, it doesn't really seem like Africa either. It's a mix, reflecting its strategic position between the two continents. Situated on the Strait of Gibraltar, Morocco has been flooded by waves of invasions over the centuries. The Berbers, the native population, have had to contend with the Phoenicians, Carthaginians, Romans, Vandals, and more.

The Arabs brought Islam to Morocco in the seventh century A.D. and stuck around, battling the Berbers in various civil wars. A series of Berber and Arab dynasties rose and fell; the Berbers won out and still run the country today.

From the 15th century on, European countries carved up much of Africa. By the early 20th century, most of Morocco was under French control; Morocco wasn't granted independence until 1956. In the late 1970s, Morocco itself became an invading country, grabbing Spain's Western Sahara territory and causing the relatively few inhabitants to clamor for independence. Western Sahara's claim has still not been settled by the United Nations.

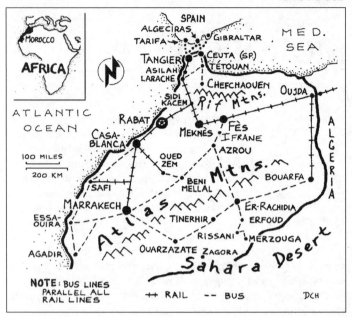

Morocco

NOTE: BUS LINES PARALLEL ALL RAIL LINES

++ RAIL   -- BUS   DCH

Most of the English-speaking Moroccans that the tourist meets are hustlers. Most visitors develop some intestinal problems by the end of their visit. Most women are harassed on the streets by horny but generally harmless men. Things don't work smoothly. In fact, compared to Morocco, Spain resembles Sweden in terms of efficiency.

When you cruise south across the Strait of Gibraltar, leave your busy itineraries and split-second timing behind. Morocco must be taken on its own terms. In Morocco things go smoothly only *"Inshallah"*—if God so wills.

Helpful Hints

Hustler Alert: While Moroccans are some of Africa's wealthiest people, you are still incredibly rich to them. This imbalance causes predictable problems. Wear your money belt. Assume con artists are cleverer than you. Haggle when appropriate (prices skyrocket for tourists). You'll attract hustlers like flies at every famous tourist sight. In the worst-case scenario, they'll lie to you, get you lost, blackmail you, and pester the heck out of you. Never leave your car or baggage where you can't get back to it without someone else's "help." Anything you buy in a guide's company gets him a 20 percent commission. Normally locals, shopkeepers, and police will come to your rescue if the hustlers' heat becomes unbearable. Consider hiring a licensed guide (I've listed referrals on page 520), since it's helpful to have a translator, and once you're "taken," the rest seem to leave you alone.

Marijuana Alert: In Morocco, marijuana *(kif)* is as illegal as it is popular, as many Westerners in local jails would love to remind you. As a general rule, just walk right by those hand-carved pipes in the marketplace. Some dealers who sell it cheap make their profit after you get arrested. Cars and buses are stopped and checked by police routinely throughout Morocco—especially in the north and in the Chefchaouen region, which is Morocco's *kif* capital.

Health: Morocco is much more hazardous to your health than Spain or Portugal. Eat in clean—not cheap—places. Peel fruit, eat only cooked vegetables, and drink reliably bottled water (Sidi Harazem or Sidi Ali). When you do get diarrhea—and you should plan on it—adjust your diet (small and bland meals, no milk or grease) or fast for a day, but make sure you replenish lost fluids. Relax: Most diarrhea is not serious, just an adjustment that will run its course.

Closed Days: Friday is the Muslim day of rest, when most of the country (except Tangier) closes down.

Ramadan: On this major, month-long religious holiday (Sept 12–Oct 11 in 2007), Muslims focus on prayer and reflection. Following Islamic doctrine, they refrain during daylight hours from eating, drinking (including water), smoking, and having sex. On the final day of Ramadan, Muslims celebrate *Eid* (an all-day feast and gift-giving party, similar to Christmas) and travelers may find some less-touristy stores and restaurants closed.

Money: Euros work here (as do dollars and pounds). Bring along lots of €1 and €0.50 coins for tips, small purchases, and camel rides. If you change money into dirhams, go to banks—or even easier, ATMs (available at most major banks), all of which have uniform rates. The black market is dangerous. Change only what you need, and keep the bank receipt to reconvert if necessary. Don't leave the country with Moroccan money unless you want a souvenir, since few places are willing to change dirhams to euros or dollars. (In a pinch, try the Bank of Morocco branch in Algeciras, Spain.)

Information: For an extended trip, bring travel information from home or Spain. The guides published by Lonely Planet and Rough Guide are good. The green Michelin *Morocco* guidebook is worthwhile (if you read French). Buy the best map you can find locally—names are always changing, and it's helpful to have towns, roads, and place names written in Arabic.

Language: The Arabic squiggle-script, its many difficult sounds, and the fact that French is Morocco's second language make communication tricky for English-speaking travelers. A little French goes a long way, but learn a few words in Arabic. Have your first local friend help you pronounce:

English	Arabic	Pronounced
Hello. (greeting)	*As salaam alaikum.*	ah sah-LAM mah-LAY-koom
Hello. (response)	*Wa alaikum salaam.*	wa ah-LAY-koom sah-LAM
Please.	*Min fadlik.*	meen FAD-leek
Thank you.	*Shokran.*	SHOW-kron
Excuse me.	*Ismahli.*	ees-MAY-lee
Yes.	*Yeh.*	EE-yeh
No.	*Lah.*	lah
Goodbye.	*Maa salama.*	mah sah-LEM-ah

Moroccans are even more touchy-feely than their Spanish neighbors. Expect lots of hugs if you make an effort to communicate. When greeting someone, a handshake is customary, followed by making a fist and placing it on your heart. Listen carefully and write new words phonetically. Bring an Arabic phrase book. In markets, I sing, "la la la la la" to my opponents. *Lah shokran* means, "No, thank you."

Getting Around Morocco: Moroccan trains are quite good. Second class is cheap and comfortable. Buses connect all smaller towns quite well. By car, Morocco is easy, but drive defensively and never rely on the oncoming driver's skill. Night driving is dangerous. Pay a guard to watch your car overnight.

Keeping Your Bearings: Navigate the labyrinthine *medinas* (old towns) by altitude, gates, and famous mosques or buildings. Write down what gate you came in, so you can enjoy being lost—temporarily. *Souk* is Arabic for a particular market (such as leather, yarn, or metalwork).

TANGIER

Go to Africa. As you step off the boat, you realize that the crossing (varying from 35 minutes to 2.5 hours, depending on the port you choose) has taken you further culturally than did the trip from the US to Iberia. Morocco needs no museums; its sights are living in the streets. Offered daily and year-round, the one-day excursions from Tarifa and Algeciras are well-organized and reliable. Given that tours from Spain (rather than pricier Gibraltar) are virtually the cost of the boat passage alone, the tour package is a good value for those who can spare only a day for Morocco. For an extended visit to Morocco, see the end of this chapter (page 525).

Morocco in a Day?

There are many ways to experience Morocco, and a day in Tangier is probably the worst. But all you need is a passport and patience (no visa or shots required), and if all you have is a day, this is a real and worthwhile adventure. Tangier is the Tijuana of Morocco, and everyone there seems to be expecting you.

You can use ATMs in Tangier to get Moroccan dirhams, but for a short one-day trip, there's no need to change money. Everyone you meet will be happy to take your euros, dollars, or pounds.

Whether on a tour or on your own, carefully confirm the time your return boat departs from Tangier. The time difference between the countries is usually two hours. Most schedules list departure times from Tangier on Moroccan time; ask when you purchase your ticket. (I keep my watch on Spanish time and get my departure time clear in Spanish time.) Plan on spending a half-hour of your day in lines (passport control and so forth). If you are traveling without a tour, you will have to show your passport

Tangier

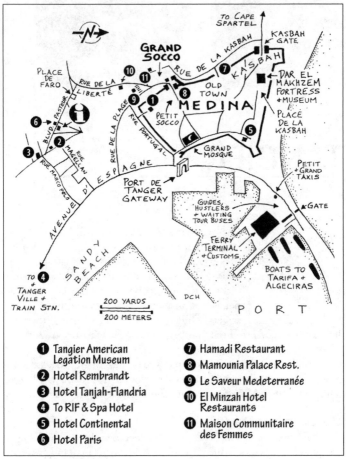

1 Tangier American Legation Museum
2 Hotel Rembrandt
3 Hotel Tanjah-Flandria
4 To RIF & Spa Hotel
5 Hotel Continental
6 Hotel Paris
7 Hamadi Restaurant
8 Mamounia Palace Rest.
9 Le Saveur Medeterranée
10 El Minzah Hotel Restaurants
11 Maison Communitaire des Femmes

and ticket, and have them stamped by a Moroccan immigration officer while on board the boat (they don't always announce this). If you're on a tour, you'll need to have your ticket—but not your passport—stamped while on board (your tour guide should remind you).

On Your Own: Just buy a ferry ticket at the FRS booth at the port or from a local travel agency. Algeciras, Gibraltar, and Tarifa have fine, modern ferry terminals, but Tarifa is by far the best launch pad, with the fastest crossing straight to Tangier in 35 minutes. Plus, Tarifa is more pleasant than Algeciras, and cheaper than Gibraltar. Coming from Tarifa, you can buy your ticket at the terminal or in any of the travel agencies I suggest (see page 516).

If you plan to sail from Algeciras, buy your ticket at the port instead of at one of the many divey-looking travel agencies littering the town. To find the right office at the Algeciras port, go to the very furthest building, which is labeled in large letters: *Estación Marítima Terminal de Pasajeros* (luggage storage available here and at train station, easy parking at port-€6). The official offices of the seven boat companies are inside this main port building, directly behind the helpful little English-speaking info kiosk (daily 6:45–21:45, tel. 956-585-463). Get your ticket here. There are 8–22 crossings daily to Tangier.

Tarifa makes a cheaper home base for a day trip than Gibraltar, but if you're not going to Tarifa, consider visiting Tangier from the Rock. However, keep in mind that you no longer can do it as a day trip—a boat leaves Gibraltar only on Friday—and returns only on Sunday (see page 490).

By Tour: You rarely need to book a tour more than a day in advance, even during peak season. Tours generally cost about €50 from Spain or €50–70 from Gibraltar. This includes a round-trip crossing and a guide who meets you at a prearranged point and hustles you through the hustlers and onto your bus. Excursions vary, but they usually offer a city tour, possibly a trip to the desolate Atlantic Coast for some rugged African scenery and the famous ride-a-camel stop (€1 to ride a camel for less than 5 minutes), a walk through the medina (old town) with a too-thorough look at a sales-starved carpet shop, and lunch in a palatial Moroccan setting with live music.

Sound cheesy? It is. But no amount of packaging can gloss over how exotic and different this culture really is. This kind of cultural voyeurism is almost embarrassing, but it's nonstop action and more memorable than another day in Spain. The shopping is—Moroccan. Bargain hard!

The day trip is so tightly organized that you'll have hardly any time alone in Tangier. For many people, that's just fine. Some travelers, however, spend a night there and return the next day (or two days later, if returning to Gibraltar). If you're interested, ask travel agencies about the two-day tour (sample cost: about €50 for 1-day tour from Tarifa; about €90 for 2-day tour). The first day of a two-day tour is the same as the one-day tour; you just go to a fancy hotel (with dinner), rather than to the afternoon boat, and then you catch the same boat—on your own—24 hours later.

Tour Tips: If you get a voucher when you pay for your tour at a travel agency, exchange it at the FRS office to get your ticket prior to boarding. Confirm where you will meet the guide. Moroccan time is usually two hours behind Spanish time, so you can take a later ferry and still arrive in Tangier at a reasonable hour. Your stomach will still probably be on the Spanish clock, so bring a snack.

Travel Agencies Offering Tours

There are dozens, particularly in Algeciras. Here are several:

In Tarifa: Marruecotur is across from the TI (about €50 for 1-day tour, daily in summer 7:40–21:00, Avenida de la Constitución 5, tel. 956-681-821 or 956-681-242, fax 956-680-256, mcotur1 @e-savia.net). Others are Speedlines Tours, across from Tarifa's bus station (Batalla del Salado 10, tel. 956-627-048) and FRSMaroc at Tarifa's dock (tel. 956-681-830).

In Algeciras: Marruecotur is at the port (about €50 for 1-day tour, open long hours, Estación Marítima C-6, tel. 956-656-185, fax 956-653-132, mcotur@e-savia.net).

In Gibraltar: Parodytur is in Cathedral Square (€50–70, tel. 76070). Most agencies are open weekdays 9:30–18:00 (closed Sat–Sun).

Ferries to Morocco

Ferries have mediocre cafeteria bars, plenty of WCs, stuffy indoor chairs, and grand views. Boats are most crowded in August, when the Costa del Sol groups come en masse. Only a few crossings a year are canceled because of storms, mostly in winter. Whether taking a tour or traveling on your own, you *must* get a stamp onboard by the Moroccan immigration officer, Take your passport and ticket with you, and look for a booth marked "Information" toward the front of the boat. If you are with a group, your passport will not be stamped but your ticket will; solo travelers will get their passport stamped. If you're returning the same day, the immigration official will also give you an exit stamp—this prevents delays at the port at departure time.

The following information is for people going to Tangier on their own. If you're taking a tour, skip this section.

From Tarifa to: Tangier (by fast ferry only, 6–8/day, 35 min, €27 one-way, €49 round-trip, no cars allowed in July, Tarifa tel. 956-681-830, www.frs.es).

From Algeciras to: Tangier (by slow ferry: 22/day in summer, 10/day in winter, 2.5 hrs; by fast ferry: 6/day, 1 hr; €35 one-way, €63 round-trip; to bring a car: €125 one-way, €225 round-trip), **Ceuta** (via Buquebus, hourly in summer, 7/day in winter, 35 min by fast ferry; €31 one-way, €62 round-trip; to bring a car: €78 one-way—€52 for the car plus €26 per person, €73 round-trip—€47 for the car plus €26 per person. Ceuta, an uninteresting Spanish possession in North Africa, is the cheapest car-entry point, but requires more waiting in line once you're in Africa, and it is not for those relying on public transport (for info on the crossing, see "Extended Tour of Morocco," page 525).

From Gibraltar to Tangier: Note that a day trip is no longer possible—there's only one departure from Gibraltar each Friday at 19:00, which returns from Tangier on Sunday at 20:00 (Morocco time) (€36 one-way, €64 round-trip).

Tangier

Artists, writers, and musicians have always loved Tangier. Matisse was drawn to the evocative light. The Beat generation, led by William S. Burroughs and Jack Kerouac, sought the city's multicultural, otherworldly feel. Paul Bowles found his sheltering sky here. In the 1920s through the 1950s, Tangier was an "international city," governed by no single nation. It attracted playboy millionaires, bon vivants, globetrotting scoundrels, con artists, and expat romantics. Tangier is always defying expectations. In this Muslim city, you'll find a synagogue, Catholic and Anglican churches, and the town's largest mosque within close proximity. Just step off the boat...you'll be surprised at what you see.

Currently, Tangier is experiencing a rebirth. Restorations are taking place on a grand scale—the beach has been painstakingly cleaned, pedestrian promenades are popping up everywhere, and gardens bloom with lush, new greenery. In the works are a new soccer stadium and a project to move the shipping port beyond the bay where the ferry docks (which will clear current traffic congestion and make Tangier a more pleasant place to live and visit). All these changes—which just began in 2006—are thanks to King Mohammed VI. Deciding to spend more time in the previously neglected north coast, the king hopes to restore Tangier to its former glory.

Planning Your Time

If you're on your own, either hire a guide upon arrival (see "Guides," below) and sightsee together, or catch a Petit Taxi from the port to the TI. They can help you get oriented. Exit the TI to the right and continue up to Place de Faro with its cannons and views of Spain. Turn right on Rue de la Liberté, and walk down to the Grand and Petit Socco. No good map exists of the confusing market area, so expect to be confused. There will be plenty of people offering to lead you wherever you want to go.

In the old town, start at the Museum of the Kasbah, then wander through the fortress (Dar el-Makhzem) and Old American Legation Museum. Then shop through the Petit Socco. Walk out of the old town into the noisy Grand Socco. From there, catch a taxi to the beach (Plage el Cano), and sightsee along the beach and then along Avenue d'Espagne back to the port.

ORIENTATION

Like almost every city in Morocco, Tangier is split into two. From the boat dock, you'll see the old town (medina)—encircled by its medieval wall—on your right, behind Hotel Continental. The old town has the markets, the Kasbah (with its palace), cheap hotels, homes both decrepit and recently renovated, and 2,000 wanna-be guides. The twisty, hilly streets of the old town are caged within a wall accessible by keyhole gates.

The new town, with the TI and fancy hotels, sprawls past the industrial port zone to your left. The big square, Grand Socco, is the link between the old and new parts of town.

Because Tangier is the fifth-largest city in Morocco, many assume they'll get lost here. Although the city could use more street signs, it's laid out simply. Nothing listed under "Sights" (page 520) is more than a 15-minute walk from the port. Petit Taxis are a godsend for the hot and tired tourist. Use them generously.

Tourist Information: Get a free map and advice at the TI. A little bit of French goes a long way here (Mon–Sat 8:30–16:30, closed Sun, Boulevard Pasteur 29, in new town, tel. 94-80-50, fax 94-86-61).

Arrival in Tangier

If you're taking a tour, follow the leader.

Independent travelers will take a five-minute walk from the boat, through customs (through the gate at the end of the port by the long, white wall), and out of the port. Consider hiring a guide (see "Guides," below).

There are two types of taxis to choose from, each with a different color: Grand Taxis are beige Mercedes which are not metered. These are generally more expensive, more comfortable, and used for longer rides. Petit Taxis, which are waiting in the same lot, are blue with a yellow stripe. Usually metered, these are more affordable than Grand Taxis, especially when shared with others. However, the port is an exception for Petit Taxis—this is the only place they don't use meters, and they can be expensive—so set your price before hopping in. The big Port de Tanger gateway defines the end of the port area and the start of the city. Leave mental breadcrumbs, so you can find your way back to your boat. Your first glimpse of the city will be a line of decent fish restaurants; restored French colonial buildings; a fancy, palm tree-lined pedestrian boulevard arcing along the beach into the

Women in Morocco

Most visitors to Tangier expect to see the women completely covered head-to-toe by their *kaftan*. In fact, only about one-quarter of Moroccan women still adhere strictly to this religious code. Some just cover their head (allowing their face to be seen) while others eliminate the head scarf altogether. Some women wear only Western-style clothing. This change in dress visibly reflects deeper, more fundamental shifts in women's rights.

Morocco happens to be one of the most progressive Muslim countries around. As in any border country, contact with other cultures fosters the growth of new ideas. Bombarded with Spanish television and visitors like you, change is inevitable. Another proponent of change is King Mohammed VI, who was only 35 years old when he rose to the throne in 1999. For the first time in the country's history, the king personally selected a female advisor to demonstrate his commitment to change.

Recent times have brought even more sweeping changes to Moroccan society. In order to raise literacy levels and understanding between the sexes, schools are now co-ed—something taken for granted in the West for decades. In 2004 the *Mudawana*, or judiciary family code, was shockingly overhauled. The legal age for marriage for women is now 18 (just like men) instead of 15. Other changes make it more difficult to have a second wife. Verbal divorce and abandonment is no longer legal—disgruntled husbands must now take their complaints to court before divorce is granted. And for the first time, women can divorce their husbands. If children are involved, whoever takes care of the kids gets the house. Of course, not everyone was happy with the changes, and Islamic fundamentalists were blamed for a series of bombings in Casablanca in 2003. But the reforms became law, and Morocco became a trendsetter for women's equality in the Islamic world.

new town; and stairs leading up into the old town and the market (on the right).

Helpful Hints

Money: The most convenient banks with ATMs are opposite the TI along Boulevard Pasteur. Nine dirhams = about $1; 11 dirhams = about €1.

Telephone: To call Tangier from Spain, dial 00 (international access code), 212 (Morocco's country code), 39 (Tangier's city code), then the local six-digit number.

Guides

If you're on your own, you'll be fighting off "guides" all day. In order to have your own translator and a shield from less scrupulous touts who hit up tourists constantly throughout the old town, I recommend hiring a guide. Stress your interest in the people and culture rather than shopping. Guides, hoping to get a huge commission from your purchases, can cleverly turn your Tangier day into the equivalent of the Shopping Channel.

I've had good luck with the private guides who meet the boat. These hardworking, English-speaking, and licensed guides offer their services for the day for €15. To avoid the stress of being mobbed by potential guides at the port, book a guide through an agency such as FRS in Tarifa or the Tangier TI before you arrive, and arrange for the guide to meet you at the port.

Aziz Begdouri is a great local guide that will show you the very best of his hometown. He's more than happy to answer questions about Moroccan society and culture. Aziz can also arrange ferry tickets from Tarifa in advance (5-hour walking tour for $18; 8-hour grand tour with minibus ride to resorts, the Caves of Hercules, and Cape Spartel for $35; easier to reach him from Spain on his Spanish mobile—tel. 607-897-967—than his Moroccan mobile, tel. 212-61-63-93-32, aziztour@hotmail.com).

Marco Polo Travel can help you with guides, hotels, and tours in other parts of the country (72 Avenue d'Espagne, tel. 93-78-99, marcopol01@menora.ma).

The **TI** also has official guides (about €15–20 for a half-day, prices vary depending on how the guide is licensed, includes lunch for the guide; tel. 94-80-50, or call guides' association directly at tel. 93-13-72, dttanger@menara.com).

If you don't want a guide and you get lost, ask directions of people who can't leave what they're doing (such as the only clerk in a shop) or of women who aren't near men. Ask "Kasbah?" or wherever you want to go, and you'll get pointed in the right direction. Fewer hustlers are in the new (but less interesting) part of town.

SIGHTS

Grand Socco—This big, noisy square is a transportation hub, market, and gateway to the medina (old town). Stroll around the square and check out the nearby market stalls. You'll see sandals, bunches of mint leaves for tea, caged chickens, and ceramic *tajines* (cone-shaped earthenware dishes for slow-cooking). Knock on the door of the Anglican church to see if someone will let you inside. From this square, you can enter the medina (go through old wall); get to the TI and recommended hotels by heading along Rue de la Liberté to Boulevard Pasteur; or reach the port and beach by taking Rue de la Plage.

The Medina and Petit Socco—A maze of winding lanes and tiny alleys weave through the old-town market area. Petit Socco, a little square in the old town, is lined with

tea shops. A casual first-time visitor cannot stay oriented. I just wander, knowing that if I keep going downhill I'll eventually pop out at the port. Expect to get a little lost... going around in circles is part of the fun. There are reports that the market is somewhat unsafe at night— but since most merchants close shop in the evening, there's no reason for tourists to hang around. During the day, plain-clothed tourist police are stationed throughout, helping to keep you safe as you explore.

Wander past piles of fruit, veggies, and olives, chickens (plucked and hung to show they have been killed according to Islamic guidelines), fresh goat cheese wrapped in palm leaves, and countless varieties of bread. Phew! Venturing right, you'll eventually come to less perishable (and less aromatic) items—clothing, recordable CDs, and lots of electronics.

When you've soaked in enough old-town atmosphere, make your way to the Kasbah (see map). Within the medina, head uphill, or exit the medina gate and go right on Rue de la Kasbah, which leads uphill along the old wall to Porte de la Kasbah, a gateway into the Kasbah.

Kasbah—This is the fortress atop old Tangier. You'll find a history museum in a former palace on Place de la Kasbah (10 dirhams, Wed–Mon 9:00–12:30 & 15:00–17:00, closed Tue, tel. 93-20-97) and a vivid gauntlet of amusements waiting to ambush you: snake charmers, squawky dance troupes, and colorful water vendors. Before descending out of the Kasbah, don't miss the ocean viewpoint, Mosque de la Kasbah, and Dar el-Makhzen—once the fortress of the *pasha* (governor) of Tangier.

Tangier American Legation Museum—Morocco was the first country to recognize the newly formed United States as an independent country (in 1777). The original building, given to the United States by the sultan of Morocco, became the fledgling government's first foreign acquisition. This was the US embassy (or consulate) in Morocco from 1821 to 1956, and it's still American property—our only national historic landmark overseas. Today this nonprofit museum and research center, housed in a 19th-century mansion, is a strangely peaceful oasis within Tangier's intense old town. It offers a warm welcome, lots of interesting paintings, and a reminder of how long the US and Morocco have had good relations (requires a guided English tour, free but donations appreciated, Mon–Fri 10:00–13:00 & 15:00–17:00, during Ramadan holiday 10:00–15:00, closed Sat–Sun, Rue America 8, tel. 93-53-17, www .maroc.net/legation, talm@wanadoo.net.ma).

Tangier Beach—Lined by lots of fun, fishy eateries, this fine, white-sand crescent beach stretches eastward from the port. It's packed with locals doing what people around the world do at the beach—with a few variations. Along with lazy camels, you'll see people—young and old—covered in hot sand to combat rheumatism. The palmy pedestrian street along the waterfront has been renamed after King Mohammed VI, since he allocated funding for the recent restorations.

SLEEPING

These hotels are centrally located, near the TI and American Express (Boulevard Pasteur 54), and within walking distance of the market. The first two are four-star hotels (by Moroccan standards). To reserve from Europe, dial 00 (Europe's international access code), 212 (Morocco's country code), 39 (Tangier's city code), then the local number. July through mid-September is high season, when rooms may be a bit more expensive and a reservation

---

Sleep Code

(9 dirhams = about $1, country code: 212, area code: 39)
S = Single, **D** = Double/Twin, **T** = Triple, **Q** = Quad, **b** = bathroom, **s** = shower only. Unless otherwise noted, credit cards are accepted, English is spoken, and breakfast is included.

   To help you easily sort through these listings, I've divided the rooms into three categories, based on the price for a standard double room with bath (during high season):

   $$$ **Higher Priced**—Most rooms 450 dirhams or more.
    $$ **Moderately Priced**—Most rooms between 400–450 dirhams.
     $ **Lower Priced**—Most rooms 400 dirhams or less.

is wise. Most hotels charge an extra tax of 6 dirhams per person per night.

$$$ Hotel Rembrandt, with a restaurant, bar, and swimming pool surrounded by a great grassy garden, has 75 clean, comfortable rooms, some with views (Sb-418–539 dirhams, Db-506–627 dirhams, breakfast-52 dirhams, air-con, elevator, Boulevard Mohammed V 1, tel. 93-78-70 or 33-33-14, fax 93-04-43, www.hotel-rembrandt.com, rembrandt@menara.net.ma).

$$$ Hotel Tanjah-Flandria, across the street with 155 rooms, is more formal, stuffy, and comfortable, but a lesser value (Sb-626 dirhams, Db-725 dirhams, breakfast-52 dirhams, air-con, elevator, restaurant, rooftop terrace, small pool, Boulevard Mohammed V 6, tel. 93-32-79, fax 93-43-47, hotelflandria@hotmail.com).

$$$ Rif & Spa Hotel, recently restored to its 1970s glamour, offers 130 plush, modern rooms with three different views: swimming pool, medina, and ocean. It's a worthy splurge (Sb-1,060 dirhams, Db-1,220 dirhams, breakfast-100 dirhams, includes taxes, air-con, elevator, 3 restaurants, Avenue Mohammed VI 152, tel. 61-32-13-96, fax 32-19-04, www.hotelsatlas.com).

$$ Hotel Continental, the Humphrey Bogart option, is a grand old place sprawling along the old town. It overlooks the port, with lavish, atmospheric public spaces, a chandeliered breakfast room, and 70 spacious bedrooms with rough hardwood floors. Jimmy, who's always around and runs the hotel and the Moroccan shop next door, says he offers everything but Viagra. When I said, "I'm from Seattle," he said, "206." Test him—he knows your area code (Sb-329–418 dirhams, Db-389–478 dirhams, includes tax, Dar Baroud 36, tel. 93-10-24, fax 93-11-43, hcontinental@iam.net.ma).

$ Hotel Paris, with 27 rooms across from the TI, is the budget option. It's noisy; ask for a room in the back (Sb-271–331 dirhams, Db-318–378 dirhams, price varies according to size, cash only, Boulevard Pasteur 42, tel. 93-81-26, run by helpful, informative manager Karim).

EATING

A few big, ornate places offer menus that include *harira* (Moroccan chickpea soup), couscous (a plain, fluffy side dish made with semolina), *pastela* (chicken pastry with cinnamon), dessert, and live Moroccan music. The first two places I recommend are in the medina. While the only locals you'll see here are the waiters, these places offer travelers a safe, comfortable break.

Hamadi is as luxurious a restaurant as a tourist can find in Morocco, with good food at reasonable prices (Rue Kasbah 2, tel.

93-45-14). **Mamounia Palace,** a fine option right on Petit Socco, is more in the middle of the action. A meal here will cost you about €9 for three courses—less if you order from the menu.

Le Saveur Medeterranée is an excellent choice for the more adventurous. Just sit down and let owner Mohammed take care of the rest. You'll be treated to a multi-course menu surrounded by lots of locals and unforgettable food. Savor the delicious fish dishes—Tangier is one of the few spots in Morocco where seafood is a major part of the diet. Ask to see how they make their juice drink; it's a mix of seasonal fruits, brewed overnight in a vat (150-dirham fixed-price meal, Sat–Thu 12:00–16:00 & 19:00–22:00, closed Fri, walk down Rue de la Liberté until you reach the stairs, then go down until you see fish on the grill, Escalier Waller 2, tel. 33-63-26).

El Minzah Hotel offers a fancier authentic experience. Dress up and choose between a continental dining area or a Moroccan lounge. Entrées in both restaurants average 140 dirhams, or $15. You'll find a cozy wine bar here—a rarity in a Muslim country (daily 13:00–16:00 & 19:00–22:00, Rue de la Liberté 85, tel. 93-58-85, www.elminzah.com).

Maison Communitaire des Femmes, a community center for women, hides an inexpensive, hearty lunch spot that's open to everyone. A three-course lunch is only 35 dirhams (Mon–Sat 12:00–16:00, closed Sun, near slipper market just outside the Grand Socco, Place du 9 Avril).

TRANSPORTATION CONNECTIONS

In Tangier, all train traffic comes and goes from the suburban Gare Tanger Ville train station, one mile from the city center and a short Petit Taxi ride away (10–20 dirhams, or $1–2). If you're traveling inland, check the information booth at the entrance of the train station for schedules for trains in Morocco. Consider the 150-dirham discount card that gives you a reduction of 35 percent on 16 rides (valid for one year). Find further info online at www.oncf.ma.

From Tangier by Train to: Rabat (6/day, 4 hrs), **Casablanca** (6/day, 5 hrs), **Marrakech** (5/day, 12 hrs), **Fès** (6/day, 4.5 hrs), **Ceuta** and **Tétouan** (hourly buses, 1 hr).

From Fès to: Casablanca (9/day, 4.5 hrs), **Marrakech** (7/day, 7 hrs), **Rabat** (9/day, 4 hrs), **Meknès** (10/day, 45 min), **Tangier** (6/day, 5.5 hrs).

From Rabat to: Casablanca (2/hr, 45 min), **Fès** (9/day, 3.5 hrs), **Tétouan** (2 buses/day, 4.5 hrs, 3 trains/day, 6 hrs).

From Casablanca to: Marrakech (9/day, 3.5 hrs).

From Marrakech to: **Meknès** (7/day, 7 hrs), **Ouarzazate** (4 buses/day, 4 hrs).

By Plane: Flights within Morocco are convenient and reasonable (about $150 1-way from Tangier to Casablanca).

Extended Tour of Morocco

Morocco gets much better as you go deeper into the interior. The country is incredibly rich in cultural thrills—but you'll pay a price in hassles and headaches. It's a package deal, and if adventure is your business, it's a great option.

To get a fair look at Morocco, you must get past the hustlers and con artists of the north coast (Tangier, Tétouan). It takes a minimum of four or five days to make a worthwhile visit— ideally seven or eight. Plan at least two nights in either Fès or Marrakech. A trip over the Atlas Mountains gives you an exciting look at Saharan Morocco. If you need a vacation from your vacation, check into one of the idyllic Atlantic beach resorts on the south coast. Above all, get past the northern day-trip-from-Spain, take-a-snapshot-on-a-camel fringe. Oops, that's us. Oh, well.

If you're relying on public transportation for your extended tour, sail to Tangier, blast your way through customs, listen to no hustler who tells you there's no way out until tomorrow, and hop into a Petit Taxi for the Tanger Ville train station one mile away (10–20 dirhams or $1–2, agree on price before leaving). From there, set your sights on Rabat, a dignified, European-type town with fewer hustlers, and make it your get-acquainted stop in Morocco. Trains go farther south from Rabat.

If you're driving a car, sail from Algeciras to Ceuta, a Spanish possession. Crossing the border is a bit unnerving, since you'll be forced to jump through several bureaucratic hoops. You'll go through customs at both borders, buy Moroccan insurance for your car (cheap and easy), and feel at the mercy of a bristly bunch of shady-looking people you'd rather not be at the mercy of. Don't pay anyone on the Spanish side. Consider tipping a guy on the Moroccan side if you feel he'll shepherd you through. Relax and let him grease those customs wheels. He's worth it. As soon as possible, hit the road and drive to Chefchaouen, the best first stop for those with their own wheels.

SIGHTS

Moroccan Towns

▲▲**Chefchaouen**—Just two hours by bus or car from Tétouan, this is the first pleasant town beyond the Tijuana-type north coast. Monday and Thursday are colorful market days. Stay in the classy old Hotel Chaouen on Place el-Makhzen. This former Spanish *parador* (historic inn) faces the old town and offers fine meals and a refuge from hustlers. Wander deep into the whitewashed old town from here.

▲▲**Rabat**—Morocco's capital and most European city, Rabat is the most comfortable and least stressful place to start your North African trip. You'll find a colorful market (in the old neighboring town of Salé), bits of Islamic architecture (Mausoleum of Mohammed V), the king's palace, mellow hustlers, and fine hotels.

▲▲▲**Fès**—More than just a funny hat that tipsy Shriners wear, Fès is Morocco's religious and artistic center, bustling with craft-speople, pilgrims, shoppers, and shops. Like most large Moroccan cities, it has a distinct new town from the French colonial period, as well as an exotic (and stressful) old, walled Arabic town (the medina), where you'll find the market.

For twelve centuries, traders have gathered in Fès, founded on a river at the crossroads of two trade routes. Soon there was an irrigation system, a university, resident craftsmen from Spain, and a diverse population of Muslims, Christians, and Jews. When France claimed Morocco in 1912, they made their capital in Rabat, and Fès fizzled. But the Fès marketplace is still Morocco's best.

▲▲▲**Marrakech**—Morocco's gateway to the south, this market city is a constant folk festival where the desert, mountain, and coastal regions merge, bustling with Berber tribespeople and a colorful center. The new city has the train station, and the main boulevard (Mohammed V) is lined with banks, airline offices, a post office, a tourist office, and comfortable hotels. The old city features the mazelike market and the huge Djemaa el-Fna, a square seething with people—a 43-ring Moroccan circus.

▲▲▲**Over the Atlas Mountains**—Extend your Moroccan trip several days by heading south over the Atlas Mountains. Take a bus from Marrakech to Ouarzazate (short stop), and then to Tinerhir (great oasis town, comfy hotel, overnight stop). The next day go to Er Rachidia and take the overnight bus to Fès.

By car, drive from Fès south, staying in the small mountain town of Ifrane, and then continue deep into the desert country past Er Rachidia and on to Rissani (market days: Sun, Tue, and Thu). Explore nearby mud-brick towns still living in the Middle Ages. Hire a guide to drive you past where the road stops, and head cross-country to an oasis village (Merzouga), where you can climb a sand dune and watch the sun rise over the vastness of Africa. Only a sea of sand separates you from Timbuktu.

APPENDIX

SPANISH HISTORY

In 1492, Columbus sailed the ocean blue—and Spain became a nation, too. Iberia's sunny weather, fertile soil, and Mediterranean ports made it a popular place to call home. The original "Iberians" were a Celtic people, who crossed the Pyrenees around 800 B.C. The Phoenicians established the city of Cádiz around 1100 B.C., and Carthaginians settled around 250 B.C.

Romans (c. 200 B.C.–A.D. 400)

The future Roman Emperor Augustus finally quelled the last Iberian resistance (19 B.C.), making the province of "Hispania" an agricultural breadbasket (olives, wine) to feed the vast Roman empire. The Romans brought the Latin language, a connection to the wider world, and (in the fourth century), Christianity. When the empire crumbled around A.D. 400, Spain made a peaceful transition, ruled by Christian Visigoths from Germany who had strong Roman ties. Roman influence remained for centuries after, in the Latin-based Spanish language, irrigation, and building materials and techniques. The Romans' large farming estates would change hands over the years, passing from Roman senators to Visigoth kings to Islamic caliphs to Christian nobles. And, of course, the Romans left wine.

Moors (711–1492)

In A.D. 711, 12,000 zealous members of the world's newest religion—Islam—landed on the Rock of Gibraltar and, in three short years, conquered the Iberian Peninsula. These North African Muslims—generically called "Moors"—dominated Spain for the next 700 years. Though powerful, they were surprisingly tolerant

Spaniards Throughout History

Hadrian (A.D. 76–138)—Roman Emperor, one of three born in Latin-speaking "Hispania" (along with Trajan, reigned 98–117, and Marcus Aurelius, reigned 161–180), who ruled Rome at its peak of power.

El Cid (1040?–1099)—A real soldier-for-hire who inspired fictional stories and Spain's oldest poem, El Cid (literally, "The Lord") fought for both Christians and Muslims during the wars of the Reconquista. He's best known for liberating Valencia from the Moors.

St. Teresa of Ávila (1515–1582)—Mystic nun whose holiness and writings led to convent reform and to her sainthood. Religiously intense Spain produced other saints, too, including **Dominic** (1170–1221), who founded an order of wandering monks, and **Ignatius of Loyola** (1491–1556), who founded the Jesuits, an order of "intellectual warriors."

Ferdinand (1452–1516) and Isabel (1451–1504)—Their marriage united most of Spain, ushering in its Golden Age. The "Catholic Monarchs" drove out Moors and Jews, and financed Columbus' lucrative voyages to the New World.

Hernán Cortés (1485–1547)—Conquered Mexico in 1521. Along with Vasco Núñez de Balboa, who discovered the Pacific, and Francisco Pizarro, who conquered Peru, Cortés and other Spaniards explored and exploited the New World.

El Greco (1541–1614)—The artist is known for his ethereal paintings of "flickering" saints.

Diego Velázquez (1599–1660)—Velázquez painted camera-eye realistic portraits of the royal court.

Francisco Goya (1746–1828)—The artist is best known for his expressionistic nightmares (see page 235 for more).

of the people they ruled, allowing native Jews and Christians to practice their faiths, so long as the infidels paid extra taxes.

The Moors were themselves an ethnically diverse culture, including both crude Berber tribesmen from Morocco and sophisticated rulers from old Arab families. From their capital in Córdoba, various rulers of the united Islamic state of "Al-Andalus" pledged allegiance to foreign caliphs in Syria, Baghdad, or Morocco.

With cultural ties that stretched from Spain to Africa to Arabia to Persia and beyond, the Moorish culture in Spain (especially around A.D. 800–1000) was perhaps Europe's most advanced, a beacon of learning in Europe's so-called "Dark" Ages. Mathematics, astronomy, literature and architecture flourished.

Francisco Franco (1892–1975)—General who led the military uprising against the elected Republic, sparking Spain's Civil War (1936–1939). After victory, he ruled Spain for more than three decades as an absolute dictator, maintaining its Catholic, aristocratic heritage while slowly modernizing the country.

Salvador Dalí (1904–1989)—A flamboyant, waxed-mustachioed Surrealist painter, Dalí and a fellow Spaniard, filmmaker Luis Buñuel, made one of the first art films, *Andalusian Dog* (see sidebar on page 112).

Pablo Picasso (1881–1973)—Though he lived most of his adult life in France, the 20th century's greatest artist explored Spanish themes, particularly in his famous work *Guernica*, which depicts Civil War destruction (see sidebar on page 240).

Placido Domingo (b. 1941)—The son of zarzuela singers in Madrid (but raised in Mexico), this operatic tenor is just one of many classical musicians from Spain, including fellow "Three Tenors" singer José Carreras, composer Manuel de Falla, cellist Pablo Casals, and guitarist Andres Segovia.

Spaniards in the News Today—King Juan Carlos I and his Greek-born wife, Queen Sofía, their son Felipe and his wife Letizia, left-of-center prime minister José Luis Rodríguez Zapatero, bicyclists Oscar Pereiro and Miguel Indurain, soccer star Raúl, golfers José María Olazábal, tennis player Arantxa Sanchez-Vicario, pop singer Julio Iglesias (father of pop singer Enrique Iglesias), and Oscar Award–winning movie directors Pedro Almodóvar and Pedro Amenábar.

Even winemaking was encouraged, though for religious reasons Muslims weren't allowed to drink alcohol. The Moorish legacy lives on today in architecture (horseshoe arches, ceramic tiles, fountains, and gardens), language (e.g., Spanish *el* comes from Arabic *al*)...and wine.

Reconquista (711–1492)

The Moors ruled for more than 700 years, but throughout that time they were a minority ruling a largely Christian populace. Pockets of independent Christians remained, particularly in the mountains in the peninsula's north. Local Christian kings fought against the Moors whenever they could, whittling away at the Muslim empire, "re-conquering" more and more land in what's known as the "Reconquista." The last Moorish stronghold, Granada, fell to the Christians in 1492.

The slow, piecemeal process of the Reconquista split the peninsula into many independent kingdoms and dukedoms, some Christian, some Moorish. The Reconquista picked up steam after A.D. 1000, when Al-Andalus splintered into smaller regional states—Granada, Sevilla, Valencia—ruled by local caliphs. Toledo fell to the Christians in 1085. By 1200, the neighboring Christian state of Portugal had the borders it does today, making it the oldest unchanged state in Europe. The rest of the peninsula was a battleground, a loosely knit collection of small kingdoms, some Christian, some Muslim. Heavy stone "castles" dotted the interior region of "Castile," as lords and barons duked it out. Along the Mediterranean coast (from the Pyrenees to Barcelona to Valencia), three Christian states united into a sea-trading power, the kingdom of Aragon.

In 1469, Isabel of Castile married Ferdinand II of Aragon, uniting the peninsula's two largest kingdoms, and instantly making united Spain a European power. In 1492, while Columbus explored the seas under Ferdinand and Isabel's flag, the "Catholic Monarchs" drove the Moors out of Granada and expelled the country's Jews, creating a unified, Christian, militaristic nation-state, fueled by the religious zeal of the Reconquista.

The Golden Age (1500–1600)

Spain's bold sea explorers changed the economics of Europe, opening up a New World of riches and colonies. The Spanish flag soon flew over most of South and Central America. Gold, silver, and agricultural products (grown on large estates with cheap labor) poured into Spain. In return, the stoked Spaniards exported Christianity, converting the American natives with kind Jesuit priests and cruel conquistadors.

Ferdinand and Isabel's daughter (Juana the Mad) wed a German prince (Philip the Fair), and their son inherited both crowns. Charles V (1500–1558, called Carlos I in Spain) was the most powerful man in the world, ruling an empire that stretched from Holland to Sicily, and from Bohemia to Bolivia. The aristocracy and the clergy were swimming in money. Art and courtly life flourished during this Golden Age, with Spain hosting the painter El Greco and the writer Miguel de Cervantes.

Six Dates that Changed Spain

711 Muslims from North Africa invade and occupy Iberia.

1492 Columbus sails Spain into a century of wealth and power.

1588 Spain's Armada is routed by the British, and the country's slow decline begins.

1898 Thrashed by the US in the Spanish-American War, Spain reaches a low ebb.

1936 The Civil War begins, killing hundreds of thousands during its three-year span, and brings on more than three decades of Franco's fascist rule.

1975 King Juan Carlos I leads the nation to democracy and the European Union.

But Charles V's Holy Roman Empire was torn by different languages and ethnic groups, and by protesting Protestants. He spent much of the nation's energies at war with Protestants, encroaching Muslim Turks, and Europe's rising powers. When an exhausted Charles announced his abdication (1555) and retired to a monastery, his sprawling empire was divvied up among family members, with Spain and its possessions going to his son, Philip II (1527–1598).

Philip II conquered Portugal (1580, his only successful war), moved Spain's capital to Madrid, built El Escorial, and continued fighting losing battles across Europe (the Netherlands, France) that drained the treasury of its New World gold. In the summer of 1588, Spain's seemingly unbeatable royal fleet of 125 ships—the Invincible Armada—sailed off to conquer England, only to be unexpectedly routed in battle by bad weather and Sir Francis Drake's cunning. Just like that,  Britannia ruled the waves, and Spain spiraled downward, becoming a debt-ridden, overextended, flabby nation.

Slow Decline (1600–1900)

The fast money from the colonies kept Spain from seeing the dangers at home. They stopped growing their own wheat and neglected their fields. Great Britain and the Netherlands were the rising sea-trading powers in the new global economy. During the centuries when science and technology developed as never before in other European countries, Spain was preoccupied by its failed colonial politics. (Still, Spain in the 1600s produced the remarkable painter Diego Velázquez.)

By 1700, once-mighty Spain lay helpless while rising powers France, England, and Austria fought over the right to pick Spain's next king in the War of the Spanish Succession (1701–1714), which was fought partly on Spanish soil (e.g., Britain holding out against the French in the Siege of Gibraltar). The rightful next-in-line was Louis XIV's son, who was set to inherit both France and Spain. The rest of Europe didn't want powerful France to become even stronger. The war ended in compromise, preventing Louis XIV from controlling both countries, but allowing his grandson to become King of Spain (Spain lost several possessions). The French-born, French-speaking Bourbon King Philip V (1683–1746) ruled Spain for 40 years. He and his heirs made themselves at home building the Versailles-like Royal Palace in Madrid and La Granja near Segovia.

The French Revolution spilled over into Spain, bringing French rule under Napoleon. In 1808, the Spaniards rose up (chronicled by Goya's paintings of the 2nd and 3rd of May, 1808), sparking the Peninsular War—called the War of Independence by Spaniards—that finally won Spain's independence from French rule.

Nineteenth-century Spain was a backward nation, with internal wars over which noble family should rule (the Carlist Wars), liberal revolutions put down brutally, and political assassinations. Spain gradually lost its global possessions to other European powers and to South American revolutionaries. Spain hit rock bottom in 1898, when the upstart United States picked a fight and thrashed them in the Spanish-American War, taking away Spain's last major possessions: Cuba, Puerto Rico, and the Philippines.

The 20th Century

A drained and disillusioned Spain was ill-prepared for modern technology and democratic government.

The old ruling class (the monarchy, church, and landowners) fought new economic powers (cities, businessmen, labor unions) in a series of coups, strikes, and sham elections. In the '20s, a military dictatorship under Miguel Primo de Rivera kept the old guard in power. In 1930, he was ousted and an open election brought a modern democratic Republic to power. But the right wing regrouped under the Falange (fascist) party, fomenting unrest and sparking a military coup against the Republic in 1936, supported by General Francisco Franco (1892–1975).

For three years (1936–1939), Spain fought a bloody Civil War between Franco's Nationalists (also called Falangists) and the Republic (also called Loyalists). Some 600,000 Spaniards died (due to all causes), and Franco won. (For more on the Civil War, see "Valley of the Fallen," page 276.) For nearly the next four decades, Spain was ruled by Franco, an authoritarian, church-blessed dictator who tried to modernize the backward country while shielding it from corrupting modern influences. Spain was neutral in World War II, and the country spent much of the postwar era as a world apart. (On my first visit to Spain in 1973, I came face-to-face with fellow teenagers—me in backpack and shorts, the Spaniards in military uniforms, brandishing automatic weapons.)

Before Franco died, he handpicked his protégé, King Juan Carlos I, to succeed him. But to everyone's surprise, the young, conservative, mild-mannered king stepped aside, settled for a figurehead title, and guided the country quickly and peacefully toward democratic elections (1977).

Spain had a lot of catching up to do. Culturally, the once-conservative nation exploded and embraced new ideas, even plunging to wild extremes. In the 1980s, Spain flowered under the left-leaning Prime Minister Felipe González. Spain showed the world its new modern face in 1992, hosting both a World Exhibition at Sevilla and the Summer Olympics at Barcelona.

Spain Today

From 1996 to 2004, Spain was led by the centrist Prime Minister José María Aznar. He adopted moderate policies to minimize the stress on the country's young democracy, fighting problems such as unemployment and foreign debt with reasonable success. However, his support of George W. Bush's pre-emptive war in Iraq was extremely unpopular with the vast majority of Spaniards. In spring of 2004, the retiring Aznar supported a similarly centrist successor, Mariano Rajoy, who seemed poised to win the election. But during the morning rush hour on March 11, 2004, three Madrid train stations were bombed, killing 200 people. The terrorist group claiming responsibility denounced Spain's Iraq policy, and three days later, Aznar's party lost the election. The new prime minister, left-of-center José Luis Rodríguez Zapatero, quickly began pulling Spain's troops out of Iraq, as well as enacting sweeping social changes in Spain.

Its political squabbles and heightened security aside, Spain is striding into the future. Though not considered wealthy or powerful, Spain is prospering, thanks in part to you and tourism.

SPANISH ART

El Greco (1541–1614) exemplifies the spiritual fervor of much Spanish art. The drama, the surreal colors, and the intentionally unnatural distortion have the intensity of a religious vision. (For more on El Greco, see page 312.)

Diego Velázquez (1599–1660) went to the opposite extreme. His masterful court portraits are studies in camera-eye realism and cool detachment from his subjects. Velázquez was unmatched in using a few strokes of paint to suggest details.

Francisco de Goya (1746–1828) lacked Velázquez's detachment. He let his liberal tendencies shine through in unflattering portraits of royalty, and in emotional scenes of abuse of power. He unleashed his inner passions in the eerie, nightmarish canvases of his last, "dark" stage. (For more on Goya, see page 235.)

Bartolomé Murillo (1617–1682) painted a dreamy world of religious visions. His pastel, soft-focus works of cute baby Jesuses and radiant Virgin Marys helped make Catholic doctrine palatable to the common folk at a time when many were defecting to Protestantism. (For more on Murillo, see page 381.)

You'll also find plenty of foreign art in Spain's museums. During its Golden Age, Spain's wealthy aristocrats bought wagonloads of the most popular art of the time—Italian Renaissance and Baroque works by Titian, Tintoretto, and others. They also loaded up on paintings by Peter Paul Rubens, Hieronymus Bosch, and Pieter Brueghel from the Low Countries, which were then under Spanish rule.

In the 20th century, **Pablo Picasso** (see his inspirational antiwar *Guernica* mural in Madrid, described on page 240), **Joan Miró,** and Surrealist **Salvador Dalí** (see sidebar on page 112) made their marks. Great museums featuring all three are in or near Barcelona.

ARCHITECTURE

Spanish History Set in Stone

The two most fertile periods of architectural innovation in Spain were during the Moorish occupation and in the Golden Age. Otherwise, Spanish architects marched obediently behind the rest of Europe. Modern architects have finally brought Spain back to the forefront of construction and design.

Spain's history is dominated by 700 years of pushing the Muslim Moors back into Africa (711–1492). Throughout Spain, it seems every old church was built upon a mosque (Sevilla's immense cathedral, for one). Granada's Alhambra is the best example of the secular Moorish style. It's an *Arabian Nights* fairy tale: finely etched domes, lacey arcades, keyhole arches, and lush gardens. At its heart lies an elegantly proportioned courtyard, where the designers created an ingenious microclimate: water, plants, pottery, thick walls, and darkness...all to be cool. The stuccoed walls are ornamented with a stylized Arabic script, creating a visual chant of verses from the Quran.

As the Christians slowly reconquered Iberian turf, they turned their fervor into stone, building churches in the lighter, heaven-reaching, stained-glass Gothic style (Toledo and Sevilla). Gothic was an import from France, trickling into conservative Spain long after it had swept through Europe.

As Christians moved in, many Muslim artists and architects stayed, giving the new society the Mudéjar style. (Mudéjar means "those who stayed.") In Sevilla's Alcázar, the Arabic script on the walls relates not the Quran, but New Testament verses and Christian propaganda, such as "Dedicated to the magnificent Sultan, King Pedro—thanks to God!" (The style of Christians living under Moorish rule is called Mozarabic.)

The money reaped and raped from Spain's colonies in the Golden Age spurred new construction. Churches and palaces borrowed from the Italian Renaissance and the more elaborate Baroque. Ornamentation reached unprecedented heights in Spain, culminating in the Plateresque style of stonework, so called because it resembles intricate silver *(plata)* filigree work (see, for example, the facade of the University of Salamanca).

The 1500s was also the era of religious wars. The monastery/palace of El Escorial, built in sober geometric style, symbolizes the austerity of a newly reformed Catholic church ready to strike back. King Philip II ruled his empire and directed the Inquisition from here, surrounded by plain white walls, well-scrubbed floors and simple furnishings. Built at a time when Catholic Spain felt threatened by Protestant heretics, its construction dominated the Spanish economy for a generation (1563–1584). Because of this bully in the national budget, Spain has almost nothing else to show from this most powerful period of her history.

For the next three centuries (1600–1900), backward-looking Spain recycled old art styles.

As Europe leapt from the 19th century into the 20th, it celebrated a rising standard of living and nearly a century without a major war. Art Nouveau architects forced hard steel and concrete into softer organic shapes. Barcelona's answer to Art Nouveau was Modernisme, and its genius was Antoni Gaudí, with his asymmetrical, "cake-in-the-rain" buildings like Casa Milà and Sagrada Família.

Much of Spain's 20th-century architecture follows patterns seen elsewhere in Europe—the minimal fascist style of the Valley of the Fallen and ugly concrete apartments. But Spain today produces some of Europe's most interesting structures. Santiago Calatrava (from Valencia, born 1951) uses soaring arches and glass to create bridges, airports, and Valencia's Opera House. One of the world's most striking buildings in recent years—Frank Gehry's Guggenheim Museum—is in Bilbao, and similarly innovative structures are popping up everywhere.

BULLFIGHTING

A Legitimate Slice of Spain, or a Cruel Spectacle?

The Spanish bullfight is as much a ritual as it is a sport. Not to acknowledge the importance of the bullfight is to censor a venerable part of Spanish culture. But it also makes a spectacle out of the cruel killing of an animal. Should tourists boycott bullfights? I don't know.

Today bullfighting is less popular among locals. If this trend continues, bullfighting may survive more and more as a tourist event. When the day comes that bullfighting is kept alive by our tourist dollars rather than by the local culture, then I'll agree with those who say bullfighting is immoral and that tourists shouldn't encourage it by buying tickets. Consider the morality of supporting this gruesome aspect of Spanish culture before buying a ticket. If you do decide to attend a bullfight, here is what you'll see.

While no two bullfights are the same, they unfold along a strict pattern. The ceremony begins punctually with a parade of participants across the ring. Then the trumpet sounds, the "Gate of Fear" opens, and the leading player—*el toro*—thunders in. A ton of angry animal is an awesome sight, even from the cheap seats (with the sun in your eyes).

The fight is divided into three acts. Act I is designed to size up the bull and wear him down. With help from his assistants, the matador ("killer") attracts the bull with the shake of the cape, then directs the animal past his body, as close as his bravery allows. The bull sees only things in motion and (some think) in red. After a few passes, the *picadores* enter, mounted on horseback, to spear the swollen lump of muscle at the back of the bull's neck. This

tests the bull, while the matador watches studiously. It also lowers the bull's head and weakens the thrust of his horns. (Until 1927, the horses had no protective pads, and were often killed.)

In Act II, the matador's

assistants *(banderilleros)* continue to enrage and weaken the bull. They charge the charging bull and—leaping acrobatically across its path—plunge brightly colored barbed sticks into the bull's vital neck muscle.

After a short intermission, during which the matador may, according to tradition, ask permission to kill the bull and dedicate the kill to someone in the crowd, the final and lethal Act III begins.

The matador tries to dominate and tire the bull with hypnotic cape work. A good pass is when the matador stands completely still while the bull charges past. Then the matador thrusts a sword between the animal's shoulder blades for the kill. A quick kill is not always easy, and the matador may have to make several bloody thrusts before the sword stays in and the bull finally dies. Mules drag the dead bull out, and his meat is in the market *mañana* (barring "mad cow" concerns—and if ever there was a mad cow...). *Rabo del toro* (bull-tail stew) is a delicacy.

Throughout the fight, the crowd shows its approval or impatience. Shouts of *"¡Olé!"* or *"¡Torero!"* mean they like what they see. Whistling or rhythmic hand-clapping greets cowardice and incompetence.

You're not likely to see much human blood spilled. In 200 years of bullfighting in Sevilla, only 30 fighters have died (and only three were actually matadors). If a bull does kill a fighter, the next matador comes in to kill him. Historically, even the bull's mother is killed, since the evil qualities are assumed to have come from the mother.

After an exceptional fight, the crowd may wave white handkerchiefs to ask that the matador be awarded the bull's ear or tail. A brave bull, though dead, gets a victory lap from the mule team on his way to the slaughterhouse. Then the trumpet sounds, and a new bull charges in to face a fresh matador.

Fights are held on most Sundays, Easter through October (at 18:30 or 19:30). Serious fights with adult matadors are called *corrida de toros*. These are often sold out in advance. Summer fights are often *novillada*, with teenage novices doing the killing. *Corrida de toros* seats range from €20 for high seats facing the sun to €100 for the first three rows in the shade under the royal box. *Novillada* seats are half that, and generally easy to get at the arena a few minutes before showtime. Many Spanish women consider bullfighting

sexy. They swoon at the dashing matadors who are sure to wear tight pants (with their *partas nobles*—noble parts—in view, generally organized to one side, farthest from the bull).

A typical bullfight lasts about two hours and consists of six separate fights—three matadors (each with his own team of *picadors* and *banderilleros*) fighting two bulls each. For a closer look at bullfighting by an American aficionado, read Ernest Hemingway's classic, *Death in the Afternoon.*

TRAVELER'S TOOL KIT

Let's Talk Telephones

Here's a primer on making phone calls in Europe. For specifics on Spain, see "Telephones" in the Introduction.

Making Calls Within a European Country: About half of all European countries use area codes (like we do in most of the US); the other half use a direct-dial system without area codes.

To make calls within a country that uses a direct-dial system (Spain, Portugal, Belgium, the Czech Republic, France, Italy, Switzerland, Norway, and Denmark), you dial the same number whether you're calling across the country or across the street.

In countries that use area codes (Austria, Britain, Croatia, Finland, Germany, Hungary, Ireland, Morocco, the Netherlands, Poland, Slovakia, Slovenia, and Sweden), you dial the local number when calling within a city, and you add the area code if calling long-distance within the country. For example, the phone number of a hotel in Munich is 089-264-349. To call it in Munich, dial 264-349; to call it from Frankfurt, dial 089-264-349.

Making International Calls: You always start with the international access code (011 if you're calling from the US or Canada, 00 from anywhere in Europe), then dial the country code of the country you're calling (see chart below).

What you dial next depends on the phone system of the country you're calling. If the country uses area codes, drop the initial zero of the area code, and then dial the rest of the area code and the local number. For example, to call the Munich hotel from Spain, dial 00, 49 (Germany's country code), then 89-264-349.

Countries that use direct-dial systems (no area codes) vary in how they're accessed internationally by phone. For instance, if you're making an international call to Spain, Portugal, Italy, the Czech Republic, Norway, or Denmark, you simply dial the international access code, country code, and phone number. For example, the phone number of a hotel in Madrid is 915-212-900. To call it from Portugal, dial 00, 34 (Spain's country code), then 915-212-900. But if you're calling Belgium, France, or Switzerland, you drop the initial zero of the phone number. For example, the phone number of a Paris hotel is 01 47 05 49 15. To call it from Madrid, dial 00, 33 (France's country code), then 1 47 05 49 15 (the phone number without the initial zero).

Country Codes
After you dial the international access code (00 if you're calling from Europe, 011 if you're calling from the US or Canada), dial the code of the country you're calling.

Austria—43	Italy—39
Belgium—32	Morocco—212
Britain—44	Netherlands—31
Canada—1	Norway—47
Croatia—385	Poland—48
Czech Rep.—420	Portugal—351
Denmark—45	Slovakia—421
Estonia—372	Slovenia—386
Finland—358	Spain—34
France—33	Sweden—46
Germany—49	Switzerland—41
Gibraltar—350	Turkey—90
Greece—30	US—1
Ireland—353	

Directory Assistance
In Spain, dial 1003 for local numbers and 025 for international numbers (expensive). (Note: In Spain, a 608 or 609 area code indicates a mobile phone.)

US Embassies and Consulates
Madrid, Spain: Calle Serrano 75; tel. 915-872-240, for emergencies after business hours, tel. 915-872-200; www.embusa.es/cons /services.html.

    Gibraltar: Call embassy in Madrid (above).

    Casablanca, Morocco: Boulevard Moulay Youssef 8, tel. 22/26-45-50, www.usembassy.ma.

European Calling Chart

Just smile and dial, using this key:
AC = Area Code, LN = Local Number.

European Country	Calling long distance within...	Calling from the US or Canada to...	Calling from a European country to...
Austria	AC + LN	011 + 43 + AC (without the initial zero) + LN	00 + 43 + AC (without the initial zero) + LN
Belgium	LN	011 + 32 + LN (without initial zero)	00 + 32 + LN (without initial zero)
Britain	AC + LN	011 + 44 + AC (without initial zero) + LN	00 + 44 + AC (without initial zero) + LN
Croatia	AC + LN	011 + 385 + AC (without initial zero) + LN	00 + 385 + AC (without initial zero) + LN
Czech Republic	LN	011 + 420 + LN	00 + 420 + LN
Denmark	LN	011 + 45 + LN	00 + 45 + LN
Finland	AC + LN	011 + 358 + AC (without initial zero) + LN	999 + 358 + AC (without initial zero) + LN
France	LN	011 + 33 + LN (without initial zero)	00 + 33 + LN (without initial zero)
Germany	AC + LN	011 + 49 + AC (without initial zero) + LN	00 + 49 + AC (without initial zero) + LN
Greece	LN	011 + 30 + LN	00 + 30 + LN
Hungary	06 + AC + LN	011 + 36 + AC + LN	00 + 36 + AC + LN
Ireland	AC + LN	011 + 353 + AC (without initial zero) + LN	00 + 353 + AC (without initial zero) + LN
Italy	LN	011 + 39 + LN	00 + 39 + LN

European Country	Calling long distance within ...	Calling from the US or Canada to ...	Calling from a European country to ...
Netherlands	AC + LN	011 + 31 + AC (without initial zero) + LN	00 + 31 + AC (without initial zero) + LN
Norway	LN	011 + 47 + LN	00 + 47 + LN
Poland	AC + LN	011 + 48 + AC (without initial zero) + LN	00 + 48 + AC (without initial zero) + LN
Portugal	LN	011 + 351 + LN	00 + 351 + LN
Slovakia	AC + LN	011 + 421 + AC (without initial zero) + LN	00 + 421 + AC (without initial zero) + LN
Slovenia	AC + LN	011 + 386 + AC (without initial zero) + LN	00 + 386 + AC (without initial zero) + LN
Spain	LN	011 + 34 + LN	00 + 34 + LN
Sweden	AC + LN	011 + 46 + AC (without initial zero) + LN	00 + 46 + AC (without initial zero) + LN
Switzerland	LN	011 + 41 + LN (without initial zero)	00 + 41 + LN (without initial zero)
Turkey	AC (if no initial zero is included, add one) + LN	011 + 90 + AC (without initial zero) + LN	00 + 90 + AC (without initial zero) + LN

- The instructions above apply whether you're calling a land line or mobile phone.
- The international access codes (the first numbers you dial when making an international call) are 011 if you're calling from the US or Canada, or 00 if you're calling from anywhere in Europe.
- To call the US or Canada from Europe, dial 00, then 1 (the country code for the US and Canada), then the area code and number. In short, 00 + 1 + AC + LN = Hi, Mom!

Festivals and Public Holidays in 2007

Spain erupts with fiestas and celebrations throughout the year. Semana Santa (Holy Week) fills the week before Easter with processions and festivities all over Iberia, but especially in Sevilla. To run with the bulls, be in Pamplona—with medical insurance—July 6–14.

This is a partial list of holidays and festivals. For more information, contact the Spanish Tourist Office (www.okspain.org, www.spain.info, tel. 212/265-8822) and also check these Web sites: www.whatsonwhen.com and www.festivals.com.

Jan 1	New Year's Day
Jan 6	Epiphany
Early Feb	La Candelaria (religious festival), Madrid
Feb 28	Day of Andalucía (some closures), Andalucía
Holy Week	Week before Easter (April 1–8 in 2007)
Easter	April 8 in 2007
Late April	April Fair, Sevilla (April 23–29 in 2007)
May 1	Labor Day (closures)
May 2	Day of the Autonomous Community, Madrid
Mid-May	Feria del Caballo (horse pageantry), Jerez
Throughout May	San Isidro (religious festival on May 15; also bullfights and zarzuelas all month long), Madrid
June 15	Corpus Christi
Late June	La Patum (Moorish battles), Barcelona
June 24	St. John the Baptist's Day
Late June–Early July	International Festival of Music and Dance, Granada
July 6–14	Running of the Bulls, Pamplona
Aug	Gràcia Festival, Barcelona
Mid-Aug	Verbena de la Paloma (folk festival), Madrid
Aug 15	Assumption (religious festival)
Mid-Sept–Mid-Oct	Autumn Festival (flamenco, bullfights), Jerez
Late Sept	La Mercé (parade), Barcelona
Oct 12	Spanish National Day
Nov 1	All Saints' Day
Nov 9	Virgen de la Almudena, Madrid
Mid-Nov	International Jazz Festival, Madrid
Dec 6	Constitution Day
Dec 8	Feast of the Immaculate Conception
Dec 13	Feast of Santa Lucía
Dec 25	Christmas
Dec 31	New Year's Eve

2007

JANUARY

S	M	T	W	T	F	S
	1	2	3	4	5	6
7	8	9	10	11	12	13
14	15	16	17	18	19	20
21	22	23	24	25	26	27
28	29	30	31			

FEBRUARY

S	M	T	W	T	F	S
				1	2	3
4	5	6	7	8	9	10
11	12	13	14	15	16	17
18	19	20	21	22	23	24
25	26	27	28			

MARCH

S	M	T	W	T	F	S
				1	2	3
4	5	6	7	8	9	10
11	12	13	14	15	16	17
18	19	20	21	22	23	24
25	26	27	28	29	30	31

APRIL

S	M	T	W	T	F	S
1	2	3	4	5	6	7
8	9	10	11	12	13	14
15	16	17	18	19	20	21
22	23	24	25	26	27	28
29	30					

MAY

S	M	T	W	T	F	S
		1	2	3	4	5
6	7	8	9	10	11	12
13	14	15	16	17	18	19
20	21	22	23	24	25	26
27	28	29	30	31		

JUNE

S	M	T	W	T	F	S
					1	2
3	4	5	6	7	8	9
10	11	12	13	14	15	16
17	18	19	20	21	22	23
24	25	26	27	28	29	30

JULY

S	M	T	W	T	F	S
1	2	3	4	5	6	7
8	9	10	11	12	13	14
15	16	17	18	19	20	21
22	23	24	25	26	27	28
29	30	31				

AUGUST

S	M	T	W	T	F	S
			1	2	3	4
5	6	7	8	9	10	11
12	13	14	15	16	17	18
19	20	21	22	23	24	25
26	27	28	29	30	31	

SEPTEMBER

S	M	T	W	T	F	S
						1
2	3	4	5	6	7	8
9	10	11	12	13	14	15
16	17	18	19	20	21	22
23/30	24	25	26	27	28	29

OCTOBER

S	M	T	W	T	F	S
	1	2	3	4	5	6
7	8	9	10	11	12	13
14	15	16	17	18	19	20
21	22	23	24	25	26	27
28	29	30	31			

NOVEMBER

S	M	T	W	T	F	S
				1	2	3
4	5	6	7	8	9	10
11	12	13	14	15	16	17
18	19	20	21	22	23	24
25	26	27	28	29	30	

DECEMBER

S	M	T	W	T	F	S
						1
2	3	4	5	6	7	8
9	10	11	12	13	14	15
16	17	18	19	20	21	22
23/30	24/31	25	26	27	28	29

Numbers and Stumblers

- Europeans write a few of their numbers differently than we do. 1 = 1, 4 = 4, 7 = 7. Learn the difference, or miss your train.
- In Europe, dates appear as day/month/year, so Christmas is 25/12/07.
- Commas are decimal points and decimals commas. A dollar and a half is 1,50, and there are 5.280 feet in a mile.
- When pointing, use your whole hand, palm down.
- When counting with fingers, start with your thumb. If you hold up your first finger to request one item, you'll probably get two.
- What Americans call the second floor of a building is the first floor in Europe.
- Europeans keep the left "lane" open for passing on escalators and moving sidewalks. Keep to the right.

Climate Chart

First line, average daily low; second line, average daily high; third line, days of no rain.

	J	F	M	A	M	J	J	A	S	O	N	D

SPAIN
Madrid

J	F	M	A	M	J	J	A	S	O	N	D
35°	36°	41°	45°	50°	58°	63°	63°	57°	49°	42°	36°
47°	52°	59°	65°	70°	80°	87°	85°	77°	65°	55°	48°
23	21	21	21	21	25	29	28	24	23	21	21

Barcelona

J	F	M	A	M	J	J	A	S	O	N	D
43°	45°	48°	52°	57°	65°	69°	69°	66°	58°	51°	46°
55°	57°	60°	65°	71°	78°	82°	82°	77°	69°	62°	56°
26	23	23	21	23	24	27	25	23	22	24	25

Almería (Costa del Sol)

J	F	M	A	M	J	J	A	S	O	N	D
46°	47°	51°	55°	59°	65°	70°	71°	68°	60°	54°	49°
60°	61°	64°	68°	72°	78°	83°	84°	81°	73°	67°	62°
25	24	26	25	28	29	31	30	27	26	26	26

MOROCCO
Marrakech

J	F	M	A	M	J	J	A	S	O	N	D
40°	43°	48°	52°	57°	62°	67°	68°	63°	57°	49°	42°
65°	68°	74°	79°	84°	92°	101°	100°	92°	83°	73°	66°
24	23	25	24	29	29	30	30	27	27	27	24

Temperature Conversion: Fahrenheit and Celsius

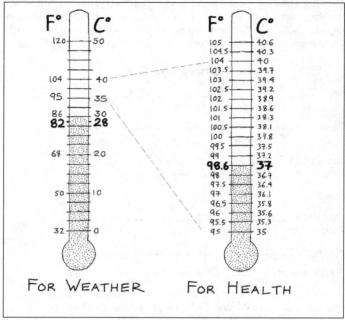

FOR WEATHER   FOR HEALTH

Europe takes its temperature using the Celsius scale, while we opt for Fahrenheit. For weather, remember that 28° C is 82° F—perfect. For health, 37° C is just right.

Metric Conversion (Approximate)

1 inch = 25 millimeters   32 degrees F = 0 degrees C
1 foot = 0.3 meter   82 degrees F = about 28 degrees C
1 yard = 0.9 meter   1 ounce = 28 grams
1 mile = 1.6 kilometers   1 kilogram = 2.2 pounds
1 centimeter = 0.4 inch   1 quart = 0.95 liter
1 meter = 39.4 inches   1 square yard = 0.8 square meter
1 kilometer = 0.62 mile   1 acre = 0.4 hectare

Making Your Hotel Reservation

Most hotel managers know basic "hotel English." Faxing or e-mailing are the preferred methods for reserving a room. They're more accurate than telephoning and much faster than writing a letter. Use this handy form for your fax or find it online at www.ricksteves.com/reservation. Photocopy and fax away.

One-Page Fax

To: _____ @ _____
           hotel   *fax*

From: _____@ _____
            name   *fax*

Today's date: _____ / _____ / _____
                  day   *month*   *year*

Dear Hotel _____ ,
Please make this reservation for me:

Name: _____

Total # of people:_____ # of rooms: _____ # of nights: _____

Arriving: _____ /_____ /_____   My time of arrival (24-hr clock): _____
             day *month* *year*   (I will telephone if I will be late)

Departing:_____ /_____/_____
              day *month* *year*

Room(s): Single _____Double ____Twin _____Triple ____ Quad_____

With: Toilet _____ Shower_____Bath _____ Sink only _____

Special needs: View____ Quiet ____ Cheapest ____ Ground Floor ____

Please fax, mail, or e-mail confirmation of my reservation, along with the type of room reserved and the price. Please also inform me of your cancellation policy. After I hear from you, I will quickly send my credit-card information as a deposit to hold the room. Thank you.

_____
Signature

_____
Name

_____
Address

_____
City   *State*   *Zip Code*   *Country*

_____
E-mail Address

Spanish Survival Phrases

Spanish has a guttural sound similar to the J in Baja California. In the phonetics, the symbol for this clearing-your-throat sound is the italicized *h*.

Good day.	Buenos días.	**bway**-nohs **dee**-ahs
Do you speak English?	¿Habla usted inglés?	**ah**-blah oo-**stehd** een-**glays**
Yes. / No.	Sí. / No.	see / noh
I (don't) understand.	(No) comprendo.	(noh) kohm-**prehn**-doh
Please.	Por favor.	por fah-**bor**
Thank you.	Gracias.	**grah**-thee-ahs
I'm sorry.	Lo siento.	loh see-**ehn**-toh
Excuse me.	Perdóneme.	pehr-**doh**-nay-may
(No) problem.	(No) problema.	(noh) proh-**blay**-mah
Good.	Bueno.	**bway**-noh
Goodbye.	Adiós.	ah-dee-**ohs**
one / two	uno / dos	**oo**-noh / dohs
three / four	tres / cuatro	trays / **kwah**-troh
five / six	cinco / seis	**theen**-koh / says
seven / eight	siete / ocho	see-**eh**-tay / **oh**-choh
nine / ten	nueve / diez	**nway**-bay / dee-**ayth**
How much is it?	¿Cuánto cuesta?	**kwahn**-toh **kway**-stah
Write it?	¿Me lo escribe?	may loh ay-**skree**-bay
Is it free?	¿Es gratis?	ays **grah**-tees
Is it included?	¿Está incluido?	ay-**stah** een-kloo-**ee**-doh
Where can I buy / find...?	¿Dónde puedo comprar / encontrar...?	**dohn**-day **pway**-doh kohm-**prar** / ayn-kohn-**trar**
I'd like / We'd like...	Quiero / Queremos...	kee-**ehr**-oh / kehr-**ay**-mohs
...a room.	...una habitación.	**oo**-nah ah-bee-tah-thee-**ohn**
...a ticket to ___.	...un billete para ___.	oon bee-**yeh**-tay **pah**-rah
Is it possible?	¿Es posible?	ays poh-**see**-blay
Where is...?	¿Dónde está...?	**dohn**-day ay-**stah**
...the train station	...la estación de trenes	lah ay-stah-thee-**ohn** day **tray**-nays
...the bus station	...la estación de autobuses	lah ay-stah-thee-**ohn** day ow-toh-**boo**-says
...the tourist information office	...la oficina de turismo	lah oh-fee-**thee**-nah day too-**rees**-moh
Where are the toilets?	¿Dónde están los servicios?	**dohn**-day ay-**stahn** lohs sehr-**bee**-thee-ohs
men	hombres, caballeros	**ohm**-brays, kah-bah-**yay**-rohs
women	mujeres, damas	moo-**heh**-rays, **dah**-mahs
left / right	izquierda / derecha	eeth-kee-**ehr**-dah / day-**ray**-chah
straight	derecho	day-**ray**-choh
When do you open / close?	¿A qué hora abren / cierran?	ah kay **oh**-rah **ah**-brehn / thee-**ay**-rahn
At what time?	¿A qué hora?	ah kay **oh**-rah
Just a moment.	Un momento.	oon moh-**mehn**-toh
now / soon / later	ahora / pronto / más tarde	ah-**oh**-rah / **prohn**-toh / mahs **tar**-day
today / tomorrow	hoy / mañana	oy / mahn-**yah**-nah

In the Restaurant

I'd like / We'd like...	**Quiero / Queremos...**	kee-**ehr**-oh / kehr-**ay**-mohs
...to reserve...	**...reservar...**	ray-sehr-**bar**
...a table for one / two.	**...una mesa para uno / dos.**	**oo**-nah **may**-sah **pah**-rah **oo**-noh / dohs
Non-smoking.	**No fumadores.**	noh foo-mah-**doh**-rays
Is this table free?	**¿Está esta mesa libre?**	ay-**stah** ay-stah **may**-sah **lee**-bray
The menu (in English), please.	**La carta (en inglés), por favor.**	lah **kar**-tah (ayn een-**glays**) por fah-**bor**
service (not) included	**servicio (no) incluido**	sehr-**bee**-thee-oh (noh) een-kloo-**ee**-doh
cover charge	**precio de entrada**	**pray**-thee-oh day ayn-**trah**-dah
to go	**para llevar**	**pah**-rah yay-**bar**
with / without	**con / sin**	kohn / seen
and / or	**y / o**	ee / oh
menu (of the day)	**menú (del día)**	may-**noo** (dayl **dee**-ah)
specialty of the house	**especialidad de la casa**	ay-spay-thee-ah-lee-**dahd** day lah **kah**-sah
tourist menu	**menú de turista**	meh-**noo** day too-**ree**-stah
combination plate	**plato combinado**	**plah**-toh kohm-bee-**nah**-doh
appetizers	**tapas**	**tah**-pahs
bread	**pan**	pahn
cheese	**queso**	**kay**-soh
sandwich	**bocadillo**	boh-kah-**dee**-yoh
soup	**sopa**	**soh**-pah
salad	**ensalada**	ayn-sah-**lah**-dah
meat	**carne**	**kar**-nay
poultry	**aves**	**ah**-bays
fish	**pescado**	pay-**skah**-doh
seafood	**marisco**	mah-**ree**-skoh
fruit	**fruta**	**froo**-tah
vegetables	**verduras**	behr-**doo**-rahs
dessert	**postres**	**poh**-strays
tap water	**agua del grifo**	**ah**-gwah dayl **gree**-foh
mineral water	**agua mineral**	**ah**-gwah mee-nay-**rahl**
milk	**leche**	**lay**-chay
(orange) juice	**zumo (de naranja)**	**thoo**-moh (day nah-**rahn**-hah)
coffee	**café**	kah-**feh**
tea	**té**	tay
wine	**vino**	**bee**-noh
red / white	**tinto / blanco**	**teen**-toh / **blahn**-koh
glass / bottle	**vaso / botella**	**bah**-soh / boh-**tay**-yah
beer	**cerveza**	thehr-**bay**-thah
Cheers!	**¡Salud!**	sah-**lood**
More. / Another.	**Más. / Otro.**	mahs / **oh**-troh
The same.	**El mismo.**	ehl **mees**-moh
The bill, please.	**La cuenta, por favor.**	lah **kwayn**-tah por fah-**bor**
tip	**propina**	proh-**pee**-nah
Delicious!	**¡Delicioso!**	day-lee-thee-**oh**-soh

INDEX

Travel smart...carry on!

The latest generation of Rick Steves' carry-on travel bags is easily the best—benefiting from two decades of on-the-road attention to what really matters: maximum quality and strength; practical, flexible features; and no unnecessary frills. You won't find a better value anywhere!

Rick Steves' Convertible Carry-On

This is the classic "back door bag" that Rick Steves lives out of for three months every summer. It's made of rugged, water-resistant 1000-denier nylon. Best of all, it converts easily from a smart-looking suitcase to a handy backpack with comfortably-curved shoulder straps and a padded waistbelt.

This roomy, versatile 9" x 21" x 14" bag has a large 2500 cubic-inch main compartment, plus three outside pockets (small, medium and huge) that are perfect for often-used items. And the cinch-tight compression straps will keep your load compact and close to your back—not sagging like a sack of potatoes.

Wishing you had even more room to bring home souvenirs? Pull open the full-perimeter expando-zipper and its capacity jumps from 2500 to 3000 cubic inches. When you want to use it as a suitcase or check it as luggage (required when "expanded"), the straps and belt hide away in a zippered compartment in the back. Choose from five great traveling colors: black, navy, blue spruce, evergreen or merlot.

Rick Steves' 21" Roll-Aboard

At 9" x 21" x 14" our sturdy 21" Roll-Aboard is rucksack-soft in front, but the rest is lined with a hard ABS-lexan shell to give maximum protection to your belongings. We've spared no expense on moving parts, splurging on an extra-long button-release handle and big, tough inline skate wheels for easy rolling on rough surfaces.

Wishing you had even more room to bring home souvenirs? Pull open the full-perimeter expando-zipper and its capacity jumps from 2500 to 3000 cubic inches.

Rick Steves' 21" Roll-Aboard features exactly the same three-outside-pocket configuration and rugged 1000-denier nylon fabric as our Convertible Carry-On, plus a full lining and a handy "add-a-bag" strap.

Choose from five great traveling colors: black, navy, blue spruce, evergreen or merlot.

For great deals on a wide selection of travel goodies, begin your next trip at the Rick Steves Travel Store!

Visit the Rick Steves Travel Store at
www.ricksteves.com

FREE-SPIRITED TOURS FROM

Rick Steves

Small Groups
Great Guides
No Grumps

Start your trip at
www.ricksteves.com

Rick Steves' Web site
is packed with over
3,000 pages of timely
travel information.
It's also your gateway
to getting FREE
monthly travel news
from Rick—
and more!

Free Monthly European Travel News

Fresh articles on Europe's most interesting destinations and happenings. Rick will even send you an e-mail every month (often direct from Europe) with his latest discoveries!

Timely Travel Tips

Rick Steves' best money-and-stress-saving tips on trip planning, packing, transportation, hotels, health, safety, finances, hurdling the language barrier…and more.

Travelers' Graffiti Wall

Candid advice and opinions from thousands of travelers on everything listed above, plus whatever topics are hot at the moment (discount flights, packing tips, scams…you name it).

Rick's Annual Guide to European Railpasses

The clearest, most comprehensive guide to the confusing array of rail-pass options out there, and how to choo-choose the railpass that best fits your itinerary and budget. Then you can order your railpass (and get a bunch of great freebies) online from us!

Great Gear at the Rick Steves Travel Store

Enjoy bargains on Rick's guidebooks, planning maps and TV series DVDs, and on his custom-designed carry-on bags, roll-aboard bags, day packs and light-packing accessories.

Rick Steves Tours

This year more than 10,000 lucky travelers will explore Europe on a Rick Steves tour. Learn more about our 25 different one-to-three-week itineraries, read uncensored feedback from our tour alums, and sign up for your dream trip online!

Rick on Radio and TV

Download free podcasts of our weekly *Travel with Rick Steves* public radio show; read the scripts and see video clips from public television's *Rick Steves' Europe*.

Respect for Your Privacy

Ordering online from us is secure. When you buy something from us, join a tour, or subscribe to Rick's free monthly travel news e-mails, we promise to never share your name, information, or e-mail address with anyone else. You won't be spammed!

Have fun raising your Travel I.Q. at
www.ricksteves.com

Rick Steves®

More *Savvy.* More *Surprising.* More *Fun.*

COUNTRY GUIDES 2007

Croatia & Slovenia
England
France
Germany & Austria
Great Britain
Ireland
Italy
Portugal
Scandinavia
Spain
Switzerland

CITY GUIDES 2007

Amsterdam, Bruges & Brussels
Florence & Tuscany
Istanbul
London
Paris
Prague & The Czech Republic
Provence & The French Riviera
Rome
Venice

BEST OF GUIDES

Best of Eastern Europe
Best of Europe

As the #1 authority on European travel, Rick gives you inside information on what to visit, where to stay, and how to get there—economically and hassle-free.

www.ricksteves.com

PHRASE BOOKS & DICTIONARIES

French
French, Italian & German
German
Italian
Portuguese
Spanish

MORE EUROPE FROM RICK STEVES

Easy Access Europe
Europe 101
Europe Through the Back Door
Postcards from Europe

RICK STEVES' EUROPE DVDs

All 43 Shows 2000-2005
Britain
Eastern Europe
France & Benelux
Germany, The Swiss Alps & Travel Skills
Ireland
Italy
Spain & Portugal

PLANNING MAPS

Britain & Ireland
Europe
France
Germany, Austria & Switzerland
Italy
Spain & Portugal

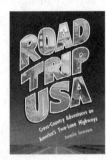

CREDITS

Researchers

To update this book, Rick relied on the help of...

Robert Wright

Robert was raised in Memphis, but now lives a bit further south—Buenos Aires, Argentina. A long-time Iberophile and a guide for Rick Steves tours, Robert spends his free time in Spain searching for the best *gambas al ajillo* and *licor de hierbas*.

Amanda Buttinger

Amanda moved to Madrid in 1998 thinking she'd be there a year. Her first reason to stay was to learn more Spanish. Then she discovered the perfect *café con leche*, travel writing, sunny city walks, massage, and professional wine tasting.

IMAGES

Spain (full page): Moorish Arches	David C. Hoerlein
Barcelona: Barcelona's Montjuïc	David C. Hoerlein
Near Barcelona: Cadaqués	Rick Steves
Basque Region: Guggenheim Bilbao	Rick Steves
Cantabria: Picos de Europa	Cameron Hewitt
Santiago de Compostela: Santiago's Cathedral	Cameron Hewitt
Salamanca: Salamanca's Plaza Mayor	Rick Steves
Madrid: Madrid's Retiro Park	David C. Hoerlein
Northwest of Madrid: Segovia's Aqueduct	Rick Steves
Toledo: Toledo Overview	Rick Steves
Granada: The Alhambra	Robert Wright
Sevilla: Sevilla Skyline	Rick Steves
Córdoba: Córdoba's Mezquita	Robert Wright
Andalucía's White Hill Towns: Arcos	David C. Hoerlein
Spain's South Coast: Nerja	Rick Steves
Morocco (full page): Camel	David C. Hoerlein
Tangier: Market Vendor	David C. Hoerlein

Rick Steves' Guidebook Series

Country Guides

Rick Steves' Best of Europe
Rick Steves' Best of Eastern Europe
Rick Steves' Croatia & Slovenia (new in 2007)
Rick Steves' England
Rick Steves' France
Rick Steves' Germany & Austria
Rick Steves' Great Britain
Rick Steves' Ireland
Rick Steves' Italy
Rick Steves' Portugal
Rick Steves' Scandinavia
Rick Steves' Spain
Rick Steves' Switzerland

City and Regional Guides

Rick Steves' Amsterdam, Bruges & Brussels
Rick Steves' Florence & Tuscany
Rick Steves' Istanbul (new in 2007)
Rick Steves' London
Rick Steves' Paris
Rick Steves' Prague & the Czech Republic
Rick Steves' Provence & the French Riviera
Rick Steves' Rome
Rick Steves' Venice

Rick Steves' Phrase Books

French
German
Italian
Spanish
Portuguese
French/Italian/German

Other Books

Rick Steves' Europe Through the Back Door
Rick Steves' Europe 101: History and Art for the Traveler
Rick Steves' Easy Access Europe
Rick Steves' Postcards from Europe
Rick Steves' European Christmas

(Avalon Travel Publishing)

Avalon Travel Publishing
1400 65th Street, Suite 250, Emeryville, CA 94608

Avalon Travel Publishing
An Imprint of Avalon Publishing Group, Inc.

Text © 2006, 2005, 2004, 2003, 2002, 2001, 2000, 1999 by Rick Steves
Maps © 2006, 2005, 2004, 2003, 2002 Europe Through the Back Door. All rights reserved.
Printed in the US by Worzalla. First printing November 2006.
Distributed by Publishers Group West

Thanks to Cameron Hewitt for writing the original versions of the Santiago de Compostela
and Cantabria chapters; and to Gene Openshaw for his writing on the Prado, Picasso's
Guernica, and other topics throughout the book.

For the latest on Rick Steves' lectures, guidebooks, tours, public television series, and public
radio show, contact Europe Through the Back Door, Box 2009, Edmonds, WA 98020, tel.
425/771-8303, fax 425/771-0833, www.ricksteves.com, rick@ricksteves.com.

ISBN (10) 1-56691-943-6
ISBN (13) 978-1-56691-943-2
ISSN 1551-8388

Europe Through the Back Door Managing Editor: Risa Laib
ETBD Editors: Cathy McDonald, Jennifer Hauseman (Senior Editor), Cameron Hewitt
    (Senior Editor)
Avalon Travel Publishing Series Manager and Editor: Madhu Prasher
Avalon Travel Publishing Project Editor: Patrick Collins
Research Assistance: Robert Wright, Amanda Buttinger, Kristen Kusnic
Copy Editor: Ellie Behrstock
Proofreader: Agatha Kim
Indexer: Carl Wikander
Production and Typesetting: Holly McGuire, Patrick David Barber
Cover Design: Kari Gim, Laura Mazer
Interior Design: Jane Musser, Laura Mazer, Amber Pirker
Maps and Graphics: David C. Hoerlein, Lauren Mills, Laura VanDeventer, Barb Geisler,
    Mike Morgenfeld
Front Matter Color Photos: p. i, children in Sevilla: David C. Hoerlein; p. viii, Sagrada
    Família, Barcelona, Spain: © Digital Vision
Cover Photos: Front image, Arcos de la Frontera © David C. Hoerlein; Back image,
    Spanish Fans © Mary Ann Cameron
Photography: David C. Hoerlein, Rick Steves, Cameron Hewitt, Robert Wright, and
    Steve Smith
Distributed to the book trade by Publishers Group West, Berkeley, California.